Fourth Edition

Introduction to Recreation and Leisure

Tyler Tapps, PhD

Northwest Missouri State University

Mary Sara Wells, PhD

University of Utah

Editors

HUMAN KINETICS

Library of Congress Cataloging-in-Publication Data

Names: Tapps, Tyler Nicholas, editor. | Wells, Mary Sara, editor.
Title: Introduction to recreation and leisure / Tyler Tapps, PhD, Northwest
  Missouri State University, Mary Sara Wells, PhD, University of Utah,
  editors.
Description: Fourth edition. | Champaign, IL : Human Kinetics, [2025] |
  "This book is a revised edition of Introduction [to] Recreation and
  Leisure, published in 2006 by Human Kinetics, Inc."--Copyright page. |
  Includes bibliographical references and index.
Identifiers: LCCN 2023017096 (print) | LCCN 2023017097 (ebook) | ISBN
  9781718212381 (print : alk. paper) | ISBN 9781718212398 (epub) | ISBN
  9781718212404 (pdf)
Subjects: LCSH: Recreation. | Leisure.
Classification: LCC GV14 .I68 2025 (print) | LCC GV14 (ebook) | DDC
  790--dc23/eng/20230513
LC record available at https://lccn.loc.gov/2023017096
LC ebook record available at https://lccn.loc.gov/2023017097

ISBN: 978-1-7182-1238-1 (print)

Copyright © 2025, 2019 by Tyler Tapps and Mary Sara Wells
Copyright © 2013, 2006 by Human Kinetics, Inc.

Senior Acquisitions Editor: Amy N. Tocco; **Managing Editor:** Jacob Roden; **Copyeditor:** Lisa Himes; **Proofreader:** Erin Cler; **Indexer:** Andrea J. Hepner; **Permissions Manager:** Laurel Mitchell; **Graphic Designer:** Denise Lowry; **Cover Designer:** Keri Evans; **Cover Design Specialist:** Susan Rothermel Allen; **Photograph (cover):** Thomas Barwick/DigitalVision/Getty Images; **Photographs (interior):** © Human Kinetics, unless otherwise noted; **Photo Asset Manager:** Laura Fitch; **Photo Production Manager:** Jason Allen; **Senior Art Manager:** Kelly Hendren; **Illustrations:** © Human Kinetics, unless otherwise noted; **Printer:** Walsworth

Printed in the United States of America   10 9 8 7 6 5 4 3 2 1

The paper in this book was manufactured using responsible forestry methods.

Human Kinetics
1607 N. Market Street
Champaign, IL 61820
USA

United States and International
Website: **US.HumanKinetics.com**
Email: info@hkusa.com
Phone: 1-800-747-4457

Canada
Website: **Canada.HumanKinetics.com**
Email: info@hkcanada.com

E8567

Contents

Preface xi

Preface

Welcome to the robust world of recreation and leisure studies. This introductory course textbook provides you with a current view of one of the top industries for the 21st century. Recreation and leisure programs serve people 365 days a year and are part of a global economy. According to the *Occupational Outlook Handbook*, between 2021 and 2031 there will be a 10 percent increase in recreation job opportunities (Bureau of Labor Statistics, 2015). These job opportunities can provide you with a challenging, yet rewarding, career path while you create crucial experiences for the lives of individuals, families, and communities.

This textbook invites you to take an amazing journey as you explore the world of recreation and leisure and the different opportunities provided in this profession. Your escorts are 47 professors and professionals from across the globe, including the United States, Canada, Europe, Brazil, China, and Nigeria. Their careers and passions mirror the various aspects of this profession. As rising stars, experts, leading thinkers, and icons in the field, the contributing authors serve as your personal guides as you begin your undergraduate studies of this exciting field. Their unique viewpoints form a foundation for understanding the industry on which your undergraduate studies will build.

Introduction to Recreation and Leisure, Fourth Edition, showcases a number of authors who are considered eminent and emerging scholars as well as some of the leading professionals in recreation and leisure education, all of whom present underlying theories, concepts, and their practical applications within the various sectors and segments of the recreation and leisure industry. The goal of this textbook is to illustrate the wide breadth of opportunities within this diverse profession and discuss a number of current issues in the world that have an impact on the field. This fourth edition delves into themes such as conservation, health and wellness, social equity, and quality of life. Also new to this edition is content that reflects the global impacts of the COVID-19 pandemic and how it has changed recreation and leisure experiences. These global themes give an indication of the direction in which the field of recreation and leisure is headed.

Furthermore, this textbook employs a robust list of ancillaries in order to enhance learning opportunities for the students and instructors who use it in their classes. These ancillaries will help students extend their learning of the chapter content into community connections and engagement, thus making them better prepared when they become recreation and leisure professionals.

For students pursuing a career in recreation and leisure or those who are considering the field as a career choice, this book offers vital information that will help in making informed career choices as well as a view of all the different career paths that are available throughout the world in the recreation and leisure industry. As you explore specific areas of this diverse profession, you will see the opportunities presented by the recreation and leisure industry:

- A field that offers lifetime career satisfaction or perhaps an entry-level start that can set you on a career path with many options
- A contemporary industry that provides employment opportunities in a wide variety of fields and associated fields
- A worldwide phenomenon that plays a large role in most of the world's economies

ORGANIZATION

Introduction to Recreation and Leisure is divided into three parts. Part I, Foundations of Recreation and Leisure, provides the foundation of this industry, including an introduction, history, and philosophical concepts. Part II, Leisure and Recreation as a Multifaceted Delivery System, introduces you to various sectors and areas of the field. Part III, Delivering Recreation and Leisure Services, presents the different types of programming found in recreation and leisure services. These interest areas include sport management; esports; health, wellness, and quality of life; outdoor and adventure recreation; and culture and the arts. This part ends with a chapter that addresses the nature of the profession and what it takes to become a professional as well as a chapter that provides international perspectives on recreation and leisure.

FEATURES

Several unique and useful features are included in the book.

- *Learning outcomes.* Each chapter lists the many important concepts that you will learn.
- *Outstanding Graduate sidebars.* Students who have graduated from recreation and leisure programs and gone on to successful careers have been highlighted in the Outstanding Graduate feature. These professionals share insights and advice on recreation and leisure as a career.
- *Glossary.* Important terms are printed in bold-face in the text, and their definitions appear in the glossary at the end of the book.

HKPROPEL

Students may access HK*Propel* by following the instructions on the key code page at the front of the book. You will find chapter summaries, glossary flash cards, research prompts, and links to websites to explore. It has been updated to support today's students' learning through entry-level learning experiences and connections to the real-world field.

INSTRUCTOR RESOURCES

Instructors have access to a full array of ancillary materials to supplement the information presented in the textbook.

Instructor guide. The instructor guide includes updated chapter overviews, learning outcomes, On the Job learning activities (assignable in HK*Propel*), chapter presentation packages, and a new reading list from current industry resources on the Internet. This updated instructor guide is intended to support today's students and bridge the gap between content presented in the book and the changing landscape of the recreation and leisure industry.

Test package. The test package includes questions in a variety of formats: true-false, multiple-choice, and multiple-response. Instructors can create their own tests.

Chapter quizzes. These ready-made quizzes allow instructors to test students' understanding of the most important chapter concepts.

Presentation package. A Microsoft PowerPoint presentation package covers the major topics and key points from the chapters. Instructors may use the presentation package to supplement their lectures. The presentation package can be adapted to suit each instructor's lecture content and style.

FINAL THOUGHTS

Introduction to Recreation and Leisure, Fourth Edition, presents a comprehensive view of the multifaceted, expansive field of recreation and leisure. Enjoy learning about recreation and leisure, reading what the principal thinkers and leaders have to say about the field, and meeting outstanding graduates from universities across the United States, Canada, and the world who share their career experiences. Let's enter the world of recreation and leisure.

PART I

Foundations of Recreation and Leisure

CHAPTER 1

Parks, Recreation, and Leisure: A Notable History and Promising Future

Ellen O'Sullivan

" Recreation plays many vital roles in modern living. For individuals, it is life-sustaining essential. **"**

Chubb and Chubb (1981, p. 2)

Mark Bowden/Getty Images/iStockphoto

LEARNING OUTCOMES

After reading this chapter, you should be able to do the following:

> Name three prominent pioneers and describe one contribution made to the field of parks and recreation

> Identify the five eras of parks and recreation, and analyze the differences between the eras

> Identify the three elements inherent of the postpandemic era of parks and recreation

> Explain three ways in which technology will influence parks, recreation, and leisure in the near future

> Create one example of your own (not cited in the book) of the blended industry

> Describe three industries related to parks and recreation that contribute to the overall economy

> Identify five less visible conditions influencing human behavior during the postpandemic era, and briefly explain how they will influence parks, recreation, and leisure

> Select any two of the emerging roles for the parks and recreation industry and describe a specific behavior related to these roles

WELCOME TO THE WORLD OF PARKS, RECREATION, AND LEISURE

Welcome to the world of parks, recreation, and leisure. Individuals pursuing a career in this field can be proud to know they join a profession with illustrious members. These include

- a Nobel Prize winner,
- the first sanitation commissioner of the United States, and
- a medical doctor whose work forms the basis for much of the YMCA movement.

Parks and recreation professionals may not reach the prominence of these pioneers, but they can still make a difference in the lives of individuals and communities. After all, it was likely anonymous staff that operated the public golf course where Tiger Woods learned the basics of golf, and similar employees who maintained and managed the public tennis courts where Billie Jean King and the Williams sisters got their start. Each of these public agencies were key to the success of these athletes, having afforded them the access and opportunity to pursue their dreams. People who worked and volunteered at Boys and Girls Clubs across the country can count among their alumni the names of

- many professional athletes;
- an Academy Award winner for Best Actor and other artists and entertainers; and

- a roster of military, political, and successful business people.

A review of the former Girl Scouts who went on to fame and success includes

- a Secretary of State of the United States;
- the first female Supreme Court Justice; and
- numerous newswomen, actresses, and pop stars.

It's apparent that after-school opportunities for youth form the basis for success later in life. Individuals exploring this professional field can rise to prominence and personal success through the expanded opportunities inherent within this profession.

ADAPTED EVOLUTION: FROM PUBLIC GOOD TO PERSONAL CONSUMPTION

How did the vast professional opportunities in parks and recreation result in supporting the needs of new urbanites and immigrants? How did the industry provide readily accessible venues so that the Williams sisters and Tiger Woods could hone their skills and rise to fame and success? When did the profession expand its reach to witness the rise of theme parks and other entities, generating substantial revenues? How did the industry go from essential, basic facilities and services for the public good to a plethora of expensive and exciting opportunities that reflect personal consumption?

The answer is adaptive evolution. *Adaptive evolution* refers to changes or modifications made over time by individuals, communities, organizations, professions, and the world in general as they respond to factors outside of their control. Such factors found within adaptive evolution could include

- changing demographics,
- social issues,
- policy initiatives,
- scientific and technological advances, and
- even geography and climate.

To grasp the significance of the evolution of parks, recreation, and leisure from a notable history to a promising future, it is necessary to consider how aspects of societal evolution shaped the industry. Parks, recreation, and leisure does not exist in a vacuum; rather, it reflects the multitude of changes and events that occur in the world in which it operates.

That's where adaptive evolution comes into play. Adaptive evolution consists of changes and modifications shaped by a wide range of factors considered outside the entity's direct control, as previously mentioned. Adaptive evolution can also occur multiple times, which is true of parks, recreation, and leisure. This section will focus on the more modern evolution of the field rather than covering the Greeks and Romans of much earlier times.

The field of parks, recreation, and leisure has likely evolved through at least five transitional stages as it went from simple sandlot playgrounds to expensive theme parks and travel experiences:

- The public good era
- The growth and expansion era
- The professional era
- The commercialization era
- The benefits era

The Public Good Era

This era likely began in the late 1880s when YMCAs emerged in England and spread to North America, creating facilities to house young men moving from the country to the city. The YMCAs aimed to fill the void for these young men who lacked the support system of an agriculturally based family and community, ensuring their well-being and explaining why so many urban Ys still offer inexpensive temporary housing.

As people migrated from rural communities to cities during the Public Good Era, large-scale developments such as Central Park in New York City brought nature and open space to densely populated areas.

Scott Dunn/Moment RF/Getty Images

As people flocked from the countryside to the cities, the need for large-scale open spaces for fresh air and nature was recognized, leading to the development of Central Park in New York City and other similar areas. It was during this era that playgrounds and playfields made their appearance as well. The basic services were directed toward the good of the general public or subsegments of the public, as was the case with the YMCAs, but were primarily intended to address social ills and human needs.

The Growth and Expansion Era

The Industrial Revolution resulted in parks, recreation, and leisure evolving with this new economic era and led to a period of growth and expansion. There were many new arrivals to the field of parks, recreation, and leisure, such as amusement parks and movie theaters, as technological advances led to silent, black-and-white flickering pictures shown in simple theaters. At this time, amusement parks were expanding to include mechanical rides and entertainment acts.

It was also during this era that federal governments had a more significant impact on the profession. Governments were motivated to set aside open space to preserve and protect it from rapidly expanding growth across the country. There was an additional influx of interest and spending by the U.S. federal government as the depression-era programs designed to put people back to work resulted in the building of campgrounds, swimming pools, and other public recreation facilities.

The Professional Era

The period following World War II was a game changer for parks and recreation. The return of the veterans, who bought newly affordable automobiles and were eager to settle down, resulted in a new lifestyle construct: the suburb. Affordable houses in nearby cities close to places of employment fueled their growth, followed by the arrival of numerous children to fully populate those suburbs. The onset of the baby boom saw an increase in the construction of schools, parks, playgrounds, ball fields, and swimming pools. New public policy made allowances for the public support of parks and recreation departments, and the professional era was born. Lessons and programs were then developed for use in these areas and facilities. Few people or government decision makers questioned why parks and recreation were necessary for a community.

This time period witnessed the growth of other areas of amusement and entertainment; Disneyland opened in California to entertain growing families, and full-blown movie palaces and drive-in movies appeared on the scene. People became accustomed to paying admission fees for amusement parks and other commercial providers. Local government continued to provide a plethora of new parks, facilities, and programs with free or low-cost services as well.

The Commercialization Era

The popularity and success of parks and recreation fueled the growth of still more programs and facilities. Soon there were centers for seniors and teens, as well as fitness centers, indoor pools, and indoor ice rinks. There appeared to be little end to the continued growth and specialization of parks, recreation, and leisure, and the addition of more professional staff. It was at this time that the early schools of parks and recreation came on the scene. Equal growth in the private and commercial sectors flourished as well.

The enormous enthusiasm for more and better buildings and programs came under siege with the passage of Proposition 13 in California. Proposition 13 was a local property tax initiative passed in 1978. It almost immediately cut those services in California that were considered "nonessential." This proposition received great publicity throughout the country and was thought to be the start of the antitax sentiment that swept across the nation. There was a similar move in Canada due to a recession and reduced national and provincial funding for parks and recreation.

The general public was already paying ever increasing fees for more sophisticated movie theaters, golf courses, amusement parks, concerts, and other entertainment opportunities. Why would they resist paying fees for public and nonprofit services?

Parks and recreation professionals, being nothing if not creative, refused to see the end of their services or closures of their facilities. Since many decision makers no longer viewed the specialized programs and facilities of public parks and recreation as a responsibility of government, and since taxpayers were accustomed to fees and charges in the private sector, parks and recreation pursued a path of cost recovery, focusing on how much of operating costs could be returned to the governmental entity that initially funded these programs and services. Many public parks and facilities (e.g., community centers and ice-skating facilities) were made possible by voter referendum to be repaid by tax dollars. However, as time ensued, many such proposals shifted to revenue bonds requiring the facility to pay for itself by generating revenue rather than using tax dollars to repay the bond over time. In doing so, public parks and recreation and some nonprofits shifted from meeting the needs of people and participants to seeking members, clients, and other user groups.

The Benefits Era

Over time it became apparent that many of the programs and services that were formerly considered a "public good" had evolved into primarily personal consumption activities that included significant prices. This shift was accompanied by several social ills, including lack of physical activity among both youth and adults, the growing obesity crisis, and the prevalence of mental health issues. While these social ills were not directly related to public and nonprofit parks, recreation, and leisure, there were many changes in the fee structure and society overall that possibly contributed to these issues.

Some examples of decreased physical activity during the benefits era, included the following:

- Children could no longer play outdoors after school since both parents were working and the local playgrounds in neighborhoods were no longer supervised.
- Youth sports leagues necessitated official-looking uniforms and major league–type fields requiring substantial funding from parents to support these activities.
- More youth abandoned team sports due to lack of affordability or the heavy emphasis on competition over fun.
- Adults also experienced decreased physical activity when motorized lawnmowers, leaf blowers, washing machines, and dryers curtailed some commonplace physical activities.

Free community special events and outdoor concerts became reliant upon commercial sponsors. These events likely solicited contributions from local businesses for many years, but it was certainly a different era when product placement and signage entered the arena. Organizations, especially public and nonprofit ones, vigorously discussed precisely what type of products would be suitable for advertising (e.g., alcohol and tobacco were likely considered unsuitable).

In the early 1990s the professionals in Canada made the first entry into this movement, referred to as the benefits approach, by getting out ahead and publishing the *Benefits Catalogue*. The benefits movement intended to ensure that the general public, taxpayers, decision makers, and partners recognized the essential benefits being provided by public and nonprofit recreation agencies. The Canadian catalogue identified four individual categories of the public good:

1. Personal
2. Social
3. Economic
4. Environmental

The catalogue also acknowledged the additional benefits of sport and recreation events, festivals, and the visual and performing arts. The National Recreation and Park Association (NRPA), the organization representing parks and recreation in the United States, soon followed by publishing *Putting the Pieces Together: The Benefits of Parks and Recreation*. This publication featured individual, community, environmental, and economic benefits of the parks and recreation offerings. In both instances, documentation of these specific subcategories was provided, offering very valuable information to parks and recreation professionals.

While the benefits era of parks and recreation was significant, it was a building block to what would come later (California Park & Recreation Society, 1999). The California Park & Recreation Society (CPRS) created a *VIP Plan—Creating Community in the 21st Century*. Its purpose was to identify critical roles that parks and recreation can and do provide. It served as the basis for the CPRS's branding project as well. One of the aspects discovered during the branding process was that decision makers could extensively list the benefits associated with themselves or their families. Still, they had difficulty stating the public good outcomes (California Park & Recreation Society, 1999).

Similarly, the national *Framework for Recreation in Canada* was an endeavor co-led by provincial and territorial governments and the Canadian Parks and Recreation Association. The four-year project began in 2011 with the National Recreation Summit and resulted in a finished document by 2015. This summit resulted in priority consideration for the framework. Among these considerations was

- the shift from those who can pay to those who need it most,

- ensuring that people live in healthy settings,
- connecting people with nature, and
- repositioning recreation as essential.

Even before the pandemic, which forced a significant shift in what was important or essential, the two national organizations were already changing their missions. Postpandemic, their evolved missions are as follows:

- The Canadian Parks and Recreation Association's (CPRA) current mission maintains that CPRA *exists to build healthy communities and enhance the quality of life and environments for all Canadians through collaboration with our members and partners.*
- The mission statement of the National Recreation and Park Association (NRPA) incorporates messages attesting to the essential nature of services provided by its members as well. NRPA's mission is *to advance parks, recreation and environmental conservation efforts that enhance the quality of life for all people.*

The National Recreation and Park Association (NRPA) supplemented its mission statement to identify three pillars of importance to the association and the professional. These three pillars are as follows:

- *Health and Wellness.* Advancing community health and well-being through parks and recreation.
- *Equity at the Center.* At NRPA, equity is at the center of everything.
- *Conservation.* Creating a nation of resilient and climate-ready communities through parks and recreation.

AND THEN, ALONG CAME COVID-19

At the end of 2019, there were only faint whispers about a deadly disease popping up in Asia and spreading globally. By March of 2020, the general public in North America was not only aware of it, but on increasing levels of high alert. Public health departments at all levels in countries across the globe were struggling to keep track of the numbers of people who had died from COVID-19 and to discern the best ways to treat the disease.

The number of cases and subsequent deaths were severe; initial changes to how people lived, worked, and played were extensive. During various instances and severities of lockdown, people were, with the few exceptions for essential workers, confined to their places of residence. Factories closed down, and offices allowed people to work from home. Schools and colleges sent students home to pursue online learning. And, of course, parks, amusements, play, and entertainment were severely affected.

The shutdowns led to the closure of parks, playgrounds, community centers, fitness centers, and swimming pools. The private and commercial purveyors of parks, recreation, fitness, amusements, entertainment venues, and travel and tourism took a big financial hit as well. Movie theaters were shuttered as were arenas, theaters, and museums. Publicly frequented facilities, namely restaurants and bars, were especially hit hard financially.

COVID-19 resulted in the beginning of a new era, not just for parks and recreation, but for everyone and every industry around the world. The preferences of and demand for services focused on personalized consumption were alive and well and assumed even greater levels due to the pandemic. There was a strong return to the commitment to the greater public good for public and nonprofit parks and recreation organizations. The essential nature of this component of the industry demonstrated its importance and role within communities. Examples included the following:

- The Canadian-based A.R. Kaufman Family YMCA provided temporary shelter to homeless men.
- YMCA of Central Ohio opened three additional shelter spaces to ensure that 250 single adult men and 60 single adult women had safe places to stay during the pandemic.
- The YMCA of Southwestern Ontario served as an emergency food drop-off and pickup site.
- Many public parks and recreation staff contacted older adults in the community to assess their well-being and identify needs. It was also an opportunity for some critically needed social interaction for the isolated seniors.
- The City of Tampa Parks and Recreation Department was especially helpful and innovative, as they created activities people could access on YouTube called "Happy at Home," which presented easily implementable crafts and activities for people restricted to their residences. The department provided space for community members to exercise, gathering in socially distant ways, and finding a bit of peace among nature. They also supported students and families by providing extended child care

hours to accommodate for virtual learning and adjusted school-day schedules, delivering Wi-Fi to support virtual learning for families without or with limited access, supplying meals, and offering spaces for Out of School Time (OST) programs (City of Tampa, 2022).

In response to societal changes due to COVID-19, the importance and impact of technology became evident. Almost overnight it seemed like most households incorporated technology as an essential part of their lives, and people who had never before used Zoom or FaceTime pursued it regularly. With no work or school to occupy this substantial amount of time, the magnetism of the screen—any screen—took hold of people's life.

- Sales of Peloton's high-end, home exercise bikes and treadmills more than tripled during the first financial quarter of the pandemic (Thomas, 2020).
- Amazon's profit doubled in 2020 due to COVID-19 (Selyukh, 2020).

WELCOME TO THE POSTPANDEMIC ERA: ESSENTIAL, BLENDED, AND ECONOMIC

The collective industry as well as many aspects of living, working, learning, and playing have entered the postpandemic era. There certainly were serious health, social, and environmental concerns prior to COVID-19, but the seemingly rapid onset of the disease caused people to focus heavily upon the illness and the less-than-desirable outcomes. Initially, and understandably so, attention was on preventing the disease and alleviating the death toll, but it was not long before people, organizations, and companies began to recognize the essential human needs affected by COVID-19.

Essential Human Needs

Human needs, especially social- and policy-related issues that had been conveniently overlooked or ignored, came to the forefront as being essential to the overall health and well-being of people, communities, and the world.

To a certain extent, the ramifications of the pandemic reminded people and society of the essential human needs addressed and served by public and nonprofit parks and recreation. Some of the catego-

ries associated with the essential needs of human beings are discussed in the following sections.

Green Space

During the pandemic, the heightened importance of green space for physical activity and mental well-being surfaced. A growing body of research and literature attests to the association between green space and mental well-being and the lowered risks for various health conditions (Louv, 2012).

Physical Activity

Regular physical activity resurfaced in people's minds as a vital element of a healthy lifestyle. Many adults spend a large portion of their time being sedentary (prolonged sitting). The Centers for Disease Control and Prevention (CDC) found that 8.3 percent of deaths of nondisabled adults ages 25 and older were attributed to physical inactivity. Being physically active and reducing sedentary behavior can benefit health (Carlson et al., 2018).

Regular physical activity (at least 150 minutes a week) is associated with reduced risk of diseases, such as

- heart disease;
- stroke;
- hypertension;
- type 2 diabetes;
- certain cancers, including bladder, breast, and colon cancer;
- dementia; and
- anxiety and depression (Piercy et al., 2018).

Physical inactivity is a significant issue in both the United States and Canada. Costs associated with physical inactivity account for more than 11 percent of total health care expenditures in the United States and are estimated at $117 billion annually (Carlson et al., 2015). According to Statistics Canada, 49.2 percent of Canadian adults get the recommended amount of physical activity (150 minutes of moderate-to-vigorous physical activity per week), resulting in half of the adult population in Canada not being active enough (Statistics Canada, 2021).

Social Isolation

People became increasingly isolated. Regardless of the pandemic, the number of single-person households had already been increasing, and the number of older adults who were housebound had been rising. Couple these conditions with the fact that many people, especially adolescents, were engaging in fewer in-person interactions and spending more time in virtual connections through technology and social media, and it is easy to see how social isolation can have a significant impact on society. Social isolation happens when a person's social participation or social contact drops.

Lack of social interaction is becoming a particular challenge among the increasing number of older adults. About 30 percent of Canadian seniors are at risk of becoming socially isolated. Reports by Statistics Canada estimate that 19 percent and 24 percent of Canadians over age 65 feel isolated from others and wish they could participate in more social activities (Government of Canada, 2022). In addition, according to a September 2020 report by the U.S. Department of Health and Human Services, the suicide rate for pediatric patients rose 57.4 percent from 2007 to 2018. Teens in the United States who spend more than three hours a day on social media may be at a heightened risk for mental health issues (Riehm et al., 2019).

Sense of Belonging and Community

Generally, a sense of belonging is a psychological construct, while a sense of **community** reflects sociological requirements. A sense of belonging tends to focus on an individual's ability to feel as if they belong to a particular group, family, or community. A sense of community reflects people's feelings that their community is important, unique, and meets their needs. Some examples are the presence of farmers markets or community bands or choruses. Community can also refer to the livability and viability of a city, town, or geographic area. Common open spaces, parks, and trails are a part of this construct as well.

New Experiences

Why do we need new experiences? Novelties are new experiences or anything new to us, including new friendships. The experience of novelty, especially within the restrictions of the pandemic, assumed many forms, such as learning a new skill, buying a new outfit, listening to new music, or traveling to a new environment. Most mammals, especially humans, naturally prefer novelty if it does not come with some perceived threat. Learning, whether academic, job related, or otherwise, continues to depend on novelty. New experiences and information stimulate the memory centers of the brain, which are closely related to the pleasure centers. We need that dopamine rush to keep us motivated and to continue going in life—to learn, work, and succeed. If we no longer feel this rush of dopamine, we will likely give up on that activity and look for pleasure elsewhere (Dean, 2019).

Environmental Sustainability

The essential need to address environmental sustainability became more apparent during the pandemic. As we continue to navigate our world, we face environmental challenges:

- Floods
- Fires
- Air pollution
- Water shortages
- Endangerment of environments to sustain certain animals
- Increased greenhouse gases
- More frequent and intense natural disasters (e.g., droughts, tropical storms, blizzards)
- Rising ocean temperatures
- The melting of glaciers and snowpack

Related to these changes in the environment is a type of disease called zoonoses, a disease or infection that can transfer from animals to humans. Zoonotic pathogens can spread to humans through direct contact or through food, water, or the environment. Zoonoses can cause major health problems globally due to our close relationship with animals in agriculture, as companions, and in the natural environment (World Health Organization, 2020). These environmental issues will affect how we pursue recreation and leisure now and in the future.

Essential Nature of Technology

Another essential category is technology. This was made apparent when life became problematic without using various aspects of technologies. The world's dependence upon technology was heightened to the point people wondered how we could survive without it.

The collective shutdown of schools, workplaces, restaurants, parks, theaters, and other public places caused people to recognize life's essential needs, particularly for contact with green and natural spaces, opportunities for social interaction, and the inherent need for engagement and enjoyment.

These closures resulted in an expanded definition of the term *essential*. Essential has shades of meanings including Merriam-Webster's related definitions (Merriam-Webster, n.d.):

- *Essential* as being something basic or necessary
- *Essential* referring to something necessary, indispensable, or unavoidable

Public parks, recreation, and nonprofits are essential because they meet basic and critical human needs. What about the world of technology and its role in the postpandemic era? The expanded world of technology, which provides a framework of services for many of those essential human needs previously cited, was deemed *essential* because technology is indispensable to how we live, work, learn, and play in the 21st century. Many millennials and members of Gen Z already considered technology as essential prior to the pandemic. Baby boomers and Gen X, in some cases, were just beginning to learn of its essential nature. If not for various forms of technology, some of the human needs unveiled by COVID-19 would have escalated once the pandemic began.

Consider the myriad ways different technologies have influenced, or in some cases dramatically enhanced or made it possible to address, human needs during the pandemic.

- The Internet alone has transformed access to places or experiences that would not readily occur otherwise.
- Mobile phones played a prominent role in keeping people connected.
- Access to medical care through telehealth allowed various forms of health care to continue.
- Zoom happy hours for friends who were unable to get together in-person became popular.
- Continuing education through online learning commenced when schools shut down.
- Fitness courses were offered on YouTube instead of in-person.

Just how dependent is society on technology?

- *Mobile phones*: The number of worldwide users of mobile phones is 7.1 billion, and this number is projected to reach 7.49 billion by 2025 (Taylor, 2023).
- *Internet usage in North America*: The estimated population of the United States and Canada in 2020 is 368,869,647. Users of the Internet in these two countries is 332,908,868, which represents 90.3 percent penetration

adamkaz/E+/Getty Images

The first decades of the 21st century saw the widespread integration of technology into everyday activities, including leisure and recreation. This integration was only accelerated by the COVID-19 pandemic.

(International Telecommunication Union World Telecommunication/ICT Indicators Database, n.d.).

Impact and Improvements of Technology

Technology has given rise to the popularity of goods and services that are for personal consumption. The impact of technology on people's leisure-time activities has been dramatically altered. Consumers can use the Internet to gather insight, suggestions, and ratings for almost any product or service, empowering previous customers and would-be customers alike.

There has been improvement in gear and equipment; practically every physical sport from archery to zoom ball has increased the proficiency and safety of participants. There is also the ubiquity of participation; people can now view worldwide competitions from home or office if they so choose, and don't need to leave their homes if they want instant entertainment, face-to-face chats with friends and family, or to visit new places through augmented reality.

Communication is an added benefit of technology for leisure. People no longer have the same level of fear when hiking if they can use cell phones for directions or to secure medical assistance. Similarly, people attending large events don't have to worry about permanently losing their friends in a crowd. A variety of apps can also identify places for enjoyment within a short distance from the app user.

Some Positive and Negative Outcomes Associated With Increased Technology

Technology positively affects a number of human needs within the category of the public good. In many instances, technology enables good things to happen for people such as

- continual contact with friends and families using Zoom or FaceTime,
- the sense of camaraderie among people playing word games or video games online with others, or
- participating in a fantasy sport league.

Consider the positive experiences of individuals who are homebound, disabled, or under financial duress to climb mountains or visit the Taj Mahal, all of which can be possible through virtual reality headsets. People are able to go places, do things, and have experiences that would have never before been possible.

The amount of time and money spent to support the proliferation of technology for leisure shows how necessary it is to many people. Some examples include the following:

- *Video gaming.* After video game purchases, in-game consumer spending accounts for the most significant share of the video gaming market. In 2020 global gaming audiences spent approximately US$54 billion on additional in-game content. In 2025 the market value of in-game purchases is projected to surpass US$74.4 billion (Clement, 2021).
- *Fantasy football.* The number of fantasy football players in the United States and Canada was 500,000 in 1988. That figure grew to approximately 15.2 million in 2003 and reached 62.5 million by 2022. This represented an over 400 percent increase from 2003 to 2022 (Sports Management Degree Hub, n.d.; Fantasy Sports and Gaming Association, n.d.).
- *Video and music streaming.* Surveys suggest that around 73 percent of Canadians with Internet access at home stream at least one hour of video, TV, or movies per day, while 43 percent stream at least one hour of music or radio per day (Canadian Internet Registration Authority, 2022).

Concerns About Technology

Technology is seen as an essential benefit to a number of people; however, some activities and outcomes are considered harmful or less than desirable. For example, the use of cell phones during family dinners may be frowned upon. Furthermore, individuals glued to their couches, watching the latest streaming opportunities, do not address the vital human needs for physical activity and social interaction. There is also a growing sense of impatience as people become more accustomed to an instantaneous world in which needs are addressed in nanoseconds. Finally, there are equity issues that have to be addressed when dealing with technology. Not everyone can access the most recent device, and many may not be able to access any device at all. This can cause an imbalance in the type of information and social connections some individuals have in comparison to others.

A Blended Industry

In this postpandemic era, we are starting to see more of a blended industry. While blending has been around for decades, it has become even more apparent today. There is rarely a good or service that is provided by only one type of agency. Involvement and participation of different industry segments are increasing over time and will form the basis of a significant portion of the industry. One of the better ways to illustrate this blending may be through examples and the benefits they provide. Consider the blending of public good and personal consumption in the following examples:

- A tour company offers organized trips through the national parks.
- A ski resort develops a complex for people who purchase ski passes on federal lands.
- A community uses tax dollars to build a large, professional-like athletic complex to rent to teams from outside of the community.
- A recreation department offers a video game tournament.
- A public or nonprofit community center closes access to a portion of its facility for a private birthday or anniversary party.
- A nonprofit museum opens its doors to the general public for free one day a week.

The preceding list is a small sample of arrangements that are currently being practiced. There will be instances of additional expanded collaborations as more private foundations, organizations, and corporations begin to realize the public good that their involvement and generosity can generate. Similarly, public and nonprofit agencies will expand upon their commitment to the public good by entering into agreements with other partners and providers.

Widespread Economic Impact

Recall how personal consumption can be defined or distinguished from a public good. Personal consumption is defined as an individual consumer's purchase of an item, durable good, service, or experience intended primarily for their use only or for the use of the person for whom it is purchased.

The problematic aspect of describing the parks, recreation, amusement, entertainment, and travel industry is the extensive listing of categories within its boundaries. ESRI is a GIS-based system that collects a wide range of data including demographics and behavior patterns for their customers to use to support business decisions. ESRI can be particularly helpful for parks and recreation services to determine the geographic location of people as well as their demographic information. In the forthcoming section that discusses the issues and conditions to be addressed in the future, please note that a number of the statistics include dollar amounts to reflect the effect positive intervention or involvement in this industry could hold for the financial health of North America.

One of numerous ESRI services that can be purchased is "Recreation Expenditures."

Under this, each of the seven major headings contain specific category expenditures.

Seven Major Headings With Examples of Expenditures

- *TV, video, and audio*. Cable and satellite services, spending on TV and other equipment and repair
- *Entertainment or recreation fees and admissions*. Tickets to theaters, movies, parks, or museums; admission to sporting events; fees for participant sports and recreational lessons as well as membership fees for clubs, etc.
- *Toys, games, crafts, and hobbies*. Toys, games, arts and crafts, playground equipment, arcade and video games, online gaming services, collecting, etc.
- *Recreational vehicles and fees*. Docking and landing fees for boats and planes; camp fees; purchase or rental of boats, campers, trailers, and RVs
- *Sports or recreation equipment and exercise equipment*. Exercise equipment and gear, bicycles, camping equipment, winter sports and other sports equipment, and repairs to this equipment
- *Photographic equipment and supplies*. Cameras, film, photo processing, and other equipment
- *Reading*. Magazines and newspaper subscriptions, individual copy purchases, and physical books and digital readers (ESRI, 2022)

U.S. data show that the outdoor recreation economy accounted for 1.9 percent ($454.0 billion) of current-dollar gross domestic product (GDP) for the nation in 2021 (U.S. Bureau of Economic Analysis, 2022). Outdoor recreation expenditures fall into three categories:

- Conventional activities, such as bicycling, boating, hiking, and hunting
- Other core activities, such as gardening and outdoor concerts
- Supporting activities, such as construction, travel and tourism, local trips, and government expenditures

In 2021 conventional outdoor recreation accounted for 35.1 percent of U.S. outdoor recreation **value added** while other outdoor recreation accounted for 17.6 percent, and supporting activities accounted for the remaining 47.3 percent (U.S. Bureau of Economic Analysis, 2022).

Outdoor Recreation by Industry

The outdoor recreation by industry data illustrate the contribution of different industries in the outdoor recreation economy. In the United States, the arts, entertainment, recreation, accommodations, and food services sector was the largest contributor to U.S. outdoor recreation value added in 2019, accounting for $128.5 billion. Other value added by industry highlights for 2019 include (U.S. Bureau of Economic Analysis, 2022) the following:

- Retail trade was the second largest sector contribution to outdoor recreation, accounting for $98.6 billion in current-dollar value added.
- Manufacturing came in as the third largest sector contributing $55 billion nationally to the outdoor recreation economy.

SIGNIFICANT ISSUES OF THE POSTPANDEMIC ERA

The postpandemic era appears to have heightened the issues critical for a healthy society. During the benefits era, professional organizations attempted to educate the public as to the critical benefits of parks, recreation, and leisure, and it is highly likely that the pandemic created either a renewed interest or an initial realization as to how physical and mental health can become at risk through day-to-day living behavior.

" The greatest wealth is health. "

Virgil

There are four critical areas of concern.

1. Physical health
2. Mental health
3. **Equity** and **equality**
4. Environmental imperative

Physical Health

During the pandemic, certain medical conditions caused extreme cases of COVID-19, or the greater likelihood of death. These medical conditions have been present and growing in number among North Americans. However, even before COVID-19, the United States had been experiencing a decline in life expectancy, but the pandemic made it even worse.

According to Worldometer, a group that tracks worldwide life expectancy, four of the five top ranking countries for life expectancy in 2023 were located in Asia and had an average life expectancy of approximately 85 years. On this same list, Canada ranked 16 at 82.96 years and the United States ranked 46 at 79.11 years (Worldometer, n.d.).

While it is not the only indicator of the overall health of a nation, life expectancy is revealing. As previously presented, the percentage of North Americans who are receiving adequate levels of physical activity can likely play a role. A role that can be readily addressed by parks, recreation, and leisure.

The resources required to provide these services is another health-related issue. The Commonwealth Fund, a private foundation aimed at promoting an improved and accessible health care system, reports this information as it relates to the United States and Canada (Alas, 2021).

CEOWorld magazine's "Health Care Index," a statistical analysis of the overall quality of the health care system worldwide, names the following ten countries as having the best health care systems in the world:

1. South Korea
2. Taiwan
3. Denmark
4. Austria
5. Japan
6. Australia
7. France
8. Spain

9. Belgium
10. United Kingdom

If you are looking for Canada and United States on that list, they can be found at number 23 and 30, respectively (Ireland, 2021).

Another significant issue related to health in both countries is the ever escalating costs of services. In 2018 the United States expended $3.6 trillion, and the Centers for Medicare and Medicaid Services project that by 2028 the costs will likely grow to $6.2 trillion, which represents about 20 percent of the GDP as opposed to 18 percent in 2018 (Peter G. Peterson Foundation, 2020). Putting this in dollar terms, health care expenditures in 2021 represented US$6,500 per capita in Canada and $12,914 in the United States (Ross University School of Medicine, 2021; Wiles, 2021).

Mental Health

In 2019 prior to the pandemic, 19.86 percent of American adults experienced mental illness, equivalent to fifty million American adults. Since then, a growing percentage of youth in the United States live with major depression, and the rates of nontreatment and suicidal thoughts continue to increase incrementally as well (Reinert et al., 2021).

In Canada one in five people will experience mental illness. By age 40, about 50 percent of Canadians will have experienced mental health illness (Canadian Mental Health Association, National, 2021).

Mental illness is likely to remain an issue for society, and the toll that mental health can have upon physical health and life expectancy is significant.

Equity and Equality

While *equity* and *equality* are often used interchangeably, the definitions are not the same.

- The focus of equality is that every person is provided with the same resources and opportunities, while
- the aim of equity is to ensure that all people have the opportunity to succeed by recognizing barriers to equitable programs and services and subsequently creating access and opportunities that support such participation (Milken Institute for Public Health, 2020).

For example, every community may have an outdoor swimming pool, but some people are unable to use the pool due to its distance from their neighborhood. If individuals or neighborhoods do not have access to walking trails, playground equipment, or swimming pools, then the ability to address physical or mental health is curtailed. These circumstances have long existed with a lengthy list of groups left out of leisure opportunities, including

- the economically disadvantaged,
- rural populations,
- Indigenous people,
- people with disabilities,
- people who are unemployed, and
- people who are undocumented.

Parks, particularly in cities, contain myriad benefits including opportunities for social interaction, the environmental influence of trees and bioswales, and space for physical activity. The City Parks Alliance published a set of case studies detailing the health, economic, and environmental effects that can be attributed to parks (City Parks Alliance, n.d.).

Identifying barriers to participation can be related to the concepts of equity and equality. For example, in the case of groups eligible for treatment for COVID-19, certain groups were eligible for treatment (equality) but were unable to do so because of real or perceived barriers (equity).

Environmental Imperative

Environmental resilience and sustainability is an additional concern that overrides all others and is the true prevailing issue for the future. If the earth can no longer supply the basic needs of human existence, then physical and mental health issues become moot. A resilient and sustainable planet is the overwhelmingly critical issue.

During the first two years of the pandemic, the world experienced a larger than average number of natural disasters, including fires, floods, food shortages, drought, and serious hurricanes and tornadoes.

Whether due to heightened visibility through media or the severity of these disasters, people's attention was captured. A recent survey conducted by The Associated Press-NORC Center for Public Affairs Research, and the Energy Policy Initiative at the University of Chicago found that approximately six out of ten Americans believe that the pace of global warming is increasing (Knickmeyer, 2021).

Another development due to environmental decline is a trend called environmental migration. Environmental migration refers to people who must physically relocate due to natural conditions or disasters in their original home. For example, homeowners in California may be unable to rebuild in their original location destroyed by wildfires. Or, in another example, starvation in an area of Madagascar can result from four years of drought. Widespread migration is typically due to war and conflict, but situations such as the one in Madagascar are likely to become more commonplace.

LESS VISIBLE CONDITIONS WITH SERIOUS CONSEQUENCES

The aforementioned overriding issues are serious in nature as are the less visible, but equally significant, conditions causing crucial consequences to societal well-being. The following additional factors play a role in physical and mental health that is not as readily recognized:

- Lack of physical activity
- Stress
- Social isolation
- Boredom

Please note that these four factors are considered conditions rather than issues. The circumstances and situations brought about by these conditions can be changed, while issues have a far greater negative impact upon the world in general. These conditions are commonplace in the world but generally not recognized, with the exception of lack of physical activity, which is widely recognized as contributing to deteriorating mental and physical health.

Parks and recreation professionals are not physicians, psychiatrists, mental health counselors, or environmental scientists, so how do these critical conditions relate to the future of the planet and the people who inhabit it? What are these less visible conditions that carry such importance to our future? Both physical and mental health can have their foundations in societal factors such as the four factors cited above. These conditions are not always associated with negative influences upon physical and mental health, yet they can be serious for those people whose lives they touch.

Lack of Physical Activity

Lack of physical activity is a condition that can be changed and falls into the skill set of our profession. Consider the following issues relevant to the work of this profession. Physical activity is different than physical exercise. People are attracted to and motivated to participate in physical activities that are fun. If they can find physical recreation that appeals to them, it is more likely that acceptable rates of physical activity will prevail.

People usually prefer some types of physical activity over others, perhaps because they have a more natural inclination toward that form of sport and recreation. Physical activity can affect more than just the body. There are potential cognitive and mental health benefits to an active lifestyle. When providing physical activity opportunities, realize that people may prefer or resist participation in some activities not because of the activity itself, but due to the format of the activity. For example, someone may love to lap swim, but may not be interested in participating in a swim meet, even if it is structured as a fun, relaxed experience. Furthermore, consider that some people find marathons a source of inspiration and enjoyment, while others wonder about the sanity of those who endure such an activity. There can be a host of other reasons that affect participation in certain physical activities, including exposure and participation to the activity as a child, or the involvement of friends and families. Being aware of the potential obstacles as well as the potential attractions to various activities helps parks, recreation, and leisure professionals plan accordingly to maximize participation.

The Impact of Stress

Stress can be serious and is becoming more recognized as a condition that can be associated with physical and mental health. Most of the bodily regulatory systems are affected by chronic stress, and the same can be said for mental health conditions. The results of a 2000 Ipsos-Reid/CTV poll revealed that 63 percent of Canadians said they were feeling at least the same (21%) or more (42%) stress in their lives as compared with five years ago. Canadians said that their work or job (45%) was the greatest cause of stress in their lives, and 50 percent said stress negatively affected their sleep (Ipsos-Reid, 2000).

Many studies and authors indicated that stress results in accidents; absenteeism; employee turnover; diminished productivity; and direct medical, legal, and insurance expenditures costing the United States an estimated $300 billion every year (American Institute of Stress, n.d.). Parks, recreation, and leisure can assist in addressing this condition since increased physical activity is associated with reducing stress.

The Serious Nature of Social Isolation

The effect of social isolation and loneliness on health and well-being is recognized globally as a public health issue. The World Health Organization recognizes the effect of social isolation on disability and death, and research generally demonstrates that social isolation is associated with increased risk of mortality (World Health Organization, n.d.). One study reports that loneliness is the equivalent to smoking 15 cigarettes a day (U.S. Department of Health and Human Services, Office of the Surgeon General, 2023).

What is the extent of loneliness? Two in five Americans report that they sometimes or always feel their social relationships are not meaningful, and one in five say they feel lonely or socially isolated. The lack of connection can have life-threatening consequences. There are also financial costs that recent studies have begun to measure. In a 2017 AARP study, the Medicare costs of social isolation and loneliness were estimated at $6.7 billion annually (Flowers et al., 2017).

This is an area that can be addressed by the parks and recreation profession; most leisure pursuits can include social contact with other people. The challenge is

- identifying these people,
- making contact with them, and
- facilitating their involvement in a group experience that appeals to them.

One of the more common roles assumed by public agencies focuses on older adults who are often isolated for a variety of reasons. Centers and programming for older adults are usually a part of their offerings. The difficulty is finding those who are often invisible to the rest of the community.

Boredom Can Result in More Than Boredom

While it is likely that everyone has been bored at one time or another, some studies suggest that transitory boredom can have positive outcomes, such as aiding creativity and enhancing productivity by allowing our minds to wander. However, research has also found that boredom can have adverse effects upon people's lives, as the following statistics illustrate:

- Sixty-three percent of American adults experience boredom at least once every ten days.

- Chronic boredom is associated with impulsivity and risky behavior, including careless driving, compulsive gambling, drug and alcohol abuse, reckless thrill-seeking, and other self-destructive behaviors.
- People who are easily bored are susceptible to depression, anxiety, anger, academic failure, poor work performance, loneliness, and isolation (Cantor, 2019).

Some of these statistics are particularly impactful. Boredom can and does lead to negative behaviors that can be self-harmful and harmful to others as well. For instance, drug and alcohol abuse usually touches the lives of the other people in a person's life, often resulting in the spread of stress, social isolation, or boredom to those people.

People can be bored at work or school, but the more obvious results of boredom are apparent during leisure time. In fact, there is even recognition of leisure boredom. *Leisure boredom* is defined as a negative mood or mindset that reflects a mismatch between the mindset and an optimal experience. (Iso-Ahola & Wessinger, 1987).

EMERGING PROFESSIONAL ROLES FOR THE POSTPANDEMIC ERA

In earlier eras, a parks, recreation, and leisure practitioner was often considered a "jack of all trades" due to the multiple areas of activity and assignments undertaken to enable the whole operation to function. Today is different and the future even more so. It will be essential, blended, and economic.

- It will meet the essential needs of people and society.
- Various forms of organizations, public, nonprofit, and commercial, will cooperate, collaborate, and find common ground in such a way that the range and impact of leisure time and pursuits can be experienced in a more integrated and blended manner with improved outcomes for people and society.
- The third component of the postpandemic era is economic. There are two distinct aspects of the economic component:
  1. First, there is the escalating revenues to be collected and managed by leisure pursuits that require a particular skill set.
  2. There is the need to recognize the economic impact of the other issues and

conditions that can be and are addressed by parks, recreation, and leisure.

Professionals need to be fully aware of the costs of

- physical and mental health,
- the environment,
- inequality,
- stress,
- lack of physical activity, and
- boredom, among others.

This working knowledge empowers the profession to devise and deliver experiences that ameliorate these conditions in a fiscal sense. For many aspects of society, money is the most telling indicator of value. The profession will need to create readily manageable ways to track the positive impact of our work and apply a dollar amount to that work. Even private and commercial organizations will need to go beyond profits and establish themselves as supporting good things, especially if an organization's operations have the potential to perpetuate environmental harm or social ills.

This means expanding knowledge beyond the rules of badminton or proper fertilization schedules for golf courses. Heavy emphasis should be on leadership skills necessary for success of the profession.

From Provider to Developer, Facilitator, and Enabler

A strategic plan for the future of recreation commissioned by the British Columbia Recreation and Parks Association, resulting in a 2007 report developed by Professional Environment and Recreation Consulting (PERC), advanced leadership adaption in the benefits era. One significant outcome of this report was the Elora Prescription. The Elora Prescription's main recommendation was that recreation professionals *should shift from being providers of services to becoming community developers-facilitators and enablers of recreation* (British Columbia Recreation and Parks Association, 2008).

If a profession is making a major shift from being a service provider to being a facilitator and enabler, it follows that the competencies and roles of those professionals will need to change as well. While this recommendation was created primarily for public and nonprofit organizations, the insights can be expanded to incorporate the entire range of opportunities within the industry.

The overriding motivation within the Elora Prescription was the shift to facilitating and enabling,

already in progress in small ways across various providers, and will form the basis for how the profession grows and thrives. Expanding its reach in the near future, it bodes well for addressing the human needs of people, blending with other entities, and creating positive economic impacts, both in real revenue and saved resources.

Potential Roles for Parks, Recreation, and Leisure

It only follows that the roles of people working in the various fields of the industry will change dramatically. Currently, job titles and job responsibilities generally refer to supervisors of facilities or program specialists, but in the future, there will be changes in both titles and responsibilities. Prospective tasks and responsibilities for this new era of parks and recreation include marketing-like approaches. In this instance, marketing does not have a commercial intent that only includes advertising and sales.

Marketing is currently defined by the American Marketing Association as "the activity, set of institutions, and processes for creating, communicating, delivering and exchanging offerings that have value for customers, clients, partners, and society at large" (American Marketing Association, n.d.). If you reread this definition, it is apparent that it can apply to all types of park and recreation organizations. Marketing is a vital, established component of our industry. Emerging roles in the parks and recreation industry include the following:

- Public good
- Barrier breaker
- Community builder
- Sustainability activator
- Experience maker
- Leisure facilitator

Public Good

Recall that the Elora Prescription and the CPRS VIP Plan projects addressed a new skill set for the public and nonprofit areas. While the public good is most often associated with the public and nonprofit sectors of the industry, there is evidence that even commercial endeavors are incorporating some aspects of public good for their participants. For example, to diminish instances of heat exhaustion and for the general public good, Epcot Center in Disney World recently added a free refreshment zone where visitors can rest and revive in a comfortable air-conditioned space and partake of complimentary refreshments. Furthermore, the commercial sector of parks, recreation, and leisure have incorporated the public good into revised cleaning and sanitation practices. Nike is one example of a corporation with a community focus; they provide funding for projects that use sports to help kids be successful and create more equality of play. Cruise lines, fitness centers, and spas, among others, have made meaningful changes not just for the public good but for persuading people to partake in their services.

With the mission of providing for the public good of residents or members, many public and nonprofit organizations are challenged by the demands to offer more specialized services, which often involve expensive expertise and costly facilities. This can be a daunting task. Many public agencies and YMCAs have found the operating cost of indoor swimming pools difficult to recover even with costly fees.

Some organizations offer a sliding scale for participation based on income or, in some cases, scholarships for programs or activities. While these approaches can work well, it often becomes a barrier for people who are reluctant to ask for or provide income information. In still other organizations, special days are offered in which certain groups can participate at no charge.

One growing approach is the use of a sliding fee based on the desired outcomes of the individual's participation or membership. For instance, the fee assigned to an activity that is primarily for the public good would be at no cost or have a nominal fee. A program or activity that indirectly benefits the community but primarily involves the participating individual would have a fee that may reflect recovering the direct costs only. If a program or activity was highly specialized and benefited individual participants specifically, then the fee would reflect the entire cost of the operation with a revenue percentage attached in some instances. See table 1.1 for examples.

The costly fees for usage or memberships often prohibit participation by individuals and families who cannot afford these services. This has resulted in equity issues and accessibility problems that prevent people from partaking in activities that are essential to their overall health and well-being and the well-being of society overall. Using sliding fee schedules can help to create a more equitable system.

Barrier Breaker

Not every American or Canadian experiences active and ongoing positive leisure participation; a number of factors can repress these behaviors. A category of barriers initially developed for adult learning has been used in a number of other fields. The most commonly cited barrier categories are dispositional, situational, and organizational.

- Dispositional barriers refer to the values, attitudes, and self-perceptions that people possess about themselves.
- Situational barriers reference the conflicts people have in attempting to balance all aspects of their lives, for instance, work and child care which organizations can find ways to ameliorate.
- Organizational barriers refer to unintentional blockages to participation such as time, location, easy access, and cost of services.

A bulletin *Look at Leisure #42: Desired Activities and Barriers to Participation* based on a 2000 survey conducted in Alberta, Canada, provides greater depth into barriers specific to recreation participation. Some of these barriers include

- awareness,
- accessibility,
- personal reasons,
- costs, and
- time conflicts, among others. (Alberta Community Development, n.d.).

Another organization that recognizes the need to improve levels of physical activity and break barriers is the American Heart Association. Acknowledging the present obstacles, they conducted a survey to reveal some of the more common barriers:

- Lack of time
- Lack of friends and family involved in physical activity

Table 1.1 Swimming Fees Based on a Sliding Schedule

Activity	Benefit level	Charge
Basic swim lessons	Public good, safety	No charge to residents or members
Swim team direct costs	Benefits individual and community	Reasonable charge to offset
Scuba lessons	Personal benefit to participant	Fee reflects full cost

Waukegan Park District of Waukegan, Illinois

One agency that provides balanced access and high-quality, specialized facilities to its residents in a fiscally responsible manner is the Waukegan Park District of Waukegan, Illinois. This award-winning agency has successfully integrated the basic needs of its residents with the ability to add world-class facilities at the same time, an excellent example of public good. Some of the facilities recently developed include

- a SplashZone featuring multigenerational water play with six slides and other play structures;
- the Field House Sports, Fitness & Aquatics Center, a modern, state-of-the-art indoor facility with great amenities at an affordable price; and
- the Greg Petry SportsPark featuring 14 soccer fields, 4 softball fields, parking and concessions for local and visiting teams, and specialized events for rental income.

The affordable facilities for residents are built intentionally to further the public good. The Splash-Zone is offered free to residents (both children and adults) while generating income from other user groups. The Field House Sports, Fitness & Aquatics Center houses a branch of the Waukegan Public Library and provides a venue for free swimming lessons for every second grader in the community. The SportsPark is a revenue producer, featuring high-quality sporting opportunities; however, it also provides 4 miles of pathways and walking trails, 16.5 acres of native plantings, and bioswales and rain gardens to provide additional beauty and water quality treatment.

While a number of these facilities are typical of park district offerings throughout Illinois, the Waukegan Park District is exceptional for two reasons. It serves a community that is very diverse and not especially wealthy, yet manages to serve residents and maintain financial responsibility (United States Census Bureau, n.d.).

- Lack of motivation or energy
- Lack of resources or equipment
- Family caregiving obligations (American Heart Association, n.d.).

Recognizing these potential barriers helps professionals adjust planning to maximize participation opportunities.

The Aspen Institute developed Project Play due to concerns that the average child spends less than three years playing a sport, quitting by age 11. This project conducted a survey in 2015 with the Utah State University's Families in Sports Lab. The survey included parents whose kids played sports and parents whose kids did not play sports, or who were forced to quit. In 2015, about one in three parents (32%) from households making less than $50,000 a year, told researchers that sports cost too much making it difficult for their child to continue participating. That is compared to the one in six parents (16%) from households making $50,000 a year or more who said the same.

The annual survey by the Sports & Fitness Industry Association (SFIA) in 2018 found that 33.4 percent of kids ages 6 to 12 from households making

$25,000 or less were physically inactive, compared to just 9.9 percent of kids from households making $100,000 or more (Solomon, 2019). It was apparent that family finances constituted a barrier.

Additionally, dispositional barriers might also exist limiting engagement in physical activity. The dispositional barriers are the most difficult to address and will require the human need knowledge and skills of professionals. Dispositional barriers include

- participants not feeling good about themselves,
- believing they lack the competency to try a particular activity, or
- feeling shy about joining an activity.

The situational barriers, such as time constraints and cost of participation, as well as the organizational barriers, are much easier for professionals to address, and it is critical that they do so.

Community Builders

Community building is a set of practices and approaches developed to address the social isolation and lack of belonging and sense of community by people across the world. Community building can include fostering connections among people or creating a collective space for people to gather (FairForce Consulting, 2021).

Parks, recreation, and leisure opportunities often involve physical spaces, which are a component of community building. These physical spaces could include parks, public squares, farmers markets, and garden plots, to identify a few. Commercial providers also host community-building activities such as the variety of birthday party packages offered at the Edmonton Mall in Canada. Birthday packages can be purchased for bowling, minigolf and adventure golf, or a water park. A sense of community, a sense of belonging, and the reduction of social isolation can also be addressed through the activities devised by the industry. Providing space for clubs and special interest groups is an example that successfully addresses these issues. The Edmonton Mall recognizes that birthday parties provide revenue, build community, bring would-be shoppers to the mall, and draw people to their facility.

In some instances, an entire community can grow and become a destination in its own right. Recognition of a community as being a special type of place has plenty of advantages. Walt Disney World, for example, transformed acres of swampland in little-known Orlando, Florida. Another example might be Branson, Missouri, which, over time, morphed into an entertainment center of the Midwest United States.

Sustainability Activator

This profession is in a unique position to share knowledge and information, provide examples, and advocate for the sustainability of the world. After all, we deal with most members of society through our programs and services. Since we provide enjoyable and worthwhile opportunities, people tend to like and respect our professionals. Plus, we have knowledge and information to share along with a plethora of opportunities that can be emulated by others. There are myriad examples in this category, including the use of recycled water for watering, the use of natural plants, and recycling of waste. It is important for sustainability activators to undertake these sustainable approaches, but they need to communicate their process and the rationale behind these efforts.

Another area in which sustainability can be enhanced is with programming, particularly

Hero Images Inc/DigitalVision/Getty Images

Outdoor programming provides opportunities for professionals to promote the stewardship of natural resources and wildlife.

programming in nature and open spaces with an emphasis on ways to continue to save these environments. Many organizations include animals and wildlife in these approaches because most people have a great fondness for them.

Experience Makers

Professionals throughout the industry have long been in the experience-making role. Special event planners who create and deliver events include planners of community and corporate activities as well as wedding and party planners. Experience makers are individuals who use their organizational and imaginative skills to immerse participants in a live event.

Neighborhoods, communities, corporations, and countries continually develop, partner with, or hire experience makers to immerse people in activities.

- Disney uses fireworks at the close of the day to extend the times people stay in the park or to provide an added perk to staying at a Disney hotel, which provides a view of the festive event.
- Private country and yacht clubs hold annual events to raise awareness of their existence to potential members and provide social opportunities for members and their guests.
- Corporations hire experience planners to organize in-house meetings, or to create more extravagant events, such as the launch of a new product or service.

The costs and economic impact of such activities and events vary extensively. For instance, the estimated total for the average wedding for 2021 stands at $22,500, but the prepandemic cost of a wedding was $28,000 in 2019 (Knueven, 2021). While this dollar amount is significant for the families and the couple, it pales in comparison to much larger events, such as the Sturgis Motorcycle Rally. The economic impact of the Sturgis Motorcycle Rally in South Dakota is in the range of $500 million to $1 billion. Reports have shown the city of Sturgis calculates that figure to be more than $800 million annually when combining Sturgis, the Black Hills, and the state of South Dakota. There could also be additional beneficiaries of the event that don't necessarily show up in official statistics such as residents who rent out homes during this time.

The Cactus League refers to baseball's spring training season in Arizona. This league contributed an estimated $363 million, with $237.7 million being part of the state's gross domestic product. If the season had not been cut short due to the pandemic, it is estimated that the economic impact would have been $644.2 million (Ruffner, 2022).

The other often overlooked role of an experience maker is the impact that slight changes or additions to programs and activities can make to positively alter the experience of the participants. A coffee station in a community or fitness center can transform the social experience of participants. Interactive games before a community concert or during a festival encourage people in attendance to meet other people and engage in family interactions.

Leisure Facilitator

Initially, terms such as *leisure counseling* and *leisure facilitation* centered on a specialized field of recreation called therapeutic recreation (TR). TR was usually assumed to be directed toward people with disabilities to teach skills and assist in opportunities for leisure. More recently, the term *leisure facilitation* has been expanded to extend beyond TR to all leisure and recreation providers with a focus on providing direction without maintaining full control.

This particular definition is seen as appropriate for the general population. If leisure facilitation is examined more closely, a number of the emerging roles previously discussed in this section are found within or support leisure facilitation.

THE VITALITY AND VIBRANCY OF THE FUTURE OF PARKS, RECREATION, AND LEISURE

It doesn't matter what aspect of parks, recreation, and leisure you select as a career option because each of the organizational configurations, whether public, nonprofit, or commercial, has the capacity to contribute to and enhance the vitality and vibrancy for the future of individuals, communities, businesses, and society.

What is vitality anyway? We use the term often, but various aspects and interpretations reveal the multifaceted meaning of the term as it relates to parks, recreation, and leisure.

People who have a sense of vitality possess the capacity to live, develop, and grow. To attain this capacity people must be physically and mentally well, which most public and nonprofit entities, as well as commercial fitness centers and athletic endeavors, can encourage and support. Vital communities are those that endure and contribute to the desirability and success of that town and its people, resources, and businesses. When professionals break barriers or facilitate leisure choices related to physical health, the health of individuals, a community, or society improves dramatically.

Similarly, vibrancy has numerous definitions that seem to build on the outcomes of vitality. Vibrancy can refer to an organism of any kind, human or otherwise. That organism must be vital in order to be vibrant because vibrancy refers to the intangible pulse of energy and activity that tends to be lively and vigorous. Whether it resonates initially or not, it is fairly easy to detect those people who are full of energy and activity, just as it would be for a community, an economy, or an organization.

What better endeavor is there than to be associated with an industry designed to enhance vitality and vibrancy? What's even more significant is the role of action within this profession. If you recall, the listing of emerging roles in parks, recreation, and leisure includes active words, those ending in "or" or "er," which means selecting this profession not only associates you with vibrancy and vitality, but indicates that you are a person who can make these qualities happen.

This concept of enhancing vitality and vibrancy is not new. The notable past of parks, recreation, and leisure led the way to helping people, communities,

© Sarah Martsolf-Brooks

OUTSTANDING GRADUATE

Background Information

Name: Sarah Martsolf-Brooks

Education: MS in parks, recreation, and tourism from the University of Utah

Credentials: AFO

Awards: Colorado Starburst Award (2016) for her Palisade Bike Skills Park

Affiliations: National Recreation and Park Association (NRPA), Colorado Parks and Recreation Association (CPRA)

Career Information

Position: Palisade Parks and Recreation (Town of Palisade, Colorado)

Organization: Upon completing my master's degree at the University of Utah, I was hired by the town of Palisade in Colorado as the recreation director. Palisade is a small, agricultural community of 3,000 people, known for abundant peach orchards, charming wineries, and plenty of outdoor recreation. Palisade also plays host to several special events, which draw in more than 40,000 tourists throughout the year. Town employees often find themselves navigating multiple jobs, with only 30 full-time employees spread out over five departments. The recreation department consists of one full-time employee, three seasonal college interns, and specialty instructors who are hired on as contractors.

Job description: Working in Palisade was most attractive because it gave me the opportunity to build a new recreation department from the ground up. The first programs I started in 2011 included basic fitness classes, DIY activities, family game nights, and outdoor activities, such as day trips and hikes. My job is rarely the same from day to day, with job duties that include marketing, program and event planning, program facilitation, grant writing, facilitating park projects, supervising interns, overseeing aquatics, attending outreach committees, merchandising for events, and coordinating volunteers. What I like most are leading outdoor adventures, bringing my dogs to work, watching new friendships grow, planning park projects, and coaching the summer swim team. However, with limited staff time, it is difficult to expand program offerings without taking away from already-successful programs.

Career path: I got my start in parks and recreation as a lifeguard with the City of Fruita, Colorado. Soon after, I progressed into pool management, worked on special events, and taught fitness classes. After completing a bachelor's degree in sports and exercise science, I worked as a personal trainer and coached rugby. I also have experience in campus recreation from both Northern Colorado and the University of Utah.

Advice for Undergraduates

The subject field of public parks and recreation offers a rewarding career because there are many opportunities to make an impact. Through trails and open spaces, people of all economic levels can be encouraged to stay active, children can be inspired to become stewards of the environment through after-school programs, and older adults can challenge age stereotypes through outdoor adventure. My advice to students is to search for jobs of interest, not based on salary range; find something that you will love getting out of bed for each day—a career that will offer challenges and opportunities to achieve new goals.

and society become both vital and vibrant. Recall the efforts of some pioneers in the field who significantly contributed to the individual vitality of immigrants, urban dwellers, and underactive children. Our beginnings were focused almost entirely on the well-being and growth of people. When considering more recent developments, it is clear that newer additions to the parks, recreation, and leisure realm (such as special events, theme parks, and travel opportunities) are part of what makes people and places vibrant. The future holds even greater opportunities and challenges for those pursuing a career in this diverse field. It is certainly a notable past and a bright future.

Review Questions

1. Which era described the period in North America when the parks and recreation profession emphasized extra support for large segments of the population?

2. Which era described a shift in perspective toward using the parks and recreation profession to improve individual lives?

3. What are some significant issues related to the parks and recreation profession relevant to the postpandemic era?

4. What are the three pillars of the National Recreation and Park Association?

Go to HK*Propel* to complete the activities for this chapter.

CHAPTER 2

History of Recreation

Tristan Hopper, Jill Sturts, Douglas Kennedy, and Jerome F. Singleton

" Those who cannot remember the past are condemned to repeat it. "

George Santayana, Spanish and American philosopher

Library of Congress, Prints & Photographs Division, LC-B2- 2956-6

─────────────────── **LEARNING OUTCOMES** ───────────────────

After reading this chapter, you should be able to do the following:

> Identify and explain the historical development of recreation and leisure in prehistoric societies
> Describe the historical development of recreation and leisure in ancient Rome and Greece, Europe, the United States, and Canada
> Describe the impact of the COVID-19 pandemic on recreation and leisure
> Explain the role of colonization in recreation and leisure within Canadian history
> Explain and describe how government and professional organizations influenced the development of recreation and leisure in Canada and the United States

History shapes what we understand today. To appreciate how recreation and leisure services are now delivered in the United States and Canada, you must understand the historical periods and societal expectations that influenced the development of these services. North American societies have been affected by the generations of immigrants that have landed, settled, and influenced recreation and leisure. By understanding how leisure has emerged, it is possible to see how history often repeats itself. What we see today is similar to what happened long ago. Whether lessons can be learned from the past undoubtedly requires an appreciation and understanding of our history.

TRACING THE ROOTS OF LEISURE

Past definitions of leisure influence our understanding of leisure today, so we will trace the development of leisure from prehistoric societies to the Protestant Reformation.

Prehistoric Societies

People in prehistoric societies were primarily concerned with survival (Shivers & deLisle, 1997). Hunting and gathering were the primary activities and provided resources to maintain life. There was little free time as we know it today. Work, survival, and rest melded to become one life-sustaining activity. Once prehistoric people could create tools and were able to store information in a larger brain, more free time became available. This free time was used for ritualization or ceremonial acts (Ibrahim, 1991). These acts often focused on celebrations of successful hunts, offerings for bountiful harvests, and beseeching the gods for their favor. It is believed that play-like activities were also critical to the needs of

emerging tribes. These activities depicted historical events, transportation practices, war games, and the use of farm tools. Play prepared children for their responsibilities as youths and adults and became a way of achieving solidarity and morality. It also became a healing experience and a means of communication, and it provided pleasure and entertainment. As societies emerged, play-like activities were also a means to relax, recover, and replenish strength after working (Kraus, 1971). These emerging societies also developed structures that allowed people to focus on specific work roles: One person could focus on being a hunter, and another could be a builder. Once such roles were established, more resources were available for activities that did not relate to sustaining life. Thus, for the first time, people had greater opportunities for leisure. We still see this pattern today: People specialize in a vocation needed by society and rely on the specialties of others for their own well-being.

Ancient Greece

Ancient Greece (1200-500 BC) is an excellent example of how societal structure influenced the development of leisure. Greek citizens, who could vote and participate in state affairs, sought to become the well-rounded ideal of that era. They embraced what was known as the **Athenian ideal**, which was a combination of soldier, athlete, artist, statesman, and philosopher. They valued developing in all areas rather than focusing on one area of expertise as is valued today. This was only possible because the tasks of everyday living were provided by laborers or enslaved people (Shivers & deLisle, 1997) who outnumbered the citizens approximately three to one. Those who were freed from everyday tasks had the opportunity to pursue the range of activities necessary to become the Athenian ideal.

Leisure was very important in Greek society. The Greek philosopher Plato and his student, Aristotle, supported this in their beliefs that virtuous and constructive leisure activities were the route to happiness and fulfillment. **Contemplation**, which involved the pursuit of truth and understanding, was thought to be the highest form of leisure (Dare et al., 1987). Athenian philosophers strongly believed in the unity of mind and body and valued each. Play was perceived to be essential to the healthy growth of children from both a physical and social perspective (Ibrahim, 1979). Citizens regarded leisure as an opportunity for intellectual cultivation, music, theater, and poetry as well as political and philosophical discussions. The concept *schole* meant to have quiet or peace. It meant having time for oneself and being occupied in something for its own sake, such as music, poetry, the company of friends, or the exercise of speculative faculties (Ibrahim, 1991). Schole embraced the experience and not the outcome. This is different from today, when the pursuit of an activity is often valued only if something tangible, such as a victory, mastery of a skill, or a specific expectation, is gained.

An important part of ancient Greek culture, and perhaps at odds with the notion of schole, was passion for games. Athletic games were held to celebrate religious rites and heroes, for entertainment, and for pleasure. Only men played the games; women were often excluded from public life (Shivers & deLisle, 1997). Four Panhellenic games were very popular among the spectators and athletes: the Olympic Games, the Pythian Games, the Nemian Games, and the Isthmian Games. These were thought to be held in honor of the gods, although others suggest that they commemorated the death of mythic mortals and monsters (Ibrahim, 1979; Mendelsohn, 2004). When athletic games were held, wars often ceased so participants could compete (Poliakoff, 1993). The early Olympic Games, which honored Zeus, included chariot races, combat events, boxing, wrestling, footraces, and the pentathlon, which was a five-sport event that embraced the Athenian ideal. Athletes also competed individually rather than on teams and represented their home villages (Ibrahim, 1991). This is similar to the modern Olympic Games in which participants represent their countries.

The early Olympics were extremely serious events. It was not uncommon for participants in aggressive sports such as *pankration* (a combination of boxing and wrestling) to be encouraged to fight to the death. This fate was seen as especially noble because it would immortalize the competitor in story for generations to come as having sacrificed his life in the pursuit of victory. So important were the Olympics that Athenians would place an olive wreath on their door when a boy was born, thus signaling the hope that he would become an Olympian (Mendelsohn, 2004). This seriousness of purpose and the use of leisure time to develop sport-specific skills are still found today. We work at getting better so we can play a sport well. Like the ancient Greeks, we claim to value well-rounded people, yet parents increasingly encourage their children to specialize in one sport, which is often played year-round, so they have the greatest opportunity to become better than their peers. Success in sports now rivals that of the adulation shown to the earliest Olympic victors, so it should be no surprise that the world finds itself facing an epidemic of competitors turning to illegal performance-enhancing drugs to ensure victory.

Ancient Rome

The emergence of Rome as a dominant society influenced how leisure was perceived at that time. Rome conquered the majority of Europe and Asia after about 265 BC and emerged as a dominant power in the Mediterranean (Shivers & deLisle, 1997). The Roman Empire influenced the judicial systems and societies it conquered by attempting to overwrite with its own culture what had come before. The Roman government was based on distinct classifications of citizens.

- Senators, who were the richest, owned most of the land, and had most of the power
- Curiales, who owned 25 or more acres (10 ha) of land and were office holders or tax collectors
- Plebes, or free common men, who owned small properties or were tradesmen or artisans
- Coloni, who were lower-class tenants on land
- Indentured slaves

Early Roman enslaved people were captured in war and served as agricultural laborers. Much later, large numbers of captive people from Asia, Greece, and central Europe became enslaved and were exploited by their owners (Shivers & deLisle, 1997). As in societies that came before it, the opportunity to participate in leisure during the Roman era was limited to those who had the appropriate resources. The greater a person's standing, the greater their opportunity was for freedom from the daily requirements necessary to live a comfortable life. Senators enjoyed almost unlimited leisure, while coloni struggled to make a comfortable life. This is not unlike the present day, in which distinct economic classes enjoy varying degrees and types of leisure.

Different from the ancient Greeks, who saw leisure as an opportunity for well-rounded development, Romans perceived leisure to be primarily rest from work. Considering that the Romans were on an almost constant crusade to dominate foreign cultures, this viewpoint was necessary and allowed recuperation before the next crusade. Play then, in the case of the Romans, served utilitarian rather than aesthetic or spiritual purposes (Horna, 1994). As the Roman Empire grew and the increasing availability of enslaved people decreased the amount of daily work people were required to do, leisure time increased and was increasingly used to control the masses. During Emperor Claudius' reign (41-54 AD), Rome had 59 public holidays and 95 game days, and by 354 AD, there were more than 200 public holidays and 175 game days. The reason for this was simple: As Romans became less occupied with work, they became increasingly bored and critical of the government. The government then attempted to pacify unrest by providing pleasurable experiences through spectacle and celebrations of holidays. What they called **bread and circuses**, which consisted of free food and entertainment, provided the framework for Roman society (Horna, 1994).

To hold people's attention, leisure activities became increasingly hedonistic and shocking. When battles between gladiators became less interesting, animals from foreign lands were brought in to become part of the savagery seen in the great coliseums. When the scale of those battles became ordinary, artificial lakes were created by enslaved people who were then used to recreate bloody sea battles depicting successful conquests. This focus on the entertainment of the masses, instead of their participation, has led some historians to argue that one of the reasons for the fall of the Roman Empire was its inability to deal with mass leisure (McLean et al., 2005). This concern is often heard today regarding current leisure habits. Increasingly, it appears that people are more content to be spectators than participants. Some sporting events, such as football and boxing, look similar to spectacles seen in ancient Rome. In fact, it isn't uncommon to hear the participants in these events referred to as gladiators. Should this be a concern? Well, with the rate of obesity greatly increasing in Canada and the United States, it is worth considering whether the focus on mass leisure seen during the Roman era (and perhaps the eventual outcome) is being repeated.

Leisure in ancient Rome focused on spectacle and entertainment for the masses instead of participation. Today, some sporting events such as boxing also take on the appearance of spectacle, and sometimes the participants are even called gladiators.

Al Bello/Getty Images

Middle Ages

With the collapse of the Roman Empire, the Catholic Church became the dominant structure in Europe (Shivers & deLisle, 1997). The Catholic Church rejected the activities that the Roman Empire had accepted, including its hedonistic ways (Horna, 1994). One example of this was the fact that people involved in theater could not be baptized. The concept of idleness as the great enemy of the soul emerged, and doing nothing was thought to be evil. During this time, the church wielded great influence over the social order, which consisted of nobility and peasants. The clergy dictated societal values whose adoption would lead to saving souls, and this was the highest goal at the time. Although the Catholic Church influenced what were acceptable and unacceptable leisure activities, many rules were so strict that at the end of this period the church went through a renaissance in which individuals within the church developed different perspectives. This renaissance saw a renewed appreciation for a variety of leisure activities.

Renaissance

Spreading from the 14th century in Italy to the 16th century in northern Europe, this era saw power shift from the church to the nobility. Previously ostracized by the church, artists were now supported and encouraged by the nobility to express their art (Horna, 1994). Play was perceived to be an important part of education. During the 16th century, Francois Rabelais (1490-1553) emphasized the need for physical exercise and games. Michel Eyquem de Montaigne (1533-1592) supported the concept of unity of mind, body, and spirit, which opposed the medieval ideal of separation, or dualism, of the mind and body. John Locke (1632-1704) was so concerned with play as a medium of learning that he made the distinction between play and recreation: Recreation was not being idle; it provided a specific benefit by easing and helping to recover the people wearied by their work. Jean-Jacques Rousseau (1712-1778) advocated for the full freedom of physical activity rather than constraint. It was during the Renaissance that an increased interest in play, both as a form of popular entertainment and as a medium of education, developed.

The following three types of parks emerged during the late Renaissance:

1. Royal hunting preserves that provided wild-game hunting

2. Formal garden parks in which participants viewed their surroundings much as you would experience a museum

3. English garden parks that emphasized interacting with the environment through activities such as picnics and other restful pursuits

These parks, developed by the nobility for their own use, were often seen as status symbols. People caught hunting in a royal hunting preserve who were not nobility were often killed. Still, the growth of parks within the nobility provided other classes with an understanding of what was possible and led to the first thoughts of parks for the masses.

Protestant Reformation

During the Protestant Reformation (16th century), Martin Luther and others questioned the accepted practices of the Catholic Church and split off into other Protestant religions. Each religious group governed the perception of what was acceptable as leisure. Play was frowned on as evil by certain churches during this transition. John Calvin believed that success on earth determined your place in heaven. With that in mind, extraordinarily hard work and lack of leisure time were signs of great success. The influence of the Protestant and Catholic churches in Europe was critical to the earliest development of leisure in Canada and the United States because settlers came primarily from Europe and brought these values and social structures to the New World. We also see that immigrant groups in Canada and the United States participate in different recreation activities, have different perspectives on leisure, and expose others to different beliefs.

DEVELOPMENT OF RECREATION IN THE UNITED STATES

Recreation developed over time in the United States and Canada. Exploration in Canada began in the 11th century and in the United States in the 15th century. It continued to develop as the populations in both colonies grew. By the late 19th century, governments in both countries began to play a role in providing recreation and leisure services. This role changed and developed throughout the early part of the 20th century. Never static, recreation and leisure in the United States evolved through wars and the depression, longer and shorter workweeks, and other periods. In Canada, the post–World War

II era brought renewed interest in recreation services, but later declines in resources meant a lack of funding for recreation. One consequence of this ever-changing face of recreation and leisure was the emergence of **professional organizations** that addressed the needs of both countries' citizens. In the 21st century, challenges such as lack of funding for recreation continue, and demographic changes, such as population aging, affect service provision.

Early Settlement

To fully understand leisure during the settlement period, it is important to recognize the purpose of the earliest inhabitants and visitors. Christopher Columbus opened up the Americas when exploration for the purposes of trade, profit, and control resulted in circumnavigation of the world (Shivers & deLisle, 1997). Europeans seeking adventure, wealth, or freedom from persecution arrived in the United States and brought their traditions and beliefs. Two early colonies founded in the United States were in Virginia and New England (Shivers & deLisle, 1997). Prior to this, Native Americans (whose ancestors had lived in North America for thousands of years before Europeans arrived) had developed their own forms of recreation. Although

their activities often celebrated religious rituals, they were also often highly competitive. One of the well-known recreation activities that is still being played today is lacrosse. Given its common name by French settlers, this activity was common throughout Native American nations in the east, the Great Lakes region, and the south; in each area were variations of the same activity. The game was often filled with traditions and ceremony, was used to release aggression or settle disputes, and often included wagering (Vennum, n.d.). Specific Native American nations developed their own unique activities. For example, the Illinois developed a straw game in which wagering revolved around who could guess the correct number of straws after a large pile was divided. Although this was often a male-dominated game, women were known to participate in their own game involving plum stones that were used like modern dice (Illinois State Museum, n.d.).

Virginia

The settlement in Virginia, established in Jamestown in the 17th century, was composed of aristocracy, adventurers, and traders. These people loved sports, games, theater, books, music, and exercise and continued to pursue these activities once they arrived. However, with little free time available as they tried

Men of the Choctaw nation playing lacrosse.

"Ball Players." Artist: George Catlin CC0

to survive, the governors banned recreational activities (Shivers & deLisle, 1997). One of the primary reasons for the strict control over these activities was the harsh conditions the colonists faced and the need for diligence to ensure survival. The conditions were so difficult that of the 8,000 colonists who arrived in Virginia by 1625, only 1,200 survived an additional 10 years (Edgington et al., 1998). The Virginia Assembly enforced observance of the Sabbath, prohibited gambling, and regulated drinking (Ibrahim, 1991). Penalties for partaking in Sunday amusements or failure to attend church services included imprisonment. Activities common to the weekend, including dancing, fishing, hunting, and cardplaying, were among those strictly prohibited (Kraus, 2001). These restrictions were lifted once survival became easier and a leisure class began to emerge through the exploitation of indentured servants and enslaved people. This societal arrangement mirrored those discussed previously in which the absence of a significant and identifiable middle class suggested the development of a leisure class. With laws and social mores relaxing in response to a social class seeking new ways to take advantage of its free time, activities such as cockfighting, dice games, football, forms of bowling, and tennis (all of which were illegal) became more common among the privileged but were still unavailable to the working class (Kraus, 2001).

New England

Although the settlement in New England also had to fight for its survival, its settlers were Calvinists escaping persecution in Europe. All forms of recreation were illegal, and the Puritan ethic restricted social activities. This philosophy valued frugality, hard work, self-discipline, and observance of civil and religious codes. Pleasure was considered to be the devil's work, and time not spent in worship or productive labor was considered wasteful (Shivers & deLisle, 1997). People were expected to behave religiously all the time, and thus work became a holy task. If daily activities belonged to God, then God's time should not be wasted in trivial pursuits. This Protestant work ethic often removed pleasure from lives. Leisure was considered a lure to sin and a threat to godliness. Puritans believed that they should avoid pleasures in their own lives and struggle against pleasure in the community (Cross, 1990). New England Puritans banned labor, travel, and recreation on Sundays. Recreation was tolerated, however, if it could help with work, such as quilting bees and barn raisings (Cross, 1990).

Eventually, the strict control over the masses could not be sustained. Towns saw construction of meeting houses and taverns. The love of games and sports

was rediscovered in these taverns. Hunting became a popular leisure activity among the men because game was abundant. Training days, in which young men learned how to serve in the militia, were held in Boston, and these were celebrated at the local tavern. Taverns were also used for cockfighting, animal baiting, dances, and orchestras. The church during this period of the 18th century, while increasingly concerned with these activities, was content to allow their participation in the relatively controlled setting of public facilities. Acceptable leisure activities included public readings and moral lectures. Amateur musical performances were occasionally tolerated. Plays were eventually accepted in Boston and Philadelphia. New York City had its own theater. The mercantile class enjoyed many leisure activities including sleigh rides, horse races, balls, and card parties (Ibrahim, 1991). The trend of allowing questionable activities to occur behind closed doors and encouraging acceptable activities to be held in public is still seen today. Blue laws restrict the sale of items such as liquor on Sundays. Laws often prohibit activities such as drinking in public, and taxes might support community events such as picnics and parades that are seen as more wholesome.

Early Park Development

An important development during the early colonial period was the realization that open space was important to growing communities. The Boston Common, a 48-acre (19 ha) oasis of nature in the middle of the city, was established in 1634 and is viewed as the first municipal park (Kraus, 2001). This influenced the creation of laws in Massachusetts requiring that bodies of water larger than 10 acres (4 ha) be open to the public for fishing and hunting (Edgington et al., 1998). As communities grew and the first organized urban planning efforts took shape, further efforts were undertaken to ensure open space was provided. The center of Philadelphia is a prime example. Several north–south streets are intersected by streets named after species of trees. Within each of the resulting quadrants is a park area that provides a touch of nature within the metropolis. The creation of Central Park in New York City is probably the best-known example of early urban open-space provision.

Frederick Law Olmsted, who is considered the founder of American landscape architecture, was hired to design New York's Central Park in 1858 and to design municipal parks in Brooklyn, Philadelphia, Detroit, Chicago, and other areas in the late 19th century. He adapted the English style of a natural park to the rectangular restrictions of

American parks (Ibrahim, 1991). He also established the initial purpose for city parks throughout the United States: to provide a space for contemplative leisure (Ibrahim, 1991). Organized and structured sports that are common in parks today were not permitted. Instead, the parks were initially intended to soothe the minds of newcomers to North America who were facing an increasingly industrial age and limited amounts of open space (Kraus, 2001). Olmsted felt that parks should be large enough to shut out the city and that green spaces could inspire courtesy, self-control, and temperance. Olmsted's parks involved walkways, natural vistas, and landscaping to create a feeling of nature in the middle of the city (Cross, 1990). Parks developed by Olmsted were an attempt to regain the country-side in the city. They had artificial lakes, regularly mowed grass, and pathways for carriages. Although the parks existed for passive use, they were full of people enjoying activities such as baseball, cycling, skating, and horseback riding. Refreshment stands and restrooms were included for people spending the day at the park (Goodale & Godbey, 1988).

The Playground Movement

The **playground movement** was first adopted by New York City when land was allocated for Central Park in 1855 (Ibrahim, 1991). Its purpose was to provide passive rest and aesthetics. In Chicago, however, Washington Park was opened in 1876 for more active sport. In Boston, Dr. Maria Zakrzewska promoted the concept of a sand garden that would eventually shape the idea of playgrounds for generations to come. In 1868, city leaders determined that an ever increasing number of children without constructive free-time pursuits needed more beneficial outlets, so they developed the first organized playground program. It grew until 1886, when the addition of a pile of sand changed the notion of playgrounds. Started by school leaders and well-meaning citizens, a sand garden was created in Boston solely for use by children. Although this may seem commonplace today, for most children it was the first time they had ever played in sand or experienced a space designed for the active use of children only. It was so successful that city leaders produced 21 more playgrounds of the type by 1889. The popularity of this effort grew until many more playgrounds were created in New York City, Chicago, and other areas (Edgington et al., 1998; Kraus, 2001).

Government Involvement

As the United States' population grew, the government became increasingly concerned with the

The sheep meadow in New York City's Central Park in the early 20th century. As you can see, the park's designer, Frederick Law Olmsted, was successful in bringing the countryside to the city.

national quality of life. In 1880, President James Garfield stated: "We may divide the whole struggle of the human race into two chapters: first, the fight to get leisure; and then the second fight of civilization—what shall we do with our recreation when we get it" (Kraus, 1990, p. 154). One major issue confronting government leaders was the amount of natural resources that would be available for future generations. Forests were being eliminated at breakneck speed to support massive amounts of construction. The conservation movement was born out of this concern and was intended to protect the national heritage of America, not to influence specific leisure behavior of Americans (Ibrahim, 1991). Mindful of what many thought was a perilous decline in available natural resources, the Forest Service was created in 1906 and the National Park Service was created in 1916. Yosemite Valley and the Mariposa Grove were granted to California to protect and preserve for future generations. Yellowstone National Park in Wyoming was the first national park, and Yosemite was taken back by the federal government and became the second (Ibrahim, 1991).

While the conservation movement sought to preserve natural resources that were typically far from the centers of the population, recreation participation within urban areas steadily increased. Perhaps no era of American history so embraced the free-spirited notion of leisure than the Roaring '20s. This era saw the widespread increase of commercial recreation and disposable income and the use of recreation as a sign of status. However, the economic pendulum swung back quickly and in a shocking reversal of fortune: The stock market crash and the ensuing Great Depression quickly ended the lifestyle of the Roaring '20s. The stock market crash led to never-before-seen levels of unemployment, poverty, and inadequate housing. With local governments struggling, the federal government assumed a larger role in the provision of parks and recreation (Goodale & Godbey, 1988). Massive unemployment stimulated a growing concern for the mass leisure that was now thrust on the unemployed. This sparked a new discussion of how people defined free time. Studies showed that people were humiliated by unemployment and that leisure was meaningless without a job (Cross, 1990).

During this period, the U.S. federal government tried a variety of actions to combat the economic peril that befell many. One effort included an attempt to spread jobs by implementing a 34-hour workweek (Ibrahim, 1991). The creation of the Works Progress Administration (WPA) had the biggest effect on the following generations. This

massive organization sought to put citizens back to work through a variety of methods. One of the most important to parks and recreation was the branch of the WPA known as the Civilian Conservation Corps (CCC). The CCC was responsible for countless construction projects that provided a variety of recreation areas, many of which are still in use today. To get an idea of the scale of the CCC's work, consider that it employed enough workers to complete the following: the building of 800 state parks, 46,854 bridges, 28,087 miles (45,200 km) of trails, 46,000 campground facilities, 204 lodges and museums, and the planting of more than 3 billion trees (Edgington et al., 1998).

The increase in facilities provided by the federal government spurred state and local governments to establish and enhance their own agencies responsible for recreation. After six CCC camps were created in Virginia in 1933, the state created its first state parks from the camps and opened them all on the same day in 1936 (Virginia State Parks, n.d.). In Missouri, after 4,000 men were employed by the CCC to construct facilities, the state developed an independent state park board in 1937 (Missouri State Parks and Historic Sites, n.d.). Other states, such as Delaware, Florida, and Georgia, also created state park systems during this time to address the increasing popularity of the new sites provided by the federal government.

Professional Organizations

Professional organizations emerged early in the United States. In 1906, Jane Addams, Joseph Lee, Luther Gulick, and others organized the Playground Association of America. In 1911, the name was changed to the Playground and Recreation Association of America. In 1926, the name was changed again to the National Recreation Association. As employment in leisure-related agencies grew and professional preparation and competence continued to be of interest, additional professional organizations were formed. Initially acting independently, the National Recreation Association, the American Institute of Park Executives, the National Conference on State Parks, the American Association of Zoological Parks and Aquariums, and the American Recreation Society merged in 1965 to become the National Recreation and Park Association (NRPA). Shortly thereafter, the National Association of Recreation Therapists and the Armed Forces Section of the American Recreation Society were added. Even after the American Association of Zoological Parks and Aquariums left to form its own organization again, the NRPA was the largest organization in the United States to serve the needs of the general public and professionals in the promotion of parks, recreation, and leisure–related opportunities (Ibrahim, 1991). The mission of the NRPA is "to advance parks, recreation and environmental conservation efforts that enhance the quality of life for all people" (NRPA, n.d., para. 3). Affiliate parks and recreation associations within each state further address this mission. These affiliates, such as the Virginia Recreation and Park Society, the Florida Recreation and Park Association, and the Texas Recreation and Park Society, serve their members through local outreach that meets the demands of professionals who serve unique populations.

The American Alliance for Health, Physical Education, Recreation and Dance (AAHPERD) was founded in 1885 when William Gilbert Anderson invited a group of people who were working in the gymnastics field to discuss their profession (AAHPERD, n.d.). In 2014, AAHPERD changed its name to SHAPE America (Society of Health and Physical Educators). The name change was initiated to provide a more inclusive and visible approach for health and physical educators and for parents, school administrators, and the media. The professional organization's mission is to advance professional practice and promote research related to health and physical education, physical activity, dance, and sport. The organization is committed to ensuring that all children can lead healthy, physically active lives (SHAPE America, n.d.).

Post–World War II Growth

After World War II, recreation and leisure saw changes, challenges, and growth in several areas. Among these were the following:

- *Therapeutic recreation*. The extraordinary increase in the number of citizens who faced disabling injuries from their wartime fighting provided a challenge. The use of recreation as therapy and the birth of therapeutic recreation as a distinct discipline occurred largely from its provision in government-sponsored Department of Veteran's Affairs (VA) hospitals. As recreation therapy grew and expanded from VA facilities to services provided in the community, a growing need for training and education evolved. Colleges and universities filled this need by creating a distinct body of knowledge. Professional organizations such as the National Therapeutic Recreation Society (NTRS) and the American Association for

Therapeutic Recreation were formed (in 1966 and 1984, respectively), although the NTRS has since disbanded. Professional certification of recreation therapists was provided by the National Council for Therapeutic Recreation Certification in 1981.

- *Concern for youth fitness*. A critical development in recreation and leisure came about in 1956. A battery of physical fitness tests comparing U.S. youth to their peers in Europe produced shocking results that showed European children to be in much better condition. Having been involved in two world wars within the last half-century, the government, under President Eisenhower, created the President's Council on Youth Fitness in 1956. Eventually changing its name in 1966 to the President's Council on Physical Fitness and Sports, this initiative promotes health and wellness for all ages by first introducing physical skill testing and awards in schools and offering active lifestyle awards for all ages. In 1983, Congress declared May National Physical Fitness and Sports Month. These initiatives mirrored a growth in mandatory physical education classes throughout the school year. Unfortunately, as time passed, the concern for youth fitness and the need for physical education were eclipsed by the concern for academic achievement in other areas. Perhaps it is worth considering whether this decreased emphasis on physical education in schools is just one factor in the sedentary lifestyle that many see as contributing to a growing obesity epidemic in the United States.

- *Concern for youth sports*. In addition to an increased concern for youth fitness, youth sports have evolved and grown. The National Alliance for Youth Sport (NAYS), a nonprofit organization that promotes the value of sports and physical activity as part of the emotional, physical, social, and mental development of children, provides support for youth sports administrators, coaches, parents, and officials. Increased parental involvement and single-sport specialization have surfaced as two trends in youth sports (NAYS, n.d.).

DEVELOPMENT OF RECREATION IN CANADA

How did recreation emerge in Canada? The following sections provide insights into the development of recreation in Canada.

Early Settlement

Canada, a frontier settlement, consisted of a few homesteads and resource-dependent rural communities (Harrington, 1996). The economic well-being of these communities was based on natural resources such as fishing, logging, and agriculture. The first European explorers arrived in Canada in the 11th century. The first permanent European settlements were founded in the 1600s (Francis et al., 1988). However, before the Europeans began to explore and settle, there were many different nations and languages among Canada's Indigenous peoples (LaPierre, 1992). The origin of Canada's first people is uncertain. Some argue that the Indigenous peoples emerged on the continent, and others argue that they migrated from Siberia. Regardless of their origin, Indigenous peoples were living in North America at least 10,000 years before the arrival of the Europeans (Francis et al., 1988). The Indigenous peoples in southern Canada enjoyed traditional games, music, and storytelling. Traditional games were based on hunting and fishing skills (Karlis, 2004). The Inuit, who lived in the North, played many games including *nalukatook*, which involved bouncing on a walrus hide held by others, and *ipirautaqurnia*, which involved flipping a whip accurately. *Baggataway,* which was played by the Algonquins and Iroquois and involved a curved, netted stick, is now called lacrosse (Karlis, 2016).

Between 1604 and 1607, the first Acadian settlement was formed when the Frenchman Samuel de Champlain and his men explored the coastline of the Maritimes and wintered at Port Royal, the first agricultural settlement in Canada. In 1606, Champlain's men took part in Canada's first theatrical production, and in 1607, Champlain founded the Order of Good Cheer, which was the first social club in Canada. However, the colony was abandoned in 1607 due to lack of money (Francis et al., 1988). In 1608, Champlain constructed a habitation, or wooden buildings forming a quadrangle, which became the center of the first permanent French settlement. The French colony existed only for trading fur, and it grew very slowly. By 1620, there were only 60 people in New France. However, by the 1650s, the French colony began growing steadily, and by the late 1700s, the language was altered by settlers to reflect traditions of the emerging country; thus, the identity of Canadians emerged.

While the French were settling New France, the British were settling colonies in Newfoundland, Virginia, New York, and Massachusetts. They also sponsored expeditions north of New France, and in 1610 and 1611, Henry Hudson discovered the Hudson Bay. Fifty years later, British fur-trading posts were established around the bay (Francis et al., 1988).

Because early settlement in Canada focused on the fur trade, and farming in Canada required a great deal of hard labor and preparation for winter, recreation opportunities were limited for the early settlers (Harrington, 1996). Men and women enjoyed activities such as curling, skating, ice hockey, snowshoeing, and tobogganing in the winter. Drama and music were also popular leisure activities at that time (McFarland, 1970).

Indigenous Assimilation Through Colonial Recreation in Canada

Recreation within Canada has a rocky historical journey. The focus of early recreation programming was targeted toward correcting improper behavior and creating a productive population, including that of Indigenous peoples. To the organizers, this was seen as an efficient and less demeaning way to shape the population. As it relates to the discussion for this section of our chapter, recreation and leisure programming have historically been, and continue to be, used as a form of colonial assimilation for Indigenous peoples in Canada (Forsyth, 2013; Forsyth & Giles, 2013; Paraschak, 2013). According to Forsyth (2013), physical practices linked to schooling constituted a new form of disciplinary society in Canada in the late 19th century. This was particularly true for Indigenous people, whose cultural traditions had increasingly been subjected to intense scrutiny in an effort by religious and government agents to understand, control, and ultimately reshape those practices. The prevalent restrictions were those placed on traditional Indigenous ceremonies, for instance, the potlatch and sun dance in the 1880s. There was a widespread belief among the broader population that these and other Indigenous customs were uncivilized, and that Indigenous people needed to engage in more productive forms of behavior so that they could contribute to the growing Canadian state (p. 21).

Indigenous children were often forcefully removed from their homes through the Indian Residential School program. Led by the Christian church, Indigenous children were forced to assimilate to Western practices. This included their participation in Westernized recreation programming. Paraschak's (2013) research shows how colonial threads still linger in Canada's approach to recreation because Indigenous understandings are actively undercut. Paraschak explained that this is done through inequitable power relations around who gets to define recreation or leisure, how sport or wellness structures operate, and how resources are allocated. As numerous Indigenous scholars have commented, it is vital that the recognition of Indigenous practices (e.g., wellness, sport, leadership) not be grounded in state affirmations of dominant Western discourse (Byrd, 2011; Coulthard, 2014; Hokowhitu, 2014). Recognition through Western discourse reinscribes inequitable colonial relations by stripping self-determination from Indigenous peoples by framing Indigenous practices and lives through a Western lens.

In response to the reverberant colonial threads within recreation and leisure spaces, the Canadian government began its path to reconciliation. In 2015, a group of key stakeholders cocreated through consultation Canada's Truth and Reconciliation Commission's (TRC) (2015) Calls to Action. Within the calls to action, numbers 87 to 91 specifically address the important role of recreation and leisure in advancing the process of reconciliation. For example, in call-to-action number 89, the TRC states the following:

> We call upon the federal government to amend the Physical Activity and Sport Act to support reconciliation by ensuring that policies to promote physical activity as a fundamental element of health and well-being, reduce barriers to sports participation, increase the pursuit of excellence in sport, and build capacity in the Canadian sport system, are inclusive of Aboriginal peoples.

At a global level, the United Nations Declaration on the Rights of Indigenous Peoples (UNDRIP) outlines the individual and collective rights of Indigenous peoples from around the world. In article 31 of their declaration, UNDRIP states the following:

> Indigenous peoples have the right to maintain, control, protect and develop their cultural heritage, traditional knowledge and traditional cultural expressions, as well as the manifestations of their sciences, technologies and cultures, including . . . sports and traditional games and visual and performing arts. (United Nations General Assembly, 2007)

Despite some traction in reconciliation in Canada, there remains more to do. Paraschak (2013) discusses how ongoing colonial influence remains a strong presence in the general community's understandings of recreation and leisure and how mainstream recreation policy undercuts and delegitimatizes Indigenous values in these spaces. Scholars have argued that culturally relevant and respectful approaches are needed when working alongside Indigenous communities (Lavallée & Lévesque, 2013).

Park Development

The first park in Canada, the Halifax Common, was established in 1763. Two hundred forty acres (97 ha) were designated for exercise for the militia in the early years (McFarland, 1970). Later the park was used for skating, lawn tennis, croquet, and archery (Wright, 1983). Municipal parks and public squares were established throughout the 19th century (McFarland, 1970; Searle & Brayley, 1993). For example, 14.9 acres (6 ha) of land in London, Ontario, were deeded from the federal government for Victoria Park in 1869. In 1875, 200 acres (81 ha) of land on the Halifax peninsula were leased from the federal government for 999 years for Point Pleasant Park, where all members of the community could enjoy exercise and recreation. Much like in the United States, however, games were often prohibited in the parks, as was playing on the grass. Parks were largely used for walking, sitting, horse-drawn carriage driving, bird-watching, and enjoying the plant life (McFarland, 1970).

As transportation improved in Canada and the railway was built, it became possible to travel for pleasure. This led to the formation of national parks. In 1885, the Canadian Pacific Railway suggested the establishment of Rocky Mountain Park in Banff (Wetherell & Kmet, 1990). Although the difficult work required of the early settlers to build the country meant that there was little time for leisure, recreation eventually became a part of the lives of Canadians.

The Playground Movement

In Canada, the playground movement developed supervised playgrounds for children. Similar to its development in the United States, the playground movement in Canada was born from an increasing sense that recreation and leisure were important in bettering citizens' quality of life. In the 1800s, municipal parks were used by the upper classes, and the lower classes did not have access to open areas. However, concern for those who lived in overcrowded areas with high crime and disease led to the creation of safe places for play (McFarland,

1970). This movement was based on the notion that play was the only appropriate method for physical development for children and was necessary for their health, strength, and moral character (Searle & Brayley, 1993). There was a belief that children required encouragement to play and that the playground could be used to teach health and social customs in a play environment (McFarland, 1970). In 1893, the National Council of Women was formed, and the council and its local groups played a major role in initiating the playground movement (McFarland, 1970).

According to McFarland (1970), there were two different justifications for the playground movement:

- The prevention of delinquency and drunkenness
- The belief that all people had the right to opportunities for leisure

However, the emphasis on preventing delinquency and drunkenness was necessary for receiving funding and to justify giving time to the playground movement. School grounds were selected for the playgrounds, and in 1908, the Toronto school board was the first to develop summer playground programs. In general, playground programs were initiated by local branches of the National Women's Council. Later, a playground association and a civic department responsible for playgrounds and recreation programming were established. In the beginning, teachers were chosen for playground supervisors, and programs included games, stories, reading, sewing, and music. Eventually, summer and winter programs merged and indoor programs were developed, which led to the hiring of full-time supervisors for public playgrounds. The playground movement led to the concept of a comprehensive parks system (McFarland, 1970).

Government Involvement

Federal, provincial, and municipal governments have long been involved in providing recreation opportunities for Canadians. The land for the first parks in Canada was often deeded or leased to municipalities from the federal or provincial governments. For example, the Canadian government authorized the Saint John, New Brunswick, horticultural society to establish gardens, a park, and a pleasure resort with 1,700 acres (688 ha) for Rockwood Park (McFarland, 1970). Also, the city of Vancouver received permission from the federal

Emerald Lake is located in Yoho National Park in the Canadian Rocky Mountains, which is one of many Canadian National Parks established by the federal government.

iStockphoto/Bart Broek

government to establish Stanley Park on part of the local harbor peninsula. In 1865, a Montreal city bylaw designated 13 open spaces for citizens to enjoy (McFarland, 1970).

In 1883, the province of Ontario passed the first legislation that affected the development of provincial parks. The Public Parks Act established parks in cities and towns with the consent or petition of the electors. The local government could appoint park management boards that included the mayor of the municipality and six board members. These park boards could purchase land for parks—up to 1,000 acres (405 ha) in cities and 500 acres (202 ha) in towns. In 1892, the province of Manitoba passed a similar act (McFarland, 1970); thus, the provincial governments played an important role in the development of parks in Canada.

In the 1940s, the federal and provincial governments, under the National Physical Fitness Act, provided recreation services that influenced municipal recreation (McFarland, 1970). In Ontario in 1945, 18 municipalities passed recreation bylaws, and within one year an additional 70 had passed bylaws (Markham, 1992). The governments focused on leadership development in schools and the community and increased awareness of the possibilities of public recreation programs. The act was repealed in 1954 (Westland, 1979). The Ontario provincial government gave grants to municipalities and encouraged the local provision of recreation opportunities for all. In the 1950s, British Columbia and Alberta supported local governments in developing municipal grant structures suitable for social and economic situations (McFarland, 1970).

All three levels of government continue to be involved in providing recreation services. The Interprovincial Sport and Recreation Council (ISRC) developed the National Recreation Statement in 1987. The statement defines the roles of each level of government. In 1978, the provinces and territories agreed that recreation was within their jurisdiction; thus, their role in recreation became significant. Once local volunteers make decisions about recreation services, provincial governments are responsible for providing the assistance, leadership, and recognition necessary to deliver these services. They provide support to community volunteers who manage recreation clubs and societies and provide leadership and instruction, raise money, and coordinate programs. The interprovincial council agreed that it is the role of the provincial governments to state policy outlining the goals and objectives and stress the importance of recreation as a social service. Some of their other roles include

- observing and analyzing trends and issues to update policy;
- providing municipal governments with resources to enhance the quality of life of a community through grants for conferences and training;
- providing programs and services to build a delivery system that links the three levels of government and voluntary, private, and commercial sectors; and
- planning and supporting recreation research.

The role of the municipality in providing recreation services is to ensure a wide range of opportunities for all community members. Municipalities are responsible for establishing a recreation authority to provide opportunities, to be aware of resources and opportunities and ensure that information is available to the public, to provide incentives and services to develop opportunities based on needs, to conduct regular assessments of needs and interests that are not being met, and to develop a council to determine the best use of community resources (ISRC, 1987).

Finally, the ISRC outlined the federal government's role in providing recreation services. The council agreed that the federal government must act to influence the scope of recreation and work closely with all recreation agents in implementing programs that affect recreation services. The federal government should provide recreation through national organizations and ensure Canadian representation in activities that serve a national purpose. The federal government should contribute to the development of recreation services through provision of resources to support public, voluntary, and commercial sectors. And finally, the federal government should provide promotional materials to encourage recreation participation (ISRC, 1987).

Parks Canada is one federal agency that provides recreation opportunities for Canadians. The mandate of Parks Canada is to "protect and present examples of Canada's natural and cultural heritage and foster understanding, appreciation, and enjoyment in ways that ensure their ecological and commemorative integrity for present and future generations" (Parks Canada, n.d., para. 1). The agency serves as the guardian of parks, historic sites, and national marine conservation. The agency guides visitors to national parks and serves as a partner in building on the traditions of Indigenous peoples, diverse cultures, and international commitments. Parks Canada recounts the history of the land and people and is committed to protecting heritage, presenting the beauty and significance of the natural world, and serving Canadians (Parks Canada, n.d.).

Professional Organizations

Professional recreation groups began to emerge in Canada in the first half of the 20th century. Both national and provincial associations serve recreation professionals and volunteers. The Canadian Parks and Recreation Association (CPRA) developed from the expanding mission and influence of the Ontario Parks Association in the later years of the war. During postwar discussions, the Ontario Parks Association called on the government to consider parks, playgrounds, and recreation a separate reconstruction project after the war. On July 11, 1944, in Windsor, Ontario, the CPRA started as a means of broadening the mandate of the Ontario Parks Association for Ontario and Quebec. Formal creation of CPRA occurred one year later (Markham, 1995). At that time, it was known as the Parks and Recreation

Association of Canada. Its purpose was to deal with changes that occurred after World War II, including the need to provide parks and recreation services. Today, the society responds to social, economic, and political changes within the country (CPRA, n.d.). The mission of CPRA is to build healthy communities and enhance the quality of life and the environment. The association serves as a national voice for parks and recreation, and it advocates on behalf of parks and recreation as essential for the health and well-being of Canadians. CPRA communicates and promotes the values and benefits of parks and recreation, responds to diverse and changing needs, and provides educational opportunities (CPRA, n.d.). In 2015, CPRA released the Framework for Recreation in Canada, which outlines five goals for achieving well-being of Canadi-

ans through recreation. These goals include active living, inclusion and access, connecting with nature, supportive environments, and development of recreation capacity (CPRA, 2015).

Another national organization for recreation professionals is Physical Health Education Canada (PHE Canada), which promotes physical activity among young children and youth (PHE Canada, n.d.-b). This organization started as the Canadian Physical Education Association in 1933. It changed to the Canadian Association for Health, Physical Education, and Recreation in 1948, added dance in 1994, and in 2008 adopted its current title Physical & Health Education Canada (PHE Canada, n.d.-a).

Provinces also have recreation associations. For example, the Saskatchewan Parks and Recreation Association (SPRA) aims to "promote, develop,

OUTSTANDING GRADUATE

Dillon Thompson

Background Information

Name: Dillon Thompson

Education: BA in recreation and leisure studies from Virginia Wesleyan University, 2017; MS in athletic administration from State University of New York, 2019

Credentials: American Red Cross First Aid Instructor Certified

Awards: STAR Award University of California, Santa Cruz

Affiliations: Member of the National Intramural Recreational Sports Association (NIRSA), NIRSA Region 6 Soccer Coordinator

Career Information

Position: Associate Director of Athletics & Recreation, Sport Programs

Organization: University of California, Santa Cruz; serving roughly 18,000 students enrolled at the institution

Job description: The program areas I oversee include intramural sports, our 30 sport club organizations, and game-day operations of our 17 NCAA Division III varsity athletic teams. I provide administrative support to several teams directly, serving as their sports administrator throughout the academic year. Along with one full-time staff member, 30 part-time student staff report to me, assisting in the operation of our sport programs through sports officiating, facility management, and on-site conflict resolution amongst participants, employees, and spectators. I'm also responsible for scheduling, training, and development of student staff, as well as our programs that serve the campus community.

Career path: While attending Virginia Wesleyan University as an undergraduate, I wasn't sure where life would take me after graduation. All I knew when I started college was that I wanted to play collegiate soccer. After declaring recreation and leisure studies as my major, my professors challenged me to look beyond an undergraduate degree and further my education by obtaining a masters degree. I followed that advice and pursued an MS in higher education, and served as a graduate assistant to further my experience in the field. From there I accepted my first full-time position at the University of Pennsylvania as the sport clubs coordinator. That experience eventually got me to my next role as an assistant director and now as the associate director.

Likes and dislikes about the job: I love that this field provides me with many opportunities to positively affect students. Without the mentors that invested in me during my time as a student and when I started my career, I don't know what path I would be on today. That commitment to student development is a huge reason why I work in higher education and why it's so rewarding to help students achieve their true potential. Seeing firsthand, and often daily, the impact I have on others reminds me how lucky I am to work in this profession.

and facilitate parks and recreation opportunities throughout the province" (SPRA, n.d., para. 1). Recreation Nova Scotia, another provincial organization, promotes the values and benefits of recreation toward a healthier future. Recreation Nova Scotia came into existence in 1998 with the merger of three organizations: Recreation Association of Nova Scotia, the Recreation Council on Disabilities in Nova Scotia, and Volunteer Nova Scotia (Recreation Nova Scotia, n.d.). A third provincial organization, Parks and Recreation Ontario (PRO), is a not-for-profit group that formed in 1995 (PRO, n.d.). The aim of PRO is to promote and develop benefits of recreation through education, collaboration, and research (PRO, n.d.).

Post–World War II Growth in Canada

Canada also experienced a host of challenges related to recreation and leisure after World War II; some were similar to and some were different from those experienced in the United States. Among those challenges were the following:

• *Concern for fitness*. The 1960s were characterized by renewed concern for physical fitness (Searle & Brayley, 1993). The Fitness and Amateur Sport Act, which was passed in 1961, redefined the role of government in sport, recreation, and leisure. In the 1960s, all levels of government became involved in financial assistance to promote recreation development. Much of this money was dedicated to building facilities (Searle & Brayley, 1993). ParticipACTION began in 1971 with the aim of increasing awareness of physical fitness (The ParticipACTION Archive Project, n.d.-a). ParticipACTION's 1973 media campaign suggested to Canadians that a 60-year-old Swede was as fit as, or more fit than, a 30-year-old Canadian (The ParticipACTION, Archive Project, n.d.-a). ParticipACTION continued until 2001, when board members decided to close the program (The ParticipACTION Archive Project, n.d.-b). However, ParticipACTION reemerged several years later with the mandate of increasing physical activity and decreasing the amount of time spent sitting (ParticipACTION, n.d.).

• *Economic challenges*. In 1973, the Arab oil embargo ended the rapid development of recreation resources and opportunities. High energy costs led to empty arenas and poorly maintained parks. The oil embargo also affected pleasure travel when gas was rationed and higher jet fuel costs made flying expensive. Provincial and municipal governments were forced to limit the growth of recreation. They needed to adopt a new style of leadership. Municipal recreation agencies became less involved in directly providing services and started playing a facilitative role instead (Searle & Brayley, 1993).

• *Changing demographic trends*. The changing nature of the family throughout the 1980s and 1990s influenced recreation service delivery and caused service providers to respond to different needs, opportunities, and constraints. Various family structures had to be considered, including blended families, single-parent families, childless families, multiple generation families, and traditional nuclear families, to name a few (Searle & Brayley, 1993). The majority of single-parent families were headed by women in the 1980s, and these families had lower incomes than two-parent families (Harrington, 1996). Common-law relationships became more common throughout the 1980s and 1990s, and marriage rates were lower. The age of first marriage rose during the 1980s and 1990s, divorce rates rose, and fertility rates declined (Harrington, 1996). All these trends affected leisure services delivery.

• *Poverty*. People living in poverty also posed a new challenge for service providers. The new poor were of particular concern and included children living in poverty, the working poor, and frail elderly community members. Leisure services were needed to help build self-esteem, develop social support networks, and teach self-reliance skills. Focus was on satisfying needs and delivering programs in the most appropriate way for clients (Searle & Brayley, 1993).

• *Multiculturalism*. This is another consideration that arose in the 1980s and 1990s, and it continues today. Canadian public policy defends the idea that differences in a nation are good for it, and the government protects the cultures of new Canadians. As a result, recreation services must provide relevant and meaningful recreation opportunities for new Canadians.

CURRENT TRENDS AFFECTING RECREATION AND LEISURE

The following emerging trends influence recreation and leisure service provision today, and they will continue to do so in the future:

• *Immigration and diverse populations*. As individuals migrate to North America, their perceptions of recreation and leisure may change the dynamics of service delivery models. Individuals who migrate from developing nations often do so for two common reasons: They leave voluntarily for a better life in a developed nation, or they are refugees who are forced to leave their country due to oppression or war (Kim et al., 2013). According to the United Nations (UN, 2015), there were 244 million international immigrants in 2015. Of these, 54 million are living in North America. Because these numbers are sure to increase with time, recreation and leisure practitioners need to be cognizant of the different experiences of immigrants compared to those who did not migrate (Kim & Van Puymbroeck, 2011). The need for recreation and leisure programming designed for these newcomers is a must, particularly programs that are provided by public parks and recreation agencies. These agencies serve the broad population within a community and must be responsive to the needs of newcomers and long-term residents alike. The increase in diversity has resulted in changes to populations served, programs offered, facilities, hiring practices, and policies.

In an effort to be more inclusive and to target individuals who were not being reached, recreation and leisure programming has been expanded to meet needs of individuals of different ages, genders, ethnicities, and ability levels. Communities have diversified programming efforts to include opportunities for increasingly diverse racial and ethnic populations. For example, the city of Seattle offers female-only swim times to accommodate women of Islamic descent who cannot wear bathing suits in the presence of men. As a result of the program, women who ordinarily would not participate in swimming have the opportunity to do so. In addition, city parks and recreation departments are diversifying their staff to mirror populations served; specifically, they are hiring employees who are fluent in languages other than English. The Washington, D.C., parks department initiated a Black History Invitational Swim Meet in an effort to increase African American participation.

- *Technology*. Rates of childhood obesity and screen time have increased in correlation with reduced time spent in physical education classes and recess. Many attribute increases in obesity rates to sedentary lifestyles associated with screen time. In response, recreation and leisure programs have been diversified to include various platforms for engagement through apps, online gaming that encourages movement, and wearable devices. These technological components can track progress and provide opportunities for competition, exploration, and information.

- *Economic challenges*. Recreation and leisure services have had to rely on fees and charges due to decreased government funding during tough times. The funds collected offset program costs and produce profits that support other programs. These fees and charges have subsidized many programs, but they have been criticized for potentially excluding those with less income.

- *Shopping as recreation*. An additional emerging trend is the notion of shopping as recreation. The term *shopping fever* was introduced to incorporate concepts such as mall mania, home shopping, online shopping, and shopping as therapy, all of which related to the "dogged pursuit of more" and a condition known as *affluenza* (DeGraff et al., 2001, p. 2). Therefore, shopping, both online and in person, provides not only a recreation activity to occupy leisure time but also a way to purchase those things that demonstrate one's economic level.

- *Population aging*. In North America, population aging has been evident for several decades as older adults comprise a larger proportion of the population (MacNeil & Gould, 2012). Increased life expectancy and declining fertility rates contribute to population aging. Baby boomers (those born between 1946 and 1965) make up a large percentage of this aging population. Pruchno (2012) argued that baby boomers are transforming what it means to be an older adult; they view retirement differently than their predecessors and seek work–leisure balance in this life phase. They tend to be more physically active and interested in outdoor pursuits than previous generations of older adults (Sperazza & Banerjee, 2010). Baby boomers are affecting how leisure services are offered to older adults because they require a broader range of options.

- *Job market trends*. Beginning in March 2020, due to the COVID-19 pandemic, most sectors within the recreation and leisure service industry experienced shutdowns of facilities and modifications to programming and employment at all levels. These changes altered the job market; new trends emerged that changed the ways in which staffing, employment, and programming exist. Recreation professionals were innovative in their approaches to the development of virtual programming and the identification of alternative methods of providing services to patrons. Due to shutdowns and cutbacks, most service providers experienced budget cuts, furloughs, and hiring freezes. In general, recreation departments were expected to do more with less. Toward the middle to end of 2021, jobs reemerged and the job market for occupations within the recreation and leisure industry is strengthening

From "Spanish Flu" to COVID-19: How History Repeats Itself

The crises brought on by COVID-19 resulted in over four million deaths worldwide by the fall of 2021. In the United States, 674,000 people had perished and an additional 27,000 in Canada had suffered the same fate. This global pandemic was seen as unprecedented by most people, but the reality is that it's the second pandemic the world has faced in the past 100 years. In many respects, the mistakes of the past have certainly been repeated.

Beginning in 1918, influenza swept across the world for two years and had several distinct phases in the same way that COVID-19 has variants. Roughly 50 million people died, including 675,000 Americans (Barry, 2005). The disease's impacts were first reported in a Spanish newspaper, hence its popular misnomer, "Spanish flu," but its origins are attributed to the United States or France; similar to COVID-19, the exact origin is unknown (Nunes et al., 2018).

In both cases, the economic impact of the pandemic has been wide scale and significant, and the number of deaths could have been reduced had steps been taken and history studied. One example from the 1918 flu pandemic comes from the city of Philadelphia. In the fall of 1918, 200,000 people packed Broad Street, the main north–south thoroughfare in the city, to watch a parade in support of the U.S. war effort. Unfortunately, because so many people were packed together, every bed in the city's 31 hospitals was filled within 72 hours. Within the week, 2,600 people had died from the flu, and, a week after that, the number had risen to 4,500, with 12,000 Philadelphians eventually dying (Davis, 2018).

Communities worldwide experienced similar super-spreader events during the COVID-19 pandemic, and history continues to point to these events' grim record of increasing infection among participants. One example is the annual Sturgis Motorcycle Rally held in South Dakota each August. After more than 365,000 people attended the August 2020 rally during the pre-vaccine era of the pandemic, hospitalizations tripled in the state and deaths increased as well (Reinman, 2020). Akin to Philadelphia in the fall of 1918, when infection spread to neighboring areas, the rally ultimately could have been responsible for over a quarter million new cases nationally, or approximately 19 percent of all cases in the United States in the two weeks after the rally (Dave et al., 2020). Astonishingly, the event was held again the following year without public health precautions, and the state's governor declared that the media should "stop spreading fear" in advance of the rally by covering the consequences of large, in-person gatherings.

Sure enough, in the two months after the 2021 event, the rally's home county endured the second largest increase in COVID-19 cases of any county in the United States. During that same time, COVID-19 cases statewide increased 300 percent (South Dakota Department of Health, n.d.). This wasn't surprising considering attendance reached over half a million people, the largest number in the rally's preceding six years (Reinman, 2021). Again, the state's governor chose to ignore the developments and refuted criticism. Even the lead singer of the band Smash Mouth chose to ignore history when he proclaimed while performing at the rally, "Now we're all here together tonight. And we're being human once again. F*ck that Covid sh*t" (Wilmon, 2020). Political leaders and others in the public eye ignoring science or history shouldn't come as a surprise. After all, a hundred years earlier, ignoring evidence to the contrary, the head of Philadelphia's Naval Hospital had this to say right before the pandemic took hold in his city: "We believe we have it well in hand" (Meier, 2018).

What can the recreation and leisure service industry learn from the 1918 flu pandemic and the COVID-19 pandemic? The health and well-being of the people served by the industry need to take precedence over service delivery when pandemics and other crises reduce societies' capacity to engage in activities without risks. Still, the human desire for recreation and leisure will persist no matter the risks, as our history of super-spreader events attest. To protect lives in the future, we must assess our past to avoid the pitfalls of our predecessors, beginning with these questions that the industry has only begun to consider:

- How will the recreation and leisure service industry ensure the well-being of participants who use their services during crises?

- How can the recreation and leisure service industry learn from the insights they have gained as a result of the COVID-19 pandemic to better ensure the well-being of their employees?

- What lessons could be gained from the experiences of universities and other institutions during the COVID-19 pandemic as they worked to ensure the well-being of their students, employees, and consumers?

and is expected to grow over the next decade (U.S. Bureau of Labor Statistics, 2021).

A specific trend within campus recreation over the past ten years has been to replace graduate assistants with entry-level coordinators. While this approach alleviates supervision time and has financial advantages, the developmental piece related to nurturing young employees while obtaining higher education is missing. An approach by Purdue University was the creation of a graduate professional internship that included a $25,000 salary, a 29-hour workweek, health and retirement benefits, and access to the education benefit that allowed the student to take masters classes online for free. This approach may gain traction within the field of campus recreation as professionals evaluate creative ways to develop staff members and save money.

SIMILARITIES BETWEEN CANADA AND THE UNITED STATES

Recreation has developed similarly in the United States and Canada. For example, both countries developed playgrounds in similar ways at about the same time. The following are among the trends that have been identified in Canada and the United States:

- Expansion of activities for children to activities for people of all ages
- Expansion of summer programs to yearlong programs
- Provision of indoor and outdoor activities
- Expansion of playgrounds into rural areas
- Shift from philanthropic to community financial support of playground programs
- Increased importance of organized play over unorganized play
- Shifting philosophy to include use of leisure and not just provision of facilities by communities
- Increased importance of community and group activities over individual interests (Rainwater, 1992)
- Creation of play spaces
- Increased opportunities for child development through play
- Growing belief in the importance of outdoor play for young people
- Increased opportunities for public recreation
- Quest for a better balance between work and play

- Appreciation of the value of play in children's lives

At the end of the 19th century the playground movement in Canada and the United States continued the trend of increased appreciation for recreation and leisure. Economic class separation in Canada and the United States was a growing reality (as it was in ancient Greece), and class structure in Western society after the industrial revolution was structured along the lines of economic wealth. The upper classes demonstrated a growing concern for those in the lower classes. Recreation and leisure were no longer seen as privileges but were rather seen as an important part of life and a way for those who were well off to help those who were less so. This sense of obligation encouraged the use of recreation and leisure as a way to address life's challenges and facilitated the playground movement.

Government has played an important role in providing recreation and leisure opportunities in both the United States and Canada. In the United States, the government began to play a role in providing social services during the Great Depression when the lack of jobs increased the amount of time available to pursue leisure activities. The federal government also developed organizations to protect natural resources and preserve them for future generations. This continued a trend of governments tackling societal problems through concern for the leisure-related issues facing their citizens.

SUMMARY

Leisure in the United States and Canada has been influenced by past definitions of leisure. Primitive societies had little time for leisure as they fought for survival. However, as their tools became more sophisticated, they gained more free time. Play was used to teach children about their roles as adults and as an opportunity for ritualization, rest, and relaxation. Among the ancient Greeks, contemplation, education, philosophy, and athletics were important leisure activities that helped people reach the Athenian ideal. However, only full Greek citizens had opportunities for leisure. In ancient Rome, leisure was time away from work, and recuperation was of great importance. Leisure was also used as a method of social control. After the fall of the Roman Empire, the Catholic Church, which restricted leisure participation, controlled what people perceived to be leisure by placing values on activities. This includes the colonial assimilation of Indigenous people of Canada through recreation and leisure participation. Further restrictions were placed on leisure and social activity during the Protestant Reformation as new churches emerged. These strict rules were relaxed during the Renaissance when artists were supported and play was considered important for education.

Early settlers in the United States and Canada brought these perceptions of what they perceived as acceptable leisure to their new countries. These views and the environmental conditions they faced have influenced leisure today. The first colonies in the United States restricted leisure because settlers were fighting for survival and had time for little else. However, as restrictions were lifted, working bees, hunting, and going to the tavern became popular pastimes. As time passed, exploration and settlement resulted in increasing recreation opportunities for European settlers. As governments established parks as early as the 1700s, participation started to grow and a concern for the appropriate use of leisure time emerged.

The playground movement in both the United States and Canada began in the late 1800s and early 1900s. The first sand garden was founded in Boston, and more playgrounds followed in New York and Chicago following Boston's success. The movement was started in Canada by the National Council of Women to give children opportunities for supervised play to prevent delinquency and promote healthy development.

All levels of government in both countries are involved in recreation. Governments provide facilities, funding, support, policy, information, and training for recreation services. The growth of organizations concerned with recreation program provision and the workers responsible for it emerged in the United States at the same time as the playground movement. These organizations evolved to become the two main national organizations today: the National Recreation and Park Association and SHAPE America. In Canada, professional organizations emerged on the national level with the Canadian Parks and Recreation Association and at the provincial level in the 1940s with Recreation Nova Scotia. As in the United States, these agencies provide support for recreation programs and promote the importance of recreation and leisure for health and well-being. In the United States, the President's Council on Physical Fitness and Sports was formed in the 1960s to address fitness, and in the 1970s the ParticipACTION program was developed in Canada to encourage citizens to become fit. As the new millennium unfolded, it became clear that many themes of the past, including how best to serve a changing society, the appropriate use of mass leisure, the government's role, and the importance of professional organizations, were as important as ever. Two decades after the turn of the century, recreation and leisure service providers continue to experience changing trends that influence service delivery. From the economic challenges with providing services to a changing population, to activities that increase and decrease in popularity, these trends and more have made recreation and leisure ever-changing and history suggests that will always be true.

Review Questions

1. How did early societies view "leisure"?

2. How did the COVID-19 pandemic affect the leisure industry?

3. Compare and contrast the evolution of the playground movement in the United States and Canada. What main purposes did playgrounds serve?

4. Discuss the Indigenous assimilation through colonial recreation in Canada.

5. What similarities and differences exist between the early Olympics and current-day Olympics?

Go to HK*Propel* to complete the activities for this chapter.

CHAPTER 3

Philosophy and Leisure

Donald J. McLean and Mary Sara Wells

David/Stone RF/Getty Images

" Happiness is thought to depend on leisure; for we are busy that we may have leisure, and make war that we may live in peace. "

Aristotle, Greek philosopher

LEARNING OUTCOMES

After reading this chapter, you should be able to do the following:

> Explain the five branches of philosophy, the relevance of each to leisure research, and the effect of each on leisure service delivery

> Compare and evaluate the concepts of leisure as a state of mind and a state of being, and apply these two notions of leisure to the provision of recreation services

> Demonstrate a comprehensive understanding of the leisure research literature by comparing theories of leisure based on empirical research and philosophical analysis

> Describe the importance of being able to logically justify conclusions and decisions in leisure services

> Discuss why aesthetics is important to our understanding of leisure and how considerations of aesthetics influence the provision of leisure services

> Apply ethical reasoning to evaluate the worthiness of leisure services

The methods of philosophy can be put to good use in the study of recreation and leisure phenomena and the delivery of leisure services. Contrary to the popular belief that philosophy provides obscure answers to theoretical issues, philosophical inquiry has many practical implications for and is important to leisure research and service delivery, because it helps focus our attention on important questions and issues related to recreation and leisure. Perhaps the best way to summarize the usefulness of philosophy to the field of recreation and leisure studies and services is that it provides us with guidance in *how* to think rather than *what* to think about issues and problems related to leisure and recreation.

WHY DOES PHILOSOPHY MATTER?

For many people, the subject of philosophy appears to have little relevance to recreation and leisure. Our stereotype of philosophers suggests that they are deep thinkers who are uninterested in matters relating to relaxation, pleasure, or fun. This highbrow image of philosophy is spoofed in the old Monty Python skit of the philosophers' soccer game: Aristotle, Kant, Hegel, and other great thinkers from the past stand like statues deep in thought on a soccer field. The ball just sits there for the whole match until Archimedes suddenly has a revelation and kicks the ball to Socrates, who then fires it into the net while the other players look on in bewilderment.

Like the immobilized philosophers in the skit, many recreation students become frozen in their seats, their eyes glazed over, when their instructor announces that the week's topic is the philosophy

of leisure. Typically, students have chosen recreation and leisure studies because they prefer active, hands-on experiences to abstract thought. What use, students ask, is there in learning what some dead white guy from long ago thought about leisure and recreation? Wouldn't their time be better spent learning how to program activities, create budgets, and market events?

Because the philosophy of leisure is often taught as a history lesson or as part of the intellectual foundations of leisure and recreation, it is understandable that students are doubtful that philosophy has any real application to leisure services. Yet philosophy affects both the study of leisure phenomena and the delivery of recreation services in fundamental ways. We tend not to recognize the importance of philosophy to recreation and leisure studies because it typically functions in the background of our thinking and practices. But when we understand what philosophical inquiry is, it is not difficult to see the contribution that it makes to the theory and practice of leisure and recreation. To learn why philosophy does matter to people interested in recreation and leisure, let's begin by first examining why philosophy has gained a reputation for being irrelevant.

The term *philosophy* translates from ancient Greek as "lover of wisdom," and originally it referred to all scholarly inquiry. Over the last several hundred years, however, the evolution of modern-day universities has seen the rise of many separate disciplines such as physics, chemistry, sociology, and anthropology as knowledge and methods of inquiry have become increasingly complex. In fact, the discipline of leisure studies follows this pattern of the increasing specialization of knowledge because most recreation curricula and departments did not exist before the 1960s.

The division of knowledge into a variety of specialized fields is an important explanation for why philosophy appears to have lost much of its relevancy. As discipline-based knowledge has grown, the scope of philosophic inquiry has been whittled away. But despite the loss of academic ownership to other disciplines, philosophy is primarily associated with five branches of inquiry:

- Metaphysics
- Epistemology
- Logic
- Aesthetics
- Ethics

Each of the five types of philosophical inquiry has relevance to recreation and leisure studies, but as will be explained later, the first two, metaphysics and epistemology, have more importance to leisure researchers, whereas ethics is more relevant to leisure practitioners. The third branch of philosophical inquiry, logic, has important implications for leisure researchers and practitioners, whereas the fourth branch, aesthetics, has received relatively little attention from either practitioners or researchers. To advance our understanding of the relevance of philosophical inquiry, let's now examine the ways in which each of the branches of philosophy has influenced thinking and practice in recreation and leisure.

METAPHYSICS AND LEISURE

Metaphysics concerns questions about the fundamental nature of reality. It is the branch of philosophic inquiry that is most likely to generate amusement and derision from nonphilosophers. Questions such as "Does a tree make a sound when it falls in the forest if no one is around?" or "Is the cup really on the table?" or "Does God exist?" are classic examples of metaphysical inquiries that can seem pointless to more practically minded people. (I remember being in a philosophy seminar in which we really did discuss whether the professor's coffee cup was on the table!) Many people have argued that metaphysical inquiry into the ultimate nature of reality is too speculative to be of any practical use. Even famous philosophers such as David Hume dismissed metaphysics as so much gibberish about nothing.

Although most contemporary philosophers do not subscribe to the view that metaphysical inquiry

is meaningless, ironically, it was advanced physics that popularized speculation about the nature of reality. Scientist–media personalities such as Carl Sagan and Stephen Hawking have done much to fuel the public's imagination about such topics as the ultimate nature of the universe and our place in it. Many people today are fascinated by theories of alternate realities as predicted by quantum mechanics, the origins of the universe, and other metaphysical speculations that stretch beyond the boundaries of empirical science.

In recreation and leisure studies, metaphysical inquiry has mainly revolved around more down-to-earth questions of how leisure should be defined. Although the average person might believe that everyone knows what leisure is, scholars and researchers have gone to great lengths debating the essential qualities of leisure. And, as many researchers have noted, the term *leisure* is difficult to define. Unlike phenomena studied in the natural sciences, in which the subject matter stays the same no matter the time or place (e.g., water has the same physical properties that it did 1,000 years ago and does not vary from one society to another), socially constructed phenomena such as leisure are continually in flux (i.e., ideas about leisure vary from culture to culture and at different periods in time). The variability of leisure as a socially evolving phenomenon of human existence makes it much more difficult to determine its essential qualities. Nonetheless, intellectual debates concerning the essence of leisure have historically fallen into two opposing theses about its fundamental nature.

- The traditional view is that leisure is a public, objective state of being.
- The modern view is that leisure is essentially a private, subjective state of mind.

Let's first examine the traditional view of leisure and then compare it with the modern definition of leisure.

The idea that leisure is a state of being—that is, a set of life circumstances—is attributable to the ancient Greeks. According to Aristotle, having leisure meant being free of the burden of work so that one could engage in more ennobling activities such as music and philosophy. For the ancient Greeks, an essential element of leisure was to possess sufficient material resources so that one could have time for leisure. Thus, if you were an enslaved person in ancient Athens, you were incapable of having leisure because you did not have the resources to engage in it.

The idea that leisure is a state of being is also reflected in contemporary conceptualizations of leisure as unobligated time. Modern economic systems, which formalized the division between work time and leisure time, have helped reinforce the idea that the most fundamental feature of leisure is that it is a time when we are free from work and other obligations of life. As well, the ancient Greek ideal that leisure time should be used to engage in worthwhile activities still resonates with many people, although research indicates that most of us do not devote much of our free time to uplifting activities. Sebastian De Grazia's book *Of Time, Work and Leisure* provides a modern-day justification for the idea that people should use their leisure time to perform worthwhile activities. For both ancient and contemporary thinkers who see leisure as a state of being, the critical point is that leisure is defined by the circumstances and actions of people that can be observed by others. Leisure, therefore, is not a private experience, but instead it occurs in a public, social context where others can judge whether we are at leisure or whether the activities we are engaging in qualify as leisurely. Leisure as a state of being thus depends on a social consensus as to what activities and living conditions qualify as leisure.

In contrast to the notion that leisure is a state of being, many leisure researchers have argued that leisure is primarily a private state of mind. John Neulinger, for example, theorizes that leisure is a psychological state in which the experience of leisure depends on how a person perceives a situation. Neulinger's theory of leisure is based on two variables: perceived freedom and motivation (Neulinger, 1974). According to his theory, perceived freedom means that a person thinks they are free in a particular instance. With Neulinger's theory, perception of freedom does not depend on the individual's actual circumstances. Even for people who are desperately poor or repressed, so long as they *think* that they have freedom, a necessary condition for leisure is satisfied. The other psychological component necessary to having leisure is whether the person perceives that their motivation is intrinsic or extrinsic, in other words, whether motivation is generated internally (e.g., one plays music because it is pleasing to oneself) or externally (e.g., one plays music to make money). Thus, when people perceive that they are free to choose to engage in a leisure activity that they find intrinsically motivating, then the resulting outcome is a state of mind whereby they experience pure leisure. According to many modern-day leisure researchers, leisure is therefore a private, subjective state of mind rather than a public, objective state of being.

Although it may seem fine and well that leisure researchers investigate and debate the fundamental characteristics of leisure, students and practitioners may wonder how such discussions could have any relevance to delivery of leisure services. But the choice between thinking that leisure is a state of being or a state of mind can have a profound influence on leisure service delivery choices (Sylvester, 1991). Sylvester states that viewing leisure as a state of mind may encourage practitioners to provide leisure experiences that are inauthentic, illusory, and even immoral:

> Regardless of the actual content, context, or consequences, *anything* counts as leisure as long as the individual avows a subjective experience of freedom. Applying to illusions as well as real events, the potential for leisure is virtually boundless. If you experience leisure, then leisure it is, for there is no disputing the truth of subjective states of mind. (1991, p. 441)

Sylvester argues that viewing leisure as a private state of mind opens the door to all sorts of horrid and depraved activities that qualify as leisure. Less shocking, but still worrisome, he says, is the possibility that leisure service practitioners may choose to provide clients who live in inequitable and repressive circumstances with leisure experiences that encourage them to accept their disadvantaged situations. And, for well-to-do clients, he also questions whether practitioners should "engineer" pleasant subjective leisure experiences. Rather than providing impetus for true personal growth, development, and achievement, subjective leisure may deceive people into thinking that their leisure lives are fulfilling and meaningful when, in fact, the leisure activities that they are engaged in lack ennobling qualities.

Although the concerns that Sylvester raises about subjective leisure are well-founded, regarding leisure as a state of mind may be beneficial in many situations. For example, some adventure recreation programming, such as high-ropes courses, deliberately uses the perception of risk to facilitate participants' personal growth. Being suspended 40 feet (12 m) off the ground can result in a perception of adventure and risk, but participants are safe because they are harnessed and belayed. Exposing participants to real danger in this situation would be not only unnecessary for achieving the benefits of the recreation experience but also irresponsible and unethical.

We can readily think of other examples in which approaching leisure as a state of mind is the proper approach. We would be unwise and insensitive to tell an enthusiastic young child that their piano playing is not very good. Nor should we disparage those who enjoy artificial leisure environments such as Disney or engage in virtual reality experiences. And what of harmless, idiosyncratic types of leisure such as eccentric hobbies that few people other than those engaged find enjoyable? Should these activities not be classified as leisure because other people do not appreciate their merit?

Even though treating leisure as a state of mind is desirable in many situations, it is equally true in other instances that it is reasonable to conceptualize leisure as an objective state of being. For example, we make the effort to visit a significant natural or cultural resource because we want to experience the authentic object or environment. No replica or simulation will suffice. We join a competitive sports program because we want to see how our skills match up with the skills of others. We set challenging goals to exercise, become fit, and lose weight. In these instances, the leisure experience is guided by the ability to achieve a particular objectively recognized state of being.

Therefore, in some situations and contexts, it is helpful to think of leisure as a state of being, and at other times it would be best to treat leisure as a state of mind. Perhaps the lesson here is not that we must define leisure in one way to the exclusion of the other but instead that we must be aware of the fundamentally different ways that leisure can be conceptualized, and understand how our presuppositions about the nature of leisure can influence our assumptions about the kinds of leisure experiences that will be beneficial to people. Thinking about the essential nature of leisure, therefore, is not simply an academic exercise for researchers. Let's now consider the next branch of philosophic inquiry, epistemology, and its influence on the field of recreation and leisure.

OUTSTANDING GRADUATE

Background Information

Name: Nicki L. Ellis

Education: BS in recreation, park, and tourism administration from Western Illinois University at Moline

Credentials: Certified Nonprofit Professional (CNP)

Awards: 2014 Anita H. Magafas Nontraditional Student Award, 2014 departmental nominee for the Lincoln Academy of Illinois' Student Laureate Award

Career Information

Position: Sales Manager

Organization: The Quad Cities Convention and Visitors Bureau (QCCVB) is the tourism marketing and management organization for the Quad Cities region of Illinois and Iowa. We increase visitor expenditures and overnight stays through strategic sales, marketing, and services to our customers, members, and communities. The QCCVB is a 501(c)(6) nonprofit organization operated by a board of directors and has just under 20 full-time and part-time employees.

Job description: I am responsible for prospecting accounts that have potential for bringing meetings, group tours, conventions, tradeshows, and sporting events to the Quad Cities. I coordinate leads, develop proposals and bid packages, track progress, and assist in closing sales while working with several levels of partnerships.

Career path: After graduating from Western Illinois University, I taught at a nonprofit preschool where I had previously interned (in their marketing department). Through networking and volunteering in the community, I kept in touch with the QCCVB.

Likes and dislikes about the job: What I like most about my job is the formation of lasting relationships that benefit my community. The least favorite part is the uncertainty that is associated with working with a nonprofit organization's budget.

Advice for Undergraduates

My advice to undergraduate students is that change is the new constant! You can't be afraid to embrace change and try something new. Also, network, network, and network some more!

EPISTEMOLOGY AND LEISURE

Epistemology is the study of knowledge itself. The term is derived from the Greek words *episteme* (knowledge) and *logos* (explanation); hence, epistemology is the branch of philosophy that explains knowledge or provides theories about how it is we know what we know. Epistemology concerns questions of how we acquire knowledge, what types of things we are capable of knowing (the scope of our knowledge), and the trustworthiness of the knowledge we possess (how certain we can be of what we know).

Traditionally, epistemological debate about the source of knowledge divides into two camps:

- Those who think that knowledge is derived from sense perceptions (**empiricists**)
- Those who believe that knowledge comes from ideas generated by our minds (**rationalists**)

Empiricists believe that knowledge must ultimately be based on evidence. Thus, empiricists place a great deal of importance on how observations are collected.

Whether we are leisure researchers or practitioners, we want to have the best information possible for advancing knowledge and making decisions. In North America, the study of leisure has been predominately data driven, but debate has been ongoing about whether observations should be collected to produce quantitative or qualitative data. Many leisure researchers believe that the investigation of leisure phenomena should use methods conducive to producing quantitative data; that is, observations of leisure should primarily take the form of numeric scores. Examples of quantitative data include the numbers generated from questionnaires that use Likert scales or the tallies from observational checklists. Researchers can then use such data to perform statistical analyses and test hypotheses about factors that are thought to influence people's leisure experiences. Often, the collection of quantitative data has a narrow focus so that the amassing of information concerning a few variables can be carefully controlled.

Other researchers take the position that observations of leisure should be gathered primarily by interpreting the meaning and significance that people associate with their leisure experiences. To understand the meaning that people attribute to leisure, researchers collect and analyze the words and statements of subjects from interviews or create field notes based on their interpretations of subjects' behavior and actions. Qualitative analysis emphasizes explaining and understanding the lived leisure experiences of the subjects being studied and tends to have a broader focus than quantitative analysis.

These two schools of thought about how observations should be collected have, not surprisingly, created an epistemological debate between the adherents who favor quantitative data collection and those who favor qualitative data collection. Although we need not trouble ourselves with the details of this lively controversy, supporters of research that produces quantitative data maintain that it is more trustworthy than qualitative data; whereas those who support the collecting of qualitative data argue that it provides a more comprehensive understanding of people's leisure experiences.

The debate is thus largely a disagreement between which epistemic qualities of knowledge are more important:

- The certainty and trust that arise from knowledge derived from observations (quantitative)
- The scope and relevancy of the knowledge derived from gathering data about people's lived leisure experiences (qualitative)

But despite these disagreements about the strengths and weaknesses of quantitative and qualitative data, note that both sides agree substantially on one fundamental point: Knowledge about leisure is based on the collection of evidence. Both believe that the source for new knowledge about leisure comes from the ability to collect observations of leisure phenomena. Thus, the debate about quantitative and qualitative data is essentially a quarrel between empiricists.

In contrast to the empiricist belief that knowledge of leisure must derive from observation, rationalist epistemology says that our minds are the primary source for our knowledge about leisure. To those of us who have been trained in empirical research techniques, it might seem inconceivable that any new knowledge about leisure could be produced by simply thinking about it. Yet many of our fundamental ideas about leisure have not been derived from empirical research. It would be absurd to believe that the classical conception of leisure was the result of data collected by questionnaires, interviews, or field notes. Although Aristotle is thought of as an empiricist philosopher for his copious observations of the natural world, his methodology when examining leisure is better classified as philosophic analysis. Similarly, many modern scholars, such as Josef Pieper, have greatly advanced our understanding of leisure without employing empirical research methodologies. The method of inquiry that these nonempiricist leisure scholars use is often referred to as *theoretical research*. Rather than looking to external sources for knowledge of leisure by collecting observations from research subjects, theoretical research generates knowledge by the internal thought processes of the leisure researcher who applies reason and logic in the form of philosophic analysis of leisure concepts and issues.

Theoretical research is particularly helpful when we are trying to come to conclusions about matters of values rather than matters of fact, as the following example illustrates. Gambling is a popular but controversial leisure activity that has been the subject of considerable empirical research, particularly since the relaxation of gambling restrictions in the latter third of the 20th century. Yet the collection and analysis of data on gambling can provide only partial answers to the practical question of whether it is a desirable leisure activity. Statistics on tax revenues generated, employment and economic multipliers, gambling addiction rates, and so on cannot fully answer the question of whether the vast expansion of the gaming industry has been beneficial. To conclude that the expansion in gambling opportunities has improved people's quality of life requires us to employ nonempirically based reasons as well. Does, for example, the enjoyment that many people gain from visiting casinos outweigh the pain experienced by the relatively few who are addicted to gambling? Should gambling opportunities be expanded because governments find themselves needing more tax revenues? Is it ethical to try to restrict and control people's access to gaming? Answers to these and other questions about gaming surely help enrich our understanding of gambling as a leisure activity and cannot be wholly determined simply by collecting information. Rather, we also need to employ our ability to reason abstractly, analyze various value issues relating to gambling, and construct arguments to justify the conclusions that we draw.

So our understanding of leisure seems to depend on both empirical data and theoretical or philosophic analysis. Given that leisure is a complex social phenomenon, perhaps we should not be surprised that it cannot be adequately comprehended by a single method of knowing. Although we naturally have our preferred method of comprehending leisure—whether by quantitative or qualitative research or by theoretical or philosophic analysis—we should be wary of excluding other ways of knowing. Simply being aware that there are multiple ways to gain knowledge and understanding of leisure can help us avoid thinking that our preferred way of understanding leisure is the only way.

Theoretical research can help us come to conclusions about matters of value as opposed to matters of fact. For example, is it right to try to restrict and control people's access to gaming?

jrphoto6/E+/Getty Images

LOGIC AND LEISURE

We have learned from our examination of the epistemology of leisure research that both empirical and theoretical or philosophic analysis are needed for comprehensive understanding of complex social phenomena such as leisure. The generation of new knowledge by empirical and theoretical or philosophic analysis is based, in part, on accepted rules of logic. **Logic** is the branch of philosophy concerned with principles and structure of reasoning. It is the study of the rules of inference that we can use to determine whether our reasons (premises) properly support conclusions that we make. Inferences (reasoning from premises to conclusions) can be either deductive or inductive.

- Deductive inferences are constructed so that if our premises are true, then our conclusion *has* to be true as well.
- In contrast, the premises of inductive inferences are structured so that if our premises are true, then it is *likely* that our conclusion is true.

Because research aims at discovering new things that we think are true, logic plays an important role in our inquiries by making sure that the conclusions we draw are properly supported. Both empirical research and theoretical or philosophical analysis place a high premium on conformity to accepted rules of logical inference. Leisure research that is deductively invalid or inductively weak is likely to be judged as fatally flawed and be rejected.

Although the rules of logical inference are important to leisure researchers, logic is also important to leisure service practitioners. While many day-to-day work tasks of leisure service practitioners can be implemented in a routine manner, other important management functions such as strategic planning, budgeting, policy creation, and evaluation and action research involve systematic processes whereby decisions must be supported by reasons and rationales. Leisure service practitioners can use inductive and deductive reasoning in these formal management processes to help structure and guide their decision making.

Besides using logic to aid their decision making, practitioners often need to be able to justify their decisions to a variety of stakeholder groups. To be effective managers and providers of leisure services, practitioners must have some understanding of the formal rules of logic for their own decision-making purposes and knowledge of rules and principles of informal logic that relate to everyday conversation. Informal logic—also referred to as *critical thinking*—assesses how people use reasoning and language to try to persuade others to accept conclusions. It focuses not only on detecting fallacies of reasoning but also on understanding nonlogical aspects of communication that may influence the acceptance of a conclusion. Thus, we use informal logic to assess both the structure of inferences and the context in which they are made (e.g., who is making the argument, in what situation is it being made, and who is the audience to which it is being directed). As philosopher Leo Groarke (2017) notes, informal logic is intended to "improve thinking, reasoning, and argument as they occur in real life contexts: in public discussion and debate; in education and intellectual exchange; in interpersonal relations; and in law, medicine and other professions." Whether leisure service providers work in the public, nonprofit, or commercial sectors, being skilled in the application of informal logic helps them effectively justify their decisions and actions to the many constituencies they serve and to whom they are accountable.

AESTHETICS AND LEISURE

Up to this point, we have primarily considered how philosophy relates to leisure in terms of generating scientific knowledge about leisure, but we have not examined our understanding of the art of leisure. **Aesthetics** is the branch of philosophy that deals with questions of the nature of beauty and the value that we associate with art and the natural environment. Our love of beauty is a primary motivation for our interest in the arts, whether we delight in dance, music, theater, painting, sculpture, or other aesthetically oriented leisure activities.

The aesthetic value of the arts has influenced public leisure policy and the development of modern cultural institutions. For example, the 19th-century Victorian era gave rise to the **rational recreation movement**, which attempted to use aesthetic appreciation as a method for elevating the character of the working class and instill middle-class values in them. It was thought that the burgeoning masses of immigrants from abroad and migrants from the farms would be a socially disruptive force in quickly growing industrial cities. Recreation reformers believed that these newcomers to urban life needed to refine their leisure so they would not resort to unsavory recreation activities such as drinking and prostitution (Cross, 1990). While restrictions were imposed on what was deemed morally objectionable leisure, it was also thought that exposure to

The aesthetic value of the arts and the belief that exposure to high culture would encourage the working class to become more responsible citizens has influenced the development of present-day museums.

high culture would encourage the working class to become more productive, responsible citizens. Thus, there was growing public support for cultivating the aesthetic sensibilities of the lower classes by encouraging attendance at cultural institutions such as museums. Art museums, in particular, were seen as well-suited to refining the character of common people by elevating their tastes. As noted by Alexander et al. (2017), these museums were designed to serve multiple purposes, including helping to educate the population, and as symbols of national glory.

Of course, whether the Victorians were correct in believing that the aesthetic value of fine art actually elevated character and reduced criminal behavior of the working class is an open question. And the agenda of raising the aesthetic taste of the lower classes to that of their "betters" is a form of **paternalism** that most people today would find offensive. Furthermore, as has been argued by leisure studies theorist Chris Rojek (1995), we now live in a **postmodern** age where "the divisions between high and low art, elite and popular culture, have collapsed" (p. 165). This dissolving of the barriers

between high and low culture has resulted in the "aestheticization" of everyday life (Featherstone, 1991), in which the regard for beauty takes on a heightened importance in the decisions of ordinary people in their day-to-day doings. Expert opinion on what constitutes the fine and beautiful is not as important as it once was. Today, people are more at ease with determining how to individually style the way they live their lives. Therefore, the idea of using aesthetic appreciation to "improve" certain classes of people has much less currency now than in the past.

As a result, while cultural institutions, such as museums, still conserve and interpret rare and beautiful objects for the public's edification, there is now more emphasis on encouraging visitors to create their own personal sense of appreciation and meaning (Falk & Dierking, 2000; Hein, 1998). This shift toward catering to the various aesthetic interests and tastes of visitors is also reflected in the adoption of new types of leisure opportunities and programming that even a generation ago would be unimaginable. It is now typical for cultural institutions to host a variety of events and activities, such as child–parent sleepovers, community festivals, themed dinners, fund-raising events, and amateur night performances, that would have previously been considered kitschy or lowbrow.

The blurring of the distinction between high and low culture has fundamentally altered the role that aesthetics play in culturally based leisure and recreation. While some are critical of this leveling of the field of aesthetic judgment (e.g., Cuno, 2004), it also presents the prospect for greater participation of students trained in leisure service delivery to work in cultural institutions. Prime opportunities include not only the creation and delivery of innovative, alternative forms of recreational and interpretative programming but also the possibility of becoming involved in the growing field of **visitor studies**, which examines and evaluates the leisure motivations, behaviors, and informal learning experiences of attendees at cultural venues.

Influencing cultural leisure and recreation, aesthetics is also an important factor in outdoor recreation, particularly for those who are attracted to wilderness. Issues concerning the aesthetic values of wilderness constitute a significant part of the outdoor recreation literature. For example, Roderick Nash, an environmental historian, argues that the aesthetic values that Western society has associated with wilderness have run the gamut from seeing nature as repugnantly ugly to sublimely beautiful. In his book *Wilderness and the American Mind*, he argues that wilderness is not a physical place so much as a "mood or feeling in a given individual" (1982, p. 1). Nash notes that ancient Greek, Western pagan, and Judeo-Christian value systems traditionally regarded wilderness as an alien, threatening environment that was repulsive rather than attractive.

- The ancient Greeks regarded the wild heath as fit only for barbarians and found beauty instead in the city and rural countryside.
- The ancient Hebrews saw wilderness as a harsh, forbidding wasteland that was the antithesis of the beautiful, idyllic Garden of Eden.
- The medieval people of northern Europe thought of wilderness as dark, sinister forests inhabited by pagan beings such as trolls and wood sprites.
- When the pioneers came to North America, they brought with them these negative images of wilderness. Combined with the fact that these pioneers were faced with the very real need for survival, wilderness was seen as a forbidding environment to be subdued and civilized.

But Nash notes that as life in North America became more "civilized" by settlement and urban development, people had less reason to see wilderness as an imminent threat to survival. In addition, in the 18th and 19th centuries, a new aesthetic judgment arose toward wilderness based on a philosophic movement called *romanticism*. Rather than seeing nature as ugly and evil, the romantics took the opposite view that wildlands represented the height of divine beauty.

The idea that nature could be aesthetically pleasing was also taken up by the 19th-century transcendentalist philosophers and essayists such as Ralph Waldo Emerson and Henry David Thoreau. The New England transcendentalists believed that profound spiritual truths must be discerned using intuition and imagination rather than rational thought, and they believed that the sublime beauty of nature was a primary pathway to understanding reality. For writers like Thoreau, who retreated to his cabin at Walden Pond, civilization rather than nature was what threatened the well-being of humankind.

Interest in the aesthetics of the natural environment waned for the better part of the 20th century as the field of philosophical aesthetics focused primarily on art, which is, of course, created by humans rather than nature. But issues concerning aesthetics and the natural environment have been revived with the rise of the field of environmental aesthetics. This renewed interest in the aesthetics of the natural environment has been driven by the growth of environmentalism and environmental legislation that can be traced back to the National Environmental Policy Act of 1969, which requires that consideration of aesthetic values be included in environmental impact assessments. Our aesthetic values and judgments concerning nature thus have some practical implications for the management of wilderness.

- Do we, for example, manage wildlands so that the aesthetic values of the landscape are not altered, much in the way that we try to preserve a fine artwork?
- Should we determine the aesthetic value of a natural environment by collecting data concerning the aesthetic experiences of visitors?
- Do we try to optimize the aesthetic appeal of natural environments by introducing nonna-

tive species, for example, if visitors judge them to be more beautiful than the indigenous ones?

- Should ecosystems that are aesthetically pleasing receive more management resources and attention than those that are unremarkable in their beauty (or perhaps even ugly) but are ecologically more important?

- Should we alter the natural environment in ways that make it less aesthetically attractive so that disabled recreationists can have access, say by paving a trail to make it wheelchair accessible?

In these and in other instances, we find ourselves in situations where we must judge the importance of aesthetic values against other important nonaesthetic values to make practical managerial and policy decisions. Given that society is becoming more sensitive to environmental issues, we can expect that environmental aesthetics will play an increasingly important role in decision making for natural resource management. An awareness and understanding of aesthetics is therefore not an abstract exercise in philosophizing; instead, it can help us make better-informed decisions about our roles as stewards of nature and providers of meaningful leisure experiences.

ETHICS AND LEISURE

Of the five branches of philosophy, **ethics** is the one most closely allied with leisure. We often do not think of ethics being that relevant to leisure and recreation. After all, leisure services provide nice things in life such as fun, pleasure, and enjoyment. Why would people working in recreation need to worry about ethical issues? (In fact, it has been suggested that both leisure researchers and practitioners themselves tend to associate recreation and leisure activities with the notion that they are intrinsically good.) But leisure service providers are likely to encounter many vexing ethical issues and dilemmas during their careers to which they must devise acceptable solutions. Consider the context in which leisure services occur. Leisure services are people oriented, and when people interact things can go awry. Leisure service providers are often put in positions of trust.

- Park rangers are charged with protecting both the natural environment and the safety of park visitors.

- Therapeutic recreation specialists are often entrusted with the care of vulnerable populations.

- Supervisors and program leaders of youth programs are expected to manage a high degree of responsibility and provide healthful activities for their young charges.

And the list goes on. Clearly, the provision of organized leisure services is not simply fun and games; it is a serious undertaking that imposes significant ethical responsibilities on service providers.

Ethics, the philosophical study of morality, is closely allied historically to the Western conception of leisure. The ancient Greeks, whose writings form the basis of the study of morality in Western culture, framed ethical inquiry in terms of how people could find happiness and how society should be organized to facilitate living a good life. For philosophers such as Plato and Aristotle, leisure played a critical role in living an optimal life.

Let's first see how Plato handled the question of how ethical behavior relates to living a good life. Then we can compare it to how his student Aristotle refined his master's teachings on the value and ethics of leisure.

Plato's Philosophy of Leisure

Plato wrote several dialogues to answer the practical question of how people should best live their lives. His dialogues read like the script of a play. In them, various characters debate with each other about a question or issue. Plato's greatest dialogue *The Republic* lays out his vision of a utopian society. He reasons that a perfectly ordered society would maximize the happiness of its citizens. To achieve such an ideal state, Plato argues that people's thoughts and actions must be strictly controlled. He proposes a harsh censorship of playful leisure activities that he believes would disrupt the order of a perfect society:

> We must begin, then it seems, by a censorship over our story makers, and what they do well we must pass and what not, reject. And the stories on the accepted list we will induce nurses and mothers to tell their children and so shape their souls by these stories.

Plato is taking aim at the telling of various Greek myths and the epics of the poet Homer. Anyone familiar with Greek mythology knows that the residents of Mount Olympus were hardly good role models. Their chief god, Zeus, is depicted as a philandering husband who seduces both mortal and divine females. His jilted wife, Hera, hatches various plots for revenge on her hapless rivals. The rest of the Olympian gods are no more admirable and are portrayed with all sorts of human failings, vices, and weaknesses. Plato believed that telling these stories of debauched and corrupt gods would harm individuals and society, so he wanted them banned.

In addition to controlling storytelling, Plato believed that other types of leisure activities should be censored. He thought some musical instruments, such as flutes, should not be allowed in his ideal society because their sound would stir the passions of listeners. Similarly, he thought music that was either dirge-like or effeminate should be prohibited because it would make people sad or weak.

Plato carefully separated good leisure activities from bad ones based on his theory of what an ideal society should be like. According to his political philosophy, leisure activities are tools to be used to shape the character of citizens of his utopian society. Only those types of leisure activities that he judged to be virtuous were allowed. He saw many forms of leisure and recreation as threats to his perfectly ordered society. He was most fearful of playful forms of recreation that excited the emotions. Plato thought an ideal society should be ruled by reason alone. The citizens of his ideal Republic were expected to behave as somber, sober rationalists. Perhaps the metaphor of an anthill would best describe his vision of how society should be structured. The workers, soldiers, and rulers who were the citizens of Plato's utopia would all go about doing their assigned **work** with the greatest seriousness. Leisure, recreation, and play would only be encouraged if they had educational or developmental value (Hunnicutt, 1990).

We can still see a legacy of Plato's political philosophy in present-day leisure services. For example, a lot of recreational programming for youth is based on the notion that activities should contribute to positive character development (Johnson & McLean, 1994). And, like Plato, many adults are concerned about the influence of music and stories on children. Even though modern-day democracies permit many freedoms, V-chips are used in televisions, sales of "adult" books and magazines are restricted, and filters are used on computers to try to prevent young minds from being exposed to the images and ideas that parents and community leaders believe are harmful.

Plato's philosophy makes it clear that leisure and recreation are important tools for influencing individuals and society. He does not regard leisure and recreation as mere fun and games, but instead treats them as critical components of a properly functioning society. Yet his vision of leisure emphasizes

repression and control. Who would really want to live in his dreary, regimented utopia? Where is the notion that freedom is an integral part of experiencing leisure? To put the freedom back into leisure, we need to turn to Plato's student, Aristotle.

Aristotle's Philosophy of Leisure

In many ways Aristotle followed Plato's political teachings. Aristotle was willing to advocate the repression of most people living in his society. Women and enslaved people were not allowed the luxury of leisure; that privilege was reserved for the male citizenry. But Aristotle did not picture this leisured class as the idle rich. Rather, the leisured elite were expected to strive for self-perfection. For Aristotle, living the ideal lifestyle was a practical matter. It required following those habits of living that were virtuous and avoiding those that were vices (Hemingway, 1988).

In *Nicomachean Ethics*, Aristotle defined *virtue* as a midpoint between the vices of excess and deficiency. Take, for example, the virtue of courage. It is an excellence of character that results from being neither cowardly (a deficiency) nor foolhardy (an excess). He recognized that every person's situation varies according to personal circumstances. However, each should live their life to maximize virtue—in other words, each person should try to be their very best. To excel in one's life requires a continual commitment to self-improvement. Aristotle therefore argues that one needs to develop habits of living that lead to excellence. It is instructive that the Greek word for ethics is derived from the word *ethos,* which means "habit"—a behavior or practice we continually engage in throughout our lifetime.

But what is the ultimate purpose of developing virtuous habits? Aristotle says that happiness results from being the best we can be. The sort of happiness that Aristotle is thinking of should not be equated with simple pleasure. Amusing ourselves can be pleasant, but he says it is childish and has the potential to cause us harm. **Amusement** for sheer pleasure degrades rather than improves us. Aristotle admits that amusement is helpful if it refreshes us from work. But amusement is never as good as true leisure, which provides a life of deep fulfillment rather than fleeting bodily pleasures.

By using leisure to become our best, Aristotle is not simply thinking of moral goodness but also those characteristics that make us uniquely human. And what did he think was our most noble quality? Aristotle says that it is our capacity for rational thought that distinguishes us from all other forms of life. He argues that the employment of reason in intellectual contemplation leads to perfect happiness. Therefore, he concludes that the person who has the most rewarding lifestyle is the philosopher who is at leisure to develop his intellect to its highest capacity.

We may disagree with Aristotle that being an intellectual is the most rewarding life people can live. It could be plausibly argued that excelling at other human activities, such as food preparation, athletics, or art, could produce equally satisfying lifestyles. But perhaps it is not important to quibble over which human activity is best. Instead, the important feature of Aristotle's theory of happiness is that it is based on the idea that human fulfillment results from achieving excellence from things we choose to do when we use our leisure appropriately.

Aristotle's philosophy of leisure, which emphasizes discipline and commitment rather than the freedom and choice we associate with our modern-day leisure experiences, may seem demanding. Nonetheless, freedom is an important element of Aristotle's concept of virtuous leisure.

- First, we need freedom from material wants so that we can have time for leisure. This means that we cannot be enslaved to our work. We need a sufficient level of material comfort (food, shelter, clothing, and so on) so we can have time for leisure at least during part of our day.

- Second, we need intellectual freedom to understand why virtuous leisure activities are good. When we are children, we can be trained to practice virtuous habits without knowing why those things are desirable. For example, we learn at a very young age not to lie. But it is only when we are older that we fully understand why lying is wrong (e.g., it is hurtful to others). So it is with the practice of virtuous leisure activities. If you are an ancient Greek freeman, you choose certain activities to excel at not because someone has trained you to do them, but because you understand and appreciate that these activities are noble.

- Third, freedom is the essential characteristic of any virtuous leisure activity. These activities are simply worthy in themselves; we do not do them because they will bring fame, wealth, or other extrinsic rewards. In other words, virtuous leisure activities are intrinsically good.

CONTEMPORARY PHILOSOPHY OF LEISURE

We might ask whether Aristotle's elitist definition of leisure has much relevance to our modern lifestyles. Perhaps we can relate to Aristotle's refined version of leisure when we think of the high level of accomplishment of professional athletes, cordon bleu chefs, and concert pianists. These people live lives devoted to perfecting their talents. But these examples are not leisure activities. Instead, they are occupations—ways of making a living. It is difficult for us to think of excellence apart from working. Typically, when we are very good at something, we want to turn it into a career. We tend to value activities that can be made productive. We are very work oriented, whereas the ancient Greeks were work averse. It was not that the Greeks thought that work was something evil, but rather they regarded it only as a necessity of life. They worked so that they could enjoy life. According to their value system, it was leisure that gave meaning and purpose to their life, not work (De Grazia, 1963).

For most of us, it is typically our work, career, or occupation that gives us our sense of self-worth.

Aristotle began his philosophic inquiry by asking himself what an ideal lifestyle for human beings should be like. What do you think?

PanosKarapanagiotis/iStockphoto/Getty Images

If you do not believe this is true, think back to the last time you met someone at a social occasion. When making new acquaintances, was it your leisure activities or your work that you primarily used to describe yourself to others? In our modern culture, the question "So what do you do?" implicitly assumes that you will respond by describing your occupation and workplace. Extolling the virtues of work would seem very odd to the ancient Greeks. We appear to have reversed that equation.

Weber's Analysis of the Work Ethic

Have you ever heard someone being praised for having a strong work ethic? This assertion is derived from Max Weber's influential book *The Protestant Ethic and the Spirit of Capitalism* (Weber, 1930/1958). The **Protestant work ethic** refers to a cultural ideal that regards work as the most important activity in an individual's life. Weber believed that a new reverence for work arose from the Protestant Reformation, when Christian religious leaders such as Martin Luther and John Calvin rebelled against the Catholic Church. Both Luther

and Calvin saw the medieval church as a corrupt institution in which the upper echelons of the clergy lived a life of wealth and leisure. Up until the time of the Reformation, the church had followed Aristotle's teachings concerning leisure and the good life. The clergy and the nobility comprised the leisured class; both were educated and wealthy enough to have the free time to engage in refined intellectual and cultural activities. The many ordinary, uneducated peasants were little more than enslaved people who provided brute labor for the upper classes. In their radical break from the church, Luther and Calvin turned Aristotle's conception of the good life on its head, making work—not leisure—the foundation of a worthy life. Both Luther and Calvin believed in the notion of a *calling*, whereby everyone had been assigned by God a certain task or occupation to perform throughout life. Answering one's calling in life was considered a virtue because you would be doing the work God intended for you. Conversely, ignoring your calling was a vice and would lead to an empty, directionless life. Thus, since the time of the Reformation, it has been work rather than leisure that culturally defines our conception of the good life.

© Human Kinetics

Weber's work ethic changed our view of the good life to value hard work over leisure.

Russell's Critique of the Work Ethic

Some philosophers have taken great exception to the notion that work can make our lives truly happy. Bertram Russell penned a tongue-in-cheek essay in the early 1930s titled "In Praise of Idleness" in which he criticizes the idea that work is virtuous. Russell argues that preindustrial societies were based on a "slave morality" used to justify the subjugation of large numbers of manual laborers so that a privileged aristocracy would have leisure to pursue spiritual, cultural, and intellectual activities. However, with the coming of the industrial revolution, modern technology created such an abundance of goods that it was possible for everyone to have sufficient resources for a leisured lifestyle. But rather than using technology to give everyone adequate leisure, Russell says we continue to support the idea that leisure should be reserved for the upper crust of society and denied to the working class.

Russell argues that it would be more rational to replace the traditional, but outmoded, slave morality with a leisure ethic that distributes work evenly. Rather than having a leisure class that does no work at all and a working class that is either overworked or unemployed, Russell proposes a work-sharing arrangement that would reduce people's working time to four hours per day and still provide the "necessaries and elementary comforts" of life (Russell, 1960, p. 17). Russell believes that with these greatly reduced work hours, humanity would enter a new golden age of leisure, giving people the freedom to pursue cultural and intellectual interests. Perhaps Russell is naive to think that everyone would use their liberation from work for ennobling leisure activities. Would not many people choose to waste their free time engaged in frivolous amusements? Nonetheless, even if many people would not use their leisure wisely, we can still ask if that is a good enough justification for keeping people busy with work. Maybe what is really needed is not only sufficient free time but also attractive and meaningful leisure opportunities that professionalized leisure services can provide.

Pieper's Critique of the Work Ethic

Josef Pieper, a Catholic philosopher, also strongly criticizes allegiance to the work ethic in his book *Leisure: The Basis of Culture* (1998). Pieper, who is writing of Europe in the aftermath of World War II, says that we no longer know what leisure is because we live in a totally work-oriented culture. Pieper argues that our fixation on work is so complete that even liberal arts disciplines such as philosophy are now treated as a type of "intellectual labor" and are only valued for their usefulness for solving practical problems. (And isn't this why many people ridicule philosophy and leisure studies, because these disciplines are thought to be useless?) According to Pieper, knowledge for knowledge's sake is devalued by our culture of work, and our leisure time is only thought to be useful if it refreshes us so that we can then resume our work with renewed vigor. Ironically, Pieper observes, our worship of work produces a meaningless, unsatisfying lifestyle. We live to work well rather than working so that we can live well.

Rojek's Critique of the Work Ethic

As the title of his book *The Labour of Leisure* (2010) suggests, Chris Rojek also argues that leisure has become a form of work. But whereas Pieper thought that modern Western society is marked by a shift from leisure to a work ethic, Rojek believes that present-day postmodern culture has blurred the traditional boundaries between work and leisure. Work, he says, now contains elements of play, whereas leisure can be a type of work. According to Rojek, leisure no longer functions as a respite from work but instead is the setting in which we learn the skills for living a successful life. He identifies **emotional intelligence** and **emotional labor** as the two key abilities that "competent, relevant and credible" people seek to develop during leisure (Rojek, 2010, p. 3).

The changes in our economic means of production from manufacturing to services means that personal interactions are now much more central to success in life. Emotional intelligence primarily refers to the capacity to accurately perceive and understand one's own emotions and the emotions of others. The closely related concept of emotional labor focuses on the ability to manage one's emotional responses when confronting work situations that are emotionally challenging, such as maintaining an appropriately professional demeanor with a rude, agitated customer. People who capably understand and regulate their emotions are, therefore, at a competitive advantage in their work and leisure lives in comparison to people who bludgeon their way through life lacking the ability to control their own emotions or are unable to respond appropriately to the emotions of others. Rojek concludes that leisure is not about freedom (which he says is for the birds), but rather it is where we school ourselves in emotional intelligence and emotional labor. If Rojek's analysis is correct, then the implication for leisure services practitioners is that emotional intelligence and emotional labor are critical competencies that they should be ready to deploy when providing leisure services and strive to build up when engaging in their own leisure.

Veblen's Critique of Consumption

Although many people believe that being a success entails working hard to achieve enough financial independence to be able to retire to a life of luxury, could our worship of work sabotage our leisure lives? Many critics argue that our economic system works against our aspirations for a truly leisured lifestyle.

Modern economies encourage ever-expanding growth in the production and consumption of products and services. As individuals, we live in a consumer culture in which our success is measured by how much we can purchase. The more luxurious and expensive the goods and experiences we can purchase, the higher our social status. The American economist Thorstein Veblen termed the ostentatious displays of wealth *conspicuous consumption* (Veblen, 1899/1998). Veblen criticized the superrich of his era—the Vanderbilts, Carnegies, and Rockefellers—as status seekers who used the great wealth they had amassed from their 19th-century business empires to give themselves an air of nobility. Their mansions, yachts, and lavish parties were symbols that these American industrialists "had arrived" at the good life.

Of course, most of us are not billionaires. We cannot hope to own executive jets, hand-built sports cars, or vacation homes on private Caribbean islands. Yet compared to the standard of living of ancient Greek freemen the lifestyle of the average person living in postindustrial societies is opulent. We have at our disposal a vast array of consumer products and services that Aristotle and his compatriots could not have imagined.

Other Critiques of Consumption

Unfortunately, being able to afford these products and services means that most of us must devote a huge portion of our adult lives to work. The flip side of a highly consumptive lifestyle is that we must also be highly productive to pay for it. During our working lives, many of us find our time for leisure is limited. Our careers require us to put in long days at work, leaving little time or energy for family and friends.

The consumerist lifestyle that most of us have adopted encourages us to think of leisure as a basket of commodities from which we pick and choose. Instead of being participants in unique and personal recreation activities, we are consumers of leisure experiences designed and mass-produced by others (Hemingway, 1996). In this market-driven context, the concept of freedom is inextricably tied to the act of purchasing: When there are many leisure products and services for sale, we have greater freedom to choose.

This free-market model of leisure services and products is undeniably attractive to most people. The leisure industry is one of the biggest and fastest growing sectors of the economy. Yet this apparent success masks several drawbacks to our commercialized leisure. As social economist Juliet Schor (1998) argues in her aptly titled book *The Overspent American*, the most obvious problem with the idea that we can buy happiness is that many of us spend more on our leisure than we can afford. Indications of overspending can be found in the level of household debt, which provides a reasonable measure of the level of stress on consumer finances. The post–World War II period has witnessed continually rising household debt levels, except for the period of the financial crisis and Great Recession that led to a one-time reduction of debt from 2008 to 2013. However, since mid-2013, debt levels have resumed their upward trajectory and, as of 2015 were back to the prerecessionary levels of 2008. While credit delinquencies significantly fell during the Great Recession, credit card, auto, and, in particular, student loan defaults are again growing. In addition, a pandemic, supply chain issues, and inflation, all of which are creating an impact on a global level, may further affect the issue of consumer debt throughout many countries of the world. So the reduction in debt triggered by the 2008 financial crisis has been a one-time event (Haughwout et al., 2017). The use of borrowing to finance the consumption of goods and services has returned us to our "normal" state of affairs in which we use debt accumulation to help finance our current standard of living that we may not be able to afford in the long run. Evidence of this overspending can be gleaned from the fact that even higher income earners may find their retirement savings insufficient to maintain lifestyles they were accustomed to while working.

The consumerist lifestyle demands that we work more to afford more goods. These shoppers hope to find happiness from the products they purchase.

Aside from the question of the long-term viability of consumerist lifestyles, the commodification of leisure may discourage personal growth by making our recreation experiences too convenient. Commercial providers of leisure services typically want to make their offerings as attractive as possible to their potential clientele. Competitive advantage can be gained by making the consumption of leisure services and products as effortless as possible. The examples are many: Golf manufacturers advertise that their clubs alone will lower your handicap and you don't have to improve your swing; resort operators provide familiar fast-food items at exotic destinations so that guests will not have to adjust to the local cuisine; movie and television producers "dumb down" the content of popular entertainment lest audiences be made to think; and the list goes on.

Although our modern leisure services and products may be convenient, we might ask whether most are worthy of our time, not to mention our money. Aristotelian leisure is based on the idea that we should devote our free time to being the best we can be. The ancient view of leisure emphasized commitment and accomplishment. In contrast, as philosopher Albert Borgmann notes, commodified

leisure appeals to our desire for comfort (Borgmann, 1984). Often, our modern leisure practices do not result in self-improvement. In fact, many of our recreational activities may cause us harm. Watching television, our most popular leisure pastime, has been linked to several modern maladies including obesity, depression, and paranoia (Gerbner, 1999; Kubey & Csikzentmihalyi, 1990). But it is attractive because of its easy access—you simply turn on the TV and then sit back and enjoy. Even our more active forms of recreation tend to cater to our desire for creature comforts. When practical and affordable, we often choose to motorize outdoor recreation activities.

- Why climb up a slope when you can use a chairlift?
- Why paddle or row when you can simply twist the throttle on an outboard engine?
- Why carry your clubs when you can ride in a cart?

These uses of machines are said to enhance our leisure experiences, but they may also disengage us from our environment and each other.

Harvard sociologist Robert Putnam (2000) argues in his book *Bowling Alone* that Americans are becoming increasingly socially isolated. He cites a wealth of statistics showing that membership in community organizations dropped dramatically at the end of the 20th century. As a result, Putnam believes that Americans have become less satisfied with their lives because they have experienced a decline in their **social capital**—the social connections that support people in times of difficulty and make life more enjoyable in times of leisure. He attributes diminishing social capital to the changes in society that alter our work and leisure values:

> Over the last three decades a variety of social, economic and technological changes have rendered obsolete a significant stock of America's social capital. Television, two-career families, suburban sprawl, generational changes in values—these and other changes in American society have meant that fewer and fewer of us find that the League of Women Voters, or the United Way, or the Shriners, or the monthly bridge club, or even a Sunday picnic with friends fits the way we have come to live. (Putnam, 2000, p. 365)

A similar decline in social capital may be happening in Canadian society, although the data are more mixed. For example, a study of social cohesion found that Canadians perceived themselves as having a high level of personal social support ("someone they can confide in, count on in a crisis situation, obtain advice from when making important decisions, and someone who makes them feel loved and cared for") but a low level of social involvement ("frequency of participation in associations or voluntary organizations and frequency of attendance at religious services") (Jackson et al., 2000, pp. 66, 68).

Putnam compares the malaise in community involvement to the problems that faced American society at the end of the 19th century when rapid industrialization created a host of social problems in large cities. He notes that people responded to these social ills by becoming more involved in civic activities and voluntary organizations, and he argues that we need to find ways to use our leisure time to be more civically engaged.

Perhaps it is because we are at least subconsciously aware that many of our leisure activities are unworthy experiences that we devise various rationales to justify our modern leisure lifestyles. We see shopping as an exciting recreational activity rather than a mundane necessity of life. We tell our employees that we value wellness, but what we are really worried about are rising absenteeism and medical expenses. We take minivacations that cause the least disruption of our work schedules and take along our laptops and handheld devices to avoid falling behind. At home, rather than spending unstructured, spontaneous time with our kids, we plan infrequent special activities and call it *quality time*. Unfortunately, this list goes on.

What we seem to lack is a sense that our leisure activities can be self-justifying. Our view of leisure as a commodity is based on the implicit premise that our leisure activities are a means to achieving some other goal. Perhaps that is not a surprising mind-set given that we live in a commercialized culture in which we are constantly bombarded with messages about products and services that promise this or that benefit. But this lifestyle is ultimately unsatisfying for many of us because it keeps us focused on our leisure as a means to something else rather than a worthy end in itself. The ancient Greeks understood very well that leisure should be reserved for activities that were good in and of themselves. Aristotle did not recommend philosophic inquiry as the best leisure activity because it made him more productive at work. Rather, he simply argued that it was the most intrinsically worthy activity that human beings could do.

Aristotle, it must be acknowledged, did not face the challenges to leisure that we do today. His social environment was far less complex than what we must deal with as leisure service providers. Of course, it may seem that there is little we can do to influence the quality of people's lives given the strong cultural and economic forces that encourage people to be workers and consumers. But we are not completely powerless. As leisure service providers, we can make a difference in the lives of the people and communities that we serve. It all begins with a clear understanding of our own leisure values. For example, if we know that people are stressed by a culture that overvalues work, then we have an obligation as leisure service providers to advocate for the value of leisure. If we see that people are stressed by an economic system that encourages the overconsumption of products, then we can offer alternative leisure activities that encourage social interaction and community building. Surely if we think of ourselves as quality-of-life specialists, then we need a philosophical understanding of some of the major problems that people and communities face; otherwise, we may unwittingly become part of the problem rather than part of the solution.

SOLVING ETHICAL DILEMMAS IN LEISURE SERVICES

So far, we have used ethical analysis to help us evaluate our leisure lifestyles. In our roles as socially responsible leisure service providers, we need this macro, or big-picture, understanding of the broad social and political issues that affect the quality of people's leisure lives. Essentially, we are using ethical analysis to continue the ancient Greeks' project of determining the role of leisure in a worthwhile life. This sort of analysis is prescriptive rather than descriptive, because it aims not simply to describe our past or current lifestyles but instead to determine how we should live our lives. But we can also use ethical analysis in a micro, or small-picture, way to help us solve problems relating to the delivery of leisure services. Consider the Philosophical Analysis: Tanning-Bed Case sidebar, which presents an **ethical dilemma** that narrowly focuses on a situation and set of individuals at a public recreation center.

Dealing effectively with the tanning-bed problem mentioned in the sidebar requires more than having a big-picture understanding of the situation. After all, the big picture tells us that skin cancer is a serious health problem, and as socially responsible leisure service providers we shouldn't provide equipment or services that are potentially dangerous. Yet, many of the people we serve don't agree with our point of view; therefore, we are left in an uncomfortable position in which a lot of people may be angry or unhappy. What we need is a way to resolve these ethical dilemmas that are common in leisure services. Fortunately, ethical analysis can help us decide the proper course of action in cases in which we are confronted with a moral conflict involving specific people at a particular time and place.

To deal effectively with ethical dilemmas, we need an ethical decision-making method we can use to justify our decisions. And as responsible leisure service providers, we are obligated to provide the people who are affected by our decisions with reasonable explanations for our actions. Not everyone will agree with our decisions, but we need to demonstrate that our decisions are not made arbitrarily. Skepticism about the wisdom of our decisions is likely to be stronger when we are dealing with ethical dilemmas, and emotions tend to run high when moral points of view come into conflict. Although it is a common belief that ethical issues are based on opinion rather than fact, we can

nonetheless apply ethical theories to help us create a rationale for our actions.

We can see from the application of the three ethical theories to the tanning-bed scenario that solutions to ethical dilemmas are not always obvious. Some might think that tanning beds should be installed, while others might be opposed to placing this type of equipment in a community recreation facility. Furthermore, we might disagree on which ethical theory is best for solving the dilemma. Some people may think consequences should decide the issue, others might believe duties are paramount, and a third group might believe that considerations of our character should dictate what to do. The important point is not that we might disagree about the proper solution to the ethical dilemma, but instead that our moral deliberations help us justify and explain our decision to people who disagree with us.

For example, suppose the people who want the tanning beds are thinking in terms of the consequences. They want the beds because they are after certain outcomes such as what they believe to be a healthy look or a sexier body. Now we can talk to them on their wavelength by pointing out negative outcomes such as skin cancer and premature aging. If they still insist that the benefits outweigh the costs, then we can also explain that we have a duty to uphold the mission of the agency to provide healthy recreation, and that according to our own professional standards, we would not feel right about providing equipment that could cause serious health problems. Of course, it is completely possible that people still will not be persuaded that we are making the right decision, but at least we have provided them with a reasonable, well-thought-out explanation for the decision. And we have accomplished this very practical task by using ethical analysis to justify it.

Serious social and ethical issues are bound to arise as we work to help people improve their leisure lifestyles. If we are unable to assess the worthiness of various leisure activities, then we run the risk of providing leisure opportunities that may not enhance the quality of people's lives. Ethical analysis can give us a macro understanding to judge the worthiness of the various leisure and recreation activities that we might choose to provide. We have seen that most of our current leisure experiences seem to be geared toward the worlds of work and commerce rather than with the provision of opportunities to engage in intrinsically satisfying activities and personal growth. But besides providing us with

Philosophical Analysis: Tanning-Bed Case

You are the recreation supervisor at a multipurpose community recreation center. The mission of the center is to promote the well-being of the citizens in the local community by providing a wide variety of high-quality recreation activities. Since the center opened, the fitness area has played an important role in satisfying the recreation center's mission. The fitness equipment and programs are popular, and they benefit participants' physical health and well-being. Recently, however, some of the patrons have asked the recreation center to install tanning beds. Many of these requests are from teenagers and young adults who say they like to work out at the center, but they also want to be able to get a deep tan. You have never wanted to install tanning beds, because you have read research that indicates that the exposure to UV rays that these beds produce increases the likelihood of skin cancer, including the deadliest form of the disease, malignant melanoma. You announce that the center will not purchase the beds because of the possible negative health effects. Unfortunately, your decision is met with dismay and even outright hostility. Many of the young people who want the beds installed say they are not worried about cancer. Some say they will drop their memberships and join a nearby private health club that has the beds. Several of the middle-aged members have contacted their representatives on the city council (to whom you report) to lobby for purchasing the beds. And a few have threatened to go to the local media and "raise a stink" about how adults should be allowed to choose whether they can tan and should not be treated like children by the recreation center staff.

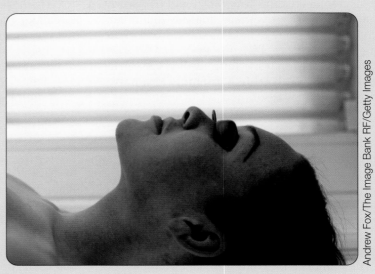

Philosophical analysis can help solve the problem of whether tanning beds should be used at a recreation center.

Andrew Fox/The Image Bank RF/Getty Images

Ethical Analysis: Three Approaches

Let's consider how you might apply ethical theory to decide what to do in the tanning-bed case. Three basic ethical theories can help you decide whether to install the beds:

1. **Consequence-based ethics**
2. **Duty-based ethics**
3. **Virtue-based ethics**

Using the first approach, you weigh the consequences of installing or not installing the tanning beds. If you install the beds, you will make many people who use the recreation center happy. You will also not lose members to the private health club because you lack tanning beds. You also will not have to deal with client complaints to the city council or the newspapers. From a consequence-based ethics perspective, the downsides would be the initial cost of the equipment and the possibility that some recreation center clients might eventually develop skin cancer. Because there seems to be several definite, immediate benefits to installing the beds, it would be reasonable to conclude that you should go ahead and spend the money on the tanning beds.

The second way you can determine the most ethical course of action is to use a duty-based ethics perspective to evaluate your duties and obligations. One important duty you have is to carry out the mission of the recreation center. You are there to serve the public, so you have an obligation to provide services that people want. But you also have an obligation to provide services that benefit people's well-being. Given that public recreation organizations receive tax monies to provide leisure services that serve the public good, it is reasonable to assume that protecting the community's well-being is a more important duty than simply providing services that people want. Therefore, from a duty-based ethics perspective, you should not install the tanning beds because that would betray your obligation to provide healthy leisure services.

At this point in the moral deliberations, you have come to opposing conclusions. Analysis from consequence-based ethics indicates that you should install the tanning beds, and duty-based ethics argues that you should not install them. How do you break this moral deadlock? You might want to turn to the third way of analyzing ethical dilemmas: virtue-based ethics. With virtue-based ethics, moral decisions are made by reflecting on your character. Instead of comparing outcomes or weighing duties, virtue-based ethics resolves ethical dilemmas using your personal integrity. For example, will you diminish yourself and have less integrity if you install the tanning beds in the fitness center? If the users of the beds are mature adults aware of the dangers of UV exposure, then possibly not. These adults have simply made a choice to engage in an activity that endangers their health. But what about the teenagers who also want to use the beds? Will you find it hard to look at yourself in the mirror before you go to work knowing you have exposed teenagers to health risks that they might not be willing to take if they were mature adults? Therefore, from a virtue-ethics perspective, you might install the tanning beds only if you have an effective way to prohibit teens from using the beds and if you can ensure that the adults at the center are well-educated about the risks of UV exposure.

a big picture of some of the social issues facing leisure services, ethical analysis can also help us deal with micro issues arising from the ethical dilemmas that we will inevitably encounter during our careers as leisure service providers. Without an awareness and understanding of the ethical issues arising from leisure and recreation activities, we run the risk of causing unintended harm to the people we serve and the resources that we have been entrusted with. Rather than having to rely solely on our intuition, we can use methods of ethical analysis to help us justify and explain our solutions to difficult moral dilemmas.

SUMMARY

We hope that our examination of the five branches of philosophy—metaphysics, epistemology, logic, aesthetics, and ethics—has persuaded you that philosophic analysis plays a fundamental role in leisure research and the provision of leisure services. Philosophy and leisure are often misperceived as being frivolous and of little practical consequence. Yet our examination of the relevance of philosophy to leisure illustrates that neither is trivial. Leisure and recreation, both as an academic discipline and as a service practice, has tremendous potential to affect the quality of people's lives and the natural environment. Leisure and recreation are complex social phenomena and are essential to living a worthwhile life. Philosophical inquiry helps us understand leisure and recreation and guide service practices in many ways.

- Metaphysics emphasizes understanding of the essential qualities of leisure.

- Epistemology teaches us that knowledge of leisure needs to be generated by empirical and rationalist methods.

- Logic helps leisure service decision makers not only avoid making faulty inferences but also persuasively defend and justify their positions to others.

- Aesthetics reveals the significance of beauty to our leisure experiences and the need to find a proper balance between aesthetic and nonaesthetic values.

- Ethics helps us deal with larger questions of what constitutes worthwhile, fulfilling leisure and provides us with theories to analyze moral dilemmas that practitioners inevitably face.

Contrary to popular opinion, leisure services is not a matter of fun and games, and philosophy is not idle speculation. Far from being either impractical or inconsequential, the study of leisure and philosophy is fundamental to helping us think and act in ways that improve the quality of people's lives and protect the natural environment.

Review Questions

1. What is epistemology?
2. Which of the branches of philosophy is most allied with leisure?
3. How is Plato's philosophy exhibited in present-day leisure services?
4. How is Aristotle's philosophy exhibited in present-day leisure services?

Go to *HKPropel* to complete the activities for this chapter.

CHAPTER 4

Leisure and Recreation for Individuals in Society

Juan Tortosa Martínez, Daniel G. Yoder, and Mary Sara Wells

Grant Faint/The Image Bank RF/Getty Images

" The person and the group are not separable phenomena, but are simply the individual and collective aspects of the same thing. "

Loran David Osborn and M.H. Neumeyer, sociologists

LEARNING OUTCOMES

After reading this chapter, you should be able to do the following:

> Show how leisure and recreation are complex human endeavors that take place within society

> Describe how leisure and recreation, whether as solitary activities or undertaken with friends, family, or larger groups, affect and are affected by society

> Describe how gender, sexual orientation, ethnicity and race, religion, and socioeconomic class affect leisure and recreation and how leisure and recreation in turn affect those factors

> Demonstrate that the values of goodness or badness can be applied to leisure and recreation

> Explain the implications of a social perspective for leisure and recreation professionals

Consider the leisure of the individual *in* society, not the leisure of the individual *and* society. Although this distinction may seem trivial, it is important. Individuals and societies do exist as separate entities in concept, but on a practical level, neither can exist independent of the other. Societies are composed of people of various

- ages,
- abilities,
- races,
- ethnicities,
- genders,
- sexual orientations,
- classes, and
- numerous other social categories.

Without these essential parts, there could be no whole. Nor do individuals exist isolated from society; human beings are social animals by nature. All human existence (including leisure and recreation) takes place at the intersection of the individual and the diverse social structures that make up our world. Even the act of thinking, which is seemingly the quintessential individual activity, is impossible without the use of mental cultural symbols. These mental images are possible only within the borders of a common cultural context.

It's worth noting again that leisure and recreation are often used interchangeably, as if they are two words for the same phenomenon. While they certainly are related, they are not the same. The term *leisure* has often been referred to as nebulous. It can be conceived as time, various activities, or even a state of mind. On the other hand, *recreation* is much more concrete or definable. Recreation is activity consciously undertaken with anticipated outcomes. Those who recreate do so with some purpose or expectation of a certain outcome. Recreation is a

type of leisure, but leisure is not a kind of recreation. Thus, it is appropriate and nonredundant to use the phrase "leisure and recreation."

We begin this chapter with a general discussion of how leisure and recreation activities take place against a social backdrop. Even when people are physically alone in their activities, **society** influences them, and their activities may in turn influence society. We also discuss the relationships between leisure and primary groups of family and close friends, secondary groups, and the following social institutions:

- Gender and sexual orientation
- Ethnicity and race
- Religion
- Socioeconomic class

It is important to note that other social institutions such as age and ability also have a great impact on how individuals engage in leisure and recreation activities. The two specific issues, however, are discussed later in the text and, therefore, will not be covered in this chapter.

Because the moral value of a leisure activity (its goodness or badness) is determined by both leisure participants and the world in which they live, we consider good and bad leisure. Finally, we discuss the implications of leisure and recreation in society for the professional practitioner.

LEISURE AS A COMPLEX SOCIAL PHENOMENON

Leisure is a wonderfully complex social phenomenon that is affected by many social institutions including economics, politics, work, technology, and war. But we must be careful in thinking that leisure and recreation are trivial pastimes that are influenced and even dictated by these social structures. In fact, leisure and recreation significantly affect the social forces just listed. Consider, for example, Las Vegas, Nevada. Without the leisure and tourism industries that pour billions of dollars into Las Vegas each year, the town would be much different (or perhaps nonexistent). Examples like this, although perhaps not as obvious, play out every day in thousands of communities across North America and around the globe.

Solitary Leisure and Society

A few leisure activities are entirely solitary, some are purely social, and most can be either private or communal.

- Reading is almost always undertaken alone.
- Playing a game of tennis always requires interaction with others.
- Playing cards is an example of an activity that can be either solitary or social, and most leisure activities fall into this category. Some people spend hours playing the classic solo card game solitaire, but you cannot play bridge without other players to compete against.

Although we might be inclined to think that our **solitary leisure** is ours and ours alone, it does not take place in a social vacuum. Indeed, other people and groups of people profoundly affect our solitary leisure activities. Furthermore, the leisure activities we undertake while we are alone have an influence—sometimes significant and sometimes not so significant—on the people and the world around us. The world around us affects our private leisure in many ways: It might support leisure, infringe on it, prohibit it, or even force us into it.

Let's consider one single act of solitary leisure and its influences. Even if you don't recognize the name, nearly everyone is familiar with the story of Aron Ralston, the young climber who was forced to cut off his arm after it became trapped between two boulders in the Utah backcountry. Thousands of dollars were spent by state and county agencies to find and save Ralston. Hundreds of volunteers sacrificed days for the search. The tragedy could have been averted if Ralston had hiked with a companion, but he chose to go it alone on this adventure. However, this story has been a tremendous inspiration to many people—not just outdoor enthusiasts. It is impossible to measure the positive consequences of this single act of courage on a solo hike in the Utah desert.

Leisure and Primary Groups

When other people are involved in a leisure activity, they are not merely bystanders but essential components of the activity. Kelly (1987) has noted that "in general, people are more important in leisure than the form of the activity" (p. 158). Especially significant are those who are part of the participant's **primary group**. Sociologists have defined primary groups as "small groups in which there are face-to-face relations of a fairly intimate and personal nature. Primary groups are of two basic types, families and cliques. In other words, they are organized around ties of either kinship or friendship" (Lenski et al., 1995, p. 48). We examine leisure activities with family and close friends only briefly here because this topic is more thoroughly considered in chapter 12.

Social customs and societal expectations profoundly affect leisure when activities are undertaken with family members and close friends. Defining the term *family* is not as simple as it may seem at first glance. Because different cultures use various forms of kinship groupings, and even the same culture may change its notion of family over time, a definition that all can agree on has been elusive. But no matter how it is defined, the family profoundly influences leisure.

The leisure lifestyle of adolescence clearly shows the effect of two occasionally competing forces: family and friends. Let's consider online behavior as an example. Kelsey is a 16-year-old from Montreal. Like many teenagers, she considers her parents to be out of touch, especially regarding her leisure activities. She is alone in her room for a night of chatting with her friends through social media. She and several of her friends do this for several hours every night. Her parents do not understand the fascination Kelsey and her friends have with apps such as TikTok and Snapchat.

Families typically move through a series of somewhat predictable stages. Not all families go through every stage, but most do or aspire to. These stages are not distinct; instead, each stage merges with those around it. Each phase of a family's development includes typical leisure activities, roles, and patterns. Consider these two scenarios:

- Many new families without children have a great deal of flexibility. Leisure activities can be spontaneous. Couples might be able to throw a few items together and get away for a weekend vacation in an hour or so.
- A family with children must coordinate their work and school schedules. Considerably more

FamVeld/iStockphoto/Getty Images

A person may participate in various athletic pursuits throughout their life because of childhood experiences of skiing with their mother.

clothing and equipment must be organized. Child safety must be considered. If the children are not going away with the parents, child care must be considered. Even the destination of the vacation is affected. A quick trip to Las Vegas is more common for a family without children, whereas a trip to visit grandparents is common for families with children.

A clear example of familial influence is found in sport. Clark (2008) used data from the General Social Surveys of 1992 and 2005 to study children's participation in sport. He found that the family affects not only children's choices of a sport but also choices through adolescence and early adulthood. Other studies support his contention that "sporty parents have sporty kids" (p. 55).

Leisure and Secondary Groups

Secondary groups affect a person's leisure activities, and a person's leisure activities have the potential to affect the secondary group. Henslin (1993) defines a **secondary group**, compared with a primary group, as "a larger, relatively temporary, more anonymous, formal and impersonal group based on some interest or activity, whose members are likely to interact on the basis of specific roles" (p. 150). Some secondary groups, such as a college classroom, a political party, or a labor union, are not related to leisure, but many are. The following examples show the obvious influence a secondary group can have on its members:

- Emira dedicates Wednesday evenings to attending a pottery class at the local park district. Instead of returning home after work on Wednesdays to spend time with her family, Emira grabs a quick bite to eat and heads straight to the pottery class.

- Miguel is a member of the National Rifle Association (NRA), and with a particularly contentious national election coming up, he receives promotional material from this organization nearly every week. Instead of watching his favorite TV shows on Wednesday night, Miguel attends NRA meetings each week. Miguel decides to vote for a candidate who supports the NRA and opposes gun control.

- Jim and Margaret, who are recently retired and fairly affluent, love to travel. They have joined a local group that organizes trips for its members. They benefit from the reduced group rates and the opportunity to interact with people with similar travel interests.

- Jamal has been playing in a cornhole league every Friday night. Not only does he enjoy playing, but he also sees a great deal of potential for this activity as a fund-raiser. When the board of the local food pantry (of which Jamal is a member) discusses fund-raisers, Jamal volunteers to organize a cornhole tournament for the community.

Although we can see how a secondary group influences the actions of individuals, the influence an individual may have on the group is not quite so obvious. It is nevertheless very real, as these examples show:

- Emira, the fledgling potter, has had a very bad week. When she attends the week's pottery session, she gets into an argument with the instructor about the schedule for firing her pottery pieces. Their heated conversation is overheard by several other class members, and it casts a pall on the evening's class.

- Although Miguel believes in most of the positions taken by the NRA, he cannot support the right of Americans to own assault rifles. It is one thing to have a rifle or a shotgun for hunting, but he believes assault rifles are just too dangerous. Thus, he begins to encourage other members to write letters to the NRA to put pressure on it to change its stance on this issue.

- Jim and Margaret believe that the local travel club has been a little too conservative in planning trips. At a meeting, they ask why the club cannot plan a trip to an exotic location such as Tahiti. Although some of the members balk at the idea, some become convinced that this is a good idea, and they assign a subcommittee to look into the possibility of such a trip.

- Jamal has convinced the food pantry's board to take on the cornhole tournament as its primary fund-raiser. The organization needs to discontinue two other fund-raising events to have enough volunteers for this activity.

filmstudio/E+/Getty Images

A member of a pottery class may have as much influence on the group as the group influences the individual. One student in the pottery class may subtly but effectively change the sessions from social events set against the backdrop of fun pottery making to serious, solo creative outlets. If most take that student's lead, fewer people will feel free to spend much time talking and laughing with their classmates.

The possibility of significantly affecting the group is more likely if the secondary group is local, such as the pottery class. Although it is difficult for an individual to change a national organization such as the NRA, it is possible.

Social categories also affect leisure activities. Lenski and Lenski (1987) note that people can be grouped into a variety of societal classifications. We become members of some of these groups voluntarily, and we are born into others. For instance, we can choose to become a member of a cooking and dining club, but our race is largely predetermined.

SIMILARITY AND DIVERSITY IN RECREATION AND LEISURE

The human race possesses a unique dynamic balance among all the fascinating characteristics that make us different and all the equally fascinating characteristics that make us similar. Diversity is an incredibly important physiological and social phenomenon, but we dare not forget or minimize our sameness. We are much more alike than we are different. In a commencement speech at Howard University, President Bill Clinton (2013) said:

We are all 99.5 percent the same. But, we spend 99.5 percent of our time thinking about the half percent of us that is different.

Such may be the case in leisure. A huge majority of people socialize as a leisure activity, but only a relative few go on wilderness excursions. Often, more attention is devoted to the difference in rates of outdoor recreation among various groups than to the commonality of socializing as leisure activity. Let's look at four examples.

- Ariché is an 18-year-old female member of the Tarahumara nation in the interior of Mexico. She is looking forward to the upcoming *tesguinado*, a festival that will celebrate the good news that the men of the tribe have won a running race against another tribe of Native Americans. There will be food and much drinking of *tesguino*, a beer made from corn. But to Ariché, what is important is not the food or the alcoholic beverage but the chance to spend time with Rahui, a young man from her nation. Young men and women customarily begin lives together at ceremonies like this (Beauregard, 1996).
- Hameed is a 73-year-old Islamic man who lives in Pakistan. Tomorrow he will go to a

large community gathering to celebrate the national team's victory in an international cricket match. The huge crowd will consist of men and women of all ages from his village. Hameed is often called on to supply trained horses for the event. One of the most popular parts of the celebration is a feast of lamb and rice. In contrast to several celebrations in other cultural feasts, the consumption of alcoholic beverages in this gathering is strictly prohibited. Few would even contemplate drinking wine or beer during this activity. For Hameed, however, the best thing about this celebration is the opportunity to gather his extended family around him. Nearly 40 of his children, grandchildren, and great-grandchildren will gather. Although the year has been difficult because of violence and a terrible drought that has devastated the local crops, Hameed will be able to forget those issues for a couple of days (Countries and Their Cultures, n.d.).
- Mabel is a 36-year-old from Pointe-aux-Chenes, Louisiana, who is working with the community on the upcoming Pride parade in New Orleans. Events in New Orleans are rarely "just" parades, and this is no exception. In addition to the parade, the event will include block parties, drag shows, and even hoedowns. Mabel has been a part of parade planning for several years and looks forward to this event with excitement and a sense of community with fellow paradegoers. Although they love their brothers and parents, this is a time they feel most at home and accepted for who they are. It will be a weekend filled with fun activities, great food, some delicious drinks, and also a chance to deepen connections with those who have become a second family to them.
- On July 6 at noon in Pamplona, Spain, the *chupinazo* (firework) indicates the start of the famous festival of Sanfermines, which honors Saint Fermin. Pablo is excited because he will be attending this large, well-known celebration for the first time. The festival lasts through July 14. Thousands of people will gather around the city hall for the *chupinazo*. There will be events all day and all night, and most of them will involve plenty of food and drinks. During this week, people will set aside work and personal problems to have a good time with family and friends. The most famous event of the week is the running of the bulls, which occurs at eight o'clock every morning. Pablo

has decided to run tomorrow morning, but he is already drinking wine and it seems that he is going to party hard. The running of the bulls is dangerous, and in some years people die. Maybe Pablo will change his mind.

On the surface, these four scenarios may seem quite different. The key characters are different in terms of age, race, religion, nationality, gender, and sexuality. In one celebration alcohol is strictly forbidden, but in others it is common. In one setting the game of cricket occupies an important place, whereas in others it does not. Closer examination, however, reveals that the similarities are profound.

- Each situation involves a person who is attending a community gathering that serves to create and maintain a shared culture involving friends, family, and others.
- Each activity involves food, although the food differs markedly.
- All four events include or allude to some type of sport or physical activity.
- Each scenario demonstrates that recreation and leisure can provide a break from the routine of life.

In the next few sections we will examine how gender, sexual orientation, ethnicity and race, religion, and socioeconomic status influence recreation and leisure.

GENDER AND SEXUAL ORIENTATION

Gender and sexual orientation are often grouped together because of a general perception that the two concepts overlap. Within the context of leisure and recreation, issues related to gender can be separate from those related to sexual orientation, but the issues can also intersect, particularly concerning the inclusion of people who are transgender or gender-nonbinary.

Gender

Gender is a social category that includes attitudes, expectations, and expressions of masculinity, femininity, and gender neutrality. Gender is one of the most defining characteristics people possess, and every person has a unique experience of their gender.

Community gatherings serve to create and maintain a shared culture through recreation and leisure. Here, the chupinazo indicates the start of the famous running of the bulls in Spain.

Pablo Blazquez Dominguez/Getty Images Europe/Getty Images

- For many people, their gender identity matches the binary assumption of "male" or "female" made at their birth based on their external genitalia. These people are cisgender (from the Latin prefix *cis-* for "on this side" or "same").

- For people who are transgender, their gender identity differs from the gender assigned to them at birth. This may mean that a person identifies with the "opposite" gender in the traditional gender binary, or the person may identify with a nonbinary gender (e.g., nonbinary, genderqueer, genderfluid, androgyne, Native American two-spirit).

- Some people identify with multiple genders, either simultaneously or at different stages in life. Others are agender, meaning they identify with no gender.

Given its centrality to personal identity, gender is linked to leisure in many complex relationships. Historically, cisgender men have enjoyed a privileged position in all Western cultures. Although patriarchy has been most evident in politics, industry, the arts, and many professions, cisgender male superiority has also been expressed and fortified in leisure and recreation. In the 1800s, many recreation activities were reserved for cisgender men only. At that time, no self-respecting woman would have gone to a tavern. In addition, binary segregation of the genders for no apparent reason was common; for example, men rode bicycles and women rode tricycles in the early years of cycling in the United States. It simply was not proper to do otherwise.

The traditional binary roles within the family also affected the leisure activities and recreation of family members. Men were breadwinners who earned the family's financial resources, and women cared for their children and husbands and maintained the home. Thus, many recreation activities for women took place in the home and included a domestic component such as cooking, decorating, or supervising activities for children.

The roles and expectations of people of all genders in Western society have changed significantly over the past century. Robinson and Godbey (1997) noted that "perhaps the most important ongoing social revolution in the United States is the change in women's roles" (p. 13). However, many authors and researchers caution that although change has been made, gender equity (the societal acceptance, support, and fair treatment of people across gender identities) has not yet fully arrived. Sociologists have pointed out that one of the barriers to a more gender diverse society is that parents and teachers tend to treat children differently based on their gender, as shown in these examples:

- A father invites his son to go hunting but never considers that his daughter might want to go as well.

- A mother teaches her daughter to bake without considering that her son might like to participate.

- Teachers might discourage students from playing with either dolls or toy trucks because it is not acceptable in their eyes, given their perceptions of their students' genders.

Such behaviors, although not meant to harm children, have the long-term effect of denying rewarding and self-enhancing activities to millions of Americans (Eshleman et al., 1993).

Today, although men are responsible for more housework than they were in the past, women still take on far more of the housework and child care responsibilities (Roberts, 2010). This circumstance limits the time available for leisure. The apparent imbalance in leisure time between men and women is somewhat offset by the fact that men, on average, work more hours outside the home than women do. Women have lower unemployment rates than men, but they are twice as likely to have part-time jobs. Furthermore, although the gap is slowly closing, employed women earn only 82 percent of what men do (Bureau of Labor Statistics, 2022).

Wage gaps also exist when taking into account members of the LGBTQIA+ community. Men in the LGBTQIA+ community (including both cisgender and trans men) typically earn 96 percent of what cisgender heterosexual men earn, and trans men specifically earn only 70 percent of what cisgender heterosexual men earn. Nonbinary, genderqueer, genderfluid, and two-spirit workers also earn 70 percent of what cisgender heterosexual men earn, while trans women earn only 60 percent (Human Rights Campaign, n.d.). Thus, regarding income, women and members of the LGBTQIA+ population are still disadvantaged. This condition affects the choices that they make about leisure time (Roberts, 2010).

Historically, sport has been cisgender male dominated, but progress has been made. It is no longer true that only boys perform and only girls cheer. One of the most important steps toward this end was the adoption of **Title IX** in the United States in 1972. This legislation directed educational institutions to develop parity between men's and women's sports. As evidence of its effectiveness, in 1971, 300,000 girls took part in high school sports in the United States; for the academic year 2018 to 2019, that number had risen to over 3.4 million (National Federation of State High School Associations, 2019). This increase in participation by girls and women shows that the gap in sport participation rates among genders is narrowing.

In Canada, progress has also been made toward gender equity in sport. The leading national organization to control sport at the university level in Canada, U SPORTS (formerly Canadian Inter-university Sport), developed a policy statement that included 12 goals to achieve gender equity (Beaubier, 2004). Some in Canada believe that the policy is incomplete and encourage Canadian sport organizations to look to the Title IX legislation in the United States for further development on this issue.

A more controversial topic in the area of sports in schools is state legislation limiting the athletic opportunities for transgender and gender-nonbinary students. This is a complex issue with strong opinions on all sides. Multiple states have passed legislation dictating what they consider to be fair in terms of competition for both men's and women's sports at the high school and college levels. Many of these laws will likely be challenged through the court system for years to come, so the issue is far from resolved.

Sexual Orientation

People of all sexual orientations have diverse recreation and leisure preferences. Although the situation has improved significantly over the last decades, people who identify (or are perceived) as lesbian, gay, bisexual, transgender, queer, intersex, or asexual (LGBTQIA+) are still at risk of being marginalized, isolated, insulted, harassed, assaulted, and, in some cases, killed by discriminatory attacks. In some countries, LGBTQIA+ people are punished severely under the law, and in Saudi Arabia and Nigeria, they are subject to the death penalty. Unsurprisingly, therefore, **sexual identity discrimination** in leisure and recreation exists in most of the world, including in the United States and Canada. LGBTQIA+ people experience constraints on opportunities to freely choose leisure activities

Tim Nwachukwu/Getty Images North America/Getty Images

After a lengthy battle for pay equity, the women's and men's national team unions signed a historic collective bargaining agreement with the U.S. Soccer Federation that guaranteed identical compensation frameworks for both teams. At the September 2022 signing ceremony, the women's team held up jerseys fittingly customized with the number "22" and the name "EQUAL PAY."

and whom they spend their leisure time with based on prejudices regarding their sexuality.

LGBTQIA+ youth and older adults are particularly vulnerable to discrimination.

- The 2019 Youth Risk Behavior Surveillance survey from the Centers for Disease Control and Prevention (CDC) indicates that LGBTQIA+ youths are at higher risk for violent victimization and suicide than their heterosexual counterparts (Johns et al., 2020). LGBTQIA+ youth are also at greater risk of experiencing homelessness (Morton et al., 2018).

- LGBTQIA+ older adults are an underresearched group despite the fact they have been identified in the U.S. national health priorities (Fredriksen-Goldsen et al., 2015). Although leisure participation by LGBTQIA+ older adults seems to be positively correlated to physical and mental health quality of life, this group often faces additional barriers due to social and historical contexts such as experiencing victimization and discrimination or coming out at an older age after living a heterosexual life for many years (Sage & National Resource Center for LGBT Aging, n.d.).

Due to discrimination, members of the LGBTQIA+ community must conceal their identities in some situations. Research by the Human Rights Campaign (2018) has suggested that almost half of LGBTQIA+ individuals remain closeted at work. Per that report, the top reasons LGBTQIA+ people stay closeted at work are to avoid being stereotyped, to make others more comfortable, and to prevent lost relationships with others. Based on this research, it seems likely that these individuals conceal their sexual identities in other environments as well, including leisure participation. Considering that leisure and recreation activities may represent the primary means by which people start forming relationships and eventually opportunities for sexual expression, these strategies protect LGBTQIA+ people in important ways but may also deny them chances for self-expression, belonging, or even sexual or love expression.

LGBTQIA+-friendly spaces including bars, hotels, bathhouses, resorts, restaurants, bookstores, and community centers are designed to provide a safe environment and to eliminate the need for code-switching or self-protection strategies among LGBTQIA+ patrons. In addition to retail businesses, nonprofit organizations, and tourist destinations, there are myriad activities in which LGBTQIA+ individuals participate that may be labeled as "LGBTQIA+-only" or "LGBTQIA+-led." These spaces and activities aim to foster community among LGBTQIA+ people and to provide them opportunities to socialize freely without feeling questioned, observed, or judged. A particularly apt example for recreation and leisure professionals is the international Federation of Gay Games (FGG), which has organized the quadrennial Gay Games—an analog to the Olympic Games—since 1982. Some argue that places or activities should not be labeled according to sexual orientation and should be accessible to everyone regardless of sexual identity; others argue that "LGBTQIA+-only" should be observed as a strict rule to guarantee the safety of LQBTQIA+ spaces; still others believe anyone can enjoy these spaces and experiences while respecting the community that created them. In the case of the Gay Games, the FGG's mission states that "the Gay Games is open to all, young or old, athlete or artist, experienced or novice, gay or straight," in service of their goal "to promote equality, diversity and inclusion through sport and culture" (Federation of Gay Games, n.d.). As with most human interactions, the key to navigating LGBTQIA+ spaces is to communicate with the participants and to respect the boundaries within the space.

Unique leisure activities for LGBTQIA+ people are the Pride celebrations in many places around the world. Pride parades started in New York City in June 1970 to honor the 1969 Stonewall riots in Manhattan and were designed to assert the rights, dignity, and visibility of LGBTQIA+ people everywhere. By the 2020s, Pride celebrations had become multiday events and had spread to locations small and large, with the festivities having important economic effects in cities such as San Francisco, London, and Madrid. Outside of Pride season, the economic impact of LGBTQIA+-friendly travel can be felt in destinations across the globe throughout the year, as LGBTQIA+ people discover, support, and create businesses that serve the specific needs of their community.

Equal rights for LGBTQIA+ people must be the goal in the entire world, and leisure and recreation should play a crucial role. Leisure and recreation professionals should be aware of the types of discrimination that LGBTQIA+ people experience and be clear that any form of discrimination against them is simply unacceptable. In order to do so, the following approaches can be used to help professionals better serve these individuals:

- Learn about the historical evolution of LGBTQIA+ bars, bathhouses, nightclubs,

Jacob Roden

Since 1969, Pride celebrations have spread from major cities to midsize and small towns throughout the world.

bookshops, neighborhoods, and tourist destinations as sites for community, advocacy, safety, and romance, then advocate for the maintenance and spread of LGBTQIA+ spaces.

- Explore the possibility of gender-neutral restrooms for your recreation facilities, and consider installing needle receptacles for transgender people who need to inject hormones while on recreational outings.

- Require LGBTQIA+ cultural competency training for the leisure and recreation professionals in your organization, so LGBTQIA+ people within and outside your staff are treated with respect.

- Collaborate with local LGBTQIA+ nonprofit organizations and advocacy groups to organize educational events and entertainment for the general public.

- Launch collection drives at recreation facilities for food, clothing, and personal hygiene items to assist the staggering number of LGBTQIA+ youth experiencing homelessness (Youth.gov, n.d.).

- Intervene when a colleague, consumer, or student makes discriminatory remarks or takes prejudicial actions within your sphere of influence.

ETHNICITY AND RACE

Race and *ethnicity* are sometimes used interchangeably, but there are important nuances to each concept: Typically, **race** refers to physical characteristics and outward signs of cultural identity shared by a subgroup within a society, whereas **ethnicity** refers to a subgroup of individuals who share a common background or descent. Henslin (1993) notes that people of the same ethnicity "identify with one another on the basis of common ancestry and cultural heritage. Their sense of belonging centers on country of origin, distinctive foods, dress, family names and relationships, language, music, religion and other customs" (p. 311). Leisure and recreation are part and parcel of these various cultural qualities.

Some social scientists and politicians argue that more equity exists among racial and ethnic groups today, whereas others contend that stereotyping, prejudice, discrimination, and racial inequality are every bit as prevalent as they ever were. The proliferation of viral videos reflecting police violence against people of color and the frequency of mass shootings that can be classified as hate crimes suggest that we do not live in a world that is as fully equal in opportunity based on race and ethnicity as it should be, and movements such as Black Lives Matter have risen in response. Still, some operate under the assumption that if race and ethnicity are issues that must be attended to, they have little relation to leisure. Phillip (2000), however, disputes this line of thinking: "Perhaps, nowhere else does race matter as much as during leisure. While schools and workplaces have been integrated over the past three decades by force of law, no similar laws have been enacted to secure the racial integration of leisure spaces" (p. 121).

Slightly more than 331 million people lived in the United States in 2020 (U.S. Census Bureau, 2020). The diversity of the population in terms of race and ethnicity has been increasing exponentially. For instance, the state of California has a population of over 39 million people, including over 15 million Hispanics or Latinos (U.S. Census Bureau, 2020). These are still considered minority groups, although in California this may need to be reconsidered. Minority groups on average still have lower socioeconomic statuses (U.S. Census Bureau, 2020) and are at greater risk of social exclusion. Not surprisingly, therefore, leisure participation rates vary according to race and ethnicity (Bell & Hurd, 2006). For example, park usage varies significantly among various ethnic groups. Most park users are Caucasian (Byrne, 2007). People from minority ethnic groups or races may feel uncomfortable or even unwelcome in some leisure settings in which their ethnic group is underrepresented. For example, some Hispanics might not participate in programs because of

- a perception of discrimination,
- fear of not being liked,
- absence of other Hispanics, and
- language difficulties (McChesney et al., 2005).

Besides variations in participation rates, usage patterns vary among races and ethnic groups. For example, African Americans may choose not

In the aftermath of George Floyd's murder and widespread protests against police brutality in 2020, companies across industries issued statements and took actions to voice their support for the Black Lives Matter movement. Sports organizations were no exception.

Pool/Getty Images North America/Getty Images

to participate in activities that are stereotypically Caucasian. Instead, they may choose activities that adhere more to their cultural norms (Shinew et al., 2004).

Beyond recognizing differences, attention has been devoted to the issue of *why* leisure is different for racial and ethnic groups. Two general explanations have come to the forefront: the marginality hypothesis and the ethnicity explanation.

- The marginality hypothesis explains lower participation in some activities as the consequence of a history of discrimination that has resulted in fewer socioeconomic resources. To explain why fewer African American children than white children join swim teams, this theory holds that African American children were historically denied access to quality aquatic facilities and coaches.

- The ethnicity explanation suggests that different rates and patterns of participation are the result of different norms, beliefs, and social organizations. According to this theory, African Americans would be more inclined to participate in track and field events rather than swimming because Black role models are common in track and field and are relatively rare in swimming.

Floyd (1998) argues that these two approaches to accounting for differences in leisure and recreation may be only a beginning. He suggests that each has serious weaknesses and that leisure researchers must continue to conduct research in this area. Although research in sport seems to be continuing, little research has been done recently in other types of recreation and leisure activities.

Furthermore, it would behoove us as professionals to look at what we can do to overcome historical systemic issues and to provide equity in opportunity to everyone regardless of racial or ethnic background. The fact is that there are examples of successful individuals from diverse backgrounds in all types of leisure and recreation activities. We need to facilitate our services in ways to help make that possible for more individuals.

RELIGION

Although religion is fundamentally related to ethnicity, it warrants further attention. For our purposes, we must differentiate between two related concepts.

- *Spirituality* is a personal belief system that may, but most often does not, have a strong social component.
- *Religion*, on the other hand, is a thoroughly and universally social institution.

According to Eshleman et al., "religion has always been the anchor of identity for human beings. Religious beliefs give meaning to life, and the experiences associated with them provide personal gratification, as well as release from the frustrations and anxieties of daily life" (1993, p. 344). In all its wonderfully diverse forms, religion pervades nearly every human endeavor, including

- politics,
- pastimes,
- child-rearing,
- marriages,
- funerals,
- hairstyles,
- diets, and
- clothing choices.

Even the recreation activities of those who do not consider themselves to be religious are affected by religion. For example, Tyrone and LaDawn are a middle-aged couple who haven't attended church for the past 20 years. One of their favorite leisure activities since their oldest daughter started high school is watching her participate in athletic events. Because of LaDawn's work schedule, she has had difficulty getting time off on Saturdays for her daughter's volleyball games. It would be much easier for her if some of them were played on Sunday afternoons. That's not likely, however, because their community, like many others, does not hold school events on Sundays to avoid conflicts with church services. In addition, the mascot for the sports teams was changed a few years ago as a result of vocal and influential Christian parents. Tyrone and LaDawn no longer cheer for the Fighting Blue Devils; now they cheer for the Lightning. One of the biggest tournaments of the season is held at the local YMCA. The Young Men's Christian Association, an international organization with its roots in the Christian faith, was one of the pioneers in developing volleyball; therefore, it is possible that the games they now enjoy watching would not exist if it were not for this faith-based organization.

We must be careful not to portray religion as simply a constraint on leisure and recreation. In fact, churches use recreation to maintain a sense of community, attract new members, and keep members from activity they perceive as harmful. For example:

- Instead of promoting traditional Halloween events such as trick-or-treating, churches across the country offer parties that emphasize other types of fun and worship.
- Many churches, synagogues, mosques, and temples have athletic teams that participate either in community leagues or in leagues with other churches, synagogues, mosques, and temples.
- Many children attend summer camps operated by faith-based organizations.

Nowhere is the relationship with religion in the United States and Canada more complex and intriguing than in the special arena of sport. This should come as no surprise given that these countries not only have significant diversity of sports but also have a vast diversity of religions. Many athletes have had to struggle with the demands of their faith and their desire to participate in sport. One of the classic examples of this struggle is depicted in the 1981 movie *Chariots of Fire*, in which devout Christian Eric Liddell must choose between the biggest race of his life and honoring his faith's admonition about running on the Sabbath. Additional examples include a girl who could not compete in a state gymnastics event because of her Orthodox Jewish family's observance of the Sabbath on Saturday, and an Iowa high school wrestler's refusal to wrestle a female competitor because of his Pentecostal religion's prohibition against contact sports between males and females.

Much attention has been given to the theory that sport has replaced religion in the lives of many North Americans. Edwards' seminal work on the topic of sport as religion continues to influence sport sociologists. According to Edwards (1973), sport and religion have 13 important similarities. Four of them follow:

1. Just like religion, sports have their saints. These are the great athletes of previous eras that serve as examples for current athletes and fans.
2. The world of sports has its "gods": those superstars that transcend time and culture and dominate the lives of individuals and even countries.

One of the similarities between sport and religion can be seen in the hall of fame gallery at the Pro Football Hall of Fame in Canton, Ohio, where former players are enshrined each year.

3. Sports have their hallowed shrines. These range from the widely recognized hall of fame sites to the trophy rooms of colleges and high schools.

4. Sports have powerful symbols of faith. The bat that Babe Ruth hit his record home run with and the ball that Dwight Clark caught to win the 1982 National Football League playoffs are examples. And who can argue that there is not a certain sacred quality of an Olympic gold medal?

In writing about the similarity between religion and sport, Prebish noted that "religion is the raft that ferries from profane reality to the realm of the sacred, that enables us to transcend ordinary reality and directly apprehend the extraordinary" (1993, p. 3). He goes on to make the case that, for some people, sport does the same thing. In the United States, the most watched television show is usually the Super Bowl, and when we watch it, we make a mental and emotional journey from everyday life to a world of fantasy.

SOCIOECONOMIC STATUS

People in nearly all societies are categorized according to some combination of

- wealth,
- power,
- party affiliation,
- life chances, and
- prestige.

Some systems, like the **caste system** in India, are very rigid. The boundaries are distinct and movement between the different categories is nearly impossible.

A **class system**, like that in many developed countries including the United States and Canada, is much more fluid, and there is overlap between classes and the possibility of movement among the classes. In many countries, classes are designated according to a combination of income, education, and occupation. This classification system is referred to as *socioeconomic status* (SES). In general terms, descriptions of these classes range from upper class, to middle class, working class, and lower class.

- The upper class consists of owners of vast property and wealth.
- The middle class is made up of managers, small-business owners, and professionals.

- The working class is made up predominantly of laborers who earn modest wages and own little property.
- The people of the lower class are those who either work for minimum wages, are periodically unemployed, or are unemployable.

Socioeconomic inequalities around the world are significant and have increased in many countries during the early 21st century. Inequalities in the United States are relatively high, and they have increased over the course of the 2000s and 2010s. According to the Central Intelligence Agency's *World Factbook* (2023):

- The United States ranks 46th on the world's inequality scale of average income as measured by the Gini index, which measures the degree of inequality in the distribution of family income in each country. Canada ranks 121st.
- African countries such as Namibia and South Africa rank as most unequal followed mostly by South and Central American countries.
- On the other end of the spectrum are countries of northern and eastern Europe such as Sweden, Hungary, Norway, and the Czech Republic, which have less difference in average family income.

There is general agreement that SES affects leisure. There is, however, less agreement on exactly *how* it affects it. Addressing a particular leisure category, Gruneau wrote: "research on sports and social equality in the United States demonstrates a general pattern of under-representation of people from the lowest income levels among active participants in organized sports and physical recreation" (1999, pp. 52-53). Recognizing some of the disagreement about the relationship between socioeconomic status and leisure, Kelly noted that "economic stratification is at least a filter, with low incomes simply eliminating the majority of the population from cost-intensive activity" (2012, p. 78).

Research supports the notion that class affects travel and tourism. As far back as the 1980s, in the President's Commission on Americans Outdoors, Mill (1986) determined that economic standing, one of the key elements of SES, affected several aspects of tourism. People in the upper and middle classes traveled more often through commercial providers, whereas the working class tended to travel by some form of public transportation. The destinations for travel were also different. The upper classes tended to travel internationally more often than other classes. The higher a person's position on the SES scale, the longer the time they spent at a destination. And, as might be expected, the upper and middle classes spent more money when they traveled for leisure purposes. Much of this information is not surprising, even today.

We should not overlook the fact that although class affects leisure, the reverse may also be true. Thorstein Veblen, in his classic 1899 treatise *The Theory of the Leisure Class*, argued that the upper class, which he called the *leisure class*, used leisure to display and maintain their prized position in society (1899/1998). Elegant and exclusive social gatherings and highly consumptive activities sent a clear message to those in lower social positions that class mattered. At the same time, many of the lower classes emulated the upper classes and tried to match their leisure styles. When a sufficiently large group from the middle class was able to participate in activities that resembled those of the rich, the upper class found even more expensive and elaborate leisure activities to maintain their status.

BENEFITS AND CONSTRAINTS OF LEISURE

Most leisure activities offer some benefit. Leisure is a voluntarily chosen activity; therefore, if nothing else, leisure activities provide participants with opportunities to express free will. However, leisure activities do have some constraints. For example, few activities (leisure or otherwise) are without cost. The following example of Winona, an active 21-year-old college student at a Midwestern university, illustrates the mixed nature of leisure:

I am mostly into leisure activities with my friends. Like during last spring break my best friend and I went to Panama City in Florida. Lying on the beach for three days and doing pretty much nothing was pretty nice. I seriously needed a break from school and work. I just wish my boyfriend could have gone with us, but he had to work. I probably should not have gone because I really didn't have the money, but I decided that I could do it if we traveled by car and stayed in a cheaper motel a few blocks from the beach. One of the things I have always wanted to do was parasail, but on the day I was going to do it, the wind came up. The people who ran the company said they could not do it if the wind was over 20 miles per hour. It was the last day, and I couldn't go. I was disappointed, but then I saw some people surfing. I rented a board and spent the rest of the day surfing. I had a great time and a wonderful workout.

One night my best friend and I wanted to go to a really great bar, but she got a little sick and could not go. I really wanted to go but didn't want to go alone. I had heard the place was a little bit wilder than I am used to. It would have been fun, but my parents always told me to be careful when I am by myself in a strange place, so I just stayed in our room that night. All in all, it was a really wonderful time, and I hope to have another spring break trip but with my boyfriend.

Winona obviously had a lot of fun and relaxation on her spring break trip. She mentioned these activities and experiences:

- She got to relax on the beach and got some exercise while surfing.
- She was able to share these experiences with her best friend.
- Winona and her friend spent money on transportation, lodging, and food. The individual benefits of recreation and leisure are easy to observe, but there were other less obvious leisure and recreation contributions as well. Their spending contributed to the economies in communities along the way and in Florida. The beaches are a main attraction to the area; thus, a great deal of effort is made to keep the beaches clean, partially as a means of attracting locals and tourists to the area, which can have a positive impact on the local economy.
- Winona alluded to the trip being restorative. After a week of fun and sun, she was revitalized and ready to go back to school and her part-time job. In turn, her increased productivity at work was valuable to her, her community, and her employer.

The National Recreation and Park Association (NRPA) recognizes that many people take recreation for granted and do not understand the contribution of this field. Thus, they developed a program called Parks and Recreation: The Benefits Are Endless to promote the role of recreation and parks to the public. Even if the benefits are not truly endless, they are certainly numerous and varied.

- The benefits are classified as individual and social (Henderson, 2010).
- Within the individual benefits category are physiological benefits and psychological benefits.

- Subcategories of the social value of recreation include economic and environmental benefits and recuperation from other activities such as productive work.

Let's also consider what this tells us about leisure and its inherent constraints. Although Winona generally had a good time on her spring break, she was certainly not operating without constraints on what she wanted to do for leisure. She was limited by

- whom she could travel with,
- how much money she could spend,
- the weather,
- a company's unwillingness to provide an activity,
- her parents' values of appropriate leisure activity, and
- her apprehension about going to a bar alone.

OUTSTANDING GRADUATE

Background Information

Name: Michael D. Lukkarinen

Education: PhD in leisure behavior (emphasis in sport management) from University of Illinois at Urbana-Champaign; MS in recreation, park, and tourism administration from Western Illinois University; BS in recreation, park, and tourism administration from Western Illinois University

Affiliations: Academy of Leisure Sciences, National Alliance for Youth Sports, National Federation of State High School Associations, National Wrestling Coaches Association

© Michael Lukkarinen

Career Information

Position: Associate Professor

Organization: Western Illinois University (WIU). The department offers outstanding and nationally accredited master's and bachelor's degrees in recreation, park, and tourism administration (RPTA). Students and faculty are engaged in service learning, research, and grant writing aimed at preparing the professionals of tomorrow. The faculty is committed to providing the tools needed to be successful in the field and in life. A career in RPTA enables students to make a positive difference in their communities.

Job description: As an associate professor, I am directly engaged in preparing students to be difference makers, both during their time at WIU and when they enter the field upon graduation. I also currently serve as the department internship coordinator. This is a position that connects our students as future professionals with their counterparts already in the field. I am both a gatekeeper and a relationship maker. I integrate my passion with sport in my classes, my research, and my life. I also serve as chair for the Western Illinois Senior Olympic Games and volunteer my time as a wrestling coach at Macomb High School and as a women's golf coach at WIU.

Career path: Like many in the field, I stumbled upon my career focus. After trying many other things, I kept coming back to my roots—as a kid who hung out at the local YMCA, ballfields, and gym. Once RPTA became my major, I was able to shine and enjoy my classes thoroughly. I have never forgotten that, and I try to share this with my students who may be unsure of themselves.

Academia wasn't on my mind until after I graduated with my master's degree and left the field briefly. Realizing my mistake, I came back and once again felt at home. I enjoy the interaction with students, colleagues, and other members of the university community. It is a great responsibility to educate others, and this is something I take very seriously.

Likes and dislikes about the job: I truly enjoy meeting students each year and seeing the world through their eyes. This can be a challenge. Bridging the gap between theory, practice, and the students of today is simultaneously a challenge and a reward. Seeing them blossom as people and become successful professionals who then go on to give internships to the next group of students is very gratifying.

Advice for Undergraduates

Be involved in as many activities as possible. Travel down many roads. These roads will help you zero in on where you belong. You may want to take the first exit ramp because you realize that road is not for you, and that puts you on another one, getting you closer to where you are supposed to be. Once you find that road, you will know, and you will not want to exit anymore.

Another lesson that we can learn from this scenario is that most of these constraints did not prevent Winona from participating. She negotiated most of them and had an enjoyable time regardless.

The great variety of possible constraints poses a challenge for categorizing; therefore, researchers have developed several models for grouping them.

Structural constraints
- Time
- Money
- Health
- Equipment

Intrapersonal constraints
- Fear
- Low self-esteem
- Attitudes

Interpersonal constraints
- Family responsibilities
- Lack of people to share the leisure activity with (Crawford et al., 1991)
- Henderson (1997) grouped constraints as antecedent limitations, such as attitudes and lack of skill, and intervening constraints, such as weather and resources.

GOOD AND BAD LEISURE AND RECREATION

If we're not careful, we may assume that leisure and recreation are unequivocally good. Who can argue that an exercise program for seniors and making parks available for picnics are not admirable and decent efforts? Certainly no one could be opposed to arts and crafts classes and family vacations. But some activities are not wholesome, and some seem to be downright wrong. We could list the bad activities, but that wouldn't be especially helpful because the list would be in a constant state of flux. It is more productive to consider how to determine the goodness or badness of an activity.

Participation in recreation cannot be forced on us. We decide to participate because we think it will be fun and possibly rewarding. In fact, the defining quality of recreation is the freedom to participate. But the same freedom in leisure and recreation can be problematic when considering the moral value of an activity. We might think that our leisure is just that—entirely and completely *our* leisure. How dare anyone tell us that our chosen activity is wrong and then try to stop us from doing it? Although that may be our initial reaction to placing moral value on recreation and leisure, we must go beyond that if we are to truly understand our society and ourselves. Let's take a moment to consider how we determine good and bad in contemporary culture.

Goodness has been discussed by every culture since the ancient Greeks. Today we have several different and competing theories about what is good and bad or right and wrong. Although there are a lot of diverse ideas, nearly all agree that goodness is not a concept simply left up to the individual to determine. Even proponents of **hedonism**, a philosophy in which individual pleasure is the chief good, recognize that our actions have consequences that affect our seeking pleasure; thus, we have to consider our behaviors in light of those around us. Other ethical theories place concerns for others at the middle of the debate about good and evil. The point is that people and the various societies of which they are a part jointly determine goodness in all things, including leisure and recreation.

Let's briefly consider a couple of contemporary theories about good and bad leisure. Nash (1953) was one of the first to tackle the issue. His model of good and bad recreation resembled a pyramid.

- The very best activities were at the peak. These activities not only provided satisfaction to the actor but also contributed to making a better society.
- In the middle of the pyramid were activities that were merely entertaining to the participants. They were not harmful to anyone, but they did not affect society either.
- Near the bottom were activities that, although freely chosen, were harmful to the individual.
- At the bottom of the diagram were activities that not only hurt the participant but also damaged society.

Curtis (1979) devised an even simpler continuum with good recreation activities on one end and bad recreation activities on the other end. Curtis labeled bad activities as **purple leisure** and defined them as activities that might bring pleasure to the individual but would cause harm to society.

Let's look at various recreation activities in light of this discussion of goodness and badness. Activities at the top and bottom of Nash's model and at either end of Curtis' continuum are easy to understand. Most of us would agree that writing and performing a beautiful song is good and vandalizing a playground is bad. But it is much more difficult to reach consensus on the goodness of many other activities. Where would you put the following?

- Hunting
- Alcohol use
- Marijuana use
- Cocaine use
- Television viewing
- Playing violent video games
- Ultimate fighting
- Going to a strip club

Then there is the thorny issue of gambling. At one time in the United States, almost every type of gambling was banned. Then it became available only in certain states and locations such as Nevada and American Indian reservations. By the 2020s, some form of gambling was available in almost every state and county. Many states have horse and dog races to bet on. Casinos are floating on almost every major body of water in the United States, and there are only five states that do not have a legal lottery (Utah, Nevada, Alaska, Alabama, and Hawaii). In Canada, gambling is legal to anyone over the age of 18. Options include scratch tickets (similar to the lotteries in the United States), horse races, bingo, betting on sport events, and gambling at one of the 121 casinos scattered across Canada.

So, is gambling good or bad? It's legal and widespread, provides jobs, provides resources for schools (and other government allocations of the money), and provides entertainment for many. But it is also associated with addiction, corruption, and other negative aspects such as the possible diminution of work ethic. As you can see, determining whether a leisure activity is good or bad is not simple. But as a society, we must attempt to because leisure activities affect us all.

IMPLICATIONS FOR PROFESSIONALS

Charged with the task of providing leisure and recreation opportunities, leisure and recreation professionals must first understand how leisure and recreation take place.

- Who participates?
- How do they participate?
- What are their motivations?

- What are their constraints and limitations?
- What are the benefits of recreation?
- Are there direct consequences or indirect consequences that will not be evident for years?

Armed with the answers to these questions, we can design programs, facilities, and open spaces that make it possible for people to flourish.

For example, knowing the demands and limitations placed on single mothers, recreation and parks professionals must offer programs that allow them to participate. Perhaps that means that some fitness programs take place in the middle of the morning and the agency offers a toddler play period at the same time. Given that money is often in short supply for this population, the agency must also subsidize the program so the mothers do not have to choose between their own physical fitness and paying the utility bills. This must all be accomplished without perpetuating the stigma that single-parent households are inferior and a societal burden that must be dealt with as conveniently as possible.

But even these efforts, as challenging as they are, are not enough. On another level, leisure and recreation professionals must be educators. They must continue to drive home the point that leisure and recreation are essential; they are so important that all people, regardless of their lot in life—color, age, ethnicity, gender, sexual orientation, religion, or class—have a right to participate. Showing the current benefits and extolling the future benefits of leisure and recreation for all will strengthen the case. The world can be better today and tomorrow for all of us through equal leisure and recreation opportunities.

SUMMARY

As we have seen, leisure is a wonderfully complex human phenomenon that is never undertaken in a social vacuum; it is absolutely inseparable from society. A multitude of social institutions—including stratification, religion, ethnicity, gender, family, and friendships—thoroughly influence leisure. But the causation arrow goes both ways. Leisure often profoundly affects the society in which it takes place. Thus, contrary to the thinking of previous eras, leisure is not a trivial pursuit relegated to the realm of leftover time and energy. Rather, it is an essential ingredient in the lives of individuals, communities, nations, and humankind. Leisure and recreation professionals venture into this rich boiling stew of the human experience.

Review Questions

1. What is one of your primary groups, and how does this group affect your leisure participation?

2. What is one of your secondary groups, and how does this group affect your leisure engagement?

3. What are some of the ways that socioeconomic status (SES) can affect leisure participation and travel in particular?

4. Are leisure activities typically seen as either all good or all bad?

Go to HK*Propel* to complete the activities for this chapter.

PART II

Leisure and Recreation as a Multifaceted Delivery System

Leisure Service Delivery Systems

David N. Emanuelson and Mary Sara Wells

© Human Kinetics

" Just call me Bond, Municipal Bond. "

Ben Wyatt, character from the television show *Parks and Recreation*

After reading this chapter, you should be able to do the following:

> Identify the three sectors that deliver leisure services to the public and the ways they operate
> Compare the challenges facing leisure service professionals in the three sectors
> Explain how various challenges require leisure service professionals to possess diverse technical skills
> Describe the educational courses that leisure service professionals should take to prepare for the opportunities that await them

Thank goodness for popular culture such as the television show *Parks and Recreation*, which provided the public with a look at how municipal governments deliver leisure services. Unfortunately, that view, although humorous, is not always accurate. Its exclusive focus on municipal governments is most misleading: There are in fact many levels of government and sectors of the economy that provide leisure services.

Leisure is a human need, which makes it inevitable that different sectors of the economy will be developed to meet that need. Of course, leisure is one need in competition with others as urgent as eating, sleeping, and working.

• A stereotypical work week in the United States and Canada is 40 hours. Because a week is 168 hours, Americans and Canadians have approximately 128 hours per week for non-work activities.

• Considering those 128 remaining hours: If the average person sleeps eight hours per night, 56 hours per week are spent sleeping, which reduces the remaining hours to 72.

• Estimates indicate that people use half of the remaining time in a week (36 hours) to do tasks essential for existence, such as cooking, cleaning, and personal maintenance.

• This leaves about 36 hours per week per person for recreation. (In this chapter, we use the term *recreation* interchangeably with the *leisure service industry*.)

Major portions of the national economies of Canada and the United States are dedicated to satisfying their citizens' desires for recreation. In fact, leisure services are the largest segment of the **gross national product** in both countries. Gross national product is the sum of total goods and services manufactured or provided by all businesses, nonprofit organizations, and government entities in a country.

The leisure service industry is a vast marketplace that includes practically anything that people do when they are not working. Because it is a diverse field, leisure service professionals need to be trained in more than one discipline, which includes:

• Travel and tourism
• Amusement and theme park operations
• Hospitality and restaurant management
• Sport and entertainment
• Community parks and recreation

This chapter

• reviews the leisure service field and the delivery systems and sectors in which it exists,
• identifies technical skills common to all sectors,
• determines which technical skills are specific to a sector, and
• suggests a course of education that will prepare professionals for success in the leisure service industry.

This chapter considers leisure service delivery systems in Canada and the United States largely because they are similar, but also because they have significant differences. The differences between governmental units are important.

• Canada is a **constitutional monarchy**, part of the British Commonwealth with allegiance to the king or queen of England. In Canada, the Crown is the foundation of the executive and judicial branches of government.

• By contrast, the United States is a **constitutional republic**, in which the executive branch is elected and the judicial branch is appointed by the chief executive.

While many of the same leisure service delivery systems exist under the two forms of government, the differences are important.

In the United States, leisure services provided by the National Park System in the Department of the Interior are considered both executive and legislative functions of the national government. The department head is a cabinet-level position and is appointed by the president, but the department was created through legislative action and its funding comes from Congress. Understanding the distinctions is important.

The United States also differs from Canada because it has a different form of federalism. In the U.S. federal system, states have substantial power. States charter businesses, nonprofit organizations, and local governmental units. A **governmental unit** is a generic term that describes a government group at any level: national, state, county, city, or other local unit. The term can be used to refer to one large unit, such as the state, or subdivisions within the unit, such as departments. In Canada, chartering of these entities is done at the national level. Yet by most other appearances, businesses, nonprofits, and local governments deliver leisure services in a similar way in Canada and the United States.

Leisure services are provided by three sectors of the economy:

- Private, or commercial, sector
- Nonprofit sector
- Public, or government, sector

The private sector was the first to provide leisure services—primarily recreation services—which is why this chapter begins with an overview of private-sector delivery systems and how they function. Discussion then moves to the nonprofit sector, which also primarily provides recreation services, because it was the second to deliver leisure services. Last discussed is the public sector, which provides a unique array of services that businesses and nonprofit organizations are not able to offer, such as parks, which were initially offered to everyone with no fee. Since the creation of government-owned and -operated parks, fees have sometimes become necessary. For example, municipal governments provide parks and open space, which the public can enjoy without paying fees. This free use of parks and open space is possible because governments collect taxes to support these services. State and federal parks, however, sometimes charge fees for admission and for specific services. The chapter touches on these services and explains why these fees and charges are necessary.

PRIVATE SECTOR

The commercial recreation sector is the largest of the three sectors. It is about 100 times larger than the public sector, and it provides students with the greatest career opportunities. In 2010, there were more than 22.5 million businesses operating in the United States and 2 million in Canada. The U.S. leisure service sector comprises more than 8 percent of the gross domestic product of the United States and nearly 2 million commercial recreation businesses. In Canada, it comprises more than 12 percent of the gross domestic product and more than 200,000 businesses.

Leisure services are part of the service industry segment of national economies, which is called the *soft sector*. Although the service industry contains other subparts including insurance, banking, retail, education, and health care, its largest segment in the United States and Canada is the leisure service industry. The service industry is not thought to produce any "hard" products such as appliances or furniture. For the most part, the leisure service industry buys and sells hard products, but it doesn't produce them. Exceptions are the sports retail, recreational vehicle, and souvenir industries, which manufacture hard products and sell them in retail outlets. This means the leisure service industry is not limited to the service industry; it can include the manufacturing of leisure service products as well as the delivery of those products.

The leisure service industry is composed of many industries, including the following:

- Travel and tourism
- Hospitality
- Resorts
- Gaming
- Amusement parks
- Restaurants
- Professional sports
- Sporting goods manufacturers and retailers
- Movie and entertainment industry
- Camping and outdoor recreation
- Video games and esports

In April 2022 the leisure service industry employed about 15.5 million Americans who earned an average of $19.75 per hour (Bureau of Labor Statistics, 2022). The leisure service industry generated $117.5 billion in annual national and state tax revenue in 2016. Economists have estimated that

$1 of every $12 in the U.S. economy is from leisure service industry spending. The total gross national product of the United States is estimated to exceed $24 trillion in 2021, so the amount of money spent on leisure services would, therefore, exceed $2 trillion annually (Bureau of Labor Statistics, 2022).

What makes the leisure service industry unique, and therefore makes leisure service delivery systems unique, is its diversity. Other than health care, a sector in which hospitals can be operated for profit, not for profit, or by governmental units, no other profession spans all three sectors. And no other profession requires the diversity of management skills required in the leisure service profession.

The leisure service industry can offer a broad array of services, even within a single industry. As an example, the cruise industry, a subcomponent of the travel and tourism industry, provides voyages to the four corners of the world. For as little as $500 per person, cruisers can

- live on a ship for a week,
- be fed gourmet meals,
- see Las Vegas–quality shows,
- purchase jewelry and other retail goods, and
- visit exotic ports of call that often offer adventure excursions.

Each of these individual services are subsets of the cruise industry, and provided individually, each could stand alone as components outside of the cruise industry.

As a growing industry that seeks to keep up with the need of Canadians and Americans to travel in comfort at an affordable cost, the cruise ship industry serves as an example of what has been taking place in the leisure service industry worldwide. Since 2000, the cruise industry has been growing by leaps and bounds. Cruise lines are introducing new ships on an annual basis, and some cost more than $1 billion to build. According to the Cruise Critic website, in 2016 Royal Caribbean Cruises launched its newest ship, which cost more than $1.2 billion and had 2,747 staterooms and a maximum capacity of 6,780 passengers. In 2017, Norwegian Cruise Line launched its newest ship, which had 1,925 staterooms. These ships employ and house almost one crew member for every stateroom, making the ships equivalent to small cities that serve the needs of customers willing to pay for the pleasure of traveling on the high seas and visiting exotic places. While the cruise industry struggled in 2020 and 2021 due to the worldwide COVID-19 pandemic, it is expected that it will rebound in strength over the coming years.

Innovation has become the hallmark of the private-sector leisure service industry. Las Vegas, founded as a place where gamblers could make wagers with no fear of breaking the law, is now a major convention center and family vacation destination. Las Vegas now has amusement parks, restaurants, entertainment venues, luxury resorts, and, of course, casinos. New hotels are regularly added to the market, and there are more than 90,000 hotel rooms available in the city.

It is easy to see why the private-sector leisure service industry keeps getting bigger: People love to play. Economists predict that leisure services will continue to grow as the middle class grows worldwide. Because the burgeoning international middle class with disposable income seeks leisure services at every life stage, the leisure service industry has the potential to be a growth industry worldwide over the long haul, just as it has been in Canada and the United States.

PRIVATE-SECTOR LEISURE SERVICE DELIVERY SYSTEMS

Private-sector delivery systems are called *businesses*. In the United States and Canada, **businesses** are organizations created to provide a service or product. They charge a higher price than the cost of producing the product or service, and the difference between the cost and the price is the profit. Businesses can be as small as a single person who sharpens and waxes skis near a ski resort or as large as the resort operation itself, which provides lift services, food, accommodations, and transportation.

Making a profit changes the power dynamic of leisure service businesses. To make a profit, managers of leisure service businesses must possess a level of power that exceeds that of government and nonprofit managers. All leisure service managers need some power; it's just that leisure service private-sector managers need more than their counterparts. Leisure service private-sector managers need the power to focus on their customers without interference from their bosses or employees, meaning that customers become more important than the employees in the private sector.

Because leisure service businesses are always looking for ways to make a profit, they are motivated to identify unmet customer needs and meet them—for a fair price, of course. In some ways, that challenge makes the private sector more exciting than the nonprofit or government sectors. Those who work for businesses always have something to do because there is always more money to be made. People who find that type of career exciting tend to gravitate to the private sector. Leisure service students need to decide whether that type of life is for them.

All leisure service organizations focus on their customers at some level. But leisure service businesses are different from delivery systems in other sectors because they focus on customers who are willing and able to pay for services. If they didn't, the businesses wouldn't profit. Being focused on profitability means that businesses cannot afford to waste their time on people who will not pay them for services. Nonprofit organizations are often established to serve those who cannot pay, and government leisure service delivery systems cannot ignore those who cannot pay.

Economists have developed a theory of the firm that suggests that everyone working for the business will act in the best interest of the business, focus on the customer, and help the business make a profit; this is in their own best interest. The economic reality is that if the business prospers, employees will retain their jobs or even share in the profits. Therefore, managers need not worry about being overbearing in their attempts to motivate employees to work hard. Employees will work hard on their own because it's in their own best interest to do so.

Challenges of Managing Leisure Service Businesses

Managing a leisure service, regardless of the sector, requires understanding the formal and informal rules for management. Each sector has its own traditions, rules, and standard operating procedures that make it different from the others and from other services in their sector.

Businesses operate in the private sector. They focus on the customer because the transaction between the business and the customer provides the business its lifeblood. This is called taking a **marketing approach**. University-level marketing programs tend to teach the five Ps of marketing:

1. Product
2. Price
3. Place
4. Promotion
5. Position

Often the emphasis is on promotion, suggesting that marketing is all about advertising. More modern marketing approaches acknowledge the importance of promotion but primarily focus on

vichie81/iStockphoto/Getty Images

Innovation is key in the private-sector leisure service industry. Las Vegas has become a family vacation destination that includes amusement parks.

creating products or services that meet peoples' needs. As the adage goes, if you build a better mousetrap, the world will beat a path to your door.

The singular focus on the customer provides private-sector managers with a challenge that doesn't exist in the public and nonprofit sectors of the leisure service industry. With no taxes or donations to sustain them, private-sector leisure service managers have no safety net; they walk a tightrope, particularly those who manage start-up businesses. Because of their dependence on revenues, commercial recreation managers confront challenges that managers in the other two sectors don't face.

- Businesses are susceptible to economic downturns and must comply with government regulations.
- Stockholders and owners expect a return on their capital.
- Lenders need to be repaid with interest.
- Customers need change, and competition is a constant threat.

Leisure service managers in the commercial sector also have advantages compared with their counterparts in nonprofit and government organizations.

- The level of transparency required of businesses is not as great as that required of government and nonprofit agencies. The media has no access to financial records of privately owned companies and limited access to those of publicly traded companies.
- Private-sector employees have fewer rights than public-sector employees, allowing private-sector labor costs to be lower than public and nonprofit labor costs. The salaries and wages of business employees can be kept secret, and in some cases, business employees can be terminated for divulging their pay. Managers can use pay as a motivational tool.
- Unlike governmental units, privately held businesses do not have public board meetings. Businesses are not required to make their decisions public; doing so would provide competitors with strategic information.
- Setting prices for services is not open to debate in the private sector as it is in the public sector.
- Board members of companies in the private sector, unlike their counterparts in the public sector, can be paid substantial sums of money for attending meetings.

Corporate board members in privately held companies are themselves the owners. Any discussion about corporate strategy occurs within that group. For publicly traded companies, corporate board members can be appointed by senior management, which is tantamount to allowing the senior executive to select their own bosses, or they can be elected by the stockholders, although the major stockholders control most of the votes.

Capital financing in the private sector is also an important difference. Leisure service managers in the nonprofit sector can solicit funds from donations to make capital improvements, and these never need to be repaid from operating funds. In the public sector, tax monies are levied to repay municipal, state, and federal bonds, but the monies are generally not repaid from operating funds.

In the private sector, almost no one makes donations to businesses. Customers pay for services. To finance capital expenses, commercial recreation managers can borrow money from banks and other lenders, but these loans are repaid from operating revenues. In addition, before lending institutions make loans to businesses, these enterprises need to demonstrate they can generate sufficient revenues to service the debt. That's why leisure service business managers as entrepreneurs face capital finance challenges that don't exist in the nonprofit or public sectors.

Skills Required for Managing Leisure Service Businesses

The most important skills that business managers need are economics, business accounting, finance, marketing, and organizational leadership. These skills are taught as academic courses in leisure studies and business programs at the university level. Traditionally, business schools have taught these subjects as having principles and formulae for success. In leisure service commercial recreation courses, some of these principles are taught as well, with the most advanced leisure service academic programs focusing on teaching them to students intending to have a career in the public sector.

NONPROFIT SECTOR

The nonprofit sector of the leisure service industry consists of organizations chartered or otherwise permitted by the national government in Canada and state and federal governments in the United States. In the United States, most nonprofits are chartered by individual states, but some are nationally chartered, such as the Boy Scouts of America. All U.S. nonprofits must follow the codes of the Internal Revenue Service (IRS). In Canada, the national government takes a more vigilant approach, making sure nonprofit organizations do charitable work.

In the United States, nonprofit organizations are exempt from paying federal taxes under section 501(c) of the Internal Revenue Code, and they file annual reports with the IRS to substantiate their tax exemption (IRS, n.d.). Numerous categories are identified under this section, but the most pertinent for leisure services are social and recreational clubs allowed under IRS code 501(c)(7) and charitable organizations allowed under IRS code 501(c)(3).

According to the Internal Revenue Code, to receive exempt status, a social club must be organized for pleasure, recreation, and other similar purposes and cannot discriminate against any person based on race, color, or religion. "A club may, however, in good faith, limit its membership to members of a particular religion in order to further the teachings or principles of that religion and not to exclude individuals of a particular race or color." The other category, charitable organizations, is for religious, educational, scientific, literary, public safety testing, national or international amateur sport competition, and animal and child cruelty prevention organizations.

The tax code defines *charitable* as including

relief of the poor, the distressed, or the underprivileged; advancement of religion; advancement of education or science; erecting or maintaining public buildings, monuments, or works; lessening the burdens of government; lessening neighborhood tensions; eliminating prejudice and discrimination; defending human and civil rights secured by law; and combating community deterioration and juvenile delinquency. (IRS, n.d.)

In the nonprofit sector, although meeting the needs of clients is important, doing it for a price to cover operating expenses, let alone to make a profit, is not always important. Whereas business organizations exist to earn and distribute taxable wealth to owners and shareholders, nonprofit corporations cannot distribute excess revenues to shareholders because there are no shareholders. Businesses retain profits and use those profits for the capital expansion of the businesses. Nonprofits strive for excess revenue over expenditures so they can reinvest into

their organizations, but they can use donations to cover operating expenses and capital improvements.

In the nonprofit sector, if donations and operating revenues fall short of covering expenses, organizations face survival issues. Nonprofit organizations are like businesses in that way, as are governmental units. In none of the sectors can organizations lose money and expect to exist in the long run. Nonprofits can solicit donations to pay for operating expenses, and governmental units can subsidize them with taxes.

As mentioned, the IRS allows various kinds of nonprofit leisure service organizations. Some nonprofit leisure service providers do charitable work, such as Boys and Girls Clubs of America, and they rely on donations rather than fees for existence. Other nonprofit leisure service organizations, such as country clubs, don't do charitable work and charge substantial fees for their leisure services. Both organizations have nonprofit status approved by the Internal Revenue Service that permits them to exist with the understanding that they will stay true to their purpose and reinvest excess revenue into the organization. Their profitability is closely monitored by the IRS because nonprofit organizations must file tax reports just like private corporations do. Nonprofit organizations walk a tightrope between generating too much in revenues and donations and generating too little.

In the U.S. leisure service sector today, tens of thousands of youth sport organizations are organized as nonprofits. They are organized to avoid paying taxes on surplus revenues in good years and permitted to solicit donations and not be taxed for them. Nonprofits are organized so that their governing boards have the flexibility of providing services without having the IRS look over their shoulders.

It has been a complaint that nonprofit organizations often compete against businesses and governmental units for clients. For instance, a local YMCA might compete with a private fitness club or the local parks and recreation department by selling memberships to their fitness club. A local youth club athletic team might compete with the local park district for youth baseball players. Because they are not taxed on their short-term profits and they are permitted to solicit donations to cover operating expenses, a YMCA fitness club will likely survive an economic downturn, whereas a private fitness club might not.

On the other hand, nonprofit leisure service providers often exist in many communities to fill a void because a governmental or private leisure service provider is not available. A charitable organization may be needed to meet the needs of children or adults who have low incomes or are disabled. People may not be able to pay fees for services, and by being able to solicit donations to cover these services, nonprofit leisure service organizations can provide services that businesses or governmental units cannot. Even where a governmental provider is available, some nonprofits exist because people want their leisure service needs met in different ways or want them met in private rather than among the public. Country clubs, tennis clubs, swimming clubs, and other athletic clubs exist because of their exclusiveness, but to maintain their tax-exempt status, they cannot discriminate by race, color, or religion.

Leisure service nonprofit organizations face a unique challenge from other nonprofits. The primary management responsibility of the charitable establishments is to seek donations so they can continue to exist, because fees from clients, who mostly have low incomes, do not generate sufficient operating revenues. The primary management responsibility of less charitable organizations, such as country clubs, is to ensure the happiness of their members so that they will continue to pay membership fees.

NONPROFIT-SECTOR LEISURE SERVICE DELIVERY SYSTEMS

Like the business sector, the nonprofit sector of the field offers many opportunities for leisure service professionals. Among the 1.85 million nonprofit organizations in the United States today, approximately 20 percent deliver leisure services, so more than 371,000 nonprofit leisure service organizations are delivering services to Americans (Internal Revenue Service, 2023).

These nonprofit organizations range from such well-known organizations as the YMCA and the Boys and Girls Clubs of America to nonprofit resident and day camps, local youth baseball and softball programs, and hospitals that provide wellness centers. Not every nonprofit provider employs full-time staff. For example, local youth baseball programs don't, but Boys and Girls Clubs and YMCAs employ full-time leisure service professionals.

Nonprofit leisure service delivery systems differ from leisure service businesses in that the nonprofit leisure service sector has boundaries that businesses do not. In search of revenue, businesses can venture into markets that are off limits to nonprofit organizations. For example, state governments will not

© Human Kinetics

Nonprofit leisure service providers, such as a private swim club, exist because either those services aren't available in the community or they meet users' leisure needs in other ways.

issue charters for nonprofit organizations to provide services such as cruising, hospitality, and gaming. Businesses are permitted in these industries because state governments recognize that these industries are profitable but are not appropriate for nonprofit leisure service organizations.

Nonprofit leisure service delivery systems are, therefore, more limited in the range of services they can provide. Athletics and fitness programs and residential and day camps are within the scope of nonprofit leisure service organization services. Bowling, amusement parks, hotels, resorts, retail outlets, and other products or services that can make a profit are not within those boundaries, as determined by the IRS when they issue nonprofit status to new organizations.

Challenges of Managing Nonprofit Leisure Service Agencies

Because fees and donations are their primary sources of revenue, nonprofit organizations need to focus on their revenues to remain financially viable. Like businesses, nonprofits must be creative in the services they provide to their clients, but setting fees that clients can afford and raising donation revenues are skills that nonprofit managers need to have.

Level of transparency is another way that nonprofits are similar to businesses. Like businesses, the records of nonprofit organizations are not readily available to the media or public, although they are required to submit reports to the IRS, but few citizens read these reports. Faking financial reports has criminal consequences in the private sector, and in the nonprofit sector, financial reports are available for donors to discern the necessity of their donations.

The boards of directors for nonprofits are similar to those of private-sector companies. When an opening on a board of directors occurs, the remaining board members select the replacement. Also, board meetings are not open to the public or regulated by state open meetings acts, so replacing board members can be done without public scrutiny. Nonprofit board members are rarely compensated for their service to the organization. In fact, their primary responsibility is to bring money into the agency through their fund-raising efforts.

Managing a nonprofit organization can be different as well. Because employees are generally not rewarded by profit sharing, managing nonprofit employees is similar to managing public employees.

Management is generally done on a group basis using sociological principles of group motivation, whereas business management of employees is more psychological and uses business leadership and organizational management techniques taught in business schools.

Nonprofit managers do not share in the surplus revenues of the organization. Big salaries or other perks are supposed to be absent. Nonprofit managers are supposed to focus on

- how much revenue the agency generates from services,
- which clients receive free services,
- how judiciously the agency spends its money, and
- how the agency can maintain an environment in which clients can be donors and employees will say complimentary things about the organization.

There has been negative publicity about large salaries and perks for executives within nonprofit organizations. There are measurements of the percentage of donations that go to administrative costs; some nonprofits spend as little as 10 percent for administration and others spend as much as 50 percent. Those comparisons are now available on the Internet, which allows donors to decide what organizations will spend their donations the most judiciously (e.g., see www.givewell.org).

The good news is that nonprofit organizations usually succeed in their missions of servicing public needs that would have otherwise gone unserved. Of the new nonprofit organizations created each year, less than 20 percent fail, partly because a safety net is present. When nonprofits are chartered by states, the people who charter them usually have established a need for their services and sources of revenue for their operations. Initially, these organizations have volunteers performing the work, and eventually donors provide a stable base of revenue. Therefore, the risk that the agency will fail is smaller, although the financial reward to management is also less.

Skills Required for Managing Nonprofit Leisure Service Agencies

Nonprofit leisure service managers need to have a blend of skills in business and public administration. Managers need to understand the following:

- Economics
- Business accounting
- Finance and marketing
- Business leadership
- Fund accounting
- Organizational theory
- Fund-raising

Several universities have emerging academic programs in public service that focus on nonprofit agency management. These programs blend business and public administration classes.

It is often said that people who pursue careers in nonprofit leisure service are not necessarily doing it for personal enrichment. They are typically intrinsically motivated people who want the security of a stable environment as they perform a service for the community. Like for-profit managers, they need financial skills, but they must have a certain level of human compassion that is not required of business managers. They need to identify what unmet human needs their organization can meet.

PUBLIC SECTOR

Government spending in the leisure service industry makes up about 1 percent of all money spent. Even so, governmental leisure services are a cornerstone of employment in the leisure service field. Many graduates from academic programs in leisure service are drawn to the public sector, particularly at the county and municipal levels. State and federal leisure service professionals attain their positions by political appointment or competitive testing.

The U.S. government is primarily in the business of maintaining national forests, parks, and recreation areas. Most recreation services are park and nature conservation–oriented, and most of the user fees charged are for admissions, parking, and use of camping, food, and accommodation facilities. The federal government provides outdoor services through many agencies in various departments. The Canadian government also provides national and provincial parks and recreation services.

The 50 state governments in the United States provide services similar to those of the National Park Service. State departments of natural resources primarily manage their state park systems, some of which have restaurants, hotels, campgrounds, boat rentals, and other supplemental services. Some parks charge fees for admission and parking, whereas others are free of charge.

For the most part, federal, state, and county agencies are not considered entrepreneurial. They exist to conserve land and, in some cases, to block public access and maintain land in its natural state.

State governments have created special taxing districts that own athletic stadiums and convention centers. The construction and maintenance of these facilities can be funded by property, sales, excise, and hotel room taxes. These facilities can be rented to professional and university sports programs and generate millions of dollars in revenue.

MUNICIPAL PUBLIC-SECTOR LEISURE SERVICE DELIVERY SYSTEMS

At the local level, the United States has more than 35,000 municipalities. At the municipal level, many structures of government provide parks and recreation services. The most common are parks and recreation departments of cities, villages, and towns. Canadian municipalities are organized similarly. Municipal departments of parks and recreation are nearly identical in Canada and the United States.

At the local level in the United States, special districts are another way of delivering public parks and recreation services. Some states have provisions within state law to create park districts at the local level (e.g., Illinois, Ohio, Colorado, Utah, California, Oregon, Washington, North Dakota). Of the states that provide park districts, the option of providing parks and recreation services as municipal departments is still available. Only in Illinois and North Dakota do park districts outnumber parks and recreation departments.

Challenges of Managing Government Leisure Service Agencies

It has been said that public administration is like managing in a fishbowl because nothing is private, and managing public employees is like herding cats who each have a lawyer. The public has the right to review all public documents and meeting notes under the Freedom of Information Act, and public employees have rights under the 1965 Civil Rights Act. The main reason for public scrutiny of government is the relationship between taxation and responsibility. Unlike businesses or nonprofit organizations in which revenues are exchanged through transactions that both parties agree on,

A park district, a public-sector leisure delivery provider, has many duties including maintaining and providing playground equipment for children.

taxation is not voluntary. Because the public is required to pay taxes, government officials bear a greater burden to explain how the taxes are spent. This principle is called ***transparency,*** which means being clear and open. To ensure that government dealings are transparent, laws adopted at the federal, state, and local levels require that

- all information, with a few exceptions, be public;
- meetings be announced and take place in public; and
- individuals or companies doing business with governmental units bid competitively for that business.

Public employees have greater rights than business and nonprofit employees do.

- In most states, public employees cannot be hired and fired by managers without consent of the elected board. Thus, every employee who is terminated has the right to a board hearing before termination.

- As in the private sector, the public sector might have employee unions to deal with, which means another set of rules for hiring and firing employees and giving pay increases.
- Except for public administrators, who usually have employment contracts, public employees are not at-will employees like private- and nonprofit sector employees are. *At will* means employees serve at the will of the administration (i.e., can be dismissed by the employer for any reason). Public employees serve at the will of the public who, in a republican form of government, elect representatives to make decisions.

Boards in the public sector are different too. The governing boards that levy taxes and approve budget expenditures must be elected. Appointed parks and recreation department boards may have advisory authority with leisure service managers, but only the elected boards have the power to decide. Directors of parks and recreation departments therefore have two boards as their bosses—the city council and their appointed advisory boards. Sometimes leisure service managers have three bosses (city council, park board, and city manager), depending on whether the municipality has a strong mayor–council system or a council–manager system. This arrangement can make managing a public leisure service agency an extremely difficult assignment.

Working for an elected board in an environment where everything that a leisure service manager does is public information adds a dimension of politics to the management process. Although nonprofit leisure service managers might worry about offending potential donors, a governmental leisure service manager who offends a member of the public may find the offended party seeking election to the manager's governing board. Disgruntled employees can run for election as well, and many of each group do.

Another challenge of managing a governmental leisure service agency is that managers need two types of financial management skills.

- One is the management of tax-supported services, typically the parks, which usually do not have admission fees and are supported entirely by tax revenues.
- The other is the operation of recreation programs and facilities, which usually generate self-sustaining revenues from user fees.

Public-sector managers are therefore running governmental units that provide both tax-supported and fee-supported services in a transparent arena in which disgruntled employees or members of the public can run for their boards, which is more difficult than running a business that needs to make a profit.

Skills Required for Managing Government Leisure Service Agencies

The skills required of leisure service public administrators are somewhat different from those required of business or nonprofit managers. Leisure service public administrators have less need to understand economics because governmental units rely heavily on relatively stable tax revenues. Financial management is less important because state governments are stringent about how governmental units handle public funds. That is not to say that economics and finance are unimportant. Working in an economic environment has political consequences, and capital funding through the issuance of tax repaid bonds requires an understanding of finance.

Government accounting is different from business or nonprofit accounting. To maintain the

---

OUTSTANDING GRADUATE

Background Information

Name: Brittany Fischer

Education: BS in corporate recreation and wellness from Northwest Missouri State University

Career Information

Position: Health and Wellness Supervisor

Organization: City of Liberty, Missouri

Job description: In my job, I manage the fitness center. I provide leadership to wellness employees: group exercise instructors, personal trainers, and wellness coaches. I create and implement corporate wellness programs and design and implement a variety of wellness programs that fit the needs of the community. My job has provided me an opportunity to network with others in the recreation field as well as in public health.

Career path: My career path began with my internship in Sioux City, Iowa, with their parks and recreation department. I then became employed with the YMCA of Greater Kansas City as a wellness specialist. I stayed with the YMCA in a variety of roles (trainer, instructor, healthy living director, youth development) until the spring of 2015, when I joined the Liberty Parks and Recreation team. I'm always striving to learn more and grow so that I can continue to move up the career ladder.

Likes and dislikes about the job: I dislike roadblocks and people who are resistant to change. I like the opportunity to have an impact on citizens while expanding the role of health and wellness in the community.

Advice for Undergraduates

My advice to undergraduates is to get as much hands-on experience as possible, because that will prepare you for the field more than any textbook or lecture.

required levels of transparency, governmental units have much more complex accounting rules than do business and nonprofit agencies, which report to the IRS and state departments of revenue and are not required to produce detailed reports. Governmental units report directly to the people, so their reports are more detailed. Such is not always the case in Canada, where public officials often report directly to the Crown or representatives of the Crown.

The skills required of public leisure service managers include the following:

- Government accounting
- Organizational theory
- Political science
- Economics
- Finance

If a leisure service manager oversees the operation of parks only, it could be argued their skills need to include those related to park maintenance and conservation. If the leisure service manager manages recreation programs or facilities, it could also be argued the skills need to be more diverse, including marketing and financial management and skills related to the recreation facility or program.

If managing a leisure service agency in the public sector can be more difficult than managing in the other sectors, why would someone choose to do it? The answer is that working in the public sector is just as rewarding as working for a nonprofit organization. Serving the public has its intrinsic rewards.

PROFESSIONAL PREPARATION FOR LEISURE SERVICE DELIVERY

Regardless of whether a student seeks a career in the private, nonprofit, or public sector of the leisure service industry, all students should pursue proficiency in certain areas. Previous discussion of the challenges facing leisure service professionals and the skills required of them suggest that every leisure service professional needs to understand how to manage money and people and how government works.

Understanding how to manage money means that leisure service professionals need to understand accounting so they can read financial reports. They need to comprehend financial management so they can take appropriate action when their financial reports are not in order. Students seeking to prepare themselves to manage finances should take

courses in financial accounting if they seek careers in business or nonprofit leisure service management or governmental accounting if they seek careers in governmental leisure service management. And all students need to take courses in finance to understand how to manage budgets.

To prepare for leisure service delivery in all three sectors, students need to take courses in marketing. Marketing teaches how focusing on product (service), price, place, and promotion leads to understanding

- what the customer needs,
- how much the customer is willing to pay,
- where and how the service ought to be provided, and
- how to communicate its availability to the customer.

Understanding these essentials of marketing is crucial for managers in all sectors.

Political science and public administration courses are essential to students pursuing careers in public-sector leisure service delivery and are useful to those seeking careers in nonprofit and business leisure service delivery. Public-sector managers need to understand how government works if they intend to be successful working in government. But because the government creates and regulates business and nonprofit entities, managers in those sectors need to understand what they will face. The government taxes businesses and forces some nonprofit organizations to provide a certain portion of their services as charitable work, suggesting that business and nonprofit leisure service managers would benefit from understanding what makes government tick.

Finally, regardless of whether you work in the public, nonprofit, or governmental sectors of the leisure services industry, all professionals will benefit from an understanding of the influence of technology on the services they provide. This includes the following:

- Software for registrations
- Videoconferencing tools
- Remote program delivery
- Security systems
- Social media marketing
- Equipment such as virtual reality devices that can be used in programming

As the world continues to progress, the expectations of consumers change with it. In order to provide the services our patrons desire, leisure service professionals must be aware of these products and opportunities as well.

PROFESSIONAL ACCREDITATION

All leisure service professionals need to consider professional accreditation not only because many agencies require it but also because accreditation teaches some of the skills required for successful careers in the field. The National Recreation and Park Association (NRPA) in the United States, in conjunction with state associations, has developed an accreditation program called the certified park and recreation professional (CPRP) program. Undergraduate students who complete an accredited NRPA curriculum with the NRPA-prescribed learning outcomes are eligible to take the accreditation test.

The NRPA also has an accreditation program for agencies provided by the Commission for Accreditation of Park and Recreation Agencies (CAPRA). The CAPRA process is based on 144 standards for national accreditation, which can be determined only after CAPRA members make an on-site visit to verify eligibility.

If an undergraduate student completes a program that is not NRPA accredited, they are required to take continuing education units (CEUs) before taking the exam. After a leisure service professional has obtained CPRP accreditation, they are required to take CEUs on a regular basis to maintain accreditation. Continuing education units need to be approved by the NRPA.

SUMMARY

Leisure service delivery systems exist in the private, nonprofit, and governmental sectors of the economy, and they account for a substantial proportion of the national economies of Canada and the United States. As subunits of the leisure service industry,

- the private sector operates businesses that serve the leisure needs of people by charging fees for services that exceed the costs,
- nonprofit organizations provide services to some people for fees and waive fees for others, and
- governmental units levy taxes for services when it is not practical to charge fees and charge fees for leisure services when doing so is practical.

The private leisure service business sector is characterized by innovation. In pursuit of profits, entrepreneurs are alert to new and changing leisure service needs of their customers. Nonprofit-sector organizations have other challenges, including fund-raising, because they seek donations to support operations that in many cases serve low-income people who cannot afford to pay fees or make donations. Governmental units provide leisure services that are necessary but cannot be provided by the private and nonprofit sectors, such as parks and open space.

Students who want to prepare themselves for a leisure service professional career in any of the three sectors need to consider taking business courses such as accounting, finance, economics, and marketing. They also need to understand government and should study political science and public administration. NRPA-accredited undergrad curricula that teach these learning outcomes allow students to become CPRPs without meeting postgraduate continuing education requirements.

Review Questions

1. What are the three sectors of the economy that provide leisure and recreation services?

2. What is 501(c)?

3. What types of professional skills are needed by leisure service professionals in all three sectors?

4. What are some examples of professional certification and accreditation that can be acquired by leisure service professionals?

Go to HK*Propel* to complete the activities for this chapter.

CHAPTER 6

Parks and Protected Areas in Canada and the United States

Paul F.J. Eagles and Jeffrey C. Hallo

> " There is nothing so American as our national parks. . . . The fundamental idea behind the parks . . . is that the country belongs to the people, that it is in the process of making for the enrichment of the lives of all of us. "
>
> Franklin D. Roosevelt, U.S. president, 1933-1945

> " The day will come when the population of Canada will be ten times as great as it is now but the national parks ensure that every Canadian . . . will still have free access to vast areas possessing some of the finest scenery in Canada, in which the beauty of the landscape is protected from profanation, the natural wild animals, plants and forests preserved, and the peace and solitude of primeval nature retained. "
>
> James Harkin, Dominion Parks Commission for Canada, director of the first national park agency in the world, 1911-1936

© Paul F.J. Eagles

LEARNING OUTCOMES

After reading this chapter, you should be able to do the following:

> Describe the history and development of Canadian and American park systems as well as their similarities and differences
>
> Differentiate and discuss various types of parks and other protected areas
>
> Name and describe the accomplishments of a few of the most prominent people who promoted and created parks
>
> Summarize current issues and trends in park resources management
>
> Define the terms *preservation, wilderness, conservation, multiple use,* and *wise use of natural resources and parks*
>
> Describe a few career opportunities in park settings

Parks and other protected areas are important parts of the cultures of Canada and the United States. Just mentioning a national park, **wildlife refuge**, or wilderness evokes strong feelings among many citizens and foreign tourists. This chapter presents the history and a current description of the major park systems and other protected areas in Canada and the United States.

The term *park* is derived from the Old French and Middle English term *parc*, which means "an enclosed piece of ground stocked with beasts of the chase, held by prescription or by the king's grant" (Runte, 2010). One of the first parklike areas was the Greek *agora*, which were plazas established and used for public assembly. Today, however, parks and other protected areas may be defined as places set aside to protect and provide for the use and enjoyment of natural, cultural, historic, or recreational resources. The movement to create parks and protected areas that emerged in Canada and the United States in the late 1800s, and continues strongly to this day, was driven by society's need to reconnect with nature after having been removed from it because of industrialization and technological advancement. It was also stimulated by a movement that recognized that outdoor recreation was good for public health.

Modern parks in the United States and Canada reflect our ideals of democracy and are managed for public use and enjoyment. Parks are places for the public to escape the stresses of life, rejuvenate, and connect with nature and history. Parks in one form or another exist in every country in the world, which indicates their widespread critical role in many societies. Their purpose may be particularly crucial in the United States and Canada, where well over a billion visits occur annually to local, state, provincial, and national parks. A substantial body of research has shown that parks and other pro-

tected areas aid considerably in child development, public health, economic growth, and quality of life. Parks also serve a critical function in protecting and ensuring the long-term sustainability of plants, wildlife, fish, historic or cultural sites, geology, and natural processes (e.g., bird migration routes and the filtration of water).

This chapter first outlines the situation in Canada and then in the United States. Those sections are followed by a summary and comparison of the two countries.

HISTORY OF PARKS IN CANADA

Canada is a large country composed of 10 provinces and 3 territories. The nation was created when four British colonies came together to form a country through confederation in 1867. Over time, other colonies joined as new provinces and other provinces were created from territories. In 1885, the national government started to create a national park system in Canada with the creation of Banff National Park in the Rocky Mountains, which became Canada's most famous national park. Also starting in 1885, Ontario, Canada's most populous province, purchased private land near Niagara Falls for the creation of a park and tourist destination. This site was the first major park created by a province in Canada. These two parks were the start of the development of the national and **provincial park** systems in Canada.

As the country grew, the provinces retained considerable land management responsibilities. One important authority was the ownership and management of all Crown land, or public land as it is called in the United States. Because the provinces owned the Crown land within the provincial boundaries, creating parks was relatively easy for them. Conversely, the federal government could not easily create parks within provinces because provincial cooperation was required. Therefore, some of the provincial park systems in Canada are as large and prominent as the **national park** systems in many other countries.

First Parks in Canada

The first parks created in Canada were in cities. The movement to form city parks in Canada was strongly influenced by city parks existing in England. The large, green, central parks of London were well known to the early populace of Canada and became a model for park creation in British North America. For example, Hyde Park, now in downtown London, England, was created in 1536 by Henry VIII for hunting. Over the next centuries, it was increasingly opened for public use and became a model in the public mind of how a city park should operate.

In 1763, the lieutenant governor of the British Colony of Nova Scotia granted the Halifax Common, former military land, to the City of Halifax. It was first used as community pasture and

for military exercises. The Halifax Common later became city parkland and is now located in the heart of the city. It is recognized as the first park created in Canada.

Toronto was the first city in British North America to formally create a public agency to manage those parks. After eight years of operation, Toronto's Committee on Public Walks and Gardens, Canada's first park management agency, took political action and asked the city council to lobby the provincial government to change the law and give cities an explicit power to create parks. The chairman of the committee spoke at a Toronto city council meeting in 1859 and said the following:

In the first place, they furnish to the wealthy places of agreeable resort, either for driving or walking, and free from exposure to the heat and dust of an ordinary road . . . thus enabling them to enjoy the inestimable blessing of the free open air of the Country—so conducive to the promotion of health and morality.

In the second place, to the mechanic and working classes, Public Grounds are of incal-

The creation of Banff National Park, the first national park in Canada, was influenced by the building of the Canadian Pacific Railway, with the promise of tourism.

© Paul F.J. Eagles

culable advantage. How much better it is for the families of such to have these places of recreation and healthful exercise, than to have them exposed on the crowded streets of the city? (McFarland, 1982, p. 258)

As seen in this speech, the committee assumed the responsibility for providing public grounds for all classes of society, especially for the working class who badly needed access to "places of agreeable resort" free of charge. This public-spirited and socialistic approach to parks—public use subsidized by community taxes—became a fundamental aspect of park management in Canada. Over the next 150 years, virtually every city and town in Canada created parks for the welfare, use, and health of its citizens. The municipalities fund these parks from income earned by **land taxes** and provide most of the parks and their facilities free to local citizens who want to use them. However, specialized programs, such as sports participation, involve a use fee.

In the initial days, city parks were managed by volunteers working on parks boards. Starting in the early decades of the 20th century, staff members were hired to manage special facilities, such as agricultural fairs and sport grounds. Many of the first park managers were gardeners. Not until the 1960s did universities and colleges in Canada start to train people specifically for working in parks and recreation in cities. The first program of this type in Canada was the Department of Recreation at the University of Waterloo, which first acquired students in 1968.

Provincial and National Parks

The origin of provincial and national parks in Canada can be traced to the 1880s and occurred simultaneously in Niagara Falls in Ontario and on the remote mountain pass of the Bow Valley in the Northwest Territories of western Canada now in the Province of Alberta.

From the beginning of European settlement, Niagara Falls attracted tourists. Because the Niagara River and Niagara Falls are in the United States (New York) and Canada (Ontario), cross-border discussions influenced the management of this rapidly developing tourist attraction. The Canadian side of the river had the best view of the falls, and by 1885 every possible view was privately owned. Entrepreneurs charged fees for visitors to enter their premises to look out windows at the magnificent waterfalls and cataracts. People in New York State proposed in the early 1880s to create reserves and organize tourism management institutions to develop public parks and foster cooperation between the two countries. Ontario adopted the idea and asked the Canadian government to fund and operate the Canadian portion as a park and tourism reserve. The idea was to create a national park on the Canadian side of the river by buying out all the private properties and replacing them with a properly designed park and tourism facility. The vast expense of the proposed land purchase and park development incited opposition from members of the Canadian Parliament from Quebec and the Maritime provinces. They objected to large amounts of federal money being spent in Ontario on this development, and this opposition effectively stopped federal involvement at Niagara. In 1885, the Province of Ontario moved alone to create a major park and tourism facility along the Niagara River and Niagara Falls. This action involved the purchase and removal of thousands of buildings on the lip of the falls and the gorge and the creation of a green parkway available for all to use. The Ontario Parliament also passed legislation for the creation of the Niagara Parks Commission, a park and tourism management body (Seibel, 1995). This was the first legislated park management body in Canada. It is still in place with largely the same responsibilities and management structure.

The Ontario actions at Niagara set precedents in three important areas.

- Niagara was the first park created by a provincial government in Canada and had the first stand-alone park management agency with its own legislation and mandate.
- The park stimulated the creation of future parks in Ontario by the provincial government, not the national government.
- It set a tone of American–Canadian cooperation in park management.

All three movements continued and strengthened in subsequent years. This book is an example of the ongoing sharing of ideas and cooperation in park management between the United States and Canada, as Canadian and American scholars work together to create a holistic image.

Simultaneous to the debates over Niagara in Ontario, the Canadian government pushed the first national cross-country railway through the Rocky Mountains to link Eastern Canada to the Province of British Columbia in the West. When hot springs were discovered near the new railway tracks in the Bow Valley in the eastern Rocky Mountains, the potential for tourism was quickly recognized. The national government acted through a cabinet

Niagara Falls parks in Ontario were created in 1885 to manage a major international tourism activity.

order in 1885 to reserve the hot springs for public use and to stop private tourism development. This action was followed in 1887 by federal legislation to create Rocky Mountain Park, Canada's first national park, which was later renamed Banff National Park. This national government activity initiated the Canadian federal government's involvement in the parks business. Many historians state that Rocky Mountain Park was the third national park in the world after Yellowstone National Park in the United States, created in 1872, and Royal National Park in the British Colony of New South Wales, now a state of Australia, created in 1879 (Marty, 1984). However, all three followed much earlier and older park developments in England, such as the creation of the New Forest by King William the Conqueror in England in 1079.

In 1887, Canada's federal government created North America's first wildlife conservation reserve at Last Mountain Lake in the Northwest Territories (now in Saskatchewan). This small reserve was established to protect the nesting and migration habitat of wildlife in the Canadian prairies (Foster, 1978). This reserve became the first of many national wildlife areas and migratory bird sanctuaries created by the national government in Canada, and later by many provinces.

In 1893, Ontario made the next important move by creating Algonquin National Park. This huge area of forested and rocky hills, lakes, and rivers in Southern Ontario became a forest conservation area and park. The government wanted to manage the logging industry in this area, protect the headwaters of five important rivers, and stop farmers from clearing the forests. This creation of a large conservation park, applying the American national park model by a provincial government, was a first for Canada. It set a precedent for Ontario and other provinces (Killan, 1993; Saunders, 1998). The name was changed to Algonquin Provincial Park in 1913, giving notice that the parks operated by provinces were unique and separate from those operated by the national government. Henceforth, the federal government moved forward in creating national parks and each province created provincial parks.

By 1900, the die was cast in Canada. The initial debates and decisions coalesced into precedents that would guide future park creation and management

© Paul F.J. Eagles

Algonquin Provincial Park in Ontario became a model for provincial park creation across Canada.

across the country. Now cities and towns throughout the country saw park creation as a normal and expected activity. Provincial parks were increasingly created for **conservation** and tourism purposes. Provincial governments also created regional parks for specific tourism and resource management concerns in regional geographic areas. Two types of federal reserves were established: national parks and national wildlife areas. The signing of the Migratory Bird Treaty with the United States in 1916 gave the federal government a powerful tool to regulate waterfowl and bird hunting in cooperation with the U.S. government. This action also gave the Canadian federal government the power to deal with wildlife management all over the country. This treaty was an early recognition of the international nature of ecology; that is, birds move widely across countries during their yearly life cycles. Therefore, international cooperation is needed for ecological conservation to be effective. The Trump administration attempted to weaken this treaty and its international cooperation, but it survived and was still in place in 2022.

Over the next century, these emerging approaches strengthened and deepened. Many more parks and reserves were created. Management institu-

tions were created. Canadians increasingly used and appreciated these areas in growing numbers. During the 20th century, parks were a major part of the culture of the country. After World War II, a massive expansion in personal auto ownership and increasing prosperity led to a vast increase in outdoor recreation, which spurred increased park creation across the country.

Long-Distance Hiking Trails

Canada has many long-distance hiking trails, all of which are operated by nongovernmental organizations called *trail clubs*. Provincial governments do not have a formal role in the creation or management of long-distance hiking trails. The oldest trail is the Bruce Trail, 900 km (560 mi) long in southern Ontario, which runs along the Niagara Escarpment from Niagara Falls in the south to Tobermory in the north on the Bruce Peninsula. This trail was opened in 1967, Canada's centennial. Initially, the trail was almost entirely on private land, but over time many landowners removed permission for public use of their land, so the trail is now on a combination of private land, parkland, and land owned by trail clubs. The Canadian long-distance trail movement was heavily influenced by earlier trail activities in the United States, especially the Appalachian Trail.

The most ambitious trail effort in Canada is the Trans Canada Trail. The creation of this trail is ongoing, and the goal is a national trail from Newfoundland in the east across Canada to the West Coast including a branch north to the Yukon, for a total length of 27,000 kilometers (16,777 mi) (TCT, 2021). The trail also involves a water route from central Alberta to the Arctic Ocean. Virtually all long-distance trails in Canada have no government funding, operating entirely through nongovernmental organizations, volunteers, and donations.

National Heritage Rivers System

Canada has a national heritage rivers system that is cooperatively managed by nine provinces and the federal government. Quebec withdrew from the system in 2006, weakening the national focus of the system. The system contains 39 rivers covering 12,000 kilometers (7,456 mi) of waterway. The goal of the system is to promote, protect, and enhance Canada's river heritage and ensure that Canada's leading rivers are managed in a sustainable manner (Leduc, 2009). The system has no legal mandate and is entirely cooperative among governments.

Wilderness in Canada (1600-2021)

In Canada, the concept of establishing large areas of uninhabited lands as designated wilderness is largely restricted to lands within national and provincial parks. This situation is markedly different from that in the United States, and reasons for the differences are important. In Canada, Aboriginal land rights have been respected, meaning that the creation of parks or wilderness sites involves negotiation with Aboriginal peoples who have land rights according to the Canadian constitution. In Canada, land is influenced by the rights of Aboriginal people. Very little land is considered vacant. A summary of the history of this situation follows.

After the American Revolution, the British government formed alliances for political and military reasons with many of the Aboriginal groups that lived in the area that is now Canada. One of the major reasons for these alliances was the shared concern of the British government and the Aboriginal peoples of the aggressive expansionist nature of the United States to the south. Shared actions were in both their interests to preserve independence.

Because the British needed the military prowess of the many Aboriginal people, their land rights were recognized and supported.

Therefore, Aboriginal people live in the wilderness in Canada. It was a living landscape composed of forests, rivers, wildlife, and Native people. In the United States, the situation was much different; Native people were killed or persecuted, removed from the land and placed into reservations, or driven into Canada, thereby creating the mythology that the area was wilderness—land without people. Widespread support never arose in Canada for the classical American view of wilderness as large expanses of land without people; Canada's wilderness contains people. These are the substantive reasons why the American wilderness concept, outside of national parks, has never gained traction in Canada.

The Canadian Constitution of 1982 recognized the existing Aboriginal and treaty rights of the Aboriginal peoples of Canada. This has meant stronger Aboriginal power in land ownership and management across Canada. As a result, all new park creation must move forward with Aboriginal involvement. Therefore, new national parks are often established under comanagement agreements whereby the parks are managed with cooperative involvement of local Aboriginal nations. This is one reason that 10 of Canada's 48 national parks are labeled as park reserves, since local Indigenous peoples will not accept full national park status and full federal government control of the parks. Also, the federal government has invested heavily, C$340 million in 2021, in funding education programs for the creation of new cadres of Indigenous Guardians who will work with Indigenous partners at Parks Canada–administered places to enhance current Guardian initiatives and cocreate new ones (Government of Canada, 2021).

Important People in Canadian Parks

During the 1870s and 1880s, Sir Sandford Fleming was the engineer in charge of the construction of the Canadian Pacific Railway, which was built to link the industrial eastern provinces through the open prairies to the west coast province of British Columbia. In an attempt to increase the use of his developing railway, Fleming proposed a series of national parks across Canada to create tourism demand and railway use. This was the first published proposal for a system of national parks in

Canada. The discovery of thermal springs in the Bow Valley in the Rocky Mountains in 1883 provided an opportunity for the national government of Prime Minister John A. Macdonald to create the first of Fleming's proposed parks. Fleming and Macdonald were central figures in the creation of Canada's first national park in 1885, which is now known as Banff National Park.

In 1887, the federal government of Canada created the first bird sanctuary in North America. Areas around Last Mountain Lake in the Northwest Territories, now Saskatchewan, were withdrawn from settlement and set aside for the breeding of waterfowl. The creation of this reserve was the work of Edgar Dewdney, then the lieutenant governor of the Northwest Territories. He feared that the extension of the railway into this area would destroy the wildlife habitat. The creation of this wildlife reserve set the precedent for the national government to set aside areas for wildlife conservation. This reserve was designated as a National Historic Site of Canada in 1987.

Starting in 1885, Alexander Kirkwood, a clerk in the Ontario Department of Crown Lands, lobbied for the creation of a national forest and park in the Algonquin Highlands of southern Ontario. Over the next eight years, his idea slowly gained the support of other government officials, influential members of the community, and ultimately elected officials. In 1893, the Government of Ontario created Algonquin National Park, which was later renamed Algonquin Provincial Park. This action created the first large provincial park in Canada partially based on the emerging American model of large, uninhabited wilderness reserves. The Algonquin Indian people retained hunting rights in the park but due to its inhospitable environment in winter, only used the park area in the summer. Thus Ontario set in motion events that resulted in the creation of thousands of provincial parks in all Canadian provinces.

In 1911, the Canadian government created the Dominion Parks Branch, which was the first national park management agency in the world. James Harkin was appointed as the commissioner and was the first national park director in the world. Harkin was an aggressive supporter of park creation and management. He was a strong supporter of parks, wilderness values, and tourism. He set out to attract Canadians to national parks and to ensure that national parks became cultural icons that rivaled the historic sites and art in Europe. He was famously successful in his goals, and as a result, he is recognized as the person who started the movement to make national parks the cultural icons that they are today.

These five people, Fleming, Macdonald, Dewdney, Kirkwood, and Harkin, set in motion ideas that resulted in Canada's national and provincial park systems. Although many of their ideas can be traced to England and the United States, they adapted them to the Canadian reality. Note the influence of politicians and government employees in this movement, which reflects that the Canadian style of government, largely borrowed from Britain, involves a powerful professional civil service reporting to elected politicians. Largely absent from the Canadian experience (unlike the American park movement described later) are writers, artists, and scholars. A possible exception to this rule is Sir Sandford Fleming, the railroad engineer who was also a planner, author, and civil servant.

PARK SYSTEMS OF CANADA

By 1900, there were five types of parks in Canada: city parks, regional parks, provincial parks, federal national parks, and federal wildlife areas. All over the country, towns and cities made park creation and management a normal role of government. In some provinces, special regional park agencies were set up to manage parks, usually around geographic features such as rivers or lakes. An example in Ontario is the St. Lawrence Parks Commission, which has a series of parks along the Canadian side of the St. Lawrence River and Seaway. All provincial governments moved forward in creating provincial park systems, often in active competition with the emerging national park system. Over the years, successive Canadian governments worked slowly but diligently to add to the two major federal systems: the national parks and the national wildlife areas.

City Parks

Parks are located in every village, town, and city in Canada. They fulfill many functions: Sport, recreation, and health are particularly important among them. In the 1980s, some cities added conservation of natural lands to these functions, such as those in river valleys and wetlands. Today, city parks are a mixture of recreation areas, parks, and green spaces. Interestingly the COVID-19 pandemic strengthened, in the public's mind, the importance of urban green space for human physical and psychological health.

Most city parks are managed by a parks and recreation department that is part of the municipal government. This department is responsible for facility construction, park maintenance, and recreation programs. Advisory groups, sport organizations, and volunteers are hallmarks of municipal parks and recreation management. Park management at the municipal level is operated by a combination of professional managers, specialized part-time employees, and many volunteers. Land taxes pay for most municipal park management. Some recreation service fees are used for special-purpose activities, such as renting a community hall or paying for sport lessons.

No national inventory of the number and size of municipal parks exists in Canada. The amount of land used for parks in cities varies from a small percentage of the city land area to nearly 40 percent. Examples of city parks include Stanley Park in Vancouver, a large natural park on the ocean near the downtown; Victoria Park in Kitchener, a traditional city park of trees, lawns, gardens, and statues located downtown; and Point Pleasant Park in Halifax, a park with impressive lawns and gardens.

In 2021, the Government of Canada launched a new program to create a network of urban parks across Canada, with funding of C$130,000,000 (Parks Canada, 2021a). Some of this money was allotted to purchase land to create new urban parks and expand existing parks. This is the first time that federal monies were used to create urban parks in Canada.

Regional Parks

In Canada, provincial governments often create regional park agencies to fulfill both conservation and recreation mandates. The province of Ontario has the most extensive system of regional parks in the country. Over many decades, the Parliament of Ontario passed legislation to create regional park agencies to establish and manage park systems in specific areas of the province. For example, the Niagara Parks Commission manages parks in the Niagara River and Falls area. The Niagara Parks have one of the highest park visitation rates in the world with as many as 16 million visitors per year. The Ontario Parliament also passed legislation to create regional planning bodies that coordinate the conservation and management of specific landscape features. The best example is the Niagara Escarpment Commission, which coordinates planning and conservation over the Niagara Escarpment that runs through southern Ontario from Niagara Falls to the Bruce Peninsula. The creation of this commission was strongly influenced by the recreational users

of the Bruce Hiking Trail that weaves throughout the Niagara Escarpment lands.

Unique in Canada, Ontario provincial legislation encourages and provides for the creation of 36 conservation authorities that manage watersheds in the populated areas of the province. Each of these local government authorities oversees a park system that is largely composed of water management projects such as dams, river valley protection areas, and wetlands. Many of these conservation areas are close to large cities and are therefore important for providing outdoor recreation near urban areas. Each year, Ontario conservation authorities serve about 5 million **visitor days** of outdoor recreation on 250 conservation areas. These parks are typically located close to urban areas and serve a valuable near-urban outdoor recreation function. They also have a major role in providing environmental education sites for local schools.

Provincial Parks

Every province and territory in Canada has a provincial or territorial park system, but the size and use of the systems vary considerably. Some provinces, such as British Columbia, Alberta, and Ontario, have developed large and well-used provincial park systems. Other provinces, such as New Brunswick, Newfoundland, and Prince Edward Island, oversee small systems. These differences result from the history and political cultures of each province.

The wealthier and more heavily populated provinces created large provincial park systems predominantly for the middle- and upper-middle-class members of their societies while concurrently discouraging federal efforts to create parks in their provinces. The poorer provinces encouraged the national government to meet the demand for parks through federal funding, creation, and management of national parks in their provinces. This approach ensured that federal tax dollars rather than provincial tax dollars were spent on parks in these provinces.

National Parks and Wildlife Areas

The national park system in Canada is large, popular, well-funded, and growing. Because most Canadians grew up visiting Canada's national parks (or at least heard about them or saw them in the media), national parks in Canada are national cultural icons. In the 1930s and 1940s, the mountain parks were backdrops for many popular Hollywood movies. This exposure created a positive profile in the minds of both Canadians and Americans that helped create a boom in tourism that continues today. The national parks are one of Canada's premier international tourism destinations, and this is especially true for the four mountain national parks of Banff, Jasper, Kootenay, and Yoho.

As of 2021, Canada had 37 national parks, 10 national park reserves, and four national marine parks managed by Parks Canada (McNamee & Finkelstein, 2021). More national parks have been proposed and are under land-claim discussions with Aboriginal groups; therefore, more parks will be created in the coming years (Parks Canada, n.d.). Parks Canada, the federal park management agency, is responsible for four park and reserve systems: national parks and reserves, national historic parks and sites, national canals, and national marine conservation areas. The Canadian Wildlife Service with Environment Canada is responsible for two park and reserve systems: national wildlife areas and migratory bird sanctuaries. Fisheries and

Oceans Canada also has a national marine protected areas program.

National parks in Canada are created according to a system plan that calls for at least one national park in each major biogeographic region of the country (see figure 6.1). This plan divides the entire country into 39 easily recognizable biogeographic regions, such as the Pacific Coast Mountains, the Prairie Grasslands, and the Hudson-James Bay Lowlands. This approach is ecologically sound in that the park creation is based on the existing biogeography of the country. This approach ensures that national parks are created in all regions of the country. Parks Canada was one of the first park agencies in the world to develop such a system plan, and the system plan idea subsequently spread all over the world. The weakness of this approach is that it does not consider outdoor recreation demand, so many of the newer parks are in very remote parts of the country that are difficult to access and therefore have low levels of visitor use.

The number of national parks continues to increase in Canada as the demands of the system plan are fulfilled. Most of these new national parks

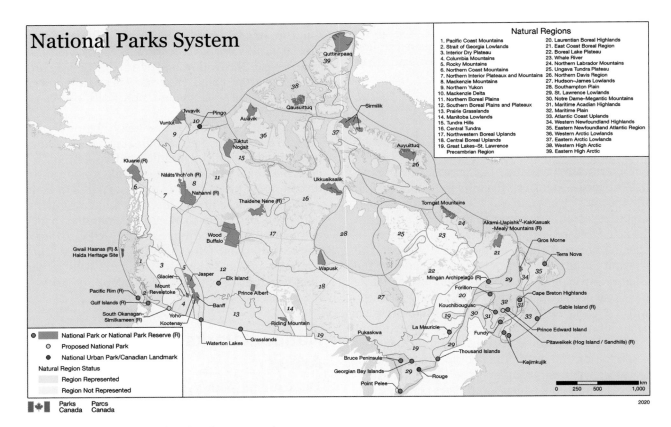

Figure 6.1   Canadian national parks system plan.

Reprinted by permission from Parks Canada, *National Parks: Map of Completing the Parks System* (Gatineau, Quebec: Parks Canada National, 2022). Available: www.pc.gc.ca/en/pn-np/cnpn-cnnp/carte-map.

are in the arctic and subarctic, but substantial parks have been created in the populated areas of British Columbia and Ontario. For example, the Rouge National Urban Park was created in 2015 on the eastern edge of Toronto, Canada's largest city.

The national parks attract approximately 25 million **person visits** per year. Because national park visitors tend to stay for more than two days each visit, the total number of visitor days is more than 50 million per year. Due to the travel restrictions caused by the COVID-19 pandemic, visitation dropped in 2020 and 2021 to the lowest level in decades: 17 million person visits (Parks Canada, 2021b).

The highly popular mountain parks of Banff, Jasper, Kootenay, and Yoho attract the most visitors. These four parks combined serve approximately 9 million person visits per year or more than 15 million visitor days. Some of the remote northern parks receive fewer than 1,000 visitors per year.

Canada also has an extensive system of national historic parks and sites. Historic sites are chosen according to a national historic sites system plan. The goal of this plan is to represent the country's important historic and cultural themes within the park and site system. The plan has five themes:

1. Peopling the land
2. Developing economies
3. Building social and community life
4. Expressing intellectual and cultural life
5. Governing Canada

All historic sites and parks are commemorated within one of those broad themes. To be recommended for designation, a site, person, or event must have had a nationally significant effect on or illustrate a nationally important aspect of the history of Canada. Places designated as national historic sites are occasionally acquired by the federal government for protection and interpretation. Of the 1004 national historic sites, Parks Canada administers 171 and contributes money to others managed by other governments or organizations. Parks Canada serves approximately 9 million visitors per year at the 171 historic sites that it manages. The number of yearly visitors to the individual sites varies dramatically from 3.6 million person visits to the historic fortifications of Quebec City to a few hundred person visits to historic sites in the far north of the country.

Parks Canada also manages a series of historic canals. These canals were originally built for military purposes but are now used for recreation and are extremely popular with boaters. The Trent–Severn Waterway in southern Ontario serves approximately 1.5 million person visits per year.

Parks Canada has the responsibility, shared with the Fisheries and Oceans Canada and the Canadian Wildlife Service, to create a system of national marine conservation areas. These areas are found off the Atlantic, Arctic, and Pacific coasts of Canada. Major reserves are also planned in the Great Lakes area. As of 2021, Parks Canada has created only five such reserves, but many more are planned. Canada has committed to place 25 percent of its marine areas in some form of protected area by the year 2025. The 2021 national budget included C$976,800,000 for marine conservation over the next five years (Fisheries and Oceans Canada, 2021). A massive establishment effort is underway to create more marine reserves in Canada.

The Canadian Wildlife Service manages two large national systems: national wildlife areas and national migratory bird sanctuaries. The national wildlife area system in Canada is large, poorly funded, and not well known by the Canadian public. Fifty-five national wildlife areas are scattered across Canada (Environment and Climate Change Canada, n.d.). These sites are important for migratory birds for both nesting and migratory stopover. The national wildlife areas have just 100,000 visitor days per year. The visitation rates at the 92 sites in Canada's national migratory bird sanctuary system are not documented and therefore cannot be reported. The very low visitation and tourism profile of these wildlife areas leads to a low political profile in Canada.

The differences between the Parks Canada systems and the Canadian Wildlife Service systems are vast. The national parks, national historic parks, and heritage canals managed by Parks Canada focus on conservation and tourism. Canadians are encouraged to visit through excellent information sources, tourism facilities, and programs. As a result, visitation is high, the public profile is high, and the government responds with substantial funds. The wildlife areas focus on wildlife conservation and hunting. Recreation is not encouraged, with the exception of hunting and fishing. Hunting is a declining activity in Canada with fewer participants every year. As a result, the public profile is low, visitation is low, and the government provides limited management funds. This demonstrates that for a park system to obtain sufficient government funding for effective management, it must have a positive public profile and a clientele that is mobilized to politically support the parks. Many people argue that a park or reserve with low visitation has fewer management stresses and therefore has more effective conservation. This position ignores the many stresses that occur in such a reserve besides recreation, including poaching, resource extraction, illegal logging, destructive farming, all-terrain vehicle use, and many other resource-damaging activities. Such stresses can be effectively curtailed only if the reserve has sufficient funds, staff, and political support. This example from Canada shows that without tourism, political support does not exist and therefore government funds are not allocated, resulting in little or no management staff. For a park to be successful, it must have users who are vocal in their support. Tourism and recreation are the mechanisms by which this use and support are created.

Budgets and Finance

Park budget allocations can be very political depending on the philosophy of the government in power. Park funding varies by jurisdiction; for example, major reductions occurred in provincial parks budgets in British Columbia and Alberta. The large park system in Ontario saw budget increases as it became dependent upon tourist fees and charges (Eagles, 2014). The national parks saw major budget increases along with substantial growth in the numbers of national parks over the 1980s and 1990s, then a massive budget reduction under the Harper government in 2012, and a major increase under the Trudeau government elected in 2015. In all jurisdictions, the trend was toward increased use of tourism fees and charges to fund parkland management. The government headed by Prime Minister Justin Trudeau, first elected in 2015, has been a strong supporter of the creation and effective management of parks and other forms of protected areas. Substantial park creation efforts are underway and substantial new funding has been allotted. In 2018, the Government of Canada announced an historic investment in nature conservation, which will support a number of national biodiversity targets. The federal budget for 2018 provided C$1.35 billion over five years to protect Canada's Natural Legacy (Canada, 2020).

Different Approaches to Park Management

Canada has a tremendous range of diversity in the approaches used in park management. The institutions include

- a government agency largely funded from taxes (e.g., Parks Canada);
- a stand-alone government agency that functions like a private corporation and is funded by tourist fees (e.g., the Niagara Parks Commission);
- a government agency that has a few supervisory staff but uses private corporations to provide most of the public services (e.g., British Columbia Provincial Parks);
- a nonprofit organization that functions like a private corporation and provides all park services (two national historic parks and some provincial parks in Ontario use this approach);
- and a mixture of public agencies and private operations that use public funding and tourism fees and charges.

This wide range of management approaches is an important area of park management that needs further investigation by scholars in the parks and recreation field. It is important to understand whether the different management approaches affect the overall management effectiveness of parks. Is one model better than another in delivering conservation and recreation services? This diversity of activity reveals that future park managers in Canada need to have a broad background in business as well as cultural and natural resource management.

One important aspect of the management of parks in Canada at all levels is the adoption of the British model of civil service. This means that the systems are meritocracies with all positions, from the field ranger up through to the agency director, assigned according to educational attainment and work experience. None of the appointments are political; they are not hired according to political experience or political party membership. At municipal, provincial, and federal levels, politicians make the overall policy decisions, but not the hiring decisions.

Parks, reserves, and other types of protected areas exist because of the acceptance and approval of society and therefore of government. For the sites to exist and be effectively managed, political support must be sufficient to counter the many societal forces that would see these lands used for other purposes. Parks need to be used and appreciated by substantial numbers of citizens for them to succeed in a competitive political environment.

OUTSTANDING GRADUATE

Courtesy of Kristine Roblin.

Background Information

Name: Emily B. Martin

Education: MS in parks, recreation, and tourism management from Clemson University

Awards: 2010 Phi Kappa Phi Certificate of Merit

Career Information

Position: Interpretive Ranger

Organization: The National Park Service is the federal agency that manages all the national park units across the country. I have spent time as a ranger in both Yellowstone National Park (Wyoming) and Great Smoky Mountains National Park (North Carolina). The mission of the NPS is to "preserve unimpaired the natural and cultural resources and values of the National Park System for the enjoyment, education, and inspiration of this and future generations." There are 417 national park units, 58 of which are national parks (the others being battlefields, monuments, historic sites, etc.). Millions of people visit the parks every year, with over 330 million recorded in 2016. The number of employees fluctuates on a seasonal basis, with part-time rangers like myself largely working during the summer. Altogether there are around 22,000 permanent and seasonal employees. At Yellowstone I worked directly with around 25 other rangers, and at the Smokies I work directly with 7 or 8.

Job description: There are three main parts to my job as an interpretive ranger:

1. *Visitor services.* I staff the visitor center to provide frontline orientation to the park, helping visitors plan their trip, distributing material, and dealing with incidents as they arise.

2. *Education.* I research, develop, and deliver engaging educational programs to the visiting public. These programs include talks, guided hikes, activities, children's programs, and special events. This is called *interpretation*, and the goal is to facilitate a meaningful connection between the visitor and the park resources.

3. *Roving.* I act as an informal presence in the park to interact with visitors who might not go into a visitor center or attend a program. I help monitor safety and renegade behavior. But more importantly, I interact casually with visitors to give them a friendly, helpful point of contact.

There are many other things I take care of as they arise, such as keeping up facilities, managing visitor–wildlife interactions, swearing in junior rangers, and helping with emergency response.

Career path: I followed my love of the outdoors into the subject field of parks and protected area management during my undergraduate career. Early on, I was captivated by the narrative and mission of the National Park Service. When Fran Mainella, the 16th director of the NPS, came to Clemson as a visiting scholar for several years, I was chosen to be her office assistant. She became an invaluable mentor and friend. Near the end of my undergraduate experience, I interned at Great Smoky Mountains National Park for a summer. After earning my bachelor's degree, I transitioned into doing graduate research on interpretive programs with the NPS. I traveled to many national parks to collect my data, which were used for developing better training tools for rangers. After earning my master's degree and taking a short hiatus to have children, I then started as a seasonal ranger in Yellowstone.

Although a permanent job would be nice, I enjoy the seasonal life and the travel and flexibility it brings. Because I have an extensive off-season, it has allowed me to spend time on my other passion: fiction writing and illustration. After a lot of hard work and rejection, I now have two novels published through a major publishing house, with a third releasing in 2018. My freelance illustration work has grown to include a children's book and many book covers. So at the moment, if I can be a ranger during the summer and an author and illustrator in the off-season, that's about as close to a dream career as I can imagine.

Likes and dislikes about the job: I love the opportunity to work in these great, storied places and be part of the tapestry of the NPS. I love the goal of facilitating an emotional connection between the visitor and the park. I feel privileged to work with incredibly dedicated, hardworking, fun-loving rangers. I also love the seasonal nature of the work because it gives my family flexibility. I get to bring along my children so they can spend their summers in some of the greatest places in our country—that's pretty special.

I dislike how difficult it can be to have a family and still work these jobs—many parks simply don't have enough housing to support a married ranger with children. I have also disliked how some professionals and academic mentors wrote me off once I had my first child, as if my degrees and career aspirations were null and void because I now had a family.

Advice for Undergraduates

People will view these professions as "fun" or "not serious" careers. The difference is that *you* make it serious. If you care about what you do and believe in the benefits you're providing for people, that makes it important and valuable.

My job isn't so much a matter of education, but of provocation and enrichment. If I can help one person develop a deeper connection to our national parks, or one child believe they have a place in the story of our national parks—whether it's as a ranger or as an author and illustrator—that is success for me.

HISTORY OF PARKS IN THE UNITED STATES

The history of parks in the United States illustrates a combination of concern for the social and psychological well-being of children and adults, the conservation and **preservation** of natural areas as the country developed and resource extraction and urbanization accelerated, and the evolution of natural areas as attractions that spurred tourism business opportunities. Improvements in transportation, the rise of the middle class, the recognition of the need for workers to renew and refresh themselves, and the fascination with the natural world increased the demand for parks and protected natural areas (Sears, 1980).

City Parks and Playgrounds

Boston Common, which was created by the British colonial government in 1634 and is now in downtown Boston, is recognized as the first parklike area created in the United States. As early American cities began to grow due to an influx of immigrants and prosperity brought on by the industrial movement, awareness grew of a need for public parks in bustling, increasingly congested, and hygienically challenged cities such as New York, Chicago, and Philadelphia. Thus began a period from about 1850 through the 1930s when city parks and playgrounds were built for the public (Cavallo, 1981; Young, 2004). Most notable among these was Frederick Law Olmsted and Calvert Vaux's 1858 plan to landscape Central Park in New York City. Olmsted felt strongly about the concept of park access for people as a demonstration of democratic principles. Olmsted believed that parks could serve as meeting grounds for people of different backgrounds and classes, unlike other developed spaces in cities that were highly stratified by social class. He also believed that great parks and open space in cities were evidence of the progressiveness of American democracy (Rybczynski, 1999). Olmsted went on to play a role in designing, planning, and building major city parks in or around Boston, Atlanta, Chicago, Buffalo, and Niagara Falls.

Federal Conservation Initiatives

Sheail (2010) points out that the creation of a park by a national government can be traced to England, where King William I created the New Forest in 1079. However, the use of this area was restricted to those of the noble classes, and public use was not allowed for another 600 years.

Early federal protection of natural areas in the United States dates from 1832 when the federal government created the Hot Springs Reservation in Arkansas as a protected area for the use of Native Americans, people traveling through on their way west, and local residents. The site was later redesignated as a national park in 1921. Yellowstone, designated by President Ulysses S. Grant in 1872 in the territories of Montana and Wyoming and often seen as the first national park in the world, was clearly an idea ahead of its time that was made possible by the incredible confluence of natural features present at Yellowstone and the prescience of prominent citizens and scientists who led expeditions into the area in 1869 through 1871 and proposed the creation of a park. The idea also received considerable support from the corporate leaders of the Northern Pacific Railroad, who understood the park's potential to attract tourists (Runte, 2010). It is interesting that in both Canada and the United States, railway leaders encouraged the creation of the earliest national parks to stimulate tourist use of the emerging cross-country railways. Progress in creating federal parks and protected areas was slow at first; by the turn of the century, only five national parks had been designated and three of those were related to California redwood or sequoia forests. Among them was Yosemite National Park, which was designated by the U.S. Congress in 1890. The seed of the idea for national parks had been sown in the 1800s but needed time and leadership to grow.

Despite the presence of national parks, there was no federal park agency in place to lead the charge for preservation of parklands or outdoor recreation. After years of advocating for such an agency by people such as Frederick Law Olmsted, J. Horace McFarland, Henry Barker, and Stephen Mather, Congress passed the law creating the National Park Service (NPS) on August 25, 1916 (National Park Service, 2003). Stephen Mather, a Chicago businessman, was named the first director of the NPS. Congress transferred the management of historic sites, army forts, battlefields, cemeteries, and monuments to the newly created NPS as well as the existing national parks and national monuments. Immediately after establishment of the NPS there was substantial growth in the number of national park sites, but their use waned during the Great Depression (1929-1939) and the U.S. involvement in World War II (1941-1945). However, during the Great Depression, the Civilian Conservation Corps (CCC) (1933-1941) was created as a separate program of the federal government to employ about 3 million young men in public works projects, which benefited many national park sites. The CCC was instrumental in building hundreds of roads, trails, campgrounds, visitor centers, and water systems that exist today in national and state parks.

Strong leadership for national government involvement in conservation came from President Theodore Roosevelt. In fewer than eight years as president he created six national parks and supported the passage of the Antiquities Act of 1906, which created an initial 16 national monuments (including the Grand Canyon). Over the years, U.S. presidents used this act to take bold and often controversial conservation action by creating national monuments without congressional approval. National monuments are often transformed into national parks through congressional legislative actions. Two major figures in land protection were advisors to President Roosevelt: Gifford Pinchot, scientific conservationist and head of what became the U.S. Department of Agriculture (USDA) Forest Service and founder of the Society of American Foresters, and John Muir, ardent preservationist, Sierra Club founder, writer, and lobbyist for wilderness and parks (Ehrlich, 2000; Keene, 1994; Miller, 2004; Zaslowsky & Watkins, 1994). The use of the Antiquities Act to protect land, and the controversy surrounding the unilateral authority it provides to the president to preserve vast tracks of land, continues today. By the end of his second term, President Barack Obama had created more national monuments than any U.S. president in history.

Two other realms of conservation, wildlife and forests, also benefited from federal action during Roosevelt's time. President Roosevelt used executive orders to create 51 bird reservations during his presidency, and he established the Pelican Island National Wildlife Refuge in 1903. This was the beginning of a system of national wildlife refuges. Their primary function is to preserve habitat and migration routes for wildlife (particularly waterfowl), but they also allow wildlife-related recreation such as hunting, fishing, and bird-watching. Roosevelt also created the U.S. Forest Service in 1905 and set aside 148 million acres (60 million ha) as national forests. Although national forests were at the time primarily viewed as a place to manage timber resources, they are now heavily used and managed for outdoor recreation.

All these efforts at creating protected natural areas—along with the increasing urbanization of the country and the increasing popularity of

Yellowstone National Park in Wyoming contains significant geothermal features that are viewed by millions of people each year.

© Paul F.J. Eagles

automobiles and the expansion of the roads associated with them starting in about 1910—gradually increased the pressure on national park and national forest managers to provide access, accommodations, campgrounds, and information for an increasing number of visitors (Belasco, 1979). The See America First patriotic movement generated public interest in America's natural wonders (Shaffer, 2001), and rangers began to expand their focus from protecting resources to accommodating and educating larger numbers of recreationists and visitors. This activity foreshadowed a massive expansion in travel and outdoor recreation that took place following the end of World War II. This era might be considered the golden age of parks and outdoor recreation in the United States.

State Park Initiatives

Several states initiated efforts to protect natural areas for public use, such as Massachusetts' Great Pond Act (1641); Georgia's Indian Springs (1825); New York's off-and-on attempts to protect the scenic attributes of Niagara Falls culminating in state acquisition in 1885; and California's failed attempt to support Yosemite State Park starting in 1864. According to Landrum (2004), in addition to Niagara Falls, other early **state parks** that have remained successful include Texas' San Jacinto Battleground State Historic Site (1883), Minnehaha Falls Park (1885) and Itasca State Park in Minnesota (1891), Miller State Park in New Hampshire (1891), and New York's Adirondack State Park (1892). Each park's story typically involved local proponents who were persistent and creative in garnering support.

Stephen Mather, as the new director of the National Park Service in 1916, saw one of his challenges to be maintaining the quality of the national park system. He was concerned about attempts to designate parks of little national significance as national parks, and he became a prime sponsor of a national conference in 1921 that promoted the idea of a system of parks that would come under the domain of each state. Although it is unclear who proposed it, the idea arose of creating a park every 100 miles (160 km) (the distance that automobiles at that time typically traveled in a day) for the public to enjoy and camp in, and it was suggested it was more appropriate for state parks to fulfill this plan (Landrum, 2004). The idea developed that state parks should preserve representative environments, preferably scenic or historical and cultural sites that were typical of each state, to provide outdoor recreation areas for residents and tourists.

© Paul F.J. Eagles

Adirondack State Park in New York, one of the oldest state parks in the United States, contains a mixture of public and private land.

Trail Initiatives

In 1921, Benton MacKaye, a forester and planner, proposed a foot trail along the Appalachian ridges from the highest mountain in the north, Mount Katahdin in Maine, to the highest peak in the south, Springer Mountain in Georgia, that passed through 12 other states along the way. The approximately 2,150-mile (3,460 km) Appalachian Trail was completed in 1937. The National Trails System Act of 1968 gave the NPS the responsibility of overseeing the Appalachian Trail and provided funds to start the process of purchasing the entire trail and buffering it where possible with federal land. The act also designated three types of trails: national recreation trails; national scenic trails; and connecting, or side, trails. The act designated the Appalachian Trail and the Pacific Crest Trail (stretching from the Mexican border to the Canadian border along the mountain ranges of the Pacific Coast states) as national scenic trails. As of 2016, amendments to the act have created 11 national scenic trails, 19 national historic trails, and more than 1,200 national recreation trails in all 50 states, most of which are in or near urban areas. National Park Service maps of these trails can be viewed at www.nps.gov/nts/maps.html.

Another form of trail park is located along rivers. In 1968, the Wild and Scenic Rivers Act was passed to protect free-flowing (not dammed) rivers, thereby assuring that white-water recreational opportunities such as kayaking and rafting could be protected. Three categories of rivers were established: wild rivers, scenic rivers, and recreational rivers. The differences were based on different levels of access, primitiveness, and shoreline development; wild rivers were the most pristine. As of December 2014, 12,709 miles (20,453 km) of 208 rivers in 40 states and Puerto Rico were protected (National Wild and Scenic Rivers System, n.d.). Most rivers are managed by the agency that manages the land through which the river flows, usually the USDA Forest Service, NPS, Bureau of Land Management, or U.S. Fish and Wildlife Service (National Park Service, n.d.-c).

Wilderness

In the 1930s, forward-thinking preservationists saw that the American **wilderness** was a rapidly diminishing resource. A paradox was becoming apparent. Protecting an area by declaring it a national park virtually assured that roads would be built to and within that park. Eventually thousands of people would visit it, and the characteristics of wilderness would be diminished or lost. In the 1960s, an oft-repeated phrase was that "Americans were loving their parks to death" as congested roads and campgrounds became the norm, at least in the summer vacation season or the autumn leaf-color season. This helped solidify the movement to protect vast roadless areas that were largely absent of both people and signs of human presence. Early proponents of creating protected wilderness areas included Aldo Leopold, U.S. Forest Service scientist and the father of wildlife ecology; Robert Marshall, an environmental lawyer; Howard Zahniser, president of the Wilderness Society; and Hubert Humphrey, a senator from Minnesota who sponsored four versions of the Wilderness Act over eight years. The fourth amended version eventually passed Congress and was signed into law by President Lyndon Johnson in 1964 (Nash, 1982).

Because wilderness designation would permanently prohibit development, roads, timber removal, and motorized activities, this bill caused considerable concern among lumber interests, some outdoor recreationists, and real estate developers. But Congress passed the Wilderness Act anyway. The process of designating new wilderness areas provided some of the most heated environmental battles in the second half of the 20th century and the first decade of the 21st century. Especially controversial were the USDA Forest Service Roadless Area Review and Evaluation (RARE) process, the Endangered American Wilderness Act of 1978, and the 1980 Alaska National Interest Lands Conservation Act. The two acts were signed and engineered by President Jimmy Carter and doubled the size of the NPS and National Wildlife Refuge lands and tripled the size of designated wilderness. Recently, in the greatest expansion of wilderness areas in 15 years, President Barack Obama signed the Omnibus Public Land Management Act of 2009 that protected 2 million acres (800,000 ha) of wilderness. In 2016, there were about 765 wilderness areas. Designated federal wilderness comprises about 110 million acres (45 million ha); 57 million of those acres (23 million ha) are in Alaska. California, Arizona, Idaho, and Washington have the next largest wilderness areas.

Era of Fiscal Restraint

Starting in the 1970s, after the rapid growth in participation in outdoor recreation and the expansion of federal programs to accommodate this growth, a series of developments led to a leveling off and even decline of federal actions. A few initiatives were associated with the nation's bicentennial celebration in 1976: the creation of bicentennial parks around the country and the Urban Park and Recreation Recovery (UPARR) program, which provided federal assistance to counteract the decline in many urban areas by rehabilitating critically needed recreation and park facilities. Recreation use in parks is closely tied to the costs of transportation. If fuel prices are high, people tend to use parks closer to home. If fuel prices are low, long-distance travel increases. In 2015 and 2016, several U.S. national parks set visitation records as low fuel prices encouraged long-distance travel. For example, Yellowstone National Park, which is remote from most large cities, set visitation records in 2015 and 2016 of 4,097,710 and 4,257,177 visitor days, respectively (National Park Service., n.d.-b).

Parks are successful when competent, dedicated, and innovative employees manage them. There is an ongoing debate on the use of private companies to provide services to the visitors. The very first NPS director, Stephen Mather, introduced concessions into the national parks. These private companies provided services such as accommodations, food, and transportation. Much later, nongovernment groups, usually called *friends groups,* became active in many parks and concentrated on providing educational services to the visitors. It has been estimated that about 75 percent of all people working in parks in the United States are employed by concessionaires and only 25 percent are government employees.

In the 1980s, the practice of hiring private companies to perform some park jobs once done by park employees (privatizing) became popular in an effort to lower the operating costs of parks. Privatization of jobs such as trash collection, vehicle maintenance, lawn care, and even staffing visitor centers or gift shops, was considered. To further reduce expenditures and generate revenue, President Ronald Reagan's Secretary of the Interior James Watt eliminated the Bureau of Outdoor Recreation, reduced the rate at which new federal lands were purchased for parks, instituted staff reductions in the land agencies, and supported natural resource extraction through mining and drilling for oil on federal lands. During this time, and in a response to these types of threats to land protection, a grassroots backlash, the Sagebrush Rebellion, began. In this, local proponents of private land rights and public access performed actions of civil (and occasionally criminal) disobedience in opposition to various threats to conservation.

In the late 20th and early 21st centuries, few federal conservation initiatives were launched and new park acquisitions were limited because federal budgets were tight. One bright spot was the Transportation Efficiency Act of 1991 and its successors, the Transportation Equity Act for the 21st Century (1998) and the Safe, Accountable, Flexible, Efficient Transportation Equity Act of 2005, which designated that 10 percent of the allocations for highway construction be set aside for alternative transportation options such as mass transit and walking, biking, and horse trails. Many localities used these funds for rails-to-trails initiatives to develop corridor park trail systems. In the 1990s, many federal agencies became better connected to and appreciated by local and state tourism promoters, and now partnerships abound between what used to be separate entities. Local tourism businesses began to better understand how livelihood in ecotourism was based on quality parks (because they attracted tourists and their money), and they became partners in supporting parks in Congress or state legislatures and in volunteering labor and services to assist parks. Congress authorized the Recreational Fee Demonstration Program in 1996 and the Recreation Enhancement Act in 2004 to allow federal lands that charged entrance fees to increase their fees and retain funds from fees collected to improve their recreation facilities and services.

After the September 11, 2001, terrorist attacks in New York City, most federal parks had to divert a segment of their tight budgets to homeland security efforts, especially the National Park Service, which manages many high-profile monuments that could present symbolic targets for possible future attacks. The cost of extra security patrols and the addition of law enforcement officers and metal detectors to the entrances of many park buildings put a strain on other operations. Another area of concern is parks on national borders, such as Big Bend National Park in Texas and Organ Pipe Cactus National Monument in Arizona. Some believe that illegal immigrants or terrorists could sneak into the country through these areas. Because of these concerns, some visitors stay away, park rangers are trained in law enforcement and border patrol strategies for 24-hour guarding, and more time and money are spent on security and less on visitor services or programs (Lovgren, 2004). By 2005, with federal budget deficits growing and gasoline prices remaining higher than in the past, funding for park agencies and programs had decreased or remained level. President George W. Bush proposed not providing grants from the Land and Water Conservation Fund to individual states. These funds have been used since 1965 to purchase parklands and develop facilities such as campgrounds, playgrounds, trails, and visitor centers (National Park Service, n.d.-c).

From 2007 to 2009, a national and global recession occurred—termed the *great recession*. This recession, followed by several years of slow economic recovery, further strained parks. Many local, state, and national parks saw additional cuts to funding for their operation and maintenance. Some parks, such as state parks in New York and California, reduced their services or were closed as cost-savings strategies. A long history of underfunding parks that created a backlog of needed maintenance, facility upgrades, and staff even before the recession hit made this problem worse. The national parks have a maintenance backlog of approximately $12 billion, which is more than three times their annual budget (National Park Service, n.d.-a). Park leaders and managers attempted to address these funding issues by reducing costs, partnering with private industries and nongovernmental organizations, and turning toward a more revenue-focused business model. Many parks use volunteers and friends groups (advocacy groups affiliated with a park that raise funds through donations) to ease constraints related to funding.

In 2006, the National Park Centennial Initiative was undertaken that created a matching fund for government and philanthropic contributions to benefit parks in the years approaching the system's centennial in 2016. In 2009, the NPS invested $750 million in nearly 800 projects to stimulate the economy through the American Recovery and Reinvestment Act. Both programs created the promise of a positive boost in funding for the national parks. Continued economic struggles from 2010 to 2012, however, resulted in declines in national budgets. In 2013, more than $150 million in budget cuts affected the NPS through a process called *sequestration,* which caused park closures and reductions in visitor services and substantial public controversy. Some states took action to reopen closed national parks, which led to a renewed debate about the importance of parks and their funding. In 2016, the 100th anniversary of the National Park Service was celebrated with a national marketing campaign called Find Your Park, and there were events in parks, substantial public attention among news and media outlets, and partnerships with corporations. In addition, the Katahdin Woods and Waters National Monument in Maine was established. This new national monument, like many past parks, was the result of a private land donation by a wealthy philanthro-

pist. This land donation came with a $40 million endowment for developing and operating the national monument. This monetary gift seemed to symbolize and solidify the place of private funding in the second century of national parks.

PARK SYSTEMS OF THE UNITED STATES

Most parks have been created on undeveloped lands and waters and reserved for public use and enjoyment; therefore, most publicly owned parks are managed by some level of the government. Similar to schools, public water supplies, and airports, parks are services that local, state, and federal governments provide their citizens for their benefit and enjoyment. Most parks have **front country** areas with facilities, roads, and primary visitor attractions, but many parks also have **backcountry** areas where nature predominates.

City Parks

Historically, city parks were created to address social needs by providing safe areas for children to play and soothing islands of green in which to escape from urban crowding, congestion, and concrete. Most city parks are smaller, closer to home, and more sport-oriented than other kinds of parks. City parks, by definition, are owned, managed, and staffed by city governments. City parks are used in more varied ways than traditional resource-based state or federal parks. For example, city parks often provide swimming pools, concerts, and food stands. Some even have small zoos, botanical gardens, or carnival rides. City parks are usually less concerned with maintaining natural resources in an undisturbed state; in most cases, the natural environment has already been heavily altered and the area artificially landscaped or designed to provide amenities such as tennis courts, golf courses, swimming pools, fountains, paved walkways, ice-skating rinks, skateboard ramps, soccer fields, and playgrounds. Despite the less-than-pristine environment, city parks often provide inner-city children with their first taste of a natural area (American Planning Association, 2007; Harnick, 2000; Taylor et al., 2001; Wals, 1994).

City parks vary greatly depending on the size of the city. Some New England towns, such as Burlington, Vermont, and New Haven, Connecticut, have classic "greens" of a few acres or less. Larger and more well-known or unique city parks are Central

Park in New York City; Boston Common; Jackson Square in New Orleans; the Riverwalk in San Antonio, Texas; the town square of Savannah, Georgia; Grant Park in Chicago; Phoenix's unusual mountain parks (including the largest city park in the United States, South Mountain Park and Reserve); and Fort Worth Water Gardens in Texas. It has been said that there are no great cities without great parks, and when you think of these large cities, this does seem to be true (Tate, 2001). But even the smallest cities and towns in the United States have parks that are often centerpieces of local pride.

County Parks

County parks are usually larger, more natural, less congested, and quieter. They are typically oriented to activities such as swimming, hiking, boating, fishing, and camping that require a more natural setting than city parks can provide. They are owned and managed by county governments and are usually operated by county employees, although there is a recent trend to subcontract park operations to private operators or groups such as the YMCA. County parks are larger and less tailored to urban uses than city parks, but they are often not as environmentally sensitive, as usage restricted, or as large as most state parks. Some county parks have larger facilities than those found in city parks, such as multiple playing fields or arenas for sports tournaments and sport events. Local school systems often conduct lessons in environmental education at county parks because they are typically close, easily accessible, and have parking. Fishing, sailing, canoeing, or water safety lessons are also conducted in county parks. In coastal states, many beach parks, especially the more developed ones, are county parks.

State Parks

State parks are typically more focused on preserving the natural or historic characteristics of an area and providing compatible outdoor recreation. Usually, they are more distant from urban population centers than most city or county parks, although in a few cases, population centers have grown around state parks. In general, state parks are larger than most city or county parks. In 2017, there were 10,336 state parks in the United States (America's State Parks, n.d.). Often state parks are associated with bodies of water, have substantial wildlife populations, and are representative of key environmental ecosystems that characterize the state, such as beaches in Florida, deserts in Arizona, prairie in Illinois and Kansas,

© Paul F.J. Eagles

Point Lobos State Natural Reserve in California protects valuable shoreline habitat and provides opportunities for nature-based recreation.

and mountains in California, Colorado, and New Hampshire. Most state parks are not unique enough, scenic enough, large enough, or filled with enough features to warrant being designated national parks. Besides highlighting natural areas, many state parks promote the state's important historical figures or events.

The character of state parks varies substantially. Some are similar to large city parks in a more natural setting, and others are as wild or wilder than some national parks or forests. Adirondack State Park and Forest Preserve in New York is the largest state park in the lower 48 states (6 million acres, or 2.4 million ha) (Adirondack State Park Agency, n.d.). Most state parks are of modest size, usually ranging from a hundred to a few thousand acres, and they provide basic facilities such as campgrounds, picnic areas, trails, visitor centers, and environmental education programs. Some are more like city parks, however, such as Eugene T. Mahoney State Park in a rural area south of Omaha, Nebraska. It has an outdoor swimming pool with water slides, a large playground area with play equipment, and an ice-skating rink (Nebraska Game and Parks Commission, n.d.).

Several states have created resort state parks to increase visitation and self-generated revenues. These parks provide resort-like services, but they are located on state parklands and are managed and funded by the state park service or a corollary association, often with subcontracts to concessionaires. Lake Barkley State Resort Park in Kentucky has a golf course, aerobic fitness center, swimming pool, tennis courts, small airport, cabins, lodge hotel, restaurant, and marina (Kentucky State Parks, 2005). Seyon Lodge State Park in Vermont provides overnight stays in bed-and-breakfast–style accommodations and guided fishing. The resort state park idea has expanded to at least 12 states, many of which are in the South.

Besides having state parks, most states, especially those in the East, also have state forests. Many of the forest areas have camping areas, hiking trails, and hunting areas. Many states, mostly in the Midwest and West, operate state fish and game or state wildlife management areas that are usually available for various forms of outdoor recreation.

Federal Parks, Forests, and Refuges

Before 1700, most of what became the United States was the domain of millions of Native Americans who were later largely exterminated in war, killed by disease, evicted from their natural territories and moved onto reservations, or forced to seek refuge in Canada (Brown, 1970; Nash, 1982). European immigrants applied for ownership of their lands from the federal General Land Office, which claimed to have the original title to the land. Tracts of land not delegated to the states or claimed by private owners were retained in federal ownership after the creation of the U.S. government in 1776. Much of this land was not suitable for agriculture or residential development or was eventually recognized as land to which the public should have access (public domain land). Growing societal needs for recreation and the preservation of dwindling natural resources prompted Congress to establish national parks, national forests, national wildlife refuges, and other federal protected areas. A variety of agencies were created to manage these places (Zaslowsky & Watkins, 1994; Zinser, 1995). Although most of these areas were initially conserved for reasons other than recreation, recreational opportunities were often a side benefit.

National Parks

The National Park Service (NPS) has been a world leader in establishing and managing national parks. The NPS operates under a principle of preservation and is funded by the U.S. Department of the Interior. Its mission is to "conserve the scenery and the natural and historic objects and the wildlife therein and to provide for the enjoyment of the same in such manner and by such means as will leave them unimpaired for the enjoyment of future generations." Maintaining a balance between allowing use and protecting and preserving resources is a constant challenge. Providing recreational opportunities that do little or no permanent harm to the park or its wildlife is one of NPS's prime missions (Sellars, 1999). With 417 National Park Service units, the national park system encompasses approximately 84 million acres (34 million ha) and manages many categories of parks (see table 6.1). In 2016, a record number of 330,971,689 recreation visits were recorded by the National Park Service (National Park Service, n.d.-b).

With such diversity of areas, many forms of outdoor recreation occur in the national park system. Activities include mountain climbing, horseback riding, boating, camping, history reenactments, hiking, white-water rafting, and driving and sightseeing, especially during spring wildflower or fall leaf-changing seasons. The more than 300 million

Table 6.1 U.S. National Park Service Categories and Examples

Categories	Total number	Examples
National parks	59	Yellowstone, Grand Teton, Yosemite, Smoky Mountains, Grand Canyon, Rocky Mountain, Shenandoah
National monuments	87	Grand Portage, Bandelier, Craters of the Moon, Coronado, Fort Sumter
National preserves	19	Big Thicket, Big Cypress, Timucuan, Gates of the Arctic
National historic sites	78	First Ladies, Fort Davis, McLoughlin House, Carl Sandburg Home, Lincoln Home
National historical parks	51	Minute Man, Women's Rights, Valley Forge, Chaco Culture, Cumberland Gap
National memorials	30	Chamizal, African American Civil War, USS *Arizona*, Mount Rushmore, World War II, Flight 93
National military parks	9	Shiloh, Gettysburg, Horseshoe Bend, Pea Ridge
National battlefields	16	Manassas, Fort Donelson, Cowpens, Antietam
National recreation areas	18	Gateway, Santa Monica Mountains, Golden Gate
National reserves	2	New Jersey Pinelands, City of Rocks
National seashores	10	Gulf Islands, Padre Island, Cape Canaveral, Cape Cod, Point Reyes
National lakeshores	4	Pictured Rocks, Sleeping Bear, Apostle Islands, Indiana Dunes
National rivers	5	Buffalo, Big South Fork, New River Gorge, Mississippi
Wild and scenic rivers	10	Obed, Ozark, Rio Grande, Farmington, Salmon
National parkways	4	Baltimore-Washington, George Washington
National scenic trails	3	Natchez Trace, Potomac Heritage, Appalachian
International historic site	1	Saint Croix Island
Other designation	11	National Mall, Rock Creek Park, Catoctin Mountain, Wolf Trap National Park for the Performing Arts

National Park Service, n.d.-a

annual visitor days to the national parks make a significant contribution to the economy of the nation and especially to rural areas that depend on the tourism that the national parks attract. Considerable adaptability and creativity are needed to manage these diverse areas, and expertise from many disciplines is needed across the system of parks. These disciplines include the following:

- Ecology
- Geology
- Archaeology
- Military history
- National history
- Fisheries
- Wildlife and resource management
- Forestry
- Outdoor recreation management
- Interpretation
- Business management
- Marketing
- Public relations
- Urban recreation programming
- Environmental education
- Alternative energy
- Public works
- Transportation management
- Tourism
- Law
- Political science

The NPS also coordinates the Land and Water Conservation Fund, which is a program that distributes federal funds to the states and federal agencies for new or continuing park or conservation projects.

National Forests and Grasslands

The Forest Service was created in 1905 and is an agency of the USDA. The Forest Service manages large forests and grasslands and follows a basic conservation and **wise-use philosophy**. The agency's mission is to achieve quality land management under the sustainable multiple-use concept to meet the diverse needs of people. Gifford Pinchot, the first chief of the Forest Service, described conservation and wise use as providing "the greatest good to the greatest number for the longest time." **Multiple-use management** means that Forest Service areas can be used for outdoor recreation, livestock grazing, timber production, watershed management, and wildlife and fish habitat. Providing recreational opportunities, which the agency tries to balance with the other uses, is a major focus of the Forest Service. The 174 Forest Service units (154 national forests and 20 national grasslands) cover 193 million acres (78 million ha) in 44 states (USDA Forest Service, 2017). National forests constitute 98 percent of Forest Service lands. These lands contain designated wilderness areas, recreation areas, national monuments and preserves, and national scenic areas. The Forest Service also manages scenic byways, wild and scenic rivers, campgrounds, alpine ski areas, boating areas, picnic areas, and over 158,000 miles (254,000 km) of trails (USDA Forest Service, 2017; Zinser, 1995).

Historically, the Forest Service gave priority to timber management, but it was induced, especially since the 1960s, through court cases, political pressure, and wilderness debates to increase the outdoor recreation opportunities in the forests. Today recreation is a primary focus and use of the national forests. From 2011 to 2015, an average of 149 million visits occurred to Forest Service lands, waters, and recreation sites per year (USDA Forest Service, 2016). Common recreation activities on national forests and grasslands include hiking, camping, wildlife watching, hunting, fishing, mountain biking, horse trail riding, skiing, and **off-highway vehicle (OHV**; e.g., all-terrain vehicle, snowmobile) use. In general, more consumptive, higher-impact forms of recreation are permitted and deemed appropriate in national forests and other federal lands compared with state and national parks.

Wildlife Refuges

The U.S. Fish and Wildlife Service (USFWS) is part of the U.S. Department of the Interior. Its mission is to work with others to conserve, protect, and enhance fish, wildlife, and plants and their habitats for the continuing benefit of the American people. Its

© Paul F.J. Eagles

Aransas National Wildlife Refuge in Texas provides winter habitat for the endangered whooping crane.

programs (including administering the U.S. Endangered Species Act and other federal wildlife laws) are among the oldest in the world dedicated to scientific wildlife conservation, although Canada created a wildlife conservation reserve in 1887. As of 2013, the USFWS manages a 150-million-acre (60-million-hectare) national system of more than 560 national wildlife refuges and thousands of small wetlands and other special management areas. Under the fisheries program, it operates national fish hatcheries, fishery resource offices, and ecological services field stations (U.S. Fish and Wildlife Service, 2013).

Most wildlife refuge areas are water related, either freshwater or saltwater, and therefore are often found along rivers, lakes, marshlands, or coastal areas. The primary focus of refuges and fish hatcheries is wildlife and fish habitat protection, promotion of breeding, and provision of safe refuge to animals. Refuges permit secondary recreational activity as long as it is compatible with the primary purpose of the refuge and funds are available to administer it. The primary recreational uses in wildlife refuges are

- hunting,
- fishing,
- wildlife observation,
- nature photography,
- environmental education and interpretation,
- hiking, and
- motorized and nonmotorized boating.

Hunting and fishing are permitted in wildlife refuges because much of the funding and support of wildlife refuges came from hunters and anglers when Congress expressed little interest in spending money on wildlife, birds, and fish. The hunting and fishing is regulated and in some areas controls the populations of animals whose natural predators have been long removed. About 30 percent of refuges are not open to recreation; these are mostly in Alaska.

Other Areas Managed by Federal Agencies

Several other federal protected areas exist that are not as well known, but many are found only in certain regions of the United States and they usually provide fewer recreation programs and facilities. The Bureau of Land Management, the U.S. Army Corps of Engineers, the Tennessee Valley Authority, the Bureau of Reclamation, and American Indian reservations manage these areas. In addition, wilderness areas are specially designated lands owned by the federal government.

National Resource Lands

The Bureau of Land Management (BLM) manages 245 million acres (99 million ha) of land (about 1/8 of the land in the United States), which is more than any other federal agency (Bureau of Land Management, n.d.-a). Most of the lands that the BLM manages are in the western United States, including Alaska, which contains about one third of the BLM-managed land. Most BLM lands are dominated by extensive grasslands, forests, high mountains, arctic tundra, and deserts. The BLM manages a variety of resources and uses, including

- energy and mineral mining;
- timber;
- grazing;
- wild horse and burro habitats;
- fish and wildlife habitats;
- wilderness areas; and
- archaeological, paleontological, and historical sites.

BLM recreation management areas include backcountry areas with minimal development of recreation facilities and special areas that provide recreation facilities such as campgrounds, boat launch ramps, cabins, and environmental education centers. BLM reports about 59 million visits per year (Bureau of Land Management, n.d.-b). Most of the land managed by BLM is desert and barren, but some of the land contains lakes, rivers, and mountains, and some of it is extremely scenic. BLM lands contain trails, campgrounds, picnic areas, boating areas, visitor centers, horse-riding trails, and OHV sites to sustain a variety of recreational pursuits.

Wilderness Areas

Areas designated under the 1964 Wilderness Act and the 1973 Eastern Wilderness Act are managed by the Bureau of Land Management, the U.S. Fish and Wildlife Service, the Forest Service, and the National Park Service. The Wilderness Act defined *wilderness* "as an area where the earth and its community of life are untrammeled by man, where man himself is a visitor who does not remain." Wilderness areas are generally open to the public for nonmotorized and nonmechanized (i.e., no bikes) recreation. Roads, buildings, and other manmade structures are typically not found in wilderness areas. Permits are often required. These areas are truly wild and contain only a minimum of facilities. Following is a summary of the 765 federal wilderness areas that cover 109.5 million acres (44.3 million hectares):

- National Park Service—61 sites, 44.4 million acres (18.0 million ha) and many other areas managed as wilderness but awaiting formal designation
- Forest Service—445 sites, 36.7 million acres (14.9 million ha)
- U.S. Fish and Wildlife Service—71 sites, 20.7 million acres (8.4 million ha)
- Bureau of Land Management—224 sites, 8.8 million acres (3.6 million ha)
- Total national wilderness—765 sites, approximately 109 million acres (44.5 million ha) (Wilderness Connect, n.d.)

These national wilderness areas are subareas designated from existing national parks, monuments, preserves, forests, grasslands, resource lands, and fish and wildlife refuges. For example, 86 percent of the Everglades National Park is designated wilderness. Some states have state-designated wilderness areas that are smaller than federal wilderness areas and tend to follow the same principles of no development or motorized access.

U.S. Army Corps of Engineers Waterways and Sites

The Army Corps of Engineers is the steward of the lands and waters at thousands of federal water resource sites like dams, reservoirs, and flood-control projects. This agency is part of the Department of Defense, but most of its employees are civilians. Its natural resources management mission is to manage and conserve natural resources consistent with principles of ecosystem management while providing public outdoor recreation experiences to serve the needs of current and future generations (U.S. Army Corps of Engineers, n.d.).

The Army Corps of Engineers is the nation's largest provider of outdoor recreation. It manages thousands of recreation areas at 403 projects (mostly lakes and reservoirs). A substantial number of these recreation areas are leased to state or local park and recreation authorities or private interests. The Corps hosts about 370 million visitors a year at its lakes, beaches, and other areas, and estimates that

1 in 10 Americans visits a Corps project at least once a year. Recreationally, the Corps manages campgrounds, boat launch ramps, fishing piers, marinas, bathrooms, and swimming areas. In total, the Corps manages 12 million acres (5 million ha) of land and water for recreation, including 33 percent of all freshwater fishing opportunities in the United States. The Corps also manages the intracoastal waterway and reservoirs that provide substantial boating opportunities in many states (U.S. Army Corps of Engineers, n.d.).

Tennessee River Valley

The Tennessee Valley Authority (TVA) is a federal agency that operates in a limited service area encompassing seven states: Tennessee, Alabama, Georgia, Kentucky, Mississippi, North Carolina, and Virginia. President Franklin Roosevelt created the TVA during the Great Depression in 1933 to create electricity, flood control, and economic development in an underdeveloped region. TVA is the largest U.S. public power company, and because it manages a major river (650 miles [1,050 km] long), many recreation opportunities are available on TVA-managed areas. Millions of people enjoy recreational activities on TVA reservoirs or rivers and adjacent land each year. The reservoirs and the surrounding 290,000 acres (117,000 ha) of land offer opportunities for recreational activities including waterskiing, canoeing, sailing, windsurfing, fishing, swimming, hiking, nature photography, picnicking, bird-watching, and camping. Recreation management has not been a priority of TVA, and it has minimized the amount of active recreation management that it does (Tennessee Valley Authority, n.d.). But because of its water-related resources, millions of people still engage in recreational activities on areas managed by TVA.

Large Western Reservoirs

Across the arid western states, water management became a critical focus as the population in those areas grew. In 1902, Teddy Roosevelt established the Bureau of Reclamation (BOR). This agency is part of the U.S. Department of the Interior and is best known for the dams, power plants, and canals that it has constructed in 17 western states. These water projects led to homesteading and promoted the economic development of the West. The mission of BOR is to manage water and water-related resources in the western United States in an economically and environmentally sound manner for the American people. BOR reservoirs serve a major role in providing water recreation opportunities to the rapidly growing but dry western states, such as boating, waterskiing, bird-watching, fishing, waterside camping, and swimming in natural areas. Over 90 million visitors make use of 7.1 million acres (2.9 million ha) of BOR recreational land and waters each year (Bureau of Reclamation, n.d.).

American Indian Reservations

The Bureau of Indian Affairs (BIA) is responsible for administering and managing 55.7 million acres (22.5 million ha) of land held in trust by the United States for American Indians, Indian tribes, and Alaska natives. Most of the land is in Arizona, New Mexico, Montana, and South Dakota, although 31 states have some Native American lands. The BIA is an agency within the U.S. Department of the Interior. Developing forestlands, leasing assets on those lands, directing agricultural programs, protecting water and land rights, developing and maintaining infrastructure, and promoting economic development are among the agency's responsibilities. As part of their economic development efforts, many Indigenous groups attract tourists to their lands by offering guided tours, camping, hunting, fishing, museums, lodges, and alpine skiing. Since the passage of the Indian Gaming Regulatory Act (1988), many tribes have opened casinos and associated resorts, hotels, shopping areas, and restaurants that attract visitors to American Indian lands (U.S. Department of the Interior, n.d.).

National Marine Sanctuaries

Two federal agencies that are part of the U.S. Department of Commerce's National Oceanic and Atmospheric Administration (NOAA) manage ocean area parks: the National Marine Sanctuary Program and the National Marine Fisheries Service. During the 1970s, when many environmental acts were passed, the Marine Protection, Research, and Sanctuaries Act of 1972 created the sanctuaries program, partially in response to oil spills and reports of toxic dumping in the ocean. Fifteen national marine sanctuaries as well as the Papahānaumokuākea and Rose Atoll Marine National Monuments protect more than 620,000 square miles (440,298 sq km) of ocean, Great Lake waters, and coasts (Office of National Marine Sanctuaries, n.d.).

The act to create these underwater sanctuaries was passed 100 years after the legislation to create the first national park on land. The primary purpose of the sanctuaries is to conserve natural and cultural marine features. These sanctuaries also provide underwater environmental education and opportunities for snorkeling and scuba sightseeing, fish and coral watching, and photography. In the late 2010s, major new marine sanctuaries were created especially in American waters around Hawaii and off the New England coast.

INTERNATIONAL TREATIES AND PROTECTED AREA DESIGNATIONS AND PARKS

Protected natural areas that transcend national borders are known as *transboundary protected areas*. Because the world's natural resources and parks are best managed on an ecosystem scale, some believe that the programs should be developed so that national borders do not interfere with good conservation practices.

Transboundary protected areas have been created around the world. Typically, these areas were created to facilitate conservation of biological diversity across national boundaries. By 2007 there were 227 transboundary complexes involving 3,043 individual parks or protected areas in many countries (Lysenko et al., 2007). North America's first international transboundary cooperation was founded in 1932 and involved the Waterton–Glacier International Peace Park World Heritage site in Alberta and Montana. Another major U.S.–Canadian transboundary protected area includes a vast complex in the northwestern Yukon and northeastern Alaska involving the Ivvavik and Vuntut National Parks in Canada and the Arctic National Wildlife Refuge in the United States. A world-renowned wilderness canoeing area is also a transboundary unit. This area comprises Quetico Provincial Park in Ontario and the Boundary Waters Canoe Area Wilderness in Minnesota. In total, Canada and the United States have nine transboundary protected-area complexes. Canada also has a transboundary area with Greenland (Denmark), and the United States has two with Mexico (Lysenko et al., 2007).

In addition, the United Nations Educational, Scientific and Cultural Organization (UNESCO) designates international **biosphere reserves**, which are terrestrial and coastal areas representing the main ecosystems of the planet in which plants and animals are to be protected and where research, monitoring, and training on ecosystems are carried out. These reserves are designed to operate as examples of sustainable land use.

Many of the larger national parks and adjacent areas in the United States and Canada have been designated as international biosphere reserves. Canada has 19 biosphere reserves and the United States had 47 (UNESCO, 2017a, 2017b).However, the Trump administration removed 17 of these biosphere reserves in mid-2017 (Smith & Greshko, 2017). The United States now has 28 biosphere reserves (Klag, 2020). Examples of biosphere reserves in Canada are Long Point in Ontario and Waterton in Alberta. Examples in the United States are the Mammoth Cave Area in Kentucky and the California Coast Ranges.

Similarly, UNESCO designates **World Heritage sites** to encourage countries to protect natural and cultural heritage sites that are of universal significance. Many of the nature sites are major national parks. In 2023, 1,157 World Heritage sites were designated globally. Canada contains 20 World Heritage sites (Parks Canada, 2017b), and the United States contains 24 sites (UNESCO, n.d.). Some sites were designated for world-class natural features, such as Dinosaur Provincial Park in Alberta, the Rocky Mountain Parks in Alberta

and British Columbia, Nahanni National Park in the Northwest Territories, Redwood National Park in California, and Everglades National Park in Florida. Other sites were designated for world-class cultural and historic values, such as L'Anse aux Meadows National Historic Site in Newfoundland, the Old Town of Lunenburg in Nova Scotia, the Statue of Liberty in New York, and Independence Hall in Philadelphia.

Another international designation for wetland areas is the **Ramsar Convention**, which designates internationally important wetlands for conservation (Wetlands International, 2023). In 2022, there were 2,471 Ramsar wetlands designated worldwide within 172 countries. Canada had 37 sites, and the United States had 41 sites (Ramsar, 2022).

The World Heritage sites and the Ramsar wetlands are designated through international conventions. Once designated, each site must be managed according to international law as outlined in the convention. The biosphere reserve designation is simply a cooperative arrangement among countries that has no international legal structure and thus requires much less conservation commitment.

© Paul F.J. Eagles

Dinosaur Provincial Park in Alberta is a World Heritage site that protects significant dinosaur fossils.

COMPARING CANADA AND THE UNITED STATES

Table 6.2 shows the status, as of 2023, of the parks and protected areas in Canada and the United States according to the United Nations Environment Programme's World Conservation Monitoring Centre (UNEP-WCMC, 2023a, 2023b). Urban parks are not included in the list because of their small size, and historic parks are not included because of their cultural focus.

Similarities Between Canada and the United States

The park systems in the countries are similar and often designate the same types of lands for protection. This resemblance is not surprising because both countries developed their park systems with constant communication and friendly competition over 200 years. The United States and Canada are similar in geographic size, so directly comparing the area dedicated to various types of parks and protected areas is possible (see table 6.2). Both countries have similar amounts of area designated as nature reserves and habitat and species management areas. Canada has much more national parkland in part because the large provincial parks are of national-park stature and size and are recognized as such in the international classification of parks. The data in table 6.2 are presented according to the **International Union for Conservation of Nature (IUCN)** categories of protected areas, not according to the official titles of the parks. For example, many provincial parks in Canada are classified in the UN list as category II parks or national parks. Therefore, table 6.2 shows 1,621 national parks in Canada, although only 47 of them are owned and operated by the national government; provincial governments own and manage the rest. Additionally, neither national historic sites nor historic canals are included in the database used for the table. The IUCN does not recognize cultural or historic sites in its classification system, and historic sites are discussed only briefly in this chapter (Chape et al., 2003).

The similarity in the form and function of parks in Canada and the United States is caused by several factors. The government structures are similar and include cities, towns, counties, provinces or states, and a federal government. Each of these levels of government develops and manages parks. Both countries have cultural roots in England, which transferred to North America the English love of nature, outdoor recreation, and the use of specialized reserves for conservation and recreation (Glendening 1997; Hudson, 2001; Jones & Wills, 2005; Ritvo, 2003). The green parks in the central areas of English cities were widely emulated across the various British colonies in North America (Sheail, 2010). As the park movement in Canada and the United States deepened and strengthened through increasing activities by cities, provinces or states, and national governments, communication of ideas between the two countries was ongoing. Many government precedents, numerous man-

Table 6.2 Parks and Protected Areas in Canada and the United States

IUCN category	Number in Canada	Number in the United States
Ia: Nature reserve	824	873
Ib: Wilderness	305	1,689
II: National park	1,621	69
III: Natural monument	705	1,073
IV: Habitat & species management area	5,393	1,091
V: Protected landscape	30	33,508
VI: Managed-resource protected area	489	2,005
Unclassified	506	2,462
Total number of sites	9,873	42,770
Total land area covered in km²	1,265,080	1,235,486
Total marine and coastal area covered in km²	516,420	1,636,523

Adapted from "Explore the World's Protected Areas," Protected Planet, accessed July 5, 2023, protectedplanet.net.

agement details, and much wording in legislation moved back and forth between agencies in the two countries over a 200-year period. Therefore, both countries have national parks, national historic sites and parks, national wildlife reserves and areas, provincial and state parks, regional parks, and municipal parks. And it is not surprising that parks in both countries have been created for everyone's use and are funded primarily by taxes.

After the parks were established, their management was done first by volunteers and later by hired professionals. Starting in the United States in the 1930s and followed by Canada in the 1960s, specialized college and university programs were developed to provide training for leisure, parks, recreation, and resource management professionals. Park managers in both countries are now viewed as professionals who have received training appropriate to the challenging tasks of conservation and recreation.

Canada and the United States both played a large role in park management internationally. Both countries have influenced the types and forms of park management that have developed around the world. U.S. government officials and academic scholars were particularly influential in spreading the U.S. model of national parks worldwide. The U.S. model is typically seen as consisting of extremely large areas from which Aboriginal people have been removed. Management is by a government agency that concentrates on conservation and outdoor recreation. Canadian officials have been influential in international activities such as creating biosphere reserves and management of the World Heritage Convention. Scholars in both countries have written abundant literature that has widely disseminated the concepts of park planning and management and outdoor recreation planning and management. The United States and Canada have consistently shown international leadership in park planning and management.

Differences Between Canada and the United States

Although the park systems in both countries are similar, there are important differences (Eagles et al., 2000). The wilderness concept is more popular in the United States than in Canada; therefore, the United States has much more designated wilderness. Through the power of the use of the Antiquities Act, the United States has a national monument designation that is not used in Canadian park law.

But the biggest differences occur in the amount of land comprising protected landscape and managed resource-protected areas. In the United States, the federal government manages these lands and has designated large areas as national forests and Bureau of Land Management–protected areas. In Canada, however, the provinces manage the forestlands, and Canada does not include all undesignated Crown lands managed by the provinces, territories, and the national government in its tabulation of protected areas. Therefore, formal lists of protected areas create the impression that the United States has much more protected land. This conclusion is misleading because massive amounts of Crown and Aboriginal land in Canada are available for outdoor recreation, but are not formally designated as some form of protected area.

One major difference between Canada and the United States is the constitutional structure of public land ownership. In the United States, the federal government owns most of the public land, especially in states that came into the union after the Civil War. Therefore, the U.S. government has the capacity to create parks and reserves on this land. As a result, many land management agencies have been created to manage the variety of reserves created on federal land. The United States has more diverse management institutions and reserves than Canada. For example, the following designations exist in the United States but not in Canada: national forests, national parkways, national scenic rivers, national wilderness areas, U.S. Army Corps of Engineer waterways, and BLM national resource lands.

Another difference between the two countries is that in Canada the provincial parks are much larger than most state parks in the United States. For example, the provincial park system in Ontario is larger in land area than all 50 of the U.S. state park systems combined. In essence, many provincial park systems in Canada are of national park stature largely because the provincial governments control most of the Crown land within their borders. Therefore, the provincial governments found it relatively easy to create provincial parks on land that they already owned and managed. Some of the richer provinces, such as Ontario, British Columbia, and Quebec, blocked national park creation while putting the best lands into their own provincial park systems. A few provinces, however, have gone a different direction. Poorer provinces, such as New Brunswick, Nova Scotia, and Prince Edward Island, welcomed national park creation because the federal government would then pay the cost of land management. In these provinces, the national parks are prominent and the provincial park systems are smaller and less developed.

Within the territories in Canada, the federal government holds Crown land and takes into account Aboriginal land rights. Therefore, national parks and wildlife areas were most easily created by the national government in territories. For that reason, the major concentration of national parks occurs in the western mountains and in the High North. In the Canadian West, the national parks were created before the provinces were created. In the North, park creation is ongoing. Canadian parks have been managed more as a system of parks with national planning, whereas in the United States, although there have been several attempts at national plans, they rarely last long, often because of changes in presidential or congressional priorities and the difficulties in coordinating 50 states.

Canada is a signatory to the Convention on Biological Diversity. Under that convention, all countries agreed that 17 percent of their land surface and 10 percent of their marine areas would be protected areas by 2020. Canada currently has 12.71 percent of the terrestrial area of the country in some form of protected area and 9.06 percent of the marine area in protected areas (Protected Planet, 2022). The area of marine coverage has seen a massive increase in the last few years as the current Trudeau government works toward achieving the Convention on Biological Diversity targets.

To reach the 17 percent and 10 percent targets of the Convention on Biological Diversity, the current federal government headed by Prime Minister Justin Trudeau created substantial amounts of new parkland. This government has been most successful in creating new marine areas, largely since offshore areas are already under federal control. The current government has created a new target of 25 percent of Canada's land and oceans by 2025 (Minister of Environment and Climate Change, 2021). Hill (2021) stated that Canadian politicians have been great at making promises to create more parkland for biodiversity conservation purposes, but have not been good at implementing these promises.

The United States is not a signatory to the Convention on Biological Diversity because the Senate refuses to approve this convention. On March 10, 2016, however, President Obama and Prime Minister Trudeau issued a joint statement that said, "Canada and the U.S. re-affirm our national goals of protecting at least 17% of land areas and 10% of marine areas by 2020. We will take concrete steps to achieve and substantially surpass these national goals in the coming years" (Trudeau & Obama, 2016). This is a dramatic example of the cooperation of the United States and Canada in park management at the highest levels possible.

It is important to note that the creation and management of parks is a political act whereby governments respond to societal interest and lobbying. Right-wing political parties tend to not favor the creation of new parks, while left-wing parties do. In Canada, the Conservative Party has been responsible in both federal and provincial governments for the defunding of park management, and in some cases the deregulation of parks. For example, in the Province of Alberta, the right-wing government proposed in early 2020 to close or delist 175 provincial parks (CBC, 2020). After massive objections from urban voters in Alberta, these plans were dropped (Defend Alberta Parks, 2020). However, the park management agency was severely weakened, as most recreation facilities and programs were given to private concessionaires.

CAREER OPPORTUNITIES

Traditionally, the operation of most public natural areas occurs within the federal, state or provincial, or municipal levels of government. City parks and recreation departments offer countless opportunities to parks and recreation specialists. Thus, employment opportunities are available with agencies such as the national park agencies, the national wildlife agencies, the forest services, and the many regional, local, and municipal parks and recreation agencies. In the United States, opportunities are also available with the AmeriCorps program, the Student Conservation Association (SCA), and many state and local nonprofit groups such as the Vermont Youth Conservation Corps. Many different job positions are available at parks, forests, and refuges (administrative, financial, clerical, secretarial, maintenance, law enforcement, educational, safety, etc.). It is important to note that in state parks, the directors are all political appointees, whose job is held at the pleasure of the governor of the state. Therefore, when governments change, the park directors change.

Park rangers carry out various tasks associated with the following:

• Forest or structural fire control
• Protection of property
• Gathering and dissemination of natural, historical, or scientific information

- Development of interpretive material for natural, historical, or cultural features
- Demonstration of folk art and crafts
- Enforcement of laws and regulations
- Investigation of violations, complaints, trespassing and encroachment, and accidents
- Search and rescue
- Management of historical, cultural, and natural resources such as wildlife, forests, lakeshores, seashores, historic buildings, battlefields, archaeological properties, and recreation areas

They also operate campgrounds, including such tasks as assigning sites, replenishing firewood, performing safety inspections, providing information to visitors, and leading guided tours. Differences in the exact nature of duties depend on the grade of the position, the size of the site, and specific needs (National Park Service, n.d.-d).

Educational requirements vary depending on the position, but a university degree is preferred for most permanent positions. Seasonal employment is available in most areas to gain experience when the employee is in college or has recently graduated. Educational training should relate to the position sought (e.g., history degree for historians; parks, recreation, and tourism degree for visitor management; biology, ecology, forestry, geology, or wildlife management degree for natural resource management positions). Except for some maintenance positions (electricians, plumbers, etc.), law enforcement jobs, or lifeguard positions, certifications are generally not required, although preference might be given to candidates who have certified park and recreation professional (CPRP) status for some positions. Information on obtaining that certification is available from the National Recreation and Park Association in Ashburn, Virginia, United States. Canada does not have a national recreation accreditation system. However, in the United States the most senior positions in park agencies are political appointees, chosen partly because of their affiliation with the political party in power.

In Canada and the United States, there is a positive relationship between universities and park managers. Many parks rely heavily on student employees for many activities ranging from biological inventories to campground management and from visitor management to environmental education. Many senior park managers and planners are university graduates. However, state park directors are political appointees, often with no specific training in park management. Maintenance and construction employees have appropriate technical training. Law enforcement staff have specialized policing training.

Many professional organizations are relevant to those interested in a park-related career. Most have student membership rates and hold annual conferences that offer opportunities to network and learn about internship or employment opportunities. Some of the better-known ones include the National Recreation and Park Association, the Canadian Parks and Recreation Association, the National Parks Conservation Association, the Society of American Foresters, Society of Outdoor Recreation Professionals, the National Association for Interpretation, state and provincial park and recreation associations, the George Wright Society, and the Wilderness Society. The best way for a young student to become permanently employed in a park is to obtain temporary seasonal work to gain experience and become known to managers.

There are also recreation employment opportunities in the private sector, both the profit-making sector and the nonprofit sector. A range of jobs are available including program planning, direct program delivery, resort-park concessionaire or lodging operations, and the sale of specialized recreation merchandise. Growing opportunities in small businesses are available for people interested in providing outdoor programs and services for activities such as rafting, birding, bicycling, and kayaking. Some resorts recognize the need for a staff naturalist or recreation employee to answer guests' questions and offer tours and sightseeing trips. Summer camps, ski resorts, tour boat companies, bed-and-breakfasts, park and beach concessionaires, park lodges, watercraft and bicycle rental companies, water parks, marinas, and outdoor equipment stores are a few more examples of potential jobsites. Increasingly, nongovernment organizations that assist with park management, such as friends groups, have become important sources of employment for parks and recreation graduates.

A glance at websites such as CoolWorks, Eco-Jobs, NRPA careers, state parks job pages, and federal job pages will show that the number and diversity of career opportunities related to parks and protected areas is immense. Perhaps the best part of these careers is the intangible benefits that a person receives from living, working, and being active in a place that others pay to see and experience.

CHALLENGES AND TRENDS FOR THE 21ST CENTURY

Parks are a product and reflection of our society, its needs, and its culture. Most citizens use, know about, and support the creation and management of parks. Over time, public demand has resulted in increasing amounts of land being reserved for parks and removed from other types of land use. Park usage is increasing in some regions but decreasing in others. Park tourism leads to two complicated problems. First, how can the cultural and ecological values of the parks be conserved and interpreted while at the same time be actively used by large numbers of tourists? Second, how can the management of all this parkland and visitor use be financed? We are fortunate to have thousands of park resources available because of the farsightedness, willingness to sacrifice, and preservation ethos of previous generations. But those resources face challenges and trends that current generations must respond to.

Carrying Capacity

Carrying capacity is a primary issue associated with parks because of the inherent conflict between providing parks for public use and enjoyment while protecting the resources that make them special. This dual mandate requires that a balance be achieved among the number and types of users allowed and the effects of their use. The point at which this balance is made is the **carrying capacity** of a park. Carrying capacity is inherently a subjective decision, but it can be informed by strong empirical science. For example, social scientists have determined public opinion regarding the acceptable level of crowds, traffic, noise, or environmental effects caused by park visitors (Manning, 2007). Likewise, experts can evaluate visitor-created effects on resources such as wildlife or plants. These opinions (both public and expert) can help inform standards for managing parks within a carrying capacity; if standards are violated, then the carrying capacity of a park has been reached and park managers should take action. These actions could include redistributing visitors to lesser used areas of the park, reducing visitor impacts, or limiting the number of visitors. The concept of carrying capacity can help ensure the sustainability of parks and their resources for future generations. Eagles et al. (2021) outline three examples, Plitvice Lakes National Park in Croatia, Point Pelee National Park in Canada, and Pinery Provincial Park in Ontario, Canada, where park visitation levels were reduced during management planning efforts in order to better match the visitor use levels to the park's carrying capacity.

International Tourism

In both countries, the impact of international tourists is becoming increasingly important; large numbers of people from other countries, especially Europe, Japan, China, and other Asian countries, visit high-profile parks. The increase in visits to national parks by international tourists can be attributed to greater awareness of environmental concerns, scarcity of natural land at home, and higher levels of travel. As international tourism increases, so does the demand for a higher quality of service management and park staff with advanced education in tourism management, cultural sensitivity, and language skills.

Funding

Over the years, government funding for public parks has become increasingly limited, and the number of park agencies that compete for these funds has grown. Some of the causes of the funding shortage include rising land prices, energy and fuel costs, and a trend toward reducing taxes. Insufficient funding hinders the provision of environmental and historical interpretation programs and the retention of sufficient park rangers or staff to maintain facilities, manage resources, and serve the public. Parks not only compete with each other for funding but they also compete with other large and popular public institutions such as education and health care for these limited public funds.

Innovative responses to funding shortfalls include increasing the use of tourism fees and charges, increasing the reliance on volunteer efforts such as friends groups, and encouraging park agencies to function like businesses by tapping all possible streams of income. Many park agencies are moving aggressively into a business model of management in which they can set prices, retain funds, hire staff, and operate programs with flexibility similar to that of a private business. Traditional income sources continue to include government appropriations and grants, campsite rentals, and day-use fees. Innovative income sources include souvenir sales, grocery sales, recreation equipment rental, specialized clothing and equipment sales, specialized accommodation rental, fees for using parks as movie-filming sites, art sales, interpretive program charges, corporate sponsorships, leases to private companies, and corporate advertising. Friends groups are also entrepreneurial. Examples of fund-raising activities include providing specialized festivals; developing activities that recognize Aboriginal traditions; encouraging film, art, and cultural development; allotting a portion of sales income from book or gift stores to the park; and encouraging donations of time and money. A complete review of Ontario's experience in tourism funding for parks was outlined by Eagles (2014). Advanced training in the business of leisure and tourism is now needed in all park agencies.

Major park management debates revolve around the types of activities that should be encouraged and allowed, the management structures used, and the source of the funding. The proportion of funding that should come from taxes or from user fees also produces heated debate. A trend has developed toward increasing the use of various types of fees and charges to fund park management, especially in state and provincial parks. There is an urgent need for park managers with specialized training in finance and business management. Many universities train resource managers, but only a few train business managers for parks.

Market Specialization

Over the years, various park agencies have increasingly specialized in providing services to a segment of the population. For example, younger people and people without much discretionary income use city parks regularly. Conversely, well-educated and wealthy older people who have the time and money to travel use national parks more frequently. The baby boom generation is a key target market. Today's park managers must plan and manage for the needs of the largest, healthiest, and wealthiest cadre of retirees in world history. For example, the picturesque landscapes of North American parks attract older travelers, but the services and facilities are typically more appropriate for young, physically active visitors. Aging baby boomers seem to prefer what has been labeled *soft ecotourism* in which they hike and sightsee in the parks in the daytime but retire to nearby lodges, bed-and-breakfasts, restaurants, and cabins at night. The boom in the development of ecolodges near parks is based on this trend of visiting parks for a nature experience but spending the evenings with good food and innovative accommodations. Resolving this competition poses a challenge to parks.

Changing Demand

The national park agencies of Canada and the United States saw a slight but steady decline in national park use until 2014, when a major increase occurred (Balmford et al., 2009; National Park Service, n.d.-b; Parks Canada, n.d.; Pergams et al., 2004). There were several key reasons for declines in park use, such as the increased cost of fuel, the global economic recession, information technology and social media increasingly taking more time (a phenomenon called *videophilia* by Pergams & Zaradic, 2006), and immigration of people to both countries who do not have a cultural background in nature-based outdoor recreation. Adapting to these challenges that reduce visitation remains one of the biggest problems on the horizon for parks. However, more fuel-efficient vehicles, decreased gasoline prices, emergence from the economic recession, and marketing and programming efforts to get more adults, diverse visitors, and children outdoors seem to have helped increase demand to visit parks of all kinds. For example, in 2015, the NPS launched an initiative to allow fourth-grade children and their families into parks for free as part of a program called Every Kid in a Park. In 2015 and 2016, the NPS set new records for the number of visitors.

The COVID-19 global pandemic caused major changes in park use. Generally, international travel to parks was severely restricted while domestic visitation increased. In Canada, park use first plummeted during the pandemic, then reached record levels in 2021 as Canadians transferred their vacation plans to local parks.

In both Canada and the United States, the pandemic resulted in a massive influx of new campers. The proportion of first-time campers exploded in 2020, with 21 percent of campers being first timers, the largest percentage in history. Camping was ranked as the safest way to travel, and RV use increased. Campers were more ethnically diverse than ever. Campers participated more often than in previous years, and adults with children expressed more interest in camping. Remote work and virtual schooling enabled these activities to continue in parks that had Internet access. Glamping, camping in semipermanent tents, boomed where it was available (Boogman, 2021).

Data from 2022 showed that park use across Canada reached record levels.

Encroachment

As private-land development encroaches on park borders, wildlife loses some of its ability to move across natural areas. Development of power plants, housing, and large retail stores adjacent to parks threatens aesthetics and air quality. Development pressures also increase the temptation for government to use public parklands for public services such as roads, power lines, cell phone towers, and pipelines. A major management focus of many agencies is to stop illegal encroachments by adjacent landowners on parklands, such as homeowners who extend their personal activities into parkland (McWilliam et al., 2010).

Environmental Threats From Outside the Park

Problems originating elsewhere can affect park resources. For example, polluted river water originates in a populated area but flows through a park, or air pollution from outside a park can spoil the fresh air and views within the park. Exotic plant species seeds are dispersed by wildlife or wind and cause nonnative plants to flourish inside park boundaries, which possibly crowds out native species. Historically, park management focused on factors within a park's boundaries. Many park managers (particularly at the regional and national levels) are beginning to recognize, plan for, and respond to these transboundary issues through partnerships and collaboration with government officials, nonprofit organizations, scientists, and other stakeholders.

Climate Change

All global environments are facing increasing threats from a climate that is affected by human forces. While once debated, climate change is widely recognized among leaders and managers as a primary influence in the future of parks and protected areas. In fact, both the NPS and the Forest Service have made understanding and responding to climate change a primary focus of their efforts. This threat is of great concern because it is pervasive and has the potential to cause significant alterations in current parks and protected areas. For example, climate change threatens glaciers that are a centerpiece of several U.S. national parks (e.g., Kenai Fjords National Park, Glacier Bay National Park, Glacier National Park), and it may cause the loss of Joshua trees from Joshua Tree National Park. Within the western United States and Canada, a warming climate has resulted in a population explosion of native bark beetles that have damaged and killed millions of trees. These dying trees have created a major forest fire threat. Alberta and British Columbia saw record levels of forest fires, including the destruction of all or parts of two cities in northern Alberta, Slave Lake in 2011, and Fort McMurray in 2016. British Columbia saw record areas affected by wildfires in 2017 (1.2 million ha, or 3 million acres),

in 2018 (1.3 million ha, or 3.2 million acres), and in 2021 (0.9 million ha, or 2.2 million acres). These were the three largest areas affected in 102 years of recorded wildfire history in British Columbia (BC Ministry of Forests, 2022). These are examples of the types of ecosystem transformations now underway due to climate change.

Illicit and Illegal Behavior

Vandalism, drug use, public sexual behavior, crime, and gang activity have made many people afraid to visit urban parks. Approaches to addressing these problems include establishing zero-tolerance zones for crimes committed within 100 yards (91 m) of a park, adding special fines or sentences for doing so, and monitoring parks with cameras. Another strategy is national night-out events to encourage large numbers of people to use the parks, which usually discourages crime. In state parks, national parks, and other protected areas, the growing of drugs (particularly marijuana) in remote regions has been an increasing concern for managers and visitors. Likewise, illegal immigration, border security, and related human trafficking at parks that share an international border (particularly with Mexico) are an increasing problem. Law enforcement is an important activity in all parks. No conservation or recreation programs can be successful if the laws underpinning these programs are not enforced.

Motorized Vehicles

Off-highway vehicle (OHV) use is one of the most prevalent and fastest growing leisure activities on public lands in the United States. From 1999 to 2005, the estimated number of OHV users in the United States grew from 36 to 51 million (Cordell et al., 2005). This figure indicates that nearly one in every five U.S. residents uses an OHV. National forests and BLM lands are frequently used as places to ride OHVs, and many of these places have trails that cater to OHV recreationists. But OHV use, particularly when not intensively managed, may lead to substantial resource impacts and controversy in these places. In 2006, the Forest Service labeled unmanaged OHV use as one of the four leading threats to the health of the nation's forests and grasslands in the 21st century. Also, inappropriate and illegal use of motorized vehicles in parks and protected areas is a concern for managers. In the province of Alberta, OHV users lobbied successfully to allow motorized vehicles in formerly protected areas. An example is the Castle Wilderness Area of southern Alberta, which is adjacent to Waterton

Lakes National Park (Alberta Wilderness Association, 2021). This Alberta example reveals how strong conflicts and public policy debates between different recreational user groups affect park use.

Coastal Development

On many coastlines, condominiums and high-rise buildings with thousands of residents are being built, which greatly increases the use of nearby coastal parks. Coastal lands have become so expensive that existing coastal parks cannot be expanded. In addition, the high density creates large human-use pressure in the parks. In October of 2022, Prince Edward Island National Park was severely damaged when hurricane Fiona caused major shoreline erosion, forest destruction, and facility damage (Parks Canada, 2023). This negative coastal impact was largely attributed to higher wind speeds associated with higher ocean levels due to climate change.

Natural Darkness and Quiet

A broadened consideration of park resources has led to both noise and light pollution becoming concerns in national and state parks (Manning et al., in press). Some parks are actively working to protect the important, yet previously unmanaged, ability to enjoy the stars in the night sky or natural sounds like birds singing or water flowing. Lightscapes and soundscapes are now recognized and managed resources in some parks. A few parks have sought and received designations as International Dark Sky Parks to certify the exceptional quality of their night sky and night environment. Other parks, like Muir Woods National Monument, have created quiet zones where people can enjoy the park without being disturbed by human-caused noise.

Multiethnic Cultural Changes

It is projected that an amalgam of minorities will make up more than 50 percent of the U.S. population by 2050. Because of immigration from a diverse set of countries, the Canadian and American populations are becoming more diverse in cultures and ideas. This transformation creates concern for park managers because some cultures have little experience visiting parks or participating in traditional outdoor recreational activities (Chavez, 2002; Johnson et al., 1997; Virden & Walker, 1999). As the ethnic balance in North America shifts, park, forest, and refuge agencies at all levels must understand the preferences and outdoor recreational behaviors of minority groups and work to introduce them to activities that they may have little experience with

or adapt facilities or programs to their cultures. This approach will be necessary to continue the legacy of public service that makes park resources available to all citizens and guests in the United States and Canada.

Workforce Changes

Many parks and protected areas are staffed and managed by a large cohort of people who are nearing retirement age. Almost half of all U.S. federal employees are within five years of retirement age, although the recent economic downturn may delay some of those retirements. Having such a large percentage of experienced park staff leaving brings with it challenges of retaining knowledge within the organization, providing adequate training, and finding qualified replacements. This change in the workforce also indicates that substantial opportunities will be available to those looking for careers in parks and protected areas.

Seasonality

Most parks in Canada and the United States deal successfully with large fluctuations in visitation resulting from changes in the seasons. In northern areas, visitation is largely concentrated in the warmer months, so many parks are staffed by short-term employees (often university students). A few parks in northern areas have snow-based recreational activities, typically downhill skiing, that enable year-round employment. But many parks in northern areas are staffed at very low levels or not at all in the colder winter months, especially in Canada. In southern Canada, warmer autumn weather in the last decades has caused a surge in visitation.

SUMMARY

The parks in Canada and the United States contain some of the most significant and attractive natural landscapes in North America. Each year, they display the ecological and cultural values of both countries for millions of people. The parks of Canada and the United States are highly valued not only by their citizens but also by many international visitors. These parks have become icons that represent the strong political, social, and cultural ideas that formed each country. Although European countries have many castles and cathedrals that mark centuries of cultural history, in North America the beauty of the wild lands—the mountains, deserts, prairies, rivers, and lakes—celebrates a major aspect of this continent and its people.

Those who work in park settings feel strongly about the value of their role, and many consider their jobs positive lifelong endeavors. In an increasingly urbanized, technology-filled, overstimulated, and fast-paced culture, people seek opportunities to connect with nature. Public parks, forests, rivers, mountains, beaches, lakes, deserts, and oceans can provide inspiration, fascination, and education. These protected natural resources, gifts from earlier generations, can provide escape from work and social challenges, peace and relaxation, and a place to spend quiet time with family and friends or alone. They are living schools for ecology, wildlife, nature, and self-discovery.

Not many places endure unchanged over a lifetime. Since the 1870s, North America has lost many farms and natural areas to development. Most parks, however, remain more or less unchanged over the years. There are places for children to swing or slide in a local park; for swimming or camping with family; for strolling hand in hand or sharing a kiss on a park bench; for celebrating anniversaries in park lodges; for hiking, fishing, canoeing, or camping; and for watching sunsets and moonrises across a scenic natural landscape. Parks are invaluable for creating personal memories as well as maintaining national heritage and culture. All citizens should visit parks, make memories in them, celebrate natural roots and connections to the animal and plant kingdoms, and play a role in protecting and sharing existing parks and creating new ones.

Review Questions

1. Where were the first provincial and national parks in Canada developed?

2. What are the five types of parks in the Canadian park system?

3. What was the impetus for creating federal land as national parks in the United States?

4. How do state and national parks differ in the United States?

5. What does a wilderness designation do in the United States?

6. What are some issues and concerns related to public lands in the United States and Canada?

Go to HK*Propel* to complete the activities for this chapter.

CHAPTER 7

Public Recreation

Mary Sara Wells and Terry Long

Ratnakorn Piyasirisorost/Moment RF/Getty Images

> " My friends, love is better than anger. Hope is better than fear. Optimism is better than despair. So let us be loving, hopeful and optimistic. And we'll change the world. "
>
> Jack Layton, leader of the opposition of the government of Canada, 2011

─────────────── LEARNING OUTCOMES ───────────────

After reading this chapter, you should be able to do the following:

> Identify the groups that helped create public recreation services in Canada and the United States

> Describe the basic types of recreation programs found in Canada and the United States

> Demonstrate an understanding of why partnerships are important in public recreation

> Recognize the trends in the changing profession of public recreation and the leadership skills needed to advance a professional career

> List and describe the various certifications available in public recreation

> Describe the philosophy of community-based recreation approaches

> Identify the role of the ADA in the development of inclusive recreation opportunities in public recreation

> Explain the role of accessibility, accommodation, and adaptation as building blocks to inclusion

> Recognize potential limits to reasonable accommodation

> Differentiate between Special Olympics, disability sport, adapted sport, and Paralympics

> Communicate the value of social inclusion to participants and community members

Public Parks and Recreation in the United States and Canada

Mary Sara Wells

❝ I am not concerned with our inability to nail down the specifics of what we do in parks and recreation. As I see it, our strength lies in our diversity. We can do anything. More specifically, I believe our job is to help people improve their quality of life through recreation and parks. ❞

Robert F. Toalson, Champaign Park District, Illinois

Public recreation continues to face numerous changes. Many public agencies that provide these valuable services are seeing their budgets cut, their resources shifted, and their priorities redefined. Public recreation is no longer always considered a staple for a high quality of life within a community. Today we need new ideas, new leadership methods, and, most important, a constant dedication to educate people about the benefits of recreation. A paradigm shift has been underway regarding the future of public recreation due to fluctuating economic issues. But throughout history, one undeniable fact is that public recreation is needed to provide fun and exciting leisure opportunities for people of all ages. The need to embrace 21st-century thinking and advance the future is upon us. The question to our profession now is how to relate to a changing environment in a modern world.

In the past, public recreation has been dependent on costly physical features such as playgrounds, trails, swimming pools, and recreation centers. These types of facilities provide valuable recreation opportunities and tend to be focused on providing something for everyone. But recreation programs are becoming more specialized for target user groups. Does this approach make sense for the public today? The public in today's world is plugged in to constant information streams that are available on their terms. The use of technology in our everyday lives has accelerated our information-based lifestyle. Knowledge is available instantly. Interacting on social technology networks has become a major form of leisure for multiple generations. In addition, many people have changed their expectations about what is possible or desired from public recreation agencies following the COVID-19 pandemic when remote programming became more accessible. How we spend our leisure time is changing. New leadership in our field is needed to reach the public in ways not considered just a few years ago.

This section explores the realm of public recreation as a possible career path. The world of public recreation has a different focus from that of our colleagues in the private sector. This section examines the pulse of public recreation and leisure services in Canada and the United States, the social and political environments in which public recreation professionals operate, the primary roles of parks and recreation professionals, and the constantly changing face of public recreation.

HISTORICAL OVERVIEW OF PUBLIC RECREATION IN THE UNITED STATES

Public recreation in the United States originated around the middle of the 19th century in the Midwest and Northeast. Although recreation in general can be found in the United States before explorers from England and other countries arrived, the mid-1800s is when government and other organizations first began providing specific services. A review of how parks and recreation developed up until this point can be found in chapter 2. Public recreation perhaps first began with the development of parks and playgrounds. Although parks and open spaces may not have been uncommon prior to this point, it is generally believed that the Boston Common and New York City's Central Park were early demonstrations of the need for intentional green space planning within urban environments. The construction of playgrounds in the mid- to late 1800s further served the needs of urban residents by providing structures on which children could engage in active and constructive play.

Among the early pioneers in the playground movement was the Massachusetts Emergency and Hygiene Association in Boston, which developed a sand garden in 1885 that led to the development of 21 more similar playgrounds by 1889. The first municipal park in the United States to have a permanent playground was Seward Park in New York City in 1903. The playground movement of this area led to the foundation of the Playground Association of America in 1906, which eventually grew to become the National Recreation and Park Association; this is the preeminent professional organization for the field today.

HISTORICAL OVERVIEW OF PUBLIC RECREATION IN CANADA

In considering the development of public recreation in Canada, people often look at the services that are closest to its citizens at the local level and primarily at the municipal level. In the early 21st century, these municipal services are supported by and driven by provincial and federal programs that operate in a system propelled by professional, community, and political initiatives. Local public recreation began as a set of independent initiatives aimed at solving problems (real or perceived) or creating opportunities for residents. The roots of today's integrated public recreation system come from parks, playgrounds, fitness, and employment initiatives; from those who wanted to reform the "sorry condition of Canada's big cities" (Rutherford, 1974, p. xv); from those who wanted to enhance the physical, mental, and moral health of all; and from those who wanted to enhance investment growth and prosperity in cities. The results were parks established to create civic beauty and promote a healthy environment, playgrounds established to provide wholesome play opportunities for children, and physical activity programs to build the fitness levels of young people so that they would be fit for work or war. The system has been advanced by those who wanted to create a better environment, although each proponent of recreation might define *better* in a different fashion.

Influences on recreation in Canada came from Great Britain, Europe, and the United States. There are readily identifiable links between British proponents of wholesome and uplifting educational and recreational programs such as the Young Men's Christian Association (YMCA) and the Young Women's Christian Association (YWCA) from England; Scandinavian promoters of physical fitness; and American advocates for supervised playgrounds and urban recreation programs. Each of these groups helped plant ideas and provide information to Canadians, but the version of each idea evolved according to the social, economic, and political influences in Canada. The expansion of eastern Canadian cities in the mid- and late 19th century, the rapid expansion of the West in the early 20th century, the depression of the 1930s, the post–World War II urban growth, and the role of government as the provider of a social safety net all contributed to the Canadian solution.

Playgrounds Came First and Then Recreation

Municipal recreation in Canada can trace its roots to the National Council of Women's (NCW) Committee on Vacation Schools and Supervised Playgrounds in 1901 after lobbying from the Saint John Local Council of Women led by Miss Mabel Peters (McFarland, 1970). The NCW focused on "'prevention' as its guiding principle" (Strong-Boag, 1976, p. 268), and by 1913 the NCW's committee was able to firmly state its mission and successes using ideas familiar to us today:

> Its work is formative as opposed to reformative. It seeks to eventually dispense with the curfew, the juvenile court, the jail and the reform school for the young of our land. Educationists are now agreed that the public supervised playground and recreational Social Center stimulates and guides a child's life in a way which no other factor of modern living can do. (Peters, 1913, p. 48)

We no longer have reform schools and seldom have curfews, but we now speak of at-risk youth. The ideas of a century ago are still with us.

Although the NCW and its local councils were advocates for playgrounds and the catalysts for their development, they were not committed to their long-term operation. They wanted to hand off responsibility to other groups such as local playground associations and municipal governments. The accompanying photo shows the publicity efforts of one playground association as its members urged visitors to try to get a playground in their neighborhood.

Recreation departments became the norm in Canadian cities in the early to mid-20th century, and they often merged with parks departments.

A local playground association's advocacy work to promote playground development in the early 20th century. The sign reads, "Try and secure one for your neighbourhood."

In the last decades of the 20th century, further mergers occurred between municipal parks and recreation and other units with similar mandates or client groups. For example, agencies that provided recreation, parks, and other social services merged with culture or tourism services into a local department of community services or community development.

Federal and Provincial Governments

The involvement of provincial governments and the federal government in recreation can be primarily attributed to the search for antidotes to unemployment during the depression in the 1930s. Two intertwined threads were involved. One developed in British Columbia, and the other included the efforts of the federal government.

In British Columbia, the government began its provincial recreation program, Pro-Rec, in 1934 to provide physical recreation for unemployed young men and women as an attempt to deal with "the large number of unemployed youth . . . who are exposed to the demoralizing influences of enforced idleness" (Schrodt, 1979, Appendix A). The first director was Ian Eisenhardt, a Vancouver Parks Board staff member who had been trained in Denmark. When the federal government established the National Employment Commission in 1936 to investigate the needs of the unemployed, it was searching for solutions to address not only employment but also leisure needs. The commission consulted experts such as Eisenhardt and devised programs to alleviate the problems of unemployment, and programs like the British Columbia program emerged. Through the Federal Unemployment and Agricultural Assistance Act of 1937 and the Youth Training Act of 1939, the provinces were given assistance to create training programs that would prepare young people to work in physical training and health education in local communities and to provide recreation opportunities for trainees in other programs such as forestry, agriculture, mining, industrial apprenticeships, and domestic and household work (McFarland, 1970). Responsibility for these training programs, including recreation workers, was delegated to the various provincial governments. Provinces that established training programs frequently relied on expert advice from Eisenhardt and staff from British Columbia.

Federal involvement in recreation had an influence on the municipal level through its programs of assistance in partnerships with most of the provinces. In 1943, the National Physical Fitness Program was established. The objective of this program was to "encourage, develop and correlate all activities related to physical development of the people through sports, athletics, and similar pursuits" (Statutes of Canada, 1943, p. 158). The program ended in 1954. It was succeeded by the Fitness and Amateur Sport Act in 1961 and the Physical Activity and Sport Act in 2003. As the federal government's involvement in recreation and leisure services evolved, various government programs came and went, such as Recreation Canada, which was established in 1971 and dissolved in 1980 (MacIntosh et al., 1988; Westland, 1979). The role of the federal government in recreation in Canada is to support sport-governing bodies, health promotion initiatives, Indigenous peoples' concerns, the provinces, recreation-related associations, and physical activity strategies including ParticipACTION, a national nonprofit initiative to promote fitness through physical activity.

DELIVERY SYSTEMS IN PUBLIC RECREATION

The public recreation system as we know it today has a variety of delivery systems in place within the various forms of governmental units. Public recreation must provide inclusive recreation and leisure services to all people, including disadvantaged and disabled patrons. This integrated approach reflects the spirit of the Americans with Disabilities Act and the Canadian Charter of Rights and Freedoms. Inclusion addresses the need to provide integration of leisure services for people of all ages, abilities, cultures, ethnicities, genders, races, and religions. This nondiscriminatory approach goes beyond the placement of special needs participants in separate recreation program settings.

In the most basic form, recreation programs found in public recreation fall into two classes of activities:

- Active recreation, which includes all types of sport, swimming, and most physical exercise recreation opportunities
- Passive recreation, which includes low-impact exercise and creative-based recreation programs such as walking, arts and crafts, and trips and excursions

American Delivery Systems

Recreation professionals in the United States provide numerous programs and services through various delivery systems, including municipal, state, and federal governmental agencies. Each type of agency serves a unique purpose or mission.

Municipal Recreation Leisure Services

Municipal recreation departments that serve communities are the primary providers of parks and recreation services. More than 2,100 community parks and recreation providers are registered with the National Center on Health, Physical Activity and Disability (NCHPAD, n.d.). These include departments at the city and county levels and through special-use districts. Services provided by these organizations often include structured programs and facilities for drop-in participation. More specifically, many municipal recreation departments have offerings such as classes, aquatic facilities, youth sports, field trips, after-school programs, golf courses, cemeteries, parks and playgrounds, and trails.

State Recreation Leisure Services

Whereas municipal recreation services provide opportunities at a local level, state recreation ser-

vices tend to focus on the wants and needs of the entire state population and the land. State recreation services typically focus on activities that take place in state forests and state parks. For the most part, there is little specific programming, and more energy is given to providing access to services and opportunities through beaches, marinas, hiking trails, golf courses, campgrounds, and other sites. By doing this, state agencies not only serve residents but also attract tourists and the economic benefits related to tourism.

Federal Recreation Leisure Services

Similar to the services provided by state agencies, the federal government also tends to focus less on specific programming in favor of providing outdoor resources for numerous activities such as hiking, camping, fishing, education, and interpretive centers. The agencies associated with these opportunities include the USDA Forest Service, the National Park Service, the Bureau of Land Management, U.S. Fish and Wildlife, and the U.S. Army Corp of Engineers.

MediaNews Group/Boston Herald via Getty Images/MediaNews Group RM/Getty Images

Municipal departments offer programs such as sport camps, day camps, and track meets.

Canadian Delivery Systems

The issue of the various levels of government jurisdiction over matters of recreation and leisure services has often been a source of debate. As a result, the National Recreation Statement of 1987 jointly signed by the Canadian federal, provincial, and territorial governments laid out the following broad principles to guide the respective responsibilities of the three levels of government:

1. The federal government focuses on national-level programs and programs within the agencies under its jurisdiction (Interprovincial Sport and Recreation Council [ISRC], 1987).

2. The provincial and territorial governments have substantial responsibilities related to recreation such as coordinating programs, providing information and financial resources to program delivery agencies, planning, and supporting research. They are very rarely the direct delivery agents for recreation and leisure services (ISRC, 1987).

3. Municipal governments are the primary suppliers of recreation services because they are close to the recipients and are perceived to be more nimble and able to respond effectively. The basic role of the municipality is to ensure the availability of the broadest range of recreation opportunities for every individual and group consistent with available community resources (ISRC, 1987).

The Canadian Constitution Act (Statutes of Canada, 1982) guarantees the following freedoms through the Charter of Rights and Freedoms:

- Freedom of conscience and religion
- Freedom of thought, belief, opinion, and expression, including freedom of the press and other communication media
- Freedom of peaceful assembly
- Freedom of association

Although the Constitution Act does not allocate legislative responsibility for recreation and leisure or state how recreation and leisure services are delivered, it does guarantee the freedoms that are essential elements of leisure. Professionals and the agencies in which they operate must uphold the Charter of Rights and Freedoms.

In keeping with the emphasis on national activities, the federal responsibility for recreation-related matters is governed by the Physical Activity and Sport Act of 2003. This act is under the jurisdiction of two departments (Justice Canada, 2017):

- The responsibility for physical activity is allocated to the Minister of Health
- The responsibility for sport is under the Minister of Canadian Heritage

That latter assignment is in keeping with that department's mandate for programs that promote "an environment in which all Canadians take advantage of dynamic cultural experiences, celebrating our history and heritage, and participating in building creative communities . . . supporting the arts, our two official languages and our athletes" (Canadian Heritage, n.d.). Several sports programs contribute to Canadian identity through high-performance and international sport. To the Canadian federal government, recreation is a physical activity that enhances health, and international sport solidifies Canada's identity. This focus often seems far removed from the day-to-day responsibilities of recreation professionals.

The various provinces and territories have different views of recreation. All have some type of government unit responsible for recreation, but the labels differ. Over the past half century, provincial governments have committed themselves to assisting recreation and leisure services through various government departments such as education and health and public welfare (McFarland, 1970). The first provincial government to establish a department whose sole mandate was recreation was Nova Scotia in 1972. Most provinces carried out similar actions in the 1970s. But just as a province can establish a recreation department, it also can change it. Provincial recreation agencies went through amalgamations and disintegrations with partners that now include departments for community services, health, seniors, sport, tourism, culture, parks, and so on, all in the interest of efficiency, effectiveness, and political expediency. Table 7.1 in HKPropel Access shows the names of provincial and territorial departments responsible for recreation.

How do government departments carry out their responsibilities? Tim Burton, former University of Alberta professor, created an explanatory model that explains the five roles that governments can take in delivering public services:

1. Direct provider
2. Enabler and coordinator

3. Supporter and patron
4. Arm's-length provider
5. Legislator and regulator (Burton & Glover, 1999)

Many recreation students will be most familiar with the **direct provider** role, which "describes the situation in which a government department or agency develops and maintains leisure facilities, operates programs, and delivers services using public funds and public employees" (Burton & Glover, 1999, p. 373). If you have been a town playground supervisor or a city swimming pool instructor, you have been part of the direct provider role. The municipality that developed the program owned the facility, ran the program, and paid you.

The next three roles involve decreasing amounts of direct involvement by the government. When a government department acts as an **enabler and coordinator**, it identifies "organizations and agencies which produce leisure services for the public and help[s] coordinate their efforts, resources and activities" (Burton & Glover, 1999, p. 374). If you have worked for a local community group that received funds and services, such as leadership training from a recreation department, you have seen a government unit acting as an enabler and coordinator.

When a government department acts as a **supporter and patron**, it "recognizes that existing organizations already produce valuable public leisure services and can be encouraged to do so through specialized support" (Burton & Glover, 1999, p. 374). If your local community festival received a government grant to assist with the production of a special event or to develop a facility, the government acted as a supporter and patron.

Furthest away from government's direct influence is the role of **arm's-length provider**, which "requires the creation of a . . . special purpose agency which operates outside the regular apparatus of government" (Burton & Glover, 1999, p. 373). Arts and culture organizations, such as museums or galleries, operate in this relationship. In theory, the government unit does not interfere with the internal operations of these organizations, but theory and practice occasionally conflict when political decision makers object to an organization's decisions to acquire a controversial piece of art or mount a controversial play using public funds.

The last role of government, **legislator and regulator**, affects many of our actions as providers and consumers of recreation opportunities. This role operates in the background of many parts of our work and leisure lives because we must abide by laws passed by various levels of government. When a government agency requires you to obtain a permit to put on an event or have a fireworks display, it is acting in this role. When you must get a fishing license or be of a certain age to enter a facility that serves alcohol, you are also experiencing these powers of government.

The municipal, provincial and territorial, and federal levels of government do not all engage in each of these five roles to the same degree. Municipal governments have traditionally operated using a direct provider role, but as cities and towns have faced financial stresses, many have shifted to a model in which they have transferred services to community groups while providing financial or in-kind support, thus moving toward an enabler and coordinator or a supporter and patron model. Provincial and federal government departments have historically used the latter two models, arm's-length provider and legislator and regulator. Provincial and federal governments have also created arm's-length agencies to carry out cultural programs. Many provincial agencies' mandates require that they operate in a legislator and regulator model.

kali9/iStockphoto/Getty Images

Various delivery systems exist for providing public recreation. This photo shows the direct provider role.

PARTNERSHIPS: CONNECTIONS TO THE COMMUNITY

Forming partnerships, cooperative ventures, and collaborative agreements or alliances has long been practiced by recreation and leisure professionals in the public sector. But today the emphasis on reviewing, revising, and renewing partnering efforts is more critical than ever. No agency or entity can thrive alone. Seeking new, inclusive, innovative, flexible, and commonly focused opportunities is imperative. Why? Because in forming partnerships, recreation and leisure professionals might be able to reduce the duplication of existing services, save money, and streamline organizations. Inevitably, they will increase the visibility of the organization, gain better networks, and develop more viable resource pools. In addition, personnel will have the opportunity to grow along with the community.

Any governmental unit can form a partnership with another governmental unit, a nonprofit organization, or a private entity. All these organizations can bring useful resources to the table to advance an opportunity, which often produces better results than going it alone. One of the most useful partnerships for a public recreation agency to develop is one with the local school district. A goal for many communities is an indoor pool. This type of facility can be cost prohibitive for most in the public environment. If the school district wants to upgrade its existing pool but does not have sufficient capital funds and the local parks and recreation agency identifies the need for an indoor pool but has limited funds as well, a partnership could be explored. This partnership would allow the parks and recreation agency to use the school's indoor pool in return for the investment of capital dollars, and the school district would get the upgraded pool. In this win–win solution, the community would recognize the benefit of the partnership. These partnerships can work wonders if the parties can produce a win–win outcome.

Most partnerships are intergovernmental agreements that outline the benefits received by the parties involved. Parks and recreation departments work with police and fire departments on safety protocols, camps, and programs such as bicycle or fire safety. Ongoing partnerships with the public works department can address building needs and general maintenance operations.

Local neighborhood groups work with parks departments to provide events, develop facilities,

Public recreation departments can cooperate with outside groups to construct playgrounds. As you discover the various aspects of recreation and leisure, community involvement with a variety of interest groups will be one of your most frustrating, and perhaps one of your most rewarding, experiences.

© Human Kinetics

and carry out cleanup programs. These partnerships not only benefit the parks and recreation department but also bring families and friends closer together because they are working toward a common goal. What better way is there to share facilities that are funded by taxpayers?

Every community can provide examples of successful partnerships. Look for examples of the following in your community:

- Programs that strengthen families such as Big Brothers and Big Sisters
- Business relationships, such as public and private partnerships, that develop or operate a facility
- Program development relationships between municipal recreation departments and universities or colleges with available facilities
- Justice departments involved in community crime prevention programs
- Volunteer groups, such as community leagues or neighborhood recreation associations, that are advocates for their communities and deliver programs
- Trails built by governments and citizen groups that link communities

The future of partnerships is bright. As agencies and communities realize the many benefits of working together, more opportunities to develop partnerships will arise.

FACES OF PUBLIC RECREATION

Most people who have chosen a career in public recreation find that they enjoy working with people through providing an essential governmental service. The need to provide recreation programs, facilities, parks, and open space for community enjoyment is a powerful mission that provides direct quality-of-life benefits. The diversity of activity types, civil servant calling, and the thrill of a variety of work environments lead to a profession that provides self-fulfillment.

Public Recreation Professionals

In the field of public recreation, many career paths include specialized areas of knowledge, such as recreation programming, facilities management, parks, outdoor education, therapeutic recreation,

and recreation administration. Professionals within the field of public recreation use a variety of skills obtained from academic study and on-the-job training. The core skills used at any level include

- ability to navigate the political environment;
- effective communication techniques;
- excellent customer service;
- ability to plan and implement programs, events, and activities;
- demonstrated leadership;
- fiscal forecasting and effective budgeting control; and
- conflict resolution.

Because recreation and leisure professionals need to be well rounded, professional training and preparation are detailed yet practical. Besides taking program development classes, recreation and leisure students take courses in environmental design and planning, leadership, and management.

The opportunity to grow professionally in public recreation is based on a variety of internal and external forces. One topic is diversification in the workplace, which is the ability to develop a wide range of job skills through on-the-job training and advancement. The ability to achieve job satisfaction can be linked to job diversification within an organization. An enhanced skill set will provide value to the organization and professional advancement opportunities for the individual. The variety of jobs within the public recreation realm sets up the opportunity for diversity within the workforce that few other careers can match. Most people still believe that the field of parks and recreation encompasses sport, fun, and games. Although these elements are certainly part of the profession, they do not begin to cover the diverse areas and links to other professions.

Public Recreation Management

Managers and leaders in recreation and leisure services plan, organize, direct, and control various areas of the agency. Managers fall into three categories: top, or executive, managers; middle managers; and frontline, or supervisory, managers. Other positions report to these managers.

Managers must possess three types of skills:

1. Technical skills that require specialized knowledge in operations, techniques, and procedures

2. Human skills that require understanding people and the ability to motivate and work with employees

3. Conceptual skills that allow the development and organization of a philosophy, mission, goals, and objectives

Besides performing organizational and administrative functions within an organization, managers are also involved in strategic planning, which encompasses community involvement and coordination with municipalities and other agencies. Managers need to work with community members to plan the many activities and facilities that are needed. By working with the community, managers help community members buy in to the activities and develop a sense of ownership. Successful collaboration draws on all the skills required of recreation and leisure professionals.

Professionals must ask themselves the following:

- What do we do as professionals in public recreation?
- Whom do we serve?
- Do we serve our career?
- Do we serve the public?
- Do we serve the politicians?
- Whom do the politicians serve?

Arriving at your own answers to these questions is a major step in your professional career.

American Professional Organizations and Certifications

As in almost any career, professional organizations provide invaluable resources for professionals. Among other benefits, professional organization membership serves public recreation providers by giving them networking opportunities, information on the latest trends and issues in the profession, education on new products and services, and, in some cases, extra services such as access to liability insurance. In the United States, the largest professional organization in the field is the National Recreation and Park Association. There are a multitude of other state and local organizations that also serve public recreation professionals.

One means of ensuring quality services is through certification of employees and agencies. These certifications demonstrate that the individu-

als holding them either meet or exceed a specific defined standard. Although certification might not be required for many positions or organizations, it does demonstrate that these employees have met the standards chosen by professionals in the field that are necessary for quality services. In some cases, such as in therapeutic recreation, certification might be required to practice. As you are looking at careers, be mindful of potential certification requirements to ensure that you meet all qualifications for employment.

The following are among the possible certifications for leisure professionals; these are offered through the National Recreation and Park Association:

- Certified park and recreation professional (CPRP) certification is granted to people employed in the recreation, park resources, and leisure services profession who meet high standards of performance.
- Certified park and recreation executive (CPRE) sets a standard for parks and recreation executives across the country in practical knowledge and real-world skills.
- Aquatic facility operator (AFO) is a state-of-the-art certification for pool operators and aquatic facility managers.
- Certified playground safety inspector (CPSI) provides the credentials to inspect playgrounds for safety and ensure that each playground meets the current national standards set by the American Society for Testing and Materials (ASTM) and the U.S. Consumer Product Safety Commission (CPSC).

To earn certification, you must demonstrate through examination that you have the basic knowledge and understanding specific to the topic. Once certification is achieved, you can improve your potential for professional advancement through your commitment to the profession and continuing education.

Canadian Professional Organizations

Many recreation and leisure service professionals work within the framework of public and governmental jurisdictions. Just as these professionals have established or worked in organizations to deliver services, they have also joined associations to promote the cause of recreation and leisure services. From the roots of the Ontario Parks Association grew

OUTSTANDING GRADUATE

Background Information

Name: Rachel Bedingfield

Education: BRM (Bachelor of Recreation Management) from Acadia University

Awards: Canadian Association for the Advancement of Women in Sport and Physical Activity 2015 list of Most Influential Women in Canada

Affiliations: Commonwealth Games Canada member, 2004-2016; Recreation Nova Scotia board member (vice president of monitoring), 2012-present; Women Active Nova Scotia board chair, 2016-present

Courtesy of Karlee Perry.

Career Information

Position: Director of Parks and Recreation

Organization: Town of Kentville, Nova Scotia, department of parks and recreation. Kentville is a municipal unit that serves a tax base of C$6,500 and a user base of 22,000.

Organization mission: Kentville Parks and Recreation's vision is a healthy, vibrant, integrated, and complete community where citizens can live, work, and play in an environment that supports a high quality of life. Kentville Parks and Recreation fosters a creative, progressive, and inclusive community where everyone belongs and everybody gets to play. We believe that recreation is the experience that results from freely chosen participation in physical, social, intellectual, creative, and spiritual pursuits that enhance individual and community well-being.

Job description: As the director of parks and recreation for the town of Kentville, I am responsible for ensuring that the vision of our department and of the town of Kentville is upheld, the standard of service is maintained, tax dollars are spent responsibly, and all members of our community, regardless of who they are, are able to access the many benefits of recreation. I manage anywhere from 10 to 40 staff daily, depending on the time of year. I report directly to the CAO as well as an advisory committee made up of elected officials and community members. I work to ensure that recreation remains relevant to all citizens of our community and that recreation is used as a way to build our community. As a recreation professional, I also ensure that we are aligning with the provincial shared recreation strategy as well as the National Recreation Framework. On this note, my main focus areas include providing opportunities to engage in active recreation; creating policies that focus on inclusion and access; connecting people with nature and building leadership capacity in this area; building, creating, and maintaining supportive environments; and building recreation capacity by focusing on leisure education principles.

Career path: I started my career working in Europe and East Africa in international development. I then worked for Recreation Nova Scotia as the inclusion specialist. I next worked for the Halifax Regional School Board as the sport animator. I then worked for the province of Nova Scotia as the regional physical activity consultant. Finally, I began work as the recreation director for the town of Kentville. I never intended to be a municipal recreation director, but I am challenged daily by this position and can certainly see myself staying here for a very long time.

Likes and dislikes about the job: The things I like most about my job are my ability to have a positive impact on my community and that every day is different. In our department we tackle everything from bike lanes to youth homelessness to facility development to community engagement and diversity training. My role is to also keep a pulse on the community, including their needs and wants. We work hard to build community empathy and provide opportunity for folks to look after one another.

There is not much I don't like about my job, but at times it requires long hours and hard decisions to be made. Despite all that, I have never held a position in which I have felt more solution oriented, nor have I ever felt more in control of being able to respond to identified needs—it's very empowering.

Advice for Undergraduates

My advice would be to simply keep trying new things. Discovering what you don't like is just as important as discovering what you do like. I graduated with the intent of becoming an inclusion specialist for people with a disability, and immediately I was taken off this track because I jumped at the opportunities that were in front of me—and I have never looked back. Be prepared to work hard, and learn to reflect on yourself as both a professional and as an individual. I have been in the field for almost 20 years and I am still very much learning from my peers, my colleagues, my community, and myself.

Being a recreation professional is one of the most rewarding and exhausting (not only exhausting physically, but also emotionally) things you will ever do. The longer I am in this field, the more powerful a tool I realize recreation is to have. And the more vulnerable I make myself emotionally, the better the results I get with regard to community development. Do not be afraid to take risks and fail. In fact, failing publicly—though scary—is a great way to endear yourself to others.

the Parks and Recreation Association of Canada (PRAC) in 1945. PRAC's mandate was "the Dominion-wide stimulation of recreation, [and] the Dominion-wide extension of parks including municipal, provincial and national parks and recreation activities" (Parks and Recreation Association of Canada, 1947). As the organization adapted to changes in the environment in the 1960s, it changed its name first to the Canadian Parks/Recreation Association (CP/RA) in 1969 and later refined it to the Canadian Parks and Recreation Association (CPRA). CPRA promotes itself as "a national organization dedicated to realizing the full potential of parks and recreation as a major contributor to community health and vibrancy," with 90% of Canadian communities containing affiliated service providers. (Canadian Parks and Recreation Association, 2023). Today CPRA provides services through its partnership with provincial or territorial organizations, each of which is autonomous and offers services in keeping with its local requirements. Table 7.2 in HK*Propel* lists the national, provincial, and territorial associations.

CHAMELEON PROFESSION: EVER-CHANGING SOCIETAL ISSUES AND NEEDS

Being a chameleon is often viewed in a negative sense, perhaps as selling out to external influences, but in the case of the public recreation profession, it is positive. We must be adaptable. We must respond to changes in physical, economic, political, or social parts of the environment. But we must not lose sight of our founding roots, our reasons for being, and our desire to contribute to the public good. What is the future of public-sector recreation and leisure? To discover where we are headed, we must understand the current reality.

Demographic Trends

Labor, leisure, and longevity trends affect how much unobligated time people have and how they use it. These trends in turn affect recreation and leisure services and professionals who provide them. Our aging, retired population is growing, and people aged 50 years and older have more free time today than they did in previous eras.

As leisure patterns in North America continue to change, one of the best predictors of change is our aging citizens, who are more active than ever before. In addition, urban areas are becoming more diverse. More people are pursuing higher levels of formal education, and women are taking on increasingly diverse roles. The gap between the haves and the have-nots is widening. Citizens expect the government to do more, but they want to pay less. People are obsessed with health, but citizens of the United States and Canada are now more obese than ever, especially the younger age groups. All this means that recreation and leisure service professionals must deal with a wide set of issues when creating programs, making plans, and obtaining resources and funding.

Trends in Canadian Public Recreation

Statistics Canada's 2021 census yields the following insights into the current population and the trends that affect employees of Canadian recreation agencies and the people whom they serve:

Age-related demographics

- The number of seniors (those aged 65 and older) increased 18 percent between 2016 and 2021 to 7.08 million. Seniors accounted for a record high of 19 percent of the population in Canada in 2021, up from 17 percent five years earlier.
- In 2021, the proportion of seniors was the highest in the Atlantic provinces (Newfoundland and Labrador, Prince Edward Island, Nova Scotia, and New Brunswick), Quebec, and British Columbia.
- In 2021, the proportion of children was highest in the Prairie provinces (Manitoba, Saskatchewan, and Alberta) and the territories (Northwest Territories and Nunavut) (Statistics Canada, 2021).

Immigration

- Almost one in four citizens of Canada are immigrants.
- Among the G7 countries, Canada had the highest percentage of foreign-born people (23%) the main source of population growth in Canada (Statistics Canada, 2021).

Aboriginal people

- In 2016, the Aboriginal population (First Nations, Métis, Inuit) in Canada reached 1,673,785—a growth of 19.5 percent since 2011.
- This growth rate is nearly four times greater than the increase for the non-Aboriginal population (Statistics Canada, 2017).

- Approximately one third of Aboriginal children are aged 14 and younger in Canada in 2016. These children represented 29 percent of the total Aboriginal population.
- Over 56 percent of the Aboriginal population lives in urban areas such as Winnipeg, Edmonton, Vancouver, Toronto, Calgary, Saskatoon, and Regina (Indigenous and Northern Affairs Canada, 2016).

Age-related demographics affect the recreation service delivery needed to provide opportunities that are innovative and stimulating to all age groups while not stereotyping seniors as a monolithic age group. While this is an opportunity, there is also a substantial challenge in many geographic areas as the proportion of the population in their working years declines often due to out-migration to growth centers in other parts of the country and abroad. This has an impact on local and provincial tax bases that support recreation services.

Despite the efforts of many communities to provide recreation services to new immigrants, the diverse mosaic of traditions, needs, interests, and expectations causes challenges. There are many barriers to participation such as high fees and related costs, insufficient funding, difficulties in finding information, and linguistic and cultural barriers (Social Planning Toronto, 2016). There are numerous examples of diverse recreation programs in cities with a substantial multicultural makeup. One example is the Sunset Community Centre in Vancouver, which serves over 36,000 residents with first languages including Panjabi, Chinese, Tagalog, Hindi, Vietnamese, and English (Vancouver, n.d.). The Centre has a vision of being "a healthy community where diverse cultures thrive, everyone belongs, and feels welcome to play, create and succeed in their own way" (Sunset Community Association, 2016, p. 8).

In much of Canada, the life experiences of the Aboriginal population are major social and political issues, and agencies and governments struggle to address the issues of a growing, young Aboriginal population on reserves and in urban areas. As noted earlier, the Aboriginal population is growing faster than the non-Aboriginal population. Aboriginal youth are not well served by the traditional urban recreation delivery systems, and new initiatives are being developed, such as the Winnipeg Broadway Community Centre's programs that serve a large Aboriginal population (Broadway Neighbourhood Centre, n.d.). Work must continue not only in delivering services on and off reserves but in training Aboriginal leaders and getting them into the recreation profession.

Trends in U.S. Public Recreation

The pace of change in today's world is accelerating, and leisure patterns and recreation needs will continue to change as well. If the public sector does not embrace the changes within recreation, nonprofits and the private sector will become the dominant providers. In some markets, such as fitness, they already are.

The biggest challenges facing leisure services in the United States today center on a changing population and the development of new programs that can meet the needs of the populace. Much work needs to be done not only in program development but also in operations and facilities to prepare for these challenges. To date, public recreation agencies have identified the need to adjust core thinking, but little real headway has been made.

Public-sector agencies need to address the following critical trends in the 21st century:

- The general population is becoming more culturally and racially diverse.
- The population is mobile, and there is substantial internal and economic migration in response to national and global economic fluctuations.
- Seniors are becoming a significant group needing innovative programming ideas that can provide rewarding leisure experiences.
- Young adults are seeking new ways to recreate.
- Health concerns due to the obesity epidemic continue to make headlines while the population becomes more sedentary.
- Children's programs are geared for active recreation activities to keep them fit.
- Nature-deficit disorder and the need to reconnect with nature are increasingly recognized issues.
- The discussion about safety versus overprotection and the perception of "bubble-wrapping" children continues.
- Agencies need to embrace private-sector product models and respond quicker to market changes.
- Governments need to invest in replacing deteriorating parks and recreation infrastructure.
- Strategies need to be developed to combat shrinking budgets relative to increasing costs.

Community Schools

Introduction to and instruction in recreation activities have long been considered essential elements of a well-rounded K-12 curriculum. Recreation activities have been vital not only to nurturing strength, flexibility, and self-esteem in young people but also to furthering educational achievement. **Community education** responds to a need to provide young people with constructive activities. Through participation in community education, such as in after-school and evening classes and activities and programs at schools, students can further enhance their strength, flexibility, self-esteem, and academic performance.

The following six components make up the philosophy of community education. Each component is vital to an effective, comprehensive community school.

1. *Community involvement*. Building a feeling of inclusion among community members by providing encouragement and opportunities for involvement and leadership in the development of community school activities
2. *Facility use*. Making use of existing school facilities that are owned by the taxpayers
3. *Adult programming*. Organizing and implementing classes and activities requested and designed by adults in the community and that appeal to their needs
4. *Youth programming*. Organizing and imple-

menting classes and activities requested and designed by young people in the community and that appeal to their needs
5. *Classroom enrichment through community resources*. Augmenting and enriching classroom curriculum and lessons by requesting the expertise and passion of knowledgeable speakers who live in the community and scheduling hands-on learning opportunities during the school day through field trips to community sites
6. *Coordination and cooperation in the delivery of community services*. Bringing together people who are involved in similar pursuits to benefit the entire community, thus avoiding duplication of effort and resolving issues

The community education concept was originally grounded in involvement and participation, and this has been the hallmark of its extended success. The practice of community education invited a new, collaborative spirit to the old model of program development. It promoted a process in which people could become involved rather than simply attending an event. This application in the development of community school services offered a seat at the table for all members of the community including adults, youth, senior citizens, people with disabilities, and people of all cultural backgrounds, and faiths.

Current Conditions of Community Education

Over the years, community education has continued to provide programs and activities that are driven by expressed community needs and has involved community members in meaningful leadership roles that enrich community living. Community school advisory councils and advisory boards have become important components of successful community schools that provide the foundation, voice, and representation for community members and community organizations (individuals, schools, businesses, and public and private organizations) to become partners in addressing community needs.

Community education advisory councils and boards became incubators for site-based leadership, a model used across the country in school reform efforts. And the influence did not end there. Community participation in education issues and

school reform has been embraced by school districts from shore to shore and has become part of the institutional culture of those organizations. In the United States, the influence of education reform has been seen in federally funded programs, such as 21st Century Community Learning Centers and the No Child Left Behind Act, all of which highlight activities that enhance academic achievement, literacy, and the unique needs of urban and rural communities.

The original community education model was founded on components that provide for the delivery of quality programs, activities, and services; the development of leadership; the shared use of school and community facilities; the integration of resources into the K-12 classroom curriculum; and the conversations necessary to achieve collaborative and inclusive relationships, all of which are

(continued)

Community Schools *(continued)*

driven by the desire to respond to identified needs. When all these components are given equal voice in a community school, the result is a balanced program that invites participation and welcomes diverse activities that meet the comprehensive needs of the community. When attention is cast on just one or two of these elements, a threat to the full capacity of the model arises.

Careers in Community Education

The following skills are needed for professional entry-level positions in community schools: volunteer management; publicity, promotion, and marketing; programming; funding and resource development; demonstrated leadership ability; group-process skills; customer service skills; positive attitude; sense of humor; and ability to build, maintain, and deepen relationships with community members, businesses, and organizations.

The following are some of the types of community education positions available: community college continuing education coordinator or director, community school coordinator or director, community education agent, school business partnership director, service learning coordinator, volunteer manager, facilities scheduling manager, community resources center manager or director, and community school or community learning center grant manager.

- Parks and recreation can become an economic engine through wise investment in increasing tourism and by providing a higher quality of life.

Parks and recreation professionals in the United States and Canada need to understand these new demographics. The traditional ways of providing park and leisure services need to change to match the ever-changing public.

Tomorrow's Leadership Skills

The changing profession and the trends facing public recreation require new leadership skills to lead public recreation into the future. What does the new breed of professionals entering the public sector look like? Can they make a difference? New leaders need to innovate as the pioneers of parks and recreation did a century ago. Now is the time for strong leadership to act. Public recreation has grown steadily because advances in technology have given people more free time. The real quest is to use ongoing research to define what public recreation will become. Making tough decisions will be easier when research is used to validate the direction on a given topic.

The ability to grow leisure service offerings by understanding the needs of the population has led many public agencies to find untapped markets. Capital construction costs are generally lower during times of recession and projects are delivered

under budget and ahead of schedule. All this is made possible by the valor to act. Now more than ever is the time to build on our ability to deliver quality of life by practicing what we do best.

The Changing Profession

While there is no guarantee of what the future might hold, the future of public leisure and recreation seems to lead to a greater interest in the environment. People now seem to be more interested in the quality of the experience and a sense of place. More diversity of leisure expression is likely to occur because the population is becoming more diverse.

The types of programs needed to meet the demands of the public are becoming more diverse based on several factors. The standard focus on youth and athletics programs is still popular, but senior, adult-only, family, and fitness-based recreation are requested more often. New ideas need to be created to address these growing interests. Communities are becoming more polarized, and recreation services that fall in the middle of the general population are less able to meet all needs.

Because state and federal funding of recreation and leisure services are declining, these services will be more locally focused. Citizens want local assistance in enhancing their quality of life. Providing parks and recreation services for all ages and diverse populations is critical. For example, citizens want the local parks and recreation agency to provide parks, various programs, and facilities. Therefore, recreation agencies need to be flexible and innovative in their work efforts including staff assignments, decision making, training programs, and the knowledge, skills, and abilities needed to do the job.

Finally, outsourcing may become the norm instead of the exception. Recreation and leisure service agencies may become more enterprising than they have been in the past. The customization of leisure programs in which people are treated appropriately, not equally, will be necessary to retain community consumers. For instance, additional strategic planning will be necessary to place appropriate, applicable facilities and programs in a community based on numbers and needs. This means that the squeaky wheel may not get the grease. In the past, different areas of a community were often treated as though their needs were all the same. This effort created more amenities but was not necessarily a strategic approach that addressed real needs.

As the members of diverse communities request more and different services, recreation and leisure professionals need to address emerging trends and issues to meet the ever-changing needs and expectations of their clientele. As services continue to evolve, parks and recreation professionals will create the future.

The Changing Professional

The profession of public recreation is at a crossroads. As with all careers, the growth of the profession is fueled by economics. Unfortunately, many public recreation agencies have had a hard time keeping budgets in pace with the demand for recreation services in times of recession or low economic growth. The amount of professional skill needed for those within the field is different from in years past. The baseline standard of education within the field is moving past a bachelor's degree to a master's degree. The public is also more sophisticated and is armed with knowledge obtained from the Internet.

The new frontier in public recreation is building an organization that can be adaptable in a changing landscape. This is a contradiction in the public recreation realm. Governments are historically slow to react and are set in a traditional hierarchical operational model. The future professional can monitor the public in ways not thought of in the past and can communicate quickly using technology applications such as social media. Research will allow professionals to understand the will of the public and produce better decisions. Public recreation professionals need to invest in continuing education to keep skills sharp and learn about new tools that will allow them to work smarter. All agencies are being asked to do more with fewer resources. Professionals in the field today face several major issues:

- How to secure financing for major capital initiatives including parks, facilities, and open spaces
- How to set spending priorities with shrinking budgets
- How to make parks safe while maintaining visitor enjoyment
- How public parks and recreation can strengthen its political position by shaping community quality of life

Parks and recreation professionals will need to understand finances and budget better than they did in years past. The ability to execute two critical activities, leading and managing, will be important. The distinction is that management is doing things right, whereas leadership is doing the right things. The ability to provide strong leadership for the organization will be a necessary trait for professional success.

POLITICAL REALITIES: NO PAIN, NO GAIN

To many novices in recreation, the words *politics* and *politicians* are incredibly negative. Why? The reality of public recreation is that the ultimate decision makers are often elected officials, and it is we who elect them. In the abstract, the challenge and the role of public recreation are to serve all of us. But does this really happen? And who is *us*? Is it realistic to believe that the public recreation system can serve all? Who takes up the challenge to try to serve all? Can they succeed? Is recreation really a public good?

Public recreation is about creating a sense of inclusion. Are you prepared to listen to and assist everyone in your community? You should be. How will you deal with competing interests? Think about a small community park. How many groups with competing interests can you imagine want to use that park? How about young soccer players and their parents, older aggressive soccer players, baseball players of all ages, parents of small children, dog walkers, neighbors who want peace and quiet, neighbors who want a pretty park to enhance their property values, kids who want a place to splash in the hot summer, teenagers who want a place to hang out, musicians who want a place to jam, skateboarders who want a place to practice stunts, pacifists who want a place to protest against a war, a theater group that wants a place to perform, a religious group that wants to perform a religious play, a new immigrant group who wants to commemorate their culture's heritage, a group of Indigenous people who want to celebrate a sacred ritual, or people experiencing homelessness who want a place to hunker down at night?

Balance will always be needed between the requests of communities and the other desires or actions that political powers believe need attention. Somewhere in the middle of the issue are the parks and recreation staff members who will try to resolve the situation or create a win–win scenario. This is what we do.

Leaders in the recreation profession need to realize that political responsiveness becomes more difficult and complex as the size and diversity of the population grow and as the polarization of politics continues to increase in our society. Problems of political responsiveness are most likely found in one of two types of settings. The first and most widely recognized is the scenario in which a new group either moves into a community or rapidly increases its percentage of community members. One example of this is the growth of youth soccer and parents' desire for more fields and amenities. Difficulties are frequently encountered in accommodating the views and attitudes of the new group in policy-making processes. The second setting is one in which the community experiences rapid population growth that outpaces the ability to provide resources and facilities. This setting further identifies the city with the haves and the have-nots.

What role can interest groups play in obtaining recreation services? Interest groups can be powerful, vocal advocates for recreation services, or they can be adversaries. They can publicly address issues that a recreation staff member cannot. They can provide a public face for those who need services. They can provide the political face for the agency. Recreation professionals must decide how they will work with interest groups. That brings us right back to the question of whom do we serve?

The public recreation profession in the United States began with the advocacy work of Joseph Lee, the father of the playground movement. In the late 1800s, he helped create the first model playground in a dejected Boston neighborhood. Lee was con-

vinced that all young people needed a place to play. He promoted a bill in the Massachusetts state legislature that required towns and cities with populations of more than 10,000 to develop playgrounds. Joseph Lee's actions set the stage for future actions by other state and local governments. This example illustrates how powerful a citizen with a cause can be and the difference a committed person can make.

When we think about developing the work that we do, we must begin with our community members. We work with many members of diverse communities to help them experience, in some form or fashion, a better quality of life. That is why we provide services, activities, and events. That is why we build facilities. That is the very reason that we exist as a profession.

BENEFITS OF RECREATION

Since the foundation work of Joseph Lee in the United States and the National Council of Women of Canada more than a century ago, we have intuitively known that recreation benefits people and their communities. But we must go beyond intuition to research. The Benefits Project collected past research about how parks and recreation helps people, their communities, and the environment. The product of this collection was the online National Benefits Hub, which took collections of research studies and packaged them into a form that could be used in the political arena. The National Benefits Hub presented benefits in four main categories and eight subcategories:

- Personal (health, human development, individual quality of life)
- Social (community quality of life, antisocial behavior, families and communities)
- Economic (prevention, economic impact)
- Environmental benefits of recreation

The Benefits Project was created to address a substantial political issue: the perception, more real than imagined, that recreation services, although important to our communities, are not considered essential by decision makers. This is our biggest challenge as we strive to contribute to the public good.

Strong public recreation delivery systems that provide the core benefits of recreation are crucial to helping people lead healthier lives and to protecting natural resources and quality of life in our communities. As parks and recreation professionals, we must educate the public about why we provide one of the most cost-effective and essential quality-of-life services around. Research is continuing to advance in this area. As noted earlier, the technology available to us is continuing to influence many facets of our lives. The natural human desire to play outside is still evident even though technology has changed the way we think about recreation. Public recreation allows us to reconnect with the outdoors. In 2007, the Outdoor Recreation Research and Education strategic plan conducted by the USDA Forest Service noted that outdoor recreation has increased in the United States. The opportunities to experience nature are becoming more valued in the 21st century.

Three core components should be noted and continually explored through research and practical practice:

1. Public recreation should provide access to recreation for all.

2. Public recreation should provide opportunities to live a healthy lifestyle through physical activity. Parks and recreation agencies have the parks and facilities to support physical activity.

3. Public recreation is essential to lifelong learning through the inherent nature of its diverse programs.

SUMMARY

Most parks, open spaces, facilities, and recreation activities that people can participate in are from the public sector. Several powerful trends are affecting public recreation. New leadership is needed to meet the future needs of the public. Special interest groups are more vocal than ever and are seeking partnerships that can advance leisure services. The political realm is not to be understated. The challenge in seeking adequate funding in tight budget cycles and severe economic downturns is causing stress in the public recreation system.

Public recreation provides an exhilarating opportunity for public service and offers challenges, benefits, and opportunities to make a difference. The profession can touch many segments of the community and provide quality moments of career satisfaction. Finally, the opportunity to become a pioneer within the industry by trailblazing new frontiers is certainly available. The countless opportunities available to make a difference mean that today is a wonderful time to be in the field of public recreation.

Inclusive Recreation

Terry Long

The importance of inclusive public recreation is a relatively new idea within society; institutionalization was the norm well into the 1980s. The latter part of the 20th century brought the American civil rights movement, which challenged norms of institutionalization and segregation, but the rights of people with disabilities were the last to be addressed in the battle for equality. Early disability rights legislation included the Rehabilitation Act of 1973 and the Education for All Handicapped Children Act of 1975, but these initial efforts fell short of addressing the concept of **social inclusion** or inclusive recreation. The Americans with Disabilities Act (ADA, 1990) was the first meaningful legislation in the United States that guaranteed the right to accessible and inclusive public recreation.

When ADA became law, the immediate focus fell mostly on physical accessibility of built environments. Municipal parks and recreation agencies scrambled to determine the financial impact of

updating facilities to meet ADA code. Despite the worry, public parks and recreation agencies were able to withstand the financial impact of the ADA mandates regarding built spaces. Older public facilities were grandfathered in, and most changes came with new construction or remodels. Codes specific to recreation facilities took over a decade to be developed and were gradually implemented. As a result, it was well into the 21st century before communities began to evolve into navigable environments for people with disabilities. Still, ADA was pivotal in the development of physically accessible recreation facilities and spaces.

The greater challenge for public parks and recreation came with ensuring that the programs delivered within the facilities were accessible. It was no longer acceptable to deny participation to a person with a disability simply because it was an inconvenience. The ADA required public recreation agencies in the United States to provide access to

Andrea Obzerova/iStockphoto/Getty Images

The ADA required public entities to improve accessibility for people with disabilities. Many facilities installed ramps and implemented other changes to built environments in order to improve physical accessibility.

all government programs. Furthermore, the law states that participation should occur in the most integrated setting possible. In essence, ADA mandated that people with disabilities be given the opportunity to participate in the same recreation programs as the general public. As a result, every public recreation facility in the United States has the responsibility of providing inclusive recreation services to all citizens, regardless of disability. As one might expect, there are limitations to the law. The following section will clarify some key terminology and elaborate on the details of what it means to provide inclusive public recreation programs.

BUILDING BLOCKS OF INCLUSION

There are three important concepts that are interrelated but uniquely important to the delivery of inclusive recreation and leisure services: access, accommodation, and adaptation. These do not ensure inclusion, but they are necessary elements of inclusive recreation.

Access

Accessibility is a building block for the provision of inclusive recreation opportunities, and it is relevant to facilities and programs. Accessible facilities allow a person to physically navigate and engage with the environment and all its elements. In the early days of the ADA, it was common to hear people explain the requirements regarding accessibility by saying, "if you turned the facility upside down, everything that doesn't fall off has to be accessible." This is an inaccurate statement when it comes to true accessibility. Accessible parking, entryways, bathrooms, and signage are all important, but so are moveable objects such as furniture and fitness equipment and written materials such as brochures. In addition, a facility can be built to be accessible, but simple mistakes such as placing a heavy step stool in front of an accessible water fountain can quickly compromise access. Another common mistake is blocking accessible routes with boxes or other items, which make it impossible to navigate a wheelchair through the area. Professionals must understand what makes a facility accessible so they do not inadvertently compromise accessibility. Of course, an accessible facility is of little use if the programs taking place inside the facility are inaccessible. The fundamental principle regarding program access is that individuals cannot be turned away simply because they have a disability. Furthermore, specialized (segregated) programming is not an automatically acceptable alternative. Every effort should be made to ensure that programs and services are provided in the most integrated setting possible.

Accommodation

Program access is often best achieved through appropriate **accommodation**, which is the removal of barriers that otherwise might prevent participation. For example, a deaf participant should be provided an interpreter during the recreation programs that they take part in; a child with an autism spectrum disorder might be accompanied by a buddy during certain activities to facilitate social interactions and behaviors; or a participant is allowed to use crutches or a wheelchair on the field during a youth softball game. The ADA requires that "reasonable" accommodations be provided to patrons of public recreation programs. Typically, accommodation requests are granted, but the following are several circumstances in which accommodations might be denied:

- The accommodation changes the inherent nature of the activity.
- The accommodation presents a safety risk to participants or others.
- The accommodation presents an undue financial hardship.
- The accommodation presents an undue administrative hardship.

Each limitation should be considered closely before declining a requested accommodation, but there are times when an accommodation might not be appropriate. For example, a tackle football league is not required to remove tackling to accommodate an individual who is at high risk of injury from being tackled. This would change the inherent nature of the game. Agencies do, however, have the option of providing accommodations beyond what the law requires. For example, some agencies choose to manage participant medications or provide diapering services during programs, both of which are beyond what public parks and recreation agencies are typically required to provide. In addition, it should be noted that any services provided

to the public should also be provided to people with disabilities. For example, if administration of medication or transportation are services provided to all program participants, then the agency must provide equivalent services to a person with a disability. Failure to do so constitutes discrimination and is a violation of ADA.

Adaptation

Adaptation is similar to accommodations but is typically tied to a specific activity. For example, providing an interpreter is an accommodation, but it does not change the way that the recreational activity is performed. Adaptations usually target an element of an activity that is problematic for the participant. Using a lighter ball to play catch, using a shorter golf club to hit a golf ball from a chair, or making a no strikeout rule during a Wiffle ball game are all examples of adaptations. Adaptations can involve the rules of the game, the equipment used, the surrounding environment, or any other factor that affects the nature of the game.

Adaptations can be counterproductive if they are not actually necessary and if they change the inherent nature of the activity beyond what is acceptable to participants. For example, it is inappropriate to alter the difficulty of a softball game by using a tee for batting if participants are perfectly capable of hitting a ball out of the air. Likewise, moving a water polo game to the shallow end would significantly change the skill set required when playing, which would be concerning to participants in a competitive polo league. Adaptations should only be made to the extent that they are necessary, and they should not compromise the experience of other participants.

DEFINING INCLUSION

On the surface, inclusion is often seen as occurring when persons with and without disabilities participate in an activity together. The ADA's mandate that programs must be provided in the most integrated setting possible affirms this perspective. Most public recreation agencies differentiate inclusive and specialized programs based on the extent to which this integration occurs. This distinction is by no means bad, but it has limitations because too much focus is often placed on physical presence rather than the lived experience of participants. Being present does not ensure true inclusion.

Successful delivery of genuinely inclusive recreation programs requires that the following considerations be kept in mind at all times. First, true inclusion involves genuine relationships that are mutually beneficial. This synergistic relationship between participants is sometimes referred to as **social inclusion**. Simply putting people into a room together will not naturally lead to positive interactions, especially if some members tend to stigmatize others based on disability.

Second, inclusion involves a mutually respectful relationship with the surrounding culture. Hironaka-Juteau and Crawford (2010) describe inclusion as a "cultural characteristic whereby that culture is characterized by attitudes and behaviors that are open and accepting of all people" (p. 4). This cultural inclusion can expand beyond the participants as an activity or event develops a place of status within society. For example, quad rugby gained a substantial fan following after the release of the *Murderball* documentary. Musical group the Blind Boys of Alabama started singing in the school chorus at the Alabama Institute for the Negro Blind in 1939; eventually other world-famous musicians sought to collaborate with this Grammy-winning group that is an inherent part of the music culture that is respected by their peers. Thus, inclusion is beyond a simple distinction between participating together (inclusion) or separately (segregated). As these examples illustrate, even programs that involve primarily participants with disabilities can be part of a broader inclusive culture as others accept the participants and their activity as legitimate and either peripherally or directly engage in associated activities.

SPECIALIZED PROGRAMS

Facilities can be accessible and accommodations can be provided, but the experiences might still occur in segregated environments. As previously noted, specialized programs can exist in the context of a broader inclusive environment. In some cases, segregated activities will be ideal when they are specialized to meet the participant's needs. In fact, specialized programs are very common and are allowed under the ADA when they are preferred by the participant or when accommodations are beyond reasonable limits; however, best practice is to strive for inclusion whenever possible.

It has been noted that the best way to provide recreation services to people with disabilities is through a continuum of opportunities ranging from most restrictive to least restrictive (Stanton et al., 2013). The level of support needed, as well as the appropriateness and desirability of an inclusive program, will vary based on the circumstances of the participant. Ultimately, we want to provide an experience that is as typical as possible without compromising participants' welfare. Knowing this, sometimes specialized programs are necessary or preferred by the participant. Keep in mind that even when participation is specialized, the surrounding culture can be socially inclusive. Competitive sport for people with disabilities is an example. Although athletes may compete in specialized divisions (e.g., wheelchair vs. traditional basketball), the environment surrounding the sport can be socially and culturally inclusive. Athletes and fans respect the accomplishments of athletes in the same manner regardless of what division they compete in. The same can be said for arts programs. Dance, theater, art, and music can all be performed or exhibited within a culture of inclusion. The following sections highlight some of the specialized programs that serve particular groups of participants.

Disability and Adapted Sport

Formal sports programs for people with disabilities exist in a variety of forms, but there are two important perspectives to consider. First, **disability sports** programs are designed specifically for people with disabilities. There is a continuum of participation levels from introductory skills to elite competition that allows an athlete to develop their ability (Davis, 2010). Various sport clubs and associations exist for athletes, providing them with opportunities to compete against others with similar competition classifications. An athlete's classification can be based on disability and skill level, depending on the sport. Athletes competing in disability sport at the highest level take part in the Paralympics, which will be discussed later.

In contrast, **adapted sports** programs are more likely to be associated with interscholastic opportunities for participation (Davis, 2010). These programs are analogous to traditional interscholastic competitions and may involve similar rewards such as earning a letter or winning a state championship. Community-based programs in adapted sport also exist through public parks and recreation agencies or nonprofit organizations like the YMCA, which offer developmental or competitive leagues to local residents. Rule adaptations are more likely to occur in adapted sport; this allows the organizers to adjust the level of challenge and competition to meet the abilities of the participants. In disability sports programs it is less likely that formal regulations will be modified, particularly at higher levels of competition.

Special Olympics

Special Olympics provides opportunities for people with intellectual disabilities and autism to participate in sport and fitness activities. The first Special Olympics event was held in Chicago at Soldier Field in 1968 through the collaborative efforts of the Chicago Park District and the Joseph P. Kennedy Jr. Foundation. As of 2022, Special Olympics is an international organization and event that includes more than 3 million athletes and almost 300,000 coaches and volunteers in over 200 countries worldwide (Special Olympics, n.d.).

Participants must be 8 years of age or older to participate, but there is a Junior Special Olympics program for kids aged 2 to 7. Competitors in individual sports play in divisions based on age, gender, and ability level. Traditional sports include track and field, team sports such as basketball and volleyball, swimming, and some wheelchair events.

In addition, Special Olympics has developed the Motor Activity Training Program (MATP), which is a basic skill-development program for individuals whose skills do not allow them to compete in tra-ditional Special Olympics programs. MATP focuses on developing sport-specific skills for individuals with severe or profound intellectual disabilities or significant physical disabilities. Coaches work with athletes to master skills associated with traditional Special Olympics competition. Areas of training include mobility, dexterity, striking, kicking, manual wheelchair, electric wheelchair, and swimming. This expansion of programming offered by Special Olympics is another example of the spectrum of specialized to inclusive recreation.

Special Olympics also offers the Unified Sports program. This program allows teammates with and without intellectual disabilities to compete together against other similar teams. It is the most inclusive of all the Special Olympics programs. Unified Sports has grown out of the societal shift toward inclusion and the recognition of the limitations that exist within specialized recreation programs that do not offer opportunities for inclusive participation. Unified Sports is sometimes delivered as part of interscholastic sport at the junior high and high school level, and it can also be delivered outside of the schools. Resources and training are available

Jeff Greenberg/Universal Images Group Editorial/Getty Images

Special Olympics allows people with intellectual disabilities and autism to compete in athletics in an affirming environment.

through Special Olympics to assist professionals who would like to develop a Unified Sports or MATP program in their area.

Paralympics

The Paralympics are the highest level of competition for athletes with disabilities. The first Paralympic games were held in Rome in 1960 with about 400 wheelchair athletes taking part. In 2021, more than 4,400 athletes from 161 countries competed in 22 different sports during the summer games held in Tokyo, Japan. Athletes are classified in a variety of divisions across six primary disability categories: visual impairment, intellectual disability, cerebral palsy/traumatic brain injury, spinal cord injury, amputation, and les autres. Athletes must join the corresponding sport association associated with

their disability to qualify for Paralympic competition and then pursue qualifying competition advancement similar to Olympic athletes.

SUMMARY

Inclusion is an ideal, but it is also a reality in the daily work of thousands of public recreation professionals around the world. We are far from finishing our work to build a fully inclusive society, but good things are happening. Through the efforts of inclusion-minded recreation professionals, participants are being empowered to engage in genuine leisure experiences in social contexts that foster acceptance, belonging, and self-concept. Providing a diverse array of inclusive recreation opportunities will ultimately allow each member of society to experience the benefits that recreation and leisure can provide.

Review Questions

1. What are some of the pioneer programs in public parks and recreation?

2. What are some typical delivery systems for public parks and recreation in the United States and Canada?

3. What are some relevant professional organizations in public parks and recreation in the United States and Canada?

4. What are the building blocks of inclusion?

Go to HK*Propel* to complete the activities for this chapter.

CHAPTER 8

Nonprofit Sector

Robert F. Ashcraft

" Nonprofit activity is everywhere. It is hard to find a neighborhood without visible nonprofit presence . . . and impossible to find a neighborhood untouched by nonprofit work. "

Michael O'Neill, professor emeritus of nonprofit management and founder and former director of the Institute for Nonprofit Organization Management, University of San Francisco

Will Lester/MediaNews Group/Inland Valley Daily Bulletin via Getty Images

LEARNING OUTCOMES

After reading this chapter you should be able to do the following:

> Clarify the overall role and characteristics of the nonprofit sector in society
> Identify the types of national and community-based nonprofit recreation organizations
> Explain the role of the professional in nonprofit organizations
> Describe challenges and opportunities for the future

An understanding of recreation and leisure services is incomplete without examining the role of nonprofit-sector organizations. In neighborhoods and communities across North America, millions of people are served by, and give service to, public and **quasi-public entities**.

It is hard to imagine that anyone goes through life without being touched by a **nonprofit organization**. Historian and scholar David Mason noted the influence of nonprofits. When he received the Distinguished Lifetime Achievement Award from the Association for Research on Nonprofit Organizations and Voluntary Action, Mason made the following remarks to the luncheon group assembled in his honor:

> My values, attitudes, and behaviors, like most of yours, have been profoundly influenced by nonprofits. . . . My parents met when they were students in a nonprofit. I was born in one. I learned about God in one, my ABCs in another, how to play ball and be a team player in another, and met my first girlfriend in another. I prepared for my career at a nonprofit university, met my wife in a nonprofit church, went on to several nonprofit graduate schools, joined numerous nonprofit professional groups, brought two newly born sons home from nonprofit hospitals, and on and on it goes, including what I read, how I vote and my avocations. It weaves its way like a golden thread through the tapestry of my life. (Mason, 1999)

Similar stories can be told by millions of citizens, well before and long after Mason's remarks, who have been affected in comparable ways. The **nonprofit sector** is ubiquitous, so it is often taken for granted. Yet an examination of the sector reveals countless examples of how nonprofit organizations affect human lives.

Nonprofits (the social sector) have grown as part of the **three-sector model** of service delivery during the early 21st century; they complement recreation and leisure services provided by businesses that include, in part, private, commercial enterprise (the economic or market sector) and by government (the public, political sector). Whether people organize to serve their personal self-interests or to promote a broader public good, nonprofits are one way in which citizens often operate along with and sometimes outside the government and business sectors to improve the quality of life in communities. In addition, as a growing career field, the nonprofit sector has emerged as a vocational choice for increasing numbers of recreation professionals. According to Johns Hopkins Center for Civil Society Studies (2019), "Nonprofit employment is much larger than expected and much more widely dispersed, outdistancing many major industries in its contribution to state employment and payrolls. Nonprofit employment is dynamic, growing more rapidly than overall employment. Nonprofit employment is spreading to the suburbs and rural areas."

This chapter reveals the characteristics of nonprofit organizations in the United States and Canada, including their goals and functions, size and scope, and resource bases. The significance of the nonprofit sector is considered in ways that differentiate its service delivery approaches from those found within government or business recreation providers. A variety of types of nonprofit organizations are discussed, as are the professional opportunities that exist within such entities. Finally, the factors that influence the future of nonprofit organizations are addressed, which provides insight into collaborative ventures developing among organizations, the impact of the nonprofit sector in the United States and Canada, and the challenges and opportunities ahead for this important dimension of recreation and leisure service delivery systems.

NONPROFIT SECTOR IN THE UNITED STATES AND CANADA

Although examples of nonprofit-sector activities exist across all regions and countries in North America, it is difficult to make direct comparisons from one country to another. There are enormous variations in how nonprofit organizations are structured, how they are registered, and how they operate within the cultural, political, civic, and economic contexts of community life. There are also major differences in the terms used to describe entities that comprise the nonprofit sector. Different terms are found in nonprofit literature, including

- voluntary sector,
- not-for-profit sector,
- charitable sector,
- quasi-public sector,
- independent sector,
- third sector,
- civil society sector,
- social sector,
- nongovernmental organization sector,
- tax-exempt sector,
- social purpose sector, and
- nonprofit sector.

The terms underscore why understanding the nonprofit sector is a challenging task, given the variety of interpretations noted. However, these variations also suggest a robust and vibrant sector that accommodates diverse forms and expressions. In this chapter, the term *nonprofit* is used.

Nanus and Dobbs (1999), Salamon (2012), Powell and Bromley (2020), among other scholars, identify three primary sectors of society:

1. Economic (commerce, private, and publicly held businesses)
2. Political (public and government at all levels)
3. Social (nonprofits)

As noted in figure 8.1, these sectors are inextricably linked, and together they represent the variety of ways to organize and deliver recreation and leisure services. The sectors exist within a milieu of forces and forms that shape society.

Some nonprofits are widely recognized and provide ready access to their programs, financial statements, governance policies, and so on. However, thousands of small, grassroots, and community-based organizations are lesser known and go largely unexamined. To fully appreciate the nonprofit sector's role, one must consider this segment of recreation and leisure services in all its vastness and vagueness. One way to understand the range of the nonprofit form is to review what nonprofit organizations hold in common.

Common Characteristics of Nonprofit Organizations

Despite enormous variations, several characteristics apply generally to nonprofit organizations in Canada, the United States, and other countries around the world. According to nonprofit scholars such as Lester Salamon (1999), Michael O'Neill (2002), Frumkin (2002), Powell and Bromley (2020), and others, nonprofit entities share six common features:

1. *Organized.* They have an institutional presence and structure; there is an identifiable entity.
2. *Private.* They are separate from the state. Although they follow laws established by legislative bodies, these entities determine their own policies, programs, and services.
3. *Nondistribution constraint.* They do not return profits to their managers (e.g., board members, staff, and directors) or to a set of owners. Whereas publicly traded corporations have shareholders and government entities have voting constituents, nonprofit organizations consider a range of stakeholders when making decisions and providing services.
4. *Self-governing.* They are fundamentally in control of their own affairs.
5. *Voluntary.* Membership in them is not legally required, and they attract some level of voluntary contribution of time and money.
6. *Beneficial to the public.* They contribute to the public purpose and public good.

These characteristics apply to a wide range of recreation and leisure entities found within the nonprofit sector. Therefore, a small running club organized and financed by and for its members in a remote New England community in the United States is as much a part of the nonprofit sector as is the Red Cross, a large, multiservice, social service agency with operating units in Canada and the United States. Nonprofit organizations, therefore, are organized to serve public purposes or mutually beneficial purposes that improve the quality of life in communities.

The nonprofit organizational form is found throughout the recreation field from sport clubs to professional associations to direct service providers. Interestingly, nonprofit organizations and their activities affect people of all ages. Often the introduction to nonprofit organizations occurs through recreation programs such as Boy Scout and Girl Scout programs, YMCAs, Boys and Girls Clubs,

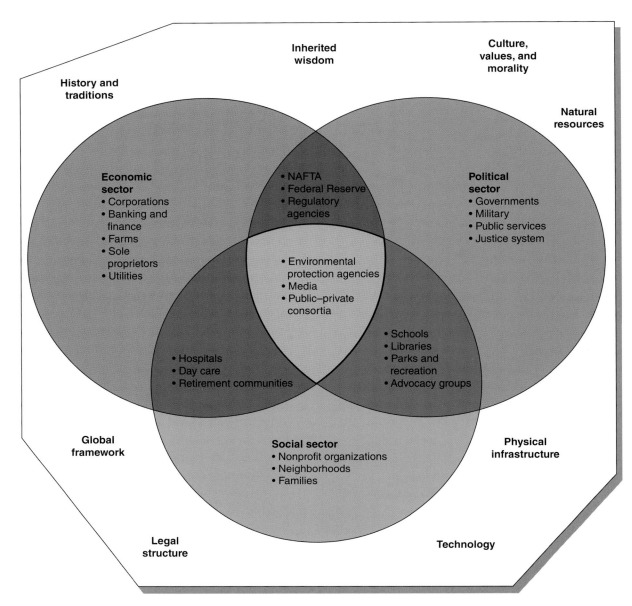

Figure 8.1 Three main sectors of society.

Adapted by permission from B. Nanus and S.M. Dobbs, *Leaders Who Make a Difference: Essential Strategies for Meeting the Nonprofit Challenge* (San Francisco: Jossey-Bass, 1999). Copyright 1999 John Wiley & Sons, Inc. Reprinted with permission of S.M. Dobbs.

Little League, and others. As interests and skills are developed through outlets such as camping programs, appreciation often grows for the outdoors. The Sierra Club, the Nature Conservancy, and the Trust for Public Land, among other environmental organizations, are nonprofit entities that advance specific mission-driven purposes that often appeal to those interested in outdoor recreation. Youth development and environmental entities are just two examples of recreation-based nonprofits that are part of a much larger collection of hundreds of thousands of organizations operating throughout

North America to advance both special-purpose and broadly based public benefit goals.

Goals and Functions

Given the vast array of activities and people that comprise the sector, it is not surprising that the goals and functions of nonprofit organizations are also varied. Such organizations often serve widely different needs and, at times, conflicting values. For example, one nonprofit may organize to protect a wilderness area by calling for the elimination of off-road vehicle use and another organizes to open the same area to such activity.

Often, however, nonprofit recreation and leisure services organizations share similar values between them and among government and business entities. After-school child care programs, for example, share overall goals regarding the education, safety, and recreation needs of children even though their delivery systems (programs, clientele, fee structure, and so on) are organized in different ways for various reasons.

Despite these variations, Salamon (1999) and Powell and Bromley (2020), among others suggest that the following two primary goals frame the orientation of most nonprofits:

1. *Public benefit*. Some nonprofits are organized specifically for social outcomes that appeal to a wide spectrum of population groups. Educational organizations, hospitals, muse-

ums, and community recreation centers are examples of public benefit nonprofits.

2. *Mutual benefit*. These nonprofits exist primarily to provide services to a limited number of members with common interests. Examples include business and professional associations, social clubs, and some golf clubs.

Nonprofits, therefore, are organized to serve both individual needs and broader community goals. Some are organized to conserve and preserve historical, cultural, environmental, and other traditions. Others are developed to advance social change with a focus on improving the well-being of disadvantaged and disenfranchised people who have been marginalized from mainstream community life. Figure 8.2 shows examples of nonprofit organizations across these various domains.

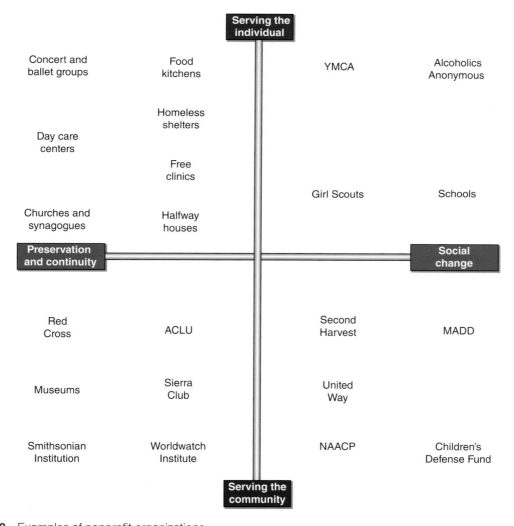

Figure 8.2   Examples of nonprofit organizations.

Organizational Framework

Because the nonprofit sector is so diverse and encompasses such a wide array of types and sizes of organizations, studying its structure and impact can be difficult. A typology known as the International Classification of Nonprofit Organizations (ICNPO), developed by researchers at Johns Hopkins University, and adopted by the United Nations in 2003 to guide global data analysis, facilitates understanding of the sector (Salamon & Anheier, 1996; United Nations, 2003). ICNPO divides nonprofits into 12 major activity groups and 24 subgroups according to the primary type of goods or services each one provides (e.g., recreation, environment, health). The following are the major activity groups:

1. *Culture and recreation*. Includes organizations and activities in general and specialized fields of culture and recreation

2. *Education and research*. Includes organizations and activities that administer, provide, promote, conduct, support, and service education and research

3. *Health*. Includes organizations that engage in health-related activities, provide health care (both general and specialized services), administer health care services, and provide health support services

4. *Social services*. Includes organizations and institutions that provide human and social services to a community or target population

5. *Environment*. Includes organizations that promote and provide services in environmental conservation, pollution control and prevention, environmental education and health, and animal protection

6. *Development and housing*. Includes organizations that promote programs and provide services to help improve communities and promote the economic and social well-being of society

7. *Law, advocacy, and politics*. Includes organizations and groups that work to protect and promote civil and other rights, advocate the social and political interests of general or special constituencies, offer legal services, and promote public safety

8. *Philanthropic intermediaries and voluntarism*. Includes philanthropic organizations and those that promote charity and charitable activities including grant-making foundations, voluntarism promotion and support, and fund-raising entities

9. *International*. Includes organizations that promote cultural understanding between peoples of various countries and historical backgrounds and also those that provide relief during emergencies and promote development and welfare abroad

10. *Religion*. Organizations that promote religious beliefs and administer religious services and rituals, including churches, mosques, synagogues, temples, shrines, seminaries, monasteries, and similar religious institutions, in addition to related organizations and auxiliaries of these organizations

11. *Business and professional associations and unions*. Includes organizations that promote, regulate, and safeguard business, professional, and labor interests

12. *Groups not classified elsewhere*.

Size and Scope

As previously noted, determining the size and scope of the nonprofit sector in North America remains difficult for several reasons. However, what is known suggests that nonprofits have played a larger role in the United States than in Canada or other countries. This fact in no way minimizes the importance of nonprofits outside the United States. However, given the size and scope of the sector in the United States, it is not surprising that nonprofit literature on recreation and leisure organizations frequently accentuates U.S. examples when examining nonprofit organizations and their purposes and approaches to service delivery.

Distinctive Characteristics of the Nonprofit Sector in Canada

Canada has no central registry for nonprofits, so what is known comes from those charities, as a subset of the overall nonprofit sector, that register with Revenue Canada (the government agency similar to the IRS in the United States). According to Imagine Canada there are an estimated 170,000 registered charities and nonprofits in Canada, and 86,000 of them are registered as official charities (Imagine Canada, 2022). According to Revenue Canada, a nonprofit organization (NPO) is "an association [that] must be both organized and operated exclusively for social welfare, civic improvement, pleasure or recreation or for any other purpose except profit" (Revenue Canada, 2021). Revenue Canada details these four categories as follows:

1. Social welfare nonprofits assist disadvantaged groups for the common good and for the general welfare of the community.

2. Civic improvement nonprofits are organized to enhance the value or quality of community or civic life.

3. Pleasure or recreation nonprofits are organized to provide a state of gratification or a means of refreshment or diversion.

4. The final category, which can serve any purpose except profit, is a generic grouping of associations that are organized for other noncommercial reasons.

As noted in the previous list, several categories account for the array of Canadian nonprofits that work to advance community life by providing services that address core social needs while advancing overall community well-being. They range from nonprofits that organize parks and museums for general community betterment to sport clubs for special interests such as golf, curling, and badminton that are organized and operated to provide recreational facilities for the enjoyment of members and their families.

An ongoing source of information about the Canadian nonprofit sector is Imagine Canada, a nonprofit launched in 2005 from a strategic alliance of the Canadian Centre for Philanthropy and the Coalition of National Voluntary Organizations. Imagine Canada seeks to fill the knowledge gap by working with charities, governments, and corporations to advance the role and interests of the charitable sector for the benefit of Canadian communities. The organization conducts and disseminates research, develops public policy, promotes public awareness, shares tools and standards, and encourages businesses to be more community minded.

Distinctive Characteristics of the Nonprofit Sector in the United States

As previously noted, the nonprofit sector in the United States is pervasive and robust. According to the National Center for Charitable Statistics (2019), there are approximately 1.54 million nonprofits in the United States. Of those, nearly 1.1 million are public charities and philanthropic organizations, encompassing about two thirds of all nonprofits. The IRS provides 27 types of tax-exempt organizations under Section 501(c) of the federal tax code. The National Center for Charitable Statistics (2015) reveals the major subcategories of the U.S. nonprofit sector as follows:

- *Charitable organizations.* Perhaps the most readily identifiable nonprofits are **charities**. As the largest segment of nonprofits in the United States, public charities are exempt from paying federal income tax under **Section 501(c)(3)** of the IRS tax code. However, most charitable nonprofits are subject to payroll and sales taxes. Diverse nonprofits comprise this category such as those that provide free services to vulnerable populations in soup kitchens and homeless shelters and those that provide wide community development and cultural enhancement activities such as hospitals, museums, and recreation centers. There are many "Friends" organizations in this category to support parks and recreation efforts. For example, the Friends of Buford Park and Mt. Pisgah in Eugene, Oregon, was founded in 1989 to support the ecological integrity of the nearly 2,400 acres (971 ha) that comprise the Howard Buford Recreation Area. Although it works in conjunction with the Lane County Parks Department, this friends group is organized separately. Thousands of such friends groups exist across the United States.

- *Foundations.* One way that individuals, organizations, and communities support causes that benefit society is through private, corporate, operating, or community **foundations**. These also operate as 501(c)(3) nonprofits, and their purposes and operating systems are as varied as those of public charities. Some foundations make grants to a range of community causes. These types of foundations encourage grant proposals from many different areas of the community including recreation and cultural causes. Other types of foundations, however, serve as a conduit for amassing resources to support their own programs and activities. Creating an operating foundation is one way that government parks and recreation programs generate private support for their public goals. There are several other structural variations of this complex nonprofit form.

- *Social welfare organizations.* Some nonprofits advocate for specific issues by lobbying legislators to advance social causes and by actively campaigning for political candidates. These nonprofits, known as *social welfare organizations,* are recognized as Section 501(c)(4) organizations. They are exempt under the tax code, but donations to these causes are not tax deductible. The National Rifle Association and the National Organization for Women are two examples of such organizations.

- *Professional and trade associations.* Nonprofits that promote business or professional interests comprise a collection of nonprofits known as *professional and trade associations.* They usually qualify for tax exemption under Section 501(c)(6) of the tax code, and they focus on the interests of specific industries or professions. They also may have broader community interests such as chambers of commerce or business leagues. Similar to advocacy organizations, donations to these associations are not tax deductible.

Hundreds of thousands of nonprofits are registered as associations in the United States, and depending on their specific mission, they fall within one of the 501(c) categories previously listed. Nonprofits formed as associations are of interest to the recreation professional and are worthy of expanded discussion in this chapter for two reasons. First, some professional associations, such as the National Recreation and Park Association, benefit the recreation professional by providing training, certifications, and a network of colleagues that assist in career success and advancement. Second, the association format is one way citizens organize around mutual interests. Frequently, these interests involve recreation, leisure, and sport pursuits.

According to the Center for Association Leadership as of 2022 nearly 67,000 trade and professional associations exist in the United States. The following are five of the largest membership associations and the total number of members for each:

- American Automobile Association (61,000,000) (American Automobile Association, n.d.)
- American Association of Retired Persons (38,000,000)
- National Education Association (3,000,000)
- National Rifle Association (5,000,000)
- YMCA of the USA (11,000,000) (YMCA, n.d.)

Several of these associations are directly applicable to recreation, sport, and leisure pursuits.

Resource Base

The resource base of a nonprofit includes all the sources of support that make its programs and services possible. Nonprofits derive their revenue from a combination of one or more sources. The following are the most common sources:

- *Membership fees*. These are fees charged to members, usually annually, in return for programs provided by the nonprofit in service to its members.
- *Program fees*. Participants pay fees for participating in specific programs. Depending on the nonprofit, program participants may or may not be members of the organization.

- *Private philanthropy*. Fund-raising from individuals, corporations, and foundations provides revenue to nonprofit organizations. The skills associated with cultivating donors, developing proposals, and securing gifts from a range of philanthropic stakeholders require increased sophistication because donations are an essential revenue source for many nonprofits.
- *Government grants*. Many nonprofits compete for and receive government grants from local, state, and federal agencies to provide services based on targeted community needs and priorities.
- *Interest income*. Nonprofits receive income from cash reserves and other unspent monies that are actively managed to maximize earnings until they are used for expenses. Some nonprofits have developed endowment funds that build assets so that the mission of the organization can continue into perpetuity.
- *Earned income*. For nonprofits that own facilities, earned income can occur through rental arrangements, admission fees, and other agreements that turn physical assets into revenue streams.
- *Sales income*. For many youth development organizations, sales from cookies, candy, and other products provide a dual benefit to the organization by providing programs through which young people learn to organize, implement plans, and reach goals, providing revenue for the organization.
- *Social enterprise*. A new and growing trend for some nonprofits is the creation of for-profit companies that channel profits back into their social cause.

Philanthropy in Nonprofit Organizations

Nonprofit organizations often intersect with our lives in deep and abiding ways through philanthropy. **Philanthropy** is the promotion of common good through voluntary action, voluntary association, and voluntary giving (Payton, 1988). Philanthropy is expressed in a variety of forms by people who freely give their money and time to the causes of their choice.

One way a sense of belonging and feelings are attached to nonprofit organizations is through acts of philanthropy. Mason (1999) noted that "when people describe their relationship to their employer, they state, 'I work for Exxon [now, ExxonMobil]. I am with Intel.'" However, he continued, "we reserve the 'belonging' for our voluntary enterprises" such as the nonprofit organizations that intersect our lives. Consider the following statements:

I *belong* to the YMCA.

I *am* a Boy Scout.

I *belong* to the Camelback Mountain Hiking Club.

I *am* a volunteer at the teen center.

The philanthropic tradition in the United States has been well documented. According to the National Center for Charitable Statistics (2019), an estimated 64.4 million American adults (25.1% of the population) volunteered, giving 7.8 billion hours of service worth $195 billion. According to Giving USA (2020), the amount of money given in 2019 is no less impressive; $490.64 billion was contributed through private philanthropy in 2019 by U.S. households when including both individual giving and bequests.

The philanthropic tradition in Canada has been studied as well. A research report released by Statistics Canada (2021) revealed that in 2018, 12.7 million Canadians (44% of the population) volunteered through a charitable or nonprofit organization. This number is the equivalent of almost 1.1 million full-time jobs. From a 2013 report, Statistics Canada reveals that 82 percent of Canadians aged 15 and older made direct financial donations to a charitable or other nonprofit organization, representing approximately 84 percent of the population and with an average annual donation amount of C$531.

These data reveal that contributors of time (volunteers) and money (financial donors) provide important resources that nurture, sustain, and bolster nonprofit recreation organizations. For example, in many nonprofit youth development organizations, volunteers serve as coaches, mentors, teachers, camp counselors, troop leaders, and board members. As financial donors they support cookie sales, donate to annual support campaigns, organize special events, and otherwise contribute income that is a vital part of organizational budgets. Such understanding of the role of giving and volunteering is an important consideration for recreation professionals in meeting the mission of their respective organization.

Given the importance of philanthropy to nonprofit organizations, a U.S. recreation professional who is responsible for coordinating volunteer programs or raising funds can benefit from a nationwide network of volunteer action centers. The Points of Light Global Network is comprised of volunteer-mobilizing organizations located in more than 200 cities and 37 countries around the world (n.d.). They help connect interested volunteers with organizations and activities. Many of the affiliates in the network operate under the name "Hands On" (e.g., Hands On Phoenix, Hands On Atlanta, Hands On Hong Kong, etc.). The centers across the United States are useful resources to recreation professionals interested in developing or expanding their volunteer program capacity.

In addition, two professional organizations advance competencies for volunteer management and fund-raising. The Council for Certification in Volunteer Administration (CCVA) articulates competencies, advances ethical practice, and promotes professional development and education to support volunteer managers. CCVA sponsors the certificate in volunteer administration (CVA) credential intended for those who lead and direct volunteer engagement in all types of organizations and settings. Similarly, the Association of Fundraising Professionals (AFP) provides training, research, and other support to those involved in fund-raising. Through AFP's credentialing program, qualified fund-raisers can earn the designation of certified fund-raising executive (CFRE), which attests to their knowledge, skill, and achievements.

TYPES OF NATIONAL AND COMMUNITY-BASED NONPROFIT RECREATION ORGANIZATIONS

As previously noted, more than a million organizations—large and small, formal and informal—exist within the U.S. and Canadian nonprofit sectors. Nonprofit organizations play a critical role in the recreational and cultural life of the United States. Salamon notes that

> many of the central recreational institutions of local communities—swimming clubs, tennis clubs, Little Leagues, country clubs—are nonprofit in form. Even more importantly, nonprofit organizations form the backbone of the nation's cultural life, producing most of the live theater, symphonic music, and opera, and providing venues for art and for cultural artifacts. (1999, p. 131)

Interestingly, the nonprofit form is often most potent when it is organized around individual special interests in collaboration with government and business to advance mutually agreed-on goals. Instances of these occurrences in the recreation field abound. One historical case example is that of Kartchner Caverns State Park located outside Benson, Arizona. The story is one of vision, leadership, and perseverance that is a lesson to those working with and through the nonprofit sector to realize long-term public good.

OUTSTANDING GRADUATE

Magdelena Saucedo

Background Information

Name: Magdelena Saucedo

Education: BS in nonprofit leadership and management from Arizona State University

Credentials: Certified Nonprofit Professional (CNP) from the Nonprofit Leadership Alliance

Awards: George F. Miller Outstanding Student Award from ASU's Nonprofit Leadership Alliance Student Association

Career Information

Position: Entrepreneur Program Manager

Organization: Boys and Girls Clubs of the Valley in Phoenix, Arizona

Organization mission: Boys and Girls Clubs of the Valley offers affordable after-school and summer programs for more than 16,000 young people. At clubs across the Phoenix metropolitan area, BGCAZ provides award-winning programs designed to change the lives of young people. For more than 75 years, BGCAZ has been creating equity and opportunity for youth through academic, social, and workforce opportunities. We help young people make healthy decisions and focus on social and emotional development to build resilient young adults. Most importantly, we work to develop strong character and leadership skills by creating positive connections to caring adults and their community.

Job description: At AZ YouthForce, a program of the Boys and Girls Clubs of the Valley, I support and manage our team who are coaching teens through paid internship opportunities with our partners in a youth workforce development program. We vet applicants and train them in essential skills in our workforce academy before they explore career pathways with a paid internship. Our case managers support them throughout the experience with a plan for success. Once an intern completes their internship, we provide alumni resources, professional development, and continued support. We work with youth aged 16 to 19, and our target populations are underresourced communities.

When I started my job, my supervisor connected me with potential mentors to meet with and interview. We're starting to build that network of mentors, people that our youth can see themselves in, whether that's a person of color or a fellow young person. Some of the mentors are people that are in the restaurant business, someone is a jeweler, another is in health and wellness as a yoga teacher. We try to reach out to people who have started their own businesses, and we also try to partner with different organizations in the space so we can work smarter, not harder.

Career path: I returned to school after working in youth mental health, at first to study public policy. But then I took a required course on nonprofits, and that class and my instructor became a turning point for me. I changed my major to nonprofit leadership and management and joined the nonprofit leadership alliance program to earn my certified nonprofit professional credential. Before I graduated, I joined Public Allies Arizona with the ASU Lodestar Center for philanthropy and nonprofit innovation. It's a national service program that partners with nonprofit organizations. When my placement was done, I got a job with St. Vincent de Paul helping them with their financials and then their homelessness prevention program. After about a year there, an alumna from Public Allies reached out about a new program they were starting at Boys and Girls Clubs of the Valley. I applied and got the job that I have now.

Likes and dislikes about the job: I enjoy being able to use my degree, certification, and experiences. I love supporting and empowering young people and seeing their growth. Our director and leadership are supportive of our team and encourage us to grow while staying within the boundaries of our mission. I'm learning so much and I'm challenged by the work, which is what I thrive on. I do not think I have any dislikes but more challenges. Our growth has been tremendous, so building our capacity to make our programs sustainable has been a challenge, and we are hoping to adapt and adjust this coming year.

Advice for Undergraduates

Be intentional about anything you do. Networking is huge. Somebody once told me to always leave a place better than when you came. I always try to do that. And understand and believe in what you do so that it never feels like a job. You're part of the solution. Adaptability is huge, especially with nonprofits. When I was in the nonprofit leadership alliance at ASU, that was always the consensus from alumni who spoke to us. If your job is program manager, well, you might also be helping coordinate volunteers and pitching in over here and over there. You have to be open to helping, learning, and growing. When you stop learning or growing, you're probably not really interested in this sector anymore.

First discovered in 1974 by Gary Tenen and Randy Tufts, the cave was kept secret for years to protect its natural and fragile beauty. Tenen and Tufts worked with several people and organizations to realize their dream of preserving their unique geological find, including a nonprofit, The Nature Conservancy, and a government entity, the Arizona State Parks Department, along with the private land owner on whose property the caverns were discovered. Following years of study and design, Kartchner Caverns opened in 1999 as a state park. Today, three sectors work together to sustain the caverns:

- Government (Arizona State Parks, which owns the land and administers the park)
- Business (Aramark Sports and Entertainment Services, which holds the contract for concessions at the park)
- Nonprofit (Friends of Kartchner Caverns State Park, which raises funds to support educational, scientific, and conservation programs)

Thousands of examples exist whereby nonprofit organizations help to nurture and sustain recreation settings in collaboration with government agencies and business enterprises.

Whether organized in direct collaboration with government and business or as largely independent entities, various types of national and community-based nonprofit recreation organizations produce significant social benefits. Some of these organizations are identified clearly by their mission, purpose, logo, and other features, and they have a history as a successful entity. Many are part of the essential delivery system of the recreation movement.

Nonprofits that are part of the recreation and leisure services arena can be generally categorized as follows:

- Voluntary youth-serving organizations
- Religious and faith-based organizations
- Social service and relief organizations
- Special populations–serving organizations
- Environmental and conservation organizations
- Associations
- Membership or service clubs and fraternal organizations

The mission and programs of some nonprofits cut across more than one category. The Salvation Army, for example, serves youth, is faith based, provides wide-ranging social services, and often serves special populations. In some communities, the local affiliate of the Boys and Girls Clubs of America resides inside a Salvation Army unit. It is helpful to consider these varied categorizations when thinking about the core missions of organizations and their targeted client or customer populations. A sampling of these organizations follows. Descriptions are derived directly from organization websites and materials provided by these organizations.

Voluntary Youth-Serving Organizations

More than 50 leading nonprofit youth and human services organizations across the United States belong to the National Collaboration for Youth, an affinity group of the National Assembly of Health and Human Service Organizations. Collectively, they serve more than 40 million young people. These organizations enlist more than 6 million volunteers to provide services and employ more than 100,000 paid staff. Many of the organizations use sport and recreation activities, community service, youth and adult partnerships, and other programming features to instill core values in their youth members. Some of these organizations are also organized with affiliates in Canada. A sampling of nonprofits with specific youth development goals include the following:

- *Big Brothers Big Sisters of America.* Founded in 1904, Big Brothers Big Sisters of America is the oldest and largest youth-mentoring organization in the United States. The organization serves over 109,000 youth aged 5 to 18 years through a network of over 230 agencies. Big Brothers Big Sisters promotes one-on-one mentoring relationships between capable adult volunteers and youth. The organization cites research studies revealing that mentoring relationships between positive adult role models and youth have lasting effects on children. Big Brothers Big Sisters of Canada was organized in 1921; similar to its U.S. counterpart, it is organized to provide high-quality volunteer-based mentoring programs to over 41,000 youth in more than 1,100 Canadian communities.

- *Boy Scouts of America.* The Boy Scouts of America was founded in the United States in 1910 with the mission of preparing young people to make ethical and moral choices during their lifetimes by instilling important values. Ranging from Cub Scouts in kindergarten to Exploring Programs through age 20, Boy Scouts strives to build character; foster citizenship; and develop mental, moral, and physical fitness in young people. In 2020, the Boy Scouts of

America had more than 2.2 million youth members and approximately 800,000 adult volunteer members. In 2019, Scouts BSA was publicly launched as the organization formally expanded membership opportunities to girls. Since the launch, the organization reports 31,000 girl members in 3,300 troops. In the same time period since the launch, the Boy Scouts reports operating through more than 260 councils geographically distributed across the United States. Scouts Canada shares a similar purpose—forming the character of boys and imparting patriotic and civic values among members.

• *Boys and Girls Clubs of America.* Founded in 1906, Boys and Girls Clubs of America annually serves approximately 4.3 million children, particularly boys and girls from disadvantaged circumstances, encouraging them to realize their full potential as productive, responsible, and caring citizens. In 4,300 club facilities that include game rooms, learning centers, and gymnasiums, trained professionals help young people learn to solve conflicts, develop study skills, and work as part of a team. Boys and Girls Clubs also offers programs aimed at developing leadership, career, health, and overall life skills. The organization planted strong

roots in Canada in 1929 and serves nearly 200,000 children and youth in 736 clubs annually.

• *Camp Fire USA.* Founded in 1910, Camp Fire USA is committed to building caring, confident youth and future leaders through its educational programs. The organization directly serves over 150,000 children, youth, and families annually with the help of volunteers and paid staff. Camp Fire is organized primarily as a club and offers age-appropriate programs for younger children. For older children, Camp Fire offers self-reliance classes aimed at building the skills necessary to resist peer pressure and cultivate healthy relationships. It also offers service-learning courses intended to instill the importance of community service and offers camping and environmental education programs for children of all ages.

• *Girl Scouts of the USA.* Girl Scouts of the USA was founded in 1912 with the purpose of helping today's girls become tomorrow's leaders. For over 100 years, the Girl Scouts program has served girls locally, nationally, and internationally and encouraged them to develop integrity, good conduct, financial literacy, and health so that they can become fulfilled and responsible citizens. Besides

Boy Scouts of America is an example of a voluntary youth-serving organization.

Inti St. Clair/Tetra images RF/Getty Images

emphasizing expression through the arts, Girl Scouts encourages girls to explore their potential in math, science, and technology. Through more than 100 councils throughout the United States, Girl Scouts of the USA has more than 1.7 million youth members and 750,000 adult volunteer members and paid staff. Girl Scouts has a strong North American presence through the Canadian organization Girl Guides.

• *Girls Incorporated.* Girls Incorporated was founded as Girls Clubs of America in 1945. There is formal history and informal history of many of the early affiliates. Technically, the first organization in the United States that was a precursor to Girls Clubs operated in the 1860s. The organization changed its name to Girls Incorporated in 1990. Its goal is to inspire all girls to be strong, smart, and bold. Local affiliates of Girls Incorporated work to help girls and young women overcome the effects of discrimination and develop their capacity to be self-sufficient, responsible citizens, and they serve as vigorous advocates for girls. The organization also works to build girls' skills and interest in science, math, and technology and to prevent girls from falling victim to peer pressure. Girls Incorporated reaches over 250,000 girls through its affiliates in the United States and Canada and through its website and educational publications. Most Girls Incorporated centers are in low-income areas and provide after-school, weekend, and summer activities.

• *Little League Baseball, Little League Softball, and Little Challenger Division.* The Little League program was derived from leagues for preteen children that were formed in New York in the 1880s. In the 1920s and 1930s, an organization began to emerge. In 1939, the first Little League game was played. Little League is the largest organized youth sports program in the world with nearly 2.4 million children participating in more than 80 countries and 6,500 communities worldwide each year. Through proper guidance and exemplary leadership, the Little League programs assist youth in developing the qualities of citizenship, discipline, teamwork, and physical well-being. By espousing the virtues of character, courage, and loyalty, the Little League programs develop superior citizens rather than superior athletes.

Religious and Faith-Based Organizations

Some nonprofits have grown to become nonsectarian organizations with historical roots in faith-based communities. The YMCA and YWCA are two examples. Other nonprofits are created and administered by faith-based or church communities. The Catholic Youth Organization (CYO), the Young Men's Hebrew Association (YMHA), and the Young Women's Hebrew Association (YWHA) are examples. The largest organizations with historical faith-based roots are as follows:

• *YMCA of the USA (the Y).* The first Young Men's Christian Association (YMCA) of the USA was established in 1851. Its initial purpose was to meet the spiritual needs of young men. That philosophy has expanded to include multiple services directed toward a much broader cross section of the population with an emphasis on families. The mission statement, "to put Christian principles into practice through programs that build healthy spirit, mind and body for all," reflects the organization's commitment to its Christian roots and its global perspective. YMCA programs are family based. Purchased memberships for individuals and families cover the use of basic services such as gymnasiums, game rooms, swimming pools, locker rooms, and lounges. Members are also eligible for reduced fees on other programs such as resident and day camp programs for children and youth sports. The Y's program offerings are virtually endless and serve members nationwide in 2,650 YMCAs and 10,000 day and overnight camps. The YMCA has a strong volunteer program that includes more than 570,000 volunteer program leaders in the United States and more than 16,500 full-time staff.

• *YMCA Canada.* YMCA Canada was founded in 1851 and is dedicated to the growth of all people in spirit, mind, and body and in a sense of responsibility to each other and the global community. YMCA Canada provides health, fitness, and recreation programs that encourage people of all abilities to pursue healthy lifestyles. Disease prevention and health promotion continue to be mainstays of the YMCA. Program offerings are similar to those in the United States. There are 39 YMCAs and four combined YMCA–YWCAs across Canada, serving 2.25 million people in 1,700 program locations.

• *YWCA of the USA.* The Young Women's Christian Association (YWCA) of the USA was established in 1858, and it reports 2.5 million members and more than 210 local associations as of 2021. The program, rooted in Christianity, is a women's membership movement sustained by the richness of many beliefs and values. Strengthened by diversity, the YWCA draws together members who strive to create opportunities for women's

The YMCA of the USA is an example of a faith-based organization.

Scott Olson/Getty Images North America/Getty Images

growth, leadership, and power to attain a common vision: peace, justice, freedom, and dignity for all people. The YWCA seeks to empower women and eliminate racism. Programs include services for women in crisis, refugee women, single parents, homeless women, women in prison, women coping with substance abuse, and other women in the general population.

• *YWCA Canada.* The YWCA in Canada was established in 1870 with the tagline "a voice for equality—a strong voice for women." The YWCA movement in Canada has provided many of the same services as the YWCA of the USA, emphasizing women's shelters and camping programs. YWCA Canada consists of 32 member associations serving one million women, teen girls, and their families through operations in more than 400 districts and communities across Canada.

Social Service and Relief Organizations

Some of the most recognizable names and logos in the nonprofit sector belong to organizations that provide social and relief services. These organizations are difficult to categorize because some are nonsectarian and others are part of faith-based communities. Each has a mission to improve the quality of individual lives in communities. They intersect in ways that bolster the goals of recreation service

providers by providing direct services themselves or by joining forces with other service providers to meet mutual goals. The Red Cross is perhaps one of the best known of any organization in this category.

• *American Red Cross.* The Red Cross was organized internationally in 1863, and the American Red Cross was founded in 1881 as a humanitarian organization to provide relief to victims of disasters and help people prevent, prepare for, and respond to emergencies. Through a network of more than 600 chapters in the United States, the American Red Cross provides numerous services to meet its mission, including disaster relief services; international services; blood, tissue, and plasma services; services to military members and families; community services; and health and safety services. The Red Cross is served by more than 500,000 volunteers and 35,000 paid employees. Local Red Cross chapters assist recreation professionals by providing water safety, CPR, and first aid training and certification.

• *Canadian Red Cross.* The Canadian Red Cross was founded in 1909. Its work is organized into over 400 branches and is supported by more than 17,000 volunteers. Services of the Canadian Red Cross include disaster relief, international services, first aid and water safety education, and home-care services in some communities (e.g., meals and general assistance for seniors).

Inclusive and Special Recreation

Although similar in structure to other types, some nonprofits are organized to meet the needs of specific population groups. For example, the United Service Organization (USO) was created in 1941 to support the needs of enlisted military personnel. Many services provided by the USO are oriented toward the leisure and recreation pursuits of its clientele. Other nonprofits work with people with specific disabilities. The following are two examples:

• *The Arc of the United States.* The Arc of the United States works to include all children and adults with intellectual and developmental disabilities in every community through more than 700 state and local chapters nationwide. Founded in

1950, the Arc is the national organization of and for people with intellectual disabilities and related developmental disabilities and their families. It is devoted to promoting and improving support and services for this group. The association also supports research into and education about the prevention of intellectual disabilities in infants and young children.

• *Special Olympics.* Special Olympics was founded in 1968 to provide year-round sport training and athletic competition in 32 Olympic-type sports for children and adults with intellectual disabilities. With the help of its strong volunteer corps, Special Olympics gives athletes aged 8 years and older opportunities to develop physical fitness, demonstrate courage, experience joy, and participate in a sharing of gifts, skills, and friendship with their families, other Special Olympics athletes, and the community. Through the family leadership and support initiative, Special Olympics offers families opportunities for sport, social interaction, and fun and also a much-needed support system. Special Olympics serves 5.5 million athletes worldwide.

Environmental and Conservation Organizations

Environmental organizations are primarily involved in lobbying and education activities for specific concerns such as wildlife protection, global warming, and safe water. They are worthy of consideration because their efforts often make possible the places and spaces in which recreational activities occur. The following are two examples:

• *Sierra Club.* Founded in 1892, the Sierra Club's purpose is to explore, enjoy, and protect the wild places of the earth; to practice and promote the responsible use of the earth's ecosystem and resources; to educate and enlist humanity to protect and restore the quality of the natural and human environment; and to use all lawful means to carry out these objectives. From grassroots campaigns to environmental law programs, the Sierra Club seeks to spread the word about the importance of protecting the planet. The Sierra Club claims more than 3.8 million members and has 64 chapters in the United States. The U.S. Sierra Club has

The Trust for Public Land works to conserve land to ensure livable communities and natural places for generations to come.

created the Mexico Project to help support and strengthen Mexican grassroots environmental and community organizations. The Sierra Club of Canada was founded in 1963 to develop a diverse, well-trained network to protect the integrity of the global ecosystems.

• *Trust for Public Land (TPL).* The TPL uses its more than 300 paid staff and supporting volunteers to accomplish its mission of conserving land for people to enjoy as parks, gardens, and other natural places, ensuring livable communities for generations to come. Operating in 30 offices across the United States since its inception in 1972, the TPL runs several national programs, such as the Working Lands Program (WLP) and Parks for People (PFP). The WLP protects farms, ranches, and forests that support local economies, and the PFP strives to ensure that every American enjoys close access to a park, playground, or other natural area.

Associations

The following nonprofit professional associations concern the recreation field and are resources for students and practitioners in the field:

- *Society of Health and Physical Educators.* SHAPE America supports and assists over 200,000 professionals involved in physical education, leisure, fitness, dance, health promotion, education, and all specialties related to achieving a healthy lifestyle. Founded in 1885, the association is the largest membership organization of health and physical education professionals. The organization operates through 50 state affiliates and provides leadership, professional development, and advocacy for its members at every level from preschool to graduate-level programs.

- *American Camp Association (ACA).* The ACA is a diverse community of approximately 12,000 camp professionals dedicated to enriching the lives of children and adults through the camp experience. For more than 100 years, the ACA has used camp programs to impart powerful lessons in community, character building, and skill development. The ACA works to preserve, promote, and improve the camp experience for 11 million child and adult campers and learners each year.

- *American Therapeutic Recreation Association (ATRA).* With approximately 2,200 members as of 2014, the ATRA is the largest membership organization representing the interests and needs of health care providers who use recreational therapy to improve the functioning of people with illnesses or disabling conditions.

- *Canadian Association for Health, Physical Education, Recreation and Dance (CAHPERD).* The CAHPERD is a national, charitable, voluntary-sector organization whose primary concern is to influence the healthy development of children and youth by advocating for quality, school-based physical and health education.

- *Canadian Parks and Recreation Association (CPRA).* The CPRA is "the national voice for the parks and recreation field." It has a national network of providers that serve in over 90 percent of Canadian communities and advances its belief that parks and recreation is essential to the well-being of individual and community life. There are also 13 provincial and territorial parks and recreation associations operating across Canada.

- *National Association of Park Foundations (NAPF).* As one of the newest associations organized to support parks and recreation, the NAPF exists to strengthen local park foundations and other "friends of the parks" nonprofit organizations across the United States to support and enhance the local park experience.

- *National Recreation and Park Association (NRPA).* For more than 100 years, the NRPA has advocated the importance of thriving, local park systems; the opportunity for all Americans to lead healthy, active lifestyles; and the preservation of great community places. NRPA enhances professional advancement and provides services that contribute to the development of its 60,000 members and advocates. Competency guidelines form the curricular content of NRPA–accredited colleges and universities that offer degrees in parks and recreation.

Membership or Service Clubs and Fraternal Organizations

Although we do not always think of service clubs and fraternal organizations as a part of the recreation and leisure services community, we should consider them for two reasons. First, many of these organizations support parks and recreation programs through their donations of time and money. Second, they provide personal and professional development networking opportunities for recreation professionals who become members. Two of the better-known service clubs are the following:

- *Kiwanis International.* Founded in 1915, Kiwanis International has a membership of professional business people dedicated to serving their communities. The organization has nearly 538,000 members and 120 paid staff in more than 8,300 adult clubs and more than 8,200 youth clubs throughout the world. The organization evaluates children's issues and community needs and conducts service projects that respond to those identified needs.

- *Rotary International.* Rotary is a worldwide organization of business and professional leaders who provide humanitarian service, encourage high ethical standards in all vocations, and help build goodwill and peace in the world. The organization was founded in 1905. Members become actively involved in hands-on projects that use their vocational skills. Rotary has 1.2 million members worldwide in more than 35,000 clubs in over 220 countries who are served by over 800 staff members.

Differences and Similarities Among Organizations

Organizations share differences and similarities according to several distinguishing variables (Hansmann, 1987; Salamon, 2012; Ott & Dicke, 2016):

- The beneficiaries of their services, such as youth, seniors, or animals
- Their function, such as service delivery or political advocacy
- Their primary source of revenue, distinguishing between nonprofits that rely primarily on sales of goods or services and those that rely largely on donations

Two additional distinctions regarding service delivery are evident within nonprofit recreation organizations:

- Whether the organization is facility based or not
- The extent to which volunteers deliver services

Facility-based recreation organizations attract participants to programs that occur at specific locations. These include Boys and Girls Clubs, YMCAs, and similar organizations. Other nonprofits, such as Big Brothers Big Sisters, are not facility based and therefore rely on community-based facilities, including parks, for their program delivery. Still other nonprofits, such as Camp Fire USA, Boy Scouts, and Girl Scouts, rely in part on their own place-based facilities, such as summer camps owned by these agencies. However, for other programming they rely on community-based facilities such as schools, churches, and neighborhood centers.

Another distinction is the role of volunteers in service delivery. Volunteers provide an essential human resource to many nonprofits. In fact, in organizations such as Big Brothers Big Sisters and in Boy Scouts and Girl Scouts programs, volunteers are the delivery system. Without them, there would be no services delivered, and the mission of each organization could not be carried out. Other organizations, such as Boys and Girls Clubs, rely more on paid staff to deliver their core programs. However, in every case, volunteers serve in a variety of governance roles, such as boards of directors and task groups, and in support roles, such as fund-raising.

PROFESSIONALS IN NONPROFIT ORGANIZATIONS

The growth in nonprofit jobs has seen a dramatic increase over the years. For example, in 1994, the nonprofit sector employed about 5.4 million people in the United States, representing 4.4 percent of all workers (Bureau of Labor Statistics, 2009). By 2016, however, nonprofits employed 12.3 million workers, or approximately 10.2 percent of all private-sector workers in the United States (Bureau of Labor Statistics, 2018). Career opportunities for nonprofit professionals are growing rapidly across all subsectors, including recreation and leisure services providers. In fact, employment in the U.S. nonprofit sector grew every year during the recession years in the decade beginning in 2000 through 2010 with both wages and employment outpacing business and government.

The trends in U.S.–based nonprofit jobs were strong at the beginning of the 2020s. According to the 2020 nonprofit employment research report released by the Johns Hopkins University Center for Civil Society Studies, between 2007 and 2017, the number of jobs created by U.S. nonprofits grew by 18.6 percent—three times faster than the country's for-profit businesses over the same period. Moreover, the research revealed that nonprofits employ more workers than a number of major U.S. industries, such as transportation, wholesale trade, finance, construction, and real estate, ranking number three in payroll income behind only manufacturing and professional services.

Nonprofits hire people with diverse skills, just as business or government entities do because there are as many different job functions as those found in other industries. However, many recreation and leisure nonprofits have relatively small numbers of paid staff in relation to their number of volunteers. Thus, the professional is often given broad responsibility for a variety of duties within the organization.

Given the unique nature of philanthropy in many nonprofits, staff members who demonstrate skills in raising financial resources and working with and through volunteers to accomplish organizational goals are particularly successful. In youth development nonprofits, some practitioners work directly with children. More likely, however, they are responsible for a geographic territory with responsibility for ensuring that financial and human resources are acquired and deployed within the mission of the organization.

A variety of job and career resources are available for those interested in pursuing careers in nonprofit recreation and leisure organizations. The national organization Action Without Borders, the operator of the Idealist nonprofit job search web platform www.idealist.org, is one of several entities that provides career guidance and posts job openings.

Trade publications such as *The NonProfit Times* and *The Chronicle of Philanthropy* are also helpful tools.

Students pursuing degree programs in recreation who have an interest in nonprofit careers may benefit from earning national certification through the Nonprofit Leadership Alliance (NLA; formerly American Humanics Inc.). NLA is a national alliance of colleges, universities, and nonprofit partners that prepares undergraduate students for careers in nonprofit organizations. Campus affiliates of NLA offer curricular and cocurricular offerings leading to the certified nonprofit professional (CNP) credential for students pursuing nonprofit professional careers. The program was founded in 1948 and is offered in the United States at 18 colleges and universities nationwide. In 2016, an alternative pathway to the CNP credential was launched through an online certification program available from NLA's Leaderosity web platform.

CHALLENGES AND OPPORTUNITIES FOR THE FUTURE

Trends revealed in a 2009 research report by the James Irvine Foundation, as conducted by La Piana Consulting, still serve as both challenges and opportunities for the nonprofit sector. These trends include

- demographic shifts,
- technological advances,
- networks that enable work to be organized in new ways,
- rising interest in civic engagement and volunteerism, and
- the blurring of sector boundaries.

In addition, issues of trust and accountability remain ongoing trends that require the attention of nonprofit leaders and managers.

The Independent Sector's 2016 report revealing results of a yearlong series of community conversations held across the United States involving leaders from more than 80 organizations also remains relevant in understanding the challenges and opportunities nonprofits face. The study brought together a diverse cross section of leaders from nonprofits of every size and mission and generated thousands of comments and perspectives about the challenges and opportunities for the charitable sector in the coming years. Key trends that are still priorities include

- disruption from inequality and environmental degradation,
- greater ethnic diversity,
- new generations of leadership, and
- technology that transforms learning, gathering, and associations.

These trends, among others, suggest new models for social change will emerge along with fundamental questions that must be answered, such as the role of government in balancing competing priorities and revenue pressures.

Each of the trends noted have been accelerated and amplified since 2020 because of the COVID-19 pandemic, which has exacerbated economic disparity among social classes, thus placing more demands for service on charities while often requiring a pivot in programming to virtual means whenever possible. The murder of George Floyd, also in 2020, is seen as a defining event resulting in some nonprofits renewing their commitment to racial equity and social justice concerns.

All of these forces and trends have direct implications for nonprofit recreation and leisure services providers. For example, as communities continue to change and grow, many will find that embracing opportunities for diversity, equity, and inclusion in staffing, boards, and programs will result in assuring relevance, impact, and sustainability. Ongoing sweeping demographic changes mean that nonprofit providers must adjust to stay relevant if they want to make a broad-based impact. This trend also speaks to the need for managing staff across generations in the workplace if organizations are to be successful. Honoring their historic traditions as they change structures, processes, and programs to welcome new and diverse populations to their organizations presents both challenges and opportunities. This tension between exclusion and inclusion cuts across many demographics including race, gender, ethnicity, culture, sexual orientation, and abilities. Using history as a predictor of the future, the nonprofit sector in North America will be composed of some organizations that change, some that remain static, and some that are created anew.

For many nonprofits, the pandemic meant embracing technology like never before in offering virtual programming to stakeholders. While certainly the case prior to the pandemic, the use of social media, online-giving approaches, and other technological advances continues to present nonprofits with ever-evolving ways to reach stakeholders, tell their stories, and engage citizens in their efforts, while serving program and service participants. The opportunity for collaboration in response to marketplace challenges addresses the need for networks that enable work to be organized in new ways. Only the rare nonprofit can afford to operate its programs without regard for other providers of similar services, be they government, nonprofit, or businesses. Issues of pricing, marketing, and consumer choice suggest that the successful nonprofit of the future must use businesslike principles without abandoning the core public service mission that earns its tax-exempt privilege. Now more than ever before there is a call for greater civic engagement and volunteerism among citizens to actively participate in the process of citizenship as a prevalent opportunity across many communities. It is through nonprofits that people frequently find their place to engage by focusing their time, money, and know-how on causes they care about.

Blurring of the lines that demarcate the sectors is a trend that directly affects the recreation field. For example, during the economic downturn that was punctuated as a result of the 2007 to 2008 financial crisis, the more recent effects of the COVID-19 pandemic, political polarization, and economic disparity, nonprofits were called on like never before to assume responsibilities previously provided by government. In the 2007 to 2008 economic downturn, the city of Phoenix, Arizona, and other cities issued proposal requests to area nonprofits, soliciting interest in having them operate and maintain parks and recreation facilities that had been closed because of budget reductions. Increasingly, networks of organizations across sectors (government, business, and nonprofit) are called on to work together to provide a common good.

At least one final trend worth amplifying concerns the issue of trust and accountability, driven by a code of ethics such as those proffered by entities like the Association of Fundraising Professionals. If nonprofits depend on the charitable giving of time and money to ensure their success, then such organizations must be led and managed effectively. Although other sectors also face accountability issues, the special trust held by nonprofits as stewards of philanthropy makes this issue especially important. Appropriate ethical conduct is an imperative for those privileged to lead and manage nonprofits.

SUMMARY

Understanding the role of nonprofit organizations is important if recreation and leisure services are to be thoroughly understood. The nonprofit form is one way services are organized and delivered. There are enormous variations in how nonprofits are organized across North America. The extent to which the nonprofit form of organization is used in one country compared to another is largely based on the economic, social, and political differences among nations.

The career field for graduates of recreation and related degree programs who seek professional opportunities is growing. A number of trends are influencing the organizations that deliver recreation services as a blurring of the lines of the three sectors (business, government, and nonprofit) occurs. Successful nonprofit managers will be those who are skillful across a range of competencies and who can span boundaries across sectors in raising philanthropic resources and working with volunteers to achieve organizational goals.

Review Questions

1. Consider the three-sector model that describes the ways in which services, programs, and activities are enacted in American society. What are the three sectors?

2. The nonprofit sector is known by a variety of terms found in literature and popular media. Name at least five of these terms.

3. Despite enormous variations, several characteristics apply generally to nonprofit organizations in Canada, the United States, and other countries around the world. What are six common features that nonprofits share?

4. Nonprofits derive their revenue from a combination of one or more sources. Describe the most common sources.

5. How are nonprofits that are part of the recreation and leisure services arena generally categorized?

Go to HK*Propel* to complete the activities for this chapter.

CHAPTER 9

For-Profit Sector: Recreation, Event, and Tourism Enterprises

Robert E. Pfister and Patrick T. Tierney

Irfan Khan/Los Angeles Times/Getty Images

" I wanted to be an editor or a journalist. I wasn't really interested in being an entrepreneur, but I soon found I had to become an entrepreneur in order to keep my magazine going. "

Richard Branson, entrepreneur and founder of the Virgin Group

---

LEARNING OUTCOMES

After reading this chapter, you should be able to do the following:

> Contrast the characteristics of for-profit service providers with other service providers in the leisure and tourism industry

> Identify the range of activities undertaken by small and medium for-profit enterprises (SME) together with larger corporations in providing services in the recreation, event, and tourism (RET) industry

> Outline strategies for success in acquiring business skills central to the delivery of valued goods, services, and experiences by for-profit enterprises

> Describe trends that influence the management, marketing, and use of technology by SME owners and operators

For-profit organizations that provide recreation, special event, and tourism services are at the center of the commercial recreation sector. The term *commercial recreation* refers to any enterprise that provides recreation or leisure experiences with the intent of making a profit. The scope of a commercial enterprise's products or services may be local, national, or multinational. Such enterprises are among the many service providers that allow consumers to choose opportunities that add to quality of life and improve productivity at work. Influenced by diverse interests and expectations, we can rely on a wide array of recreation, travel, event, and tourism enterprises when it comes to our leisure choices. Consider, for example, the following scenario:

Reflecting on the past 12 months, you and your long-term partner recognize that it was a memorable year. As outdoor enthusiasts, the two of you enjoyed all your favorite outdoor activities together—downhill skiing, mountain biking, kayaking, and even an unexpected Caribbean cruise. It's December, and you are comfortably relaxed in a ski lodge, ready to celebrate the joy and rewards associated with a series of well-organized mini vacations.

You first remember the surprise Caribbean cruise received as a rewards certificate from your favorite ski equipment retail outlet that you have frequented for over a decade. A letter stated that in their drawing you had won first prize in a customer loyalty contest, which was an all-expenses-paid, four-day Royal Caribbean cruise sailing from Miami.

You discovered that the vacation package was prepared by an incentive travel company that works with commercial enterprises to reward loyal customers and productive employees. The timing of the trip even allowed you to take in a professional NBA game, because the Miami Heat was playing a home game before the trip departure.

In late spring, you went on a kayak trip on the Green River in your home state of Colorado. Then later in the summer, it was off to California for a multiday mountain bike experience put together by the Downieville Adventure Company. You had the opportunity to bike the course of one of the best-known mountain bike races in the country. Your guide urged you to stay on designated trails and demonstrated how to practice low-impact recreation. In the fall, you went back to your favorite retail outlet store to equip yourself for the upcoming ski season. Now you find yourself at your favorite local ski area, thinking about how great it was to do what you enjoy most with the support of a variety of key service providers.

Regardless of their services, products, or size, the commercial enterprises identified in this scenario tend to function in a similar fashion in terms of their legal status and operational practices. In addition, they share attributes that clearly distinguish the for-profit sector from the nonprofit and public sectors. Commercial business enterprises fit into a standardized statistical category under the provision of the United States-Mexico-Canada Agreement (USMCA).

ATTRIBUTES OF FOR-PROFIT SERVICES

When you look closely at the memorable experiences in the scenario, you'll see that some were delivered by large corporate resort properties and others by small businesses. These businesses share some attributes that distinguish them from other service providers; see table 9.1 for a summary.

The pricing of services can be the same for domestic and international customers, but this is rarely the case for tax-based (e.g., public) or membership-based (e.g., nonprofit) service providers. Moreover, variable pricing, such as higher prices during peak demand times, is a marketing feature that can be designed to appeal to a targeted market and to maximize revenue.

It is common for commercial enterprises to create travel packages that appeal to certain market segments, which include specialized food, accommodations, and attractions. Packages can increase the length of stay for travelers because they offer convenience, value, and specialization, thus encouraging additional time at a destination or on vacation. These packages can serve other purposes, as in the case of incentive travel whereby companies specialize in creating specific programs that motivate and reward high-achieving company staff.

The ability to buy and sell an enterprise is particularly unique to the commercial sector. In many cases, legal ownership of a business is one of the reasons why diligent and hardworking entrepreneurs invest considerable effort in building the reputation, assets, and customer base of their businesses. This type of commitment represents value that can be appraised when selling the business.

The need to be responsive to changes in the marketplace is central to maintaining a competitive edge in the commercial sector. This attribute reflects an inherent capacity in the design of the business to respond quickly to customer preferences to remain profitable and even capture new and evolving markets. Some commercial recreation businesses may choose to operate seasonally, and this may reflect their ability to be entirely profitable on a seasonal basis or to shift their services and products in response to cyclical patterns in certain regions.

Legal Status, Business Name, and Operational Practices

The legal status of an enterprise is indicative to its choice of a name, and it is fundamental to its ability to be bought, sold, or transferred. For small and medium businesses, the most common forms of ownership are sole proprietorship and general partnership. In such cases, it is common for the venture to carry the name of those involved in the formation of the enterprise or its owners. An alternative would be for the business to carry a name that reflects its base of operation or its service territory (e.g., Downieville Adventure Company).

The third legal status is to incorporate, and this form of doing business is evident in destination resorts, corporate properties, cruise ship lines, and so forth. With incorporation, companies often invest substantially in branding and trademarks for the business because its identity is vital to name recognition in the marketplace. Naming conventions refer to the choices available to a business given its legal status; these are displayed in table 9.2.

For-profit service providers carry out a set of operational practices and systematic decisions to ensure that the range of goods and services they advertise are available to the people they serve. Their operational practices involve the following integrated steps:

1. Planning that goes into assessment of demand and the creation of value-added products and programs (e.g., goods and services) for the consumer

2. Marketing the products, goods, services, and programs in a well-designed communication plan

Table 9.1   Five Characteristics That Distinguish For-Profit Enterprises From Other Service Providers

	For-profit	Public	Nonprofit
Pricing of services	Single competitive price	Based on resident fees	Limited to members
Tour packaging	Commonplace	Rarely undertaken	Done for members
Business can be sold	Yes	No	No
Ability to respond quickly to changes in the market	High capability	Limited capability	Some capability
Seasonal products or programs	Outdoor operators shift between geographic regions	If facility based, programs often change	Shift based on member preferences

Reprinted by permission from R.E. Pfister and P. Tierney, *Recreation, Event, and Tourism Businesses: Start-up and Sustainable Operations* (Champaign, IL: Human Kinetics, 2009), 11.

Table 9.2 For-Profit Legal Status and Implications for Naming Conventions

Legal status	Implications	Process
Sole proprietorship	No formalities are necessary if a person named John Gow wants to use the name John Gow Guide Service. A surname can also be used alone.	If a business name does not show the owner's surname or implies the existence of additional owners, many states require the owner to file a fictitious business name statement and publish notice. See DBA.
General partnership, joint venture, limited liability partnership	Two names generally appear in the business name.	If surnames are not used in the partnership, the owners most likely will file for a fictitious business name. See DBA.
Corporation, limited liability corporation, S corporation	When the owners create a recognized legal entity, the naming process is more involved. Laws and fees governing corporations vary from state to state. Most owners incorporate in the state in which they will conduct business. Some other considerations may be important. Nevada does not charge a state corporate income tax or personal income tax, and it allows a higher level of privacy for businesses. Business-friendly states do this to attract corporations to have offices in their jurisdiction.	Although the owners may have considerable choice for a name, guidelines for naming conventions are established by the laws of incorporation, which will vary by federal and state statute. Some words will be restricted because they are reserved for nonprofit societies or associations. More important, owners will have to research the availability of the name selected because it may not be available to be registered if an existing business has filed for it.
Doing business as (DBA)	Owners can choose a name that simply sounds good, such as Aardvark Adventures, Dianne's Dance Studio, Frank's Fly-Fishing Shop, or Bertha's Restaurant, and the owner's name does not have to be Aardvark, Dianne, Frank, or Bertha.	A business name that is not the owner's name is an assumed or fictitious name. The owner will have to complete the DBA process, which varies from one jurisdiction to another. DBA advertisements appear in the business section under DBA. Several states have online services that make the search process considerably easier.

Reprinted by permission from R.E. Pfister and P. Tierney, *Recreation, Event, and Tourism Businesses: Start-up and Sustainable Operations* (Champaign, IL: Human Kinetics, 2009), 66.

3. Delivering the goods and services in a timely manner

4. Monitoring the results of their efforts after the consumer has purchased the goods or services

All successful businesses have a vital interest in monitoring consumer satisfaction in one form or another. The services that recreation, event, and tourism (RET) businesses provide must be valued by customers, and they must meet the consumers' expectations; otherwise, competitors are likely to capture the unsatisfied market. This topic of consumer satisfaction is reflected in the earlier scenario in which a retail outlet implemented a customer loyalty reward and provided a Caribbean cruise to a loyal customer. In other cases, incentives might involve discount coupons, a cash prize, air miles, or gift cards. RET businesses must also develop cash flow statements, a plan of the projected sources, and uses of cash over the year. In figure 9.1 the operational practices are displayed as a set of integrated steps performed by an enterprise, often as part of their business plan.

USMCA and Recreation, Event, and Tourism Activity

The nature and attributes of the for-profit sector become even more differentiated as we look at a variety of recreation, event, and tourism enterprises in the context of their services to the consumer. The adoption of the RET label originates from a monitoring or data-collection need to standardize the coding of industry sectors for statistical purposes combined with the approach contained in the United States-Mexico-Canada Agreement (USMCA). Within USMCA, the **North American Industry Classification System (NAICS)**, which is applicable to the United States, Canada, and Mexico, recognizes arts, entertainment, and recreation, as well as event, meeting, and convention planning sectors of the economy in a uniform way (U.S. Census Bureau, 2020). Thus, when professionals describe RET businesses, the acronym encompasses a diverse set of businesses responsible for a wide range of commercial leisure services in urban, rural, and even remote locations that attract

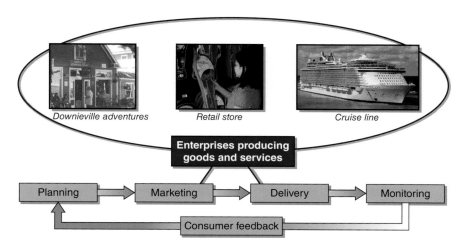

Figure 9.1   The four basic operational practices (planning, marketing, delivery, monitoring) are represented in the RET operations model.

Photos left to right: © Patrick Tierney, © Human Kinetics, and Baldwin040/Wikimedia Commons/CC BY-SA 3.0

Reprinted by permission from R.E. Pfister and P. Tierney, *Recreation, Event, and Tourism Businesses: Start-up and Sustainable Operations* (Champaign, IL: Human Kinetics, 2009), 183.

people to participate in leisure or a combination of business and leisure activities and to travel to new destinations. An RET enterprise generally refers to a business that provides a set of leisure-oriented goods or services and intends to be profitable within a reasonable time.

For-profit leisure enterprises vary from those that provide indoor batting cages in East Coast urban areas to those that rent outdoor equipment in remote barrier islands off the coast. Event businesses might arrange large spectator festival events in urban venues or small family weddings in rural communities. Small tourism businesses may offer special services to large time-share resort destinations or offer dogsled trips in the Yukon Territory. Any new term seeking to capture the diversity of the aforementioned commercial activities is likely to be met with some resistance, because it is a departure from previous terminology and typologies. The following section addresses the rationale for recognizing the RET category of businesses and provides a description of how previous models or typologies chose to group types of businesses.

RET INDUSTRY MODEL

Travel is said to require

- a motive,
- information about opportunities,
- an affordable means of travel,
- destination attractions,

- something to do, and
- a place to eat and sleep.

Using this idea as an organizing principle for a travel-commerce model, we can examine the primary function of each business, agency, or organization within the overall tourism industry. Synthesizing earlier theories and numerous research studies on the RET industry, we have developed the **recreation, event, and tourism (RET) industry model** shown in figure 9.2. There are three basic functional areas:

1. Attractions
2. Support and facilitation
3. Hosting functions

The model also contains two integrated functional groups that merge elements of the attraction and hosting functions.

Attractions

At the top of the pyramid, attraction businesses and public-sector facilities provide the motive and stimulation for travel and draw people to specific destinations. A basic premise is that tourism industry **attractions** provide the services and products that lead people to travel, and they power the demand for businesses in the other two functional areas by creating memorable visitor experiences. Attractions consist of three general types:

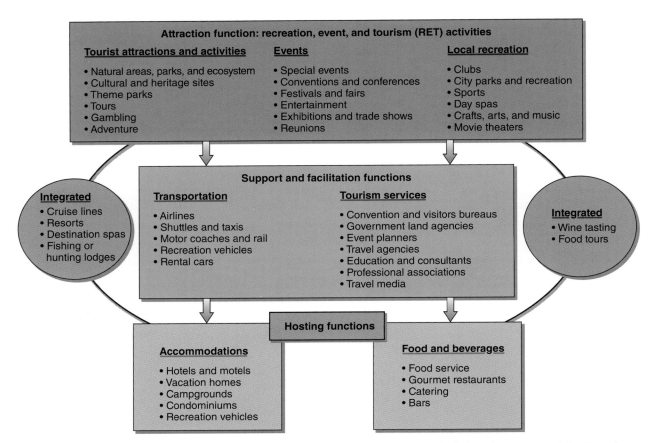

Figure 9.2 The recreation, event, and tourism (RET) model shows businesses of all sizes that represent the three functional areas of the RET industry: attractions, support and facilitation, and hosting.

Reprinted by permission from R.E. Pfister and P. Tierney, *Recreation, Event, and Tourism Businesses: Start-up and Sustainable Operations* (Champaign, IL: Human Kinetics, 2009), 15.

1. Tourist attractions primarily lure nonresident tourists. They range from natural and cultural attractions to theme parks, gaming casinos, and family and friends.

2. Event experiences are short-duration activities that are not generally repeated frequently and that attract both residents and visitors. They include special events, conventions and conferences, festivals, exhibitions, and reunions.

3. Local recreation consists of facilities and activities that provide residents with frequently repeated, nearby leisure experiences. Examples of local recreation organizations include clubs; city recreation departments; sport organizations; day spas; arts, craft, and music suppliers; and movie theaters.

Figure 9.2 clearly illustrates the importance of the private and public recreation and event attractions, because without them, transportation services or hospitality elements, such as accommodations and food services, would be unnecessary. The length of stay at a destination is also directly related to the number and quality of attractions. The model also shows the wide range of businesses and organizations found in the RET industry, which illustrates how vital, essential, and valuable RET is to our economy and lifestyle and the wide range of job providers within it.

Support and Facilitation Functions

The **support and facilitation function** contains two components: transportation and tourist services. Transportation providers such as airlines, taxis, railroads, recreational vehicles (RVs), and rental cars deliver tourists to the destination. Without reasonable prices and safe transportation, people would not get to the desired destination and use other elements of the system.

Countless services are geared toward assisting visitors including the following:

- Travel facilitators (e.g., travel management agencies)
- Convention and visitors bureaus
- Event planners
- Government land management agencies (e.g., National Park Service and Parks Canada)
- University tourism programs
- Research consultants
- Equipment rental firms, rental and retail businesses
- Travel media

Without these support services, other businesses would function less effectively, and people might choose another destination or be less satisfied with their experiences.

Hosting Function

The **hosting function** consists of accommodations and food and beverage services. Overnight lodging is provided to visitors by

- hotels and motels,
- vacation homes,
- campgrounds,
- RVs,
- bed and breakfasts, and
- family and friends.

Lodging is a basic visitor necessity, and its quality can greatly influence the visitor's experience. A variety of accommodation options are available, some of which are free (homes of friends and relatives) or low cost (hostels and campgrounds).

The food and beverage functional area includes restaurants, fast food, event catering, bars, and coffee shops. Like accommodations, food and beverage services are a necessity and vary greatly in cost and quality. They can have a large effect on visitor satisfaction.

Integrated Functions

A number of RET businesses integrate or combine attractions and hosting functions at one site. Examples of the **integrated function** in accommodations include

- resorts,
- cruise lines,
- destination spas, and
- hunting and fishing lodges.

Most integrated accommodations also provide food and beverage products.

An array of food and beverage businesses have an integrated function within RET because food and beverage service is a primary attraction for travel rather than a supporting service. Food and beverage services integrated with attractions include

- activities such as wine-tasting tours,
- food tours,
- catering for events, and
- gourmet restaurants for "foodies" or people who travel specifically to eat at a particular restaurant.

A wide variety of travel packages are created around wine-tasting tours and food experiences, such as the Taste of Chicago or the Boston Seafood Festival.

A cruise ship is a great example of a fully integrated RET business. Clients buy cruise vacations because of the activities and events on board and ashore. Passengers use a variety of tourism services, stay in cabins, and eat most meals on board while the ship transports them to new destinations.

You can use the RET model shown in figure 9.2 to identify links and understand how various types of RET businesses fit together. By doing so, you can better understand the RET industry and start to envision which part of the RET businesses you might consider working in.

CONSIDERING AN RET CAREER

The pathways to a successful and rewarding RET career can be as diverse as the industry itself. The following questions will offer insights into the choices you have in the years ahead:

- Are you inclined to be in business for yourself or do you prefer to be an innovator and deliver services in a corporate setting?
- What are the essential education opportunities available to you that match your interests?
- How can you acquire the leadership skills that will be vital to a successful career?

MOKreations - Fotolia

A cruise ship illustrates a fully integrated RET business that offers accommodation, transportation, and attractions. Clients are attracted to buy cruise vacations because of the appealing route, activities and events on board, and often the food services.

- Which of the many professional associations or marketing organizations will most benefit your career development?

Entrepreneur or Intrapreneur

Preparing for a career in the business field will certainly include developing some skills that differ based on a position title and your status within an enterprise. Within the RET industry model (figure 9.2), you might choose to be a proactive, self-employed person who operates a small or medium business (e.g., **entrepreneur**), or you might choose to be a proactive, forward-thinking employee (e.g., **intrapreneur**) within a larger enterprise or corporation. The term *intrapreneur* was coined and advocated in a book by Pinchot and Pellman (1999, p. ix); they say it comes from the words *intra*corporate and entre*preneur*.

Whatever your employment status, you should have common knowledge of personal leadership skills that contribute to success. If you are employed in a corporate setting, you will need to be mindful of major changes occurring in the industry and ensure you have an innovative perspective to respond to the change. In both employment situations, knowledge about managing change will be a springboard for success, as discussed in subsequent paragraphs.

Career Preparation

Many postsecondary curriculums focus on preparing graduates to start as employees. Beginning in such a capacity offers notable benefits. Several common characteristics are found across the various RET employment opportunities. Areas of emphasis that are foundations in both entrepreneurship and intrapreneurship pertain to leadership skills and appreciating the language of business (a combination of accounting, business law, and practice related to contingency planning). Experience suggests there will be dramatic changes in the industry over time due to new markets, products, laws, and the nature of competition.

A logical first step is to identify personal opportunities that will strengthen your knowledge of leadership and its practice in the industry. Formal education combined with practical, progressive, and innovative work experiences provides a time-tested and sensible combination of activities. The content and focus of any formal or informal work experience program can occur at various points in time. If we were to reflect on Richard Branson's quote at the beginning of this chapter, we could note that his career goal to become a journalist at a young age started him on an educational journey to understand what is required to become a successful entrepreneur. His experiences are instructional and often quoted today (GrowThink Consulting 2021; Wolff-Mann, 2015; Flory 2015; Murphy, 2015).

Foremost among the leadership skills revealed by Richard Branson is the mind-set exhibited in dealing with a changing and challenging business environment. Many authorities stress the importance of visionary leadership qualities in business (Covey, 2020; Nahavandi, 2021; Tedlow, 2021; Western, 2019). The authors uniformly identify the need to look at challenges with a particular perspective and to adopt skills that ensure flexibility and adaptability to a changing environment. Entrepreneurial skills associated with success in a business are anchored in understanding and applying leadership practices. Moreover, these qualities and practices are portable to each of the diverse RET work environments described in figure 9.2.

The Leadership Factor

In the distinctly service-oriented RET industry covered herein, the ability to discover, adopt, and excel at acquiring basic attributes of leadership should be a priority. Covey (2020) sets out eight fundamental and notable principles in this regard. He states that a principle-centered leader is continually educated by their experiences and sees life as an adventure in which to chart new territory with confidence. Thus, it is not uncommon to hear principle-centered entrepreneurs say that they learned more from their mistakes than from their successes. It is a commentary on their outlook that life is an adventure, and they see all experiences as learning opportunities.

Two other valuable principles for people who choose to work in this field are the commitment to being service oriented and belief in other people. Leadership, in Covey's view, is about service to others and recognizing the unseen potential in those with whom the leader works. These principles focus on the people skills linked to effective communication and call for each of us to build capacity to see the best in everyone.

Additional leadership principles include embracing an attitude of optimism and being productive in creative ways, which is described as being synergistic. A positive and hopeful spirit when tackling the things that need to be done lays the foundation for successful leadership. This optimism can be revealed through a sense of humor. When the need arises to negotiate win–win solutions or create change, the capacity to demonstrate synergy is invaluable. It begins with exploring options and expands into seeing new alternatives. It is an asset to every leader.

Finally, a leader needs to demonstrate a balanced lifestyle and commit to some form of regular exercise program. The balanced lifestyle is linked to seeing life as an adventure and savoring life experiences. Leaders are commonly active in many ways outside work, and they recognize the need to exercise the mind, body, and spirit.

Altogether, each of these principles for acquiring leadership qualities can be experienced in both formal and informal education programs. These are preparatory commitments that will serve those seeking to be entrepreneurs or intrapreneurs in the RET industry.

Investing in Professional Networks

Volunteering or obtaining membership in professional associations expands a person's knowledge and skills and is part of building a professional network. There will be opportunities to network with nonprofit industry organizations and specific career-related associations. Nonprofit industry associations

- facilitate the exchange of information,
- educate the travel public, and
- develop programs to promote professionalism within the industry.

Professional and **tourism associations** have been around for a long time and exist for nearly every sector of the industry. The same can be said for **entrepreneurial associations**.

Tourism industry associations provide great opportunities for students entering the field and for established entrepreneurs to network, attend educational sessions, earn certifications, meet other

OUTSTANDING GRADUATE

Lori-Ann Shibish

Background Information

Name: Lori-Ann Shibish

Education: Masters of Tourism Management, Edith Cowan University (ECU), Western Australia (WA), and Bachelor of Tourism Management, Vancouver Island University (VIU)

Credentials: Community Engagement Certification (International Association of Public Participation), SuperHost, Mentorship, Peer Supporter

Awards: Governor General's Academic Medal, Tourism Industry Association of British Columbia's Pat Corbett Leadership Award, VIU President's Scholarship, Morvah Award for International Development, Zonta International Jane Klausman Award for Women in Business, Rotary Club of Nanaimo North Humanitarian Award, Malaspina University-College Scholarship for Academic Excellence, Forum Advocating Cultural and Ecotourism student award, International Tourism Studies Association Presentation Award, Parks and Wildlife Nature-Based Tourism Award, WA Graduate Woman's Scholarship, ECU Post Graduate Scholarship, Tourism Council WA customer service finalist.

Career Information

Position: Community Engagement and Information Officer, Parks and Wildlife Service, Esperance, Western Australia (WA)

Organization: The Parks and Wildlife Service is part of the Department of Biodiversity, Conservation and Attractions (DBCA). The Parks and Wildlife Service works to ensure the natural assets of WA are conserved, protected, and valued. The agency manages parks, forests, and reserves for wildlife conservation and sustainable recreation and tourism, while protecting communities from wildfire. The state government's Plan for Our Parks aims to add 5 million hectares to WA's conservation estate over five years. To be successful with the creation of parks including marine parks, DBCA and other state government agencies consult widely with a broad range of stakeholders, including traditional owners, industry, and local government.

Career path: I initially followed in the footsteps of my farming family, graduating high school and staying on the farm. Having no family member who had undertaken studies beyond high school, I was without a role model until my experience as a Rotary exchange student opened my eyes to the possibility of pursuing postsecondary education. I felt terrified about entering university as a mature-aged student, but with encouragement from my Rotary host families, I took the leap of faith and enrolled at Vancouver Island University (VIU). Surrounded by nature on the side of a mountain, this university made me feel at ease, which enabled me to settle into studies. The world-class teachers at VIU provided me many opportunities to learn practical skills while working on community projects. The field studies were extremely valuable and helped to diversify my education, which enabled me to connect my passions for the environment to working with communities, especially Indigenous people. I was able to study in rural British Columbia, including traveling to Haida Gwaii, in rural Ghana, West Africa, and the Antarctic. My teachers brought out the best in me and I graduated, winning the Governor General's award. I was fortunate to be awarded a scholarship for a master's program at Edith Cowan University in WA. My thesis examined the evolution of joint management of protected areas with Indigenous people and the nexus of tourism development. To undertake the research, I needed permission from Parks and Wildlife, and the lasting relationships I developed with the agency set me on a trajectory for my dream job. Upon graduation, work in my preferred area was not immediately available, so I undertook volunteer work, followed by part-time work, and then contract work. These jobs and connections helped build my skills and credibility in the community, and when a position to be part of a team to create a new marine park came available, I had the confidence and skill set to be the successful applicant.

Likes and dislikes about the job: I love working with a passionate team on the creation of a legacy: A new marine park ensures an ongoing healthy marine ecosystem on the south coast of WA for future generations to enjoy, and safeguards the environment so it can be resilient to the challenges of climate change, pollution, and extractive pressure. I feel privileged to be assisting traditional custodians to reconnect with their country and creating opportunities for them to continue their culture and their important role in caring for country. There are no dislikes in my dream job.

Advice for Undergraduates

I highly encourage students to embrace every opportunity that university provides; be an active participant in your education; aim for the stars; work hard; and balance it with sport, recreation, and clubs to get the most out of your university years. These are precious years. Your best future opportunities depend on becoming the best you can be. I stress the importance of being willing to take small steps in a career while you patiently work toward your dream job.

professionals, and possibly find jobs or mentors. Tourism associations also conduct research on the industry. These benefits are extremely helpful for people starting out in a career. Some groups, such as the Resort and Commercial Recreation Association (www.rcra.org) are dedicated to professional development and networking with professionals, students, educators, vendors, and all others involved with the commercial recreation field.

Numerous professional associations have been created to support young entrepreneurs. Members are challenged to address real-world business and economic issues in their own ventures as well as in their communities. Involvement in one or more of these associations would certainly help aspiring business-minded people obtain timely information and build valuable networks.

Destination Marketing Organizations (DMOs)

Regions, states, provinces, and even countries create organizations to promote themselves as preferred tourism destinations. Because membership in these organizations often includes small and medium

businesses as well as national corporations, it is instructive to observe how businesses collaborate with visitor service bureaus. It is worthwhile to investigate in a directed studies course how they work, the career options associated with them, and their influence in creating destination images. In the United States and Canada, states and provinces commit funds to tourism offices, welcome centers, visitor information centers, and their corresponding DMOs. They often provide members with opportunities for cooperative marketing by displaying company brochures in racks at visitor information centers, placing company information on the DMO website, and providing educational opportunities to attend tourism outlook meetings for the region.

Exploring websites will provide an overview of how destination marketing targets the traveler directly, the nature of the relationships with the tourism partners, and ways in which events and attractions are positioned to build a travel itinerary. Some websites have sections on how to start a business within the state or provincial jurisdiction being examined. In addition, many state and provincial DMOs have regular electronic newsletters that keep subscribers up to date on new initiatives, changes in the programs, funding initiatives, and

UIG via Getty Images

Leisure travel accounts for nearly 75 percent of all international travel, and tourism is now the world's largest employer.

scheduled meetings of professional groups. Their websites tend to keep up with the latest in website technology because the marketing environment is competitive. It is worth the effort to search local websites for information; it will become apparent that the benefits of an RET career are endless.

For-Profit Enterprises Are Global and Diverse

When you examine for-profit RET opportunities and review each sector in figure 9.2, you will find an exciting array of global and diverse settings that are open to entrepreneurs or intrapreneurs of all backgrounds. Tourism was the fastest growing economic sector in terms of foreign exchange and job creation prior to the COVID-19 pandemic. Then the pandemic struck and shut down most international travel, but travel is returning (United Nations World Tourism Organization [UNWTO], 2021). Tourism can function as a double-edged sword. For example, when travel conditions are favorable, the global economy benefits. However, when a travel crisis occurs, such as during the COVID-19 pandemic, each of the commercial sectors has to respond to the circumstances.

The RET industry managed to enjoy a substantial period of growth, even through ordeals such as the terrorist attack of September 11, 2001, and the global financial crisis of 2008. However, COVID-19 affected the RET industry globally, unlike any other crisis. In an effort to monitor the influence of the pandemic and other factors, like the war in Ukraine, the UNWTO developed the tourism recovery tracker website to better understand the degree to which the industry was able to restart. The website dashboard displays data on tourism sectors by region and by destination (UNWTO, 2021). The UNWTO program has been an embryonic effort to see where sectors and destinations can get back on their feet.

Global Reach

For the business-minded person, the opportunity exists to explore many places around the world where your goal for a commercial enterprise might be a good fit. Leisure travel in 2020 accounted for 82 percent of all domestic and international travel spending in the United States, according to the U.S. Travel Association (2022). Domestic travel and commercial recreation have been important for a long time. Although economists began talking about the emergence of a global economy at the end of the 20th century, leisure travel, special events, and domestic tourism have been worldwide activities for more than three centuries.

Diversity

Leisure interests and tourism continue to be very important to U.S. society, and were so even during the COVID-19 pandemic. At the height of the pandemic in 2020, Americans flocked to outdoor recreation sites and took up new recreation activities in significant numbers. For example, the number of Americans who went hiking in April, May, or June in 2020 grew 8.4 percent compared to the same period in 2019 (Outdoor Industry Association, n.d.). New outdoor participants were more diverse than the overall outdoor participant base and are driving increasing diversity not only by ethnicity but also across age groups (Outdoor Industry Association, 2021). There are always opportunities and new markets every year. The numerous small businesses providing diverse products and services to society are vital to leisure experiences. If societal demand is present, an opportunity is available for an entrepreneur to fill it. Although no classification can reveal all the commercial enterprises that are encompassed by the leisure or tourism industry, figure 9.2 presents components of the tourism industry. Entrepreneurship is critical to tourism and travel:

> Entrepreneurships associated with small businesses are regarded as the key vehicle for creating new enterprises in a country as they generate more job opportunities and stimulate competition. Small businesses play an important role as the lifeblood of the economy. In many countries, they are at the forefront of government's efforts to promote innovation, enterprises and increased productivity. Small business firms are particularly important because of their role in supply chain. They are important for the competition they stimulate and ideas, products and services they bring to the market place. (IPL, n.d.)

Economic Impact

The commercial RET sector has contributed significantly to the world economy, with international tourism alone hosting 333 million jobs in 2019, following ten years of job growth (World Travel and Tourism Council, 2022). When the pandemic surprised the industry, almost all international travel came to a halt. Governmental and business-sector actions resulted in border closures, supply chain disruptions, staff shortages, and public health precautions such as social distancing within enclosed spaces and wearing masks. After this worldwide recession and slowing of travel due to COVID-19, international tourism arrivals are projected to bounce back to near prepandemic levels by 2023 (Economic Intelligence Unit, 2022). It is clear every sector of the industry has to make adjustments to address the significant changes occurring in international and domestic markets.

Openness

The public marketplace is open to anyone who is able to acquire the knowledge, skills, and capital necessary to participate in the leisure and tourism industry. The free enterprise system is the cornerstone of the open economy and is one of the reasons that the commercial sector thrives in the leisure and tourism field. You may have interpersonal abilities in dealing with people based on family history, personal travel experiences, language training, recreational lifestyle preferences, or even cultural heritage that will be an asset in an aspect of the industry. For example, the cultural aptitude of entrepreneurs from India may explain their inclination to dominate the SME in the U.S. lodging sector:

> Many young people immigrated to the United States from India and participated in forming the AAHOA in the late 1980's [sic] which today is the largest hotel association in the world. The association today has more than 19,000 members who together own over 20,000 hotels representing more than 40 percent of all hotel properties and 50 percent of the economy lodging properties. The membership of AAHOA is individual entrepreneurs who each have a myriad of personal success stories. The market value of hotels owned by AAHOA is around $38 billion and they create at least a million jobs. (Asian American Hotel Owners Association, n.d.)

TRENDS AND CHALLENGES

Local, regional, and global trends are constantly changing and will affect recreation, event, business, and employment prospects in the future. In response to these trends, there will always be micro- and macroadjustments within the industry. While it is possible to identify some predictable adjustments, the continuing global response to the COVID-19 pandemic will transform the international travel sector for some time to come. The following are a few of the key trends along with the challenges and opportunities that they present.

Reflection, Reorganization, and Change

Unexpected events are inevitable and create conditions for innovation and new opportunities. The pandemic dramatically accelerated reflection and reorganization in the RET industry. Within each of the five functional groups of the RET industry model, there has been, and will continue to be, a thoughtful and careful assessment of the impact of the pandemic and the degree to which changes will occur in order to remain viable. Moving forward, we will see contractions and expansions of specific businesses based on their costs of operation and the motivations of the market. For example, visitation to national parks and natural areas saw substantial increases in attendance between 2020 and 2021 (National Park Service, 2022) and some park concessionaires had record sales in the summer of 2022 (J. Placer, personal communication, October 18, 2022).

With border closures in 2020, the transportation sector, particularly airlines, experienced the disappearance of international and business travel. When a worldwide ban on cruise ships occurred, the entire cruise industry came to a standstill in early 2020. Every country in which the cruise industry played a role was affected. The accommodation sector quickly adjusted to adopt new cleaning standards for their rooms to ensure health protocols were met and concerns from their markets were addressed. By the end of 2022, each of the key industry functions were adapting and finding strategies to become more resilient to heath and financial crises.

Increasing Requirements for Specialized Skills and Certifications

Today the RET industry demands greater professionalism and higher skill levels of workers in the field than ever before. Until the last two decades, most professionals did not have specialized RET college degrees. Likewise, few universities offered specialized RET degree programs, and almost none offered master's degree RET specializations. In addition, managers frequently came from other industries besides RET. This situation is changing rapidly because the industry is becoming more competitive and demanding specialized skills from its workers (except for some frontline and entry-level positions).

Being trained on the job for two weeks does not provide sufficient preparation to perform professional job functions. Job announcements for professional positions now have minimum degree requirements and long lists of preferred skills and experiences that are often specialized to the RET industry (e.g., hospitality accounting or legal issues in the RET field). An array of university undergraduate and graduate degrees now provides appropriate RET training, and not just hotel management. In addition to obtaining a general RET degree, a common way to demonstrate competency in the field is through specialized certificates. These assure potential employers that you have met minimum skill and experience requirements. Examples of RET-related certifications include the following:

- Certified special events professional (CSEP) available through the International Live Events Society
- Certified lodging security supervisor (CLSS) available through the American Hotel and Lodging Educational Institute
- Certified park and recreation professional (CPRP) available through the National Recreation and Park Association

An RET-related degree or certification does not guarantee a job in the field. Combined with industry experience, however, it often provides an advantage and may qualify the applicant for additional job interviews. In addition, RET graduates frequently advance more quickly than nongraduates after they are hired.

Work–Life Balance and Wellness

Along with the trend toward specialized skills and professional certifications, the push for more work hours has historically been ubiquitous in American and Canadian societies. Work in some segments of RET is focused on nights, weekends, and holidays, which can isolate workers, affect wellness, and place extra stress on the worker's physical and mental health, family and partner relationships, and quality of life. Therefore, a new professional in the RET industry must take proactive steps to achieve a work–life balance, such as selecting an employer and supervisor who do not have unrealistic work expectations and do not push salaried staff to put in large amounts of uncompensated overtime. Some employees now work from home for at least part of the week. Workers and employers must realize that staff members need time to be physically and socially active if long-term health and productivity are to be maintained.

Likewise, the RET industry is in a unique position to offer services that greatly improve the health and long-term wellness of its clients. Health-promoting services in the RET industry have seen significant growth. Professionals should consider facility, food, scheduling, and activity alternatives that promote wellness. Health is a basic demand that is nearly recession proof. During the 2008 to 2010 recession and the COVID-19 pandemic, spas that focused primarily on pampering lost out to those offering programs that fostered health as well as personal service (Mindbody Business, 2021). Professionals need to evaluate their services and products to ascertain how they can be modified or how new ones can be developed to enhance client health.

External Forces Increasingly Affect RET Services

There have been significant factors influencing the global demand for RET services such as safety, economic, and climate events (Zou & Yu, 2022; Layne, 2017; WTTC, 2021).

- As previously discussed, the COVID-19 pandemic almost entirely shut down international travel during 2020 and 2021. International tourist arrivals between January 2020 and May 2021 declined 85 percent compared to the same period a year earlier (UNWTO, 2021).
- In contrast, visitation to local parks near urban centers increased 63 percent at the onset of the pandemic, dipped when many parks were closed, then returned to elevated levels once they reopened in late 2020 (Volenec et al., 2021).
- During the 2008 great recession in the United States and Canada, hotel occupancy in the United States dropped 56 percent (Sheel, 2008). This forced numerous bankruptcies and layoffs.
- The Russian war with Ukraine will produce a notable impact for its maritime neighbor, Turkey. Forecasts of fewer than two million Russian tourists in Turkey in 2022 could result in a multiple billion dollar loss of tourism revenue (O'Regan, 2022). The war in Ukraine and the devastating 2023 earthquake have had profound impacts on tourism in nearby Turkey. Between these two factors, tourism in Turkey is expected to decline significantly (Rizzi, 2023).

- Supply chain issues affected the travel industry like it did in other areas of the economy. For example, car rental companies had returned their vehicles following the COVID-19 pandemic and subsequently faced inventory shortages, due to supply chain disruptions, when trying to replace them (Baldanza, 2022).

These data show how volatile discretionary travel and recreational expenditures can be to safety and economic forces. This instability presents significant challenges to RET businesses to plan and operate their companies and to retain staff and strong relationships with their suppliers. Add the increasing severity of impacts from global climate change, and RET operators will need to respond quickly to changes in demand and impacts to crucial natural and cultural resources. Tourism and travel bounce back after downturns, and this presents opportunities for new RET businesses to emerge and job seekers to fill openings. But new entrants into the RET job market will have to be creative, develop a network of contacts, and exhibit entrepreneurial and interpersonal skills to find a job that best matches their interests, values, and skills and that is financially sustainable.

Sustainability and Stewardship

Growing concern about the dire environmental impacts of human activities, such as global climate change (International Panel on Climate Change, 2022), has caused many citizens to call for significant changes in businesses' operations to become more environmentally and socially sustainable. Federal and state or provincial government agencies in the United States and Canada require companies operating with permits in public facilities and on public lands to have comprehensive environmental management systems and to report their performance on moving toward sustainable operations. Resorts and other businesses need to be responsible stewards of natural resources and enlist their clients in these efforts. The modern consumer is well educated and will select a provider based not only on price, value, and quality of the services but also on the company's record of ethical behavior as well as its efforts at reducing environmental impacts and helping the local community. A survey of travelers found that 48 percent were willing to pay 10 percent more for services that employ green practices in the travel industry (Tierney et al., 2011). But in the study, only 12 percent could identify a green

The Hornblower Hybrid, the nation's first hybrid ferry, takes visitors to Alcatraz in California.

Courtesy of Alcatraz Cruises, LLC.

product or service that they had recently purchased or used in the last year, and most of those were low in cost and commitment.

Support for green practices is broad, but RET companies need to educate consumers about their genuine efforts toward environmental and social responsibility. Green business certification has been one way some firms have tried to distinguish themselves and verify their commitment to potential users. Companies with strong environmental and community records and certifications in these areas have competitive advantages, stronger growth, and higher profitability than firms that do not. Therefore, ethics, green practices, and sustainability are bottom-line considerations for how a business plans and operates. Workers in the RET industry who have passion as well as hard skills in delivering green practices will be in demand by employers.

Adventure and Entertainment

Large segments of the population are sedentary, and their daily routines are rather mundane. Many people, from seniors and families to childless young adults, look toward RET activities to compensate for inactivity and boredom through adventure and excitement with safety. Others look to be entertained while in the care of an RET company. Loathe to lie around the pool for three days, many people require resorts and other RET providers to offer active, educational alternatives and entertainment. RET providers must offer participatory alternatives despite the potentially greater initial costs, risks, and legal liability. The need persists for highly trained leaders who are technically skilled in delivery of a specific adventure or entertainment activity and are service oriented with the ability to create a quality experience for the customer.

SUMMARY

The for-profit, or commercial, sector of the tourism and travel industry encompasses a diversity of small, medium, and large enterprises largely focused on attractions, hosting, and support functions for domestic and international travelers. In addition, many SMEs also depend on serving the leisure needs of residents in the communities in which they are located. The structure and key elements of this industry are identified in the model presented in this chapter.

By the nature of their financial structure, the business enterprises described in this chapter differ in a variety of ways from public and nonprofit organizations. The fact that recreation, event, and tourism business ventures can be sold, bought, and transferred from one owner to another is one distinguishing characteristic. Businesses also adopt pricing strategies best suited for their target markets that ensure profitability in the long run. One important aspect of serving the travel market is combining products and services with other commercial operations to create an all-inclusive package that appeals to customers seeking one-stop vacation shopping. Packaging products and services can be profitable because it commonly increases the length of stay for the traveler.

Consumer preferences can shift quickly based on personal or economic factors and social turmoil; therefore, businesses must be responsive to unexpected changes in the marketplace. The for-profit sector must be entrepreneurial and be prepared for contingencies that arise on short notice. Seasonality of demand for products and services often dictates when attractions are in full operation and when major events are scheduled. Enterprises that rely on seasonal services must include details that address the financial implication of the seasonal nature of leisure and travel activities in their cashflow statements.

Preparation for employment in the for-profit sector can come from work experience and formal education. Cooperative education and internship programs allow students to be placed in a work setting where they can gain valuable experience. Entrepreneurs will say that good judgment in business comes from experience, and most admit that valuable experience comes from prior bad judgment. In other words, working in a business setting allows you to learn the lessons acquired by the owner over time. In addition, knowing and applying the language of business practices (topics such as accounting, law, leadership, and contingency planning) enables a potential entrepreneur or intrapreneur to contribute to an informed business decision and, at the very least, to be an astute observer of successful practices in the industry. Working in the commercial for-profit sector of the RET industry offers numerous benefits, such as travel during employment and working in the business of fun. Most important, knowledge and experience are portable across the work setting among the small, medium, and large enterprises that make up the RET industry.

Review Questions

1. An example of a tourism service in the recreation, event, and tourism (RET) model is
   a. an airline
   b. a hotel
   c. a theme park
   d. an event planner

2. A key difference between a tourism service and a tourism activity in the RET model is that a tourism service
   a. is a primary reason for visiting a destination
   b. is more likely to be assisting or facilitating a tourist before their outing
   c. always includes guided tours
   d. provides transportation for visitors from their home to a destination

3. Leisure travel in 2020 accounted for less than half of all domestic and international travel spending in the United States, with business travel providing the majority of spending.
   a. true
   b. false

4. According to research of U.S. residents by the Outdoor Industry Association, during the COVID-19 pandemic in 2020
   a. Americans were less likely to visit outdoor recreation sites compared to the previous year
   b. recreationists engaged in more new types of recreation activities than they personally had in 2019
   c. participants in outdoor recreation were less ethnically diverse than the year before
   d. all of the above

5. Federal land management agencies, such as Parks Canada, are considering but do not yet require companies they permit to operate in public facilities and on public lands to report their performance on sustainable operations criteria.
   a. true
   b. false

6. For-profit businesses have three legal organization choices under which they can operate.
   a. true
   b. false

(continued)

Review Questions *(continued)*

7. If you would like to be successful in an RET business, the authors identify four basic operational practices to implement:
   a. purchasing, inventory, monitoring, sales
   b. marketing, sales, inventory, staffing
   c. planning, marketing, delivery, monitoring
   d. staffing, purchasing, sales, taxes
   e. none of the above

8. In general, businesses tend to focus on a single service function such as transportation, accommodation, or something linked to major attractions such as an entertainment, a guided tour, or a theme park. However, there are some integrated businesses that offer two or more of those functions such as
   a. travel agencies
   b. resorts
   c. theme parks
   d. cruise lines
   e. b and d

Go to HK*Propel* to complete the activities for this chapter.

CHAPTER 10

Therapeutic Recreation

Frances Stavola Daly and Robin Kunstler

> " The improvement of the quality of an individual's life through a focus on the leisure component is much more complex than the provision of enjoyable activity or the delivery of some segmented therapy utilizing activity as the medium. . . . The focus on leisure and its outcomes is the contribution of TR services to the mission of health and human service providers. "
>
> Norma Stumbo, Illinois State University, and Carol Peterson, University of Illinois, Professors Emeriti

RyanJLane/E+/Getty Images

———— LEARNING OUTCOMES ————

After reading this chapter, you will be able to do the following:

> ❯ Distinguish between therapeutic recreation and recreational therapy, and describe the profession's purpose and benefits

> ❯ Explain the history of therapeutic recreation, including key legislation, and its influence on current therapeutic recreation services such as inclusion

> ❯ Comprehend the scope of therapeutic recreation services including settings, programs, interventions, and clientele

> ❯ Analyze the steps in the therapeutic recreation process

> ❯ Evaluate the components of professionalism and its significance to the therapeutic recreation profession and future professional opportunities

> ❯ Identify trends and societal changes that will affect therapeutic recreation services in the 21st century

Learning how therapeutic recreation (TR) can help people is relevant to students and professionals working in any area of recreation and leisure services. People with disabilities and health conditions participate in recreation programs in all types of settings, and knowledge of how to support their successful participation is essential for all recreation majors. Recreation can be a powerful tool to help improve many aspects of people's lives and contribute to an optimal state of health and well-being. Recreation activities are a major vehicle to attaining this optimal state because they involve

- challenge,
- excitement,
- rewards,
- choices,
- concentration, and
- pure fun.

Also, because recreation activities are pleasurable and satisfying, freely chosen, and intrinsically rewarding, people are highly motivated to engage in them. Therefore, recreation can motivate people to change, grow, and improve their health. Recreation has *re-creative* powers; in other words, people can renew, restore, and refresh themselves and develop their abilities and skills through recreation participation. People with illnesses, disabilities, or limiting conditions have the same rights to healthy and satisfying recreation participation as people without disabilities.

Approximately 56.7 million Americans, or one out of every six people (16%), have at least one **disability**. The percentage of Canadians with dis-

abilities is a little less than in the United States, at 14 percent (Bullock & Mahon, 2017). Because conditions such as disease or disability may impose barriers on people's ability to engage in recreation, professional assistance such as TR may be required. Although only half of the people with a disability consider some aspect of their functioning to be impaired (Bullock & Mahon, 2017), millions of people could potentially benefit from TR services. In fact, most of us can probably recall a situation in which our ability to participate in the things we love to do was impaired by a physical, emotional, or social condition or situation.

Research on recreation experiences has found that participation

- provides physical, cognitive, social, and expressive benefits;
- promotes growth and development; and
- contributes to life satisfaction and well-being.

For the health care system and society, successful outcomes of TR services can lead to

- lower health care costs in the least costly settings of home and community (McCormick et al., 2020),
- decreases in disability and rehospitalization (McCormick et al., 2020), and
- increases in community inclusion (CTRA, 2022).

In addition to the treatment role of TR, its role in preventing illness and disability is now recognized: "Recreational therapy has the potential to not only provide services within the hospital environment, but also to integrate prevention and treatment-oriented services directly into the community" (Snethen & Mitchell, 2019, p. 442). This aligns with TR's roots in the recreation profession, which had its beginnings in what can be considered public health according to the American Public Health Association: "promoting and protecting the health of people and the communities where they live, learn, work and play" (Colman, 2020, p. 43).

This chapter will explain

- how the practice of therapeutic recreation developed,
- key concepts related to providing TR services, and
- the scope of TR settings, programs, interventions, and populations.

A discussion of the TR process outlines the daily duties of a therapeutic recreation practitioner. Professional issues, trends, and future challenges are examined to provide concrete information that will help you understand TR and evaluate its suitability as a career choice.

DEFINING THERAPEUTIC RECREATION

What exactly is therapeutic recreation? This question may be the hardest one that you answer when family and friends ask, "What is your major?" For TR students, the answer is not simple. Many definitions of TR have been put forth over the years, each with slight variations in language and emphasis, which leads to a lively debate about the true definition of TR. However, all TR definitions include the following common components that capture the essence of TR (Negley, 2010):

- Purposeful selection of recreation activities to reach a goal or **outcome**
- Enhancement of independent **functioning** through recreation participation
- **Quality of life**, wellness, and optimal **health** as core concerns
- Focus on the individual in the context of their own environment, including support and resources provided by the family and community

A composite definition of TR that brings together these common components has been developed. It states that TR is "engaging individuals in planned recreation and related experiences in order to improve functioning, health and well-being, and quality of life, while focusing on the whole person and the needed changes in the optimal living environment" (Kunstler & Stavola Daly, 2010, p. 4).

The **American Therapeutic Recreation Association (ATRA)**, the national professional organization for **certified therapeutic recreation specialists (CTRSs)**, explains the relationship between key terms used in the profession:

- *Therapeutic recreation* is the field.
- *Recreational therapy* is the practice.
- *Recreational therapists* are the practitioners.
- *Certified therapeutic recreation specialists* (CTRSs) are the qualified providers. (ATRA, 2015)

ATRA presents the following definition:

Recreational therapy, also known as *therapeutic recreation*, is a systematic process that utilizes recreation and other activity-based interventions to address the assessed needs of individuals with illnesses and/or disabling conditions, as a means to psychological and physical health, recovery and well-being. Further, "Recreational Therapy" means a treatment service designed to restore, remediate, and rehabilitate a person's level of functioning and independence in life activities, to promote health and wellness as well as reduce or eliminate the activity limitations and restrictions to participation in life situations caused by an illness or disabling condition (ATRA, 2015).

The Canadian Therapeutic Recreation Association defines therapeutic recreation as "a health care profession that utilizes a therapeutic process, involving leisure, recreation, and play as a primary tool for each individual to achieve their highest level of independence and quality of life" (n.d.).

We can see from these definitions that TR has a focus on improving health and quality of life, regardless of setting.

You will find that the terms *therapeutic recreation, recreation therapy* (RT), and *recreational therapy* are often used interchangeably, as shown in the previous ATRA definition (ATRA, 2015). Some professionals prefer RT because it seems to emphasize the treatment aspects of the field; others prefer the broader term therapeutic recreation. For the purposes of this chapter, we will use therapeutic recreation (TR) as more all encompassing of the range of the field, but we will refer to the practitioners as recreational therapists or recreation therapists (the Canadian preferred terminology) (RTs) throughout the chapter.

Therapeutic recreation is provided to people of all ages, demographic characteristics, and abilities regardless of health status or level of functioning. This includes children, teenagers, adults, and older adults with physical, developmental, psychiatric, and cognitive conditions as well as those who are affected by social conditions such as homelessness, war, poverty, incarceration, natural disasters, and risky environments. In short, any individual who can benefit from TR can be a recipient of TR services. TR has strong roots in humanistic philosophy, which asserts that people are capable of growth and change, that they strive to meet their needs and goals, and that they are autonomous (capable of making their own decisions and choices and directing their own lives), and are inherently altruistic (desire to do good for others). TR is based on a system of beliefs about human nature, needs, and behaviors as well as about the meaning and purpose of recreation, leisure, and play in people's lives. Interaction with others in recreation activities is a strength of TR because it provides emotional and social support, opportunities to learn from others facing similar challenges, and a shared positive experience. For some clients, TR may be their most successful therapy because it is enjoyable and provides opportunities to make choices, set goals, and develop feelings of self-confidence, competence, and belief in their abilities.

HISTORY OF THERAPEUTIC RECREATION

Studying history can help us understand how our profession evolved to its current state, and identify the trends and changes that have occurred in TR over time. Most students are fascinated to learn that although the TR profession is less than 100 years old, the benefits of participation in recreational activities for people with illnesses and disabilities were recognized thousands of years ago. The ancient Greeks, who believed in a sound mind in a sound body, built curative temples where activities such as walking, gardening, exercise, boating, and music were offered. The Egyptians created a positive environment using music and dance to treat mood disorders. In India, Charaka, a surgeon, had patients play games and drink wine while he operated on them because he knew that those activities would distract them from the pain. Nonetheless, history provides few examples of compassionate care for those with disabilities until after the Middle Ages.

In Europe, the Renaissance (1400-1600) and the Age of Enlightenment (1700s) brought a greater concern for the rights of all people. The first schools for the deaf and the blind were established in Paris in the late 18th century. In the United States in the early 19th century, hospitals were built to serve people with mental illness, and they provided recreation activities as part of more humane treatment. During the mid-19th century, Florence Nightingale, an English woman who was considered the founder of modern nursing practice, wrote that wounded soldiers should be in beautiful environments or "recreation huts," listen to music, and have visits from family and pets to comfort them and speed their recovery. During the same period, Dorothea Dix advocated for better treatment of people with disabilities and illnesses in U.S. asylums and prisons. The latter half of the 19th century brought many immigrants to North America, and this contributed to the growth of cities and social problems and led to the establishment of settlement houses, which were community centers that provided social services, education, and recreation.

The history of TR from 1889, when the first settlement house was founded, to the present day is presented in the Timeline sidebar.

Maskot/Getty Images

An art class is one type of intervention that a therapeutic recreation specialist might use to improve functional skills, develop a new leisure interest, or contribute to overall well-being.

Timeline: History of TR 1880s-Present Day

1880s—Hull House, the first settlement house (opened in Chicago by Jane Addams), uses recreation to improve the lives of people with substance abuse and people living in poor circumstances.

Early 1900s—Agencies begin to provide recreation to children with disabilities living in the community.

1917-1918—The American Red Cross provides recreation to convalescing soldiers at military bases during World War I.

1920s—Recreation personnel are hired to work in military and veterans' hospitals.

Recreation services are offered in state mental hospitals.

1930s—One of the first experimental research studies is published that demonstrates the value of recreation participation in teaching social skills to children with intellectual disabilities.

Recreation is used as a treatment in psychiatry at the Menninger Clinic in Topeka, Kansas.

1940s—The Red Cross establishes a training program in basic recreation for workers during World War II.

The U.S. Veterans Administration establishes its Recreation Service.

The first organization for wheelchair sports, the National Wheelchair Basketball Association, is founded.

1950s—Three professional organizations emerge to serve the needs of recreation practitioners working in hospitals and schools and with people with disabilities in varied settings: the National Association of Recreation Therapists (NART); the recreation therapy section of the American Alliance of Health, Physical Education and Recreation (AAHPER); and the hospital recreation section (HRS) of the American Recreation Society (ARS).

Development of standards for practice, personnel, and curricula is underway.

1960s—Special Olympics are founded.

The disability rights movement begins.

Deinstitutionalization is initiated at state and federal levels.

The National Therapeutic Recreation Society (NTRS) is formed from NART and HRS and is established as a branch of the National Recreation and Park Association (NRPA) in 1966.

1970s—Landmark U.S. federal legislation is passed regarding equal access to education, provision of recreation services, and accessibility of public facilities (including recreation facilities) for individuals with disabilities.

Federal education grants fund programs, education, and research on therapeutic recreation.

1980s—The age of **accountability** in health care brings stringent documentation requirements.

The American Therapeutic Recreation Association (ATRA) is established in 1980.

The National Council for Therapeutic Recreation Certification (NCTRC) is formed in 1981.

1990s—The Americans with Disabilities Act is passed in 1990.

The inclusion movement gains momentum.

The Canadian Therapeutic Recreation Association (CTRA) is incorporated in 1996.

Evidence-based practice in health care is initiated.

2000s—CTRA and NCTRC agree that the CTRS will be the recognized credential in Canada.

Committee on Accreditation of Recreational Therapy Education (CARTE) is established as the ATRA-supported accreditation program for RT curricula.

The NCTRC establishes a specialty certification program.

The NRPA changes its organizational structures and eliminates branches including the NTRS.

Five U.S. states enact licensure for RT/TR.

(continued)

Timeline: History of TR 1880s-Present Day   *(continued)*

RT/TR services further expand to serve people with disabilities in community settings, schools, and disease prevention and health promotion programs as well as expanding to serve wounded veterans.

2020s—COVID-19 pandemic accelerates the use of technology to enable participation and increases programming options.

ATRA ramps up monitoring and lobbying efforts to influence federal legislation affecting TR.

TR expands its commitment to social justice and equity issues in service provision.

Legislation

The sociopolitical movements of the latter half of the 20th century led to the passage of landmark legislation in the United States and Canada that not only broadened opportunities for people with disabilities but also reflected and promoted a societal change to more positive attitudes toward people with disabilities. Table 10.1 identifies key U.S. and Canadian laws that have significantly affected the lives of people with disabilities, their rights, and their access to recreation services, which led to the inclusion movement. As of 2022, Canada does not have a federal law like the Americans with Disabili-

Table 10.1   Key Laws of the United States and Canada

Law	Description
United States	
PL 90-480 Architectural Barriers Act, 1968	Mandated physical accessibility and usability of buildings and facilities
Section 504 of the Rehabilitation Act, 1973	Mandated program accessibility for people with disabilities
PL 94-142 Education for All Handicapped Children Act, 1975	Stated that all handicapped children were entitled to a free and appropriate public education in the least restrictive environment and may receive recreation as a related service
PL 101-476 Individuals with Disabilities Education Act, 1990	Reauthorization of PL 94-142 that emphasized family involvement, required transition planning, and provided for assistive technology
PL 101-336 Americans with Disabilities Act (ADA), 1990	Comprehensive civil rights law intended to eliminate discrimination against people with disabilities in all aspects of American life including employment, government services, public transportation, public accommodations, and telecommunications; required that reasonable accommodation be made to facilitate participation by people with disabilities in these five areas by removing barriers and providing auxiliary aids and services as necessary
ADA Amendments Act, 2008	Expands interpretation of disability, major life activities, and major life functions to make it easier for individuals to seek protection under the ADA
Affordable Care Act (2010)	Gave people with disabilities greater access and flexibility in their health care
Canada	
Vocational Rehabilitation for Disabled Persons Act, 1962	Provided rehabilitation services for people with disabilities
Canadian Charter of Rights and Freedoms, 1982	Stated that all people have the right to equal protection and benefit of the law without discrimination based on mental and physical disability
In Unison: A Canadian Approach to Disability Issues (government report, not a law), 1998	Provided the basis for asserting equal rights for people with disabilities to achieve full integration and access to supports, services, employment, and income
Accessible Canada Act (2019)	To make Canada barrier-free by 2040 by systematically and proactively identifying, removing and preventing barriers to accessibility

ties Act in the United States, although individual provinces such as Ontario and Manitoba have their own laws protecting the rights of individuals with disabilities.

Inclusion

Inclusion refers to empowering people with disabilities and health conditions, people from marginalized groups, and others deprived of equitable access to become valued and active members of their communities through involvement in socially valued life activities of their choosing. A key tenet of inclusion is that the community offers support, friendship, and resources to facilitate the equal participation in everyday life by all its members. Inclusion philosophy and practices evolved from the core principles and concepts identified in table 10.2. The inclusion movement has broadened the traditional view of TR from focusing solely on the person to serving the person in the context of the total environment and the settings the person inhabits throughout their life. The role of RTs in facilitating inclusion is to help clients achieve their goals of living in the most inclusive environment possible through minimizing and removing barriers to inclusion and promoting diversity and equity in all services. A more recent concept in inclusion phi-losophy is **identity-first language**, as in "disabled person." Identity-first language puts the disability first in the wording referring to the person and reflects the concept that disability is part of one's identity and is not shameful (Hawley, 2020). While person-first language advanced the principle that people with disabilities are people first, and was seen as the most respectful way to refer to them, the most recent usage of inclusion language should be based on the individual's personal preference.

THERAPEUTIC RECREATION SETTINGS AND SERVICES

Each of us is responsible for basing our professional practice on our readings, reflections, and values that will support our efforts and deepen our understanding of and commitment to our chosen field. For TR students and professionals, it is vital to understand

- humans and their development throughout the life span;
- the variations in human development and experience;
- the effects of these variations on lifestyle;
- the potential contributions of leisure, recreation, and play to healthy human development; and

Table 10.2 Building Blocks of Inclusion

Building blocks	Definitions
Deinstitutionalization	The move away from large-scale, institution-based care to small-scale, community-based facilities; began in the late 1960s
Accessibility	Equal entry into, and participation in, physical facilities and programs by all people; accomplished through the elimination of architectural, administrative, and attitudinal barriers to create a usable environment
Normalization	Making available to people with disabilities the patterns and conditions of everyday life that are as culturally normative as possible
Integration	Physical presence and social interaction of people with and without disabilities in the same setting
Mainstreaming	Movement of people into the activities and settings of the wider community
Least-restrictive environment	The environment that imposes the fewest restrictions and barriers on a person's growth, development, and participation in a full life
Supports	Friendships, social networks, assistance, and resources that enable a person to participate in the full life of their community
Person-first language	Language that puts the word *person* or *people* first in the sequence of a phrase or sentence to emphasize a positive attitude toward the individual (e.g., a person with a disability rather than a disabled person)
Inclusion	Empowering people who have disabilities to be valued and active members of their communities by making choices, being supported in daily life, and having opportunities to grow and develop to their fullest potential

- the wide range of activities and interventions that are useful to RTs.

By now you're probably wondering where you can work as an RT and what a typical workday would look like. One of the exciting aspects of the TR profession is the range of settings and populations served by RTs. People of all ages with all types of disabilities, health conditions, or social challenges are potential recipients of TR services, which can include seemingly infinite types of recreation activities. Students contemplating this profession can consider many possibilities ranging from acute medical or psychiatric treatment in the hospital setting, to residential facilities for individuals with developmental disabilities or HIV/AIDS, to long-term care for people with multiple sclerosis, Huntington's disease, or dementia. TR is offered at the following sites:

- Hospice programs
- Physical rehabilitation centers
- Military bases
- Prisons
- Assisted-living facilities
- Adult day cares
- Partial hospitalization and outpatient programs
- Drug treatment programs
- Homeless shelters
- Group homes
- Schools
- Early intervention programs
- Community recreation centers
- Camps
- People's homes

RTs may serve as inclusion specialists in transition and community-based programs using their knowledge of disability, accessibility, assessment, and activity analysis to facilitate the participation of people with disabilities in their communities.

Job Duties and Responsibilities

The RT is recognized as a vital member of the interprofessional health care team. The team meets regularly to develop and review the plan of care or services for the client. Depending on the setting, the other members of the team might be physicians, nurses and nursing assistants, dietitians, social workers, and physical, occupational, or speech therapists. In addition, rehabilitation counselors, mental health staff, creative arts therapists, teachers, and exercise specialists might be members of the team depending on the type of setting and the services offered. Each RT should be an active participant in the team process by accurately reporting on the client's status and progress toward goal-achieving outcomes. The RT has a significant contribution to make to the team's understanding of the client because the RT works with the client in the most natural and relaxed setting in the service environment. The RT can observe the client's strengths and needs during typical activities.

To achieve the outcomes of TR, the RT

- develops a rapport and interacts therapeutically with clients,
- conducts individual assessments,
- develops treatment plans,
- plans a schedule of TR programming,
- motivates clients to participate in TR activities,
- leads individual and group programs,
- observes and documents client participation and progress, and
- attends treatment team meetings (also known as *comprehensive care-planning meetings* or similar names) and in-service training.

Other duties include

- maintaining equipment and supplies,
- supervising volunteers and interns,
- providing support to family members,
- advocating for the rights of clients, and
- organizing special events and community outings.

Management responsibilities may include

- budgeting,
- risk management,
- marketing, and
- participating in strategic planning and performance improvement projects.

TR Programs and Modalities

RTs use a range of modalities, including the following:

- Traditional recreation activities such as the arts, sport, fitness and exercise, games, crafts, social activities, outdoor recreation, horticulture, aquatics, and community outings

- Activities not traditionally considered recreation, such as **leisure education**, volunteering, adult education, and animal-assisted (pet) therapy
- Therapeutic interventions such as cognitive stimulation, sensory awareness, assertiveness training, anger management, pain management, stress management, and leisure counseling, depending on the mission and goals of the agency and the needs of the population being served

Agencies may utilize a treatment approach, such as cognitive behavioral therapy or milieu therapy, that RTs, along with all staff, will follow in their work with clients. Complementary and alternative medicine (CAM) is also becoming an area for TR practice. Interventions such as relaxation, meditation, aromatherapy, guided imagery, yoga, and tai chi are popular.

Use of technology in programming grew tremendously with the onset of the COVID-19 pandemic. In health care facilities, TR staff were called upon to provide individual activities to those confined to their rooms, using cell phones and tablets to assist clients with communicating with their loved ones and engaging in individual interests. In TR programs that had limited budgets to obtain additional technology, staff often used their own cell phones, tablets, or laptops to organize group viewings of streaming television programs. Staff facilitated many virtual sessions for clients who did not have the skills or resources for personal technology use. The pandemic taught us that almost any category of activity can be adapted for virtual participation. Online programming has expanded to include

- fitness,
- dance,
- games,
- discussions,
- arts and craft sessions,
- music performances, and
- movies, among many other activities.

These formats, powered by videoconferencing software, allow RTs to offer both individual and group activities. This enabled participation during the pandemic as well as increased options for those unable to leave their rooms or homes.

Fitness and exercise is just one modality a therapeutic recreation specialist may implement.

Ariel Skelley/Digital Vision/Getty Images

In addition, hallway programming, in which residents and clients sit in the doorway of their rooms while maintaining social distancing, was a popular means of supporting clients' social and emotional needs by playing group games, exercising, enjoying animal visits, listening to live music performances, and more. TR staff prepared individual kits with crafts, puzzle books, no-bake cooking, and aromatherapy to distribute to clients. All these programs served as the foundation for fulfilling the purposes of TR and meeting client goals in a true time of crisis.

THERAPEUTIC RECREATION PRACTICE MODELS

Depending on the setting, the TR department may follow one of the TR **practice models** that have been developed over the years. A practice model is a visual representation of the relationships between philosophy and theory and the real world, and serves as a guide for practice. The benefits of providing TR services according to an appropriate practice model are that a model

- directs the types of programs and services offered,
- communicates the purposes and services of TR to other disciplines, and
- ensures that clients are provided the services and interventions best suited to their needs and goals.

Practice models often reflect the political and social realities of the period in which they were developed. In all models, TR emphasizes the abilities and strengths of the client to overcome or alleviate the limitations imposed by disability or illness. TR also stresses that people have the right to live in the optimal environment of their choice with appropriate supports. These supports may be provided by the person, their family and friends, community agencies, and other sectors of the environment as needed. This ecological perspective recognizes that the person's family, friends, and community are significant factors in their health and well-being.

The predominant TR practice models include

- the leisure ability model,
- the health protection and health promotion (HP/HP) model,
- the TR service model,
- and the TR outcome model.

Each model represents TR practice in a unique way. For example, in the leisure ability model, TR is provided along a continuum encompassing three types of services—functional intervention, leisure education, and recreation participation—to develop one's leisure lifestyle. According to the HP/HP model, the purpose of TR is to achieve optimal health in a favorable environment by using prescriptive activities, recreation, and leisure as interventions. The TR service model describes a role for TR in four areas of health care provision, including diagnosis and needs assessment, treatment and rehabilitation, education, and prevention and health promotion. In the TR outcome model, the purpose of TR is to increase quality of life by improving functioning in one or more of the behavioral domains, which should result in improved health as well.

Many of the trends since the mid-1990s, such as inclusion, a shift to community-based health care, an increase in chronic conditions, people living longer with severe medical problems and disabilities, a focus on spiritual health, and strengths-based approaches to services, have led to the development of additional models.

Trends such as positive psychology and the strengths-based approach have reconceptualized the traditional TR frameworks by emphasizing using one's strengths and resources and facilitating positive experiences to achieve one's potential rather than focusing primarily on individual limitations and deficits (Hoffman & Long, 2020). Other models reflect this thinking, including the leisure and well-being model (Hood & Carruthers, 2007), the leisure-spiritual coping model (Heintzman, 2008), and the flourishing through leisure model (Anderson & Heyne, 2012). The increasing global perspective of TR has also brought about a rethinking of the models in light of varying cultural beliefs and practices related to health care and individual versus collective values, and has led to increased focus on developing cultural sensitivity (Dieser, 2020). Future models will take into consideration advances in technology (Ross & Ashton, 2017) that enable greater participation and expand programming options. The International Classification of Functioning, Disability and Health, a framework developed by the World Health Organization to standardize a worldwide approach to health care, is being utilized by a number of agencies and organizations. This framework takes a holistic approach to health, including a person's activity, participation, and environmental and personal factors. It supports the person-centered and strengths-based approaches (Devine & Bennett, 2020) and may lead to the development of new TR models.

OUTSTANDING GRADUATE

Veronica Spinden

Background Information

Name: Veronica Spinden

Education: BA in recreation administration from Kean University, with a concentration in therapeutic recreation, and MS in recreational therapy from Temple University

Credentials: CTRS (Certified Therapeutic Recreation Specialist)

Affiliations: American Therapeutic Recreation Association (ATRA), member at-large

Career Information

Position: Allied Clinical Therapist–Recreational Therapist

Organization: Penn Medicine Princeton House Behavioral Health is a 110-bed inpatient behavioral health hospital providing detoxification, psychiatric, and dual diagnosis services for adults. This facility provides a variety of therapeutic services within the allied clinical therapies department including recreational therapy, art therapy, music therapy, and dance movement therapy. Princeton House utilizes evidence-based practice and innovative approaches to behavioral health treatment.

Job description: Recreational therapists plan and administer high-quality clinical therapies to adult patients in individual or group settings. Their most significant role is to plan and implement recreational therapy interventions to address client's psychosocial functional needs throughout their treatment at Princeton House. Through assessment, observation, and development of treatment goals they are able to address client's functional needs and effectively document client outcomes and progress. Allied clinical therapists are a crucial part of the treatment team and present necessary clinical information during multidisciplinary meetings.

Career path: My first exposure to the therapeutic value of recreation began when I volunteered with children with varying disabilities at an inclusive summer camp. I recognized the impact recreation had in producing positive health and wellness outcomes for campers and began exploring academically how recreation can be used in other therapeutic formats. From there, I discovered recreational therapy and knew this was the field I wanted to pursue. Throughout my studies I saw the potential implications of using leisure and components of psychotherapy in behavioral health treatment. I discovered my passion for practicing recreational therapy with clients with substance use disorders during my internship at Princeton House. Following graduation, I was hired as a recreational therapist with the allied clinical therapies department. After completing my undergraduate degree, I pursued a graduate degree in recreational therapy to further my knowledge of recreational therapy practice and explore evidence-based practice for behavioral health settings and populations.

After finishing graduate school, I wanted to find other ways to stay involved in recreational therapy outside of my everyday practice. I became involved in the American Therapeutic Recreation Association (ATRA) working on the leadership development team. Since then, I have been fortunate to join the ATRA Board of Directors as a member at-large to further explore my interests in innovative recreational therapy practice and support other leaders within the profession. Additionally, I have joined a community of recreational therapy professionals at Kean University as an adjunct professor to share my knowledge and skills with developing therapists. I'm looking forward to finishing my alcohol and drug counseling license and pursuing a PhD in Public Health to unite my passions of recreational therapy and community health initiatives.

Advice for Undergraduates

Out of all the advice I was given throughout college, the two pieces that I found to be most helpful were to take advantage of the expertise of your professors and to treat your internship like your first job. Learning from a textbook and learning from real-world application are two very different approaches to developing skills. Your professors are experts in the field and have knowledge from years of experience. They are an invaluable resource who will provide advice and feedback that a textbook can't teach you; use them! Your internship is your first glimpse at real-world practice; take it seriously. Ask questions, step out of your comfort zone, and absorb all you can while you're still a student. There will come a time when you won't have all these resources at your disposal. Don't waste them!

In Canada, the primary model during the 2010s and early 2020s has been the leisure ability model, which reflects the nation's long-standing commitment to integration of people with disabilities into all aspects of society and its recognition that recreation is a part of the vision of full citizenship for all Canadians. However, with the increased emphasis on health in the Canadian definition of TR (Canadian Therapeutic Recreation Association, 2022), other models such as HP/HP are being increasingly utilized. Practitioners in the United States also follow the leisure ability model as well as the HP/HP model, which has become more prevalent in clinical settings. The strengths-based approach and the leisure and well-being model are also becoming more widely adopted and incorporated into many aspects of the TR process in all settings.

THERAPEUTIC RECREATION PROCESS

The TR process is a series of steps used to carry out the purposes of TR. The National Council for Therapeutic Recreation Certification (NCTRC) periodically conducts a job analysis to identify the job tasks of a CTRS, most of which are functions of the TR process. A handy acronym for the four steps in the TR process is APIE:

- Assessment
- Planning
- Implementation
- Evaluation

Some scholars and experts have advocated adding documentation as a fifth step in the TR process (Long, 2020); however, others believe that documentation is an essential component of each step and should not be excluded from any of the original four steps (Austin, 2018). While the TR process is unique to TR practice, the steps are included in the work of most professional disciplines focused on clients' health and well-being. The TR process can be applied in any setting where recreation is used with therapeutic intent to help a person achieve specific outcomes. Let's examine the four steps more closely and apply them to the case of Mr. Perez, shown in the sidebar.

Assessment

The first step is **assessment**, which is a systematic process of gathering and synthesizing information about the client and their environment using a variety of methods, such as interviews, observation, standardized tests, and input from other disciplines and significant others, to devise an individualized treatment or service plan. The information the RT seeks includes the client's strengths and areas that need improvement, and their levels of physical, social, emotional, and cognitive functioning related to two areas:

1. Capability to participate in different types of TR programs
2. Aspects that can be improved through TR participation

The RT also obtains information related to the client's leisure functioning including

- interests,
- needs,
- perceived problems with leisure,
- patterns of participation,
- available leisure partners,
- planning and decision-making skills, and
- knowledge of and ability to use leisure resources.

The client may be asked to identify their goals to best understand motivations and develop the most appropriate plan. Obtaining input from the client, to the best of their ability, is an essential component of conducting an assessment so the client feels invested in the TR process.

Planning

Planning refers to the development of the client's individual treatment or program plan. By participating in the planning process with the assistance of the RT, clients are at the center of their services. This approach increases the client's feelings of control over decisions affecting their care and treatment and enhances their motivation to participate, thereby maximizing the benefits of TR. RTs also use individuals' strengths in planning to overcome their limitations and to reinforce their abilities and perceived competence, which are components of the strengths-based approach. Utilizing this approach, the RT helps people reach their goals and aspirations through active participation in planning their services to build on and develop their strengths. "Strengths may be internal, within an individual, or external, within the environments and contexts in which an individual lives, works, or plays" (Anderson & Heyne, 2012, p. 108). Once developed, the

Illustration of the TR Process: The Case of Mr. Perez

As part of the TR process, the RT might design a specific intervention that targets a client's functional limitations. For example, Mr. Perez had a stroke that resulted in muscle weakness and stiffness. The team identified his goals as strengthening his muscles and increasing his range of motion. During the TR assessment, Mr. Perez stated that he enjoys swimming and spending time with his grandchildren, and he wants to continue to do these things. The RT collaborated with the physical therapist to make a plan, using evidence-based practice and active treatment to help Mr. Perez reach his goals. Identifying research that showed the positive outcomes of adapted aquatics to address muscular limitations from stroke, the RT planned active treatment for Mr. Perez, consisting of adapted aquatics three times a week (frequency) for 30 minutes each time (intensity) for four weeks (duration). Mr. Perez agreed to participate in this program. He first needed to learn how to use a flotation device to support himself in the pool. The expectation was that at the end of the four weeks, he would have made predetermined improvements in his muscle strength, range of motion, and ability to use the flotation device.

The RT can also identify and indicate in the written plan specific leadership and therapeutic approaches to use with the client. Mr. Perez required frequent positive reinforcement, physical assistance, and a demonstration of the appropriate use of the adapted equipment to promote his progress. Mr. Perez's discharge plan included information and scheduling about an adapted swim program for senior citizens at the local YMCA, and other activities he could do with his grandchildren.

During the implementation phase, the RT evaluated Mr. Perez's progress in the adapted aquatics. Formative evaluation revealed that Mr. Perez was scheduled for aquatics in the morning, but it became apparent that he was too tired at that time, so the program was moved to the afternoon. He stated he was a little fearful about entering the pool because of his muscle weakness and stiffness. Using **active listening** (the process of carefully paying attention to the information someone shares with you, and reflecting back—through questions and body language—that you heard them), the RT provided much emotional support. Additional assistance from two staff members rather than one, as was originally planned, was provided. This change was made as soon as the need was recognized. At the end of the four weeks, the summative evaluation identified that Mr. Perez had made a 25 percent increase in his range of motion and minimal improvement in muscle strength. He also expressed feelings of relaxation because of the aquatics and a desire to invite his grandson to participate with him, thereby gaining the benefits of family recreation. Mr. Perez was successful in making measurable progress toward his functional goals and gained additional qualitative benefits from the TR experience.

Active listening is the process of carefully paying attention to the information someone shares with you, and reflecting back—through questions and body language—that you heard them.

plan is placed in the client's chart as the official record of the TR services that the client will receive. The plan generally includes

- an assessment summary,
- the client's goals and specific objectives (or steps) to reach the goals,
- a schedule of the client's planned participation in the TR program, and
- a discharge plan, if required.

Based on the assessment, the RT specifies goals or outcomes, in cooperation with the client, that the client will work toward while participating in the TR program. These goals can be related to changing leisure-related behaviors, reducing health concerns, improving functional ability, and increasing quality of life. Goals are statements that provide direction for the client's services. Client goals may be identified by the professional health care team for appropriate intervention in one or more disciplines. For example, goals could be to increase range of motion, attention span, or social interaction.

As a member of the treatment team, the RT addresses team-specified goals and develops goals, with input from the client whenever possible, for client use of recreation-based interventions. In addition to addressing functional goals, the RT sets goals related to leisure behavior. These goals could include acquiring knowledge of community resources for recreation participation or learning how to use adapted equipment to enable participation in a recreation activity. The RT then specifies a series of behavioral objectives, also known as *measurable goals,* which are steps toward achieving the overall goal. The successful accomplishment of each behavioral objective or measurable goal in the progression will lead to meeting the overall client goals. The terms used to describe goals and objectives may differ from setting to setting. Some settings use *behavioral objectives* instead of measurable goals or *outcomes* instead of goals. The intent and purpose are the same regardless of terminology.

A major component of the planning step is the selection and scheduling of specific TR interventions or activities. Recreation activities are the primary means through which RTs serve clients, so they need to understand which recreation activities produce which outcomes. Just as a doctor knows which medications to prescribe to treat an illness, RTs work with their clients to select the recreation activities that offer the best chances of producing results. A very important point to remember is that most TR programming occurs in groups. Each group will have multiple participants with both similar and differing needs. Understanding which needs can be met by each activity or program allows the RT to tailor the group experience for maximum benefit of the participants and select appropriate activities to enable clients to reach their desired goals.

An important TR practice is to have clients be as involved as possible in planning the TR services that they will receive. This is known as ***person-centered planning.*** In person-centered planning, the client is actively involved in choosing the life they want to live and the supports they will need to realize their vision of their future. The RT should work with the client to choose activities that the client is interested and willing to participate in. Using **activity analysis**, the RT analyzes the behaviors required to participate in an activity. The RT can then prescribe a specific activity or a group of activities in the **individual treatment plan** or care plan. A given activity may help a client progress toward more than one goal, or several activities may address a single goal. For an older nursing home resident with dementia, playing computer games can help increase attention span, improve eye–hand coordination, stimulate cognitive functioning, and promote feelings of accomplishment. This resident may participate in a sewing group in addition to, or instead of, the computer games and be working toward the same goals. Both of these activities also can be sources of recreation, fun, and enjoyment for the resident.

Collaboration among disciplines at team meetings can help develop the optimal plan for the client. The RT is often responsible for developing a weekly or monthly calendar of all TR programs and activities that are offered. To plan a feasible calendar for maximum participation, the RT might coordinate with other disciplines to schedule facility use and avoid conflicts in scheduling services such as a physical or occupational therapy session, a meeting with a social worker, or a consultation with a dietitian.

Implementation

The third step in the TR process is implementation. To implement the program, the RT puts the client's individual TR plan in action. This step involves motivating the client to participate in individual and group TR activities. The RT may use various therapeutic strategies to both motivate the client and to enable progress toward achieving goals during participation. These might include active listening, cognitive-behavioral techniques, and positive psychology strategies. Implementation considers the overall facility schedule, available space and resources, needed equipment and supplies, needs of the client, and staffing requirements of programs. Successful implementation may require adjustments to the plan to maximize the benefits to the clients.

Evaluation

Evaluation is the final step in the TR process. Evaluation is both formative and summative.

- **Formative evaluation** is ongoing during the implementation phase and leads to immediate changes and improvements in the treatment plan.
- **Summative evaluation** occurs at the completion of the program to determine whether the program helped the client reach their goals and whether changes are needed before implementing the program with other clients.

A plan might not produce the desired results due to

- changes in the client's condition,
- use of new medications,
- lack of support from family,

.shock/iStockphoto/Getty Images

Implementing a program involves motivating the client to participate in individual and group TR activities.

- failure to obtain important information during the assessment,
- lack of skill on the part of the RTs,
- inappropriate leadership approaches, or
- inconsistency on the part of the team.

Determining the factors that may have impeded the client's progress is an important evaluation task.

The client will probably achieve the outcomes according to the treatment plan. Planned health care outcomes are generally measured in quantitative terms such as the amount of time spent in activity or improvement in the ability to perform a certain task. A client may experience some unintended benefits as well, such as feelings of relaxation or pleasure in social opportunities. These unplanned benefits may be just as significant and are often more subjective, meaning that they are unique to the participant and relate to the quality, enjoyment, and personal meaning of the experience for the client. They should not be overlooked when reporting a client's progress in TR because they can provide a fuller picture of the client's accomplishments.

Documentation

It is critical that the RT document the client's assessment and progress. TR **documentation** is the written or electronic recording of a client's participation and progress in the TR program. This information is recorded in the client's record or medical chart, which is considered a legal document, and supplies evidence of the TR services provided and the outcomes of participation for the client. The accuracy of the RT's documentation should be above reproach. Documentation occurs at regularly scheduled intervals and is reviewed by auditors, surveyors, and regulators of accrediting bodies and governmental agencies. Every RT must be well informed of agency policies regarding documentation.

PROFESSIONALISM

You may now be asking yourself whether TR is right for you and what you can look forward to if you decide to become an RT. Approximately 20,000 people are employed as recreational therapists in the United States (Bureau of Labor Statistics,

2021). Thousands more work as recreation leaders in therapeutic settings. Most CTRSs work in hospitals (34%) and skilled nursing facilities (16%), and about 70 percent work with adults and older adults (NCTRC, 2020). Job growth may also continue in community-based settings, as opposed to hospital and inpatient treatment facilities as services expand for people in their local communities. The average salary for the 18,600 recreational therapists in the United States is $51,000 (Bureau of Labor Statistics, 2021), although this includes non-CTRSs as well. According to the National Council for Therapeutic Recreation Certification (2020), almost half of all CTRSs earn over $60,000 per year. Earning potential can go as high as $100,000 per year for directors of departments who have advanced degrees and extensive experience, depending on setting and location, with almost 4 percent of CTRSs earning over $100,000 (NCTRC, 2020).

Keep in mind that being a professional entails more than just carrying out your job duties and responsibilities. Being a professional in any field means

- obtaining an education,
- possessing the credentials recognized by your profession,
- being an active member of professional organizations at local and international levels,
- providing services based on professional standards of practice,
- adhering to a code of ethical behavior, and
- updating your professional knowledge through reading, research, and continuing education.

Education

The first step in becoming a TR professional is to obtain an education in TR, which provides a philosophical and theoretical foundation related to TR service provision and extensive knowledge in areas essential to TR practice. Knowledge areas include the nature of illness and disability, the effects of disability on functioning, the role of TR in addressing the limitations imposed by disability, and the procedures and methods used by RTs in developing treatment plans and implementing TR services. TR curricula may be an option or specialization in a recreation degree program or its own degree program at the associate, bachelor, master, or doctoral level. College programs may apply for **accreditation**, a process by which the academic program is evaluated according to a set of standards for curriculum content. Although accreditation of curricula is not required by law, accreditation ensures that the content areas cover essential information for college students. The Committee on Accreditation of Recreational Therapy Education (CARTE) was formally initiated with the Commission on Accreditation of Allied Health Education Programs (CAAHEP) in 2010. The Council on Accreditation of Parks, Recreation, Tourism, and Related Professions (COAPRT) has also developed and issued outcomes for curriculum content areas for TR academic programs. Regardless of the accreditation status of a college program, the value of a sound education in TR cannot be overstated and is a component of requirements for obtaining appropriate professional credentials.

Credentialing

Credentialing is the process by which a profession or government certifies that a professional has met the established minimum standards of competency required for practice. Credentialing is intended to protect consumers when they receive services. The three types of credentialing programs are registration, certification, and licensure.

1. Registration is a voluntary listing of people who practice in a profession according to established criteria.
2. Certification requires meeting a set of predetermined criteria and usually includes a written examination.
3. Licensure is a process by which state governments legally mandate qualifications for practice and administer a licensing program.

In TR, the largest credentialing program is administered by the **National Council for Therapeutic Recreation Certification (NCTRC)**. To be eligible for certification as a CTRS according to NCTRC, applicants must meet a combination of education and experience requirements and pass the certification examination. In 2010, NCTRC established a specialty certification program to recognize advanced levels of practice in five areas: physical medicine and rehabilitation, geriatrics, developmental disabilities, behavioral health, and community inclusion services. Utah, North Carolina, New Hampshire, Oklahoma, and New Jersey have passed licensure laws, and several other states are actively pursuing this legislation.

The credentialing process attests that you have met the standards to practice your profession and that your judgment and decision-making skills as a professional can be trusted. To maintain your credentials, most credentialing programs require TR professionals to participate in continuing education activities to update their knowledge and skills for practice. Workshops and conferences that cover a wide range of topics are offered by professional organizations at the local, state, regional, national, and international levels.

Professional Organizations

By becoming a member of a professional TR organization or association, you are joining your peers to

- promote the value of TR;
- participate in education, communication, and advocacy; and
- establish and maintain standards of professional practice and behavior.

The national TR professional organizations are the ATRA in the United States and the CTRA in Canada. Almost every state and province has either a TR organization or a TR branch of the state or provincial recreation association. Examples include the New York State Therapeutic Recreation Association (NYSTRA) and Therapeutic Recreation Ontario (TRO). Local TR chapters of ATRA have also been formed, such as the New Jersey/Eastern Pennsylvania chapter. Joining professional organizations demonstrates your commitment to advancing the profession. Many RTs agree that one of the most valued benefits of membership is the interaction with peers through networking, sharing ideas, and forging lasting friendships based on common interests and needs.

Standards of Practice

Standards of practice define the scope of services provided by TR professionals and state a minimal, acceptable level of service delivery. Adherence to these standards ensures consistent practice across service settings and helps establish the credibility of the profession. ATRA and CTRA have both developed sets of standards that cover the following core practices:

- Assessment
- Treatment planning
- Documentation
- Management

You will find that these standards are valuable guides in designing and implementing quality services and helping ensure ethical practice and behavior.

Ethics

A hallmark of a true profession is a **code of ethics**, which is a written description of the established duties and obligations of the professional to protect the human rights of recipients of services. ATRA and the provincial Canadian TR associations have codes of ethics for TR professionals. All codes cover the four major bioethical principles:

1. *Autonomy.* The client has the right to self-determination, which may conflict with what you, the family, other staff members, or the agency thinks is best for the client.
2. *Beneficence.* Only do good for your clients.
3. *Nonmalfeasance.* Use care and skill in service so you prevent and do not cause harm.
4. *Justice.* Allocate resources in a fair and equitable manner.

Other ethical concerns include

- confidentiality (the client has the right to control access to their own information and to know who will have access to that information),
- maintaining a professional relationship with clients (not overstepping boundaries into friendships or personal relationships), and
- cultural competence (understanding and respecting diverse beliefs, identities, and values and how they influence clients' behaviors).

Keeping Current in the Profession

The foundation of a profession is a body of knowledge derived from research. Professionals have the obligation to read and apply relevant research findings. Reading research helps practitioners become more reflective and thoughtful in their work and can enrich their practice as they apply proven techniques. TR research is published in professional journals such as the *Therapeutic Recreation Journal*, *Annual in Therapeutic Recreation*, and the *American Journal of Recreation Therapy*. In addition, new textbooks are published every year and present best practices and analysis of current thinking in the profession that are invaluable to career development even after one graduates.

In addition to reading and applying research, professionals should actively participate in the research process to contribute to the body of knowledge in the field by writing books, chapters, and magazine articles for the TR field and for publications geared to other professions and the public. There is a need for efficacy research in TR, which is research that demonstrates that TR can produce the outcomes it claims to produce. This research leads to a refinement of TR interventions targeted to specific health care problems and goals. Many TR settings offer the opportunity to implement a research project.

Right now, you might not be interested in conducting research, but an important trend in health care, which started in Canada, uses practitioners' expertise and research findings to select the best programs and services to achieve outcomes. This approach, known as *evidence-based practice* (*EBP*), enables practitioners and researchers to collaborate on systematically collecting data to provide evidence for the optimal type of client care. Practitioners can write up the results of their research and publish it in appropriate journals and present their findings at professional conferences. Increasing the body of knowledge of TR through research continues to be a major objective of the TR profession.

Being a professional implies a sense of calling to do more than just go to work every day and carry out assigned responsibilities and duties. Professionalism implies dedication to the beliefs and values of your chosen field, lifelong learning, and commitment to the highest standards of practice. As you explore the TR profession and meet TR practitioners, observe the demeanor and behaviors of people who demonstrate admirable qualities. Can they articulate the meaning and value of TR? Are they enthusiastic and positive about the work they do? Do they demonstrate their love of TR through professional activities outside work and keep up to date with the latest developments? To have a rewarding and fulfilling career, you may wish to emulate these professional qualities.

YOUR FUTURE IN THERAPEUTIC RECREATION

Students are often attracted to a TR major because of their interest in being part of a helping profession that works with people in health or human service settings. Sensitivity, compassion, patience, com-

munication skills, and the desire to help people are essential to working as an RT. Much of the RT's work involves communication and emotional support of clients, which helps promote clients' well-being and successful goal achievement. Many students are also attracted to recreation as a major because of their interest in activities such as sport, fitness, outdoor pursuits, music, or art, and then they discover TR. Although no one personality type is best suited to TR, people who enter helping professions such as TR often possess certain attributes. Within TR, the following are highly desirable qualities that facilitate a relationship focused on helping the client achieve their goals:

- Being self-aware
- Having the desire to learn new things and to communicate with people
- Being comfortable with taking initiative
- Being flexible and adaptable to change and unexpected events
- Having creative ideas, energy, enthusiasm, and compassion for people

Whatever has led you to the TR field, essential elements to continued professional success and satisfaction are knowledge of a wide range of traditional recreation activities, the ability to implement credible programs, and the motivation to learn new activities and therapeutic techniques. Although RTs must have general knowledge of recreation opportunities, they must also be skilled in nontraditional facilitation techniques, such as cognitive behavioral therapy and positive psychology, as well as the wellness and **health promotion** modalities described at the beginning of the chapter, which may include stress management, assertiveness training, sensory stimulation, and a variety of wellness and relaxation techniques. You will learn about many recreation activities as part of your TR curriculum.

Attending workshops and conferences is a valuable way to gain exposure to and learn about innovative programs and techniques. Taking noncredit, continuing education or adult education courses helps you stay up to date with fresh program ideas. Certifications are offered in specialty areas such as adapted aquatics, horticulture therapy, personal training, aromatherapy, and yoga. Some jobs may require a driver's license or certification in first aid, CPR, or lifeguard and water safety instruction. Obtaining specialized training and credentials will enhance your qualifications as an RT and enrich your job performance. One of the wonderful features of TR is that your personal interests can be

© Jon Feingersh/Blend Images/Corbis

Attending workshops and conferences is a valuable way to gain exposure to and learn about innovative programs and techniques.

incorporated into professional practice. You should strive to keep your work interesting and participate with your clients with a sense of joy and fun. If *you* are bored by the programs that you lead, think about how your clients will feel!

In addition to learning new interventions and therapeutic methods, you will benefit from acquiring competency in management techniques and administrative processes, including skills such as

- budgeting,
- grant writing,
- marketing,
- public relations,
- oral and written communication, and
- the use of technology.

These are essential for RTs who wish to become supervisors and administrators of TR services. Collaboration skills are needed to work with other disciplines, departments, and agencies to improve client outcomes, maximize resources, and reduce duplication of services. **Cross-cultural competence**, which refers to the ability to understand, respect, and communicate with diverse groups of people, is essential in the culturally diverse nations of Canada and the United States. Although 85 percent of CTRSs are white (NCTRC, 2021), the client populations served are extremely diverse. Cross-cultural competence is a social justice issue and essential for successful interactions with staff, clients, and their families.

TRENDS FOR THE 21ST CENTURY

What does the future hold for the TR profession? As you have read, TR is a broad and varied field that operates in numerous settings and with diverse groups of people with all types of disabilities, health conditions, and disadvantaged situations. Changes in health care, economic pressures, social trends, demographic characteristics, and technological advances are influencing society to focus on health promotion, independent functioning, quality of life, and quality and effectiveness of services. Continued calls for creating welcoming, diverse, and inclusive environments for both clients and workers have presented challenges and opportunities for growth and innovation in the TR field. Health promotion and disease prevention, particularly in the areas of obesity, lifestyle conditions, and stress-related illness, and reducing the impacts of disability, can be achieved through participation in recreation activities such as exercise, dance, gardening, art, social recreation, games, and sport. Wellness practices such as tai chi, yoga, massage, and aromatherapy are being incorporated into many TR programs. Encouraging people to take responsibility for their health can improve health status and lead to independent functioning.

The shift from the institution to the community as the primary residential setting for people with disabilities has opened the doors for TR practice in schools, day programs, group homes, community centers, military bases, and individuals' homes. Emphasis in these settings is on promoting independent functioning and finding joy and meaning in life through recreation participation in the optimal living environment. RTs have responded to these changes by offering retirement planning, early intervention, family leisure counseling, caregiver support groups, and community reintegration. The inclusion movement will continue to expand, offering opportunities for RTs to function as community inclusion specialists, accessibility consultants, and trainers in leadership techniques, adaptations for people with disabilities, and cross-cultural competence. Public parks and recreation departments have increased their emphasis on promoting parks for public health (Colman, 2020), expanding professional opportunities for RTs in the community. More and more RTs have opened their own RT businesses as private practitioners to utilize their expanding skills and service a diversifying client base with a more personalized approach tailored to their needs. In the political arena, TR organizations have lobbied to include TR in legislation and regulations concerning health care, education, and disability. Several states are pursuing government-sponsored licensure to strengthen the value of the credentialing process for TR practitioners.

Those who enter the profession will confront several challenges. Although many professionals participate in professional organizations, obtain their credentials, keep current with the latest developments, and continually improve their programs and services, greater involvement in these professional activities industry wide is vital for the full recognition of TR as an essential service. Membership in professional organizations at every level does not reflect the number of people who identify themselves as working in TR. Many who are eligible to obtain professional credentials have chosen not to do so. Employers continue to hire people to work in TR positions who are not educated in TR. Curricula in college and university TR programs vary. Inconsistency in using the best practices of the field still exists across TR settings. These challenges need to be addressed by all professionals to ensure the most effective and meaningful services for the people we serve.

As the 21st century progresses, the following trends will continue to shape discussions about health policies and human services, including TR:

- Increasing cultural diversity in North America that represents various values and interests, and recognition of the need to create welcoming, diverse, and inclusive environments for staff and clients
- An expanding aging population of active and recreation-oriented seniors, and older and frailer people who live into their 90s and beyond
- The continuing impact of both the ADA in the United States and the Accessible Canada Act on the lives of people with disabilities
- Increased visibility of the LGBTQIA+ population and the imperative to respond to their needs
- Wounded veterans who return from war zones with severe and involved injuries and conditions (such as traumatic brain injury,

post-traumatic stress disorder, military sexual trauma, and amputations) who will be served in Veterans Administration hospitals and facilities as well as community-based programs
- Millions of people taking personal responsibility for their health and well-being, increased use of complementary and alternative approaches, and recognition of the role of recreation and leisure in public health
- An increasing obesity crisis, declining levels of physical activity and fitness, and increases in diabetes, hypertension, and other lifestyle-associated conditions
- The spiraling cost of health care and the enormous demands placed on the health care system
- Technological innovations, including telehealth; increased reliance on technology for programming and as assistive devices; the costs, benefits, and risks associated with technology usage; and the need for additional training of staff and clients to utilize tech effectively
- Responding to newly emerging health crises and their long-lasting impacts

SUMMARY

This chapter described the scope and range of clients, settings, and services that make up the TR profession. The populations served by RTs and the settings in which RTs work will continue to multiply, and the purposes and role of TR will continue to evolve. Studying the TR definitions, models, philosophy, and benefits is essential to fulfilling a role as a TR professional. Understanding the TR process and the components of professionalism will help prepare you to make your professional choices and plan for a satisfying and meaningful career. As TR faces the challenges of the future, well-educated and credentialed practitioners will hold the key to ensuring that the benefits of therapeutic recreation are experienced by people from diverse backgrounds whose lives have been affected by disability, health conditions, and social disadvantages. TR offers a perspective and service that is unique and rewarding for practitioners and the people they support.

Review Questions

1. Distinguish between therapeutic recreation and recreational thera-py. Regardless of terminology, describe the purposes and benefits of the profession and the settings and populations served.

2. Identify and explain the steps in the TR process. Why do some professionals think it has four steps and others think it should have five steps?

3. How has inclusion philosophy evolved since the passage of the first laws regarding accessibility? Include in your answer reference to the legislation, building blocks, and recent trends.

4. What are the characteristics and behaviors of a TR professional? Which professional behaviors do you plan to develop as you ad-vance in your education and career?

5. Discuss trends in TR practices related to programming, settings, and credentialing.

Go to HK*Propel* to complete the activities for this chapter.

CHAPTER 11

Unique Groups

Nicole Green, Augustus W. Hallmon, John Byl,
David Kahan, Mary Parr, and Yating "Tina" Liang

> **"** If bread is the first necessity of life, recreation is a close second. **"**
>
> Edward Bellamy, American author

Tara Moore/DigitalVision/Getty Images

——— LEARNING OUTCOMES ———

After reading this chapter, you should be able to do the following:

> Understand the purpose of campus recreation

> Summarize the history of campus recreation

> Describe the benefits and value of campus recreation

> Compare the programs and components associated with campus recreation

> Describe the growth of esports since the first video game competitions in the 1970s

> Understand the debate surrounding the status of esports within the context of traditional sports

> Identify job opportunities and programming possibilities that esports present to recreation and leisure professionals

> Understand that Christian, Jewish, and Muslim communities are interested in using recreation to enhance their communities and to bring outsiders in

> Understand there is considerable variability within Christianity, Judaism, and Islam

> Know that the three pillars of NRPA are upheld by Christianity, Judaism, and Islam, but those pillars are tempered with the larger goals of maintaining group affiliation and proselytizing

> Appreciate that many Muslims do not view their requisite behaviors (e.g., fasting during Ramadan, covering for modesty) as obstacles to recreation and that recreation professionals can provide conditions that allow for universal access to services

> Compare the definitions of community health and individual health

> Describe a step-by-step process for the development of a corporate wellness program that addresses health concerns for a business

> Describe the employer benefits of investment in employee wellness and health promotion programs

> Understand the role recreation plays in the U.S. and Canadian Armed Forces

> Compare the different programs and services offered in a military recreation setting

---

Campus Recreation

Nicole Green

 You can discover more about a person in an hour of play than in a year of conversation. **"**

Plato, Greek philosopher

Campus recreation provides facilities and programs for campus communities to engage in recreation, sport, and wellness opportunities. Recreation services offered on a college or university campus are commonly called *campus recreation*, *university recreation*, or *recreational sports*. The structure and offerings of campus recreation vary based on the size of the institution, the reporting structure, and whether it is a **residential campus** or **commuter campus**. Campus recreation is unique because of the population it serves. There is regular turnover in this group and an influx of new users each fall. Programming and hours of operation tend to follow the academic cycle with high participation during the academic terms and low participation during final exams and break periods.

The primary consumers of campus recreation are students and other members of the campus community, which could include faculty, staff, alumni, and sometimes the local community. Campus recreation is unique in that the main user group is traditional college-aged students ranging from 18 to 24 years old (Wallace-Carr, 2013). Another distinctive factor is that a portion of this audience turns over every year. Colleges and universities have seen an increase in nontraditional and veteran students returning to campus, and this has diversified programming. This continual turnover requires campus recreation departments to rely heavily on marketing and communication. Often, campus recreation departments partner with student orientation programs to familiarize students with the facilities and programs during the orientation process.

HISTORY OF CAMPUS RECREATION

Campus recreation has an exciting and innovative history. Unbeknownst to most, intramural sports were the first initial form of structured, competitive sports for college students on colonial campuses in the early 19th century. Intramurals were organized for students and by students with the goal of being a diversion from the rigors of academic life (Mueller, 1971). Intramural competition was the gateway to the creation of intercollegiate athletics, which were created in the middle of the 19th century (CAS, 2015). Athletics progressed to be the dominating activity presence on campuses, and intramural sports continued to develop, change, and expand as institutions created intramural programs on their campuses.

In 1913, The Ohio State University and the University of Michigan were the first two flagship institutions to create intramural sports programs and dedicate staff members to these program areas. Additional institutions followed soon after, such as Kansas State, Oregon State, the University of Illinois, and the University of Texas. The University of Michigan was the first to build a facility exclusively for the use of intramural sports in 1928. Dr. Elmer Mitchell, the first director for intramurals at the University of Michigan, is fondly considered the "father of intramural sports" (University of Michigan, n.d.).

Dr. William Wasson is another significant leader in campus recreation. In 1950, Dr. Wasson, the director of health, physical education, and recreation at Dillard University, formed an intramural

institute and workshop for Black colleges and universities. This was the first workshop of its kind, including 22 African American male and female intramural directors from 11 historically Black institutions. This resulted in the formation of the National Intramural Association (NIA) (NIRSA, n.d.).

In 1975, the NIA was renamed the National Intramural-Recreational Sports Association (NIRSA) because the scope and focus of recreation were changing, and the organization was no longer exclusive to intramural programs (Wallace-Carr, 2013). The range of services and programs has expanded tremendously, and campus recreation centers now include a diverse and dynamic array of offerings including intramural sports, fitness, youth and family programs, aquatics, club sports, outdoor recreation and climbing, activity classes, adaptive recreation, and other innovative program areas. NIRSA has evolved to be a significant, holistic organization that is distinguished as a "cornerstone of students' overall collegiate education and experience" (Wilson, 2008, p. 27). In 2009, the organization name was changed again due to the scope of program and facility offerings becoming even broader and more encompassing. It is now called NIRSA, Leaders in Collegiate Recreation. NIRSA's mission is to be "a leader in higher education and the advocate for the advancement of recreation, sport, and wellness by providing educational and developmental opportunities, generating and sharing knowledge, and promoting networking and growth for members" (NIRSA, n.d.-b). There are over 4,500 career staff, students, and businesses that make up the association. There are over 8.1 million students at colleges and universities across the United States and Canada that are participating in campus recreation programs (NIRSA, 2022).

ORGANIZATIONAL STRUCTURES

There are a wide variety of organizational structures found across campuses depending on the needs of the institution and its population, funding sources, and model. Traditionally, a department will include three areas: administration, facilities and operations, and programs.

Administration

Administration is the supporting structure of the department. The functions of administration include leadership, business services, marketing

OUTSTANDING GRADUATE

Courtesy of Kamala Ersson.

Background Information

Name: Christin Everson

Education: BA in psychology from the University of Oregon, MS in kinesiology from Indiana University

Credentials: Certified Personal Trainer, Health Coach, and Group Fitness Instructor

Awards: 2016 NIRSA Foundation Scholarship

Affiliations: Subject matter expert for American Council on Exercise (ACE)

Career Information

Position: Assistant Director of Fitness and Marketing

Organization: Seattle University (SU) is a private Jesuit institution located in the urban setting of Seattle, Washington. University Recreation (UREC) provides employment to over 120 students and is the third-largest employer of students on campus. Through sport, fitness, and outdoor programming, UREC inspires, educates, and empowers the SU community to live happier, healthier, and more successful lives. UREC serves nearly 8,000 members, made up of students, faculty, staff, alumni, and their partners and dependents.

Job description: I oversee all fitness programming and operations as well as all marketing for the department. I also have an adjunct faculty role with Seattle University in the sport and exercise science department. My specific responsibilities are to

- mentor, supervise, hire, train, and evaluate a group fitness staff of 20, a personal training staff of 10, and two part-time group fitness program managers; and

- oversee all marketing operations for the university's recreation department, including four student marketing managers.

Career path: My career path is truly the result of what can happen when mentors believe and invest in you. I started as a former competitive athlete who came to college no longer belonging to a specific community. I found the rec center at the University of Oregon and was hooked from day one. My supervisors quickly began pushing me to challenge myself in new ways, advocating for me to attend regional and national conferences and preparing me for what a career in this field might entail. With their help, I secured a graduate assistant position at Indiana University working specifically in group exercise. As a first-generation college student, I never anticipated continuing my education past a bachelor's degree; recreation helped me achieve a goal that I didn't even know I had. Since finishing my master's degree, I have held three different professional positions in fitness. I have begun teaching for Seattle University as an adjunct faculty member, and I work with the American Council on Exercise as a subject matter expert, assisting in the creation of both the health coach and personal trainer exams.

Likes and dislikes about the job: My job is about two things: creating safe and effective programs for members to enjoy movement and reach their goals, and creating a safe and effective space for students to learn and grow. Campus recreation is the only field that combines both those items into one daily job. One drawback is the monetary value (or lack thereof) assigned to our work.

Advice for Undergraduates

Know your passion and act on it! Work hard and take every opportunity given. Each experience is useful, even when you don't think it is. Working in recreation provides so many incredible experiences, both professionally and personally. I've met some of my best friends and favorite people working in this field.

and communications, budget and finance, purchasing, human resources, and information technology. Campus recreation departments most often align or report to one of the following units: **student affairs**, athletics, enrollment management, or business affairs. In most cases, building, operations, and programming costs are paid for by student fees associated with tuition. In some cases, the cost to students can be offset or reduced for departments that can sell memberships, rent spaces, and provide additional programming.

Best practices, standards, and guidelines for the administration and programming of campus recreation are established by the Council for the

Advancement of Standards in Higher Education (CAS). These standards and guidelines are created by professionals working in the field of campus recreation.

Facilities and Operations

Facilities are the physical buildings, fields, and equipment used for campus recreation programs. **Operations** relates to the management of the spaces and the people in them. Campus recreation facilities are state-of-the-art, multifaceted buildings developed to meet participant needs. There is great variance in the types of facilities managed by campus recreation departments. The average facility has cardio and weight-training equipment; multiuse courts for basketball, volleyball, and badminton; multipurpose rooms for fitness classes, instruction, and meetings; locker rooms; and staff offices. There are a variety of spaces that might be found in the main facility or in a separate location often referred to as an **auxiliary facility**, such as a racquetball and squash court, indoor turf field, aquatic center, indoor and outdoor climbing and bouldering wall, ice rink, bowling center, field house, lounge, tennis center, theater, and more.

There are dedicated staff assigned to the management of these facilities. People who work in facilities and operations positions are responsible for building and equipment maintenance, supervision of patrons and activities, scheduling activities and group usage, sales and services, equipment checkout and rentals, controlled access and security, employment of student staff, and **open recreation**.

Programs

The programs are the leagues, special events, activities, classes, and services. **Intramural sports** allow students to participate in teams they assemble and to compete in organized, often officiated, league sports, special events, and tournaments. Leagues include traditional sports such as flag football, basketball, volleyball, soccer, and other smaller or new and innovative sports such as Spikeball, Battleship, soccer golf, and cornhole.

Fitness programs offer students a wide variety of fitness-related activities and classes, such as group fitness classes, personal training, small-group training, fitness assessments, and strength and conditioning competitions and events. For example, at the University of Oregon, innovative and trending

Intramural sports allow students to participate in teams they assemble and to compete in organized, often officiated, league sports, special events, and tournaments.

Stephen Zenner/SOPA Images/LightRocket via Getty Images

programs include TRX, kettlebell, Olympic lifting, playground circuits, and an affiliation with Cross-Fit. Group exercise programming is enhanced with unique choreographed classes such as POUND, UrbanKick, ballet strength, and top 40 dance. "Incorporating new technology in programming, such as group cycling consoles that measure and display intensity through power output, improves the user experience and increases participant success in reaching their fitness goals" (C. Russell, personal communication, June 23, 2016).

Club sports are athletic programs that are run by student leaders and compete against other universities or colleges. Many club sports are associated with regional and national governing bodies (such as USA Ultimate, USA Rugby, National Club Softball Association). Club sports often practice regularly, follow an organized schedule, and can be recreational or competitive in nature. Most often teams are allocated a budget and also fund-raise to be able to travel, register, and purchase gear and equipment. Most club sports are recognized student organizations, part of the social network throughout their campus, and the students who take on leadership roles in these organizations gain invaluable experience organizing their peers.

Outdoor and climbing programs provide exciting educational and hands-on learning opportunities for outdoor enthusiasts ranging from novice to expert levels. Programs can include climbing and bouldering walls, equipment rentals, bike and ski shops, outdoor clinics and education sessions, and guided outdoor adventure trips, such as mountaineering, backpacking, rafting, ice climbing, mountain biking, and canyoneering. An exemplary program is the Adventure Leadership Institute (ALI) at Oregon State University. ALI was founded in 1947 and is the "authority in adventure leadership education, providing awe-inspiring, transformative experiences to more than 9,500 students each year." ALI spends a staggering 20,000 contact hours teaching outside the classroom each year, and it offers over 300 facilitation opportunities for students annually (Oregon State University, n.d.).

When resources are available, program areas can also include specialties such as aquatics, inclusive programs, and youth and family initiatives. Aquatics programs provide an assortment of activities and services such as formal swim lessons and classes, family swim time, lap swim, water aerobics, club sports practice (swim, diving, water polo), and open recreational swim. Many facilities have pool space dedicated to informal recreation such as diving boards, slacklining, water slides, climbing walls, lazy rivers, and other innovative elements.

Inclusive recreation programs help address the needs of individuals that feel or identify that current programming does not meet their needs. Portland State University (PSU), for example, has inclusive recreation programs that include adaptive climbing and swimming, sitting volleyball, goalball, and wheelchair basketball. PSU also offers adaptive trips that include alpine skiing, paddling, and cycling (Portland State University, n.d.). It is important to be cognizant when implementing these programs that modification, additional assistance, and support may be required to help people participate. A few factors include accessibility to facilities, modified equipment, and appropriate resources to properly relay critical information.

A unique and beneficial partnership has formed between NIRSA and Special Olympics. Students on campuses throughout the country, also known as Unified partners, are joining together with Special Olympics athletes to compete in Special Olympics Unified Sports competitions. Unified Sports is an integral part of Special Olympics Unified Champion Schools—a program that strategically creates sports, leadership, and whole school engagement opportunities for students with and without intellectual disabilities.

Youth and family programs offer a dynamic range of activities to serve the entire community in a safe, energetic environment. These programs target nontraditional students with families and are also open to the community. These programs also provide great opportunities for student employment because the instructors and camp counselors are predominantly college students. Programs can include swimming, climbing, and tennis lessons; creative dance; adventure runs; day and sport camps; gymnastics; and ninja warrior training.

BENEFITS

Individual involvement in campus recreation programs and services produces three major benefits: improved overall emotional well-being, reduced stress, and improved happiness (NIRSA, 2004). Campus recreation centers are more than just facilities for physical activity; they also provide spaces where students can meet new people, hang out, study, and relax. Recreation centers are a focal point for community building and socializing.

Seventy-five percent of students report using on-campus recreation center facilities, programs, and services (Forrester, 2014). Clearly, campus recreation is a tremendous platform and has an opportunity to affect students, get them involved on campus, and provide a sense of belonging. Astin's theory of involvement (1984) states that the more a student is involved in their university, the more learning that will take place. Being involved on campus directly affects student success. Astin (1993) also believes that participation in intramural sports is related to students' overall satisfaction with college.

Participating in campus recreation programs and facilities is also linked with higher academic success. A study conducted by North Carolina State University examined the relationship between exercising and graduation rates. They found that for every extra hour that students exercised, their odds of graduating (or returning the following year) increased by 50 percent (Wexler, 2016). This is supported by Ratey's (2008) findings, which state that "exercise influences learning directly, at the cellular level, improving the brain's potential to log in and process new information" (p. 35).

In addition, as demonstrated in figure 11.1, students that participate in campus recreation facilities, programs, or services report increases in time management (75%), respect for others (71%), academic performance (68%), and sense of belonging (68%) as well as other important characteristics (Forrester, 2014).

CAREER OPPORTUNITIES

There are several career opportunities in the field of campus recreation, and there are numerous paths to entering this field. Many students obtain jobs in campus recreation centers as undergraduates to make money, meet new people, or gain skills; then, they realize they have a passion for working in a recreational setting and pursue it full-time. Many professionals have also entered campus recreation after working in city or commercial recreation, resort or tourism, or an athletic field.

Universities vary in how they use student employees. Many employ undergraduates to work as intramural officials, facility operations staff, personal trainers, lifeguards, area attendants and supervisors, and camp counselors, to mention a few. Student employment is an excellent opportunity to expose students to the variety of career positions. Other opportunities exist after graduation, including professional internships, fellowships, workshops, certification courses, and graduate assistantships. **Graduate assistantships** are common in the field of campus recreation and are one of the best ways to move into the profession following graduation. In this type of position, full-time graduate students work part-time as paraprofessionals. They are paid a stipend for their work, and the department covers their tuition. This experience is valuable to future employers who want to fill positions in their campus recreation departments (Wallace-Carr, 2013). All these professional-level experiences provide hands-on learning, mentoring, evaluation, and networking opportunities to help students reach the next level.

Organizational structures can look very different depending on the institution. Figure 11.2 illustrates this arrangement in a midsized university and shows the three main areas discussed previ-

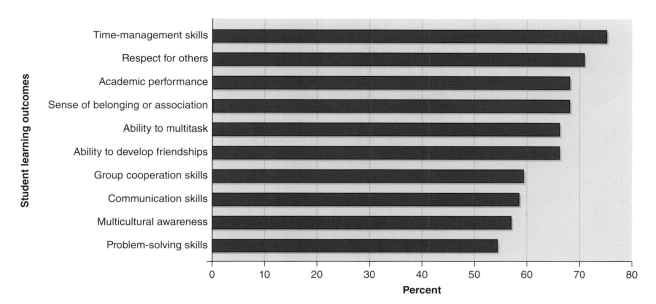

Figure 11.1 Students that use campus recreation facilities, programs, or services report increases in soft skills.

Reprinted by permission from S. Forrester, *The Benefits of Campus Recreation* (Corvallis, OR: NIRSA, 2014).

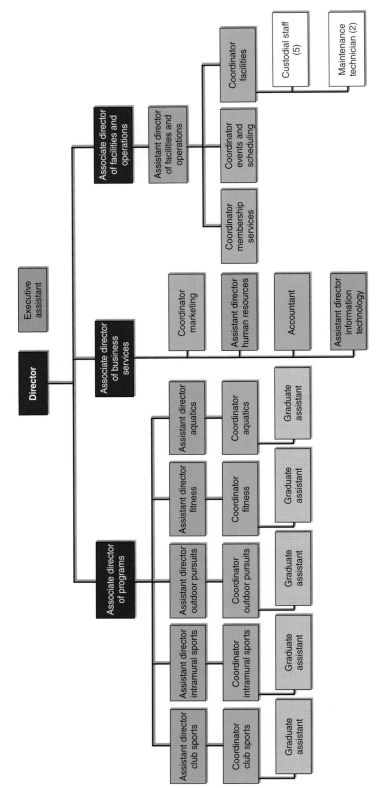

Figure 11.2   An organizational chart for a midsized university shows the three fundamental components of the campus recreation department: administration, facilities and operations, and programs.

ously: administration, facilities and operations, and programs. At this institution there is a multilayer hierarchy that includes a director, associate directors, assistant directors, coordinators, and graduate assistants. Additional staff can include personnel in specialty facilities (e.g., ice arenas, bowling alleys), marketing, information technology, community outreach, and public relations.

Professional certifications may be required, preferred, or recommended depending on specific areas. Commonly, CPR (cardiopulmonary resuscitation), AED (automated external defibrillator), and first aid certification are required of all personnel working in supervisory or administrative roles at a recreation facility. Blood-borne pathogen (BBP) training is also typically required and provided by the employer. Additional certifications may be required for specialized areas. Examples include lifeguard certification from StarGuard or the American Red Cross for aquatics staff. Fitness programs require or recommend that personal trainers, health coaches, and group exercise instructors have American Council on Exercise (ACE) certifications. Outdoor and climbing programs might require staff to obtain certifications from the American Mountain Guides Association (AMGA) or the Climbing Wall Association (CWA).

TRENDS IN CAMPUS RECREATION

There are many facility amenities and program offerings that have been in high demand for the past few decades. As the field of recreation progresses and the campus community evolves, so do the expectations regarding management, spaces, equipment, and programs. Departments are expected to collect and report participant statistics and also demonstrate the effects on student success. There is an increase in the demand to provide students with opportunities to learn stress management skills. Facilities and operations practices are becoming more sustainable and efficient. Recreation facilities are being built more like collegiate athletic facilities that include a wow factor and university branding. Spaces are being built with an open-concept and flexible approach for space usage so that if one activity is no longer popular, the space can be transformed for another use for minimal cost. Facilities have increased the amount of open space, high-tech equipment, and natural light. Marketing has evolved to include social media.

Campus recreation programs lead and respond to trends more so than any other area of the field. These trends often require additional expertise and

Many campus recreational facilities implemented temporary setups for cardio and weight equipment to allow for social distancing during the COVID-19 pandemic.

Ben Hasty/MediaNews Group/Reading Eagle via Getty Images

certifications so program staff continually diversify and increase their levels of knowledge. Following are a few of the program trends:

- *Fitness programs.* Functional training, Latin dance, ballet strength training, CrossFit, Olympic lifting, Pound, TRX suspension training
- *Youth and family programs.* Break camps, different types of summer camp offerings (e.g., classic camp, sport camp, sport science camp, climbing and outdoor adventure camp)
- *Activity classes.* Lecture-based classes such as coaching, group exercise, and personal training certification
- *Intramural sports.* Inclusive and adaptive recreation
- *Esports.* Video game tournaments

The COVID-19 pandemic challenged campus recreation in many ways. For a period of time, gathering was paused. Many states and localities prohibited indoor recreation out of concern for health and safety. As people began to resume activities, recreation looked very different in some places around the country. Sports, teams, and group events were limited due to social distancing guidelines. Instead, workout spaces were set up for a single person and spaced 6- to 10-feet apart from another participant. Gymnasiums, which would typically be packed with pickup basketball games, became repurposed with widely spaced cardio and weight equipment. Some fitness centers relied on a reservation system to help maintain facility user capacities and prevent overcrowding. Many group activities moved outdoors and creatively used fields, tennis courts, or tracks. One of the positive unintended consequences of the pandemic resulted in enhanced cleaning protocol by both employees and participants.

SUMMARY

Campus recreation has become an important part of college campuses and of the student experience. Campus recreation provides opportunities for students and the campus community to stay physically and mentally healthy and to engage in play and community building. Providing recreation, fitness, and sport in the higher education field is exciting, challenging, and rewarding.

Esports

Augustus W. Hallmon

HISTORY

Electronic sports, more commonly known as *esports*, is defined as video gaming competition that involves individuals or teams of players. Various entities have had a role in shaping how the esports world is conceptualized today. Riot Games, Blizzard, and Valve Corporation are a few organizations out of many that have had their history tied to the rise of esports.

Riot Games Inc.—an American video game developer, publisher, and esports tournament organizer—was founded in 2006 by Brandon Beck and Marc Merrill in Los Angeles, California. The company's debut title was *League of Legends*, which was released in 2009 and has received worldwide acclaim. As this company has grown, the annual League of Legends World Championship has featured qualified esports teams from 12 international leagues. *League of Legends* is among the largest and most popular gaming and sporting events in the world today (Riot Games, 2022).

Blizzard, another American video game developer and publisher, is based in Irvine, California. This company is a subsidiary of Activision Blizzard, which was founded in 1991. One of their notable games was the highly popular multiplayer online role-playing game *World of Warcraft*. Their other notable esports games include *Call of Duty* (*COD*) and *Overwatch* (Blizzard, 2022).

Valve Corporation was founded in 1996 by former Microsoft employees Gabe Newell and Mike Harrington. Their original creation was a first-person shooter game called *Half-Life*. In 2010, Valve Corporation began to produce fewer games and focus more on developing hardware and virtual reality (VR) equipment. They produced *Half-Life: Alyx*, a VR game that was a return to the series (Valve Corporation, 2022).

The histories of the previous organizations are important to know, but in an article by Kim et al. (2020), the authors describe the esports movement as being part of society since the 1970s, when students at Stanford University hosted the first esports tournament; the Intergalactic Spacewar Olympics focused on the early video game *Spacewar!* Twenty-four players participated in this tournament, with the winner receiving a year's subscription to *Rolling Stone* magazine. By 1980, the first consumer video game competition was held, playing the game *Space Invaders*. The Space Invaders Championship had 10,000 participants and was a popular topic in the media due to the fact that *Space Invaders* was a known brand at that time (Bountie Gaming, 2018). By the 1990s, technology had advanced enough that the Internet was readily available. This technology allowed gamers to connect with each other and provided an online competitive gaming environment. Companies such as Nintendo and Blockbuster began sponsoring video game championships worldwide (Bountie Gaming, 2018). Through Blockbuster's influence from 1994 to 1995, 16-bit war video game tournaments were running on the Super Nintendo (SNES) and Sega Genesis systems, with qualifying rounds being held in Blockbuster stores and the winner going to a final competition in Fort Lauderdale, Florida.

The 2000s to early 2020s saw the shift of esports from being a local video gaming community to becoming a global entity with increased technological developments. Games evolved from 16-bit systems to advanced video game systems (e.g., PlayStation, Xbox, Nintendo Switch) and powerful personal computers (PCs) that could run more sophisticated and complex video games. By the 2010s, not only could video games look very realistic but gamers could also communicate with individuals from different parts of the world in real time. In the 2020s mobile gaming has become a big contributor to the video gaming community, so players don't need to invest in a costly video game system or a PC in order to participate in some esports competitions. The growth is not only in the systems and video games but how individuals can be spectators.

Kim and colleagues (2020) provide the following examples of the popularity of esports:

In 2022, the South Korean team DRX became the first play-in qualifier ever to win the League of Legends World Championship tournament.

Riot Games/Getty Images

Over 80 million watched [the] 2017 League of Legends World Championship, which is comparable with the 111.3 million who watched [the] 2017 Super Bowl match. Its revenues reached $1 billion in 2019 and were projected to hit $1.5 billion by 2020. The total prize money awarded out for E-sports events was $110.6 million from 3,765 tournaments in 2018. Consequently, the number of companies who invest on E-sports sponsorship and launch E-sports leagues is growing rapidly. (p. 2)

Not only has the viewership trend grown over the years, but it has become a lucrative form of revenue that has supported the growth of several video game companies. New jobs and businesses have been created to support its continued growth as well. In 2018, over $4.5 billion was invested into the esports industry, and it grew a global fan base of $380 million, with 37 percent representing males ages 21 to 35 and 16 percent representing females ages 21 to 35 (Deloitte, n.d.). This fan base has continued to increase, showing growth in 2019 ($397.8M), 2020 ($435.9M), and 2021 ($465.1M), and it is projected to grow in 2024 ($577.8M) (Geyser, 2022).

The Saudi Esports Federation announced in September 2022 that it was joining Saudi Arabia's Vision 2030, with the goal of investing about US$38 billion to become a global hub in esports and gaming, according to Prince Faisal bin Bandar bin Sultan Al Saud (Cooke, 2022).

ESPORTS IN PARKS AND RECREATION

Several parks and recreation agencies have been very progressive in incorporating esports into their services. For example, San Marcos Parks and Recreation, South Suburban Parks and Recreation, and Kansas Recreation and Park Association have programs that focus on promoting esports tournaments. This rise in competition suggests there is more room to grow in this area. Previous tournament formats required minimal resources. Comparing previous needs to the current needs and roles of a 2022 esports tournament, there is a drastic difference. The following are some positions and companies that specialize in providing esports.

Opportunities in esports include the following:

- Esports athlete or player
- Event manager (managing esports tournament venues)
- Coach
- Shoutcaster (both a play-by-play and color commentator)
- Analyst
- Team manager
- Owner
- Marketing or public relations (PR) executive
- Community and social media manager
- Sales manager (e.g., ticket sales, sponsorship)
- Administrator (e.g., oversee tournaments, enforce rules)
- Broadcaster
- Agent

Some top organizations in esports are these:

- OpTic Gaming
- FaZe Clan
- G2 Esports
- Team Liquid
- FURIA
- Cloud9
- Fnatic
- Natus Vincere
- TSM
- Spacestation Gaming
- EDGE (Esports Development and Growth Enterprise)

This list, while not comprehensive, represents the most popular and well-known aspects of esports jobs and agencies focused on this industry. These agencies are great examples of successful management and have supported esports during its increased popularity in recent years.

Going in a different direction, Columbus Recreation and Parks Department has launched a youth esports program in which they are "striving to break misconceptions around esports and provide participants with an experience currently not found anywhere else" (Columbus Recreation and Parks Department, 2022). The program will not only be focused on video games and competition but will also feature a classroom experience involving a STEM-certified curriculum. These examples illustrate the growing popularity of esports as a leisure experience. In addition, we see that the concept of esports could be transformed into an educational experience. The provided examples show the versatility of esports as a leisure experience and how it can be used by various recreational agencies.

ARE ESPORTS REALLY SPORTS?

When we consider the role that sports play in society, the focus has primarily been on the physical ability of the players and the athletic competition. With the continued growth of esports, the question has arisen: Are esports actually sports? The various ideological views that follow will be discussed for years to come, but the literature on esports is still justifying its status as a sport as of 2023.

- Parry (2019) provides a compelling argument that esports are not sports based on our current understanding. They believe that, while there is a certain level of athletic ability needed in esports, if we must question whether an activity is a sport, it most likely isn't a sport. Parry used the example of the Olympics: If an activity is considered an Olympic sport, then it is a sport.
- Kim et al. (2020) present a narrative to suggest that esports are just as financially viable as other recognized sports. In addition to the fact that esports are a popular activity, athletes can be paid millions of dollars to compete against their peers, similar to other sports.
- Esports athletes need to have developed dexterity, quick reflexes, and physical stamina. Schutz (2016) conducted a study on esports athletes in Germany and described that the skills needed to participate in traditional sport competitions and esports competition would be similar. We have to be reminded that esports are still a competition and thus not only do athletes need to have athletic ability but they must also practice, hydrate well, and properly stretch in addition to participating in athletic competition.

When considering esports' role in health and well-being, we see that as our research evolves our understanding of health does as well. Esports are commonly considered a sedentary leisure activity. Indeed, chess, *Magic: The Gathering*, first-person shooter games (e.g., *Call of Duty*), and similar competitive activities lack much of the physical movement associated with traditional sports, but they are psychologically, socially, and spiritually stimulating in ways that can rival and exceed traditional sports. Combined with the requisite athletic ability described by Schutz, this stimulation provides overall positive benefits for the individuals that participate in esports and similar activities.

Before COVID-19, the popularity of esports was a niche market. However, as more people have become familiar with esports and its recent consideration as an Olympic event, it may be difficult to argue its status as a sport. Instead, a more productive discussion may focus on how it can be more beneficial to society.

FUTURE OF ESPORTS

The future of esports will likely continue to expand and be driven by sponsorship revenue more than it has been previously. We will continue to see the growth and increased monetization of esports through sponsorships and technological advancements. BMW, Levi's, Marvel Entertainment, and IBM provide noteworthy examples.

- The BMW group initially invested millions of dollars into esports logos and events; as of 2023, they have begun investing in in-car gaming technology and the metaverse.
- Levi's and Marvel have both become involved with esports not only by designing apparel for some esports teams but by allowing their brands to be used in social media ads that feature esports athletes wearing their apparel during everyday activities. This revenue stream will most likely continue to grow as the popularity of esports continues to rise.
- IBM's language processing, machine learning, and Watson AI technology have led to improved *Overwatch* league ranking systems and created live and in-broadcast predictive analysis.

Esports are trending toward a more diverse and inclusive environment. Nordland (2021) argues that 35 percent of esports viewers in 2019 were women, which is vastly different from the percentage of women watching traditional professional sports. This statistic is encouraging because it highlights a potential market for esports. Along with these statistics, we see an increase in advocacy groups that are encouraging women to get involved in esports (e.g., AnyKey, Women in Games, British Esports Association initiatives, and Female Esports League). The parks, recreation, and sport industry has observed that individuals may want to have other competitive activities besides traditional sports (e.g., football, basketball, baseball, soccer). This interest in new or alternative activities may be an environment that esports could thrive in and recruit new viewers.

Another trend in esports relates to the way that people participate in competition. Mobile gaming has grown in popularity and contributed to the success of esports. Nordland (2021) suggests that with increased accessibility of smartphones, mobile gaming could help reduce barriers to participation in esports, especially considering the popularity of free-to-play games. Esports tournaments have historically required a significant financial investment for proper facilities and equipment (e.g., computers, monitors, keyboards, and more). With smartphones, tournament organizers would not necessarily have to make as significant a financial investment into facilities.

A final trend is streaming TV's response to the growth of esports (Saini, 2021). As esports become more accessible to the mainstream population, this opens up more opportunities for streaming TV to be a crucial part of the growth. Currently, most esports tournaments and shoutcasters are using Twitch as their media platform to share not only the content of the competition but also commentary on the games so viewers can feel invested in the material. But, thinking futuristically, the possibility of streaming esports tournaments across the Internet or holding esports tournaments using virtual reality (VR) technology to give participants a more intimate gaming experience could be an evolution of this industry. This approach to esports would only be achievable if streaming services see the usefulness in increasing their infrastructure to accommodate the player base. Time will tell how this area evolves over the next 5 to 10 years.

SUMMARY

When we consider the rich history of esports, there are many components to consider. Esports have been part of our society since the 1970s; yet, when COVID-19 dominated our society, esports asserted their benefits not only to a society confined to their homes but to the sports industry as a whole. The pandemic boosted the profile of esports as a competitive and athletic market. As we move forward, the popularity of esports has an opportunity to grow and attract new spectators, players, and business sponsors. This growth will require emerging recreation and sport professionals to be prepared to engage with esports.

COVID-19 has forced leisure professionals to reconsider how we offer, participate in, and enjoy our leisure experiences. Esports are leisure activities that benefited greatly from the shift toward socially distant pastimes during the pandemic. Esports will not overtake other traditional sports, but as a society we must conduct serious dialogue about esports within our culture.

Faith-Based Recreation

John Byl and David Kahan

" The city streets will be filled with boys and girls playing there. **"**

Zechariah 8:5 (*New International Version Bible*, 2011)

People of faith often engage in recreational activities through their religious institutions. These activities are often designed to enhance internal community cohesion and used as recruiting tools to engage community outsiders (Baykara et al., 2021; Bynum, 2003; Karlis et al., 2014). In the United States in 2014, 76.5 percent of those 18 and older identified with a religious group (Pew Research Center, 2015). At 76.5 percent of the U.S. population, religious organizations should be recognized as legitimate providers of recreation activities in the leisure service delivery system.

In Canada, a 2015 Angus Reid Institute poll analyzed four broad segments in their survey: "The Non-Believers (19% of the total population), the Spiritually Uncertain (30%), the Privately Faithful (30%), and the Religiously Committed (21%)" (2017). Religion in Canada plays a lesser role than it does in the United States. However, Canadian recreation providers may find themselves more quickly reaching out to the religiously committed since it is reported that those with "higher levels of belief are correlated with higher levels of personal happiness, charitable giving, volunteerism, and overall community engagement" (Angus Reid Institute, 2017). While those born in Canada have lessened their commitment to religion, immigrants have kept the number of committed religious folks somewhat constant. For example, 400,000 people identifying as Muslim came to Canada from 2001 to 2011. The median age for this group was only 29 (Angus Reid Institute, 2017). For those working with religious groups in Canada and the United States, collaborating with immigrants with strong religious affiliations is an important part of the task. Religious institutions play an important role in providing satisfying recreational opportunities within their communities. Next, we examine differences within and between faith traditions and then explore employment in faith-based recreation.

DIFFERENCES WITHIN FAITH TRADITIONS

Religious groups may emphasize differences from other religions and sameness within their own religious group, but not all religious groups are homogeneous units. Some of the differences are fostered because of alternate ways of thinking about beliefs, and some are fostered because of varying ethnic roots. For example, in one study, a Mennonite cookbook was used as a metaphor for the themes of Canadian Mennonites. The author explains, "Two of my favourite cookbooks—*More-With-Less* and *Mennonite Girls Can Cook*—are perhaps metaphors for increasingly divergent ideological tones amongst Mennonites that we see during this era: one might describe it as left-wing versus right-wing thinking" (Epp, 2019).

The cookbook study demonstrates that Christians within a denomination can hold significantly different views about the purpose of cooking. The same is true in other faith traditions. Within Judaism there is a whole range of different beliefs between liberal Jewish believers and ultra-Orthodox Jewish believers (My Jewish Learning, n.d.; Sheskin & Hartman, 2019). The same is true in defining Islam. Gholam Khiabany wrote,

> Operating on the assumption of a monolithic Islamic totality suppresses the internal diversity, division and political, social, cultural and ideological rifts in a religion that encompasses one billion people from North Africa to Indonesia as well as a variety of minority communities (increasingly under attack) throughout the Western world. (2007, p. 111)

Some of the differences between religious groups relate to individual commitments and ethnic backgrounds. Some people's religious beliefs intentionally and fully shape their recreation choices, whereas others express beliefs that unintention-ally and partially shape their recreation choices. Nationality also shapes unique differences between religious groups. The intersection of nationality and religious beliefs encourages some people to recreate with others with similar interests, backgrounds, religious affiliations, and languages. Being in this comfort zone within a subculture and being shaped by the subcultural values are examples of **selective acculturation** in leisure (Taylor & Toohey, 2001; Ambrosini, 2016).

DIFFERENCES AMONG FAITH TRADITIONS

North America is home to many religious groups, but we discuss the three largest faith groups—Christians (70.6% of the U.S. population in 2014), Jews (1.9%), and Muslims (0.9%)—to provide insight into how various traditions value and engage in recreation (Pew Research Center, 2015).

Christianity

The largest and most popular, but quickly declining, religion in the United States and Canada is Christianity (Clarke, 2021; Cornelissen, 2021).

- In the United States, 70 to 76.9 percent of the population declares Christianity as their faith (PEW Research Center, 2015; Jeff Diamant, 2019).

- In Canada, 59 to 71 percent of the population declared Christianity as their faith in 2012, depending on the polling method used (Bibby & Grenville, 2016; Cornelissen, 2021).

Since the beginning of the Christian church, living in community with fellow believers has been valued. Togetherness as a congregation has been enjoyed in church fellowship halls through coffee socials, youth clubs, annual church picnics, dances, and competitive leagues with teams from similar congregations since the early 1900s. The purpose of this recreation is to enhance a sense of community between people of the same faith and to be a place of connection for immigrants.

Typically, church programs, particularly those for kids, include a refreshment break that provides an opportunity for leaders to speak briefly about Christian principles or to share personal testimonies and invite participants to accept Jesus as their savior. Special kids' programs such as KidsGames are modeled after the Olympics and take place during church summer camps during the years when the Summer Olympics and the World Cup occur. Competitions are held in various sport events, Bible knowledge, poster design, and essay questions. KidsGames began in Barcelona in 1985 as an evangelical Christian program in preparation for the Olympic Games in that city, and it is now used worldwide (Bynum, 2003).

Besides offering programs for kids, many Christian churches organize adult church sport leagues. These leagues generally do not permit alcohol use at games, and they include time for prayer, fellowship, and talking with others about their relationship with God. Many churches in the United States have built large fitness centers to serve their members and to serve and reach out to others in the community. Christian music is often played in the fitness centers, and during breaks in the activity people can share personal testimonies and pray. However, according to Shoemaker,

> there often exists a tension between sport and religious commitments in the South. On the one hand, sport is understood as an opportunity for discipline, evangelism, and further social interactions of the religious community. On the other hand, sport can interfere with religious participation and practice. (2019)

Several examples of Christian organizations that use sport in a positive way in the United States are Germantown Baptist in Tennessee, Kroc Salvation Army in Memphis, Red Rocks Sports in Colorado, and Southeast Christian Church in various locations. For Canada, check out Don Christian Recreation Centre in British Columbia, and Upper Canada Camp in Ontario.

Several for-profit companies have organized to fill a niche in the fitness market for Christian fitness centers that train both the body and soul. Many of these centers offer classes in yoga, Pilates, KickFit, stretching, and self-defense, and other amenities such as personal training and cafés.

Some churches have turned to organizations like Upwards to assist them in rolling out sport programs by "leveraging the power of sports to achieve and increase the impact of their mission" (Upward Sports, n.d.). Another organization that helps churches use sports and recreation programs to reach out to their communities is the Association of Church Sports and Recreation Ministries (CSRM). CSRM provides support by "working with local church leaders to use sports, recreation, and fitness as evangelistic and discipleship tools" (Association of Church Sports & Recreation Ministries, Inc., n.d.). CSRM's motto is "Equipping Local Churches.

Changing Lives Through Sports, Recreation & Fitness Outreach Ministries."

To help churches, other organizations, and individuals, *Faith & Fitness Magazine* launched in 2003 and has been producing bimonthly online issues since 2007.

Judaism

Those who identify as Jewish form the second largest religious group in the United States, representing 2.4 percent of the U.S. adult population (Pew Research Center, 2021). Although Christians and Muslims see all of life as affected by their religious commitments, Jews distinguish between sacred and secular activities, thereby providing an interesting and alternative perspective on faithful living in one's recreation.

For Jews, religion affects what happens in the synagogue and in personal and family devotional life but has less impact on what happens on the soccer pitch or in the boxing ring. The nation of Israel binds many Jews together; therefore, some recreation activities are based more on national commitments than on Jewish faith commitments. For example, the quadrennial Maccabiah Games are held in Israel the year following the Olympic Games. The Maccabiah Games are meant "to promote the physical strength of Jews while fostering a sense of nationalism among Jewish athletes" (American-Israeli Cooperative Enterprise, n.d.).

The Maccabi World Union developed the idea of holding a sort of Jewish Olympiad every four years in Israel, and the first Maccabiah Games were held in 1932. In addition, the Pan American Maccabi Games are held every four years in various South American cities. The JCC Maccabi Games, sponsored by the Jewish Community Centers, are held each summer in the United States and are the largest organized sports program in the world for Jewish teenagers (Jewish Community Center Maccabi Games, n.d.).

Another important influence on the recreation habits of Jews in the United States and Canada was the establishment of organizations to help recent immigrants adapt to their new surroundings. During the late 1800s and the early- to mid-1900s, Jewish settlement houses, immigrant aid institutions, and Young Men's and Young Women's Hebrew Associations were established in cities such as Boston, New York, and Chicago. The Young Women's Hebrew Association offered programs in calisthenics, basketball, baseball, track and field, tennis, physical culture, domestic education, aquatics, "religious work, gymnastics, social work, and educational work to promote social and physical welfare for Jewish families" (Borish, 1999, p. 248). These centers were concerned with the Americanization of Eastern European immigrants (Borish, 1999). They provided places where Jews could participate in new activities and learn about North American culture without losing their Jewish culture. These organizations merged with the Jewish Community Center (JCC) Association of North America in 1990.

The JCC Association of North America guides the Jewish community centers across North America, serving over one million American Jews annually. This organization is a movement that uses community camps and community centers to promote Jewish culture and community (Jewish Community Centers Maccabi Games, n.d.). These centers, like the Maccabiah Games, are concerned with "Jewish living" rather than **Judaism** as a religion.

Islam

Islam, which has its roots in present-day Saudi Arabia, was spread by the Prophet Muhammad (PBUH) beginning in approximately 610 AD. (Prac-

ticing Muslims say "Peace be upon him" upon the mention of Muhammad and write the abbreviation "PBUH" with his name.) In Canada, the estimated Muslim population numbers roughly 1.78 million persons (Statistics Canada, 2022). Meanwhile, the Pew Research Center (2018) estimates that there were about "3.45 million Muslims of all ages living in the U.S. in 2017, and that Muslims made up about 1.1% of the total U.S. population." The expectation is that these numbers will double by 2050 to 2.1 percent of the population, due largely to higher fertility rates among Muslims and higher immigration rates. About as many people are converted to the Muslim faith as leave the Muslim faith (Mohamed, 2018).

According to the Muslim American Survey (Pew Research Center, 2011), 78 percent of American Muslims are first-generation immigrants or second-generation Americans. Immigrants hail from 77 different countries, with most from Pakistan. The same survey reported that a plurality of American Muslims expresses a medium level of religious commitment, which takes into account frequency of mosque attendance and daily prayer, and the importance of religion in one's life. Additionally, 60

Camps are a popular activity for faith-based organizations.

Jeff Gritchen/MediaNews Group/Orange County Register via Getty Images

percent of women reported wearing a hijab all, most, or some of the time (Pew Research Center, 2011).

The diverse cultural backgrounds and religious beliefs and attitudes of American Muslims pose unique opportunities and responsibilities for recreation researchers and practitioners. In a recent study, it was deemed that "sports according to Islam are emphasized. Because recreation, which is a part of community life, can increase the quality of life of people," and quality of life is valued by Islam (Baykara et al., 2021).

Awareness of observant Muslims' behaviors is an important step toward accommodating recreation schedules, facilities, and programs. For example, sawm (fasting) may be practiced daily during daylight hours during the month of Ramadan. Thus, many adherents may not be able to engage in regular recreational or leisure activities during this time, and program options that are available after sunset would be preferable. The **hijab**, which is worn for modesty and privacy in conformance with verses in the Quran (Surah 24:30-31), and which was originally intended for the Prophet's wives, presents a more complex issue for recreation specialists. Given that the second caliph (Umar/Omar) specifically enjoined adherents to teach their children archery, horseback riding, and swimming as well as the many modern-day ethnic games and national sports ascribed to Muslim countries, every effort should be made to offer egalitarian access to leisure and recreation services. Keep in mind that for more observant females, gender-segregated activity spaces, where females cannot be seen by males, may be required to allow for full participation in dance, exercise, and sports.

Much of the research conducted in Muslims' physical activity beliefs, attitudes, and behaviors has originated outside North America. Early research frequently used a deficit lens in identifying what Muslim girls and women could *not* do. Contemporary international literature shows empowered Muslim women who are frequently supported in their physical activity habits by parents, immediate and extended family, and changes in community expectations and standards (e.g., Bhatnagar & Foster, 2021; Agergaard, 2016; Knez et al., 2012; Miles & Benn, 2014; Soltani et al., 2021; Stride, 2016). These women negotiate their degree of participation by finding a balance point between their religious, cultural, and personal identities.

In the United States, Hamzeh and Oliver (2012) proposed the *hijab discourse* as a means by which Muslim girls could discover the types and circumstances of physical activity in which they felt comfortable participating. Girls in their study overcame visual, spatial, and ethical hijabs (i.e., hijabs used as metaphors for distinctiveness) when participating in swimming, basketball, and indoor rock climbing. This unveiling required them to cross religious, cultural, and self-imposed boundaries that dictated what (visual), where (spatial), and how (ethical) they could do physical activity. In light of these findings, recreation specialists should at least understand that Muslim girls want to participate in activities of their choosing, and they engage in a complex process of relativism in which they judge the ways and means by which they can be comfortable participating. In Canada, Shia Muslim young women were found to encounter and engage in similar internalized struggles while figuring out their place within and their positionality toward physical activity (Jiwani & Rail, 2010). To these women, physical activity was viewed as a way to enhance one's health and self-esteem but subservient to the importance attached to religion. They specifically recommended creating affordable and accessible activity venues within and outside the Muslim community and educating recreation providers about the needs and alternative representations of hijab-wearing women.

Muslim children need quality physical activity experiences that meet U.S. guidelines of 60 minutes per day of moderate-to-vigorous physical activity. However, family dynamics and cultural or religious norms may pose barriers to achieving this goal. In Minnesota, Somali parents expressed (1) need for community-based indoor programming that respected a requirement for gender-segregated activity; (2) reliance on schools to provide adequate physical activity during the school day; and (3) adaptations for engaging in home physical activity in limited indoor spaces during winter months (Arcan et al., 2017). Also in Minnesota, Somali and Sudanese adolescents identified several culture-specific facilitators (e.g., family and community members available as role models, motivators, and coparticipants) and barriers (e.g., gender-role expectations for girls to assist in household chores and child care, which limits time available for physical activity) that affected physical activity engagement (Wieland et al., 2015).

Rules are helpful in understanding what is and is not permissible. One scholar argued that "as long as sports protect the basic principles and elements of Islam and do not lead to the neglect of worship and ethical duties, it is considered permissible" (Baykara, 2021). An exhaustive how-to guide for creating environments conducive to Muslim Americans' recreation needs, and specifically for the religiously observant, is beyond the scope of this section. Generally, some guidelines include surveying clients' interests and participation requirements, which may include

- alleviating time-specific conflicts associated with prayers, holidays, and fasting;
- relaxing dress codes, especially for aquatic activities;
- conducting physical activity programming within the mosque space;
- ensuring that changing areas offer complete privacy and that performance venues restrict physical and visual access to the same sex; and
- staffing aquatic, dance, exercise, and sport classes and sports programs with same-sex personnel (e.g., lifeguards, referees).

The following programs have implemented the preceding five guidelines:

- Muslim Youth of North America camps (MYNA, n.d.)
- An independent summer day camp for Muslim youth in Irvine, California (American Camping Association, 2010)
- Requested swimming programs that conform to Islamic propriety (Brown, 2009; Burks, 2012; Moore et al., 2010)
- A six-month exercise intervention for adult women held at a Toronto mosque
- A basketball league for East African male teens located in metropolitan Seattle, Washington (Stutteville, 2015)
- Karate and soccer programs for Muslim girls in Columbus, Ohio (Gordon, 2014)

JUDAISM, CHRISTIANITY, AND ISLAM AND THE NATIONAL RECREATION AND PARK ASSOCIATION PILLARS

Our view of the world is shaped by what we believe in. What we believe in often blends with our cultural norms, other significant events in our lives, and the times and place we live in. Every faith tradition has distinct views on the National Recreation and Park Association (NRPA) pillars of conservation, health and wellness, and social equality. However, it is important to realize that how individuals or specific groups understand and practice these views can vary greatly.

Judaism

In terms of conservation, the Torah begins with the words that God created the "heavens and the earth" (Genesis 1:1). What God created was "very good" (Genesis 1:31), and people were instructed to work and protect the earth (Genesis 1:28). There are many examples in the Torah in which the environment was protected (e.g., not cutting down fruit trees [Deuteronomy 20:19] and allowing land to lie fallow every seven years [Leviticus 25]). Related to conservation is a positive view of health and wellness. People were made in the "image of God" (Genesis 1:27) and therefore ought to care for themselves and each other. If anyone causes injury to another, helping that person heal is that person's legal responsibility (Exodus 21:19). It also follows that if all people are created in the image of God and come from the same parentage (Genesis 3:20), all people should be viewed equally. The Torah instructs that when a foreign person lives among them, they are to be treated as "Native-born" (Leviticus 19:34). Different cultural expectations were placed on men and women, but both are viewed as created in the image of God and therefore socially equal (Genesis 1:27).

Christianity

Christianity is also based on the Torah, but it significantly includes the lives of Jesus as Messiah and the writings found in the New Testament. The New Testament reminds its readers that "all things were created: things in heaven and on earth . . . all things have been created through him and for him" (Colossians 1:16), and therefore all things need to be cared for (Colossians 1:16-20). Jesus himself tells his followers to "go into all the world and preach the gospel to all creation" (Mark 16:15). Physical health was also still important, as readers are reminded in the welcome from one of the apostles: "Dear friend, I pray that you may enjoy good health and that all may go well with you" (3 John 1:2). Furthermore, one of the New Testament writers argues that people want to bring God a holy and pleasing worship by exhorting, "offer your bodies as a living sacrifice" (Romans 12:1-2). In terms of social equality, the New Testament states that "there is neither Jew nor Gentile, neither slave nor free, nor is there male and female, for you are all one in Christ Jesus" (Galatians 3:28). In addition to viewing all people as one, the New Testament also encourages a respect for diversity among people (1 Corinthians 12:12).

Islam

Islam is based on the Quran, which was divinely revealed to Prophet Muhammad (PBUH) by the angel Gabriel in the month of Ramadan 610 AD. Muslims also follow the Sunnah, which details Prophet Muhammad's (PBUH) application of the Quran's principles in his daily life. Both sources provide codified guidance for a life that upholds Christian and Jewish traditions. Support for the NRPA pillars is clearly stated within these two sources. Environmental stewardship is referred to in the Quran verse 6:165 as translated by Yusuf Ali: "It is He Who hath made you (His) agents, inheritors of the earth." Muslims are enjoined to take personal responsibility for their health and wellness, which in the Quran is alluded to in verse 4:79 as translated by Muhammad Sarwar: "Whatever good you may receive is certainly from God and whatever you suffer is from yourselves. We have sent you, (Muhammad [PBUH]), as a Messenger to people. God is a Sufficient witness to your truthfulness." Though the Quran does not specifically mention physical activity, the hadith (oral tradition about Prophet Muhammad's [PBUH] words and behavior) states that parents are to teach their children swimming, archery, and horseback riding. Regular practice of these specific activities would have resulted in military fitness, which was important at the time. In modern times, recreational pursuit of these activities would be valued as a means to emulate the Prophet. Islam's followers are likely the most ethnically heterogeneous among the three Abrahamic religions because Islam's spread over seven centuries reached into Northern and Sub-Saharan Africa, Europe, the Middle East, Central and South Asia, and other regions.

In his final sermon in 630 AD, Prophet Muhammad (PBUH) preordains Islam's egalitarian stance toward gender and race:

> O People, it is true that you have certain rights with regard to your women, but they also have right over you. If they abide by your right then to them belongs the right to be fed and clothed in kindness. Do treat your women well and be kind to them for they are your partners and committed helpers.

> All mankind is from Adam and Eve, an Arab has no superiority over a non-Arab nor a non-Arab has any superiority over an Arab; also, a white has no superiority over a black nor a black has any superiority over white except by piety and good action. You know that every Muslim is the brother of another Muslim. Remember, one day you will appear before Allah and answer for your deeds. So beware, do not stray from the path of righteousness after I am gone.

EMPLOYMENT IN FAITH-BASED RECREATION

Professionals in faith-based recreation must meet three requirements. First, a passionate commitment to the faith is central and is the first entry point into any position. For Jewish leaders, faith is not critical, but a positive disposition to Jewish culture is important. Second, although some people with ecclesiastical training are hired, most of those hired have training in recreation and leadership. Academic training might consist of a recreation diploma from a college, or a recreation, physical education, or leadership degree from a university. Third, a faith-based recreation leader must nurture the faith (or the culture, in the case of Jewish leaders) through recreation with people of various backgrounds. Although some of this nurturing involves specific spiritual instruction, the nurturing may also be primarily focused on encouraging friendships within the group.

LGBTQIA+ people are both accepted and prohibited from employment in various religious places of work. In Canada and the United States, the United Church of Canada, the Anglican denomination, some Presbyterian congregations, various Lutheran traditions, and Unitarians affirm LGBTQIA+ identifications and support employment of LGBTQIA+ people.

SUMMARY

Most North Americans identify with some form of religion. Each ideology presents clear and unique ramifications on the ways followers engage in recreation. Religious institutions play important roles in advising their members on the importance of recreation and, in many cases, in providing opportunities for their members and those from the broader community to take advantage of recreational activities.

Worksite Recreation and Health Promotion

Mary Parr

" Physical fitness is not only one of the most important keys to a healthy body, it is the basis of dynamic and creative intellectual activity. **"**

John F. Kennedy, U.S. president, 1961-1963

Corporate wellness programming has become a billion-dollar industry. Whether operated through the company or offered to employees contractually through a separate organization that specializes in prevention work, these programs afford corporate health and wellness promotion professionals with opportunities to make a difference for employers' bottom lines and employees' lives.

CORPORATE WELLNESS AND HEALTH PROMOTION

According to research compiled by the Centers for Disease Control and Prevention, 60 percent of adults in the United States are living with a chronic disease such as heart disease, risk of stroke, cancer, type 2 diabetes, arthritis, and obesity, and a little more than 40 percent have more than one (CDC, 2022, para. 1). While aging is a strong predictor of chronic illness, many chronic diseases are associated with risky behaviors such as smoking and exposure to secondhand smoke, poor nutrition, a lack of physical activity, and excessive alcohol consumption (CDC, 2022). According to a report by Buttorff et al. (2017), average health care expenditures for those with three or four chronic diseases are 8.5 times higher than the average expenditure for those with none. The upside is that chronic disease can often be prevented or delayed through positive health behaviors.

Individuals managing and medicating chronic diseases incur high health care costs and health insurance premiums. Employers pay a large share of these costs, and they can curb health insurance premiums by implementing corporate wellness and health promotion programs in the workplace. These programs also benefit companies through reduced sick leave and increased employee productivity.

HISTORY OF WORKSITE WELLNESS

Employers have been providing recreation in health promotion programs for more than 150 years. Two of the first documented programs were library resources and singing classes offered by the Peace Dale Manufacturing Company in Rhode Island in the 1850s (MacLean et al., 1985). As the United States continued to industrialize during the late 1800s and the early decades of the 1900s, more companies began to offer employee recreation and fitness programs. In the 1860s, the YMCA became one of the first private agencies to work with business and industry to provide positive recreation alternatives to industrial workers (Cross, 1990). The YMCA built gymnasiums and offered fitness-related programs to the young men who were moving to the cities in ever larger numbers to work in the factories. The Playground and Recreation Association of America (now the National Recreation and Park Association) began assisting companies in the provision of employee recreation and wellness programs in the early 1900s. In 1941, the National Industrial Recreation Association was formed to help address concerns related to the provision and management of employee recreation services (Sessoms et al., 1975). In the 1930s, labor unions began to play an increased role in the provision of employee recreation and health promotion services. The growth of employer-provided recreation and health promotion services has continued since World War II.

The types of services provided have gone through many iterations, and services continue to evolve in the 21st century. Typical services offered by employers through the first 100 years of employer-sponsored recreation and health promotion programs included the following:

- Company-sponsored picnics

- Athletic teams
- Hobby clubs and classes
- Bowling leagues
- Aquatics programs
- Exercise breaks
- Group vacations

In the decades since World War II, many more companies have provided recreation and fitness facilities with amenities such as gymnasiums, pools, tennis courts, walking trails, golf courses, athletic fields, aerobic and strength training areas, and child care.

Today's corporate wellness and health promotion programs vary greatly in scope from social activities for employees to systematic, **evidence-based programs** focused on chronic disease prevention activities. According to the 2019 Employee Benefits Survey conducted by the Society for Human Resource Management (SHRM), company offerings of programs, clubs, and classes showed small increases compared to previous years. Companies reported offering community volunteer programs (51%), organization-sponsored sports teams (20%), and company outings or picnics (68%). Let's look at how a corporate health and wellness promotion professional might approach the development of systematic, evidence-based programs targeted at reducing chronic disease.

COMMUNITY HEALTH, POPULATION HEALTH, AND INDIVIDUAL HEALTH

When operating worksite wellness and health promotion programs, it is important to have a basic understanding of community health, population health, and individual health as well as the core principles related to chronic disease prevention.

The term *community health* is used to describe the health status of a defined group of people; that group might be defined by proximity, gender identity, race, or another common factor. The term can also include the actions taken to address health concerns for the defined group. Often used interchangeably with community health, *population health* refers to the health outcomes of a defined group of people and the distribution of such outcomes within the group. In contrast, *individual health* focuses on the health of one person.

The fitness industry has long focused on the individual. An exercise physiologist typically conducts a battery of fitness tests on an individual, discusses fitness goals, and prescribes an exercise routine, nutritional changes, and other positive healthy behaviors to achieve specific goals. Unfortunately, this individual health focus is not always successful in the long term. In the prevention world, there is a parable of the diseased pond. A sick frog is removed from the pond, assisted in becoming healthy, and then placed back into the same diseased pond, where it becomes ill again. It is thought that only when the pond itself is treated can the sick frog become truly well. Even more, creating a healthy pond can improve the health of all the frogs in the pond. This parable helps explain why corporate wellness and health promotion programs focus on both the individual and the corporate environment to achieve the best possible outcomes for community health.

BENEFITS OF CORPORATE WELLNESS AND HEALTH PROMOTION PROGRAMS

The breadth of work necessary to improve the corporate environment (the pond) is wide. Efforts can be categorized across eight dimensions of wellness (see figure 11.3):

- Physical
- Social
- Emotional
- Environmental
- Spiritual
- Financial
- Intellectual
- Occupational

These efforts work together to create a community in which health care and workers' compensation insurance costs to the employer are contained, use of sick leave is lessened, and employee productivity is increased.

Rapid increases in the incidence of chronic diseases combined with current economic trends in the health care industry have resulted in significant increases in health care costs, which makes a company's focus on wellness and health a priority. Benefits range from increased employee satisfaction to financial benefits to the company. Researchers have found that employees who work for companies that offer health and wellness programs are more likely to have higher levels of job satisfaction than those who work for companies without such programs (Marshall, 2020).

Figure 11.3 The eight dimensions of wellness.

WELLNESS AND HEALTH PROMOTION PROGRAM PLANNING AND OPERATION

In most corporations, the human resources department plays a lead role in the design and implementation of wellness and health promotion programs. This makes sense because human resources staff members manage a corporation's health insurance and workers' compensation insurance programs and employee benefit programs. When a corporation implements more complex wellness programs, more staff are needed to support the programs in areas such as medicine, exercise science, nutrition, counseling, and event management.

There are many private organizations designed to assist human resources managers. Hospital organizations often have the medical personnel needed to conduct **health risk appraisals (HRAs)** that assess individual and environmental needs of the identified population. These organizations frequently hire staff with backgrounds in nutrition, exercise science, health promotion, and corporate wellness to manage the postassessment program implementation. Many corporations contract with businesses (wellness vendors) that provide comprehensive health solutions to assist an in-house wellness coordinator. The comprehensive services typically include a program app and website, marketing materials, incentives, team-based fitness challenges, and participation and outcome reports. Corporations of all sizes can implement corporate

wellness and health promotion programs by partnering with these organizations. Facilities used for assessment can be on-site for larger corporations or off-site for smaller companies.

Corporate health professionals that use best practices will operate programs aimed at improving health risk behaviors related to a higher incidence of chronic disease. The **strategic prevention framework (SPF)** is a planning process created by the Substance Abuse and Mental Health Services Administration (SAMHSA, 2019) and used to prevent substance use and misuse (see figure 11.4). The process includes

- assessment of the current condition,
- capacity analysis,
- selection and planning for program and service prescriptions,
- implementation of those programs and services, and
- evaluation.

Following evaluation of program outcomes, the cycle is repeated. This cycle can be adopted by the corporate wellness and health promotion professional to develop corporate wellness and health promotion programs. The five steps in the process are guided

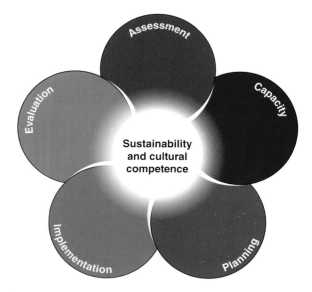

Figure 11.4 The strategic prevention framework (SPF) is a prevention model that can be used by the corporate health and wellness promotion professional to plan a corporate wellness and health promotion program.

Reprinted from Substance Abuse and Mental Health Services Administration, *Applying the Strategic Prevention Framework (SPF)* (Rockville, MD: SAMHSA). Available: www.samhsa.gov/capt/applying-strategic-prevention-framework.

by two principles: cultural competence and sustainability. SAMHSA's planning model is distinguished from other planning processes in that it is dynamic and iterative, data driven, and team oriented.

Assessment

Without an assessment of the individual and community health needs of employees, programs intended to target improvements in health and wellness are more likely to miss the mark. Programs in all areas of prevention begin with an assessment of current conditions. Assessments conducted by corporate wellness and health promotion professionals might include the following:

- Review of workplace accidents, injuries, and workers' compensation claims
- Review of health insurance premiums and employees' use of health care services, compiled in aggregate form to protect personally identifiable health information
- Review of the use of **employee assistance program (EAP)** services in aggregate form
- Review of employee HRA results
- Review of corporate policies, programs, and services that might affect health

Following best practices, including assessing which health issues significantly affect employees, allows the corporate health and wellness promotion professional to plan effective programs.

Identification of Capacities

Once the corporate health and wellness promotion professional has reviewed the data and determined which health issues are of greatest concern for the organization and its employees, resources available to the organization can be determined. Who can help from inside the organization? What partners might be available to offer assistance? What facilities can be used? Are there other companies that might be working on the same issues? Ensuring that the organization's administration understands and is ready and willing to address the issues is a key part of this process.

Planning

Once the corporate health and wellness promotion professional has determined what resources are available, the most promising, evidence-based strat-

egies for the organization are selected. Often these strategies are not programs. The corporate health and wellness promotion professional can look at policy changes such as vending services, on-site cafeteria offerings, and employee break policies, and company practices and culture can be targeted toward positive health behaviors. Adding facilities for physical activity can be expensive, but the return on investment is good if employees use them.

Implementation

Implementation of health and wellness programs is often the simplest step in the strategic prevention framework. An understanding of employee motivation and publicity strategies that will encourage participation is key at this stage. If only a few employees participate, the programs will not produce the desired results.

Evaluation

The final step in the process is to evaluate the success of the programs. The corporate health and wellness promotion professional should focus primarily on changes in the aggregate health data rather than reviews of employee satisfaction. Reviews are important in that employees are more likely to continue with programs that are satisfying, but it's possible that programs might be well liked but have little impact on aggregate health data. Assessing the effects of the programs on health status will help the corporate health and wellness promotion professional adjust the programs offered to ensure they are meeting the goals of the organization.

WELLNESS AND HEALTH PROMOTION: OTHER PROGRAM TYPES

The public often considers fitness to be the sole path to leading a healthy life. However, well-rounded worksite wellness and health promotion programs target the broader spectrum of health by including recreational activities for socialization, EAPs for mental health, and other programs that address all aspects of wellness.

Recreation Programs

Athletic programs and social activities such as corporate sport challenges, lunchtime basketball games, softball teams, company picnics, and other pastimes offer opportunities to be active, interact with coworkers, build relationships, and improve morale across the company. Social and emotional wellness play a role in employee satisfaction on the job. A body of research on the relationship between workplace team sports and workplace benefits showed that team sports not only improved individual health but also improved group cohesion and performance and increased work performance (Brinkley et al., 2017).

EAP

An employee assistance program (EAP) is a benefit offered by a company that helps employees manage personal issues that can affect their job performance. Typical services include counseling or referral services for a wide range of mental and emotional health issues such as alcohol and substance abuse and misuse, stress, grief support, financial troubles, legal issues, and family problems.

General Wellness Programs

Corporate health and wellness promotion professionals can choose from a myriad of programs across the wellness wheel (see figure 11.3). Examples of such programs are listed in table 11.1.

Table 11.1 Types of Wellness Programs

Physical	Social	Environmental	Occupational	Spiritual	Emotional	Intellectual	Financial
Fitness class	Company picnic	Stewardship program	Lunch and learn program	Self-esteem reflection	Employee assistance program	Book club	Financial planning service
Back injury prevention seminar	Holiday party	Recycling program	Cross-departmental or division training	Sabbatical program	Mindfulness awareness	Tuition assistance program	Retirement savings program
Walking club	Corporate challenge participation	Safety and loss control program	Attaining work–life balance	Stewardship program	Stress management seminar	Leadership training program	Flexible spending account

Corporate health and wellness promotion professionals can improve the health of a company's employees by enacting programs such as worksite fitness classes.

Andresr/E+/Getty Images

IMPACTS OF RECENT LEGISLATION

The field of corporate wellness and health promotion has been affected by health care reform initiated by the passage of the Affordable Care Act in 2010. The legislation puts a stronger emphasis on disease prevention and early intervention and creates opportunities for corporate health and wellness promotion professionals to include health screenings covered by group health insurance as a part of the data collection process. More comprehensive data collection may result in a more targeted selection of evidence-based programs for a corporate wellness and health promotion program. In addition, the Health Insurance Portability and Accountability Act of 1996 (HIPAA) includes provisions that protect people's health information. Professionals who work with medical information, even in the development of corporate wellness and health promotion activities, need to be cognizant of the privacy law and exercise due care when using and handling health information. Professionals most often use the data in aggregate form, meaning data are compiled into a single set and any references to individuals are removed.

CAREER PREPARATION

People seeking careers in worksite recreation and health promotion will need knowledge, skills, and experience in a variety of areas to remain competitive in the job market. Successful job candidates must be competent in

- public relations,
- human resource management,
- budget development and management,
- facility design and management,
- risk management,
- recreation and fitness programming,
- advocacy,
- health promotion and exercise science, and
- recreation sport management.

Job candidates can enhance their prospects by completing a university-approved internship and by obtaining professional certification through a recognized professional association.

Numerous accredited health promotion and fitness organizations offer certification programs such as the American College of Sports Medicine's Health Fitness Instructor (HFI) or the National Commission for Health Education Credentialing's Certified Health Education Specialist (CHES). These organizations have various requirements that candidates must meet prior to application for certification. All these organizations require successful passage of a written exam, and some require candidates to pass a practical exam. The programs that have the highest degree of recognition among health promotion professionals also require a college undergraduate degree in exercise science, kinesiology, health education, wellness, corporate recreation and wellness, or a related field of study. The following accredited associations offer certification programs:

- American College of Sports Medicine (ACSM)
- National Strength and Conditioning Association (NSCA)
- American Council on Exercise (ACE)
- National Commission for Health Education Credentialing (NCHEC)
- World Instructor Training Schools (W.I.T.S.)
- National Exercise Trainers Association (NETA)
- National Exercise and Sports Trainers Association (NESTA)
- Athletics and Fitness Association of America (AFAA)

SUMMARY

Corporate wellness and health promotion programs vary as greatly in scope and complexity as the number and sizes of companies that offer them. Corporate health and wellness promotion professionals have an opportunity to affect employees' lives and contribute to their happiness and productivity at work. In addition, health and wellness programs have positive effects on employee absenteeism, use of workers' compensation, use of sick leave, and health care premium costs. The best-performing programs will follow a planning process that includes data collection, capacity assessment, program planning, implementation, and evaluation. Students interested in the field should have a combination of health-related and service-delivery competencies and plan on enjoying a rewarding career in a growing field.

Model Program: Worksite Recreation and Health Promotion

We are all familiar with Google since it is one of the most widely used search engines on the Internet. Google is so ubiquitous that we often refer to searching the Internet as "googling." But what is it like to work for Google in 2023? Google's mission is to organize the world's information and make it universally accessible and useful, along with a commitment to "significantly improving the life of as many people as possible," which includes their employees (referred to as "Googlers") (Google, n.d.).

We strive to provide Googlers and their loved ones with a world-class benefits experience, focused on supporting their physical, financial, and emotional wellbeing. Our benefits are based on data and centered around our users: Googlers and their families. They're thoughtfully designed to enhance your health and wellbeing, and generous enough to make it easy for you to take good care of yourself (now, and in the future). So we can build for everyone, together. (Google Careers, n.d.)

Google provides benefits in the following categories:

- Health and wellness
- Financial well-being
- Family support and care
- Community and personal development
- "Googley extras"

Besides the traditional benefits provided by most companies, they offer student loan reimbursement and one-on-one financial counseling, paid time off including reset or well-being days, a hybrid work model option, four "work from anywhere" weeks per year, and time off to volunteer. They feature an internal network of Googler community groups and local clubs; fitness centers; healthy on-site meals; at-home fitness, well-being, and cooking classes; and art programs.

Information from Google (https://careers.google.com/benefits/).

Recreation in the Armed Forces

Yating "Tina" Liang

" The Canadian Armed Forces know that physical activity, recreation, and sport are essential for promoting well-being and operational readiness at home and while deployed. Whether it be organized sports, individual activities or participation in recreational clubs, the CAF knows these types of activities provide support to our families, build capacity in our communities, and ensure our quality of life. "

Lieutenant-General Christine Whitecross, commander, Military Personnel Command

" We are dedicated to providing support and leisure services that are as outstanding as the people we serve. "

U.S. Army Morale, Welfare and Recreation

Recreation programs in the United States and Canadian Armed Forces are based on two basic philosophies:

1. Members of the military and their families are entitled to the same quality of life that is afforded to the society they protect.

2. Quality recreation programs have a direct effect on mission readiness.

Recreation programs are designed to maintain a positive quality of life that leads to a sound mind and body, a productive community, and a strong family environment. Recreation programs for the U.S. and Canadian Armed Forces have unique requirements that set them apart from other public-sector programs. These programs must support military personnel and their families at their home stations as well as in deployed environments at remote sites around the world (Canadian Forces Morale & Welfare Services, n.d.).

HISTORY

Recreation programs have existed in the United States and Canada for hundreds of years. In the United States, organized programs started on the battlefields of the Revolutionary War where sutlers were assigned the responsibility of providing for the personal needs of the soldiers. These itinerant merchants provided many of the services of the present-day exchange stores, and a portion of their profits were returned to the units. These unit funds were used to provide services to soldiers in the battlefield. Today, revenues generated by the profit-oriented services are still used to fund a variety of leisure activities, including libraries, financial assistance programs, bands, and school projects (Canadian Army, 2017b; USA Government, 2017).

By the Civil War, sutlers had priced themselves out of business, and their roles were assumed by canteen associations, which became essential social clubs for the units and authorized by Congress in 1893. These had naturally become centers for command-sponsored social events and were recognized as important for promoting esprit de corps ("the common spirit existing in the members of a group and inspiring enthusiasm, devotion, and strong regard for the honor of the group" [Merriam-Webster, n.d.]). Organized programs started on the battlefields of World War I, where the Salvation Army and Red Cross members ministered to the needs of soldiers as the forerunners of today's recreation specialists (US Army MWR, n.d.).

In 1941, at the beginning of World War II, the U.S. Morale Division, named Special Services, was established in the U.S. Army. Between 1946 and 1955, core recreation programs were established and staffed by a combination of active-duty military personnel and civilians. Until the mid-1980s, active-duty personnel held occupational specialties in Special Services at every level of command. As those specialties were discontinued, civilians continued to operate programs with military oversight as the program requirements grew and the senior commanders came to understand the value of recreation in mission readiness (U.S. Army MWR, n.d.).

In Canada, it has long been recognized that the success of the military depends on the physical, emotional, and spiritual well-being of the **military community**. Throughout the history of the Canadian military, morale and welfare programs have been available to all serving members and their families with the goal of enhancing the quality of life of the military community and contributing to the **operational readiness and effectiveness** of the armed forces. In 1969, the Canadian Treasury Board set out the basic principle that "a reasonable level of goods, services and recreational facilities should be available to Canadian Forces personnel in their areas of service" (CFMWS, n.d.). In 1996, the Canadian Forces Personnel Support Agency (which was later renamed to Canadian Forces Morale and Welfare Services) was created with the mission of providing the military community with morale and welfare programs and services (CFMWS, 2016).

As of 2022, in the United States and Canada, recreation programs within the military environment are broad in scope and are constantly evolving to meet the ever-changing needs of the military community. The U.S. Armed Forces use the common acronym **MWR** for **Morale, Welfare and Recreation** to refer to those programs, whereas in Canada, the **Personnel Support Programs (PSP) Division** of the **Canadian Forces Morale and Welfare Services (CFMWS)** is the key provider of recreation services within the military environment (PSP, 2017; US Army MWR, n.d.).

MILITARY VERSUS CIVILIAN RECREATION

Military recreation departments are administered similarly to civilian recreation departments. Many of the programs, such as swimming lessons, leadership certifications, and recreation club activities are conducted in partnership with, or are modeled on the products of, civilian agencies. Like their civilian counterparts, military recreation departments employ many operational tools to efficiently manage and profile programs and services. From recreation management software to online recreation brochures, military recreation strives to encourage participation, increase patronage, and enhance the benefits of recreation participation.

Although military recreation is modeled after civilian recreation programs, the unique environment and requirements of the military community result in several distinct differences between the two. One of the key differences is the transient nature of the clients. Military families relocate frequently. Programs and services based on the expressed needs of the military community one year might be quite different the next year because the families who make up the community relocate. Recreation professionals must constantly survey the military community to be aware of the changing needs and interests of military families.

Second, many military communities are located in remote or unstable places around the world. Recreation opportunities are as important to the serving members in isolated or combat environments as they are to members and their families at the home station. Recreation professionals must be prepared and willing to provide services under difficult and sometimes dangerous conditions.

A third difference between civilian and military recreation is the scope of the recreation department. Civilian recreation departments provide services to residents and other interested users. Military recreation departments are exclusive and provide services to military members, their families, and other members of the military community such as veterans and their families. MWR and PSP often offer services to each other's primary clients when military personnel from the other country are stationed in the United States or Canada (Military Benefits, 2017).

A fourth difference is the culture in which recreation programs are conducted. Many military installations are located in foreign countries, and the recreation programs blend activities and events with the local, regional, and national culture of the foreign country. In many countries, joint activities and events are offered between the military and the host community. Programs such as volksmarches (organized walks) and volksfests (regional festivals) are popular activities with military families stationed in Germany (Military Benefits, 2017).

Last, volunteer management can be challenging within the military community. Volunteers are key contributors to the success of the military community recreation program. Without volunteers, many programs would be unsustainable, and with the high turnover of military families, managing volunteers is often difficult. MWR and PSP have developed viable volunteer management programs that strive to develop, support, and nurture the involvement of volunteers in recreation programs (Military Benefits, 2017).

U.S. ARMED FORCES

The **U.S. Armed Forces** provide a variety of recreation programs to maintain individual, family, and mission readiness during peacetime and in times of declared war and other contingencies. The U.S. Armed Forces consist of the

- U.S. Army,
- U.S. Marine Corps,
- U.S. Navy,
- U.S. Air Force, and
- U.S. Coast Guard.

Although the scope of each MWR program might vary slightly, the mission is to provide quality recreation programs to the U.S. fighting forces at home and abroad.

Military MWR programs are an integral part of the military benefits package, encouraging positive individual values, and building healthy families and communities. They provide consistently high-quality support services that are commonly furnished by other employers or state and local governments to their employees and citizens. MWR programs promote esprit de corps and provide for

- physical, cultural, and social needs;
- general well-being;
- quality of life; and
- community support of service members and their families.

Recreation programs are a vital factor in maintaining each force's ability to fight and win its nation's wars. The fighting forces need a balance of work and leisure to be ready to fight when needed, especially during frequent contingency operations. A *contingency operation* is a military operation that is either designated by the secretary of defense in which members of the armed forces are or may become involved in military actions, operations, or hostilities against an enemy of the United States or against an opposing force. Families left behind during a deployment to a contingency operation must be cared for so that the service member can fight without worrying about those left at home (Military MWR, 2012).

Military mission readiness depends largely on the resilience of service members and their families. Resilience is important to the military because it helps people overcome traumatic experiences such as those encountered in contingency operations, helps family members better cope with deployments, reduces stress, and boosts energy levels. Resilience is often described as the ability to respond to and cope with difficult or stressful experiences, situations, environments, people, and setbacks common to all people in life. Although everything we do involves stress, how we respond to a particular stressor is important. Increasing the ability to handle stress and bounce back from the strains of daily life increases resilience (Military MWR, 2012).

MWR provides well-balanced recreation that normalizes behavior after a stressful experience. Participating in exercise and recreation programs reduces stress and builds mental and physical resilience. Besides building resilience, MWR enhances mission readiness. This conclusion was demonstrated by findings from the Department of Defense customer satisfaction survey conducted in 2009 and 2011 to assess MWR programs. The survey findings indicated that MWR satisfaction has the greatest effect on mission readiness. This correlation is critical to understanding the importance of MWR recreation in building resilience and influencing military mission readiness throughout the armed forces (Military MWR, 2012).

During contingency operations, MWR equipment and deployed personnel deliver MWR programs and activities that build unit esprit de corps, increase morale, relieve stress, and provide greatly needed mental diversion during these operations. Internet cafés with computers are operated by MWR at no cost to service members. MWR Internet cafés also offer webcams and headsets for making videos and phone calls using voice over Internet protocol (VoIP), which costs only a few cents per minute. In addition, service members have access to all the popular social networking websites to communicate with family and friends. Portable morale satellite units provide free Internet access to remote, forward operating bases. Fitness, recreation, and social activities include cardiovascular and weight equipment, suspension training systems, sports, recreation, games, outdoor recreation equipment, large screen TVs, DVD and CD players, and current video games. Armed Forces Entertainment, in cooperation with the United Service Organizations (USO), provides much-welcomed celebrity and professional entertainment. The Department of Defense MWR online library is available through the military services library portals and offers 24/7 one-stop shopping for all library resources in print, electronic, and downloadable formats. Free downloads of thousands of ebooks and audiobooks and free access to comprehensive databases for recreation, lifelong learning, reference, and career

transition are available for all ages and all interests. In addition, digital books and paperback books are provided monthly to deployed units (Military MWR, 2012).

For service members returning from contingency operations with severe injuries, the MWR program provides recreation inclusion training for recreation programmers from all military services. Recognizing that recreation and sport play an important role in the recovery process, training concentrates on

- post-traumatic stress disorder,
- limb amputations,
- traumatic brain injury,
- spinal cord injuries,
- adaptive and specialized equipment,
- accessible design,
- age-appropriate inclusive recreation programming, and
- societal and cultural issues.

Trained recreation programmers and recreation therapists develop or expand inclusive recreation programs at their installations, which enables wounded service members to develop their abilities and continue their military mission (Military MWR, 2012).

The MWR program provides recreation opportunities for people of all abilities to exercise and recreate. With programs such as outdoor recreation, fitness classes, team sports, and bowling, just to name a few, MWR helps individuals and units maintain physical fitness, alleviate combat stress, and foster total family fitness. By promoting exercise and recreation, MWR enables service members and families to build physical and mental resilience to stress, which affects military mission readiness. The oversight for providing recreation services in the United States is governed by specific agencies within each branch of the military (Military MWR, 2012).

- *U.S. Army.* The U.S. Army Family and Morale, Welfare and Recreation, is the G9 Division of the U.S. Army Installation Management Command. They administer the MWR program through its headquarters in San Antonio, Texas, with more than 500 staff members. It is a comprehensive network of quality support and leisure services that enhance the lives of soldiers, civilians, families, military retirees, and other eligible participants. MWR services and activities offer soldiers and their families opportunities to enrich their lives culturally and creatively. The programs relieve stress, build strength and resilience, and help people stay physically, mentally, and financially fit. The unique challenge to the army is the requirement to provide the same level of support to troops around the world regardless of the existence of a viable installation (locations can vary from a military garrison in the United States to a tent in the desert) (Military.com, 2017; U.S. Army MWR, n.d.).

- *U.S. Marine Corps.* The marine corps manages the MWR program through Marine Corps Community Services (MCCS) at its headquarters in Quantico, Virginia. "Marines are the youngest, most junior and least married of the four military services" (MCCS, n.d.). MCCS provides fitness and recreation programs, personal services, and business activities to support individual and family readiness and retention. MCCS delivers services to its over 2,000 facilities with more than 12,000 staff worldwide. The mission of MCCS is to "take care of Marines and their families by providing quality of life programs, products, and services in support of the Marine Corps objectives" (MCCS, n.d.).

- *U.S. Navy.* The U.S. Navy Morale, Welfare and Recreation Division, located in Millington, Tennessee, and the Commander, Navy Installations Command, in Washington, D.C., administer the MWR program to active-duty, reserve, and retired navy personnel and their families. The mission is to provide high-quality, customer-focused programs and services that contribute to resiliency, retention, readiness, and quality of life. The navy serves the needs of its members around the world at installations and on board ships at sea. Civilian recreation specialists carry out this mission work on installations in the United States and overseas and are assigned on board most of the navy's larger ships to manage MWR programs and services (Military.com, 2017).

- *U.S. Air Force.* The U.S. Air Force operates MWR programs through its joint headquarters in San Antonio-Lackland, Texas, under the title of Services Center (AFSVC). "AFSVC ensures successful operation of essential food, fitness, childcare, lodging and recreation opportunities for military members and their families" (Air Force Installation & Mission Support Center, n.d.). The mission of the air force's MWR program is to contribute to mission readiness and improve productivity through programs that promote fitness, esprit de corps, and quality of life for air force people and to provide policy and direction for the worldwide services program to help sustain the air force mission. Although not normally considered recreation programs, activities such as mortuary services and wartime feeding are included under the umbrella of MWR services, which makes its program delivery broader than that of the other service branches (Military.com, 2017).

- *U.S. Coast Guard.* The U.S. Coast Guard in the Department of Homeland Security provides recreation programs to its members worldwide. Although it is the smallest of the service branches, it offers a critical element in the quality-of-life programming for its members and their families. The mission of the Coast Guard Morale, Well-Being, and Recreation (MWR) program, operating out of Chesapeake, Virginia, is to "uplift the spirits of the coast guard family and be an essential element of coast guard readiness, retention, and resiliency through customer-owned and customer-driven MWR programs and services" (U.S. Coast Guard MWR, n.d.).

The U.S. Armed Forces have unique recreational opportunities for active-duty military and their families. One such service that is mirrored throughout the armed forces is special recreation programs for single service men and women. About 40 percent of service members are age 25 or younger (National Academies of Sciences, Engineering, and Medicine, 2019). For many of these people, it is the first time they have been separated from their families, and they are stationed in communities or countries that are vastly different from their own. This creates unique needs that are different from families with children. Programs such as the Better Opportunities for Single Soldiers (BOSS) Program, Navy Liberty Program, Airman and Family Readiness, and Single Marine Program (SMP), provide a voice for this segment to advocate for their unique needs and desires (Military Health Service, n.d.). These programs are composed of advisory councils that include a staff member and address quality-of-life issues such as recreation, volunteerism, and living situations in the barracks. Each council tailors its activities to the needs and unique opportunities of the local community or country (Army Study Guide, 2017).

An additional service provided by the Department of Defense is the Armed Forces Recreation Center (AFRC) resorts. These centers are located in Garmisch, Germany; Walt Disney Resort in Florida; Seoul, Korea; and Waikiki Beach in Honolulu, Hawaii (Armed Forces Recreation Center Resorts, n.d.). Each of these centers is a full-service resort with an array of programs, services, tours, and recreational opportunities unique to their location. Service personnel and their families use these centers for family vacations, as areas to reunite with a family member who has been deployed and is on leave from the combat area, or as regional destinations for getaway weekends. The AFRC facilities meet various needs for recreation, relaxation, rest, and restoration from various life situations and combat (Army One Source, 2017).

CANADIAN ARMED FORCES

The **Canadian Armed Forces (CAF)** are separate and distinct from the Department of National Defence. The CAF are headed by the Chief of the Defence Staff (CDS), which is Canada's senior serving officer.

The CAF serve on the sea, on land, and in the air through the Royal Canadian Navy, the Canadian Army, and the Royal Canadian Air Force.

- *Royal Canadian Navy.* The Royal Canadian Navy (RCN) consists of approximately 8,400 regular force and 4,100 reserve sailors supported by about 3,800 civilian employees. The mission of the RCN is to generate combat-capable, multipurpose maritime forces that support Canada's efforts to participate in security operations anywhere in the world as part of an integrated CAF (Government of Canada, n.d.).
- *Canadian Army.* The Canadian Army is the land component of the CAF, and it consists of approximately 22,500 regular force and 21,500 reservists supported by about 3,500 civilian employees. The mission of the Canadian Army is to "posture for concurrent operations by generating combat effective, multi-purpose land forces to meet Canada's defense objectives" (The Canadian Army, 2022).
- *Royal Canadian Air Force.* The Royal Canadian Air Force (RCAF) includes approximately 13,000 regular force personnel and 2,400 air reserve personnel. Approximately 2,000 civilian public servants are also employed within the RCAF organization. The RCAF provides the CAF with relevant, responsive, and effective air power capabilities to meet defense challenges. PSP recreation services vary wing to wing, but they are geared toward family activities. Recreation departments also participate in organizing annual wing air shows that include face painting and food concessions (Royal Canadian Air Force, 2022).

The Canadian Armed Forces Recreation Program

Canadian Forces Morale and Welfare Services (CFMWS), with over 4,000 employees, works under the authority of the defence minister. It is a separate agency of the defence team and operates under the nonpublic property framework. The Personnel Support Programs (PSP), a division of CFMWS, is responsible for fitness, recreation, sports, and health promotion for the CAF members and their families (CFMWS, 2022).

With up to 20 percent of the military population living in the residential housing on bases and wings in fiscal year 2019 to 2020 (Government of Canada, 2021), PSP partners with civilian agencies to ensure that their needs are met in the neighborhoods in which they live. The Canadian Forces Appreciation Program offers rate reductions and incentives that are exclusive to CAF members, particularly in the areas of family attractions, leisure, travel, and entertainment (CFMWS, 2022).

CAF Recreation Program Operations

Unique to the CAF recreation program are the services provided to ill and injured soldiers and those who are deployed. Soldier On is a CAF program that supports currently serving members and veterans in overcoming physical or mental illnesses or injuries through sport, recreational, and creative activities. Since its inception in 2007, Soldier On has helped more than 8,800 ill and injured members obtain sporting or recreational equipment and gain access to high-level training from world-class instructors, and has supported their participation in a wide range of structured activities from alpine skiing to fishing to adventure expeditions. This reintroduction of an active lifestyle provides members with opportunities to develop new skills, build confidence in their abilities, and meet peers with similar challenges. Many ill and injured members credit Soldier On with helping them adapt to their new normal and realize their full potential (CFMWS, 2022).

Since August 2000, PSP has been deploying morale and welfare staff to manage and deliver programs for CAF personnel on overseas missions. Depending on the needs of the mission, staff members support deployed personnel by offering services such as retail operations; mass services; fitness, sports, and recreation programs; barber services; and more. Programs are often similar to ones offered at home, although recreation professionals must be creative and flexible in their approaches to traditional offerings due to lack of facilities and challenging environments (CFMWS, July 2017).

To assist with decompression from missions, CAF provides reintegration programs for military personnel that resemble social and travel activities at the military installation. To complement the mental health services provided by CAF through the decompression activities and services, PSP organizes recreation and social activities to help members unwind and relax. During longer missions, PSP can also support rest and recreation centers in which deployed members are given a few days away from the operation. PSP at these centers organize tourist excursions and provide services similar to a hotel concierge by arranging everything from spa packages to dinner reservations (CFMWS, July 2017). The Canadian Forces have dedicated music programs where musicians are allowed to join the military force full-time or part-time. Under the artist programs, artists are invited to be in residence with the military for a certain period of time, and they often create artistic work for Canadian military forces (Canadian Armed Forces, n.d.).

A comprehensive, varied, and universal recreation program assures military members that their families are well cared for in their absence and provides the military family with opportunities to engage in the community while maintaining or enhancing their personal morale and welfare. Military Family Resource Centers (MFRCs) are committed to enriching the lives of individuals and families in CAF communities through positive action, education, and support. They provide relevant programs and services that empower and encourage strong, independent individuals and families within the CAF (CFMWS, July 2017).

MFRCs encourage and facilitate the voluntary participation of CAF families, particularly spouses, in all facets of their operations from program planning and delivery to organization governance and leadership. In Canada, MFRCs are incorporated, not-for-profit, third-party organizations. They work in partnership with the local commanding officer (CO) and are governed by elected boards of directors (SPS, 2017).

MILITARY RECREATION PROGRAM AREAS

In Canada and the United States, the recreation mandate operates to serve the following MWR and PSP program offerings:

- *Sports and fitness.* At the heart of every recreation program is the sports and fitness program. Because of the need to maintain a strong and healthy force, sports and fitness programs have long been recognized by military leadership as a key to mission readiness, and they have become the centerpiece of every MWR and PSP organization. These programs offer state-of-the-art gymnasium and fitness facilities as well as organized sports competitions from intramural to competitive levels (CFMWS, July 2017; U.S. Navy, n.d.).

- *Skill development.* A staple of the military recreation program's inventory is skill development through instructional classes. Classes are organized in response to a community's interest in skill development and leadership opportunities. The classes include specialty cardio workouts and aerobics, arts and crafts, camps, swimming lessons, weight training for youth, sport clinics, and leadership development. Programs are available for all ages and interests and are developed and implemented in consultation with members of the military community (CFMWS, July 2017; U.S. Navy, n.d.).

- *Libraries.* Libraries remain a vital part of most MWR programs in areas that cannot provide adequate or convenient services to the military population. Libraries vary in size and offerings but generally provide standard recreation reading inventories, reading programs, educational studies, research materials, Internet and email services, and support services. Library programs have become especially crucial in supporting troops in deployed locations and on ships at sea around the world where no local civilian resources are available (CFMWS, July 2017; U.S. Navy, n.d.).

- *Outdoor recreation.* Outdoor recreation programs provide outdoor equipment and access to campgrounds, parks, beaches, and lakes as well as adventure programs and other activities that promote the care and protection of our natural resources. Because of the huge land masses placed under the care of military installations, numerous outdoor recreation opportunities are available. Military organizations are entrusted with the care and preservation of valuable natural resources, and that responsibility provides the opportunity for military personnel to develop new skills while preserving and enjoying natural resources around the world (CFMWS, July 2017; U.S. Navy, n.d.).

- *Child and youth activities.* Child and youth programs and services are offered at all military locations where family support is provided. Programs extend various levels of support that include child development centers, youth centers, and youth activities such as skill development and sports programs. All programs are age appropriate and offer activities that focus on supporting transition, easing the stress of relocation, building and sustaining meaningful relationships, and developing a sense of belonging within the community. Activities that provide universal access to information, tools, resources, and services that support youth; activities that focus on the promotion of healthy and fulfilling life choices; and activities that encourage the development of leadership and assets in youth (40 assets developed by the Search Institute) are also central to the recreation mandate (CFMWS, July 2017; U.S. Navy, n.d.).

• *Recreation centers*. Each military community offers a variety of drop-in opportunities for casual participation in unorganized recreation. Recreation centers are available to military members and their families and provide safe and comfortable environments for self-directed activities as well as for designed programs (CFMWS, July 2017; U.S. Navy, n.d.).

• *Special events and entertainment*. Each military community offers a variety of annual special events to profile military community activities and accomplishments and honor the contributions of volunteers and community partners. Many services host worldwide concert series tours that provide live entertainment to troops, and others focus on local events and festivals (CFMWS, July 2017; U.S. Navy, n.d.).

• *Business activities*. A variety of pay-as-you-go activities geared toward leisure and fitness pursuits are available at most military locations. Theaters, golf courses, special-interest clubs, restaurants, nightclubs, and bowling centers are popular activities enjoyed by military families. These commercial services are generally offered when no local off-base resources are readily available. These operations provide military members with the types of services that are available in most civilian communities and provide a revenue source to support other morale and welfare activities (CFMWS, July 2017; U.S. Navy, n.d.).

• *Recreation clubs and private organizations*. Recreation clubs or private organizations are self-governing and self-funded entities operated for and by specific-interest groups in accordance with established constitutions and bylaws. Recreation club constitutions and bylaws are military directives that outline club operating principles and member codes of conduct. All recreation clubs are managed by a volunteer executive council and governed by its membership. Examples of recreation club activities include specialty arts, scuba, running, woodworking, sailing, martial arts, gymnastics, swimming, figure skating, and dancing and activities for auto and motorcycle, saddle, and rod and gun enthusiasts (CFMWS, July 2017; U.S. Navy, n.d.).

ADRIEL REBOH/Patrick McMullan via Getty Images

Soldiers take time out to dance at a special event. This necessary recreation helps build physical and mental resilience to stress.

EMPLOYMENT OPPORTUNITIES

Military recreation provides vast employment opportunities because of the thousands of civilian employees around the world that make up the various MWR and PSP organizations. MWR employs more than 100,000 people in the United States and overseas. They have positions available for professionals in areas such as child development, sports and fitness management, outdoor recreation, NAF (nonappropriated funds) contracting, marketing, financial management, professional golf management, and food and beverage (MWR employment, n.d.). People entering employment in military recreation programs generally begin in a specialty such as outdoor recreation, club management, or child development specialist and then move into general management positions within the personnel system. The personnel system might be paid with federal tax dollars (appropriated funds) or with revenue-generating activity funds (nonappropriated funds); both systems are parallel and are considered civil service with portability between each. Careers in MWR are varied but generally start out at the entry level or through an internship with progressions to the top of the civil service ladder (PSP, 2017; Military 4 Life, 2017).

MWR assigns people to a variety of locations from the beaches of California to the sands of the Afghan desert to the icy rivers of Alaska and the high seas of the Atlantic. Variety in jobs and location means there's little opportunity for boredom in the business of providing recreation programs to the armed forces. MWR employees work hard so that others can have fun and enjoy life, and they do it seven days a week and sometimes 24 hours a day. The benefits of a career in MWR range from the great potential for upward mobility to the opportunity to travel and live abroad.

Army MWR programs can be found all over the United States and other parts of the world. Within the United States, MWR programs can be found in 30 states. Outside the United States, programs are available in Puerto Rico, Japan, Korea, Germany, Belgium, Netherlands, and Italy (Army MWR Installation, n.d.). Various naval bases can be found in 20 states within the United States where internship or employment opportunities related to MWR services and programs are available. Internationally, such opportunities are available in Bahrain, Cuba, Guam, Greece, Italy, Japan, Korea, and Spain (Navy MWR Careers, n.d.). Marine Corps Community Services (MCCS) can be found in nine states within the

United States. Outside the United States, services are available in Japan and Korea (MCCS Careers, n.d.). Internship opportunities and employment with Coast Guard can be located in seven states and Puerto Rico (Coast Guard MWR, n.d.).

In Canada, the CFMWS is the largest employer of physical education, human kinetics, and leisure study graduates. The variety of positions and the potential for mobility between Canadian military locations contribute to the attractiveness of a career in the Canadian military recreation field. Most recreation positions within the CFMWS require an undergraduate degree or college diploma plus specific qualifications, such as lifeguarding and first aid certifications or volunteer management certificates to match the position's requirements. Some senior management and director positions require postgraduate degrees, specialty knowledge, and experience in the field of military morale and welfare. Furthermore, in recognition of Canada's linguistic diversity, most positions with the CFMWS require proficiency in French and English (PSP, 2017; Military 4 Life, 2017).

Each Canadian military recreation department is composed of a manager, community recreation staff, and various program-specific support staff such as an aquatics supervisor, a youth programmer, or an administration coordinator. Part-time staff, such as lifeguards, camp staff, and youth center monitors also provide programs directly to the military family. Throughout Canada, the CFMWS employs more than 6,000 staff to deliver and support morale and welfare programming.

COVID-19'S IMPACT ON MWR

Like many other businesses and operations affected by the COVID-19 pandemic, MWR programs and their operations were interrupted during this time. "Over 55,500 employees in the services' MWR programs are facing immediate risk of furlough resulting from COVID-19 closures of morale, welfare and recreation facilities," according to the documents by Department of Defense (Jowers, 2020). The Department of Defense provided more than $300 million to MWR programs to ensure MWR employees were not furloughed and were paid even though many facilities were shut down, particularly during the first few months of the pandemic in 2020. Facilities affected by the pandemic in MWR included child and family centers, fitness centers, theaters, libraries, golf courses, bowling alleys, lodging facilities, and food and beverage operations, just to name a few. Most of these programs rely on customer visits and fees to be self-sustained, so the temporary closures of these facilities due to the pandemic resulted in significant revenue reductions. Under the federal, state, and local guidelines, states started phased reopenings starting May 2020 (National Governors Association, 2021). Like many other recreation-related businesses, MWR programs had to invest additional expenses in personal protective equipment (such as face masks or coverings, face shields, goggles) and cleaning supplies for prescribed cleaning and disinfecting procedures, which put additional constraints on the MWR programs with already reduced budgets (Jowers, 2020). In fiscal year 2022, the U.S. Navy was facing a $280 million budget shortfall and planning to cut 1,000 civilian jobs, which included staff cuts on MWR beaches, in gyms, in base libraries, and at base swimming pools (LeGrone, 2021).

With the development of the COVID-19 vaccine, many facilities started to reopen to a more regular capacity. The secretary of the Department of Defense issued mandates for the COVID-19 vaccine in August 2021 (Vergun, 2021), although the mandate was rescinded in early 2023 (Department of Defense, 2023). Depending on the types of programs and where they were located, the reopening started in 2021 with some programs going back to normal operations, such as golf courses and lodging facilities, while other programs were still operating at a limited capacity or limited hours, such as child centers and swimming pools (Navy MWR Pax River, n.d.). Reopening of facilities were affected by the nature of the programs, the characteristics of their participants, the type of facility, and other factors. The Department of Defense has protocol for public health emergencies like the COVID-19 pandemic, known as health protection condition (HPCON) levels. Commanders review and update these HPCONs based on risk levels within a local community in cooperation with local, state, or host nation guidance (U.S. Department of Defense, 2020). All MWR programs have recovery plans and reopen their facilities after closure with the approval of higher authorities (Navy MWR Great Lakes, 2021).

The Public Health Emergency caused by COVID-19 ended on May 11, 2023 (U.S. Department of Health and Human Services, 2023), and all MWR services returned to normal operations at that time.

Besides the physical health threat that COVID-19 posed, concerns about mental health have also grown due to lockdown, social distancing, and uncertainty of the virus. "It is our shared responsibility to ensure the continued health of our collective soul and identity," describes General David Berger, commandant of Marine Corps (Marine Corps Family Programs Division Campaign Plan, 2021-2024). MWR programs play an even more important role to maintain physical, emotional, and social wellness for service members and their families. Just like other sections in the parks and recreation field, MWR services will need to make revenue recovery plans and create sustainable revenue resources in order to provide postpandemic support and programs to service members and their families.

SUMMARY

Most people in the profession of armed forces recreation feel they make a valuable contribution to the mission of the armed forces and are proud to serve military personnel and their families. Armed forces recreation professionals work around the world and strive to improve the quality of life for soldiers, marines, sailors, air force personnel, and coast guard personnel and their families who are serving their countries in difficult and challenging times.

Armed forces recreation professionals are proud to support their country's military mission because they believe in the importance of what they do for the armed forces and understand the effect they have on mission readiness and, ultimately, the defense of their country. Much like their counterparts in the civilian sector, military recreation professionals must strive to ensure that the programs they provide are beneficial.

Review Questions
Campus Recreation

1. What is the definition of campus recreation?
2. What are the benefits of graduate assistantships?
3. What was the original focus of NIRSA, and how did this evolve?
4. Name some benefits of participating in campus recreation programs.
5. What are two funding sources for campus recreation?

Esports

1. What was the location of the first esports tournament? Which game was played?
2. How has the Columbus Recreation and Parks Department used esports in their services?
3. Describe how literature has discussed whether esports should be considered a sport.
4. What impact has COVID-19 had on esports?
5. How have Levi's and Marvel Entertainment contributed to the prominence of esports in society?

(continued)

Review Questions *(continued)*

Faith-Based Recreation

1. What is the second largest faith group in the United States?

2. When considering religion-based activities, what are some examples of items that recreational activities should not interfere with?

3. Name for-profit companies that organized to fill a niche in the fitness market for Christian fitness centers that train both the body and the soul.

4. What are the three faith-based recreation requirements that professionals must meet?

5. What is the definition of selective acculturation?

6. How do religious institutions support the three pillars of the NRPA?

7. What two gender-specific requirements are necessary to maximize participation by very religious Muslim women when they exercise?

Worksite Recreation and Health Promotion

1. What are some advantages of offering health and wellness benefits to your employees?

2. What department typically designs and implements health and wellness programs in an organization?

3. List and describe the steps a professional would follow to develop a worksite wellness program targeted at the most significant health issues of a company.

4. Compare individual health and community health.

5. What accredited associations offer certification programs that would be helpful for the corporate wellness and health promotion professional?

6. List three types of programs that can be implemented by a corporate health and wellness promotion professional to address social wellness.

(continued)

Review Questions   *(continued)*

Recreation in the Armed Forces

1. What two philosophies are the recreation programs of U.S. and Canadian Armed Forces based on?

2. *MWR*, *PSP*, and *CFMWS* are the common acronyms used to refer to the recreation providers of the U.S. and Canadian Armed Forces. What do they stand for?

3. Name two differences between military and civilian recreation.

4. Which military forces make up the United States and Canadian Armed Forces?

5. Provide at least three examples of program offerings by MWR or PSP.

6. Describe the impact of COVID-19 on MWR programs.

Go to HK*Propel* to complete the activities for this chapter.

CHAPTER 12

Leisure and Recreation Across the Life Span

Mary Sara Wells and Tyler Tapps

Patryce Bak/Stone RF/Getty Images

"There is a fountain of youth: it is your mind, your talents, the creativity you bring to your life and the lives of people you love. When you learn to tap this source, you will truly have defeated age."

Sophia Loren, Italian film actress

LEARNING OUTCOMES

After reading this chapter, you should be able to do the following:

> Describe recreation and leisure programs that effectively align with the developmental characteristics of each stage of the life span

> Identify significant milestones throughout the life span and their implications for recreation and leisure service provision

> Describe programs from the recreation industry that address developmental characteristics across the life span.

Recreation and leisure is one of the largest industries in the world, and it plays a role as a form of social development over the course of one's life. As the recreation and leisure industry continues to grow, a shift has occurred in the mission of recreation and leisure services. It is no longer an atmosphere of only fun and games; a new focus emphasizes the health benefits of participating in recreation and leisure activities. For example, since 2014, the National Recreation and Park Association (NRPA) has implemented new health and wellness and social equity aspects to their strategic plan to align with the shift in the profession. As children grow and adults age, recreation and leisure interests, activities, and definitions must also evolve and change. Therefore, changes in our recreation and leisure behavior directly reflect developmental changes.

Psychologists and other recreation and leisure researchers describe development in seven **life stages**:

1. Infancy (birth-2 years)
2. Early childhood (3-6 years)
3. Middle and late childhood (7-12 years)
4. Adolescence (13-19 years)
5. Early adulthood (20-39 years)
6. Middle adulthood (40-59 years)
7. Late adulthood (60 years and older)

When recreation and leisure programmers consider how to manage the components of the recreation and leisure experience (e.g., leadership, staffing, facilities), they must line up with the developmental stage of the target audience. This increases their ability to implement successful recreation and leisure experiences and programs (Neulinger, 1974).

LEISURE FUNCTIONS ACROSS THE LIFE SPAN

If we examine the various life stages, it becomes evident that recreation and leisure fulfill different social functions:

- Some recreation activities are done alone.
- Some are done with members of the same or opposite sex in the traditional gender binary.
- Some are done only with peers.
- Some are done with spouses, parents, children, or relatives.

Many people choose to participate in recreation or leisure activities not only because of personal preference but also to facilitate the maintenance or strengthening of social bonds with friends, neighbors, or kin (Kleiber & McGuire, 2016). For example, one person might prefer a game of golf to a game of Scrabble, but the family's group decision might be to play Scrabble to be with one another, to enjoy one another's company, or simply to show respect to one another. The extent to which people participate in recreation and leisure activities varies throughout the life span. For example, when an individual reaches old age, involvement once again is likely to become unconditional, chosen because it's enjoyable (Kleiber & McGuire, 2016).

INFANCY

Infancy is the time from birth until approximately 2 years old. There are many changes that occur during this period. Infants make large gains in their motor skills such as rolling, sitting, and crawling. Their memory and recognition also develop; these are often seen in an infant's reaction to seeing a parent or hearing a parent's voice. Infants start to demonstrate their personality development through their interactions with others and their toys.

Infants are often interested in the social world around them, and babies try to communicate with others (Erikson, 1950). By age 2, they exhibit signs of peer play. Infants will often show their toys to one another and offer to share their toys. This is part of their development of basic communication skills. As communication becomes more developed, they will start to show signs of cooperative play. *Cooperative play* is often defined as the organized recreation of a group of children in which activities are planned to complete a desired outcome such as placing blocks in a basket.

Considerations for Programming

Infant development is rapid; infants develop **gross motor skills** and begin to recognize people, places, and objects. Recreation and leisure–based programs should foster development and prepare the infants for early childhood. It is vital that programmers develop a safe and conducive atmosphere for play. The most important aspect of play for infants is freedom. They must be permitted to make mistakes and messes. Developed play spaces that have a lot of rules, regulations, and restrictions are typically considered nonconducive to play (Kagan, 2002). Also, an environment in which adults are constantly monitoring the noise levels, trying to keep clothes clean, or trying to correct play is not considered a conducive play environment. In short, it is important to let infants and toddlers discover their limits and make their own decisions about where the play-based activities should be. This is how they develop their imaginations and discover desired outcomes to activities (Kagan, 2010).

Recreation and Leisure Program Example

Parks and recreation agencies often offer programs and services for parents and their infants. These are often centered around physical movement because it is fun and helps the infants develop and master fundamental motor skills. The following is an example of a program designed for infants that is enjoyable but also developmental.

Parent/Tot Classes. In these classes, the activities alternate between circle time, music, songs, dance, rhythm, stories, obstacle courses, Play-Doh, and parachutes. Children at this level thrive on rapidly expanding their vocabularies, and they do so at lightning speed through songs, stories, and one-on-one and group interactions. Often there is also exposure to outdoor recreation and the natural world, which children love to explore. These classes also include parent or guardian discussion that covers a range of child-related issues such as sleep and bedtime rituals, children's storybooks, or cultures and traditions. During the instructor-led discussion period, adults are encouraged to ask for help or ideas in specific child-rearing areas. Adults

vgajic/E+/Getty Images

Recreation and leisure programs for infants focus on classes with parents.

in the class may also inspire others as they share their own experiences with the group. In interacting with other families, those raising the infants are able to network and share helpful information regarding young children, siblings, and family and community events.

CHILDHOOD

When children have some independence and freedom, they are likely to play or interact with siblings and peers. Erik Erikson, a famous developmental psychologist, suggested that children's playful progression from being concerned with self to being more focused outward or focused on others is a way to learn to fit into the outside world. This requires children to

1. sufficiently interact with others within a social context,

2. create their own opportunities for enjoyment, and

3. show an interest in wanting to relate to others.

When adults organize and structure children's free time, such skills cannot develop properly or are not tested. Also, if children become accustomed to having their free time structured, they are more likely to feel bored on the rare occasions when they are unsupervised.

The desire to be part of the wider world also moves children beyond their neighborhood friends. The latter years of childhood are devoted to establishing **relative competence**. Restrictions on free or play-based leisure at this age can lead to a sense of inferiority. In this **age of instruction**, children are attracted to groups in which they can develop skills alongside others who show the same interests. For example, the Girl Scouts, Boy Scouts, Girls and Boys Clubs, public parks and recreation sport teams, and 4-H clubs are all examples of popular organizations children often participate in. Through these activities, children find their leisure identities and begin to take their expressive abilities seriously in ways that will likely define future leisure interests. It is the most likely starting place for what Stebbins (1992) refers to as **serious leisure** pursuits.

Developing Interests at School

Children usually rely on their families or guardians for guidance throughout childhood. Nevertheless, some cultures have established practices and opportunity structures for moving children out of dependence on families and into preparation to be self-sufficient members of society. The ages at which children do this can vary, but when they begin school they begin the task of separation from family that will continue through adolescence. The systems of school and community coincide with a child's natural inclination to establish competence and to connect more effectively with others. Leisure activities move away from purely child-directed play and games to activities that have some connection to the wider world.

The influence of schools on the development of leisure interests and orientations is inherently problematic. The knowledge base developed in schools combined with the cognitive skills discussed previously provide a strong foundation for learning activities outside of school. However, children all too often leave such interests at the school door. Most schools use an elaborate system of extrinsic motivation, primarily in the form of grades or benchmarks, to ensure the development of the knowledge and skills necessary for continuing in school, participating in the workforce, and contributing to society. However, this process often undermines the intrinsic interests that children bring to learning in the same way that rewards and emphasis on winning can take the fun out of children's games and sports. At the same time, many schools provide exposure to a wide variety of activities through art, music, physical education, recess, and extracurricular activities.

The effects of recess on leisure interests are particularly interesting. Recess has frequently been the focus of discussion and an often-questioned part of the school day. These breaks are only approved because they support the academic objectives of the school or curriculum. There is some evidence to suggest that recess activity might enhance classroom performance. Recess does, however, create a unique context in which play and social interaction can be shaped by the children within the constraints of a limited, timed break within the school environment. Although children might have afternoons and weekends free for self-directed activity, the defining of limits of time, space, and play groups gives recess the great potential for allowing children to create their own social worlds.

Childhood can generally be broken down into two stages: (1) early and (2) middle and late. During these stages, children continue to increase their abilities to reason, and they are increasingly aware of relationships with others (e.g., they recognize gender differences). Play is still unstructured, but by the age of 5, children begin to understand competition. They continue to develop physically, mentally, and emotionally, but at a slower, steadier pace than in infancy. Through recreation and leisure activities, they can form their first close relationships outside the family. Younger children are more interested in having fun and learning skills, whereas older children may be more interested in competition.

Recreation and Leisure

Children do not often use the words *recreation* and *leisure*, but they certainly understand what you mean if you say, "let's play." Children also develop an understanding of recess, after-school time, vacation, and weekends. When they begin attending school, they start to experience a struggle between freedom and constraint in their time. Playtime, however, is an idea that most children learn before they start school as they come to distinguish it from activities such as cleaning up, bathing, brushing teeth, and going to bed. The youngest children tend to live in the present; they can commit themselves to the moment as if nothing else matters at that given time. Patterns of play clearly reflect changes in development that reveal the reasons for participation or intrinsic motivations as children grow. Play expresses freedom and occupies a great deal of time. Play should not be mistaken with *exploration*, which is specifically oriented to reveal the true nature of things. Play is considered a nonliteral behavior or a transformation of reality; for example, a child's doll might represent a baby, or an empty wrapping paper tube might represent a laser gun. Play shares the quality of intrinsic motivation with other forms of leisure, and because it is considered transformative, it represents the qualities that make leisure different from the realities of everyday life.

Play is considered a practice of free choice and provides a growing need to seek out motives and abilities. Thus, a child exercises whatever functions they can to create an effect and then make it change. Infants begin playing by putting everything into their mouths to experience it, and they repeat sounds and actions almost endlessly. The world of play at this time is considered autocosmic, or a private world within the sphere of the body. In early childhood, children enter into the microsphere when they focus their attention toward the nearest environment. This is where **pretend play** emerges and reflects the development of intelligence. Due to the increased focus on environment and intelligence, children at this stage (3-6 years old) typically show tremendous growth in language development.

During early childhood, play is often done alone, but as children become more aware of others, their play expands from the microsphere to the macrosphere, where the world extends beyond family. Initially, children relate to others through parallel play, or playing next to but not with others. However, they eventually learn to play together in associative play in which they share, imitate each other, and engage in pretending through the use of new social skills and physical skills. Children in early childhood have not yet learned to make decisions about the perspectives of others. It is in middle and late childhood that children engage in truly **cooperative play** and can play games with rules.

Early Childhood (3 to 6 years old)

Early childhood is the time between 3 and 6 years of age. There are many significant physical (e.g.,

growing taller and getting stronger) and behavioral (e.g., increasing attention span and increasing pretend play over parallel play) changes in this stage. During this period there is also significant improvement in motor skill development. Cognitively, children's attention spans increase, and they start to develop reasoning skills. They also start to think about toys or objects that are not present, which is referred to as *symbolic thinking*.

Physical Abilities

During the preschool years, children may shed what is often referred to as *baby fat*, and their bodies lengthen. It is at this stage that physical gender differences related to the body become apparent. For example, most girls at this stage have more fatty tissue and most boys have more muscle. Brain maturation permits greater control and coordination of the arms, legs, and neck. Children in this stage show an increase in **fine motor skills**, and by the end of this period, they can construct towers out of blocks and draw pictures using multiple colors. However, due to the nervous system not being fully developed, children in this stage may have difficulty with other tasks that require fine motor skills.

kali9/E+/Getty Images

During the early childhood stage, children show an increase in fine motor skills.

Cognitive Abilities

Brain growth slows in this stage compared to the infancy stage; however, children's ability to pay attention grows during the preschool years. They can spend longer periods of time doing one activity or watching a video. Also, as they age, they can process information more quickly. Their language ability continues to evolve rapidly, and they progress from saying single sentences or repeating sounds to creating more complex statements that combine multiple words. For that reason, children in this age group begin to have conversations with their parents, other adults, and their peers and may show an increased interest in writing and reading.

Socioemotional Characteristics

As children age, the relationships they develop with others consume more of their time. At this stage, they can compare themselves to others and, therefore, can start to process and understand differences. This understanding allows them to achieve a greater understanding of who they are and where they fit in relation to their peers. Many recreation researchers have suggested that play with peers has significant results in relationship building for children in this stage (Sutton-Smith, 1971). For example, researchers have stated that play with peers

- releases tension,
- develops increased self-efficacy,
- increases cognitive development,
- increases exploration,
- increases comfort in an environment,
- promotes attachment to others, and
- helps children learn to cope.

It also has been described as an outlet for children to learn to expel anger or learn how to deal with emotions (Larson & Verma, 1999). This stage of childhood is often described as the years of pretend or make-believe or, as most recreation researchers call it, play. At no other time in life is a person so thoroughly involved in the world of fantasy or play. Pretend play makes up approximately two thirds of all play in this stage of childhood (Larson & Verma, 1999).

Considerations for Programming

With the increase in childhood obesity, preventative health is becoming more popular in programming for children. According to the Centers for Disease Control and Prevention, obesity is a major concern during this stage of childhood (Fryar et al., 2021); research has indicated that being overweight in preschool is likely to carry over into adolescence and adulthood. An important part of combating childhood obesity is building active play elements into recreation and leisure programs. Whether structured or unstructured, all programs should have a physically active portion that also educates participants and, if possible, parents about the benefits of being active in everyday life. The recreation professional can play a significant role in designing programs that allow for active play and educational opportunities. The NRPA website has information and resources related to the benefits of being physically active and active programming related to health and wellness.

Recreation and Leisure Program Example

Recreation programs at this stage of childhood should focus on using materials such as blocks, crayons, balls, and gym mats. Materials should be used imaginatively or in any way children think is fun. Early childhood is a time when children enjoy new challenges to test their developing skills. Children should be active and explore. The promotion and implementation of active play pursuits within programs is a great way to encourage a healthy lifestyle and can result in benefits that extend to the middle childhood stage and beyond. The following is an example of a program for children in this age group.

Kids' Corner. Kids' Corner is a recreation program designed for children aged 3 to 6 years. The main objective is to strengthen children's self-image and feelings of competence through physical, cognitive, and socioemotional activities. Children are encouraged to actively and creatively explore the world around them through arts and crafts, music and rhythms, field trips, storytelling, and many other learning experiences. The Kids' Corner activities are age appropriate and include music, stories, art, indoor and outdoor play, negotiating physical elements, and language development. Social skills are most important. Play is a child's work; therefore, children are encouraged to play.

Middle and Late Childhood (7 to 12 years old)

Children who are 7 to 12 years old are in **middle and late childhood**. The development during this stage is more complex than in previous stages because motor skills and cognitive functions become much more refined. Although children's physical development slows down, cognitive and physical changes are dramatic. School-age children can skillfully handle objects, have much longer attention spans, and think logically. The social aspect of being accepted by their peers is also important during this stage.

Physical Abilities

Physical growth is slow but consistent during this stage. Muscle mass gradually increases and muscle tone improves. Children in this stage double their strength capabilities, which allows them to run faster, jump higher, climb, and move their own weight more easily. Fine motor skills continue to improve, and by ages 10 to 12 children can demonstrate skillful handling similar to that of adults. The complex movements needed to create high-quality crafts or play music can begin to be mastered at this stage.

Cognitive Abilities

One of the most important cognitive developments of middle and late childhood is the ability to reason logically about ideas and events. Children acquire and understand principles associated with logic and learn how to apply them to specific situations. Increased thinking, knowledge, and ability to communicate clearly are significant developments in middle and late childhood. Children in this stage have thought processes that involve considering evidence, planning, thinking, and formulating guesses.

Socioemotional Characteristics

During this stage, children are interested in learning how things are made and how they work, and they can sometimes struggle to master cultural values or norms of society. Children in middle and late childhood also spend increasing amounts of time with their peers, which leads to their perceptions of how competent or smart they are compared to their peers. In this stage, children tend to be more dependent or reliant on each other for companionship and self-validation.

Personal friendships in middle and late childhood are more important than being accepted by the entire group. Increases in emotional understanding lead to the ability to control emotional responses so they are more situationally appropriate. Children can now demonstrate empathy; for example, they can have sympathy or feel sorry for a friend who is feeling down. According to research, the follow-

ing are the six functions of children's friendships at this age:

1. *Companionship.* Friendships provide playmates who will spend time and interact with a child during activities.
2. *Stimulation.* Friendships provide interesting information, excitement, and amusement.
3. *Physical support.* Friends offer time, resources, and assistance.
4. *Ego support.* Friends provide encouragement and feedback, which helps the child develop and assess self-efficacy.
5. *Social comparison.* Friendships provide information about where the child stands in relation to others and whether the child is OK.
6. *Intimacy and affection.* Friendships offer warm, close relationships based on trust.

These functions are important because peers may play a more central role in a child's life at this stage than parents do, primarily because of the consequences of peer isolation. Children at this age are highly susceptible to bullying. Being the target of a bully can have long-term effects such as social withdrawal, depression, and anxiety. Recognizing the critical value of social interaction and friendships at this age is vital in the design and implementation of recreation and leisure programs.

Considerations for Program Design

Children at this age usually participate in organized after-school activities. Unfortunately, many children do not participate in after-school programs that involve physical activity; instead, they engage in more sedentary activities such as watching television, playing video games, and scrolling through smartphone apps. Children should still be heavily involved in various active programs and activities, which provide physical and behavioral benefits. Recreation programmers should recognize the importance of designing and providing fun and active programs for children of this age.

Recreation and Leisure Program Example

Programs that accommodate this age group's desire to be with friends are good ways to get them involved. Recreation programs should allow for multiple social and physical opportunities. The following program is an example of one that allows for socializing, being active, and staying entertained.

Programming that emphasizes fun and physical activity is important for children at the middle childhood stage.

Don't Get Caught With the Cookie. This recreation activity is done in a gymnasium or large outdoor space. Two children are designated as taggers, and the other participants are divided into two groups. Each student in one group receives a ball (cookie); the other group does not receive any balls. The taggers are only allowed to tag people who are holding balls. To avoid being tagged, a child with a ball can throw the ball to someone who does not have a ball, making this child a target for the tagger. If the ball is dropped while being thrown, both the thrower and the receiver must do five jumping jacks. When a child with a ball gets tagged, they must also do five jumping jacks. A child cannot throw a ball back to the person who threw it to them. This program is a great way to promote the physical needs of children in this age group.

ADOLESCENCE

Adolescence occurs between the ages of 13 and 19. During the early part of this stage, adolescents begin to experience puberty, although this has become more common at younger ages as well (Epstein, 2019). Puberty has dramatic effects on individuals' physical, cognitive, and socioemotional development. It is during this stage that adolescents begin to become more independent from their parents and form intimate friendships and romantic relationships. These are just a few factors that recreation and leisure professionals need to account for while designing and implementing appropriate programs.

Recreation and Leisure

The term *teenager* did not appear in the American vocabulary until the 1930s. It has been argued that increases in urbanization and technology have produced problems that are either exclusive to this age group or affect teens more intensely than others. Perhaps because of this, the relationships made in adolescence are more compelling than in other periods of life; friends and peer groups become all-important. This has good and bad consequences. If all a teen's friends smoke, for example, it will be difficult for the teenager to avoid smoking. Teenagers experience a great confusion of value. Although there is a strong trend toward social conformity with the peer group, teens also shift between childish and more adultlike behavior. In some ways, teenagers suffer from the same lack of clearly defined roles that the elderly do (this is discussed later in the chapter).

As children enter adolescence,

- their independence from parents increases,
- they are more affected by the influence of peers,
- some take part-time jobs,
- their mobility often increases, and
- they begin to have a greater range of recreation and leisure options.

Many of these situations bring teenagers closer to each other, sometimes through social groups that develop recreation and leisure patterns that are detrimental to personal and public health and safety. Juvenile crime, substance use, and distraction-related activities such as texting while driving reflect this reality.

During this period, teenagers also go through small successive shifts in status and roles that often make them uncertain about how they should behave. With increasing age and education, generally, comes increasing freedom and access to resources. Adolescents also have more time for leisure and higher participation rates in leisure activities than their older counterparts. Teenagers are more likely to participate in most forms of outdoor recreation compared to those who are older. At this stage of the life span, separate "cultures of youth" emerge, complete with their own values, music, clothing, hairstyles, social concerns, language, attitudes, and sexual orientation. Furthermore, while all of these cultures are youth focused, each of them can vary based on numerous factors, including region, economics, personal identity, or religion. Members of such cultures can be segregated from

Maskot/Getty Images

During the late childhood stage, teenagers often appear to withdraw into a separate society, and they enjoy hanging out with one another.

the rest of society. Hanging out on street corners, in cars, in coffee shops, in online multiplayer games, or on social media, these teenagers often appear to withdraw into a separate society, one that typically has neither younger children nor adults.

Many activities are abandoned during adolescence. In the case of sports, for example, there is an enormous drop-off in participation. The peak of youth participation in sports is age 11, which can be explained through a combination of multiple factors, including

- an overemphasis on winning,
- a lack of fun,
- an unwillingness to endure school-like discipline,
- the perceived lack of ability to be competitive at a high level,
- the lack of social interaction with a broader range of friends outside of the sport, and
- growing preferences for other activities.

However, the desire to move on and away from adult direction is part of it as well.

During this period of life, teenagers experiment with how to relate to people to whom they have an attraction. Dating as socialization produces the opportunity for commitment between two individuals. The factors that can produce commitment to a relationship include love for the partner, the status that comes with the relationship, and the feeling of obligation to sustain the relationship. Commitment is reduced by anxiety about the relationship, the attractiveness of alternative relationships, or internal and external pressures (e.g., family or friends) to try other alternatives.

Social Development

As previously discussed, adolescents begin to form many different types of relationships, and many of their relationships will become deeply involved and more emotionally intimate. During adolescence, teens' social networks become larger and include many different types of relationships. Therefore, adolescent social development involves a more dramatic change in social relationships than in other periods of the life span.

Adolescents must learn to balance multiple relationships that compete for their time, energy, and attention. For example, as children in school they commonly had one teacher for all subjects or one coach for most sports, but as adolescents there are typically several teachers and multiple coaches that maintain their own requirements.

Communication technologies enable teens to create and to maintain social bonds virtually (e.g., BeReal, WhatsApp, Snapchat, Instagram, Reddit, TikTok, X [formerly known as Twitter]). These technologies have dramatically expanded the size and complexity of social networks by

1. increasing the amount of time people spend staying connected with others,
2. changing the way adolescents relate to one another, and
3. redefining what it means to be a "friend."

It has grown common to have virtual friendships without ever having in-person interactions.

Physical Development

Adolescence is often described as the time when teenagers transition into adults. During adolescent growth spurts, the arms and legs lengthen and eventually become proportional to the rest of the body. Teens may suddenly feel awkward and uncoordinated during this time because growth does not always occur at a proportional rate, which can frustrate young teenagers.

Adolescents also experience changes in body composition (i.e., the ratio of body fat to lean muscle mass). Factors such as genetics, nutrition, and muscle-building exercise influence muscular development. If adolescents play sports, lift weights, or routinely work out in other ways, they are more likely to gain muscle mass. Many teenagers feel self-conscious about their bodies when compared to their friends and classmates, which can lead to body image issues and other negative consequences.

Cognitive Abilities

According to Piaget (1970), the adolescent years are remarkable because youth move beyond the limitations of concrete mental operations and develop the ability to think in a more abstract manner. Piaget used the term *formal operations* to describe this new ability. Formal operations refer to the ability to perform mental operations with abstract, intangible concepts such as justice or poverty and to be able to estimate or describe the effects of these intangible concepts. For example, formal operational stages is the answer to the question, "If Christy is taller than Landon and Landon is taller than Carter, who is tallest?" This is an example of inferential reasoning, which is the ability of a child to think about things they have not actually experienced but can draw conclusions from.

Socioemotional Characteristics

For many parents, the adolescent period can seem like a whirlwind of rapidly changing emotions. Early theories about adolescent development proposed that a period of "storm and stress" was to be expected and suggested that adolescents characteristically tend to overreact to everyday situations. Developmental experts have since learned that what may appear as "storm and stress" is the natural outcome of youth learning to cope with a much larger array of new and unfamiliar situations (Larson & Ham, 1993).

In addition to navigating the new and uncharted territory that inevitably comes with growing up, teens in the early 21st century are subjected to increased demands on their physical, mental, and emotional resources. Social relationships outside the family have exponentially increased with the advent of social networking. Academic standards have become more stringent. Sports and other recreational pursuits are more competitive. Therefore, while teens are learning to cope with these challenges, it should be expected that they will have a diverse range of emotions that might fluctuate.

Teens must learn how to respond to new and unfamiliar situations while navigating the increased demands on their physical, mental, and emotional resources (Tapps & McKenzie, 2014). This can increase stress for teens, and the ability to cope with stress is influenced by many factors. Certain genetic factors, such as temperament, make some people more sensitive to stress. And traumatic life events, including abuse, bullying, teen dating violence, and community violence and instability can further exacerbate the issue. Environmental factors such as family and community, however, can help mitigate the effect of stress by enabling youth to become more resilient when faced with stressful situations.

Considerations for Program Design

Program design should follow the identified needs of adolescents. Programmers should consider a developmental approach that encourages teenagers to see themselves as resources rather than problems that need to be fixed. Historically, researchers have

used a youth development model for teenagers to encourage growth in competencies. The following are the five basic competencies that should be included in programs developed for adolescents (Baltes et al., 2006):

1. *Health and physical competence.* Youth need to have appropriate knowledge, attitudes, and behaviors to ensure future health.
2. *Personal and social competence.* Youth need to have skills and traits such as self-discipline, ability to work with others, coping skills, and problem-solving.
3. *Creative competence.* Youth need to be able to participate in creative expression and develop language skills.
4. *Vocational competence.* Many degree programs focus on experiential learning and service-based learning; adolescents need to develop skills that will help them prepare for their careers and understand the value of work and leisure.
5. *Citizenship competence.* Teens need to understand community history and values and be encouraged to contribute to their communities.

Recreation and Leisure Program Example

In addition to the previous competencies, recreation and leisure programmers should incorporate the teen's own desires in their leisure choices. The following is a recreation program developed specifically for teenagers.

Swat the Fly. The objective of this recreation activity is for teams to gain the most points possible by swatting correct answers. Participants are divided into teams of about five. Each team is given one fly swatter. A participant from each team comes to the middle of the room, and participants stand back-to-back. The leader of the program asks a question about a topic such as nutrition. When the leader shouts *go,* the participants run as fast as possible to the wall or the projection on the wall to locate the correct answer. The participants must swat the correct answer with the fly swatter. The first person to hit the correct answer gets a point or prize for their team. This is a great activity to address the health and physical competency. The competitive aspect is often attractive to the adolescent population.

ADULTHOOD

Movement from adolescence to adulthood usually aligns with the achievement of emotional independence from the family. Young adults tend to be more accommodating than they were when they were younger, which is often associated with transition into the adult world. In U.S. culture, the assumption of roles of worker, spouse or partner, and parent for those moving into adulthood bring dramatic changes in behavior and experience that are reflected in leisure choices.

Adulthood should be viewed as several periods with different interests and patterns of leisure. While early theories of aging assumed that adulthood was characterized by either stability or decline, subsequent theories recognize the potential for age-related gains and losses in adulthood. Although adulthood has often been considered the eventual decline of skills developed in childhood, it is actually a time of further skill development. The term *plasticity* is used to refer to the continuing development of skills for adults. There are many influences on adults such as psychological, biological, community related, and historical. These influences mix together to form a path for each adult. Although plasticity can occur at any time during the life span, the potential decreases with age.

Recreation and Leisure

The adult life shapes leisure motivations, constraints, and ways of participating. Recreation and leisure also shape adult life. For example, recreation and leisure are contexts within which friendships are developed. Therefore, leisure with friends and family is highly valued throughout adulthood. Through recreation and leisure people also discover self-identity, and those in early, middle, and later adulthood gain a sense of self-determination. Specifically, recreation and leisure can be a context for

- self-expression,
- challenge,
- learning,
- credibility,
- recognition, and
- accomplishment.

Recreation and leisure may also provide opportunities to disengage from everyday demands and concerns and reengage in experiences that are more personally meaningful. Psychologically, there tends to be a shift from an external to a more internal sense of meaning in middle adulthood that continues into later years. Perhaps this is because of a shifting time perspective and concerns of middle adulthood and exclusion of older adult's productive roles. Recreation and leisure provide opportunities to step back and reengage.

The extent to which recreation and leisure experiences hold meaning for each adult varies according to their understandings of leisure and what society allows for them. The life conditions of adults vary widely in recreation and leisure resources and constraints. Some adults place a high value on leisure and construct life patterns that make a major and consistent place for recreation and leisure. Others fit recreation and leisure into their relationships. Throughout adulthood, there seem to be rhythms of leisure that rise and fall as other elements of life become the focus. New relationships, becoming a parent, caregiving, career changes, retirement, loss of a partner, and other conditions have effects on what is possible and what is desired. For example, the athlete might become the coach of their child's baseball team and down the road may participate in senior league softball. For most of the life course, recreation and leisure are part of the balance that adults seek in expressional, relational, and productive activities.

Early Adulthood (20s and 30s)

Early adulthood comprises the years between 20 and 39. During this time, most people begin roles in employment and become intimate partners and parents. Research suggests that young adults typically establish themselves in three distinct areas:

1. Work
2. Family
3. Social identity

Researchers have suggested that as youth move into early adulthood, they begin developing a dream. This dream typically has to do with career-related aspirations. For example, the dream may be to become an executive director or recreation director or to be in an administrative position within the first 10 years with a company. By their mid-30s, however, young adults often report reaching a plateau, and they become more realistic about limited opportunities that affect what it will take to realize their dreams. It is at this point that some decide to return to school to change occupations or obtain certifications or specializations in specific areas of work (Schaie & Willis, 2016).

Young adults also establish themselves in family or intimate relationships. Erikson (1950) described *intimacy* as the ability to share oneself emotionally (and often sexually) and to sustain a committed relationship with another person without fear of losing their own identity. He described *isolation* as the dread of getting emotionally and sexually close to another person. Intimacy is not something young adults are automatically capable of establishing. Rather, the art of dating is practice in intimacy, and through these relationships people learn how to share themselves without losing their self-identities.

Individuals in early adulthood are also seeking to establish social identities. Young adults are seeking a sense of competence and recognition for accomplishments. A lot of the expectations for success are placed upon people as social norms, or what is considered the right thing to do in society (Edginton et al., 2004). For example, one historical societal norm is that after college people are expected to start a career and get married. It is not a necessary event sequence, but has been common and is, therefore, a societal norm. Being competent as a worker, a lover or friend, and as a community member are all ways that people develop social identities in early adulthood. Competence is highly related to establishing focus on productivity in family, work, and community (Tapps, 2012).

Considerations for Program Design

The young adulthood stage often lends itself to commercial and school-based recreation and leisure experiences. As people establish families and settle down, leisure and recreation pursuits tend to become restricted due to time. People, then, select fewer, more specific activities that are more about the comfort of performing the leisure activity and less about the experience itself. Public recreation agencies can become important as families begin sharing leisure experiences. Therefore, programmers can focus on encouraging interaction and development of families. It is important to note, however, that not all individuals in this age group follow this trajectory. Many can be single, widowed, divorced, without children, or have a multitude of other life circumstances. Professionals should keep this in mind in the programming process in order to develop opportunities for all individuals to engage in leisure services.

Recreation and Leisure Program Example

Oftentimes, programming for parks and recreation is associated with children. However, it is important to develop programs and services that are targeted to adults in the community. There is a specific growing need for adult programming or whole family programming. The following program is one that young adults and families might enjoy.

Concert in the Park. Family-friendly concerts in the park are common events hosted by parks and recreation departments. These evening or night events provide an entertaining social environment for families. Some places have developed theme-based concerts to target specific groups. Another great attraction is inviting local food truck vendors to provide refreshments or dinner for people who are attending the concert.

Programming in early adulthood reflects the growing need for whole family programming such as concerts in the park, which appeal to both children and adults.

Douglas Mason/Getty Images North America/Getty Images

Middle Adulthood (40s and 50s)

As individuals move into **middle adulthood**, their focus shifts from employment, parenting, and intimate partner relationships to two specific themes. The first involves order, security, and stability. The second involves what Levinson (1978) describes as "making it," which includes striving to reach major goals. Many of those who fail to reach their professional goals will turn to leisure as a way to add meaning to their lives. This helps explain why hobbies might be renewed or developed at this stage.

For this group, exercise is important to maintain good health as individuals become more aware of their mortality. When people reach their 40s, they often realize their bodies will not last forever, and the need to take care of them becomes more important. This stage of adulthood lends itself toward a consumer model of leisure behavior such as buying a boat or camper, traveling on planned vacations, and going out to eat. As a result, leisure and recreation take place within the commercial rather than public sector. In other words, the focus becomes more intrinsically rewarded (Pittman, 1991).

Toward the end of the middle adulthood stage, many people experience a midlife transition. For some, this becomes a midlife crisis, but for most it is a time when people evaluate life and make minor adjustments for the late adulthood stage. This stage of life can see a number of major life changes, such as children going to college or work, reaching a career peak, and noticing physical changes and slow recovery from physical exertion. However, there are some positive changes related to leisure as well. For example, this stage of life often comes with more free time from work and a greater financial security, which leads to a high self-expression in leisure that was not yet available in previous life stages. To this end, leisure and recreation participation has been known to serve three basic functions in middle adulthood.

1. It brings acceptance from others, which replaces the focus on achievement from young adulthood.
2. It helps people avoid despair or depression, which is often a major concern at this stage of life.
3. It allows for structured time when people are starting to have more free time.

Considerations for Program Design

Although every adult is different, programs for people in this stage of life should encourage self-directed behavior (Edginton et al., 2005). Adults in this stage are generally more self-directed than during any other times of their lives. Their leisure and recreation behaviors are more likely to be

The middle adulthood stage lends itself toward a consumer model of leisure behavior such as buying a boat or camper, traveling on planned vacations, and going out to eat.

Thomas Barwick/Digital Vision/Getty Images

- self-motivated,
- experientially based,
- related to life tasks,
- focused on the present, and
- internally motivated.

Recreation and Leisure Program Example

Programming for those in middle adulthood should focus on activities that allow people to express themselves. Programming for this age group should address a work–life balance. During the later stages of middle adulthood, there is an increase in free time. Thus, middle adulthood is an opportunity for people to focus their interests on leisure activities for themselves as opposed to focusing on their families' needs. The following is an example of a program for people in middle adulthood.

Painting and Wine Class. These classes are designed specifically for adults who want to learn or express artistic skills. It combines an art lesson in painting with the light consumption of wine. This is a fun, social, and group setting in which an artist guides participants in replicating the night's featured painting. Typically, it is an adults-only event, and it is perfect for adults who are looking to express themselves.

Late Adulthood (60s and older)

Those in **late adulthood** are the fastest growing segment of the U.S. population. People in this stage of life are typically identified as 60 years old or older (Administration on Aging, 2020). They are also referred to as boomers because most of them were born in the baby boomer generation from 1946 to 1964.

The three most common theories associated with later adulthood are disengagement theory, activity theory, and continuity theory.

- **Disengagement theory** suggests that people in late adulthood start to withdraw from the world on social, physical, and psychological levels.
- **Activity theory** suggests that successful aging occurs when people maintain the interests, activities, and social interactions they were involved in during middle adulthood.
- **Continuity theory** suggests that people need to maintain their desired level of involvement in society to maximize their sense of self-esteem and well-being (Baltes, 2005).

Researchers have suggested that leisure is associated with well-being in later life mainly because leisure opportunities provide engagement and are meaningful (Cochran et al., 2009).

Active people in later adulthood are a major market for leisure professionals. In a study conducted in 2009, leisure and recreation researchers revealed the top 10 leisure and recreation activities that people over the age of 60 enjoy participating in. Interestingly, they had recreation professionals who work with this group rank their top 10. The results are very interesting (see the sidebar), and they indicate that programmers are not really in tune with the current interests of this group (Cochran et al., 2009).

Top 10 Leisure Activities Ranked for People Over 60

People who participate	Recreation professionals
1. Reading	1. Travel
2. Walking	2. Fitness
3. Gardening	3. Walking
4. Travel	4. Golf
5. Hiking	5. Social activities
6. Bicycling	6. Taking university courses/education
7. Social activities	7. Reading
8. Movies	8. Investments and finance
9. Camping	9. Music
10. Sewing/listening to music (tie)	10. Gardening

Leisure and recreation programming in later life is a large market that includes

- senior centers,
- social clubs,
- residential communities,
- outreach programs,
- adult day-care facilities,
- nursing homes, and
- traditional leisure and recreation sites (Leitner & Leitner, 2004).

There have been numerous studies that suggest many benefits that leisure and recreation activities have on people in later adulthood. These include lowered depression (Tapps et al., 2013), reduced risk of falls (Nied & Franklin, 2002), increased laughter, lower anxiety, higher functional independence, and higher feelings of achievement and accomplishment (Leitner & Leitner, 2004).

Ariel Skelley/Digital Vision/Getty Images

Gardening is a popular leisure pursuit during the late adulthood stage.

Retirement

Throughout our lives, very few days can cause so much joy or anxiety as the day of retirement. It signifies freedom and an opportunity to pursue lifelong dreams, but it can also represent a feeling of uselessness or cause depressive symptoms. Growing old in a world of youth can be a scary idea, but many people also find retirement to be everything they dreamed about. It is often perceived as time earned through dedicated years of employment to focus on self, family, and happiness.

It is easy to overestimate the impact of retirement on leisure and recreation behavior. Most people continue to pursue their same leisure activities, but they now have more free time to participate in them; as a consequence, some of these pastimes become serious leisure pursuits (Liu et al., 2013). In addition, older adults are often said to be "aging in place," meaning they do not move from where they resided when they were working. There is a misconception that older adults will retire, pack up, and move to a retirement community. Of those aged 65 years and older, only 1 percent move to a different state in a given year. Suburbs are becoming increasingly inhabited with older adults even though they were designed for families with children. However, older adults are discovering that these suburbs lack housing, transportation, and health care options.

The idea that people retire at age 65 is increasingly less common. In fact, the boomer generation often associates with their jobs so much that they struggle to give up that identity and work until they are in their late 60s or into their 70s (Administration on Aging, 2020). Others work past age 65 because they can't afford to retire or can't afford health care. Often it is those with a broad range of leisure and recreation skills that seem to adjust the best to retirement; those who have limited leisure interests and skills often struggle to resurrect old leisure interests and learn new leisure skills. In the same context, those whose leisure activities are an extension of their work will have more work to do to reorient themselves to the idea that these activities are for leisure purposes only and they are no longer associated with work or no longer spill over into work (Godbey, 2008). When work ends for these people, they often discover that many of their leisure activities are not satisfying replacements to their work. Therefore, a successful retiree must have or develop leisure skills just like they developed successful work skills.

Considerations for Program Design

Recreation and leisure service organizations should be concerned about the growth and well-being of individuals in their programs. Therefore, programs should be developed around the premise of the activity theory. Programs for people in later adulthood should include the following five elements (Cochran et al., 2009):

1. *Choice*. People want to pick their own activities and their own level of participation.
2. *Participant involvement*. Leisure and recreation professionals should provide opportunities for seniors to be involved in the planning process. After all, this is the group that is historically known for their leadership skills.
3. *Integration*. One common mistake is that recreation professionals believe that older adults don't want to interact with others and they only want to be with others their age. However, generations are starting to work together and be integrated even more. Lack of education and experience working with other age groups is prevalent, but leisure can bridge those gaps.

OUTSTANDING GRADUATE

Background Information

Name: Laura Covert

Education: MS and BS in therapeutic recreation from Northwest Missouri State University

Credentials: Certified Therapeutic Recreation Specialist (CTRS)

Affiliations: American Therapeutic Recreation Association, Kansas Recreation and Parks, Kansas Recreation and Park Association Young Professionals

Career Information

Position: Assistant Professor

Organization: The health, human performance, and recreation (HHPR) department at Pittsburg State University (PSU) in Pittsburg, Kansas. There are about 7,500 students who attend PSU.

Organization mission: The mission of the Pittsburg State University HHPR department is to provide science- and field-based training in physical education, recreation, and exercise science to

- prepare graduate students for careers in K-12 education, athletic coaching, and collegiate athletic coaching; for careers as recreation and leisure professionals; or for future doctoral studies;
- prepare undergraduate physical education majors to be physical educators, athletic coaches, and exercise fitness specialists;
- prepare undergraduate recreation majors in the fields of therapeutic recreation, recreation administration, and community, corporate, and hospital wellness; and
- prepare undergraduate exercise science majors for graduate and professional schools or clinical health and wellness professions.

Job description: I teach general recreation and therapeutic recreation courses, advise recreation students, and am involved with various university committees.

Career path: I first started my therapeutic recreation career working as a personal trainer and group exercise instructor in a wellness center specifically for older adults and special populations. I then became a wellness coordinator within a retirement community. While working, I decided I wanted to become more involved with educating future therapeutic recreation specialists while pursuing my passion of studying aging and the aging population. This job is a long-term goal that I was able to achieve early on in my career.

Likes and dislikes about the job: The number of items I like about my job outweighs the number of things I dislike about the job. Top likes: interaction with students and the daily opportunity to motivate and educate students about the world of recreation and therapeutic recreation. Dislikes: all the grading.

Advice for Undergraduates

There are never-ending opportunities in the field of recreation. Find an area that you are passionate about, and pursue it as a career. Every day presents a new challenge. Have an open mind and be willing to work with others.

4. *Innovation*. Older adults have usually spent years in the workforce and did the same job for many years. They may have raised children, and many have grandchildren. They do not want the same old programs. Therefore, programmers should not be bound by traditional rules when providing activities for older adults. Instead, traditional sports or games should be modified to facilitate senior needs.

5. *Sensitivity*. Programmers should be aware of the needs of older adults by providing user-friendly, barrier-free, and accessible facilities.

Recreation and Leisure Program Example

Older adults are a diverse population in terms of interests and abilities. Although recreation programmers might be challenged to meet the needs of such a diverse group, the idea of creating social interaction opportunities can be essential to an age group often associated and prone to disengagement. The increasing dependence of society on technology and the need for social interaction are great examples of programming needs that should be met by programmers for older adults. Social media apps and other communication technology are common and practical applications that are used today, and older adults want to learn how to use these systems. For example, a great way to enhance the ability for older adults to experience increased social interaction is through Zoom.

Zoom for All Ages. This course teaches older adults how to connect with old classmates and friends by using online communication technology on a laptop, tablet, or smartphone, and can increase participant confidence. The class requires a room with a computer and overhead projector, but it is ideal if everyone has their own laptop, tablet, or phone. Partnering with a local library or school is a great way to access these resources. The facilitator must know and understand Zoom. Handouts and visual instructions are also beneficial.

GENERATION EFFECT

As shown in this chapter, there is a relationship between leisure behavior and stage of life. It is important to examine the traits of each generation, because each faces different challenges. In addition, specific events from each generation can shape people's behavior. For example, one generation of older adults will behave differently from another

because they had different life experiences; 60-year-olds today work more closely with other generations than 60-year-olds did in 1980.

The following are the five identified generations that are currently living together in the United States (Howe & Strauss, 1997):

1. The oldest current generation is called the *greatest generation*. It is broken into the GI generation and the silent generation. The GI generation was born between 1901 and 1924 and is a term used for Americans who fought in World War II. The silent generation was born between 1925 and 1945 and is identified as the generation born between the two world wars who were too young to join the service when World War II began.

2. The second-oldest generation in the United States is the baby boomer generation. This generation includes people born between 1946 and 1964. This period saw a 14-year increase in birthrate worldwide following World War II. Some members of this group were associated with the 1960s counterculture movement, or the hippie subculture, which began in the United States during the 1960s and was considered a worldwide phenomenon. Civil rights and the women's movement were also issues addressed in this generation. People started their own communities, embraced the sexual revolution, and experimented with drugs that altered states of consciousness. For recreation and leisure programmers who work in assisted living, the effects of the hippie culture might still show in increased drug- and alcohol-related dementia among residents from this generation.

3. The third generation is Generation X. This generation was born between 1965 and 1985. They are commonly broken into two subgroups: baby busters and the boomerang generation. Generation X is known for being connected to pop culture of the 1980s and 1990s. Most people in this generation are children of the boomer generation. Baby busters are defined as the post-peak boomers due to the long slow decline of the birth rates of the boomer generation. This generation made its mark on society through festivals such as Lollapalooza, grunge bands such as Nirvana, and MTV (prior to the reality show movement). The boomerang generation is so named due to how often they chose to live

with their parents after having lived alone. Researchers have suggested that this was due to the financial success and security afforded to them throughout their childhoods from their boomer parents (Howe & Strauss, 1997).

4. The fourth generation are Millennials. This generation was born between 1980 and 1994. These are children of the boomer generation and of early Generation Xers. This generation is commonly associated with the public display of arguments between progressive and conservative perspectives within news media and public discourse (Howe & Strauss, 2000).

5. The fifth and final generation is Generation Z. These individuals are said to have been born between 1995 and 2001. This generation is much more difficult to identify because researchers cannot agree on when the earliest members of Generation Z were born. This generation is known for being born into technology and the Internet. This generation spends less time outdoors, but research suggests that those who spend time outside have higher feelings of happiness and

increased self-confidence (Louv, 2005; Howe & Strauss, 1997). This generation has also demonstrated political and social awareness often focused on issues of climate change and equity across diverse populations including race, gender, and LGBTQIA+ issues.

SUMMARY

There are many variables that affect leisure and recreation across the life span. The concept of the life span implies that life is a series of interconnected stages in which each one has an effect on the next but remains distinctive (Kelly & Godbey, 1991). Recreation and leisure service organizations play an important role in offering programs and activities to members of the public, and they must be creative in programming for people across the life span. As people change, so must programs, and recreation and leisure professionals are responsible for meeting the recreational needs of the people they serve. As researchers have pointed out, and as you have probably discovered in this chapter, leisure is not a product but rather a process that is a vital part of the life span development (Edginton et al., 2006).

Review Questions

1. What are some developmental characteristics for individuals in each of the primary life stages?

2. What are some significant milestones across the life span that might affect recreation and leisure programming?

3. What attributes can you include in recreation and leisure programming to align with the developmental characteristics of each stage within the life span?

4. Please describe the past five most recent generations.

Go to HK*Propel* to complete the activities for this chapter.

PART III

Delivering Recreation and Leisure Services

CHAPTER 13

Program Delivery System

Diane C. Blankenship and Rachel Kollasch

LWA/Stone RF/Getty Images

> **"** We do not remember days, we remember moments. **"**
>
> Cesare Pavese, Italian poet of the 20th century

After reading this chapter, you should be able to do the following:

> Develop a program delivery system based on leadership
> Design a program delivery system across the program classifications
> Revise a program delivery system based on program format and skill level

Recreation professionals create moments for people to meet their personal needs through the programs and services provided by an agency. The program delivery system is the comprehensive model used to develop an agency plan to meet the needs of individuals and groups within the community, provide various experiences for people with diverse skill levels and interests, and meet the agency's mission. Developing a program delivery system is an art and a science that requires a creative thought process and methodical planning. The process of developing a program delivery system requires the recreation professional to use three different yet interrelated processes:

1. Leadership considerations
2. A program classification system
3. A program format system

These three components are used together while considering the mission, vision, goals, objectives, needs, and resources of the organization to enhance the quality of life of the people served within the community or region. This process is used across private, nonprofit, commercial, and public recreation agencies to meet diverse needs based on skills, abilities, interests, and desires within the community using the available resources ethically, efficiently, and effectively (Rossman & Schlatter, 2011).

PROGRAM DELIVERY HISTORY

The professional program delivery process of today evolved along with the progression of society in general from the agricultural era. During the 1800s, Canada and the United States consisted of agricultural communities and a limited number of urban centers. Within rural agricultural communities, recreation was planned and provided by either the family or the church. The isolation of families on their farms demanded that recreation be a family affair conducted at home. The church

and local agricultural community planned and coordinated special gatherings around holidays and harvest festivals. These events provided an opportunity for families to socialize with others in the community. As urban centers developed, recreation was still family focused but occurred within local park systems and involved some limited commercial entertainment. Local parks provided space for people to recreate on their own with little supervision. As time passed, the necessity for trained leaders at local playgrounds was realized. The professionalization of planning programs and services began on the playgrounds within urban centers during the industrial revolution (Human Kinetics, 2019).

The process of professionalizing recreation and park management developed through the 1930s. Colleges and universities established programs to train people for parks and recreation management positions. The process and art of planning comprehensive recreation delivery systems continued to develop along with the formalizations of community recreation departments, school recreation programs, local parks, and national destinations for vacations. The conclusion of World War II in 1945 was followed by a great expansion of wealth, roadways, and labor-saving devices. Demand further grew for trained recreation professionals who could systematically and creatively develop program delivery systems to meet expanding needs, interests, and population segments such as people with disabilities, seniors, and children (Human Kinetics, 2006).

This developmental process continued for decades and culminated in the development of program standards that address program leadership, participant outcomes, and the variety and diversity of programs and services within diverse communities. Agencies and professionals must know how to meet community needs, provide a diverse menu of programs and services, and assess outcomes of those programs. Recreation professionals enjoy and embrace these opportunities by positively affecting the lives of those served by their agencies.

© Human Kinetics

Special events that appeal to a broad-based audience, such as mud runs like the Tough Mudder and Warrior Dash, are popular activities in the recreation industry for program systems. Runners and walkers are looking for new activities to try, and these events combine running or walking with a series of seven or more physical challenges.

MISSION AND OUTCOMES

When recreation professionals face the task of developing a program delivery system, they may feel overwhelmed with the endless options and choices. The guiding lights for every organization's program delivery system are the mission and vision statements of the organization. The **mission statement** is a broad statement that defines the purpose of the organization in regard to the group of people it serves. It helps determine the scope of the program delivery system, such as fitness, health, or quality of life. The vision statement is a statement about the future of the organization and has a long-term focus. The difference between the mission statement and vision statement is the focus. The mission statement guides programs and services in the present while the vision statement guides programs and services for the future. The vision statement guides decisions within the organization with the future goal in mind. This could be financial decisions, large projects, future facilities, and services for the community.

The two mission statements noted in figure 13.1 contain the phrase "quality of life" along with statements concerning parks and open space. The reality of the profession is that the agency cannot be all things to all people. With that in mind, the agency determines the scope, the boundaries, and the area for the program delivery system, based upon needs, partnerships, and allocated financial, human, and physical resources. For example, a quality-of-life area for both City of Toronto Recreation and for the Maryland-National Capital Park and Planning Commission is wellness. Both agencies approach wellness by offering a wide variety of fitness activities and fitness-related facilities. Both agencies have pools, fitness centers, and numerous fitness classes for various ages and fitness levels. The boundaries of programs can be naturally determined by the facilities that the agencies manage and operate.

The mission and vision statements guide the composition of the program delivery system and outcomes sought by the programs and services in the form of goals and objectives.

MISSION STATEMENTS

Toronto, Canada Parks and Recreation Mission Statement

Toronto's parks, recreation facilities and natural spaces are places where Torontonians come together to build community and play, celebrate and explore. In Parks, Forestry & Recreation Division's role as stewards of these spaces, we contribute to the city's social and environmental resilience by ensuring that our parks, playing fields, recreation centres, ice rinks and pools, along with tree-lined streets, trails, forests, meadows, marshes, and ravines, are beautiful, safe and accessible, that they expand and adapt to meet the needs of a growing city, and are filled with vibrant, active, and engaged communities.

Reprinted from Toronto Canada Parks, Forestry and Recreation. Available: https://www.toronto.ca/city-government/accountability-operations-customer-service/city-administration/staff-directory-divisions-and-customer-service/parks-forestry-recreation/.

Maryland-National Capital Park and Planning Commission Mission Statement

Throughout 80 plus years of service, The Maryland-National Capital Park and Planning Commission has endeavored to improve the quality of life for all of the citizens of the bicounty area it serves and of the communities in which these citizens live, work, and raise their families. This mission is embodied in three major program areas. These major program areas respond to the vision of our founders and are incorporated into our charter. The mission of The Maryland-National Capital Park and Planning Commission is to:

- Manage physical growth and plan communities
- Protect and steward natural, cultural, and historic resources
- Provide leisure and recreational experiences

Reprinted from Maryland National Capital Park and Planning Commission. Available: https://www.pgparks.com/176/Mission-Vision-Value-Statements.

Figure 13.1 A mission statement helps an organization determine what the program delivery system should include in areas such as fitness or health by keeping the organization focused on why it exists, what it intends to do, and whom it serves.

- **Goals** are broad-based intended outcomes related to the mission and are not measurable, but guide the program delivery system development, evaluation, and revision.
- **Objectives** are the measurable steps that need to be taken to achieve the agency and program goals.

In the case of the Maryland-National Capital Park and Planning Commission, a goal for the aquatics program could be "to advance the swimming skills of the residents." One objective for the goal could be "60 percent of the participants in beginning swimming will pass the class requirements by the end of the session."

All elements within the agency are interrelated and depend on each other; therefore, the recreation professional must consider the following elements when developing the program delivery system:

- Mission and vision
- Resources
- Needs

- Goals
- Objectives

The program delivery system requires recreation professionals to create opportunities that vary in leader interaction, program area, and format. The leadership options within the program delivery system are examined next (Moiseichik, 2016).

LEADERSHIP WITHIN THE PROGRAM DELIVERY SYSTEM

The leadership used within programs and services is the backbone of all **program delivery systems** within public, private, nonprofit, and commercial agencies. Leadership characteristics vary from program to program and service to service, such as teaching a class versus directing the use of public parks. The leadership used for programs affects the participants' experiences. For example, in an instructional class, the leader has higher control over the experience compared to the leader of a visit to a park. Four options are available for leadership of programs and services:

1. General supervision leadership
2. Indirect leadership
3. Facilitated leadership
4. Structured leadership

As one reviews the leadership options on a continuum from general leadership to structured leadership as shown in figure 13.2, the various levels of control of experiences by the leaders is evident.

General Supervision Leadership

General supervision leadership focuses on providing facilities and areas in which people can recreate, play, and socialize independently. Additionally, the leader serves as a resource to the community and guides people to amenities that are available. General supervision is used in facilities and spaces such as

- parks,
- trails,
- picnic areas, and
- sports fields.

These facilities and spaces provide opportunities for self-directed leisure experiences. People determine what they will do at these facilities based on their own needs, wants, desires, and personal schedules (Moiseichik, 2016).

Think back to an experience at a park, gym, or trail and examine why you were there, what you did, and what other people were doing. For example, Brice enjoys going to the local state park and spending time at the lake beachfront enjoying the warm weather and swimming. During one of her trips to the park, she looked around to see what other people were doing. She saw

- a man scuba diving in the lake,
- families enjoying the shade trees and cooking out,

- people on the hiking trail,
- people riding bikes,
- people playing soccer, and
- others simply reading books.

She was amazed at the variety of activities occurring in one location. This experience is enjoyed while under general supervision. The lifeguards were on the beach area ensuring the safety of the swimmers, and rangers came through the area regularly to ensure visitors were enjoying themselves. Both the lifeguards and rangers were providing general supervision during Brice's visit to the park (Mulvaney & Hurd, 2022).

Consider the region in which you live: What are the facilities, programs, and open spaces available to the public free of charge or for a small fee? These facilities are generally owned and maintained by local, state, or regional government agencies. Playgrounds, athletic fields, trails, and parks provide seasonal or year-round recreation opportunities. For instance, local trails can often be used year-round by different user groups.

- Hikers, dog walkers, and runners can readily use the trails during spring, summer, and fall.
- During winter, trails may be used for snowmobiling, cross-country skiing, and snowshoeing.

The general supervision and maintenance of the areas permit people to use the facility or space to create their own experience based on their personal goals, objectives, and needs. This leadership option is a vital component in the program delivery system that permits people to determine and control their own recreational experiences. When revisiting figure 13.2, you'll see that structured leadership is on the opposite end of the continuum from general supervision leadership.

Structured Leadership

Structured leadership is used when programs require face-to-face instruction. This approach is used in all types of classes, and the participant's experience is controlled, guided, and facilitated by

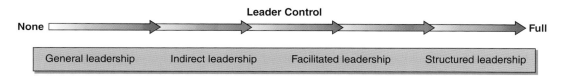

Figure 13.2 The leadership continuum shows four different leadership options available for programs and services.

General supervision leadership *(a)* provides spaces for people to recreate; structured leadership *(b)* requires a leader to deliver instruction.

the leader. It involves leaders who have a strong skill set or credentials in a specific area that meet the leadership requirements of the program. These types of leaders can be instructors hired by the agency or contractors to provide specific programs. This provides participants confidence in the program leaders, and they may be more inclined to sign up for future programs. For example, a fitness instructor has specific skills, knowledge, and certifications to safely move people through a complete workout, including a warm-up, the intense exercise portion, and the cool-down.

Structured leadership is used to assist people in moving through an experience when they lack the knowledge to do so independently. Participants want to learn to do something, but they need help learning the skills. This type of leadership is used throughout the recreation profession within public, private, nonprofit, and commercial recreation. Each type of agency has skilled leaders and offers a variety of structured leadership programs to meet people's needs (Moiseichik, 2016).

Facilitated Leadership

Facilitated leadership serves a different need within the community from other leadership positions. This leadership option helps groups to become independent, self-operating, and able to provide programs and services for themselves. With facilitated leadership, the recreation professional

within the community works with the group leaders to set up

- a place for activities,
- a process for the league or club, and
- procedures for operating the group.

The recreation professional and the group leadership work hand in hand to formalize the operations of the group. After the operations are established, the recreation professional is not involved with the group and the group operates independently. An example of facilitated leadership is a recreation professional working with a group to create a club or league that independently operates out of a recreation facility (Moiseichik, 2016).

Youth sport leagues such as soccer, football, hockey, lacrosse, and cheerleading are some of the most common group types that rely on facilitated leadership within communities. With facilitated leadership, the recreation professional within the community works with the group leaders to set up a place for activities, a process for the league or club, and procedures for operating the group. The recreation professional and the group leader work hand in hand to formalize the operation of the group. After the operations are established, the recreation professional is not involved with the group and the group operates independently. For example, due to limited personnel and financial resources, a local recreation department does not have the staff to coordinate and conduct a youth soccer league for

OUTSTANDING GRADUATE

Background Information

Name: Gideon Peterson

Education: BS in recreations and parks management with a concentration in adventure sports management from Frostburg State University

Credentials: Certified climbing/zip-line instructor, certified wilderness first responder, certified in CPR and first aid, certified mountain bike instructor, and certified Leave No Trace instructor

Awards: Eagle Scout; dean's list spring semester 2020, fall semester 2020, and spring semester 2021

Affiliations: National Recreation and Park Association (NRPA)

Gideon Peterson

Career Information

Position: Assistant Adventure Manager

Organization: In 2002, the Maryland board of public works approved a request from the Baltimore-based Erickson Foundation to lease 97 of the 2,200 acres (890 ha) within the Elk Neck State Park in Cecil County, Maryland. The product of a unique public and private partnership between the Erickson Foundation, the Maryland State Department of Education, and the Department of Natural Resources, NorthBay opened its doors to students in 2005. The Maryland State Department of Education approved NorthBay's curriculum which was specifically designed for sixth grade students from a variety of demographics backgrounds. The goal of the program is to provide a high energy, academically rigorous and engaging science curriculum that inspires students to take responsibility for their surroundings and decisions. The state-of-the-art NorthBay facility also serves as a retreat center for groups both large and small. From small corporate retreats and weddings to large youth retreats, NorthBay's location, facilities, and staff create a perfect setting for our guests.

The program has grown from serving 4,400 students in its first year of operation to serving over 10,000 public school students each year in NorthBay's intensive five day and four night environmental education and character development program. Additional educational programs such as the Chesapeake Wilderness Institute and the NorthBay Extended (NEXT) programs, serve an additional 8,000 students, while over 14,000 retreat guests stay at NorthBay each year. The programs serve diverse groups ranging from corporate staff to youth-at-risk. The COVID-19 pandemic provided a new opportunity for the NorthBay academy to serve 6th grade students from Baltimore City through an onsite residential academic program.

Job description: As the assistant adventure manager, I have three main duties. First, I am responsible for the safe operations of all adventure activities and elements at the camp. This is accomplished by training staff members on how to operate each one properly, conducting safety inspections of all of the elements, and performing maintenance. Second, I am responsible for overseeing staff during operations, for groups, and the academy students, and being a shift manager for various times during the day and evening. Finally, I conduct team-building activities with guest and education groups, which progress from games, to low ropes course elements and then to high ropes elements, using the "Challenge by Choice" philosophy.

Career path: My career began at Rodney Scout Reservation where I worked for five summers in the first-year scout program called *Brownsea*. Through this program, I learned that I love working in outdoor education and it heavily influenced my future decisions. In my junior year of high school, I began working as an adventure staff member at NorthBay; first for two years as a part-time employee during the school year while continuing to work at Rodney Scout Reservation during the summers. Once I began at Frostburg State University working toward my degree in recreation and park management, I returned to NorthBay during my winter break to work as a seasonal educator and during COVID-19. During the onset of the pandemic, I discovered that the assistant manager of adventure position was vacant. I was seeking an internship opportunity to complete my bachelor's degree and the NorthBay manager agreed to use my internship as a trial period for the position. I am happy to say that I was offered the position and accepted it at the completion of my internship. My current plan is to continue working at NorthBay as I work on my master's degree in the online program in recreation and parks management at Frostburg State University. The management experience I am gaining at NorthBay, along with my master's degree, will prepare me for my ultimate goal, which is to become a National Park Ranger at one of the top 30 outdoor National Parks in America.

Advice for Undergraduates

My number one advice to undergraduate students is to cultivate and maintain good relationships with your professors. Your faculty are your allies, they want you to succeed, and will help you to do so by opening doors for you, both personally and professionally. Also, be honest with your professors and other people, if you mess up or don't understand something, do not create an excuse, or blame others. The faculty will understand and help move you forward in school and life. This is all part of the professional development process.

the community. To meet this need, parents volunteer and formalize a board of directors that takes on the leadership role for the youth soccer league. This board works with the local recreation department to schedule field use and field maintenance. Beyond the use of the facilities, the board runs and coordinates the community youth soccer league to meet the need within the community.

The facilitated leadership option is a useful technique for working with groups who have special interests, manpower, and the necessary skills. These groups can conduct programs and events for the community by representing the agency, but they place few demands on the agency. In local communities, facilitated leadership commonly creates sport leagues, arts councils for performing and visual arts, and clubs for recreational interests such as skiing and reading.

Indirect Leadership

Indirect leadership falls on the continuum between general supervision and facilitated leadership in figure 13.2. The indirect leadership option provides the agency with an opportunity to augment programs and services by providing people with equipment or services for a fee, such as equipment rental or picnic shelter rental (Moiseichik, 2016). The only interaction between the participant and the leader occurs during the reservation, rental, and use process. The recreation experience is determined by the participant, not the leader. Many agencies have picnic shelters for rent to accommodate people who need a place for large gatherings such as family reunions, school picnics, birthday parties, and church functions. Other centers rent bikes, canoes, and paddleboats.

Indirect leadership provides ways for people to pursue activities or have group gatherings that might not otherwise occur. The recreation agency meets the diverse needs of people within the community and provides the resources for these groups to create their own experiences using agency resources. Within indirect leadership, the leader must be able to provide excellent customer service since the interactions are generally brief. This will create a positive interaction and increase the likelihood the customer will return to the agency for future services.

The four leadership options are blended together in a program delivery system. This mixture of leadership helps ensure that the agency meets its mission, but leadership is not the only element in the program delivery system that recreation professionals need to consider in meeting the mission.

To plan the program delivery system, two other elements must be reviewed:

1. The program classification area
2. The program format

PROGRAM CLASSIFICATION

The second area of the program delivery system is **program classification**, which guides the development of diverse program options. The profession of parks and recreation divides all programs and services into 15 classification areas that are highlighted in table 13.1. Each classification area includes hundreds of opportunities for programs and services depending on the resources of the agency. The program classifications listed in table 13.1 can be used with the leadership options to evaluate the current program delivery system and generate additional ideas for programs and services that most efficiently and effectively meet the needs of the community and align with the mission, vision, goals, and objectives of the organization (DeGraff & Jordan, 2019).

Let's examine the aquatics area in detail to demonstrate the wealth of program options within the program classification system. Within the aquatics area, agencies use all the leadership options to meet a wide spectrum of needs within the community that the agency serves. The type of aquatic programs provided determine the type of leadership needed. For example, swim teams are common in public, nonprofit, private, and commercial agencies. Because this activity requires face-to-face leadership with swim coaches, the supervision leadership option is used to conduct a swim team program.

Agencies with pools provide a variety of program options, such as open swim or free swim times, swim team practices, pool parties, and adults-only events. Table 13.2 has a sample of activities that could be conducted in pools and the leadership options used for these programs. Recreation professionals should ask the following three questions while reviewing a list like this one:

1. Do these programs meet the mission and goals of the agency? Yes. The programs address improving the quality of life or wellness of the community.
2. Do these programs serve the various segments of the community in terms of age, group, ability, gender, sexual orientation, race, and ethnicity? Yes. The programs listed in table 13.2 provide opportunities for all ages with the open swim and class options.

Table 13.1 Program Classifications

Classification	Description	Examples
Arts	Creative process of making items	Painting, sculpture
Performing arts	Activities or programs that focus on self-expression in music, dance, or drama	Concert in the park, community play
Crafts	Making something of decorative value	Pottery, knitting
New arts	Using technology such as digital cameras or computers	Photography class
Literary activity	Activities involving books, writing, or speeches	Book club
Self-development activity	Activities or programs that promote personal development	Stress management class, retirement seminar
Aquatics	Activities or programs done in the water	Swimming lessons, water aerobics, swim team
Outdoor activity	Activities or programs done in the outdoor environment	Hiking program, kayaking program, camping
Wellness program	Programs that focus on comprehensively improving wellness	Fitness classes, nutritional seminars, stress management seminars
Hobbies	Activities in which people collect something, create something, or educate others	Coin collecting, model railroading, garden clubs
Social recreation	Programs and services that promote social interaction	Dances, festivals, teen clubs
Volunteer services	Programs in which people provide services to others	Working the front desk, greeting customers, taking care of roadways and parks
Travel and tourism	Trips that take people to attractions	Ghost tours, biking tours, visiting casinos or national parks
Sports, games, and athletics	Activities with some rules that involve competition	Card games, soccer leagues, swim teams
Virtual	Online programs and events	Training and conditioning classes

The lessons, swim team, and parties focus on children, and the master's swim program and water fitness focus on seniors, athletes, and others. The open swim can meet the needs of people of any age, group, ability, gender, sexual orientation, race, and ethnicity.

3. Do these programs serve a continuum of skill levels from introductory to advanced levels? Yes. The programs, classes, and services provide opportunities for people from the beginner level to the advanced level. Swimming lessons are the first step in learning skills. Swim lessons serve as the foundation for staff to recruit children into the swim team program and introduce them to a lifetime sport that they can continue as an adult through the master's program. The current aquatic programs provide opportunities for a variety of skill levels.

As table 13.2 highlights, a pool provides numerous opportunities for programs and services that use each of the leadership options to meet the agency's mission, serve a broad base of customer needs, and provide activities for people of various skill levels to develop their abilities for various activities with beginner, intermediate, and advanced levels.

Table 13.2 Aquatic Programs and Leadership Options

Leadership option	Aquatic programs
General leadership	Open swim Lap swimming Dive-in movie
Structured leadership	Swim lessons Water fitness Arthritis water fitness Swim team
Facilitated leadership	Triathlon workout club Master's swim club Water walking club
Indirect leadership	Swimming birthday parties Fins and flotation devices

The process of developing a program delivery system depends on this creative planning process to generate and evaluate the programs and services within the program delivery system. To further create program options to evaluate for the program delivery system, program formats help determine the program structure. This technique takes the planning effort from the leadership options and classification options one step further to generate different program formats within the classification areas.

PROGRAM FORMATS

Program formats are the methods through which the program is structured for participants, and assist the recreation professional to further develop the program delivery system into a comprehensive plan. The nine program formats are listed in table 13.3 with virtual programs included. The use of the virtual program format soared during the 2020 pandemic as professionals adapted to continue to provide needed programs and services to the community. The various formats can be used within any of the program classification areas to generate program options and associated leadership needed for each option. This next step in developing the program delivery system helps determine the specific scope and variety of programs and services. This assists the recreation professional in determining whether a program should be offered only once or on a continual basis, or whether the program should be leader directed or self-determined (DeGraff & Jordan, 2019). This type of detailed analysis is necessary to ensure that a balance of program classifications and formats are provided to best meet the needs of the community. This also aids in determining where the financial, human, and physical resources should be allocated within the program delivery system.

Take a closer look at how the program formats, leadership options, and classifications can be used to build program delivery systems for aquatics and soccer. What programs could be offered in aquatics and soccer using the eight formats? For many of the formats, listing a program is easy, whereas for others it is more challenging. For example, what programs could be developed for interest groups and outreach in aquatics and soccer? This task is the challenging and creative part of developing a program delivery system. Table 13.4 lists examples of various programs and services based on program formats that could be offered by recreation agencies for aquatics and soccer.

Table 13.5 pulls together the three major areas of a program delivery system: program leadership, classification, and format. The table format can be used to generate additional program or service options or evaluate existing programs or services. The items listed in this table comprehensively represent different leadership options for programs to provide choices for participation in leader-directed programs to self-directed activities. The activities go far beyond providing competitive formats, which are not always appealing to beginners. Finally, a review of the activities in this table demonstrates a logical progression of programs is available to attract new customers and retain current customers. This progression provides participants with opportunities to further develop their skills and use new skills

Table 13.3 Program Formats

Format	Explanation	Program examples
Competition	Program that involves a competition or a contest	Indoor soccer league
Class	Instructional sessions over a series of weeks	Aerobics class
Club	Group that is self-conducted with regular meetings	Running club
Drop-in or open area	Area in the facility left for people to use freely	Open gym time
Interest group	Similar to a club but organized around an issue or program	Arts council
Outreach	Taking programs to people or reaching people not normally served by the agency	Playground day camp program, mobile arts bus
Special event	One-time large program	Arts and crafts festival
Workshop or conference	Programs that focus on learning a skill	Digital photography editing workshop
Virtual	Online courses or activities	Online cooking class

Table 13.4 Program Formats for Aquatics and Soccer

Format	Aquatics	Soccer (or other sport)
Competition	Dual swim meets	Indoor youth soccer league
Class	Lifeguard classes	Soccer skills class
Club	Master's swim club	Travel team
Drop-in or open area	Open swim	Area open for practice
Interest group	Swim team advisory group	Soccer league advisory group
Outreach	Special Olympics training program	Wheelchair soccer
Special event	Pool water carnival	Soccer tournament
Workshop or conference	Stroke-and-turn judge clinic	Coaching clinic
Virtual	Online certification program	Online coaching seminar

Table 13.5 Program Formats and Leadership

Leadership type	Format	Aquatics	Soccer (or other sport)
Structured	Competition	Dual swim meets	Indoor youth soccer league
Facilitated	Class	Lifeguard classes	Soccer skills class
General	Club	Master's swim club	Travel team
Indirect	Drop-in or open area	Open swim	Area open to practice
General or structured	Interest group	Swim team advisory group	Soccer league advisory group
Indirect or general	Outreach	Special Olympics training program	Wheelchair soccer
Structured	Special event	Pool water carnival	Soccer tournament
Structured	Workshop or conference	Stroke-and-turn judge clinic	Coaching clinic
Structured	Virtual class, class, or workshop	Conditioning dry land exercises	Stretching and flexibility exercises

in new programs. The essence of every program delivery system is to offer diversity in programs and services, as well as diversity in classification, leadership, and format options, to meet the varied needs and abilities of the people who are served by the organization (Moiseichik, 2016).

SUMMARY

This chapter explores the program delivery system in several ways. The backbone of the program delivery system is the mission and vision of the organization, which guide its planning efforts. The leadership options provide a variety of participant experiences, from instructional classes to open use of facilities, to allow people to do what they want to do when they want to do it. The next area of consideration in developing a program delivery system is the classification of the programs and ser-

vices. This step ensures that a well-balanced array of programs and services exist for the participants to meet their needs. The final step in developing a program delivery system involves using program format options to develop specific programs and services for participants across formats and classifications. This step also ensures that one format is not overrepresented in the delivery system while others are neglected. All these considerations lead to providing a balanced menu of programs and services to participants. After the program delivery system is developed, planned, and conducted, the professional can examine the outcomes for the participants, determine whether the system is meeting the mission and vision of the organization, and then make the necessary revisions to provide quality programs and services to the community or customers while optimally using the human, financial, and physical resources of the agency.

Review Questions

1. What is the purpose of the mission statement for a parks and recreation agency?

2. How does the mission statement guide the program delivery system?

3. How does the mission statement influence the program goals and objectives of the organization?

4. How are general leadership and indirect leadership similar and different?

5. How can facilitated leadership be used in a parks and recreation department?

6. How can structured leadership be used to engage people in a series of developmental programs and move people to general leadership situations?

7. How do the program classification and leadership options interact while developing a program delivery system?

8. Why is it important to use the program classifications while developing a program delivery system?

9. When developing a program delivery system using the program classification option, what are the limitations for not offering various programs?

10. How do the mission, leadership, program classification, and program format interrelate while developing a program delivery system?

11. Why is it important to use the program format options when developing a program delivery system?

12. What program options and leadership are needed for a hiking program across the program formats?

Go to HK*Propel* to complete the activities for this chapter.

CHAPTER 14

Recreational Sport Management

H. Joey Gray, Robert J. Barcelona, and Kelsie N. Roberts

" Sports for all means sports for all ages, all racial and ethnic groups, all ability levels, all genders, and all social strata. "

Andre Carvalho, former program manager at United Nations Development Programme

Halbergman/E+/Getty Images

LEARNING OUTCOMES

After reading this chapter, you should be able to do the following:

> Describe the components of the foundation of recreational sport management

> List the broad scope of recreational sport activities and events

> Describe the trends affecting recreational sport management

> Analyze and evaluate the scope of participation in recreational sport

> List career opportunities in recreational sport management

Recreational sport, or sport for the masses, is a popular and appealing form of leisure and recreation to many American adults. In 2021, approximately 76.3 percent of Americans (232.6 million people) aged 6 years or older participated in some type of sport, fitness, or outdoor activity (Physical Activity Council, 2022). More than half of 6- to 12-year-olds (56.2%) actively participated in team sports (National Survey of Children's Health, 2019). Often seen as a subset of both the sport management and recreation and leisure industries, recreational sport professionals provide sport opportunities for the masses, and their job functions and the recreational sport settings in which they work are incredibly diverse (Barcelona et al., 2016).

Sport in American society has experienced tremendous change and increased popularity over the 20th and early 21st centuries. As of 2022, sport and physical activity are as much a part of American culture as other institutions such as work, marriage, and the family. Once simply considered a diversion from work and a tool for recreation, sport has grown to be a multibillion-dollar industry. For some people, sports such as baseball, football, and basketball are like a civil religion—what Forney once called the "holy trinity" (2010). Avid fans spend thousands of dollars on tickets, paraphernalia, fantasy camps, and the myriad expenses associated with travel and fandom. In 2023, the average ticket price for the Super Bowl peaked at $8,837, according to an article published in Sporting News (Al-Kahteeb, 2023), the second-highest average of all time. Sports fans and participants alike currently possess unfailing devotion to sport with both their discretionary time and their money.

Sport is indeed a business, and the industry has had a significant influence not only in the United States but also around the globe (Szymanski et al., 2020). This increased popularity and devotion to sport globally has significantly affected the way sport and leisure services have been delivered in the past and will continue to be delivered in the future.

As of 2023, sport has become very entertainment and spectator oriented, and record numbers of people have been watching or attending professional sporting events. Social media provides sport entertainment at the fingertips of fans, who can check scores, pore over stats, and stream both live and recorded games at any time from an array of smart (i.e., Internet-enabled, computer-powered) devices including phones, TVs, speakers, laptops, and watches. NFL Sunday Night Football was the most watched television program in 2022 with 18.4 million views in the United States (Al-Kahteeb, 2023). Professional athletes are considered folk heroes and paid astronomical salaries.

In addition, many people across social categories routinely participate in recreational sports themselves by engaging in individual and team sports and fitness activities. In this regard, sport has become participant oriented, involving diverse populations in a variety of programs and activities. Sport touches almost every facet of society, from the economy to youth development and leisure pursuits. Delaney and Madigan said it best, "sport is interconnected with every major social institution in society" (2015, p. 393).

EXAMINING SPORT MANAGEMENT FROM A RECREATIONAL PERSPECTIVE

The discipline that manages sports programs has been referred to by a variety of different terms and titles over the years. Although there is no consensus on the name of the field, the term *sport management* is generally the umbrella term used to identify professional careers in planning, organizing, leading, and controlling sport events, programs, personnel, and facilities (Barcelona et al., 2016). The most widely accepted definition of **sport management** is provided by Pitts and Stotlar (2013) stating "the study and practice of all people, activities, businesses, or organizations involved in producing, facilitating, promoting, or organizing any sport-related business or product" (p. 3). Pitts and Stotlar, according to the North American Society of Sport Management (n.d.), state that sport management addresses the application of business to the professional side of sport, which includes the following topics:

- Sport marketing
- Employment competencies
- Management competencies
- Event management
- Sport and the law
- Personnel management
- Facility management
- Organizational structures
- Fund-raising

Professional sport management focuses on **sport performance**, and professionals often work with elite athletes (e.g., as sport agents) or in the planning, promoting, or managing of professional sporting events (e.g., sport promotion, sport communication, sport equipment sales, ticketing agents). Settings include the following:

- Professional sport
- Intercollegiate athletics
- Sport marketing firms
- National sport governing bodies

The primary emphasis or goal in this area is to win championships with elite athletes and to increase revenue and profits for team franchise owners or stakeholders through

- ticket or sports equipment sales and promotion,
- stadium and arena facility management, and
- entertaining spectators.

The major defining characteristic of recreational sport management that separates it from professional sport management is its focus on **sport participation** for the masses. Recreational sport provides diverse sports programs, facilities, equipment, and services that promote and enhance greater appreciation for lifelong involvement in sport and fitness. Over the years, there has been a significant increase in the demand for broad-based recreational sports programming that meets the needs and interests of all participants regardless of age, race, ethnicity, gender, sexual orientation, religion, or athletic abil-

ity. It is important to identify and understand the components of recreational sport and the role they play in the realm of sport management.

Recreational sport management emphasizes the leadership and management of people and resources in a variety of participatory or recreational settings. In this delivery, the key principle of active sport participation is represented by various degrees of competitive activity within many sectors:

- Collegiate parks and recreation
- Municipal parks and recreation
- Commercial recreation
- Corporate recreation
- Correctional recreation
- Military recreation

From this perspective, recreational sport is a major component of people's lifestyles, either as participants in or spectators of sports during leisure (Mull et al., 2019). Figure 14.1 provides a leisure sport management model that illustrates the concepts of participation and spectatorship in sports programming ranging from **educational sports** at the lowest level to **professional sports** at the highest.

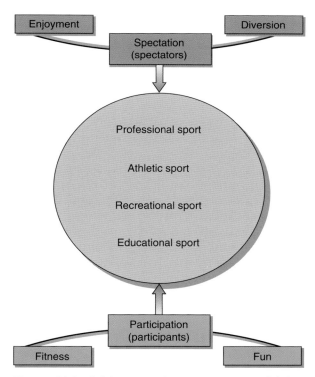

Figure 14.1 A leisure sport management model that illustrates the concepts of participation and spectatorship.

Reprinted by permission from R.F. Mull, K.G. Bayless, and L.M. Jamieson, *Recreational Sport Management,* 4th ed. (Champaign, IL: Human Kinetics, 2005), 9.

Many people, ranging from youth to older adults, actively participate in sport at the educational or instructional and recreational levels. Then, as participants progress upward in the model toward the apex, participation in the leisure experience shifts from being actively involved to being a spectator. For example, at the professional level of sport, the leisure experience of most people consists of watching professional athletes perform and compete rather than being actively involved in the sport.

DEFINING RECREATIONAL SPORT

Traditionally, recreational sport has been described as

- intramural sport,
- physical recreation,
- physical activity,
- nonvarsity athletics,
- open recreation,
- intramural athletics, and so on.

However, none of these accurately reflects what recreational sport is. The basis of recreational sport is a person's involvement during leisure time either as an active participant or as a spectator at one of the levels of the leisure sport hierarchy. The major characteristic of recreational sport management that separates it from other sport disciplines is its focus on sport participation for the masses. Recreational sports programs are designed to give *everyone* an active role regardless of sport interest, age, race, ethnicity, gender, sexual orientation, or athletic ability. It truly is sport for all. Because recreational sports programs are participant driven, sport programmers and managers put significant effort into defining and meeting participants' wants and needs. The complexity and magnitude of recreational sport management are a result of societal demands for more and better services that target mass participation in recreational sport.

FIVE PROGRAMMING AREAS OF RECREATIONAL SPORT MANAGEMENT

Five basic program delivery areas comprise the recreational sport spectrum:

1. **Instructional sports** are the recreational sport activities that teach skills, rules, and strategies in a noncredit or academic environment.

2. **Informal sports** involve self-directed participation with an individualized approach focused on fun and fitness.

3. **Intramural sports** involve structured sports in the form of leagues, tournaments, and contests conducted within a particular setting.

4. **Extramural sports** consist of structured sport activities between winners of various intramural sports programs.

5. **Club sports** are undertaken by groups of participants that organize because of a common interest in a sport.

Instructional Sport

Most traditional recreational sports programs are based on sport competition, and they appeal primarily to people who are already familiar with a sport or have some degree of skill and involvement with sport. The instructional sports program area focuses on an even larger segment of the population that needs to learn basic sport skills and how to incorporate the physical activity and fitness components of sport into daily life.

This program area was developed to encourage participants to gain the core skills in various levels of sport activities and to provide a way for people to have fun and enjoy the many benefits of participating in the sport activity. The primary emphasis, then, is on participant skill development, enjoyment, and learning how to play the game.

Historically, instructional sport was offered only through educational settings such as physical education classes and varsity athletics. But with the increased interest in and popularity of recreational sport participation, instructional sport has expanded into these nonacademic settings:

- YMCAs
- YWCAs
- Boys and Girls Clubs
- Municipal parks and recreation
- Commercial recreational sports
- The armed forces recreation sector

Practically every setting (campus, military, municipal, youth, etc.) offers instructional sports that teach individuals or groups through classes, lessons, clinics, and workshops and usually at three instructional levels:

1. Beginning
2. Intermediate
3. Advanced

Examples of instructional sports include exercise and conditioning, gymnastics, martial arts, swimming, golf, bowling, tennis, racquetball, and squash.

Informal or Self-Directed Sport

Informal sport, which is probably one of the most misunderstood and misrepresented program delivery areas in recreational sport management, is self-directed sport participation for fun and fitness. This program area is at the other end of the spectrum from coordinated intramural sports and possesses the least structure. Informal sport activities include things like the following:

- Backyard volleyball or softball at the family picnic
- Pickup basketball games at the local park
- Early-morning swim
- Lunchtime run
- Lifting weights at a fitness facility

This program area emphasizes self-directed participation. The participant designs and develops the specific personal program and goals, and the recreational sport staff facilitates the involvement or experience through appropriate and available facilities and equipment. In most sectors (municipal parks and recreation, armed forces recreation, educational recreation), informal sports involve the largest number of participants. Because informal sports are the least structured, sport takes place whenever there is an available facility or interest in the activity.

For recreational sport programmers, many elements go into informal sports programming and management. Because the primary goal is to facilitate sport participation, perhaps the biggest concerns for informal sport programmers are facilities and equipment management and scheduling. Having available and accessible facilities and equipment is essential to creating a satisfying and positive experience for all participants.

Although the benefits of fitness and wellness are part of all the program delivery components, managing specific fitness and wellness programs has become a special programming area in informal sports. Especially popular are

- group exercise programs, such as step aerobics, trekking, indoor cycling; and
- mind and body activities, such as Pilates, yoga, and tai chi.

These programs help participants enhance or achieve overall well-being through sport and fitness activities and play an integral role in the overall management of recreational sport.

Intramural or Structured Sports

Intramural sports involve structured participation *within* a specific setting such as leagues, tournaments, and matches. The word *intramural* is derived from the Latin words *intra* (within) and *mural* (walls). Intramural sports, then, are structured activities between teams and individuals within an agency's limits or boundaries such as the city, university campus, YMCA branch, and so on. Intramural sports are generally limited to participation among the participants served by a particular agency and should provide opportunities for men, women, and mixed competition with a variety of rule modifications to meet the needs and interests of the participants in that setting. Intramural sports can include the following:

- *Individual sports.* Events that generally allow people to participate alone (e.g., fishing, golf, swimming, diving, trap and skeet, cycling, hunting, boxing, archery)
- *Dual sports.* Events that require at least one opponent (e.g., badminton, table tennis, tennis, squash, handball, racquetball)
- *Team sports.* Events that require a specific number of players who play as a team of either men, women, or mixed intramural divisions (e.g., baseball, basketball, softball, kickball, lacrosse, field hockey, rowing, soccer, volleyball, wallyball, water polo, flag football)
- *Meet sports.* Separate events occurring within a larger event and usually conducted over a period of one or two days (e.g., swimming, gymnastics, diving, wrestling, golf, track and field)
- *Special events.* Nontraditional activities usually not practiced regularly by the participants (e.g., Wacky Olympics, sports all-nighters and festivals, superstar competitions)

Intramural sports are typically the signature programs or mainstays of recreational sport agencies. In many instances, they provide the basic sport opportunities from which agencies build and expand their overall program offerings. This is because of

- the familiarity and high-profile nature of traditional sports programs,
- the large participation base,
- a well-organized and highly structured program delivery,
- the competitive (but wholesome) atmosphere, and
- the recognition and awards for participants and teams who excel.

Historically, the term *intramural sports* has been associated with recreational sports programs at colleges and universities. However, as of 2022, several entities offer a variety of sport events that are very similar to collegiate recreational sport but with participants who are not 18- to 22-year-old college students, including

- municipal and community recreation departments,
- churches,
- YMCAs,
- military bases,
- elementary and secondary schools,
- industries, and
- private clubs.

These events, although not thought of as intramural sports, in fact meet the definition of sport played "within the walls" of an agency.

Extramural Sports

Extramural sports refers to structured recreational sport participation in which participants compete against those from other agencies or organizations. Competition takes place between winning teams from several programs. Extramural sports include sports programs and activities in which teams from winning programs are invited to represent their home agency and compete for an overall championship. Examples include the following:

- Little League Baseball World Series
- A navy basketball team representing its base
- The Morale, Welfare and Recreation (MWR) department playing in the local municipal parks and recreation tournament
- A collegiate intramural flag football championship team from one university playing

against other collegiate champions for national champion recognition

Many times, the extramural sports program fills the gap between varsity athletics and intramural sports and provides additional opportunities for many higher-skilled athletes to compete.

Club Sports

Club sports involve any group that organizes to further its interest or skill level in a specific sport activity. These interests range from very competitive club teams that travel and play in various high-level competitions to the recreational, social, and instructional clubs that conduct activities such as basic-skill instruction and tournaments among themselves.

The history of club sports is long. It is believed that club sports are the forerunners of college athletics, intramural sports, and formal physical education classes. The main purpose of a club sports program is to provide various degrees of interaction and sport participation to its members. In many instances, club sports are formed

- for the social aspects that incorporate practices, informal get-togethers, and philanthropic functions;
- to offer instruction and skill development for beginning to advanced skill levels; or
- for the sole purpose of competition and tournaments.

Because clubs are not limited to the college setting, they can be found in the public, military, commercial, private, and correctional settings. Club sports programs have become popular because they generally operate with fewer administrative resource needs such as staffing, facilities, referees, and so on than other types of organized recreational sports programming. Many clubs are self-sufficient and generate all needed funding.

The nature of club sports allows members to direct their interests both within and outside the recreational agency. Characteristics that distinguish club sports from intramural sports, informal sports, and extramural sports include the following:

- They are self-administered and regulated to some degree with participant-developed operating policies.
- Members can conduct their club sport without substantial administrative support from the agency.

- Club sports offer opportunities for regular and ongoing year-round participation.
- Club sports provide a more structured design than informal sports.
- Unlike the staff-structured intramural sports program, club sport members develop, operate, and administer the club.

SCOPE OF PARTICIPATION IN RECREATIONAL SPORT

Participation in recreational sport has grown steadily over the past several decades. Millions of people around the world participate in team, individual, or dual sports in

- municipal parks and recreation programs;
- campus recreational sports programs;
- nonprofit agencies, such as the YMCA and Boys and Girls Clubs;
- employee recreation programs;
- private clubs;
- commercial recreational sport facilities and sports programs; and
- armed forces MWR programs.

Recreational sport has even evolved to include online sport participation such as fantasy sports leagues. The following brief descriptions of participation in recreational sports programs and sport facilities provide an overview of the scope of participation that should meet the needs of people who want to participate in recreational sports.

Active Participation Choices

Active participation, as discussed earlier, is more integral in recreational sport management than it is in varsity **athletic sports** and professional sports. The key principles of active participation are the choice to participate in structured sports (instructional, intramural, extramural, or club) or self-directed sports (informal) and the wide variety of participation opportunities. This wide assortment of recreational sport, which should be afforded to *all* people, is the distinguishing feature that differentiates it from athletic and professional sports.

Participants

It is essential for recreational sport programmers to recognize to whom they provide services so they can better meet the needs and interests of the participants. Recreational sport management is intended for the enjoyment of all age groups. These groups include children, youth, adolescents, adults, and senior citizens. Today, more than ever, it is paramount that organizations be knowledgeable about the needs of various cultures, religions, races, genders, ethnicities, sexual orientations, and varying abilities. We must know our constituents and make a concerted effort to educate those we serve. Sport programmers need to consider what accommodations or considerations should be in place to ensure all participants have a safe and optimal experience. Some religions do not allow women to wear pants, which would affect uniform policies. One of the most debated topics in sport today is transgender athlete participation in sports. Consider what your organization's policies are for transgender athletes. Keep in mind that your personal views may sometimes differ with organizational policy or popular opinions. Participation policies are driven first and foremost by federal, state, and local laws. In addition, participation policy should consult with participants, staff, and the organization's board of directors. The number one priority of recreational sports is participation for all, and to do so we must focus on how to ensure participant inclusion.

Location

Very simply, participation in recreational sport occurs in both indoor and outdoor sport facilities. Indoor recreational sport facilities include

- bowling centers;
- handball, racquetball, and squash courts;
- gymnasiums for volleyball, basketball, badminton, and floor hockey;
- billiard rooms;
- roller- and ice-skating rinks;
- aquatic centers;
- strength and conditioning weight rooms; and
- exercise rooms.

Outdoor recreational sport facilities include

- softball and baseball diamonds;
- golf courses;
- trap and skeet ranges;
- fields for soccer and flag football;
- tennis courts; and
- outdoor aquatic centers.

Recreational sport can take place in a multitude of facilities and settings.

Outdoor facilities may also include natural features such as white-water rivers and streams, caves, lakes, and mountains.

Sport Settings

Recreational sport management is programmed in a variety of sport settings such as the following:

- Recreation departments on armed forces installations around the world
- Boys and Girls Clubs
- Churches
- City and community parks and recreation departments
- Commercial recreational facilities such as racket clubs, bowling centers, and roller- and ice-skating rinks
- Correctional institutions (city, county, state, and federal)
- Educational institutions (public and private elementary, secondary, and higher education)
- On-site industrial and corporate recreational sport facilities
- Private clubs (country clubs and fitness and health clubs)
- YMCAs and YWCAs
- Vacation resorts (hotels, motels, and cruise ships)

These settings represent thousands of employment positions in recreational sports programming and open the door to numerous job opportunities for those who want a career in this field.

Benefits

Recreational sport participation can provide one of the most important sociocultural learning environments in our society, and it provides a substantial range of benefits for participants and the community, organization, or agency that sponsors it. While active participants gain many health and physical benefits, the community or agency can also benefit from an economical or environmental perspective. By providing sport opportunities and encouraging participation, recreational sports programs can develop participants' interests, knowledge, and skills to enable participation in recreational sport and fitness activities over the course of a lifetime.

Personal Benefits

People who regularly participate in recreational sport activities can gain improved health, physical fitness, and self-esteem. Although physical benefits are easy to detect, active participation can also provide

- positive and enjoyable experiences that can decrease stress and psychological tension;
- the opportunity to burn excess energy and emotional stress not released in other aspects of life; and
- a positive social environment where people can relax and enjoy the company of others.

Competition and winning and losing help many people learn to control their emotions and express aggression in a positive way. Cooperation is fostered because people must work together to achieve a goal. By working with others, people gain interpersonal skills, learn to tolerate differences, and acquire time management and goal-setting skills. People can develop integrity by establishing their own values and behavior patterns and testing them against the values and behaviors of others.

Community Benefits

By providing opportunities for social interaction, recreational sports programs can help increase community cohesion and encourage community interaction by engaging different segments of the community in wholesome sporting activities regardless of age, race, ethnicity, sexual orientation,

ability, or gender. Participation can also help deter antisocial behavior such as vandalism, violence, and crime. Communities can benefit economically from well-planned and well-managed sport facilities. These economic benefits include

- direct and indirect employment in recreational sports programs,
- income from sales of recreational sporting goods and services, and
- the revenue generated from hosting local, city, state, regional, or even national recreational sports tournaments and sport events.

Tourism-related activities, through the promotion of recreational sport opportunities and the quality of sporting facilities, can contribute significantly to the local economy.

Agency, Organization, or Setting Benefits

Participation in recreational sports programs can have a direct effect on the agency, organization, or setting that provides the activities. The following are examples:

- The Employee Morale and Recreation Association (EMRA) suggests that "Sports leagues and special interest clubs allow employees to express themselves as individuals. Through involvement in these activities, employees develop a broader range of skills, learn to be leaders and enjoy coming to work" (2023, para. 4). Recreational sports programs can deliver tangible benefits in terms of workplace safety and improved productivity from happier and healthier employees.
- Studies indicate that in the collegiate setting, active engagement in recreational sports and fitness programs supports the value of recreational sports programs at colleges and universities (Hashemi et al., 2021). The benefit is improved mental health, including reduction in depression, improved sense of belonging, and student retention.
- Navy MWR fleet recreational sports programs and equipment support the quality of life of sailors on land and on board navy ships. These mission-essential MWR programs consist of voluntary fitness and recreational sport activities conducted to promote morale and physical and mental combat readiness (Navy MWR, n.d.).

Rainer Martens/Human Kinetics

Participation in recreational sport can benefit the individual as well as the community. Individuals can boost self-esteem and decrease stress, and the community can see economic benefits from a large event as well as increased community cohesion.

- Through the YMCA mission of putting "Christian principles into practice," recreational sport, a mainstay of the YMCA's offerings, emphasizes fun, teamwork, and friendly competition in a supportive community for all ages and skill levels (YMCA of the Triangle, n.d.).

TRENDS IN RECREATIONAL SPORT MANAGEMENT

To be able to fully plan and make projections properly, it is essential to examine current issues and concerns. Examining current challenges and problems and forecasting their impact on the future are of great value to any profession, and recreational sport management is no exception. By identifying and studying future trends, professionals and practitioners in the field can prepare and explore many aspects of their current programs and activities. Although it is not possible to predict exactly what will occur, observing and identifying future trends might allow us to redefine the nature of what we do and how we do it.

It is also important for recreational sport managers to understand that the programs they direct and the organizations they manage operate within larger social, economic, health, educational, and political systems. Even though recreational sport participation represents a leisure activity for many people, sport is affected by larger issues and trends in society. Understanding how sport interacts with these larger socioeconomic and political trends is a key competency for recreational sport managers.

Funding

One of the top trends in administering recreational sports programs is income generation for programs and facilities. The COVID-19 pandemic had a major financial effect on many sports programs and businesses. Publicly funded programs must often seek additional revenue streams to support their programs through sponsors, registration fees, and grants. Because of this, additional revenue and sources of income must be generated. The challenge for the recreational sport manager is to find creative ways to overcome these economic constraints. Private organizations and businesses have the potential to be lucrative, depending on the financial model, structure, and consumer market.

Legal Aspects

It is imperative for recreational sport administrators to educate not only themselves but also their staff and participants in various legal aspects. Recreational sport administrators must be responsible for developing sound risk management plans and programs that reduce the likelihood of accidents and injuries that might lead to participant lawsuits against the agency. Administrators should become familiar with the laws of their state that apply to recreational sports programs and sport facilities. Effective risk management planning is essential for reducing losses and avoiding lawsuits. The following steps will help reduce the potential for lawsuits:

- Risk management plans and reporting
- Record keeping
- Facility inspections
- Training
- Event supervision
- Emergency procedures

Further, DeSensi and Rosenberg (2010) note that "sport management leaders must view social responsibility as an integral aspect of decisions they make with regard to organizational concerns, the management of funds, the treatment of those in the sport community, and the basic integrity of sport" (p. 10).

Sport Facilities

Facility construction is a growth area in recreational sport management. Over the early 21st century, recreational sports programs in a variety of sectors have witnessed tremendous growth in the number of new sport facilities being constructed. Collegiate recreational sport is leading the way in the number of new recreational sport complexes on campuses across the country. Experts believe that participants will continue to demand larger and more specialized recreational sport facilities, which will result in even more new construction well into the 21st century. The sport industry continues to change and expand to meet the demands of current and future participants. Administrators will need to be prepared in many areas related to sport manage-

ment including securing funding for existing and new sport facilities.

Technology

Computing technology has significantly affected the way sport businesses and agencies deliver sports and tournament programming. Selecting appropriate technology may have the biggest effect on improving the efficiency of a sports program. Although technology is not the panacea for a quality recreational sports program, using technology, including hardware and software components, is clearly an important trend and tool that can improve the quality and speed of daily operations. Software and web-based programs make it easy for sport administrators and sports programming staff to

- create round-robin and single-elimination schedules for single or multisport leagues,
- register teams and accept payments online, and
- manage websites and facilities.

For sport facility managers, computer-aided facility management technologies help them do their jobs more effectively and efficiently.

Technologically advanced exercise gadgets and equipment innovations ranging from gaming consoles and 3D technology to sophisticated fitness machines are transforming not only how participants exercise but also how they stay motivated to exercise. Exergaming is used by both children and adults and is a common form of exercise for those who do not want to go to a gym (Hwang et al., 2023). Electronic activity trackers such as Fitbits and Apple watches are also becoming more accessible to children whose parents can afford them, and motion trackers on cell phones can provide feedback on physical activity.

While there is still considerable debate about whether esports can truly be considered sports in the traditional sense of the word (see chapter 11), they undoubtedly share several common characteristics, such as

- competition,
- players,
- referees,
- tournaments,
- technical skills, and
- spectators.

Hedlund (2021) maintains the future of esports will include virtual reality (VR), augmented reality (AR), and mixed reality (MR) devices. The incorporation of VR, such as use of the Oculus Quest virtual reality headset, has made a large impact on the ability to participate in recreational sport, particularly during the COVID-19 pandemic. Those limited by transportation, ability, or time can use these technologies to participate in sport. The pandemic also created space for a sharp rise in the popularity of esports. After major limitations on the participation, consumption, and attendance of traditional sporting events began in March 2020, esports quickly became a popular alternative for millions around the world.

In fact, esports were announced as an official medal sporting event for the 2022 Asian Games in China. The event was canceled due to COVID-19, but the announcement itself was groundbreaking: The Asian Games is one of the world's largest multisport events, second only to the Olympics. The International Olympic Committee (IOC) is considering esports for the 2024 Olympics. The adoption of esports at such events provides the industry unprecedented worldwide visibility as it continues its trend of remarkable growth.

From avid baseball enthusiasts to Brad Pitt superfans, the story of the Oakland Athletics and their use of data analytics during their 2002 season is well known, thanks to the 2003 book and 2011 movie, *Moneyball*. Michael Lewis' story about the Oakland A's is a remarkable account of sport analytics and is often credited as a catalyst for introducing the benefits of data-driven decision making in athletics (Fry & Ohlmann, 2012). While the movie may have helped popularize the idea of sport analytics, it provides viewers with only a small glimpse into a continuing trend.

Sport analytics has been defined as

the management of structured and historical data, the application of predictive analytic models that utilize the data, and the use of information systems to inform decision makers and enable them to help their organization in gaining a competitive advantage on the field of play. (Alamar & Mehrotra, 2011)

OUTSTANDING GRADUATE

Background Information

Name: Qi Wang

Education: BA from Central South University of Forestry and Technology, College of Tourism

Awards: Third prize in the Hunan Tourism Innovation Contest

Career Information

Position: Procurement Manager

Organization: Tuniu is a leading online leisure travel company in China that offers a large selection of packaged tours, including organized and self-guided tours, as well as travel-related services for leisure travelers through its website (www.tuniu.com) and mobile platform. It has over 1,700,000 stock keeping units (SKUs) of packaged tours, covering over 140 countries worldwide and all the popular tourist attractions in China. Tuniu provides one-stop leisure travel solutions and a compelling customer experience through its online platform and offline service network, including a 24/7 call center, 180 regional service centers, and 11 international centers. There are 24 branches in China and 20 all over the world.

Job description: I design and plan outbound packaged tours for the Changsha region and coordinate the operation of different sectors.

Career path: I began as a procurement staff member and was promoted to procurement manager. I have witnessed the ups and downs of the company and have worked at different sectors.

Likes and dislikes about the job: What I like the most are the strict rules, streamlined guidelines, and equal opportunities to move up the career ladder.

Advice for Undergraduates

Pay attention to the development of Internet technologies and online travel. Keep an eye on the general trends of the tourism industry and learn about rivals and partners. Go to frontline sales desks to understand the supply and demand aspects of the market.

With continuing advancements in technology, sport industry professionals have access to more data than ever before. These data have been used as a valuable resource in

- injury prevention,
- team and player performance enhancement,
- increasing revenue, and
- evaluating sponsorship effectiveness, just to name a few applications.

Sport analytics is a field with opportunities emerging at all levels of play. There is widespread use of sport analytics by professional and collegiate sport, as well as by competitive recreational sports teams, and even by dedicated fans.

Personnel

Because technology is ever changing and its use is growing, recreational sport managers must hire additional staff to maintain up-to-date computer applications to assist with registration, scheduling, facility use, and marketing efforts. The ubiquity of technology and social media has yielded an increased demand for staff with unique skill sets in these areas. Individuals who are knowledgeable in web programming and communication on social platforms will be critical to sports programs. Sport agencies use social media platforms to advertise and monitor programs, and to communicate with their participants. Specialists will be needed to create and maintain an agency's online presence in the face of a volatile social media landscape.

Marketing has become a core activity for recreational sport management due to the diversity and rapid expansion of programs and facilities to meet the growing needs of participants. Recreational sport staffing now includes marketing specialists with the skills, experience, and dedicated time to plan and implement marketing strategies to support the sports programs and services. These staff members have a significant effect on the success of the agency because marketing can have a direct effect on participation, revenue, and program expenditures. National Recreation and Park Association's (NRPA) 2019 Marketing and Communications Report discussed the importance of increasing public awareness of programs for revenue generation and to sustain agency funding. Marketing is so vital in fact, NRPA published a free marketing and promotional tool kit on their website (2022).

Parental Concerns

Top parental concerns consist of

- long-term injury,
- quality or behavior of coaches,
- cost,
- time commitment, and
- overemphasis on winning and competition.

A major concern of parents regarding sport participation is injury. In the 2000s, news media began covering the alarming number of head injuries and related concussion issues that occur primarily in professional football but also in other sports and at the youth and collegiate levels. Parents and sport administrators are concerned. Many parents have chosen to not allow their children to participate in football, basketball, or other contact sports because of the increased risk of these types of head injuries. Sport administrators from the NFL down to the neighborhood youth sport association are now reviewing and updating sports rules, regulations, and standards for sports equipment, especially helmets used in football. The key to injury prevention, or reduction, is proper policy, education, and training of sport staff and volunteers. Increasing costs including travel, equipment, and fees can limit participation for children who are from a lower socioeconomic bracket, live in rural areas (Fleming et al., 2023), or have single-parent families and often a combination of these barriers. *The Cost of Winning* documentary provides a realistic view of the pressures of winning over fun in youth sports. Coaches, parents, and fans all too often lose sight of the purpose of youth sport, which is to learn and have fun playing the game. An overemphasis on winning can lead to stress, burnout, low self-esteem, poor self-concept, and many more negative outcomes. If winning is the only measure of success, then 50 percent of children that play are failing. Winning, when kept in proper perspective, can be a fun and important part of the game. Keeping these key issues in mind, sport administrators must ensure best practices and policy are established, communicated, and followed.

Paramount to recreational sport is staff education and the use of background checks among youth sports programs. Recreational sport agencies must ensure that all staff and volunteers be properly trained by providing educational sessions such as workshops, certification opportunities, educational materials, and routine supervision. In addition, screening staff and volunteers is no longer an option;

yearly criminal **background checks** should be mandatory for all coaches and volunteers for youth sport agencies (Gould, 2016). Despite the 2016 call from Gould, background checks were not mandated by federal law or policy in youth sports as of 2023.

Costs for background checks can be a concern for youth sport agencies. Ways to offset these costs are to

- require the staff member or volunteer to pay for the background check,
- have the agency pay part of the fee,
- use free sources (web, local, and state agencies), or
- seek grants or private funding to assist with costs.

Regardless, each youth sport agency must ensure the safety of its participants by requiring background checks.

Programming

Recreational sports and fitness programs are immensely popular and usually attract large numbers of participants. Millions of Americans partake in a variety of recreational sport and outdoor recreation activities throughout the year. *Sports, Fitness and Recreation Participation—Overview Report* (Physical Activity Council, 2022) summarizes data related to physical activity and sport participation and spending in the United States for people aged 6 and older. The 2021 study consisted of 18,000 interviews and included 122 sports and activities.

School physical education programs continue to be the key pathway to regular participation among youth during their school years as well as when they reach adulthood. Adults who reported having physical education are more likely to be active as adults with 80 percent reporting they were still active in 2021 (Physical Activity Council, 2022).

From a programming perspective, recreational sport programmers must stay abreast of key trends as well as account for postpandemic changes to marketing when planning and developing sport activities for their agencies. Table 14.1 provides the estimated number of participants in several recreational sport activities. Knowing and understanding participant trends can provide a better understanding of participant needs and interests, which can enable agencies to better plan, design, and implement comprehensive recreational sports programs.

Participation in outdoor sports such as stand-up paddleboarding is increasing.

Cavan Images/Getty Images/Getty Images

Table 14.1 Participation Rates by Activity Category

Rank	Category	Participant rate
1	Fitness sports	67.3%
2	Outdoor sports	53.9%
3	Individual sports	41.9%
4	Team sports	22.4%
5	Water sports	14.0%
6	Racket sports	14.0%
7	Winter sports	8.1%

Physical Activity Council (2022).

INTERNATIONAL PARTICIPATION IN RECREATIONAL SPORT

Although participation in recreational sport is immensely popular in the United States, it is just as popular in many other countries. A new report predicts by 2025 global sport participation will include 3.5 billion people, resulting in a US$1.1 trillion sports market (SIGNA Sports United & Boston Consulting Group, 2021). Approximately 67 percent of Canadian children aged 3 to 17 years participated in organized sports (Solutions Research Group Consultants Inc., 2023). In England, 28.6 million people aged 16 years and older participated in recreational sports at least once per week in 2019 (Sport England, 2020). According to the Global Matrix 3.0 on Physical Activity, of the 49 counties surveyed, Denmark scored the highest on organized sport participation (Active Healthy Kids Global Alliance, 2022). Recreational sport participation continues to be a priority for these countries and others. Many have made sport and active recreation a key policy priority in order to improve national concerns such as fitness, health, economic development, community cohesion, and social equity.

CAREER OPPORTUNITIES

Although a general core of sport management competencies is required to work in the sport management profession, the various career settings and venues will dictate specific competency areas. Those interested in working in professional sport management will need advanced knowledge of business and marketing principles and techniques, whereas recreational sport professionals will need more knowledge in sports programming, including

- tournament scheduling,
- personnel management (e.g., officials, supervisors, lifeguards),
- training and scheduling, and
- facility management.

Regardless of the career path chosen, the growing popularity of sports programs will create significant demand for competent professionals, both full- and part-time, who can deliver and oversee sport management programs and services in diverse employment settings. The number of positions and specific job responsibilities will vary depending on the sport setting.

Five Sectors of Recreational Sport Organizations

With the growth and interest in recreational sports programs, there have been increased opportunities for employment ranging from leadership positions working face-to-face with participants to top administrative positions. The following five general levels of personnel (figure 14.2) are commonly found in settings that provide recreational sport management (Barcelona et al., 2016):

- *Upper-level administration*. The administrative staff personnel are the ultimate authorities and provide the overall direction and leadership for the entire recreational sports program and its resources including staff, budget, facilities, and equipment. Specific duties of the administrator are to
  - determine the nature, scope, and direction of the program;
  - evaluate overall program efficiency in terms of goals and standards;
  - provide guidelines, establish priorities, and determine schedules for the acquisition and construction of recreational sport facilities; and
  - explain policy and major program changes to staff and the public.

Typical job titles at this level are administrator, director, or executive director. Because of the wide range of recreational sports programs and the need for experience in decision making, top administrators usually hold a master's degree and have a minimum of 10 years of experience.

- *Middle management*. Middle management are full-time professionals who support upper-level administration. They also help formulate and administer policies, guidelines, and resources while monitoring programs, facilities, and program staff. People in this role serve as liaisons between the top administrator and the program staff in day-to-day decision making. Job titles are often specific to the sport setting, but general titles at this level include

- associate director,
- program director,
- fitness director,
- public relations director,
- operations director,
- facility manager, and
- sport coordinator or director.

People in these positions usually hold bachelor's degrees and many hold master's degrees in recreation, sport management, or a related field and have a minimum of five years of programming-related experience.

- *Program staff.* This refers to many entry-level positions within an organization. Work responsibilities require specialized skills and training in organizing and conducting various sports programs. People in this role may initiate publicity and promotion, purchase and inventory equipment, and implement policies for safety, participant control, and governance. The program staff is also responsible for recruiting, hiring, training, and scheduling support staff, including sport officials, lifeguards, and supervisors. Typical job titles are

- assistant director,
- marketing assistant,
- coordinator,
- building manager,
- personal trainer,
- pool operator,
- leader, and
- activity specialist.

Many of these positions require a bachelor's degree, but many employers prefer candidates with master's degrees.

- *Contingent staff.* The contingent staff are part-time, hourly, or volunteer positions that engage in face-to-face contact with the program participants. The contingent staff primarily consists of seasonal or part-time positions such as

- officials,
- scorekeepers,
- supervisors,
- aerobics and group exercise leaders,
- equipment room attendants,
- aquatics instructors,
- fitness consultants,
- facility entry attendants,
- lifeguards,
- maintenance crews, and
- youth sport coaches.

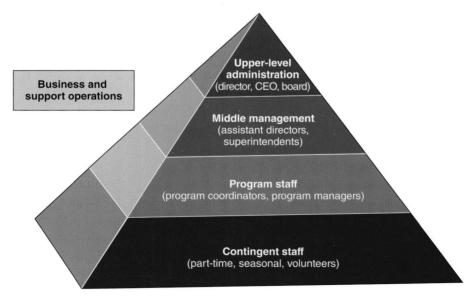

Figure 14.2 Five sectors of recreational sport organizations.

Reprinted by permission from R. Barcelona, *Recreational Sport: Program Design, Delivery, and Management* (Champaign, IL: Human Kinetics, 2016), 152.

Although this is the level at which many program staff members gain experience, people seeking employment at this level usually do not have degrees but might have some type of specialized sport credential or certification such as first aid, water safety instructor, CPR, sport official, or youth sport coach.

- *Business and support operations.* Business and support operations provide technical assistance to the other four sectors to help the recreational sport organization achieve its core mission. Support staff
  - provide administrative assistance,
  - perform maintenance duties,
  - coordinate transportation, or
  - handle hospitality and business services, such as vending or merchandising.

Additional support could also come in the areas of marketing, accounting, purchasing, or human resources management depending on the size and scope of the recreational sport organization. Most recreational sport organizations will use business and support operations staff in some capacity, although the exact positions will differ depending on organization and setting. Some of the job functions of business and support operations may be embedded in other staff positions such as marketing, financial accounting, program evaluation, or human resources management.

Job Outlook

Finding a career in recreational sport management is a promising prospect for those willing to pursue it. There are various levels of recreational sport management positions in thousands of for-profit and nonprofit institutions throughout the United States. These institutions support recreational sports programs that serve millions of people of all ages. In many settings, the demand for qualified recreational sport management specialists far exceeds the supply, which provides great job opportunities for students interested in this field. According to the Bureau of Labor Statistics (2021), employment of recreation workers is projected to grow 10 percent from 2021 to 2031, faster than the average for all occupations. Moreover, with the projected growth of global sports participation and market, finding employment in sport management is very promising. Employment opportunities in recreational sport management include the following:

- The Amateur Athletics Union (AAU), founded in 1888, has a philosophy of "sports for all, forever" that is shared by nearly 700,000 participants and more than 150,000 volunteers in the United States. The AAU is divided into 56 distinct associations that annually sanction more than 34 sports programs, 250 national championships, and over 30,000 age-division events across the country. These activities and events provide employment opportunities involving sport facilities, programming, and operations (Amateur Athletics Union, 2021).

- Armed forces recreation supports a full range of sport and recreation services for military service personnel and their families in all branches of the U.S. military. Sport programmers and sport directors run programs and manage facilities on military bases and installations in the United States and throughout the world. The personnel support division of the Canadian Forces Personnel Support Agency is the key provider of recreational services within the Canadian military environment.

- Boys and Girls Clubs of America serve more than 4.6 million youth in more than 4,700 chartered clubs in the United States. It is one of the fastest growing youth services agencies and has nearly 64,000 trained full-time professional staff members (Boys and Girls Clubs of America, 2021). The Boys and Girls Clubs of Canada serve 200,000 children and youth in 736 community-based locations nationwide. The organization has more than 6,800 trained full-time and part-time staff (BGC Canada, 2020).

- The Association of Church Sports and Recreation Ministers (CSRM) serves a network of church recreation and sport ministry professionals.

- The Canadian government funds the National Sport Organizations (NSOs), which oversees 58 sports programs in Canada. Alpine skiing alone has over 50,000 volunteers and 200,000 supporting members (Government of Canada, 2021).

- Collegiate and campus settings offer a variety of recreational sport career opportunities across the United States.

- Commercial sports offer thousands of job opportunities in country clubs, bowling centers, theme parks, health and fitness spas, racket clubs, tennis centers, ski resorts, golf courses, aquatic centers, hotels, and natural settings for boating, rafting, and fishing.

- Correctional recreation programs are staffed by practitioners at the federal, state, and local levels who work in juvenile, medical, and community-based facilities. A growing emphasis in this specialty is on promoting inmate health and fitness and providing sport opportunities.

- Employee recreational sports provide career opportunities for sport programmers in business, commercial, and industrial employee recreational sports programs.

- As of 2023, fitness is a $30.8 billion industry in the United States alone and expected to increase by 6 percent by the end of the year (Ibisworld, 2023).

- The International Health, Racquet and Sportsclub Association (IHRSA) is a global trade association that represents more than 200,000 health and fitness facilities around the world. The IHRSA predicts a rebound of health clubs, gyms and studios (IHRSA, 2021).

- Municipal parks and recreation departments provide recreational sports and physical activity programming for children, youth, adults, and seniors in towns and cities throughout the United States and Canada.

- State games festivals are organized by the State Games of America, a property of the National Congress of State Games (NCSG), which is a membership organization composed of 30 summer state games and 10 winter state games organizations. The NCSG is a community-based member of the U.S. Olympic Committee. Nearly 200,000 athletes of all ages, backgrounds, and skill levels participate nationwide (National Congress of State Games, 2021). Job opportunities are available at the national and state levels for full-time sport directors and event management coordinators as well as thousands of volunteers needed to conduct these large, multisport events across the United States.

- The Y (formally known as the YMCA and YWCA) employs approximately 230,000 professionals. The Y serves more than 64 million participants in 120 countries and employs over 2,000 people (YMCA, 2021). YMCA Canada is a federation of all 39 Ys in Canada and serves 2.25 million members and hosts 424 staff. Each of the 47 clubs is independent, hires its own staff, and recruits its own volunteers (YMCA Canada, 2021).

Professional Associations and Organizations

Sport management professionals need to remain current in theoretical and practical concerns in the field. Many sport practitioners hold active memberships in a variety of professional associations and organizations that sponsor a wide range of continuing education courses, institutes, workshops, regional and national conferences, and other in-service training for people working in this field. The National Intercollegiate Sports Association (NIRSA) is comprised of over 4,500 members and promotes the importance of collegiate recreation for lifelong wellness (n.d.). Associations and organizations provide practitioners and students with opportunities for conferences, workshops, seminars, and management schools that help them stay abreast of trends and practices and their implications for program delivery in the rapidly changing sport management field.

Here are some related professional sports organizations:

- Club Management Association of America (CMAA)
- International Facility Management Association (IFMA)
- International Health, Racquet, & Sports Club Association (IHRSA)
- National Association for Girls and Women in Sport (NAGWS)
- National Association for Campus Activities (NACA)
- National Association of Sports Commissions (NASC)
- National High School Athletic Coaches Association (NHSACA)
- National Institute for Fitness and Sport (NIFS)
- National Interscholastic Athletic Administrators Association (NIAAA)
- National Ski Areas Association (NSAA)
- North American Society for the Psychology of Sport and Physical Activity (NASPSPA)
- North American Society for Sport Management (NASSM)
- Sports Field Management Association (SFMA)
- Sportsplex Operators and Developers Association (SODA)
- Stadium Managers Association (SMA)
- Women in Sports and Events (WISE)
- Women's Sports Foundation (WSF)

SUMMARY

The role of recreational sport as an integral part of human enjoyment and vitality is well established and recognized. Participation in sport for fun and fitness is a very popular leisure-time pursuit among Americans and Canadians. Active participation in recreational sports is an important part of day-to-day existence for many people and involves an individual's choice of participating in structured sports (instructional, intramural, extramural, club) or self-directed sports (informal) in a multitude of sport settings. These settings, which range from municipal parks and recreation, campus recreation, YMCA, esports, and military installations to youth service organizations, offer recreational sports programs and events that provide mental, physical, social, and emotional benefits to all participants.

With the increasing interest in recreational sport participation and fitness activity for all age groups, there is a need for broad-based recreational sports programming that reflects these needs and interests. This will continue to spur the growth of recreational sport management and provide a variety of exciting and fulfilling job opportunities in diverse settings.

Review Questions

1. What is a major defining characteristic of recreational sport management that separates it from professional sport management?

2. What are the major concerns of parents in youth sport?

3. Discuss the five areas of recreational sports.

4. Name and discuss at least five areas of employment in recreational sport management.

Go to *HKPropel* to complete the activities for this chapter.

CHAPTER 15

Health, Wellness, and Quality of Life

Rhonda Cross Beemer, Matthew Symonds, and Terrance Robertson

" The first wealth is health. "

Ralph Waldo Emerson,
American poet, lecturer,
and essayist, 1803-1882

Mike Harrington/Stone RF/Getty Images

LEARNING OUTCOMES

After reading this chapter, you should be able to do the following:

> Describe at least three current trends in health

> Share the four factors that affect health

> Explain the interconnectedness of the dimensions of wellness

> Discuss at least three roles that parks, recreation, and allied professions play in developing and maintaining healthy lifestyles

As one of three pillars of the National Recreation and Park Association, health and wellness promotion plays a critical part in the daily activities of effective parks and recreation professionals. This role facilitates the development of healthier communities, healthier citizens, and improved quality of life. This chapter provides a broad overview of three areas where parks and recreation professionals have widespread influence:

- Health
- Wellness
- Quality of life

The personal and professional growth opportunities in these areas are limitless for future parks and recreation professionals who are committed, motivated, academically prepared, and appropriately credentialed. Although people generally appreciate the benefits of good health, many take it for granted until it is gone. Health experts have long advocated for the implementation of diverse behaviors to prevent disease and disability, a view that importantly goes beyond clinical treatment of signs and symptoms of illness. As long ago as 1946, the World Health Organization (WHO) adopted the following definition of health: a "state of complete physical, mental, and social well-being and not merely the absence of disease and infirmity" (Grad, 2002) in their constitution. This definition still stands and can be found in the WHO Constitution.

While education has improved for many populations, income levels have risen, and life expectancies have changed, societal, technological, and behavioral changes have led to increasing incidence of lifestyle-related diseases such as obesity and diabetes. In North America, adult obesity is increasing (CDC, 2022a). This singular health concern presents many challenges and opportunities for people entering parks and recreation and related professions. As you learn more about health, wellness, and quality of life in this chapter, think about the important

foundational information you can gather and use as a future parks and recreation professional. Also consider the fact that parks and recreation professionals are uniquely positioned in communities to

- have a widespread impact on a community's physical and mental health,
- assist in building more healthy communities, and
- improve the quality of life for the diverse communities served.

There are also related career opportunities specifically focused on health and wellness promotion. This chapter provides an overview of each of these areas for future parks and recreation professionals to examine.

PERSONAL HEALTH

Individual or **personal health** is a specialized discipline. Those interested in this area professionally can find careers in the health sciences, such as

- primary care physician,
- physical therapist,
- athletic trainer,
- health educator,
- dietitian, and many other career paths.

While the career opportunities are broad, there is often specialized education or training, requiring unique professional preparation. Other careers with a health connection include epidemiology, geographic information systems, and emergency and disaster preparedness, to name a few.

Personal health and wellness are often assessed using a standard set of indicators and **anthropometric** (or biometric) **measurements**, including

- blood pressure,
- body mass index,

- cholesterol screening,
- amount and intensity of physical activity,
- dietary consumption,
- alcohol and tobacco use, and
- access to health care.

Ultimately, each person's health affects both **community health** and population health.

Current State of Health in the United States and Canada

People in many locations are living longer than previous generations. According to data published in 2019, the life expectancy in the United States is 78.7 years (Kochanek et al., 2020). In contrast, the life expectancy in the United States during 1940 was 62.9 years, meaning life expectancy has increased nearly 16 years in about eight decades. Similarly, Canada is experiencing changes in its population. Life expectancy at birth in Canada has significantly improved, peaking in the 2014 to 2016 period with men reaching 79.9 years and women reaching 84 years (Statistics Canada, 2018). Globally, the life expectancy has also increased to over the age of 72 since 2019 (Roser et al., 2019). However, life expectancy and death rates will likely be affected by the global COVID-19 pandemic. For example, preliminary estimates project that COVID-19 is expected to lower life expectancy by nearly 18 months (Czeisler & Czeisler, 2022).

As life expectancy provides one view on population health, the health status of the youngest members of society also provides a picture of overall health. U.S. infant mortality rates have shrunk to historic lows of just under six deaths per 1,000 live births (Xu et al., 2021). Infant mortality rates in Canada have decreased to less than five deaths per 1,000 live births, with more than half of the infants dying within 24 hours of birth (Statistics Canada, 2018). According to the WHO (The Global Health Observatory, n.d.), global infant mortality rates have declined from 65 deaths per 1,000 live births in 1990 to 29 deaths per 1,000 live births in 2018. Since 2020, neonatal deaths have dropped from 5 million to 2.4 million (WHO, 2022a). Generally, lower infant and child mortality rates equate to healthier communities and clearly have a positive effect on life expectancy at large.

According to the 2019 Youth Risk Behavior Survey results, many U.S. high school students still engage in behaviors that can lead to compromised health, and some of these behaviors can have health implications that last into adulthood. Some behaviors, such as sexual risk behavior among high school students, have improved due to the decrease in the number of high school students reporting having sex as well as a decline in the number of multiple partners of four or more for those high school students. Although sexual activity may have decreased, other behaviors like condom use have also decreased, presenting serious health risks for sexually transmitted diseases. Other health risk behaviors that continue to be areas of concern include

- not wearing a seat belt,
- texting and driving,
- riding in a car with a driver who has been drinking,
- using marijuana or alcohol, and
- smoking cigarettes (CDC, 2020).

In addition, many violence and safety issues exist for this segment of the population.

High school students' nutrition and physical activity practices continue to be of concern. Poor eating habits and low physical activity levels are associated with obesity, type 2 diabetes, and heart disease, all of which are increasing in children and young adults in the United States. Data indicate that people with obesity, compared to those at a healthy weight, are at an increased risk for multiple serious illnesses, including overall mortality, high blood pressure, cholesterol and triglyceride issues, and type 2 diabetes (CDC, 2022a). Childhood obesity concerns may be associated with low socioeconomic status and education level. Data indicate that there is less obesity among families in the highest income grouping (CDC, 2022b). Health literacy may play a role in this. By improving knowledge and skills (health literacy) through primary care–based intervention, weight gain will be reduced in the first 18 months of life (Sanders et al., 2021).

The economic impact of obesity is staggering. In 2008, the annual medical costs related to obesity in the United States were $147 billion. In fact, a large portion of the nation's total health care costs is incurred by treating lifestyle-related chronic diseases. In addition, there is growing concern regarding obesity as a national security issue. For example, as many as 71 percent of people between the ages of 17 to 24 do not qualify for military service due to obesity (CDC, 2022a). Despite dialogue and public attention, lifestyle-related health concerns remain a

Poor eating habits and low physical activity levels are associated with obesity, type 2 diabetes, and heart disease.

pressing issue. These health-related issues result in many opportunities for parks and recreation professionals. Addressing health-related issues affect all parts of comprehensive parks and recreation operations, including facilities and programs in rural, suburban, and urban settings.

Issues of health, wellness, and quality of life are of interest to professionals, educators, and people at community, national, and global levels. Health assessment and surveillance have taken place for many years throughout the world. Similarly, parks and recreation professionals around the world are interested in analyzing health status and implementing health promotion and disease prevention strategies. In its 2020 charter, the World Leisure Organization (WLO) includes several concepts directly related to health promotion and recreation:

- Ensure availability and protection of open spaces for recreation in residential areas
- Ensure suitable space and facilities for children's play

- Support for health-enhancing amenities, such as facilities for sport and exercise
- Ensure that all members of the community have access to leisure facilities and services
- Support training of a workforce for the leisure, sport, and cultural service industries
- Support research on the benefits and costs of leisure activity
- Recognize leisure-related legislation, policy, and regulations
- Support for community access to food, clothing, housing, medical care, necessary social services, and security (World Leisure Organization, 2020)

The ideas in the WLO charter indicate that the organization continues to focus on several factors that affect health and well-being, including an emphasis on a number of the components of wellness outlined in this chapter.

Factors That Affect Health

The four major categories that affect health are

1. genetic and personal factors,
2. health behaviors,
3. health care factors, and
4. environmental factors.

Although it is not an exhaustive list, table 15.1 outlines several important items in each of these categories.

Positive changes in health behaviors are important for developing a healthy population and economy. Research has demonstrated that even moderate changes in health behaviors, such as decreased smoking, increased fruit and vegetable consumption and physical activity, and decreased alcohol consumption, can have significant health benefits that can lead to improved **morbidity**, even if **mortality** is not affected (Irvin & Kaplan, 2016).

A Global Perspective

Many indicators of health are monitored globally by experts who look for triangulation of causes or indicators. Individual indicators are direct or leading indicators, whereas others are considered secondary or contributing indicators or factors. Examples of leading indicators include low birth weight and genetic risk factors. For example, as seen in figure 15.1, **body mass index (BMI)**, which is a secondary indicator of obesity, is tracked by the WHO (2021)

Table 15.1   Selected Factors That Affect Health

Genetic and personal factors	Health behaviors	Health care factors	Environmental factors
Age Body mass index Body type Sex Height Race and ethnicity Weight	Alcohol consumption Fruit and vegetable consumption Hours of sleep Physical activity Seat belt use Stress management Tobacco use	Access to health care Regular physical examinations Blood pressure Blood glucose levels Preventative age- and gender-specific screenings Total cholesterol (HDL & LDL)	Access to fitness facilities Access to healthy food sources Access to parks and trails Access to public transportation Living environment Working environment Air and water quality

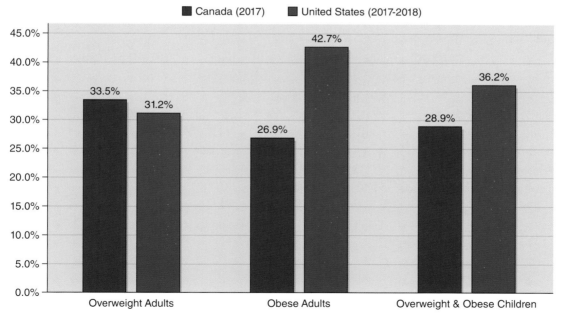

Figure 15.1   Overweight and obesity prevalence of adults and children in Canada and United States.

Data from data.worldobesity.org (2021).

and shared globally. Globally, obesity has almost tripled since 1975. More than 1.9 billion adults were overweight with over 650 million of them being classified as obese in 2016. Worldwide in 2020, 39 million children under the age of 5 were considered overweight or obese, and over 340 million children and adolescents aged 5 to 19 were overweight or obese. We have now reached the point at which more people are dying from being overweight than from being underweight (WHO, 2021).

Leading causes of death are another common way to monitor health and often vary by geographic region and income level. However, the majority of the top global causes of death are associated with cardiovascular diseases, respiratory diseases, and neonatal conditions. These causes can be grouped in communicable diseases, noncommunicable diseases, and injuries (WHO, 2020). A comparison of the top 10 leading causes of death for 2019 in Canada and the United States is shown in table 15.2 (WHO, 2020). It should be noted that this table does not include data in regard to the COVID-19 pandemic. According to the Centers for Disease Control and Prevention (2021b), the leading causes of death are similar; however, heart disease and cancer are the top two leading causes, while COVID-19 is the third leading cause of death in 2020. Due to the morbidity and mortality across the globe related to COVID-19, it is expected that the leading cause of death as well as years of life lost will change in the coming years once more data are collected.

Health can be illustrated from multifaceted perspectives. One example of a multifaceted model includes personal factors, environmental factors, and situational factors; this PES model attempts to address the previously mentioned major factors that affect health:

- Genetic and personal factors
- Health behaviors
- Health care factors
- Environmental factors (see figure 15.2)

There are also communication and health logic models and complex plotting and factoring models to understand factors such as relationships, timelines, causation, and so on. Ideally, model development would allow

- the prescription of services (assessment, monitoring, treatment, etc.) and
- the implementation of potential interventions to decrease morbidity and mortality.

Parks and recreation professionals should approach the development of health promotion programs from a multifaceted perspective.

Historically, the United States has focused on diagnosis and treatment of disease. Only in the last decade has it moved to adopting a health promotion or prevention perspective that includes a more holistic wellness approach. Other countries have previously adopted the prevention or well-

Table 15.2 Top 10 Leading Causes of Death (2019), Canada and United States

CANADA		UNITED STATES	
Cause	Death rate per 100K population	Cause	Death rate per 100K population
Ischemic heart disease	107.1	Ischemic heart disease	153.4
Alzheimer's disease and other dementias	82.8	Alzheimer's disease and other dementias	87.3
Trachea, bronchus, lung cancers	56	Chronic obstructive pulmonary disease	59.4
Chronic obstructive pulmonary disease	38	Stroke	48.2
Stroke	37.8	Trachea, bronchus, lung cancers	47.3
Colon and rectum cancers	25.8	Kidney diseases	26.1
Lower respiratory infections	19.9	Drug use disorders	22.6
Breast cancer	15.8	Hypertensive heart disease	20
Diabetes mellitus	15.3	Colon and rectum cancers	18.8
Lymphomas, multiple myeloma	13.8	Diabetes mellitus	18.7

From: World Health Organization (2021). Available: https://www.who.int/data/gho/data/themes/mortality-and-global-health-estimates/ghe-leading-causes-of-death.

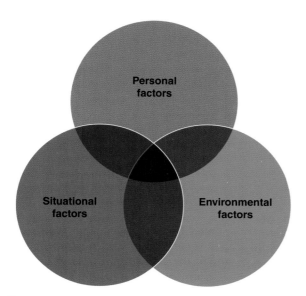

Figure 15.2 In the PES model, health can be viewed as interaction of personal factors, environmental factors, and situational factors.

ness model. Regardless of the treatment or prevention activity, service providers usually focus their activities on people within prescribed geographic areas, sometimes expanding based on patterns of individuals or diseases.

Assessment and monitoring of disease and the use of evidence-based diagnosis and treatment are collaborative global efforts. The WHO is generally considered responsible for collection and dissemination of these data on a global level. Both the United States and Canada utilize agencies such as Health and Human Services, National Institutes of Health, Health Canada, or the World Health Organization for

- monitoring and researching health,
- communicating with the public about health issues, and
- assisting the public with maintaining and improving health.

In addition, local public health departments also assist in the collection and dissemination of health data and the provision of health services.

THE WELLNESS PERSPECTIVE

In thinking about the WHO's early definition of health, the current state of health, and the factors that affect health, we begin to see that achieving optimal health is a multidimensional endeavor. This

whole-person approach can be referred to as **wellness**. The wellness perspective includes examining health across several interrelated components or dimensions, including

- physical wellness,
- intellectual wellness,
- emotional wellness,
- social wellness,
- environmental wellness,
- occupational wellness, and
- spiritual wellness.

This holistic approach helps us make a connection between our health, wellness, and quality of life. This holistic approach to health also demonstrates a clear role for parks and recreation professionals in the health promotion process for individuals and communities at large.

Even though a great deal of information is available at our fingertips, not all consumers have the same level of health literacy. **Health literacy** can be defined as the degree to which people have the capacity to obtain, process, and understand basic health information and services needed to make appropriate health decisions. The degree of health literacy affects every dimension of wellness (see figure 15.3), and it is an important consideration for those entering parks, recreation, and other health-related professions. Here we explore these interconnected wellness dimensions.

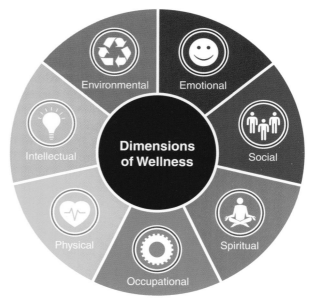

Figure 15.3 The seven dimensions of wellness.

Physical Wellness

Nutrition and physical activity provide foundations for overall wellness. People control several components of physical wellness such as eating and activity habits. Let's explore some accepted guidelines as well as the roles that parks and recreation might play in physical wellness.

Proper nutrition has many health benefits, such as decreasing the likelihood that a person will become overweight or obese and decreasing the risks for some chronic diseases, such as high blood pressure, type 2 diabetes, and some cancers. The amount and types of food people eat greatly affect health. For example, a child will have different calorie and nutritional needs compared to an adult. If calorie guidelines are met but there is poor nutrition, detrimental health impacts are still likely. In addition, calorie requirements vary based on other factors such as physical activity levels.

Commonly accepted dietary practices

- recommend a healthy diet that emphasizes fruits, vegetables, whole grains, and low-fat or fat-free dairy;
- include lean meats, poultry, fish, beans, eggs, and nuts; and
- are low in certain fats, cholesterol, sodium, and added sugar.

Although people might understand the importance of proper nutrition, many do not meet recommended dietary guidelines. You can learn more about proper nutrition, develop an individual nutrition plan, and track your progress at MyPlate: http://myplate.gov.

Being physically active is not an all-or-nothing proposition. Health benefits can be derived even from low levels of physical activity. According to the WHO (2022), one in four adults do not meet the global recommended amount of physical activity, and more than 80 percent of the world's adolescents are lacking sufficient physical activity. Inactive individuals have a 20 to 30 percent increased risk of death compared to those completing recommended physical activity requirements. Per estimates, up to five million deaths could be prevented annually if the global population was more physically active.

The World Health Organization offers specific physical activity recommendations for all ages.

- For the youngest children, physical activity guidelines range from "tummy time" prone positioning activities for infants to vigorous intensity activity for children nearing age 5.

- For children and adolescents aged 5 to 17, 60 minutes of moderate to vigorous intensity of physical activity (MVPA) per day, primarily in the form of aerobic activity, should be completed. In addition, for this same age group, three days per week should be dedicated to vigorous-intensity aerobic activities and muscle strengthening activities.
- For adults (aged 18-64), a range of 150 to 300 minutes of moderate-intensity aerobic physical activity or 75 to 150 minutes of vigorous-intensity aerobic physical activity (or a combination of moderate- and vigorous intensity activity) should be completed throughout the week. Additionally, two or more days of muscle strengthening activities throughout the week are recommended.
- Finally, adults 65 and older should meet the MVPA requirements as outlined for other adults and also incorporate functional balance and strength training three or more days per week.

Across the life span, sedentary activity should be decreased (WHO, 2022b). This creates many opportunities for recreation professionals to develop and implement physical activity programs for all ages and skill levels. Moreover, there are additional opportunities to provide targeted programming in women's health, to address specific recommendations for pregnant and postpartum women without contraindications (WHO, 2022b).

Physical activity requirements present several opportunities for parks and recreation programs. Efforts must be made to create community programs for youth that instill a healthy mind-set for the future. Separate programming for aging populations should also be included. Combining physical activity and nutritional programs will further enhance people's health.

There are many benefits to leading a physically active lifestyle, such as

- controlling weight;
- decreasing the risk of cardiovascular disease, type 2 diabetes, metabolic syndrome, and some cancers;
- strengthening bones and muscles;
- improving mental health and abilities to complete activities of daily living;
- increasing life expectancy;
- improved sleep quality;
- fall and other injury reduction; and
- overall enhanced quality of life.

Improving the physical dimension of wellness can assist in improving many other dimensions as well.

Physical activity, nutrition, and weight management programs are commonplace in all sectors of the parks and recreation profession, including worksite wellness programs, health clubs, public parks, hiking and biking trails, and aquatic facilities. Programs and facilities managed by parks and recreation professionals provide outlets for physical activity for individuals, families, and communities. Physical activity and nutrition trends point toward a continued focus on these programs and services for parks and recreation professionals. People will continue to visit spas, national parks, and other destinations to improve personal health.

Intellectual Wellness

One of the many benefits of physical activity is improved cognitive function. Intellectual wellness focuses on learning throughout life. We live in a

---

OUTSTANDING GRADUATE

Danae Holtman

Background Information

Name: Danae Holtman

Education: BS in applied health science with an emphasis in exercise sport from Northwest Missouri State University (NWMSU), College of Health Sciences; doctorate of physical therapy from Des Moines University, physical therapy department

Credentials: PT, DPT

Career Information

Position: Physical Therapist

Organization: Mosaic Life Care-Maryville, Missouri. Mosaic Life Care is a physician-led health care system serving 35 counties in northwest Missouri, northeast Kansas, southeast Nebraska, and southwest Iowa. The Maryville location has 81 certified beds, is a level III stroke center, and has four rural health care clinics. Services provided include inpatient, outpatient, primary, specialty, emergency, and behavioral health. With hospitals, clinics, and medical centers in St. Joseph, Maryville, and Albany, Missouri, the organization serves a population of approximately 270,000 and is the largest employer in the region with more than 4,000 employees.

Organization mission: To improve population health outcomes in the region by providing the right care, at the right time, place, and cost.

Job description: I currently work as an outpatient and inpatient physical therapist. In the outpatient setting, I work with a variety of patients from 0 to 99 years old with musculoskeletal impairments, surgical revisions, and generalized weaknesses. I take a special interest in treating a majority of our pediatric patients. I also work in the inpatient setting on the med/surg floor working with a variety of conditions including cardiac, respiratory, and musculoskeletal conditions. I focus on returning the patient back to their previous quality of life, making recommendations toward assistive devices that could aid them, or help patients and physicians determine discharge plans such as assisted living, skilled nursing facilities, or returning home independently based on patient safety. In both settings, we focus on pain relief, flexibility, strengthening, stabilization, mobilization, and use of modalities to serve each individual patient.

Likes and dislikes about the job:

- I love helping others achieve their personal goals regarding their health, quality of life, and level of activity. Helping someone go from 0 to 100 percent improvement is so rewarding. I also love educating the general public regarding anatomy, importance of exercise, and ways that physical therapy can improve overall well-being.

- One dislike of the physical therapy industry is the amount of time that we dedicate to documentation. Although very necessary, it reduces the amount of time we spend with patients.

Career path: My first job was babysitting throughout my summers with kids ages 0 to 10 years old. I then coached junior high softball for three years. In college, I worked for the mail/copy center on campus at NWMSU and was also a cake decorator at Hy-Vee.

Advice for Undergraduates

Don't be afraid to get involved. The best way to learn is to ask questions and get hands-on experience. Volunteer as much as you can in a variety of settings to gain diverse outlooks on a multitude of populations.

dynamic, changing, fast-paced world; to adapt, we need to continue to read, think, and reflect throughout our lives. Our minds require frequent stimulation. The adage "use it or lose it" applies to our bodies and our minds.

Although parks and recreation professionals may not consider intellectual development their primary goal, there are many programming and service opportunities for intellectual wellness development. A book club during which people discuss books while walking on a community trail contributes to physical and intellectual wellness. Creating a scavenger hunt in which children learn about the various plants and animals that can be seen in a park and then identify them on a map while exploring the environment is another example that incorporates learning and physical activity.

Using educational manipulatives will also enhance understanding and problem-solving. For example, a recreational professional can compile a list of items that can be seen while hiking on a nature trail. The professional can show learners a maple leaf, and they can touch it and ask questions about it, draw it, and identify which tree it belongs to. Once all objects are found and discussed, the learners can see how many they can identify on the next hike.

Adding a reflective portion to any parks and recreation activity will enhance learning. Professionals can embrace facilities as centers for lifelong learning where individuals, families, and communities gather to learn new skills and apply their knowledge and skills in recreation settings. The possibilities are limitless.

Emotional Wellness

Mental health issues and mood disorders are on the rise and can be directly linked to emotional well-being. In fact, more than 50 percent of people in the United States will be diagnosed with a mental illness or disorder at some time in their life (CDC, 2021a), and one in five Canadians will experience a mental health issue in a given year (Canadian Mental Health Association, National 2021). The National Institutes of Health (2015) notes that people who are emotionally well have fewer negative emotions and can bounce back from these challenges. The wellness perspective includes a component that encourages people to develop a skill set that will allow them to effectively handle these emotional encounters. New friendships, relationships, job challenges and opportunities, and the death of friends and family members are examples

of events that present emotional challenges. Parks and recreation programs can offer outlets that foster emotional development with many of these challenges; the programs can take place in urban and built environments as well as rural and wild areas, considering that spending time outside has been shown to have a positive impact on mental health of both adults and children.

Abundant research supports the link between emotional health and overall health. Stress has been linked to the six leading causes of death. Moreover, positive emotional health has been shown to increase longevity and increase productivity at work (American Psychological Association, 2011). Emotional health and the ability to cope with stress are important parts of a healthy life. People can deal with emotional situations in many ways that reinforce the interconnectedness of health and wellness such as

- learning stress management or meditation techniques;
- participating in physical activity, such as a running program or yoga class;
- eating a healthy diet;
- developing a support system of friends and family; or
- relying on religion or spiritual growth.

Although an improved outlook and attitude may not seem like a primary goal of many parks and recreation programs, because of the interrelated nature of the wellness perspective, emotional benefits are oftentimes a secondary outcome of many programs. Because exercise, dietary consumption, relationships, and stress management affect mental and emotional well-being, we can easily see the influence that parks and recreation can have on this important component of wellness.

Social Wellness

Humans are, by nature, social creatures. Social interaction is an important part of leading a well-rounded, healthy lifestyle. Social wellness represents a person's ability to interact and participate effectively in a variety of environments and includes

- communication skills,
- meeting new people and building relationships,
- showing respect for self and others, and
- developing a supportive network of family and friends.

Social wellness is also important in allowing people to participate effectively in the workplace, in communities, and in society.

Often, the concepts of compassion, volunteerism, fairness, inclusivity, and justice are viewed as parts of social wellness, and as part of social wellness, all aforementioned concepts can exist in parks and recreation programs. As leisure professionals, we frequently use volunteers in our programs. In addition, fairness and programming for everyone are fundamental to our efforts. Finally, we provide many opportunities for people to interact with one another while being active in leisure pursuits. Incorporating buddy systems, team challenges, and social ice breakers are just a few examples of these interactive opportunities. Parks and recreation professionals and programs provide social wellness opportunities across the life span.

Environmental Wellness

Environmental wellness has received increased attention over the past decade. As communities focus on green initiatives, the impact that the environment has on health has become more evident.

Ranging from access to parks, trails, and community fitness and recreation facilities to the products that we buy and the services that we use, everyone makes measurable contributions to the state of the environment. Conversely, environmental factors have an important effect on the wellness of people, communities, and regions.

For example, the natural environment in a state like Colorado may influence or lead to lower rates of obesity due to lifestyle activities, nutritional practices, type of career, and even cultural influences when compared to the environmental conditions in a major metropolitan area like New York City. In Colorado, many people are active in the natural environment, whereas in New York City (or other urban areas), individuals may need to attend a fitness center or exercise on sidewalks to be physically active, or travel to other locations to be active in the natural environment. In other words, built and natural environments affect multiple dimensions of wellness.

In many cases, parks and recreation professionals develop activities in natural and built environments all the time. Whether a built environment is used for developing parks and trails, campaigning for

One aspect of environmental wellness is access to community fitness and recreation facilities.

FG Trade/E+/Getty Images

a bond issue to build new facilities, or renovating existing parks and swimming pools, the built environment is often used to improve access to and use of public areas for physical activities. Clearly, these purposeful contributions are important to developing an environment that can promote wellness. In addition, developing environmentally friendly building and energy practices and providing prosocial opportunities, such as recycling programs or go-paperless programs, within parks and recreation sectors can instill a sense of purpose, fulfillment, and accomplishment for participants. This will also affect emotional wellness.

The Robertson and Robertson (R&R) model is helpful in understanding the relationships between a person's (or organization's) behavior, the environment, and the resources available (see figure 15.4).

- A person who has high regard for their environment and resources will interact with the environment and thus exhibit healthier behavior.

- A person who has low regard for their environment and resources will be inactive and thus exhibit behaviors that are less healthy.
- A person could have high regard for the environment and low regard for available resources and thus be reactive in exhibiting healthy behaviors.
- A person could have high regard for their resources and low regard for the environment, in which case the person would be proactive in exhibiting healthy behaviors.

To help someone move from one area to another (e.g., move from being inactive to proactive), a service provider would need to help the person increase their regard for resources or help improve or increase available resources. To help someone move from reactive to interactive, a service provider would need to help the person increase or improve available resources (real or perceived).

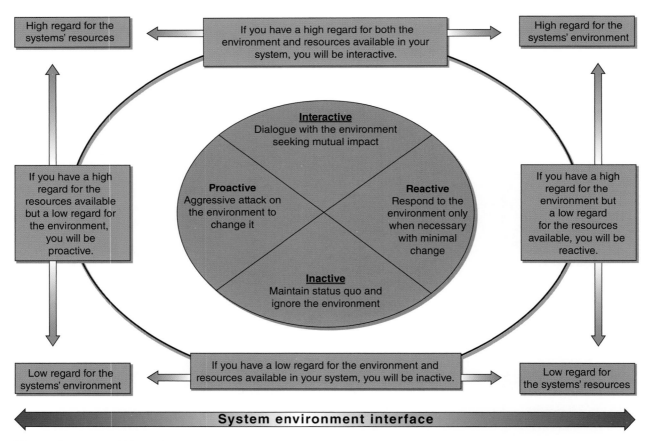

Figure 15.4 The R&R model of interaction between the environment and resources.

© Terry Robertson and Clifford Robertson.

Occupational Wellness

Occupational wellness is interconnected with many of the other dimensions of wellness. A person's occupation, as well as how that person performs in the occupation, is important and can directly affect physical health and emotional well-being. If a person is unable to balance their work activities with leisure time, then workplace stress can occur. Work performance can decrease and dissatisfaction in the workplace can increase, and this can also lead to an increase in illness. Health can decline due to poor occupational habits such as improper or risky techniques (causing physical injury), sedentary behavior, and poor dietary decisions during the workday. If a person is completely dissatisfied with the job, then emotional well-being is hindered.

What role can parks and recreation professionals play in improving occupational wellness? Programming can offer an outlet for employees before, during, or after work. Communicating programming efforts and teaming up with constituents in the area will improve the health and well-being of employees and will foster healthy relationships. By incorporating the physical dimension of wellness in the job (such as teaching and encouraging employees to be physically active and eat proper nutritional portions), the occupational well-being of workers and their production may also improve.

Parks and recreation professionals can team up with others in the community to promote healthy activities throughout the workday such as stress management, physical activity, and nutritional programming and education. Not all occupations and personnel will incur the same work-related health problems; therefore, it is important to have many programs available that allow for healthy activities and awareness throughout the workday. The health promotion activities can also directly relate to improvement of **health risk assessments (HRAs)**. Activities implemented by a parks and recreational professional might include exercises that can be done at the office, fitness challenges, or education on the importance of nutrition and hydration with an accompanying water or nutritional challenge. The programming is limitless, but it must address the specific needs of a community.

Spiritual Wellness

The spiritual wellness component is different for everyone because it involves values, ideals, beliefs, and purpose in life. Often, spiritual wellness is viewed as the concept of balance between what we need as individuals and our interactions with the world in which we live. According to the National Wellness Institute (2011), "you'll know you're becoming spiritually well when your actions become more consistent with your beliefs and values, resulting in a 'world view.'" Spiritual wellness follows these tenets:

- It is better to ponder the meaning of life for ourselves and to be tolerant of the beliefs of others than to close our minds and become intolerant.
- It is better to live each day in a way that is consistent with our values and beliefs than to do otherwise and feel untrue to ourselves (National Wellness Institute, 2011).

Each person can follow a different route to spiritual wellness. It may involve prayer, meditation, or other practices that support the person's progress toward a spiritual place or connection.

Measuring Health-Related Quality of Life

A growing field of research is concerned with developing, evaluating, and applying quality-of-life measures within health-related research (e.g., randomized controlled trials) and especially health services research. Many of these investigations focus on the measurement of health-related quality of life (HRQOL) rather than a more global conceptualization of quality of life. They also focus on measuring HRQOL from the perspective of the patient or person and thus take the form of self-completed questionnaires. The International Society for Quality of Life was founded in response to this research and is a useful source of information on the topic.

Many groups and agencies around the world, including the United Nations and the WHO, have tried to develop ways of assessing quality of life. In addition, many disciplines and individual researchers have studied or are currently studying quality of life, but few are studying this for people who have disabilities. Why do you think this is?

The roles of parks and recreation professionals in spiritual wellness promotion may be more passive than their roles in other areas. Although they may actively offer yoga or meditation classes, a sanctuary of escape, or travel, their roles in the development of spiritual wellness may be more about providing safe and positive places for people to practice their spirituality at their own pace and in their own way.

QUALITY OF LIFE, HEALTH, AND HEALTHY COMMUNITIES

The term *quality of life*, while frequently used, is sometimes overused or abused. Similarly, the term *healthy community* is familiar to many and can also be overused or abused. Combining these two terms when speaking of health (think about the definition of health previously provided) can further confuse issues, purpose, and intent, so each topic is briefly discussed here.

Quality of life (QOL) is often considered the degree of well-being felt by a person or group of people. Unlike a standard of living (SOL) approach that primarily uses socioeconomic measures to determine relative health or **health status**, QOL examines broader conceptual and theoretical constructs to describe it. As such, QOL is not a physically tangible concept, so it cannot be measured directly. Instead of using a single, direct type of measure (say economic status), an examination of QOL uses indicators that represent various aspects of health and wellness. QOL generally consists of two components:

1. The physical aspect includes items such as health, dietary consumption, physical activity (frequency, intensity, and time), and protection against pain and disease.

2. The psychological aspect includes stress, worry, pleasure, and other positive or negative emotional states.

Environmental QOL indicators often include

- air, water, and soil quality;
- dietary consumption and nutrition;
- access or lack of access to fresh foods;
- built or natural environments; and
- diseases caused by environmental exposure.

Holistic wellness, health, and health status are conceptually linked to QOL, and they have similar measures. Although these are all related, they are different in some key ways.

Another method for measuring differences in QOL is to examine differences in the standard of living (SOL) between individuals or groups based primarily on economic indicators. For example, income would be an indicator of health and a predictor of health status; therefore, the more a person earns, the better their health and health status should be. Further, according to the technical application of health status, people in rural areas and small towns, who generally have lower income levels, might be reluctant to move to larger urban areas even if doing so would mean a substantial increase in their standard of living (income). Conversely, some people living in urban areas might prefer a higher SOL in exchange for a lower QOL. Thus, the QOL experienced by living in a rural area may or may not be of enough value to offset a lower standard of living. Similarly, people are sometimes paid more to accept jobs that would lower their QOL. Night jobs, jobs that require extensive travel, or jobs that are potentially hazardous might pay more, so the difference in salaries can also be a measure of the value of QOL.

QOL, SOL, and wellness are integrally related. The measures or indicators can be similar or the same. In each of these areas, an ecological or holistic approach is preferred. Professionals and participants (individuals, patients, people with disabilities, seniors, organizations, cities, etc.) are interested in and concerned about affecting at least three things in order to make positive sustained changes or improvements:

- The **p**erson (or organization)
- The **e**nvironment
- Any leading or causal **s**ituations (PES)

The R&R model (figure 15.4) is an informal model that a person or organization can use for self-examination in relation to resources, environment, and interactions with each.

Predicting the QOL of a specific person is virtually impossible, because the combination of attributes that leads one person to be content is rarely the same for another. But we can presume with some confidence that better-than-average dietary consumption, shelter, safety, freedoms, and rights in a general population will result in a better overall QOL. As mentioned before, health literacy is one of the primary predictors of health status, and both health status and its predictors can be measured directly. Further, those who teach or provide health and recreation or wellness services are not the only ones who are interested in it. For instance, the magazine *International Living* focuses on quality of life for retirees (International Living, 2022).

Other examples of QOL indexes also exist, applying a variety of methodologies, including things like job security, the political environment, individual freedom, education, and the natural environment to determine an overall index. These indexes illustrate that there may be more to overall quality of life than thought of at first glance.

Economist Robert Putnam's seminal work *Bowling Alone* (2000) looks at the economic and civic effects of changing trends within communities. In the book, Putnam presents evidence from more than 500,000 interviews on how we have become increasingly disconnected from family, friends, neighbors, and our democratic structures. The issue of social capital (who we know) is also a major element of this book. Putnam warns that our stock of social capital has plummeted, impoverishing our lives and communities. As evidence, Putnam says that as a society we belong to fewer organizations that meet face-to-face, do not know our neighbors as well, meet with friends less frequently, and even socialize with our families less often. His evidence also indicates that we are bowling alone: Although more Americans are bowling than ever before, there are fewer self-described "bowlers," and they are not bowling in leagues. Bowling leagues and their tournaments have shrunk, thus providing their participants with less social capital. Factors that have contributed to this decline in social capital include changes in

- work,
- family structure,
- age,
- suburban life,
- social access,
- television,
- computers, and
- gender roles.

Putnam's metaphor of "bowling alone" is especially apt in 2023, given the prevalence of communication that occurs via the Internet (often anonymously) rather than in person (Hudson, 2020).

Alongside the previously listed factors, social media, technology, and the impact of social isolation since the start of the COVID-19 pandemic have all influenced socialization in the 2020s. Clearly, each of these factors is related to QOL. Given that civic engagement is a major part of the original thought behind the healthy communities movement, it is logical to surmise that those interested in civic engagement could also have interest in QOL.

More than having an interest in civic engagement, those interested in healthy communities are interested in

- the health of each person,
- the health of specific groups,
- the health of the community, and, of course,
- the health of the general population.

So what is a healthy community? A healthy community is one in which people (volunteers or paid personnel) come together to make their community (a place where they live, work, or play) better for themselves, their families, their friends, their neighbors, and others today and in the future. It is a community where citizens purposefully work together to create a healthier, more livable, and more sustainable environment. Creating such an environment takes time and commitment. A healthy community

- creates open and ongoing dialogue,
- generates leadership opportunities for all,
- embraces diversity,
- connects people of all ages and backgrounds, and
- fosters a sense of community.

More important, it shapes its future through a shared vision, shared work, and shared learning. Healthy communities are self-developed, self-guided, and self-directed. Most use common language and concepts, whereas others try to create unique terminology to help establish a specific identity or to brand themselves and their work.

Parks and recreation professionals should recognize that a healthy community is about more than physical activity; clean, safe, and nurturing programs, services, and environments are also essential. As a professional, you need to consider how your programs, services, and environments can contribute to the health of your community and its citizenry. Further, you should look at how you can do more than offer passive support. Instead, try to build the promotion of health and well-being into your place of work, the place where you live, and the leisure that you enjoy. Be a role model. Assess yourself, your family, and your environments, and identify opportunities to make a difference within the lives of others now and in the future.

Cooper Neill/Getty Images North America/Getty Images

Easily accessible playgrounds can increase the quality of life within a community.

HISTORY IN THE MAKING: HEALTHY COMMUNITIES

The term *healthy communities* owes its origins to a 1984 conference organized by Trevor Hancock in Toronto, Ontario. The conference, called Beyond Health Care, had one day set aside for discussion of the health of cities that developed into the concept of *healthy cities*. The healthy cities concept proposed the use of a comprehensive, community-based approach to improving public health. More specifically, a healthy city was defined as "one that is continually creating and improving those physical and social environments and strengthening those community resources which enable people to mutually support each other in performing all the functions of life and achieving their maximum potential" (Hancock & Duhl, 1988). As a result, a healthy cities network began in Europe. Subsequently, the U.S. Public Health Service facilitated a comprehensive nationwide examination for ways to improve the health of communities. The result was the start of the U.S. healthy communities movement.

From 1987 to 1997, two primary groups of actors were active within the movement:

1. Hospitals and health care providers
2. Related professionals and community problem-solvers (volunteers, civic leaders, investors, entrepreneurs, etc.)

Businesses, governments, educational institutions, and organizations of all types have adopted the healthy communities terminology and approach, sometimes as part of their approach to quality or customer service standards and other times as part of human resources or training efforts. The growth of the healthy communities movement may result from the fact that living or working in a healthy community is surely more desirable than living or working in an unhealthy community. Progress in these areas was accelerated when the CDC funded 331 communities and 52 state and territorial health departments through its Healthy Communities Programs from 2008 to 2012 (CDC, 2017). However, this program is no longer funded.

CAREER OPPORTUNITIES

Career opportunities, continuing education opportunities, and research opportunities within the health and wellness area are too extensive to comprehensively cover here. Health-related career fields are expected to experience growth. In addition, the widespread growth in outdoor activities experienced during the COVID-19 pandemic has rekindled recreation interests for many people. Hiking, cycling, running, camping, and golf all experienced growth during the pandemic. As such, an increased need for facilities and equipment will likely have a positive impact on career opportunities for the foreseeable future. A list of potential careers related to the seven dimensions of wellness appears in table 15.3. Within an area of interest, you can investigate opportunities that are specific to individual wellness component areas. The potential employment opportunities are diverse in terms of role expectations, potential political and fiscal support, mobility, and longevity.

These opportunities are just starting points. As in every viable profession, the dynamic nature of the area combined with increased knowledge, changes in technology, population trends, and evolving public policy creates constant change in the sci-ence and application of the profession. Continuing education, training, and research are essential. Opportunities will come and go, although not as quickly as in less robust and diverse professions.

SUMMARY

This chapter introduced a variety of concepts related to health, wellness, and quality of life. An understanding of the factors that affect health, the current health status and risks in communities, the components of wellness, and other quality of life issues provides a basis for many parks and recreation programs and activities. Professionals have many opportunities to study, apply, or create new ways to contribute to the health and well-being of their communities. The time is right and the key elements are in place, so the opportunities to explore, contribute, and provide services are wide open. They are available only to those who are motivated to pursue a common vision: a healthy, sustainable, accessible, and livable community.

Table 15.3 Career Opportunities Categorized by Wellness Component

Wellness area	Potential employers	Possible position titles
Physical	Municipalities, community centers, health clubs, Boys and Girls Clubs, YMCAs and YWCAs, health departments, schools, universities, private companies	Fitness instructor, group exercise leader, personal trainer, nutritionist, massage therapist, athletic trainer, researcher, community health professional
Intellectual	Schools, colleges, universities, federal governments, state and local governments, private companies, nonprofit organizations, web design firms, public relations firms, professional associations	Teacher, leader, researcher, writer, consultant, graphic designer, musician
Emotional	Home health agencies, hospitals, community health care organizations, municipalities, nonprofit organizations, religious organizations, churches, synagogues	Therapist, counselor, religious worker, hospice worker, researcher, community worker, advocate
Social	Private companies, not-for-profit organizations, cruise ship lines, travel organizations, tourism bureaus, hotels, municipalities, country clubs, amusement parks, specialty camps	Special event manager, tournament director, researcher, game designer, manufacturer, social media developer, public relations specialist, social justice advocate, cruise ship director, activity director
Environmental	Health departments, federal governments, state and local governments, parks, developers, private organizations, schools, universities	Emergency management officer, community health professional, public health professional, researcher, environmental health professional, resource manager, health officer, solid waste manager
Spiritual	Churches, synagogues, hospitals, nonprofit organizations, private companies, military branches	Church or religious worker, life coach, personal advisor, pastor, youth leader, 12-step program director, motivational speaker, product developer, landscape architect, funeral service provider
Occupational	Businesses and industries, hospitals, universities, governments, military branches, schools, national parks	Health promotor, wellness director, health educator, safety coordinator

Review Questions

1. How do you assess personal health and wellness?
2. What are the concepts included in the World Leisure Organization charter?
3. What are the four major factors that affect a person's health?
4. What makes spiritual wellness different for every individual?
5. What is a healthy community?

Go to *HKPropel* to complete the activities for this chapter.

CHAPTER 16

Outdoor and Adventure Recreation

Bruce Martin, Garrett Hutson, and Marni Goldenberg

" Those who contemplate the beauty of the earth find resources of strength that will endure as long as life lasts. "

Rachel Carson, American conservationist and author of *Silent Spring*

——————————— **LEARNING OUTCOMES**———————————

After reading this chapter, you should be able to do the following:

> Provide an overview of outdoor and adventure recreation in the United States and Canada

> Summarize the history of outdoor and adventure recreation in the United States and Canada

> Describe outdoor and adventure recreation in various settings

> Outline career opportunities in outdoor and adventure recreation

> Identify and discuss contemporary trends and issues related to outdoor and adventure recreation in the United States and Canada

What comes to mind when you think about time spent outdoors that has shaped your life in positive ways? What made those experiences fun, impactful, educational, or even therapeutic?

- Was it time spent alone by a quiet lake at dawn with the smell of pine trees in the air?

- Was it an activity, such as skiing or snowboarding, that required intense focus as cold snow hit your warm face?

- Was it a person that you became friends with by sharing a canoe during a university outdoor orientation program?

Perhaps you learned about resilience while hiking down a mountain in the wind and rain. Or maybe meaningful outdoor experiences in your life combine themes from some of the scenarios mentioned. This chapter will encourage you to think further about these questions by providing an overview of outdoor and adventure recreation (OAR) in the United States and Canada.

Broadly speaking, participation in OAR activities is on the rise in Canada and the United States, and it profoundly affects the leisure landscapes of both countries. In 2019 and 2020, Parks Canada reported over 25 million person visits to Canadian national parks and national historic sites (Parks Canada, 2021). In 2020, over 160 million Americans aged 6 and over participated in outdoor recreation in some way (Outdoor Industry Foundation, 2021).

The U.S. Congress recognized the growing significance of outdoor recreation to the U.S. economy through the passage of the Outdoor Recreation Jobs and Economic Impact Act, which was signed into law by President Obama in December 2016. Due to this law, the outdoor recreation economy is considered part of the national gross domestic product of the United States. The outdoor recreation economy made up $454.0 billion (1.9%) of the United States gross domestic product in 2021 (U.S. Bureau of Economic Analysis, 2022).

In 2020, the Great American Outdoors Act was passed by the United States Congress and signed into law by President Trump. Designed to provide $1.9 billion per year for five years to support maintenance of key facilities and infrastructure in America's parks and protected areas, the Great American Outdoors Act was hailed as "landmark conservation legislation" (National Park Service, 2022). The economic outdoor recreation climate as of 2022 and beyond means opportunities for businesses big and small.

Not only is outdoor recreation good for the economy, but it is also good for our health. The health benefits of participating in OAR activities and programs continue to be uncovered by researchers. These benefits include

- enhanced psychological well-being and social functioning;

- increased self-esteem, self-respect, and self-confidence;

- the development of pro-environmental behaviors; and

- the promotion of active lifestyles (Dustin et al., 2010; Duvall & Kaplan, 2014; Ewert et al., 2021; Goldenberg & Soule, 2014).

OAR influences American and Canadian societies in powerful and positive ways that are clearly aligned with the three pillars of the National Recreation and Park Association: conservation, health and wellness, and promoting social equity (NRPA, 2022). The purpose of this chapter is to explore why and how this happens through a discussion of OAR definitions, values and benefits, history, settings and delivery systems, and trends within various contexts. We start by offering a definition of terms.

DEFINITION OF OUTDOOR AND ADVENTURE RECREATION

There are many terms associated with the outdoor industry. The title of this chapter encompasses two of these terms: *outdoor recreation* and *adventure recreation*. Other commonly used terms include *experiential education*, *adventure education*, *outdoor education*, *environmental education*, and *environmental interpretation*. However, we focus on the terms *outdoor recreation* and *adventure recreation* because they represent the focus of this chapter.

Outdoor Recreation

Outdoor recreation is considered a form of leisure and recreation (Cordes & Hutson, 2015). It is commonly defined as participating in intrinsically motivating outdoor activities during free time that depend on human–nature interaction and an appreciation of the natural world (Cordes & Hutson, 2015; Huddart & Stott, 2019; Plummer, 2009). The natural elements involved (mountains, rivers, forests, canyons, etc.) are the defining features that outdoor recreation depends on.

- Sea kayaking is outdoor recreation because it depends on the rhythms of the ocean, wind conditions, and tides that are affected by the position of the moon in relation to the earth.
- Skiing and snowboarding are forms of outdoor recreation because they rely on mountains, winter weather patterns, precipitation rates, and the moisture content of the snowpack.
- Rock climbing is outdoor recreation because it depends on millions of years of geologic history that produced unique formations of limestone, sandstone, and granite cliff lines.

All these examples are tied to nature, which is the key ingredient of the outdoor recreation experience. Therefore, conservation (wise use) of the natural environment is another important aspect of outdoor recreation that will be discussed later in this chapter.

Adventure Recreation

To adventure means to dare, to take a chance, and to be bold. **Adventure recreation** may or may not occur outdoors. Adventure recreation is commonly defined as "a variety of self-initiated activities often

Adventure recreation involves an interaction with the natural environment that contains elements of real or apparent danger.

Tillia Smith/iStockphoto/Getty Images

utilizing an interaction with the natural environment that contains elements of real or apparent danger in which the outcome, while uncertain, can be influenced by the participant and circumstance" (Ewert, 1989, p. 6). Danger connotes risk and uncertainty and is commonly discussed in terms of objective and subjective dangers (Martin et al., 2017; Priest & Gass, 2018).

- Objective dangers are observable, measurable, and generally agreed upon by those familiar with certain environments and activities. Weather, river levels, the height and age of a ropes course element, avalanche conditions, and the time the sun sets are all objective dangers.

- Subjective dangers relate more to human dimensions and perceptions of risk. For example, those new to whitewater kayaking may perceive a high subjective danger or risk of drowning, but under appropriate supervision and instruction of a trained outdoor leader, the actual chances of drowning are very small. For the novice whitewater kayaker, being on the water for the first time might feel like quite the adventure. The seasoned paddler, however, likely does not experience it this way; for them, a day on the water might simply be casual outdoor recreation with friends.

Whether a participant experiences a sense of adventure during recreation is largely in the eye of the beholder. Uncertainty, fear, a realistic understanding of competence, and perceptions of risk are all necessary parts of the adventure recreation experience. In fact, many people "enjoy the emotions that are tied up in setting their own abilities against such activities" (Bunyan, 2011, p. 10) and are intentionally seeking the ideal balance between competence and danger. Martin and Priest (1986) called this optimal balance *peak adventure*, and for many, it is the major thrust to continued participation in adventure recreation activities.

HISTORY OF OUTDOOR AND ADVENTURE RECREATION IN CANADA AND THE UNITED STATES

The history of OAR in Canada and the United States is rich, complex, and intertwined. This section begins with an overview of Indigenous people of North America and the ways they shaped and cre-

ated the foundations of OAR. It then addresses the romantic origins of the conservation movement in the United States and Canada and the way in which the romantic era framed more modern notions of the value of OAR activities and spaces and why these spaces are worth protecting. It then focuses on the emergence of the camping movement in the United States and Canada. Finally, it highlights how railroads, automobiles, and air travel expanded opportunities for OAR in North America and around the world and helped OAR become mainstream within the tourism sector.

Indigenous People of North America

Many OAR pursuits common in North America today are rooted in the Indigenous traditions of the American Indians, First Nations, Métis, and Inuit (among other peoples) of North America. It has been theorized that the first people of North America traveled over a land bridge between present-day Russia to Alaska and then throughout the continent between 14,000 and 20,000 years ago. The values, traditions, rituals, and spiritual beliefs of the first people of North America influence the ethics often associated with OAR today.

For example, many Indigenous beliefs rely on the concept of interdependence, or that all things within the natural world depend on one another without any one thing being considered more important than the other. Indigenous ceremonies, celebrations, and rituals brought the concept of interdependence to life by coinciding with harvests, hunting patterns, the changing of seasons, and rites of passage involving survival in outdoor environments. What we might consider outdoor recreation activities today often overlapped with everyday life patterns of Indigenous people because no real division between work and play necessarily existed (McClean et al., 2017).

The use of the canoe by Indigenous people of North America has shaped the outdoor recreation identity of Canada and the United States to some degree, especially given that other modes of travel during those times were out of the question due to the challenging landscape and climate. In fact, the French word *voyageur*, or traveler, was used to identify French Canadians who traveled great distances by canoes during the fur trade era. The ethos of the Canadian voyageur explorer lives on today in part due to Indigenous and early European use of the canoe (Cordes & Hutson, 2015).

The framing of the history of outdoor and adventure recreation comes with acknowledgment that North American outdoor settings are contested historical lands with associated violent histories of colonization and widespread mistreatment of Indigenous peoples. As of 2022, a movement advocating for sharing the full truth of Indigenous history and how Indigenous people have been negatively affected is underway and touches every sector of modern society including outdoor and adventure recreation. The Truth and Reconciliation Commission of Canada is an example of a federal response to Canada's Indian Residential School system, which among other things, aims to document the scale and impact of past injustices committed against Indigenous communities as an attempt to begin repairing the harm caused by residential schools. Another related example is the United Nations Declaration on the Rights of Indigenous Peoples in Canada, which affirms the rights of Indigenous peoples to manage their future including protection and preservation of Indigenous lands, waters, and

traditions (Government of Canada, 2021). The U.S. Department of the Interior released an investigative report in May 2022 as part of the Federal Indian Boarding School Initiative efforts to bring to light and rectify the similarly negative legacy of federal Indian boarding schools in the United States (Newland, 2022).

Romantic Origins

Views of the natural world from the 19th century American romantic era shaped modern thinking about why nature should be thought of as sacred, special, and spiritual (Cordes & Hutson, 2015). Most well-known among these visionaries were Ralph Waldo Emerson and Henry David Thoreau, who championed the transcendentalist movement that began in the northeastern United States. Transcendentalism relies on the notion that universal truths can be accessed through experiences in nature with strong emphasis on intuition and individual experience. These ideas were contrary to the

Westend61/Getty Images

The romantic origins of outdoor and adventure recreation are still seen today where participants view nature as a place for spiritual renewal and a place where one's character can be tested.

prominent religious beliefs of the time. Perhaps the most famous of all American transcendentalist writing was Thoreau's book *Walden*, which chronicled his two years living in a cabin near a Massachusetts' pond on Emerson's land. Thoreau's purpose for living near Walden Pond was to practice self-reflection and simple living and to develop a broader understanding of the world. These beliefs about the value and benefits of nature-based experiences were novel and rare for the time and contributed to the conservation movement of Canada and the United States that followed (Plummer, 2009).

Literary figures such as Emerson and Thoreau gave voice to the aesthetic and spiritual values that draw so many of us to wilderness environments and natural areas to engage in OAR pursuits. With the rise of industrialism and urbanization, traditional views of nature as forbidding and dangerous spaces were flipped, and nature became viewed as a place for spiritual renewal and a place where one's character could be tested and forged. Nature became a place that could inspire a sense of adventure and provided opportunities to test one's abilities and challenge one's limitations.

The Emergence of the Conservation Movement

The conservation movement in the United States and Canada was the result of shifting philosophical beliefs and attitudes toward nature such as those reflected within the transcendentalist movement led by Emerson and Thoreau. The conservation movement was also a result of natural science advancements such as Charles Darwin's theory of evolution and Alexander von Humboldt's well-documented observations of interconnected life systems. Perhaps most important, the conservation movement in Canada and the United States was due to witnessing the destruction of natural resources, especially as the American and Canadian frontiers came to a close. Clear-cutting of forests, abandoned mines, observable loss of species such as the passenger pigeon, and catastrophic fires all contributed to shifting mind-sets about the relationship between people and nature (Dennis, 2012).

City planners, landscape architects, and others began to recognize the value and necessity of green space within rapidly expanding cities. Frederick Law Olmsted (considered by some to be the father of the American park) and Calvert Vaux designed New York City's Central Park, which was established in 1857. Toronto, Canada's largest park within city limits, High Park, was officially opened in 1876. Conservationist, John Muir, had the foresight to recognize what would be lost if large expanses of nature in the western United States were not protected. Muir played a major role in helping protect Yosemite Valley, California, through legislation passed in 1864; this legislation later helped Yellowstone in Wyoming become the world's first national park in 1872 (Nash, 2014). Muir also helped form the Sierra Club in 1892, which has a history of protecting wild places in the American west. Canada's first national park, Banff National Park, was established in 1887 near hot springs that were discovered in the province of Alberta four years prior (Campbell, 2011). Parks Canada was established in 1911 as the world's first federally managed park service, and the U.S. National Parks Service was established in 1916 (Martin et al., 2017). Overall, these major events signaled the beginning of a movement based on wise use and protection of outdoor environments that continues to shape how Americans and Canadians think about places where OAR takes place today.

The Emergence of the Camping Movement

Somewhat concurrently with the conservation movement, the camping movement gained momentum as a way to positively affect youth development beginning in the late 1800s and continuing throughout the industrial revolution. Historically, children in U.S. schools had summers off to help with the family farm. As populations in North American cities increased, many suggested that camping helped reconnect children to nature and taught valuable life lessons that no longer occurred on the family farm during the summer. Furthermore, camp programs were increasingly viewed by social reformers as useful to counteract society's shortcomings and were considered part of the progressive education era (Ozier, 2018).

William Frederick Gunn of Connecticut's Gunnery School is often credited with starting the first summer camp for boys in 1861. The YMCA opened its first known summer camp, Camp Dudley at Orange Lake, New York, in 1885 (YMCA, 2022). Between 1900 and 1915, well-known youth-serving organizations such as the American Camp Association, Boy Scouts, Girl Scouts, 4-H, Campfire Girls, and Boys Club emerged. The Canadian Camping Association was founded in 1936. In the United States, there were

OUTSTANDING GRADUATE

Kelsey Bracewell

Background Information

Name: Kelsey Bracewell

Education: Master of business administration (MBA) from University of Mary Washington in Fredericksburg, Virginia; MS in recreation and sport sciences from Ohio University in Athens, Ohio; BA in wilderness leadership and experiential education from Brevard College in Brevard, North Carolina

Credentials: Wilderness First Responder; Certified Whitewater Kayaking Instructor; Leave No Trace trainer; U.S. Center for SafeSport trained; Management Concepts, grants management certificate

Awards: Annual Safety & Rescue Award, ACA President's Award, Brevard College Wilderness Leadership and Experimental Education Department Student of the Year

Affiliations: American Canoe Association, National Boating Safety Advisory Council, U.S. Army Corps of Engineers, National Association of Boating Law Administrators, USCG Auxiliary, International Whitewater Hall of Fame, National Safe Boating Council, University of Mary Washington Athletics, University of Mary Washington Campus Recreation Program, Friends of the Rappahannock, Friends of the Dahlgren Railroad Heritage Trail

Career Information

Position: Director of Safety, Education, and Instruction

Organization: American Canoe Association. Founded in 1880, the American Canoe Association (ACA) is a 501(c)(3) national nonprofit organization serving the broader paddling public by providing education related to all aspects of paddling, stewardship support to help protect paddling environments, and sanctioning of programs and events to promote paddle sport competition, exploration, and recreation. The ACA has a network of members spanning every U.S. state and 45 countries, who range from elite level competitors and internationally recognized instructors to recreational novices and beginner paddlers. Since 2017, the ACA has served as the national governing body for paddle sports (sprint, slalom, and paracanoe) for the United States Olympic and Paralympic Committee and as the U.S. National Federation to the International Canoe Federation. The heart of the ACA is the people who paddle, cherish, and protect the rivers, lakes, streams, bays, and oceans of the United States and beyond.

Job description: The Director of Safety, Education, and Instruction (SEI) department manages all facets of the ACA national paddle sports instruction program and serves as the liaison between the ACA instructor cadre and the safety education and instruction council (SEIC) and subcommittees. This position is responsible for outlining, publishing, and disseminating pertinent policy and curriculum information as well as managing the course management database, which contains more than 20,000 individual credentials. The position authors and delivers presentations to the ACA board of directors and SEIC members, as well as attendees of ACA's educational and outreach events. This position also has the responsibility of writing and overseeing the execution of grant-funded projects while managing other staff members and contractors.

Career path: After graduation from Brevard College in 2009, I pursued a master's degree from Ohio University in Athens, Ohio. With this combination of education and paddling experience, developed and refined while attending both institutions, I earned the role of SEI department coordinator at the American Canoe Association in 2011. I was promoted to department manager in 2016, and advanced to department director in 2021. This progression was made possible not only by work ethic and belief in the ACA mission and vision, but was also supplemented by dedicated volunteer work, community engagement, and devotion to professional growth. I also serve as the staff liaison to the ACA diversity, equity, and inclusion board committee and am the program manager for the International Whitewater Hall of Fame, which is a project of the World River Centre.

Advice for Undergraduates

For students out there who are not always fans of group work, embrace every opportunity to collaborate. Having been a student who preferred to control the grades and ultimate outcomes of their work, I shied away from delegating and sharing the load of a project with others, but I have really learned the value of sharing both the accomplishment and the burden. The depth, meaning, value, and diversity of the world is made up of people; we cannot accomplish anything alone. I am proud of the work I have done and the people I have served, but I could not have achieved any of it without someone first offering mentorship, expertise, or partnership to me. Learn to let go of "your way" of accomplishing a task, join energy with others, and you will realize that the results are far greater than you had ever thought possible.

- 106 camps by 1910,
- 1,248 camps by 1924, and
- 3,485 camps by 1933, and most were located in the northeastern United States (Bernard, 1999; DeMerritte, 1999).

The Emergence of Outdoor and Adventure Tourism

The emergence of outdoor and adventure tourism is directly related to access to transportation. The expansion of railroads across the United States and Canada increased opportunities for recreation. The first transcontinental railroads opened in the United States in 1869 and in Canada in 1886. When Canadian Pacific Railway workers discovered hot springs near Banff, Alberta, the Canadian government realized they could use the same railway to profit from transporting Canadians to Banff National Park for outdoor recreation tourism. However, it was transportation by automobile that had the greatest influence on outdoor and adventure tourism growth in the United States and Canada.

Automobiles began to become more widely available and affordable to the masses beginning in the early 1900s. Although city parks provide much-needed green space within densely populated urban centers, outdoor recreation facilities such as ski resorts and state, provincial, and national parks all required travel outside of cities either by railroad or car. By 1920, auto touring and car camping in America's national parks began to blossom. Travel by airplane became commercialized during World War I and opened further opportunities for outdoor and adventure tourism on a global scale. Air travel shaped the development of outdoor adventure tourism activities such as snow skiing, high altitude mountaineering, and surfing by giving a greater number of people access to such activities. Transcontinental highway systems in the United States and Canada combined with the continued growth of parks in both countries from 1920 forward created further opportunities for outdoor and adventure tourism.

SETTINGS AND DELIVERY SYSTEMS

OAR incorporates many different settings and delivery systems. Settings range from park systems to commercial ski resorts, retail shops to summer camps, and from wild rivers to open spaces used for mountain biking or rock climbing. This section introduces the various OAR settings, delivery systems, and career opportunities, and participation trends in these settings.

Parks and Protected Areas

Most of the OAR field operates within parks and protected areas. Consequently, an understanding of parks and protected areas is essential for anyone interested in working in the OAR field. Parks and protected areas are often managed by government agencies such as the U.S. National Park Service, the U.S. Forest Service, the U.S. Bureau of Land Management, or Parks Canada. Each organization operates differently, but all have the goal of maintaining natural land and open spaces. Most countries have their own systems to protect and preserve natural areas, and most countries have passed national laws and acts that protect and preserve natural spaces for future generations. Parks and protected areas are also managed by state, provincial, and local agencies such as state parks and municipal parks and recreation departments. Managing agencies and the legal frameworks under which they operate determine the purpose and uses of the public lands and other natural resources. Some public land is set aside for multiuse purposes, such as grazing for livestock, mining, or lumber, whereas other land is strictly set aside for preservation. As a user of the land, it is essential to know the regulations and rules that the managing agency uses to govern the land. Protection of cultural and natural resources is an integral part of maintaining parks and protected areas.

Various career opportunities in parks and protected areas include

- park rangers,
- interpreters,
- land managers,
- biologists,
- researchers, or
- law enforcement agents.

Some careers require certain education and training, and others might be more open, such as a seasonal park aide. Various park ranger academies exist that offer training needed for the various jobs. If a person loves and appreciates the natural areas, working in parks and protected areas may be a very rewarding career option. The various government agencies have web pages that provide career information.

Resorts

Commercial resorts are for-profit enterprises that focus on the economic potential of an area. Resorts centered around OAR can be focused on any outdoor activity such as skiing, river running, or fishing. Commercial resorts can be either public or private.

Public commercial resorts are typically operated through concession programs within public parks and protected areas systems. They are often based on a pay-to-play system and can include commercially managed rivers or ski resorts. An example of a public commercial ski resort is Mammoth Mountain Ski Area in California. Mammoth Mountain offers skiing during the winter and is considered the "premier bike park in the U.S." during the summer, offering terrain for all levels of bikers, lessons, rentals and demos, lift tickets, and more (Mammoth Mountain Ski Area, 2022). They also offer an adventure center and gondola rides.

Private commercial resorts are typically operated on privately owned land. Many private commercial resorts, such as country clubs, hunting clubs, and other club resorts, require a membership. Martis Camp in Lake Tahoe, California, is considered "possibly the best four-season private community in the U.S." (Olmsted, 2013). This resort offers golf as well as a full-sized ski mountain, lakes, 16 miles of hiking and cross-country ski trails, and various other outdoor amenities. Adventures on the Gorge in West Virginia, located adjacent to the New River Gorge National Park and Preserve, is another example of a resort that offers adventure tourism opportunities, including river rafting trips on the New and Gauley Rivers, aerial canopy tours, mountain biking, rock climbing, and more. Career opportunities in commercial resorts can include

- resort manager,
- instructor,
- marketing expert, and many others.

Guide Services

Many outdoor adventure activities require specialized equipment or training. For example, white-

Ski resorts provide a classic example of outdoor adventure recreation opportunities for a fee.

Gary Coronado/Los Angeles Times/Getty Images

water rafting uses equipment such as rafts, life jackets, paddles, and wet suits. In addition, specific knowledge of rivers in general, knowledge of the specific river they are running, water safety skills, and group dynamics skills are all needed. To make various outdoor activities accessible to the public, guides are available to enable participants to experience the activity.

One example of a guiding company is Alaska Mountain Guides and Climbing School Inc. (AMGCSI), which guides expeditions in Alaska, the Yukon, and other international destinations. AMGCSI takes groups on expeditions involving mountaineering, ice climbing, white-water paddling, trekking, and other outdoor activities. Another example of a guiding company is the Wildland Trekking Company, which provides hiking vacations in the United States, Canada, and elsewhere around the world. Various types of hiking trips are offered, such as backpacking trips, stock and porter trips, inn-based trips, and photography tours.

People in the outdoor adventure guiding industry work long hours to take participants through an outdoor experience and are responsible for safety, education, and providing a meaningful experience. Guides typically have expertise in an area and a passion for sharing that expertise with others. Guides can provide introductory experiences, such as rock climbing or surfing for a few hours to a day, as well as multiday experiences for a group on a long expedition.

Summer Camps

Summer camps range in location, price, availability, and numbers of days. Some are day camps and others are overnight camps. Some camps cater to a specific population, such as adults with specific religious affiliations, whereas other camps are open to anyone. Many of us grew up attending some sort of camp experience such as an overnight experience in a different state or city or in a local area. This first exposure to a camp setting could be why you are interested in the field of recreation, parks, and tourism. Some camps operate year-round, even if they are primarily summer camps. Year-round operations could include a challenge course, retreat center, or lodging facility. Careers in summer camps can start with your first summer as a camp counselor, and you can work up to a director or programmer. Some career paths in summer camp settings are seasonal, but others might be longer.

The American Camp Association (ACA), one of the largest nonprofit organizations for camps, serves over 12,000 members in providing a community for camp professionals to share knowledge and ensure quality programs through setting standards and accreditation. The mission of ACA is to enrich "the lives of children, youth and adults through the camp experience" (American Camp Association, 2022). Many camps inside and outside the United States run under the ACA standards. Camp Mardela in Denton, Maryland, is an accredited member of ACA that offers various options such as camps for those with little camping experience, camps for those who wish to learn about equestrian safety and riding, and camps that focus on outdoor adventure activities.

Outdoor Adventure Programs

National Outdoor Leadership School (NOLS) and Outward Bound are two of the leading outdoor organizations that provide instructors for groups to have a shared learning experience in the outdoor context. NOLS, a nonprofit organization that focuses on outdoor leadership development, is based in Lander, Wyoming, but offers courses throughout the world including in locations such as New Zealand, Patagonia, and East Africa. Skills learned in courses can range from

- backpacking,
- caving,
- Leave No Trace,
- wilderness medicine,
- rock climbing,
- mountaineering, and
- sea kayaking.

NOLS's mission is to "be the leading source and teacher of wilderness skills and leadership that serve people and the environment" (NOLS, 2022).

Outward Bound has 10 regional schools in the United States and operates in over 35 countries. Outward Bound teaches similar skills as NOLS but the focus of the organization is on changing lives through discovery. Many other programs exist, such as the Wilderness Education Association, the International Wilderness Leadership School, or Alaska Mountain Guides, and programs vary by country.

In outdoor adventure programs, the outdoors is used as the classroom environment to teach technical and interpersonal skills to individuals and groups. The emphasis in these programs is on providing educational experiences and maximizing learning for the participants. Some groups are predetermined, and members know each other in advance, whereas other group members may be from a variety of backgrounds and locations. These programs focus on the educational component of the experience, which may include

- cooking,
- working with a group,
- leading a group,
- preparing a campsite,
- experiencing navigation, or
- a variety of other outdoor skills.

Often programs will vary in terms of length, location, and skill development. Among the many desired outcomes are development of leadership skills, personal reflection and development, and positive group development.

Career opportunities in the outdoor adventure programming field include

- directors and managers,
- course instructors and educators, and
- logistical operators.

Some organizations, such as NOLS and Outward Bound, offer instructor training programs and courses that provide students the opportunity to learn skills needed for the organization while also assessing whether the individual would be a good fit as an instructor.

The Retail Industry

The retail industry is an integral part of the outdoor and adventure field and includes apparel and equipment needed to operate a program or activity. Several retail stores are available in cities and on the web for purchasing equipment. There are small local companies that design and sell equipment, and there are also national retail chain stores that serve the industry. Some larger retail companies include REI, Patagonia, The North Face, and L.L.Bean. Some retail companies have also developed trip programs, such as REI Adventures, that offer organized adventure trips to their customers. Career opportunities in the retail industry can include

- equipment designers and testers,
- store owners and managers, or
- working as a representative or sales manager.

Many companies now have sales, marketing, special events, and design teams. Many students get their start in the retail industry by working for a company as an intern running their special events or assisting with marketing.

Military Recreation

The United States and Canadian militaries both sponsor outdoor and adventure recreation programming to support the morale and welfare of their service members and veterans as well as their service members' and veterans' families. In Canada, this service is known as the Canadian Forces Morale and Welfare Services (CFMWS). In the United States, it is known simply as Morale, Welfare and Recreation (MWR). These services offer a broad array of general recreation and leisure activities intended to help military service members and their families navigate the unique challenges of life in the military. Among these activities are opportunities for outdoor and adventure recreation, many of which are designed to take advantage of resources of the locales where military personnel are based. For example, MWR in Italy offers escorted and guided cultural trips, high adventure activities, skiing and snowboarding, water sports, hiking, and biking (U.S. Army MWR, 2022). Traditionally these activities are offered at discounted rates and are meant to encourage military personnel and their families to have well-balanced lives. Careers in CFMWS and MWR are available for civilians and military personnel. Internships, entry-level positions, and director positions are available. A desire to see the world, work with people, and provide recreational opportunities are musts for these positions.

Ecotourism and Adventure Travel

OAR includes the areas of ecotourism and adventure travel. Ecotourism is a form of nature-based tourism focused on learning about and developing an appreciation for ecosystems that have rare, fragile, and unique ecological characteristics. A popular ecotourism destination for North Americans is Costa Rica, which has protected approximately 25 percent of its lands through a system of parks and protected areas intended to draw tourists to the country. There are numerous companies in Costa Rica that promote ecotourism opportunities throughout the country, and there are a variety of professional opportunities within the industry, including working for guide services, eco-lodges, national parks, and management positions. The International Ecotourism Society is a nonprofit organization that supports over 15,000 active members in over 190 countries with a mission that supports "uniting communities, conservation and sustainable travel . . . in facilitating economic, social, and environmental sustainability" (The International Ecotourism Society, 2022).

Adventure travel is a travel experience in which risk is a central component of the experience. White-water rafting on the Colorado River through the Grand Canyon is an example of adventure travel. Mountain climbing in places such as the Pacific Northwest is another example of adventure travel. There are numerous companies in both Canada and the United States that specialize in guiding clients down raging rivers and up mountain summits throughout North America and around the world.

CONTEMPORARY TRENDS AND ISSUES IN OUTDOOR AND ADVENTURE RECREATION

Societies around the world have evolved dramatically since the outdoor and adventure recreation industry first began to emerge in the 18th and 19th centuries. With these changes have come changes to the outdoor industry itself. With the rapid expansion of nature-based tourism in the 1950s and 1960s, the natural spaces that served as venues for outdoor and adventure recreation pursuits began to be negatively affected by overuse. Many parks and protected areas began to experience a "tragedy of the commons" (Manning, 2007, p. 7). As the modern environmental movement emerged in the 1960s, so too did an expression that characterized our new relationship with natural areas: We were loving them to death. One of the key reasons for the negative impacts of OAR pursuits at the time is that many visitors to parks and protected areas operated on the principles of the woodcraft movement (Turner, 2002). The woodcraft movement

represented a traditional approach to camping that entailed cooking over open fires, building lean-tos and other natural shelters, hunting and foraging for food, and so forth. The carrying capacity of a given area tends to be low when visitors engage in these practices while visiting.

To address the dilemmas posed by the woodcraft movement, a new outdoor ethic began to emerge that emphasized wilderness living and travel techniques that resulted in minimal environmental impacts. This movement ultimately culminated in the establishment of the Leave No Trace Center for Outdoor Ethics, an organization devoted to protecting the outdoors by educating the public to use natural and open spaces in environmentally responsible ways. The emergence of Leave No Trace represented a shift from an environmental ethic that prevailed during the late 19th and early 20th centuries that emphasized the virtue of living off the land to an ethic that emphasizes minimizing our impact on recreation resources and preserving them for successive generations of users. This new ethic, embodied in the seven principles of Leave No Trace, has prevailed since. However, scholars and practitioners in the field of OAR have begun to question the efficacy of this approach in the face of new environmental dilemmas resulting from global climate change. They are beginning to ask about the effects that we have on the recreation resources that serve as venues for OAR pursuits and question the effects of the retail industry that supports this minimal-impact approach to outdoor and adventure recreation (Simon & Alagona, 2013).

Just as the transition from a predominantly rural and agrarian economy to a predominantly industrial and urban economy resulted in dramatic societal changes during the late 19th and early 20th centuries, new economic and technological developments are yielding equally dramatic changes in society. The development of new technologies, the global dynamics of trade and commerce, and global climate change will continue to perpetuate changes that will redefine the ways we engage in OAR pursuits. The following explores some of these trends.

The Seven Principles of Leave No Trace

1. Plan ahead and prepare.
2. Travel and camp on durable surfaces.
3. Dispose of waste properly.
4. Leave what you find.
5. Minimize campfire impacts.
6. Respect wildlife.
7. Be considerate of other visitors.

For more information on the Leave No Trace Center for Outdoor Ethics, visit their website: https://lnt.org.

The Challenge of Global Climate Change to the Outdoor Industry

A phenomenon that has emerged in the tourism industry is last-chance tourism (Lemelin et al., 2012; Woosman et al., 2022). Tourism destinations threatened by global climate change have become destinations for tourists who hope to experience their unique environmental and cultural attributes before they disappear or are drastically altered as a result of climate change. Examples of last-chance tourism opportunities include

- polar bear viewing in the Hudson Bay region of Canada,
- glacier viewing in the Waterton-Glacier International Peace Park along the U.S. and Canadian border in northern Montana and southern Alberta, and
- skiing in certain alpine areas in the United States and Canada.

In many cases, entire ecosystems are at risk of being drastically altered or disappearing altogether. Coastal wetlands are a prime example of this. Sea levels are projected to rise by as much as six feet over the next 100 years. Freshwater wetlands in coastal areas around the world stand to be inundated by rising sea levels. With the loss of these freshwater wetlands will come the loss of tourism opportunities associated with them. Many coastal resort communities, such as those on the Outer Banks of North Carolina along the east coast of the United States, will be inundated. As these areas are deluged by rising waters, much of the tourism industry that currently flourishes there will diminish and, in some cases, disappear.

There are many dire consequences that are likely to result from global climate change, and perhaps the implications of these consequences for the tourism industry should be the least of our worries. However, the reality of global climate change raises important questions for those professionally engaged in the outdoor industry and for citizens who participate in outdoor and adventure recreation activities and tourism opportunities.

- In what ways does our participation in these activities contribute to global climate change?
- Short of forgoing participation in these activities altogether, what can we do to help mitigate the problem of global climate change in the outdoor and adventure recreation field?

Simon and Alagona (2013) have highlighted an uncomfortable paradox in the adoption of Leave No Trace as an approach to mitigating the environmental impacts on natural resources from recreation and tourism activities. They argue that Leave No Trace has been effective in mitigating direct effects of users on these resources. However, in doing so, Leave No Trace has merely displaced these effects, which helps perpetuate a consumerist outdoor retail culture focused on supplying equipment and goods needed to participate in OAR activities without negatively affecting the land. Tents and other forms of synthetic shelter have taken the place of lean-tos built from natural materials found on the land. Camp stoves have eliminated the need for campfires in the camp kitchen.

Visit any REI store in the United States or Mountain Equipment Co-op store in Canada and you will find a plethora of equipment and clothing produced by manufacturers such as Patagonia, Sierra Designs, Marmot, and others that is intended to help you experience the outdoors in an enjoyable and comfortable fashion while minimizing your impact on the land. Patagonia is an example of a company that has dedicated itself to mitigating the negative environmental impacts of the consumer-based economy of which it is a part. In 2022, Yvon Chouinard, the founder of Patagonia, made the monumental decision to transfer ownership of his company, valued at approximately $3 billion, to the Patagonia Purpose Trust, which is designed to ensure that the company remains independent and uses all its future profits to promote wildland preservation and to combat climate change (Gelles, 2022). Although Chouinard's generous act of philanthropy is intended to promote a more socially and environmentally conscientious form of capitalism, the outdoor retail industry at large continues to contribute to broader environmental problems that are a result of the consumer-oriented economy of which they are a part. There are numerous issues related to environmental and social justice that arise because of the roles that Leave No Trace and the outdoor retail industry play in contributing to environmental degradation around the globe.

Few would advocate returning to the woodcraft movement to which Leave No Trace was a response. Leave No Trace has been successful in fulfilling its mission of protecting outdoor recreation resources from the direct effects of their users. However, the question becomes, what can we do to mitigate the broader environmental effects that have resulted from the outdoor industry over the past half century or more? We are now facing indirect environmental

Sshepard/iStock/Getty Images

While Leave No Trace has been effective in mitigating environmental impacts, it has contributed to a consumerist outdoor retail culture.

effects to our parks and protected areas that threaten the existence of the very environmental and cultural attributes that make them unique.

To address this shortcoming of Leave No Trace, Alagona and Simon (2012) proposed adding an eighth Leave No Trace principle: Leave No Trace starts at home. They suggest extending the ethos embodied in the Leave No Trace principles to our daily lives. Indeed, although not embedded in its list of principles, Leave No Trace has promoted this idea over the years with the mantra "from our backcountry to your backyard." Perhaps it is time to formalize this idea by including it as an explicit Leave No Trace principle, as Alagona and Simon (2012) suggest. In any case, we must all begin to consider participating in OAR activities in ways that minimize our contributions to the broader environmental effects of the industry.

The Influence of New Technologies on the Nature of OAR Experiences

New technologies developed over the past century have redefined and will continue to redefine the ways and the extent to which humans experience nature. Prior to the development of modern modes of communication (e.g., radio communication, cell phones, satellite phones, and satellite two-way communication devices with integrated GPS navigation and SOS features), explorers and adventurers were on their own when venturing into the wild. Explorers and adventurers would step into uncharted territory with no means of communication with the outside world. The success of an expedition was unknown until the explorers returned (or failed to return).

George Mallory and Sandy Irvine, for example, disappeared while attempting a first ascent of Mt. Everest in 1924. Their fate was shrouded in mystery for 75 years until Mallory's frozen and mummified body was found at the base of the Northeast Ridge of the mountain. They had ventured into a remote and harsh environment without any means of communication with the outside world, without the ability to communicate distress, and without any hope of rescue from an outside party should they suffer a mishap. Edmund Hillary and Tenzing Norgay made the first successful climb of Mt. Everest in 1953, and, since that time, over 4,000 climbers have reached the summit. The mountain is no less dangerous than it was when Mallory and Irvine attempted to summit it in 1924. Ripper (2023) reports that, according to the Himalayan database, at least 322 people have died on Everest between 1922 and 2023. However, the development of new technologies has revolutionized how climbers experience the mountain. These new technologies include not just modern modes of communication but also more modern clothing and equipment, modes of transportation, weather forecasting systems, and so on, that have increased the safety of climbers on the mountain and have made the mountain more accessible to expert and amateur climbers alike. The influence of new technologies on OAR experiences is not unique to mountaineering. The same is true for nearly every OAR pursuit from white-water kayaking to sailing to adventure trekking.

Welser (2012) argues that the development of new technologies has diminished the quality of OAR experiences and threatens to end wilderness experience as we traditionally conceive it. He argues that new information technologies have created a ubiquitous bridge to civilization and consequently "reduce our opportunity to experience the self-reliance, isolation, adventure, exposure to the wild, and natural consequences that define the wilderness experience for recreationists" (p. 153). These technologies tend to inhibit our ability to disconnect with the modern realities that define our lives and consequently diminish the restorative value of the environments into which we venture to participate in OAR pursuits. Welser (2012) also argues that modern communication technologies have resulted in increased awareness of remote and exotic recreation areas, thus promoting the popularity and overuse of these areas.

On the other hand, Hitchner et al. (2019) view modern communication technology in a more positive light, highlighting the role that it has played in enhancing the experiences of thru-hikers on the John Muir Trail. In particular, they examined "how the communication medium of travel blogs becomes a vehicle for both self-reflection and for sharing spiritual experiences, and how the act of blogging merges virtual and corporeal communi-

ties formed among hikers" (p. 353). They view the storytelling reflected in these blogs as an extension of the tradition of travel narratives found in such popular books as Bill Bryson's (1999) *A Walk in the Woods* and Cheryl Strayed's (2012) *Wild: Lost and Found on the Pacific Crest Trail*. Hitchner et al. (2019) recognize that further research is needed to more fully understand the social impacts of more modern forms of storytelling. However, rather than viewing them as a bad thing, they see them "simply as a reconfiguration of the relationships of a subset of tech-savvy and highly connected hikers, commonly called flashpackers, with the natural world" (p. 363). Needless to say, the use of technology in natural spaces continues to be contentious and will likely remain so as it continues to evolve.

SUMMARY

This chapter introduces you to the field of outdoor and adventure recreation and offers definitions of outdoor and adventure recreation and various terms associated with the field. The chapter illustrates ways in which the practice of OAR in the United States and Canada can be used to promote the three pillars of the National Recreation and Park Association: conservation, health and wellness, and social equity (NRPA, 2022). The chapter provides an overview of the history of the field as well as an introduction to various sites and settings through which OAR goods and services are delivered. In doing so, we present many career opportunities associated with the field. Finally, the chapter presents a discussion of contemporary trends and issues that have significantly affected OAR over the past half century and will continue to affect the field for generations to come.

At the start of this chapter, we posed a series of questions and challenged you to consider these questions as you progressed through the chapter. We hope this chapter offered you an opportunity to revisit some of these experiences, to consider them in a new light, and to continue to draw lessons from them. We also hope that you will find inspiration and meaning in future OAR experiences, whether as an outdoor professional or as an OAR enthusiast.

Review Questions

1. Identify three health benefits associated with participation in outdoor and adventure recreation.

2. Describe ways in which one or more outdoor recreation activities rely on and are influenced by the natural environment.

3. What words of wisdom did Kelsey Bracewell offer to undergraduate students?

4. Discuss the uncomfortable paradox that Simon and Alagona (2013) highlighted in the adoption of Leave No Trace as an approach to mitigating the environmental impacts on natural resources from recreation and tourism activities as well as their recommendation for addressing this paradox.

Go to HK*Propel* to complete the activities for this chapter.

Arts and Culture

Julie Voelker-Morris and Kim Lyddane

" The arts have the remarkable ability to create a sense of togetherness, belonging and community. They can help decrease stress, loneliness and anxiety. They can provide opportunities to reflect, process experiences and feelings, imagine what our future might look like, and connect us through our common humanity. These are all things echoed in parks and recreation. The park and recreation field has the unique opportunity to create a bridge of access to arts and culture for the community by making it attainable. "

Devin Graham, 2020, National Recreation and Park Association

Helen H. Richardson/MediaNews Group/The Denver Post via Getty Images

LEARNING OUTCOMES

After reading this chapter, you should be able to do the following:

> Demonstrate an understanding and awareness of the types and the importance of arts and cultural experiences in North America

> Identify components of arts and cultural programming

> Describe some meanings, benefits, constraints, and opportunities affecting organizations, individuals, and communities through arts and cultural experiences

> Compare the amount, type, breadth, and impacts of arts and cultural experiences

> Describe some roles and benefits of diversity, equity, and inclusion efforts in arts and cultural programming

Provision for arts and cultural experiences has a long tradition in recreation and leisure settings. More than 65 years ago, Meyer and Brightbill (1956) advocated that arts and crafts, dancing, dramatics, literary activities, and music activities be standard in comprehensive recreation programs and settings. Arts and cultural opportunities have been valued as means of improving peoples' lives, livelihoods, and neighborhoods via connection to others through cultural experiences, positive economic contributions, and development of skills as a result of lifelong arts offerings (Americans for the Arts, 2010; Arnold, 1976; Carpenter, 2008; International Labor Organization, 2013; Leroux & Bernadska, 2014, National Endowment for the Arts, 2020a; National Governors Association, n.d.; Powell Hanna, 2016; Sherman & Morrissey, 2017). Healthy communities are built when recreation

Albany Parks and Recreation River Rhythms concert. Community members enjoying a free, national act concert in Albany, Oregon, put on by the city's parks and recreation department. The River Rhythms series has brought thousands of visitors to Albany each Thursday night in the summer for the last 38 years.

Kristi Crawford Photography

specialists build relationships between artists, arts programs, and diverse members of a specific community. **Arts and cultural activities** in recreation settings engage and honor a variety of skill and interest levels while emphasizing health and wellness through psychomotor, cognitive, and affective skills development.

Arts and cultural recreation opportunities endure as part of public agencies' responsibilities to support and enliven communities and to provide citizens with viable offerings in self-support programs. This chapter discusses the importance of providing arts and cultural experiences to the broad public as part of life in a democratic society. Benefits of arts and cultural programming for individuals, organizations, and communities are explored. Contemporary arts and cultural programs, with a focus on the United States and Canada, are highlighted throughout the chapter to show the broad range of organizations and types of programs, provide context for historical and contemporary participation, and show trends in the field. Select constraints are included when the benefits of such programming are discussed. Each shared example seeks to build social equity or contribute to the health and wellness of residents, tourists, and others in the communities described.

TYPES OF ARTS AND CULTURAL EXPERIENCES IN RECREATION AND LEISURE

Leisure is sometimes considered a nonactivity—the time in which one rests, relaxes, or steps out of the rest of life. However, planned and active leisure also includes experiences that bring about activities and opportunities of engagement found in recreation services (Carpenter, 2008; Seibel & Volmer, 2021; Stebbins, 2017). Such engagement and participation can and should include arts and cultural experiences within community settings.

The **arts and cultural sector** in North America is a large, heterogeneous set of individuals, entrepreneurs, and nonprofit, private, and unincorporated organizations engaged in creation, production, presentation, distribution, preservation, and education about aesthetic, heritage, and entertainment activities, products, and artifacts (Americans for the Arts, 2017; Cherbo et al., 2008; Taylor & Littleton, 2012; Wyszomirski, 2002; Zuidervaart, 2011). Organizational contexts such as parks and recreation, leisure education, and tourism are all viewed as part of the arts and cultural sector in North America. Leisure behaviors (e.g., collecting, cuisine) and pursuits (e.g., gaming, sports) are other components in the sector.

In 2019, the National Endowment for the Arts, in partnership with the U.S. Census Bureau, completed the most recent iteration of the Survey of Public Participation in the Arts (SPPA). The SPPA has been conducted about every five years since 1985 and examines how adults engage with the arts. The most recent survey was conducted in 2022 with reports from the study to be published in 2023 and beyond. The study covers the multiple ways that people participate in leisure activities around the arts such as

- consumption of the arts through digital media (music, dance, illustration, critiques of art, interviews with artists, etc.) and at discipline-specific venues (cinemas, galleries, performing arts centers);
- voluntary reading and art making as individuals or through clubs or interest circles;
- art sharing via social media, blogging, or other means (Instagram, YouTube, non-fungible tokens [NFTs]); and
- arts production and learning through individual or group performances, exhibitions, classes, and workshops in a specific instrument, dance style, theatrical performance, creative writing, photography, and the like.

This study has continued to confirm much of Chartrand's (2000) well-regarded and often cited referenced mapping of arts and cultural industries that includes

- parks and recreation,
- leisure,
- education,
- tourism,
- antiques and collectables,
- cosmetics,
- cuisine,
- funeral practices,
- furniture and fixtures,
- gaming,
- multiculturalism,
- native cultures,
- languages,

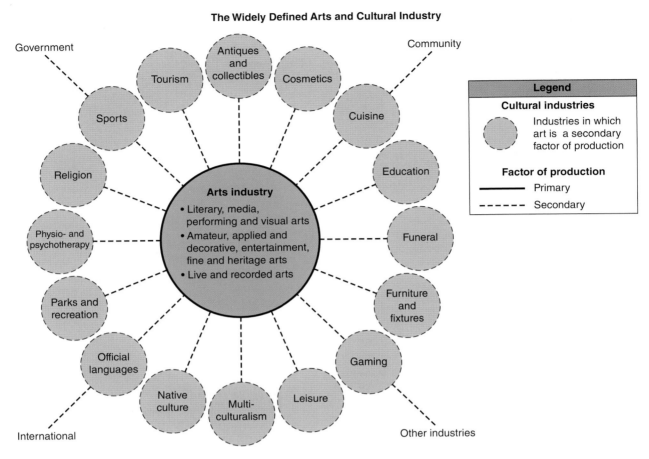

Figure 17.1 Chartrand's art and cultural industry map.

Adapted by permission from H.H. Chartrand, "Toward an American Arts Industry," in *The Public Life of the Arts in America*, edited by J.M. Cherbo & M.J. Wyszomirski (New Brunswick, NJ: Rutgers University Press, 2000), 22-49.

- physiotherapy and psychotherapy,
- sports, and
- religion (see figure 17.1).

As such, a wide variety of leisure organizations, activities, and behaviors are considered part of the contemporary arts and cultural sector.

Multiple authors (Andina, 2017; McCarthy & Jinnett, 2001; Zuidervaart, 2011) remind us that defining the arts can be challenging because many people make a distinction between

- the classic arts (opera, ballet, dance, theater, classical music, painting, sculpture, literature),
- the more popular arts (photography, hip-hop, graffiti and murals, digital illustration, computer arts, NFTs), and
- entertainment enterprises (film, radio, television, social media, mobile phones).

Given what we know from the SPPA study, it seems reasonable to conclude that the arts include notions associated with auditory, visual, movement, and experiential factors and might also include ethnic activities, religious ceremonies, specific types of athletics, crafts and culinary arts, fine arts or photography, film or web design, or horticultural practices (Arnold, 1976; Deshays, 2022; Dissanayake, 2008, 2018; Rennie, 2020). Popular arts, a term suggested by Arnold (1978) to categorize arts experiences, includes 11 content areas. Table 17.1 depicts ways the arts have often been defined by activity category. Arnold's categories were the first definitions of various popular arts experiences found in parks and recreation programs. Over the years, Arnold's categories have been adapted by and continue to prove valuable to recreation professionals.

Table 17.1   Categories for Popular Arts

Category	Description
Horticulture arts	Gardening, topiary, flower pressing
Craft arts	Weaving, crafts, fabrics, decorating, design
Athletic arts	Martial arts, gymnastics, fencing
Folk arts	Fairs, festivals, circuses, horse training
Cultural arts	Taiko drumming, Kpanlogo dancing, Wasco/Klamath basket weaving
Fine arts	Painting, sculpting, photography, architecture
Performing arts	Ballet, opera, theater, symphony
Communication arts	Theater or music arts for television, podcasts, radio, speech, film, writing, web or social media design
Sensual or sensory arts	Finger painting, Play-Doh, calligraphy, cooking

Adapted from Arnold (1978).

TYPES OF ORGANIZATIONS AND ROLES AVAILABLE

Traditions for supporting popular arts and cultural experiences in leisure and recreation organizations and programs are numerous (Deshays, 2022; Dissanayake, 2008; Littleton, 2012; Meyer & Brightbill, 1956; Zuidervaart, 2011). Most arts and cultural organizations are nonprofit, public, or quasi-public organizations that have their own missions and resources for meeting their goals (American Assembly, 1997; Americans for the Arts, 2017; Canada Review Agency, 1991; Lynch, 2017; Nathan et al., 2016). Such organizations include

- community arts centers and recreation centers,
- art museums and performing arts organizations,
- art commissions and councils,
- historic sites and folklore associations,
- museums and reenactments,
- libraries and literary organizations,
- arts and cultural festivals, and
- youth and senior citizen organizations that offer special arts and cultural programs.

Arts organizations often have a mix of

- paid permanent and temporary staff,
- volunteers and governing boards, and
- ongoing and one-time project-based programming.

Before training and education in specific arts and cultural activities were available, people had to learn on the job. Table 17.2 lists current jobs that provide arts and cultural programming across categories. Positions are categorized by type (i.e., museums and visual arts, performing arts, **community arts**, media, education and public programs). Most of these positions are in arts and cultural organizations that may be connected to parks and recreation agencies, government agencies and regional tourism groups, as well as nonprofit and private entities that add economic, tourist, and labor benefits to specific locations. These professionals work in

- performing arts centers,
- community arts organizations,
- government-affiliated sites,
- for-profit production companies, and
- museums and galleries.

The positions depicted are typical of options available to graduates of degree programs that emphasize **arts**, **culture**, arts management, and community. Arts and cultural organizations often have many types of employees who work with professional and amateur performers, artists, crafters, teachers, and facilitators to offer arts and cultural experiences. The diversity of positions further illustrates the growth that has been taking place in arts and cultural programming. Part of this growth stems from changes in participation in arts and cultural activities that we touch on next.

Table 17.2 Examples of Professional Positions in Arts and Cultural Organizations

Public and education programs	Government parks and recreation	Community arts	Museums and visual arts	Performing arts	Media
Museum educator, Midway Village Museum, Rockford, Illinois	Events and programs coordinator, Albany (Oregon) Parks and Recreation	Youth programs manager, Santa Cruz Museum of Art and History, California	Memberships and visitor services, University of New Mexico Art Museum	Events coordinator, Lied Center, Lawrence, Kansas	Content marketing specialist, Gallery Systems, international locations
Public programs and marketing assistant, Isabella Stewart Gardner Museum, Boston, Massachusetts	Community engagement manager, City of Eugene Cultural Services, Oregon	Community engagement coordinator, United Way of Lane County, Oregon	Collections manager, Pratt Museum, Homer, Alaska	Marketing coordinator, Portland'5 Centers for the Arts, Oregon	Assistant manager, digital communication, Hammer Museum, Los Angeles, California
Education outreach coordinator, Metro Arts Alliance, Des Moines, Iowa	Art instructor, Prince George's County Parks and Recreation, Maryland	Director of programs, The Art of the Rural, Kentucky and Minnesota	Curator, National Mining Hall of Fame and Museum, Leadville, Colorado	Director of annual fund, Baltimore Symphony Orchestra, Maryland	Studio producer, Swift Agency, Portland, Oregon
Development associate, Volunteers of America (remote)	Theater manager, Venice Island Performing Arts and Recreation Center, Philadelphia, Pennsylvania	Project manager, Art in Public Places, Washington State Arts Commission, Olympia	Coordinator of youth and community engagement, High Art Museum, Atlanta, Georgia	Theater arts department chair, Umpqua Community College, Oregon	Manager and web developer, University of Oregon-Eugene
Public programs coordinator, Hollywood Theatre, Portland, Oregon	Data analyst, City of Portland Bureau of Parks and Recreation, Oregon	Community arts coordinator, Utah Department of Heritage and Arts, Salt Lake City	Development manager, Boise Art Museum, Idaho	Lease relations and events manager, Gallo Center for the Arts, Modesto, California	Web development and graphic designer, Backcountry Gear, Eugene, Oregon
Director of marketing and music education, Eugene Concert Choir, Oregon	Analyst, Maryland-National Capital Park and Planning Commission, Washington, DC	Director, Alzheimer's Glass and Iron Project, Beacon, New York	Gallery assistant, Cultural Arts Council of Estes Park, Colorado	Communications Coordinator, Eugene Symphony, Oregon	Software trainer, Making Everlasting Memories, Cincinnati, Ohio

PARTICIPATION IN ARTS AND CULTURAL ACTIVITIES

Arts and cultural recreation opportunities are increasingly sought by individuals, families, and groups who want to connect with a variety of people in their communities, whether these experiences are in person, fully remote, or hybrid. Many activities compete for people's time: sports, concerts, birthday parties, meetings, community picnics, hikes in the woods, cultural celebrations, and religious commemorations. Why is interest in arts and cultural events increasing? Reasons cited include

- the number and variety of experiences available,
- organizational initiatives and arts education,
- inviting venues, and
- varied delivery formats, as well as participant expectations (Carpenter, 2013; National Endowment for the Arts, 2020b).

Participation in arts and culture must also be viewed outside organizational or agency contexts. From vlogging to knitting or bicycle repair to individually created modifications in Minecraft and other forms of maker culture, people are participating directly in group and individual activities of creative expression. Quantification of this change in venues and definitions for arts participation was first identified in a report by the National Endowment for the Arts (2011b). For almost 30 years, this report has tracked the numbers of public participants in the arts. The report was previously based on art forms such as opera, theater, and ballet, but in 2008, participation criteria were revised to include access to the arts via the Internet and digital tools as well as creating arts and crafts. After this revision, the data indicated that at least 75 percent of Americans participate in the arts. Contemporary participatory culture and **participatory arts**—in which the public assists in contributing to or making art—reduces barriers to artistic expression and civic engagement. The most recent public participation brief from the National Endowment for the Arts (2020a, 2020b) upheld the earlier data, noting that up to 74 percent of U.S. citizens participate in the arts.

As interest in arts and cultural participation has proliferated, ideas regarding who provides arts and cultural experiences and where such experiences are encountered have expanded (Americans for the Arts, 2017; Carpenter, 2008; National Endowment for the Arts, 2020a). Individuals and communities are claiming both digital and physical public spaces in new ways and for new purposes. As Rosewall (2014) reflected, "arts participation has moved out of arts-specific venues like concert halls and museums and into bookstores, community centers, homes, and city streets" (p. 3). In response to the recent COVID-19 pandemic, individuals and their related social groups interested in arts and cultural activities have moved to a variety of digital platforms and methods to engage in performing arts online or to create artwork at home or over video streaming platforms and social media, or through hybrid events mixing digital and in-person activities. Both fully virtual and hybrid event formats allow for multimodal engagement and social distancing while forming connections across geographic time and space. The National Endowment for the Arts (2020b) asked which arts activities or art forms between online and in-person arts and cultural activities were most closely linked and found that

Adults who used media to consume visual art or music, dance, or theater performances were at least five times as likely as other adults to attend in-person arts events. This ratio holds after accounting for differences in race/ethnicity, gender, age, and educational background. (p. 2)

Information about participation in arts and cultural activities can support recreation and leisure settings and programmers in enhancing and diversifying participation in the arts at national, regional, and local levels.

Whether one experiences maker spaces hosted in libraries or community centers, or festivals and performances held in a mix of traditional, digital, and outdoor settings, such sites bring audiences, artists, and arts administrators together. Public squares, plazas, and gardens as well as videoconferencing and social media platform meetups are seen as democratic spaces where conversations and performances occur and diverse members of society mingle. People are seeking arts experiences in their everyday lives within their local neighborhoods or homes or public outdoor park or recreation facility settings, or otherwise easily accessible locations. Individuals and communities also want to connect through local and global experiences. Recreation professionals are essential to providing meaningful arts and cultural activities within specific neighborhoods or regions for all audiences.

A particularly interesting example regarding local community public space for offering arts and cultural leisure experiences is the City of Paducah, Kentucky. Paducah, a city of about 30,000, needed to address a loss of population, sense of community, failing infrastructure, and other problems of decay following national and regional economic changes in the late 20th century. In 2000, Paducah began the Artist Relocation Program (ARP). ARP incentivized artists to invest in the Lowertown neighborhood of Paducah. Incentives included full financing for purchase and renovation of properties, marketing and promotion, moving expenses, and even rehabilitation assistance. By 2017, over 75 artists had participated in the program, generating $30 million in investments and significant community engagement through addition of new businesses, tourism, and pride in community (City of Paducah, n.d.). ARP's influence within the community has expanded as the Paducah Arts Council has further activated its member designation as a United Nations Educational, Scientific & Cultural Organization (UNESCO) Creative City of Craft and Folk Arts. Through their membership in this international body, they have hosted internationally acclaimed artists and creative influencers, including an artist residency with fellow UNESCO Creative Cities artists from Jingdezhen, China, for a residency around the creation of both ceramics and craft beer (Steele, 2019).

Arts and cultural programs have become more visible because of administrative initiatives, such as the one provided by the City of Paducah, to provide arts and cultural experiences. Creative placemaking plans like these as well as smaller-scale arts programming opportunities have been responsive to the desires of people for more choices of things to do during their discretionary time. Though sometimes constrained by funding parameters, outlets for marketing, and limited staffing, successful efforts to build arts participation have resulted from restructuring efforts undertaken by small nonprofit and community-based arts organizations as well as large nonprofit and commercial arts institutions (Americans for the Arts, 2017; Friedenwald-Fishman & Fraher, 2016; Lynch, 2017; McCarthy & Jinnett, 2001; National Endowment for the Arts, 2020b). Such practices show ways that the arts and cultural sector contributes to and benefits a healthy economy and diverse and healthy society.

BENEFITS OF ARTS AND CULTURAL RECREATION OPPORTUNITIES

Arts and cultural activities may initially appear to be in competition with social service providers and programs. However, individual and group-based arts and cultural activities provide benefits in their own right and offer additional support for health and human service programs and the social needs of mental, physical, spiritual, and occupational support by providing skill development and social connection. In community centers across North America, arts and cultural programming is available in a variety of free or paid activities. Free activities may include card making, puzzles, book groups, quilting circles, and community jam sessions. Paid recreation programs include everything from orchestra to pottery, memoir writing to water coloring.

City of Eugene Cultural Services Division.

Community residents join artist Michael Moloi in a pop-up Gumboot and Pantsula dance workshop in a city square. These dance forms originated in Johannesburg, South Africa, as communicative expressions of Black identity and politics before being adopted as physical dance expressions of status, style, and swagger by young South Africans.

Studies have shown multiple benefits associated with personal, social, economic, play, spiritual, and environmental leisure (Kirkpatrick & Romens, 2015; Canadian Parks Council, 2011; Cherbo, 2007; Deshays, 2022; Ontario Ministry of Heritage, Sport, Tourism and Culture Industries, 2021; Parks and Recreation Federation of Ontario, 1992). For individuals, such rewards may be

- the personal pleasure of the immediate experience,
- individual growth,
- social connection, or
- skill building through involvement in focused learning.

For communities, we find increases in economic strength, social identity, and shared values. Access to arts and cultural activities creates more attractive, livable communities.

Individual and Group Benefits of Arts and Culture

Examining how people in a democratic society choose to spend their discretionary time has been of interest to recreation professionals and arts managers whose jobs are to develop and produce arts and cultural programs. It is important to understand the expected benefits that people realize during leisure engagement. Feelings of individual freedom and choice characterize leisure and are central to the nature of creative activity (Animating Democracy, 2022; Carpenter, 2013; Ione, 2016; Kelly & Freysinger, 2000; Stebbins, 2017). Further, the arts add excitement and joy to our lives, and arts-related experiences can create an understanding and appreciation of the arts and storytelling throughout our lives (Deshays, 2022; Dissanayake, 2008, 2018; Friedenwald-Fishman & Fraher, 2016; Ione, 2016; Orend, 1989). Arts experiences also provide an opportunity to devise visual, auditory, or other creative responses or critics of society (Blandy & Congdon, 1987, 1991; Karwowski & Kaufman, 2017; Tavin, 2003). By offering programs in crafts and culinary arts, music and dance, poetry and weaving, hiking and tree climbing, parks and recreation professionals provide people with the best opportunities for enjoyment and engagement through creative endeavors, quiet contemplation, and adventuring.

Benefits realized from arts and cultural participation vary by individual and type of experience (Carpenter, 2013; National Endowment for the Arts, 2020a; Zuidervaart, 2011). Individual artists or groups of artists may benefit from direct sponsorships of their art practices. This is a long-held tradition from historical commissions by nobles of Western European or African kingdoms or entities such as the Catholic Church to current commissions by corporations, foundations, government entities, or more recently through funding platforms such as Kickstarter. The U.S. National Endowment for the Arts sponsors the Traditional Arts Apprenticeship Program (TAAP) grants in several states to support preservation and passing down of traditional practices from skilled crafters and artists to those who are apprentices in the art or craft.

For example, by hosting specific events at parks and recreation sites to celebrate and showcase specific artists, Traditional Arts Indiana expands public awareness of traditions and cultural values in Indiana's traditional arts practices through

- interviews,
- audio or video recordings,
- photographs,
- archives and publications,
- webinars,
- exhibits, and
- other public programming.

Based on the success that Traditional Arts Indiana (n.d.) has had in parks, the Indiana Arts Commission began a new $300,000 Arts in the Parks initiative in 2015 that encourages public participation in state parks and forest systems through arts activities such as artist residencies, performing arts events, exhibitions, creative hands-on activities, and educational residencies (Indiana Arts Commission, n.d.). Traditional Arts Indiana (n.d.) continues to provide opportunities for the next generation of artists through apprenticeship programs. In 2021, apprenticeships teams were formed around quilting, weaving, hoop net making, beadwork embroidery, glass art, and playing the five-string banjo (Traditional Arts Indiana, n.d.).

For other participants in arts and cultural leisure activities, repeat participation is due, in part, to the unique benefits people receive from participation. Though many people might participate in the same experience, such as playing in a community jazz band, it produces different benefits for each participant. One person might relish the music while another might delight in the friendships that jamming with others facilitates.

such specific events invite artists, fans, academics, and other interested participants to engage with contemporary and historic impacts of popular culture and related art forms (e.g., Comic-Con International: San Diego, 2022). Cosplayers design, create, and present their costumes because they enjoy it just as other individuals enjoy leisure activities such as sports, hobbies, or needlework. Events such as Comic-Con also host audiences who will very likely appreciate the skill, time, and attention taken to create such costumes and who will celebrate individual interests.

Beyond attendance and participation with friends and family, volunteering in arts and cultural activities provides direct individual and group benefits. Volunteering is a serious leisure pursuit that has gained increased importance in arts and cultural agencies (Stebbins & Graham, 2004). Stebbins (1992, 2005a, 2005b, 2017) found that serious leisure is the systematic and determined pursuit of an activity by an individual or group of amateurs, hobbyists, or volunteers. Volunteering affects arts and cultural organizations and participants because

- volunteers donate hours and expertise to advance an organization's mission and programs,
- volunteers advance their own skills and knowledge through sharing their expertise with others, and
- volunteering serves as a leisure experience for the individual and for groups who volunteer together around a purpose or cause (Carpenter, 2013; Stebbins, 2017).

In particular, Stebbins (2005a, 2017) has been the leading researcher and theorist studying the concept of **project-based leisure** as contributing to an understanding of group behavior and benefits. Group project-based serious leisure provides clear purpose, drive, and social connections; an example of this can be found at Lotus World Music and Arts Festival (Holladay & Lowenthal, 2014) in Bloomington, Indiana, which has more than 600 volunteers bring a four-day annual event to life. The connections and sense of contribution to the larger Bloomington community maintain cohesive group behavior that then generates successful outcomes for the volunteers and for the festival. Additionally, staff and volunteers work together to develop educational resources, such as the Lotus Blossoms World Bazaar Virtual Resources (2022) website, that informs both in-person and virtual festival participants about styles of music, cultural information,

Courtesy of Michelle McKeon.

Doctor Who cosplay fans. This family won awards and widespread social media recognition for their design and creation of costumes and props for a regionally sponsored cosplay contest. Most importantly, they were individually satisfied with the leisure time labor and artistic skill they applied in development of this work.

An example of joy in arts participation is cosplay (costume play), which can be seen at Comic-Cons (comic conventions), Beyoncé fan clubs, Star Wars nights at sport events, or live symphony performances of a film score while the film plays, among other experiences. For example, the Abilene (Texas) Public Library (n.d.) has developed specific events that invite participants to cosplay or participate in ancillary art activities such as comic book design, game creation, caricature drawing, and similar activities. Though anyone can cosplay anywhere,

and artist backgrounds featured at each festival. Without the support of these annually consistent, committed project-based volunteers, Lotus would not hold the same strong national and international reputation, or local and regional educational and economic collateral.

Professionals in recreation and leisure have recognized individuals' desires to participate in arts and cultural activities and other recreation and leisure activities with friends, family, and other community networks (Arnold, 1978; Bhatt, 2020; National Recreation and Park Association, 2016). This notion has been further corroborated by national U.S. data:

> Of all adults who attended a visual or performing arts event in the years surveyed, roughly 80 percent cited "socializing with family or friends" as a key reason for going. Indeed, across all generational groups, the youngest ("Generation Z") and the oldest ("The Silent Generation") were the most likely to report the lack of someone with whom to attend as a reason for not going to an arts event in general. (National Endowment for the Arts, 2020a, preface)

Shared experiences are a common ingredient of many recreation events (Gray, 1984; National Endowment for the Arts, 2011b, 2019, 2020a; Stebbins, 2005b, 2017), and they often bring people together who might not share other interests or relationships. Not only do recreation organizations assist in educating the public about leisure options in the arts and cultural sector, but they also play a key role in

- defining and perhaps establishing social values, and
- addressing social inequalities that reinforce the idea that creative opportunities and pleasure for all is a good thing (National Recreation & Park Association, 2021; Roth, 2021; Van Deursen & Van Dijk, 2014).

Shared live and digital activities that involve others can be beneficial in forming and validating friendships and relationships that revolve around shared passions for arts and cultural experiences.

For example, to reach a wide audience from many regions and many walks of life, the Washington National Opera, a program of the Kennedy Center in Washington, D.C., has long partnered with the Washington Nationals baseball stadium to simulcast select performances. As of 2022, the program

moved to Audi Field, host of Major League Soccer in the D.C. area (Fraley, 2022). Through partnerships with corporate sponsors and other generous donors, audience members attend "Opera on the Field" for free and can sit in the lawn (normally for members of the sports team), enjoy a picnic, and watch the opera on the stadium's jumbotron. This allows a diverse group of people to experience the same musical performance at the same time in the same location. For individuals who are unable to access the stadium, online digital access to productions is available via live streaming. These events also increase access to an art form that can sometimes appear staid, incomprehensible, or less desirable than current popular forms. Having broad exposure to a lesser-known art form can

- increase people's desire for more engagement with the art form,
- increase ticket sales for both the event producer and host site,
- spread word-of-mouth praise for the performance or the producing organization,
- bring audience goodwill and desire to return to the venue for future leisure events, and
- provide other tangible and intangible benefits to both the art organization and the venue.

Organizations such as the Washington National Opera are engaging audiences where and how they live in contemporary society by providing updated programming in

- classic physical gathering spaces (e.g., theaters, dance halls, public squares, stadiums), as well as
- digital gathering spaces (e.g., live-streaming sites, Zoom, Instagram).

Community Benefits of Arts and Culture

Arts and cultural recreation experiences are socially significant beyond the friend, family, or volunteer group benefits previously described. Fostering the arts in specific localities helps create a sense of togetherness, belonging, and community. Connections through arts and cultural activities allow for members to combat loneliness, fight stress and anxiety, and imagine a better future (Graham, 2020).

Community benefits of arts and culture in recreation and leisure abound. For example, researchers in Philadelphia, New York, and other cities found that local cultural activity has a dramatic influence on neighborhoods (Stern & Seifert, 2002, 2015, 2018). Their findings showed that cultural activity creates positive social environments and results in

- greater civic participation and gradual residency growth;
- reduction of neighborhood, ethnic, and class divisions; and
- lower truancy, delinquency, and poverty rates.

Stern and Seifert (2015, 2018) further found that a sense of community values and connection, school effectiveness, and greater safety can arise with arts and cultural offerings in public settings. This can be seen when arts, recreation, and community come together around **creative placemaking**, which is when public, private, not-for-profit, and unincorporated community sector entities strategically partner and plan to shape the economic, physical, and social character of a neighborhood, town, city, or region around arts and cultural activities (Animating Democracy, 2022; Markusen & Gadwa, 2010).

Totally Cool Totally Art (TCTA), coordinated by Austin Texas Parks and Recreation Department, was created in 1996 to "provide positive and safe spaces for teens to curb gang violence, teen pregnancy, teen alcohol and drug use, and just general teen negative behavior." The program empowers teens by connecting them with professional artists who use creative tools to make interesting things happen. Every day, teens use art to establish themselves with peers through their taste in fashion, music, social media videos (TikTok), television and movies, and graffiti. Teens participating in TCTA are mentored in painting, sculpture, short film, fashion, screen printing, jewelry, and more so that they can be involved in the process of making the art they see around them. When given opportunities, even hard-to-reach demographics will rise to the challenge and channel their energy into positive and productive behaviors. In the last 25 years, TCTA employed over 150 artists to mentor thousands of teens. During the COVID-19 pandemic, classes moved online to continue to provide service to this demographic. An online option provided additional access for some teens and as a result, the program hopes to run a virtual model in conjunction with traditional classes in the future (Hofmeister personal correspondence, October 13, 2021).

Festivals are another form of creative placemaking. Festivals bring a temporary sense of social connection, identity, or value to a specific geographic location or cultural group, as well as economic impact to communities. Arts managers and parks and recreation agencies often produce large-scale public festivals, and may hold art fairs and celebrations as part of significant promotional and fundraising efforts. Participants' beliefs about the social benefits of a festival may include

- an enhanced image of the community,
- a sense of community well-being,
- the ability to have a variety of cultural experiences, and
- increased interest in future art and cultural-related or identity-specific programming (Bachman et al., 2022; Chang & Hsieh, 2017; National Council for the Traditional Arts, 2022).

These positive effects can be weighed against social costs such as

- reduced local community privacy,
- overcrowding,
- increased noise levels during the festival, and
- concerns about crime and safety (Bosse, 2015; Chang & Hsieh, 2017; Delamere et al., 2001; Rollins & Delamere, 2007; United Nations World Tourism Organization, 1997).

Whether at large-scale festivals such as Coachella or Burning Man or arts fairs in local parks, socially responsible tourism must be practiced when developing festivals. Building partnerships

- honors the host community's identity and values,
- solidifies financial operations and benefits, and
- provides a social service (International Labor Organization, 2013; Zhang & Deng, 2022).

A 2016 National Recreation and Park Association survey of 1,107 Americans aged 18 and older, showed the popularity of community-based arts and cultural events. The following percentages of survey respondents planned to attend an event over the summer months:

- 34 percent—Outdoor concert and movie
- 33 percent—Carnival/fair
- 31 percent—Food festival
- 25 percent—Arts/craft fair
- 16 percent—Cultural festival

Attendees enjoy an evening of music from Opera Edwardsville in a local park in Edwardsville, Illinois.

Educational Benefits of Arts and Culture in Recreation

Historically, general knowledge of arts and culture and appreciation for and aptitudes in the many forms of artistic and cultural expression were developed in school, craft workshops, or family settings. Research shows that early exposure to recreation and arts experiences, arts learning, growth in a skill set, and valuing of arts and recreation by family members and peers leads toward continuing participation in adulthood (Blandy, 2019; Iso-Ahola, 1980; Kleiber, 1999; Orend, 1989; Powell Hanna, 2016; Zakaras & Lowell, 2008). Further, knowing oneself and how to understand, participate in, critique, solve problems, and seek change in the varied cultural values and orientations in democratic civic life are benefits of education in arts and cultural activities in leisure settings (Chapman, 1978, 2003; Darts, 2004; Freedman & Stuhr, 2004; Kelly, 1996; Lanier, 1969; McFee, 1961, 1978; Tavin, 2003).

Arts education in public schools dates back to the late 1800s and typically included drawing, painting, music, dance, and theater at the elementary and secondary levels. Values, funding, and priorities about arts and education ebb and flow in North American schools and community leisure and recreation settings. American public schools have often inadequately prepared students to participate in rich lives associated with arts and cultural experiences, as evidenced by

- issues with arts and education student training and teacher preparation,
- adverse shifts in teaching practices and goals in the arts, as well as
- budget constraints (Cascone, 2020; Dehner, 2021; National Endowment for the Arts, 2011a; Wallace Foundation, n.d.; Zakaras & Lowell, 2008; Wolff, 2022).

As these cycles have evolved for schools, partners outside of school settings have emerged to advocate for, support, stimulate, or restore the loss of school arts programs (Hall & Thomson, 2021). This has resulted in an expansion of

- arts education programs offered in community arts centers,
- arts council professional artist residencies in schools, and
- after-school classes offered by recreation and nonprofit organizations.

Those working in schools, community centers, or after-school programs might be trained as arts education specialists, education generalists, professional or amateur artists, or interpreters of art (Dehner, 2021; Hogan et al., 2018; Hall & Thomson, 2021).

For example, the Youth Art Exchange in San Francisco provides free classes, in-school residences, internships, field trips, and events in fashion design, architecture, photography, dance, music, and other art forms to low-income high school students. Participants learn from local professional artists about ways of thinking, creating, and leading through creative practice (Youth Art Exchange, 2022). Through opportunities for expressive activity, participants apply their creative abilities and further their potential (Sternberg et al., 2004; Sheridan et al., 2022; Sternberg et al., 2002), and ultimately, they begin to think like studio artists. This allows students to

- acquire and apply specific techniques;
- persist in sustained work even when it is challenging;
- visualize new ideas, forms, or practices;
- express personal voice and ideas;
- observe and critique; and
- better understand art, themselves, and the world by trying new things, taking risks, and building on mistakes (Csikszentmihalyi, 1990; Hetland et al., 2007; Sheridan et al., 2022).

Students also have opportunities to host public exhibits and performances of their creative work, participate in youth arts summits, and work with neighborhoods throughout San Francisco on public art and architecture projects such as the Art/Lit Living Innovation Zone on Fulton Street, the Excelsior Neighborhood Art Cart, the Persia Triangle Kiosk, and the Bayview Asian Garden. In addition, through events and pop-up exhibits on street corners and other public and private spaces, these students are able to democratically "talk back" to the community about locally needed social change to support low-income and racially disadvantaged teenage youth within a city that is almost 80 percent white, with 16 percent of the population under the age of 18 being Asian (MTC-ABAG Library, n.d.).

As Vincent Lanier (1969), the influential 20th-century art educator, stated, "art education must engage the 'guts and hopes' of youngsters [and] give the art class a share of the process of exploring social relationships" (p. 314). This combination of opportunities provides students who would otherwise be unable to access these resources with time, space, and tools to

- build individual skills in an art form,
- learn how to self-critique and reflect,
- collaborate with others toward end goals,
- experience real-world practice, and
- network with local institutions.

Economic Benefits of Arts and Cultural Recreation Opportunities

Studies by the National Recreation and Park Association (2015, 2017) show the important economic effects of local and regional park agencies. Information generated by various studies have shown that when community leaders invest in the arts and parks, they also invest in the economic health, tourism, and livability of their local communities (Bourdieu, 1986; City Parks Forum, 2008; Coleman, 1988; Edin & Kefalas, 2011; National Recreation and Park Association, 2020; Portes, 1998; Putnam, 2000; Roth, 2020; Stack, 1975; Zhang & Deng, 2022).

Cultural activities

- attract tourists and
- spur the creation of ancillary facilities such as restaurants and hotels and the services needed to support them.

Cultural facilities and events enhance

- property values,
- tax values,
- tax resources, and
- overall profitability for communities.

In this way, the arts are direct contributors to urban and rural revitalization (Americans for the Arts, 2010; Conference Board of Canada, 2008; Lynch, 2017; National Governors Association, n.d.; Stern & Seifert, 2015, 2018, 2022). Further, arts and culture and park activities not only offer individual and social health and wellness, but they also attract companies and educated workers to geographic regions. This results in greater economic health and wellness for communities, local governments, and business enterprises (Americans for the Arts, 2010, 2017; City Parks Forum, 2008; Florida, 2002; Nathan et al., 2016; National Recreation and Park Association, 2017).

The following examples describe some aspects of recent **economic impacts** of arts and cultural activities and the participation in parks in the United States and Canada:

- The total economic activity in the nonprofit arts industry in the United States was $166.3 billion in 2015, which included the total spending by organizations ($61.1 billion) and spending by arts audiences ($74.1 billion) (Arts Consulting Group, 2017; Lynch, 2017).

- The U.S. Travel Association (2022) showed that domestic leisure and tourism travel remained strong throughout COVID-19 shutdowns and restrictions between 2020 and 2021; however, recovery remains uneven across other travel sectors including international inbound travel spending (78% below 2019 levels), affecting economic and labor impacts associated with arts and cultural programming through tourism.

- Tourism spending is increasing overall. The Canadian Tourism Commission (2022), for example, identified that a year after the onset of the COVID-19 pandemic, tourism spending rose 44.4 percent over the second quarter of 2020.

- Over 55 percent of U.S. travelers participated in arts and culture–related leisure activities as the tourism industry regained participants in more crowded event settings following COVID-19 travel restrictions. Most frequent travelers were considered baby boomers and members of Gen Z. Members of the older generations typically had more money and leisure time, staying in locations longer. Affluent visitors of all ages were able to participate in more expensive arts and cultural activities (e.g., concert tours featuring famous artists, multiple days at amusement parks); the less affluent participated predominantly in pop-up or short-term events (e.g., single-day festivals, pride parades, local museum self-tours) (Miller, 2021). All financial levels of cultural tourists spend more and stay longer than other types of U.S. tourists (Mandala Research, 2013). Further, nonlocal U.S. arts patrons who attend performances, festivals, and other events spend almost twice as much as local attendees do.

- Canada had the largest creative economy employment as a percentage of the workforce at 12.9 percent compared to the United States and the United Kingdom (Nathan et al., 2016). Statistics Canada (2016) estimated that the direct economic impact of culture industries (arts, cultural, library and archives, media and film, and heritage) was C$53.1 billion in 2017, or 2.7 percent of the country's gross domestic product, which is higher than agriculture, accommodation and food service, or utilities. The economic impact is eight times larger than the sports estimate (Hill Strategies, 2019).

- Local and regional public park agencies in the United States generated $166.4 billion in total economic activity and supported over 1.1 million jobs in 2017 (National Recreation and Park Association, 2022). In Canada, terrestrial parks and associated visitor spending support 64,000 jobs, generate a return of 6 to 1 in GDP, and return 44 percent of government investment back in taxes (Canadian Parks and Wilderness Society, 2020).

- Canada's Budget 2021 dedicated C$500 million over two years to Canada's internationally renowned festivals, outdoor theaters, local museums, and related venues and experiences. These funds support reopening and recovery of in-person performances, events, and activities and the tourism, labor, and other economic benefits associated from these sources (Canadian Parks and Recreation Association, 2022).

- In the United States, the American Rescue Plan Act designated $135 million in support of the recovery of the arts and culture sector. Forty percent of the allocation was given to 62 state, jurisdictional, and regional arts organizations; 60 percent of the allocation supported jobs in nonprofit and local arts sector agencies nationally (National Endowment for the Arts, 2021).

As these examples show, arts and cultural activities and participation in parks, tourism, and recreation make significant contributions to the economic health of communities, regions, and countries.

CONTEMPORARY TRENDS FOR RECREATION PROFESSIONALS WHO IMPLEMENT ARTS AND CULTURAL ACTIVITIES

Contemporary strategies improve the planning and implementation of arts and cultural activities and enhance participation. Such practices include

- recognizing changing generational values and lifestyles,

- offering connections in a variety of digital and physical public spaces, and
- addressing access and opportunity as well as concerns of equity, inclusion, and diversity.

To gain a clearer picture of current trends in arts and cultural programming, this portion of the chapter looks at roles played by

- parks and recreation,
- festivals,
- artists,
- government and foundations, and
- private enterprises.

The last portion of the chapter examines several contemporary strategies in providing arts and cultural experiences.

Managing Arts and Culture in Parks and Recreation

Parks and recreation agencies have traditionally provided a number and variety of arts and cultural opportunities for people of all ages. Arts and cultural activities have been part of comprehensive recreation programs and training offered to the public at community, state and provincial, regional, and national levels since the beginnings of arts-related recreation programs at Hull House in Chicago and the playground movement in Boston (Carpenter, 2013; National Recreation and Park Association, 2022). Programming in public recreation settings requires planning and design, administration and management, access and inclusion, ethics and accountability, and leadership and creativity, whether focused on

- arts and culturally integrated environmental activities,
- sports and games,
- volunteering,
- education or social recreation,
- wellness or identity, or
- typical categories such as art, crafts, dance, drama, and music (Corbin & Williams, 1987; Farrell & Lundegren, 1978, 1983, 1991; Kraus, 1966, 1979, 1985; Litwiller, 2021; Nelson & Rich, 2022; Van Wyk et al., 2022; Weissman et al., 2022).

No matter the type of programming, the programmer's task is facilitating individual and group engagement in leisure based on their understanding of how leisure is experienced (Litwiller, 2021; Nelson & Rich, 2022; Rossman, 1995; Rossman & Schlatter, 2009; Seibel & Volmer, 2021; Weissman et al., 2022).

To be most successful in providing individual and community impacts for creative expression or embodying and motivating change, arts and cultural activities—whether festivals, historical reenactments, musical or theater performances, or culinary events—must focus on

- needs assessments with community involvement,
- program development for civic and social engagement,
- implementation for inclusion and diversity,
- reflection and evaluation, and
- ongoing modification for improvement (Animating Democracy, 2022; Carpenter & Howe, 1985; Simonds, 2020).

One successful program example is the Cumberland Trail State Park (CTSP). Extensive fieldwork completed over the past 40 years via the Tennessee State Parks Folklife Project (Tennessee State Library and Archives, n.d.) has been highly influential in continuing opportunities for arts and cultural engagement throughout the park system in Tennessee. Modifications in programming based on findings from this fieldwork have led to opportunities for individuals and groups to engage with

- permanent and temporary exhibitions;
- digital and physical archives;
- publications and recordings;
- special events, such as the presentation of African griots to America's leading banjoists through the Tennessee Banjo Institute;
- multiple folklife festivals across the state (some of which have operated for 20-30 years);
- specific local traditions, such as the rolley hole marbles of Clay County, Tennessee, which has attracted more national coverage than any other event in Tennessee State Parks for 40 years;
- over 20 oral history projects;
- more than 15 regular park-sponsored jam sessions; and
- specific cultural and identity groups, such as commercial fisher storytelling, African American fife and drum bands, white oak

basketry, quilting, and foodways agricultural lore (Fulcher, B., personal communication, May 10, 2016; Fulcher & Orr, 2022).

The Tennessee State Parks Folklife Project is believed to be the world's only active recording label connected with a park. Along with the recording label, the park features the only known state or national park with a consistent weekly, lengthy, interpretive broadcast that features local and regional musicians who play bluegrass, gospel, rockabilly, ballads, vintage country, western swing, blues, and other unique music styles specific to the location of this park system (WDVX, n.d.). For the past 20 years, this weekly radio program has been broadcast on local airwaves and available via webcast. This broadcast and the recording label, along with the live radio performances, were developed based on the desire for a regular outlet to celebrate Appalachian and bluegrass music in regional parks and leisure settings. As Fulcher noted, "I've considered it [the recording, broadcast, preservation, and broad reach of our arts programs] fundamental work for responsible management of state park resources" (personal communication, May 10, 2016).

Arts and Cultural Festivals in Parks and Recreation Settings

The social and economic benefits of community festivals highlight the importance of individual, group, organizational, and community engagement in arts and culture (Chang & Hsieh, 2017; Delamere et al., 2001; Davies, 2020; Lynch, 2017). Urban and city parks have been important settings for arts and cultural programs. In the late 19th century, parks commonly hosted parades, festivals, cultural celebrations, and musical events. By the beginning of the 20th century, dance, theater, and the new medium of film began to be represented in parks programming (Carpenter, 2013; City Parks Forum, 2008). As of 2022, parks are home to chalk art festivals, literary events, farmers markets, and even fitness competitions that incorporate local cultural elements.

Festivals and other gatherings throughout North America have shown the rich diversity of cultures, landscapes, and interests in topics that range from mushrooms, to wool, to fisher and cowboy poetry, to world music, to local heritage. Congdon and Blandy (2003) found that participating in the culture of everyday life through art—broadly conceived of as *folklife*—is something all of us do.

Kristi Crawford Photography

Children and adults watch as hot air balloons take off at the Northwest Art & Air Festival in Albany, Oregon. In a city of 50,000, the event attracts over 65,000 attendees, and includes balloon launches, arts and craft vendors, children's activities, local bands, and a national headliner concert.

The authors describe a direct relationship between arts and culture and everyday life that includes the myriad ways in which people assemble, work, and act together for a variety of political, aesthetic, economic, familial, religious, and educational purposes. Within this context, the inclination to make and appreciate art is so ordinary that its extraordinary contributions to commonplace activities such as cooking, fishing, keeping house, gardening, computing, and the many other endeavors of daily life are often overlooked.

Such folklife practices are honored at cultural events such as the National Folk Festival and the Smithsonian Folklife Festival in the United States that are well known internationally. The Niagara Folk Arts Festival (NFAF) in St. Catharines, Ontario, is billed as "Canada's oldest continually-running Heritage Festival" celebrating the "blend of the cultures and people that make Canada a nation to be envied" (NFAF, n.d., para. 1). Diverse forms of entertainment from the variety of ethnicities and cultural backgrounds are on display in the parks and other recreational settings throughout the month of May each year and include

- culinary arts,
- music,
- dancing,
- visual arts,
- balls or galas,
- tours of historic sites,
- parades, and
- costuming.

Further, the festival hosts a Canadian citizenship ceremony for those members of the region newly recognized as formal Canadian citizens. This is a celebration of rich cultural diversity and immigration in the largest city of the Niagara Falls region.

Government-Sponsored Arts and Culture in Public Spaces

Governments support the creation of arts in public spaces. For example, 28 states and territories in the United States have Percent for Art programs that designate a certain percentage of funds toward public art when building or remodeling new public structures or related activities (National Assembly of State Art Agencies, 2022). In addition, we find that public art can assist in building attractive, livable, interesting communities and neighborhoods, particularly if residents are involved in decision making and claim ownership of public art in their

regions (Knight Foundation, n.d.). Municipal, state, regional, and national art and culture recreation sponsorships include specifically tourist attractions such as the World's Largest Czech Egg in Wilson, Kansas (Wilson Chamber of Commerce, n.d.), or the many Smithsonian museums in Washington, D.C., to ongoing support for events, educational programs, and other activities at venues such as outdoor amphitheaters, ice rinks, performing arts centers, or nature centers.

Public art support in local communities includes the long-standing traditions of murals and other visual public arts design, submission, and placement programs in metropolises such as Los Angeles and Philadelphia. Since the 1970s, for example, Philadelphia, Pennsylvania, has operated the Mural Arts Program. Originally started as an antigraffiti movement under Wilson Goode, the first African American mayor of Philadelphia, the program has expanded exponentially to almost 3,000 murals

The Tuskegee Airmen were a group of African American military pilots who fought in World War II in the 332nd Fighter Group and the 477th Bombardment Group of the United States Army Air. This mural is on the side of the building above a corner parking lot in Philadelphia. It commemorates notable individuals from the community, provides a sense of history, and invokes civic pride.

created by local, national, and international artists based on specific neighborhood goals and identities. Public art installations like these assist in

- engaging and interesting the public in democratic processes and activities,
- encouraging discussion and debate about public policy or site-based work, and
- developing a space as dynamic, exciting, and inviting for neighbors to meet with one another in public spaces (Blandy, 2008; Walsh, 2018).

Financial Constraints and Opportunities in Parks and Recreation Settings

Arts and cultural programs are not free to produce. Most parks and recreation organizations operate on a shoestring budget with multiple competing priorities. Even prior to the COVID-19 pandemic, organizations were tasked with doing more with less, as budgets failed to recover from the great recession. Often, arts, cultural, and recreation programs compete for the same dollars as

- public safety (police and fire),
- infrastructure projects (roads, water, sewer), and
- other essential services (schools, utilities, etc.) (Roth, 2020).

A Penn State and National Recreation and Park Association study (Mowen et al., 2017) shows parks and recreation agency funding plummeted after the great recession at higher rates than any other local government service and has been slow to rebound. It is no secret that government officials look to parks and recreation departments when there are financial constraints (National Recreation and Park Association, 2020). As a result, organizations must look beyond subsidy in order to remain relevant and to keep providing valuable, desired services.

Cost recovery is a tool many parks and recreation agencies use to allocate resources for community needs while taking into account the organization's financial reality. Cost recovery is a strategy that allows organizations to allocate funding based on operational priorities regarding services and programs. In parks and recreation, programs or facilities are typically subsidized at a higher rate when they provide a free or low-cost community service. Often, as services become more individualized, subsidy drops, and the individual pays a higher proportional fee (Amilia, 2020). In parks and recreation, cost recovery is a methodology that

is becoming increasingly more popular as tax and bond dollars subside, costs for services rise, and interest and need for services increase. GreenPlay describes cost recovery as a "complex subject, but essentially, it represent[s] a parks and recreation agency's decision to generate revenues by charging fees for some, or all, of its programs and services" (110%, n.d.; Dropinski, 2020). An example would be an organization may charge more for an adult intermediate painting class so that there are more funds available to provide a free or reduced cost youth art camp. Each organization will have a different model, but the framework provides programmers and managers a way to quantify and qualify which programs should receive the most subsidy and how to develop and implement accordingly.

Private-sector enterprises support public and nonprofit organizations through sponsorships and grants. Businesses provide money to organizations that helps provide arts or cultural offerings through

- advertising sponsorships,
- general fund sponsorships, or
- grant funding.

Sponsorships are a way for businesses to advertise themselves and their roles in international, national, or local communities by aligning themselves with respected arts organizations or cultural initiatives. Arts and recreation managers, as well as public school professionals, have become very skilled in securing sponsorships that allow for planning and implementing a wider variety of arts experiences for general and specific publics. Businesses have learned that it is good for business to contribute to their communities in this way.

U.S. Bank (n.d.), for example, offers a robust network of arts and culture partnership opportunities that support low- and moderate-income adults and children in playing and creating. The company notes that they want to support areas in which populations are potentially underserved or have less access to museums, aquariums, botanic gardens, visual and performing arts education and events, and other cultural activities. They note that supporting arts and cultural activities enhances the economic vitality of communities they serve. U.S. Bank further piloted a program in conjunction with the Minnesota Vikings to improve the quality, safety, and accessibility of a variety of trails, athletic facilities, playgrounds, and parks. Support by private enterprises such as U.S. Bank lowers entry costs for certain types of leisure experiences. As more arts and culture–related leisure experiences become accessible to more people, the choices and opportunities increase; this, in turn, increases the number of people who are able to participate in more, although not necessarily the same, experiences.

Additionally, private enterprises can take risks to pursue new markets and new arts and cultural experiences whose outcomes are sometimes too uncertain for nonprofit organizations or public entities. Because of this ability to take calculated chances, businesses and industries add to the number and variety of art and cultural opportunities for people of all ages. Entrepreneurs in particular have created multiple ways for people to spend their discretionary income during their leisure time. Corporate and small entrepreneurial endeavors exist everywhere, from Nashville, Tennessee, to Vancouver, British Columbia, and from Disneyland to Las Vegas to Toronto. Individuals, families, and social groups

- support local businesses that combine carousels, pizza parlors, and music for birthday parties;
- buy early access tickets to a favorite touring Broadway production;
- experience a talented impression artist's performance at the local casino; or
- watch the Metropolitan Opera at the local cinema.

Each of these activities is a form of engagement with arts and cultural programming that is provided by private businesses.

Access, Equity, Diversity, and Inclusion in Arts and Culture

Access for all is a goal for park and recreation professionals. It is widely recognized that Indigenous peoples, communities of color, and other marginalized groups (LGBTQIA+ people, immigrants, people who experience disability, people with low incomes) have not had the same access to recreation opportunities due to systemic inequities (National Recreation and Park Association, 2021). Moving forward, many organizations are working to address the gaps in service. A 2021 study found almost half of surveyed organizations were taking action to

- determine the impact of operational and programmatic decisions on marginalized communities;
- increase antiracism, access, and cultural diversity and inclusion education for staff;
- improve internal and external messaging; and
- reach out to stakeholder groups (Roth, 2021).

Current access to and opportunity for arts participation in public spaces is a social and cultural equity issue more necessary than ever to be addressed (Elsabagh et al., 2022; Guinard & Margier, 2018; Mauldin et al., 2016; Walsh, 2018). Art in public spaces has been shown to reduce stress and improve moods, build social connection and cultural understanding, and reinforce connections to place and a sense of individual and community belonging and identity (Elsabagh et al., 2022; Walsh, 2018). Organizations, managers, programmers, and educators who provide arts and cultural activities have legal, moral, and social obligations to serve the public as a whole (Cuyler, 2007, 2013; Stein, 2000). Citing examples such as Jim Crow laws, which prohibited the integration of arts audiences, Cuyler (2007, 2013) reminds us that we "need to anticipate and understand the financial, historical, individual, psychological, and social barriers that may prevent underrepresented students from participating in arts and cultural activities or organizations" (p. 103).

To meet these needs, recreation and parks professionals should address the diversity of experience of community members served related to

- educational background,
- economic class,
- country of origin,
- first language,
- sexual orientation,
- physical ability,
- employment history,
- gender identity,
- ethnicity, and many more aspects that make up intersectional human identity (Loden & Rosener, 1990; National Recreation and Park Association, 2021).

For arts and cultural programming to be equitable, diverse, and inclusive of many in our communities, recreation and leisure professionals need to

- read literature on these topics;
- speak thoughtfully with and listen to community members on the board, staff, and in audiences; and
- reexamine policies, practices, and procedures.

Such practices can then lead to changes in our organizations, programs, marketing, and education for specific and general audiences (Mauldin et al., 2016; National Recreation and Park Association, 2021).

Providing access to spaces and activities that might otherwise be inaccessible due to finances, time, location, or opportunity is a goal of the Prince George's County Department of Parks and Recreation Arts (PG Parks) division in Riverdale, Maryland (a suburb of Washington, D.C.). Their mission is to "celebrate the arts and embrace the cultural diversity of Prince George's County and value the contributions of the artists and arts organizations who make this an electrifying and inspiring place to live" (Prince George's County Department of Arts and Recreation, n.d., para. 1). As part of this nationally award-winning programming, the venues of arts and cultural experiences offered by the division range from traditional performing arts and visual arts spaces with exhibits, performances, workshops, camps, and classes to an equestrian center and a local radio station. Opportunities abound to attend free concerts, plays, and festivals in parks, community centers, historic sites, museums, and nature centers.

PG Parks also features unique programs such as

- Arts on a Roll, which brings visual and performing arts to groups who want to create and engage in their own creative expression but may not have access to transportation to participate in other locations;

- Café Groove, which provides monthly opportunities for teens to share their own creative works and meet with a professional artist; and

- Art on the Trails, which asks "local artists [to] re-purpose materials found along nature trails to create sculptures, totem poles, and other park fixtures that reflect the wildlife and environment of the trail" (Prince George's County Department of Arts and Recreation, n.d.).

OUTSTANDING GRADUATE

Bri Mellott

Background Information

Name: Lizz Wells

Education: BA in photography from East Carolina University; Master of Fine Arts (MFA) in studio art from Rutgers University; Master of Nonprofit Management (MNM) and graduate certificate in arts management from the University of Oregon

Awards: Graduate teaching fellow, Rutgers University; graduate teaching fellow, University of Oregon

Affiliations: Resiliency task force of New Hanover County, education committee of Cameron Art Museum, both in Wilmington, North Carolina

Career Information

Position: Program Director

Organization: DREAMS Center for Arts Education is a youth development organization that utilizes its high-quality, multidisciplinary, tuition-free arts education program to achieve its mission of creating a culture of confidence for youth and teens ages 12 to 17. For 25 years, DREAMS has provided art education in downtown Wilmington, North Carolina, through after-school classes and summer camps and at outreach sites in parks and other recreation settings throughout New Hanover County. The program is located in the historically underserved Northside of Wilmington and over 80 percent of DREAMers come from low-income households. DREAMS currently offers over 25 different classes ranging from jewelry making to spoken word poetry to comic book making to podcasting. Fifty-three percent of enrolled students are young artists of color.

Job description: As program director, I oversee the successful design, implementation, and evaluation of all DREAMS programs. I ensure that programs and community collaborations serve our major programmatic initiatives: youth entrepreneurship, family engagement, public art, cultural connections, and teen engagement. I am also responsible for the continued expansion of all programs with a focus on ensuring equitable access for underserved groups.

Career path: Through my own education and experiences in the arts, it became clear to me that I wanted to pursue a path that would help ensure more folks and communities were provided access to all the benefits that the arts offer. A master's degree in nonprofit management helped prepare me to take on more of the administrative and finance sides of a position such as program director.

Advice for Undergraduates:

Be sure to give equal attention to cultivating your soft and hard skill sets. The ability to collect and analyze data is very important, as is feeling confident in communicating your findings in a way that is understandable and engaging to multiple stakeholder groups.

PG Parks has strategically planned and built programs based on the availability and desire of participants for sharing arts experiences, ideas, dialogue, and connections with others. Such programming aids in addressing the continuing calls for cultural equity and the rights of audiences as producers and consumers of culture and the arts (DeLaure & Fink, 2017; Goldberg-Miller & Heimlich, 2017; Mauldin et al., 2016).

As another example, the city of St. Louis, Missouri, wanted public involvement in reviewing and responding to municipal data. To promote engagement by diverse stakeholders, the city invited artist and author Jer Thorp (2017) to create a public art project. Thorp worked with the city to develop the public art project, St. Louis Map Room. The St. Louis Map Room included 29 groups of residents who came together and created maps reflecting their lived experiences of the city. Groups mapped routes they used to get to work, school, religious centers, parks and recreation facilities, food banks, governments, and other services and centers, as well as regions of the city they identified as either safe or dangerous from their own experience. These maps, created by city residents, were overlaid with city data ranging from poverty statistics to tree numbers and bus routes to crime statistics. These map overlays provided a sense of demographic change over time and helped the city think about gaps in services, opportunities, and spaces in arts and cultural recreation programs, among other issues (Moffit, 2017). This type of public art project has now been re-created in other cities to

- further community engagement in community planning decision-making processes and neighborhood changes and
- hear stories of other residents' experiences and perspectives that may differ from those of the parks, recreation, or other city staff.

Research shows us that there are important access, health, and social benefits to this type of arts and culture community engagement. Polley and Sabey (2022) suggest that health benefits of involvement in arts and cultural experiences include

- supporting child development;
- affecting social cohesion;
- encouraging healthy lifestyle;
- improving life satisfaction, confidence, and purpose; and
- enhancing well-being and mental health.

As Rosewall (2021) noted, "arts programs . . . bring together diverse groups of people . . . young and old, people of different ethnic backgrounds, and people of different socioeconomic groups" (p. 251). Additional **social benefits** that contribute to community building include

- reduction of alienation or antisocial behaviors for youth and adults,
- promotion of ethnic and cultural harmony,
- bonding for families and neighbors who participate in recreation together,
- community pride in the quality of the local leisure programs and facilities, and
- opportunities to increase civic engagement and shared management and ownership of local resources (Guinard & Margier, 2018; National Endowment for the Arts, 2019, 2020a; Rosewall, 2021; Roth, 2021; Walsh, 2018; White, 2009).

The COVID-19 pandemic has changed the way arts and cultural organizations do business. UNESCO (2021) estimated that the gross value added from arts and cultural industries fell by US$750 billion and that 10 million creative sector jobs were lost globally, as compared to 2019 information. They note that this loss is larger than the entire gross domestic product reported by countries such as Poland, Thailand, or the United Arab Emirates. Many arts and cultural programs and events went online during the pandemic in order to continue to produce, distribute, and provide services, events, and activities within health guidelines. Prior to the pandemic, a marginal number of agencies provided consistent online programming. As of April 2020, over 60 percent of organizations provided some virtual programming and resources (Bhatt, 2020) and many continue to provide online programs and events (UNESCO, 2021). While some organizations like Clearview Recreation and Leisure in Canada provided a collection of links for various cultural experiences, programmed and hosted by other organizations (e.g., maple syrup making, castle and museum tours, and performance series by national artists), other agencies created video or virtual programming to provide additional opportunities for engagement (Discover Clearview, 2021). The Township of Esquimalt (2021) in Canada, for example, offers an online art gallery, virtual ukulele lessons, puppeteering, and painting through videos and blogs. Many organizations have invested in technology so that programs can be offered in hybrid format, as well as entirely in person or fully virtually. Attendees might sign up for a cooking class at their local recreation center and choose if they want to participate in person or at home through Zoom with a take-home ingredients kit. The hope is that community members of all abilities, age and health levels, interests, and schedules—and with access to reliable, high-speed Internet—will continue to be able to have time and ability to engage in arts and cultural recreational experiences.

SUMMARY

As we have seen in this chapter, informal groups, nonprofit organizations, private companies, municipalities, and state and national sites across North America are offering more arts and cultural activities in digital spaces as well as in parks, forests, gardens, libraries, sidewalks, and other public settings. Audiences are seeking and requesting more diverse and inclusive events and activities in public spaces rather than in formal buildings. Virtual, hybrid, pop-up, and mobile arts and cultural events and programs are highly popular because they are inexpensive and readily accessible and offer a quick sampling of experiences that provide a sense of innovation, quality, and novelty.

This chapter provided evidence of the importance of arts and cultural activities throughout the history of leisure in parks and recreation. People have enjoyed arts through recreation and parks programming for a lifetime of engagement, learning, individual health, and social networking. Programmers of arts and cultural recreation throughout North America need to remain open to alternative ways of bringing experiences to traditional and new audiences in unanticipated or previously unimagined ways. Recreation professionals with interest in providing arts and cultural experiences need to keep abreast of current trends in the field and find multiple partners for funding and programming that provide individual, group, and community benefits. Arts and cultural experiences continue to communicate and critique our social values, help us understand contemporary and historical life, and be vital to our individual and social well-being.

Review Questions

1. Why is interest in arts and cultural events increasing?

2. How have arts and cultural programs in recreation and leisure settings become more visible?

3. What are some of the social benefits of arts and culture?

4. What are some economic effects of arts and culture?

5. Describe participatory arts in recreation and leisure settings.

6. What are characteristics of arts and cultural programming?

7. Describe three advantages of planning for greater audience access and opportunity and including concerns of equity, inclusion, and diversity for arts and cultural programming.

8. What are some reasons for volunteering in support of arts and cultural activities?

9. How are recreation and leisure organizations responding to changes in programming due to COVID-19 and related sociocultural shifts?

Go to HK*Propel* to complete the activities for this chapter.

CHAPTER 18

The Nature and Future of Recreation and Leisure as a Profession

Tracy L. Mainieri

> " We don't build bridges; we build the people who build bridges. "
>
> Fran McGuire, professor, Clemson University

Gremlin/E+/Getty Images

The author would like to thank Dr. Denise Anderson for her contributions to earlier versions of this chapter.

————— LEARNING OUTCOMES —————

After reading this chapter, you should be able to do the following:

> › Describe how the field of recreation and leisure services exemplifies the seven criteria of a profession
> › Describe how recreation and leisure is a human services profession
> › Explain the steps you can take now to position yourself for a career in recreation and leisure services
> › Identify methods to stay up-to-date on trends as a recreation and leisure services professional
> › List four current trends affecting the recreation and leisure services profession

Let's be honest. How often have you had a conversation with your parents, mentors, aunts and uncles, or roommates about your career choice in recreation and leisure services only to have them say, "Well, that sounds like fun"? Or have you ever tried to explain to your grandmother what recreation and leisure service management is only to have her stare at you blankly and ask why you aren't studying something meaningful like medicine or engineering? Although these comments may be well intentioned, they shed a great deal of light on the misconceptions associated with the recreation and leisure services profession. This chapter provides you with the answers to your friends' and family members' questions and a framework with which to move toward a successful career in the recreation and leisure services profession.

CHARACTERISTICS OF THE RECREATION AND LEISURE SERVICES PROFESSION

Part of the skepticism of parents, grandparents, or mentors for your chosen career path may have stemmed from the all-too-common confusion about working as a professional in the field. But a strong case can be made that recreation and leisure services is indeed a noble profession. The following seven commonly accepted markers explain what makes a job not just a job but a profession, and recreation and leisure services measures up (Hurd, Anderson, & Mainieri, 2021).

Social Values and Purpose

The first criterion recognizes that a profession must have a social value and purpose. That is, the field in question must contribute to the greater good of

society. Recreation and leisure services easily meets this requirement with its emphasis on

- health,
- wellness,
- youth development,
- quality of life,
- community and economic development,
- the environment, and
- sustainability (Hurd, Anderson, & Mainieri, 2021).

Public Recognition

The second standard is that the field has public recognition. That is, the public acknowledges the importance of recreation and leisure and, perhaps more important, is willing to pay for it. Certainly, the acknowledgment differs among the various sectors of the field. Spending patterns related to travel and tourism and other forms of commercial recreation differ from those of government-sponsored (or public) recreation. Of course, the means of funding for each are also different.

- The private sector, also known as commercial recreation, depends entirely on the willingness of people to choose one product over another (e.g., Disney World versus Six Flags).
- Public-sector organizations such as local parks and recreation agencies get at least a portion of their funding through appropriated government funding, such as property and hospitality taxes (Hurd, Anderson, & Mainieri, 2021).

Whether through direct payment of fees or through payment of their taxes, the public is willing to pay for recreation and leisure services.

Specialized Professional Preparation

The third necessary component of a profession is specialized professional preparation, which refers to the degree to which the profession has requirements that those working in the field must meet before they can practice, or the degree of professional authority that a practitioner must possess.

In recreation and leisure services, three areas are related to this criterion:

1. Professional preparation in recreation and parks
2. Specialized body of knowledge
3. Accreditation in higher education (Hurd, Anderson, & Mainieri, 2021)

Professional Preparation

Professional preparation refers to the college and university curricula that have been developed including two-year associate degrees, four-year bachelor's degrees, and master's and doctoral degrees. The four-year bachelor's degree is the most common requirement for entry into a full-time position within the field, although the degree specifications can vary from program to program depending on a student's specific area of interest. For example, in many recreation and leisure services university programs, students have a choice of concentration areas that might include

- community recreation management,
- sport management,
- camp management,
- travel and tourism,
- therapeutic recreation,
- recreation resource management, and
- professional golf management.

Therefore, although most programs develop their core curricula around accreditation standards, which are discussed next, course requirements following completion of the core delve more specifically into the concentration area requirements.

Specialized Body of Knowledge

The specialized body of knowledge refers to whether the field has a unique knowledge base that a practitioner must have to be effective. A cursory look at any recreation and leisure services curriculum might suggest that the field has simply absconded with knowledge from a variety of areas, including communications, management, marketing, and finance, and added a parks and recreation spin on the content. On closer look, however, it becomes apparent that this spin, as well as an increasingly specialized research base that contributes to the overall body of knowledge in the field, has assisted the recreation and leisure services field in developing its own specialized body of knowledge. In fact, an examination of our growing base of literature,

Students who major in recreation and leisure services often get large amounts of hands-on learning to build their specialized knowledge of the field.

Christopher Futcher/iStock/Getty Images

exemplified by books about recreation and leisure services and journals focused on the field of leisure research, illustrates the advancements that have been made in understanding how the field is unique.

Further enhancing this body of knowledge are practical, defined internship experiences that are required of recreation and leisure services students. These internships allow students to put this knowledge into action. This hands-on experience combined with our growing understanding of the nature of recreation and leisure services as a human services profession provides students and practitioners with the confidence to identify recreation and leisure services as a profession that has a specialized body of knowledge.

Accreditation in Higher Education

Finally, this specialized professional preparation is enhanced through a commitment to accreditation in higher education. Accreditation requires academic programs to meet standards set by a governing body that has identified the critical skills and knowledge needed to work in a profession. Although not all university recreation and leisure programs are accredited, those that are have demonstrated to the governing body that their curriculum is designed to teach those skills and has been successful in doing so, as verified by outcome measurement. For recreation and leisure programs in the United States, Canada, and Mexico, the Council on Accreditation of Parks, Recreation, Tourism and Related Professions (COAPRT) is the accrediting body for recreation and leisure services curricula. In 1986, COAPRT was officially recognized and accepted into membership by the Council on Postsecondary

Accreditation (COPA), now called the Council for Higher Education Accreditation (CHEA) (COAPRT, 2021). Specific disciplines within the recreation and leisure services field also have accreditation opportunities, such as the Committee on Accreditation of Recreational Therapy Education (CARTE).

Existence of Related Professional Associations

The existence of a professional culture and related professional associations is the fourth indication that a field is recognized as a profession (Hurd, Anderson, & Mainieri, 2021). Professional associations are membership organizations that provide a variety of services related to the development and advancement of the field. Professional associations can serve as advocates for the goals of the profession and provide opportunities for networking and continuing education of their members to advance the profession. For instance, the National Recreation and Park Association (NRPA) has identified three pillars of focus:

1. Health and wellness
2. Equity
3. Conservation

NRPA serves as an advocate nationally and internationally through interaction with government officials and partnerships with public- and private-sector agencies (NRPA, 2021b). In addition to their advocacy efforts, professional associations provide individual and organizational members with

- guidelines for professional standards,

Sample List of Professional Organizations in the Field

- American Camp Association
- American Therapeutic Recreation Association
- Association of Outdoor Recreation and Education
- Canadian Camping Association
- Canadian Parks and Recreation Association
- Canadian Therapeutic Recreation Association
- International Association of Amusement Parks and Attractions
- International Festivals and Events Associations
- National Recreation and Park Association
- NIRSA: Leaders in Collegiate Recreation
- North American Society for Sport Management

- opportunities for professional development and training,
- networking events like conferences, and
- grant and funding opportunities, as well as much more.

All of these activities contribute to the growth of individual members and the profession as a whole. The sidebar provides a sample of the numerous professional associations in recreation and leisure services.

Credentialing, Certification, and Agency Accreditation

True professions will recognize credentialing, certification, and agency accreditation as key indicators of quality within the field. *Credentialing* refers to qualifications that professionals must meet before they can practice in a field. Although recreation and leisure services, as a diverse field, has no unified credentialing system, various arms of the field have certification processes designed to set standards for practice. Numerous certifications exist for a variety of specific areas ranging from meeting planners to playground inspectors to special events professionals to aquatics to interpretation.

Two of the most well-known certifications are the certified park and recreation professional (CPRP) and the certified therapeutic recreation specialist (CTRS). Certification ensures that a practitioner in the field has attained a certain level of skill and knowledge as measured by a standardized exam. Practitioners must

- meet certain education or experience guidelines to sit for the certification exam, and, upon successful completion of the exam,
- earn a predetermined number of continuing education units over a specified time to retain certification, thereby ensuring that their knowledge remains current.

Detailed information on the certification processes can be found online for both the CPRP and CTRS.

Like academic programs, public parks and recreation agencies can also undergo an accreditation process through the Commission for Accreditation of Park and Recreation Agencies (CAPRA) to ensure that they are practicing at a high level with respect to the services they offer. This type of accreditation process also ensures higher levels of professionalism in the recreation and leisure services field (Hurd, Anderson, & Mainieri, 2021).

Code of Ethical Practice

The sixth criterion for a profession is that it has developed a **code of ethical practice**. This code outlines the responsibilities of the field to the public and the ways professionals will carry out services in the field. Although the recreation and leisure services profession does not have an overarching code of ethical practice such as that found in the medical field, individual agencies typically develop their own codes, or, more commonly, professional associations for the various sectors of the field develop codes of ethical practice that agencies then follow (Hurd, Anderson, & Mainieri, 2021). For instance, the code of ethics for the American Therapeutic Recreation Association addresses issues such as autonomy, justice, fairness, and confidentiality.

Codes of ethics are also commonly developed by individual agencies or for particular projects, exemplified by the Gwaii Haanas National Park Reserve, National Marine Conservation Area Reserve, and Haida Heritage Site. Gwaii Haanas is cooperatively managed by the Council of the Haida Nation and the Government of Canada. When crafting their land-sea-people management plan, the planning team collaborated with advisory committee members, Indigenous and local communities, and a variety of stakeholder groups. The plan was grounded in a set of guiding principles based on ethics and values from Indigenous Haida law. The sidebar displays the guiding principles for the Gwaii Haanas Land-Sea-People Management Plan.

Existence of Extensive Professional Development Opportunities

The final criterion for a profession is that practitioners have numerous opportunities to continue to learn, grow, and evolve via professional development. In recreation and leisure services, these opportunities include conferences, workshop series, webinars, and professional magazines offered at the local, state, regional, national, and even international levels. For example, the Association of Outdoor Recreation and Education (AORE) offers members the following:

- Annual conference
- Global University
- Women-centered professional development
- Wilderness medicine courses
- Mentorship program

Example of a Code of Ethics: Guiding Principles of the Gwaii Haanas Land-Sea-People Management Plan

These guiding principles are based on ethics and values from Haida law. They were adapted to support planning on Haida Gwaii and have been modified for the Gwaii Haanas context. They align with principles of ecosystem-based management described in scientific, planning and management literature.

- *Yahguudang—Respect*. We respect each other and all living things. We take only what we need, we give thanks, and we acknowledge those who behave accordingly.

- *'Laa guu ga ḵanhllns—Responsibility*. We accept the responsibility to manage and care for the land and sea together. We work with others to ensure that the natural and cultural heritage of Gwaii Haanas is passed on to future generations.

- *Gina 'waadluxan gud ad kwaagid—Interconnectedness*. Everything depends on everything else. Healthy ecosystems sustain culture, communities, and an abundant diversity of life, for generations to come.

- *Giid tlljuus—Balance*. The world is as sharp as the edge of a knife. Balance is needed in our interactions with the natural world. Care must be taken to avoid reaching a point of no return and to restore balance where it has been lost. All practices in Gwaii Haanas must be sustainable.

- *Gina k'aadang.nga gii uu tll k'anguudang—Seeking Wise Counsel*. Haida elders teach about traditional ways and how to work in harmony with the natural world. Like the forests, the roots of all people are intertwined. Together we consider new ideas, traditional knowledge, and scientific information that allow us to respond to change in keeping with culture, values and laws.

- *Isda ad dii gii isda—Giving and Receiving*. Reciprocity is an essential practice for interactions with each other and the natural and spiritual worlds. We continually give thanks for the gifts that we receive.

Reprinted by permission from Gwaii Haanas Archipelago Management Board, "Gwaii Haanas Gina 'Waadluxan Kilguhlga Land-Sea-People Management Plan," last modified January 25, 2021, https://parks.canada.ca/pn-np/bc/gwaiihaanas/info/consultations/gestion-management-2018.

- Numerous trainings
- Weekly enewsletters, and more (Association of Outdoor Recreation and Education, n.d.)

The Canadian Camping Association offers its members an enewsletter, access to a resource database, provincial conferences, and numerous workshops (Canadian Camping Association, n.d.). Having extensive professional development opportunities for a profession ensures that its practitioners remain relevant, innovative, and connected.

RECREATION AND LEISURE SERVICES AS A HUMAN SERVICES PROFESSION

Another response to family members and friends questioning the legitimacy of recreation and leisure services as a profession is to share the human impact of our field. The recreation and leisure services field is associated with enhancing the quality of life for participants. The goals and outcomes associated with programs, facilities, and services are designed to improve individuals' lives and enhance communities in a variety of ways. For these reasons, a career in recreation and leisure services is a career in a **human services profession**.

The human services field has the objective of meeting human needs through an interdisciplinary knowledge base by focusing on prevention and remediation of problems and maintaining a commitment to improving the overall quality of life of those they serve. Human services professions also promote improved service delivery systems not only by addressing the quality of direct services but also by seeking to improve accessibility, accountability, and coordination among professionals and agencies in service delivery (National Organization for Human Services, n.d.).

Recreation and leisure services agencies certainly fit this profile. Whether the service population is interested in youth programs, a cruise around the world, a game of tennis, camping, or rehabilitation services, our field is about improving people's lives through recreation and leisure. So what does that mean for you?

Recreation and leisure services professionals provide numerous services to the public in a variety of ways. In the provision of services, professionals can be

- direct service providers,
- information providers,
- advocates, or
- facilitators (Henderson, 2014).

A **direct service provider** is a professional who is responsible for a program from start to finish and leads the participants through the program. In other words, the direct provider controls the program, and participants are responsible for little more than participating in the program.

A professional who is an **information provider** focuses on facilitating engagement in recreation by serving as a conduit through which information about opportunities available in the community can flow. In addition, this service delivery method may include making direct referrals to specific programs or people so the agency can meet the recreational and other needs of community members. No single person or agency can provide everything that a community wants in terms of recreation. Therefore, an agency that is committed to providing information about other services not provided by its own staff is delivering a needed service to the community, although it is not engaged in direct service provision.

A third way that professionals serve the public is by becoming advocates. An **advocate** is a professional who recognizes an injustice that prevents community members from engaging in recreation and leisure services. For example, advocating for people with disabilities is just one role that

South_agency/E+/Getty Images

Professionals in recreation and leisure services often wear a variety of service provision hats while doing their jobs.

professionals in recreation and leisure might play. Although the information referral approach would provide people with disabilities with information about activities available to them, it may not recognize the significant barriers to participation beyond lack of knowledge about available opportunities. The advocate would work to gain a better understanding of these barriers and try to help that group overcome the barriers. Therefore, if the barrier to participation in a wheelchair sport was the cost of a sport wheelchair, an advocate might work with local agencies or funders to provide those chairs for people with disabilities to increase their participation in recreation and leisure programs.

The final type of service provision is that of a **facilitator** or educator. This type of professional facilitates participants' engagement in leisure such that they are responsible for many of their own leisure experiences. The provision of leisure education is an excellent example of this type of service delivery. A practitioner who can improve the public's attitudes, knowledge, skills, and awareness toward leisure provides the necessary components for community members to meet their leisure needs on their own outside the context of programs offered by direct service providers (Henderson, 2014).

All four of these types of services can be found in the numerous sectors of service provision in the recreation and leisure services profession. From travel and tourism to outdoor recreation to therapeutic recreation, all recreation agencies will likely incorporate direct service provision, information referral, advocacy, and enabling services (Murphy et al., 1991). For example, the nonprofit sector of the field, which includes agencies like the Y, is well known for its direct service provision in which

A Day in the Life of Jenny Worth, a Marketing Event Specialist With COUNTRY Financial

There is never a dull moment in my role as an event specialist with COUNTRY Financial. The goal of my job is to grow brand awareness and in turn gain business for the company through in-person and virtual events.

- A typical day starts with catching up on email for any pressing events. During a busy time, I start by diving into the project plan for my next event. This document houses my event's budget, timelines, packing list, asset list, and roles and responsibilities list, as well as insurance reps from the field that will be involved. It's crucial to stay on top of keeping this detailed plan up to date so that essentially anyone could piece together the event if I wasn't there.

- Next, I reach out to and request updates from vendors that are a part of the event. I may need to send a floor plan to the tent rental company, process an invoice from the design agency, or approve a banner for print. This is where problem-solving skills are key as well. If a vendor can't follow through with something that was previously promised, I have to improvise what to do instead.

- On a weekly basis I am in touch via email or a quick Microsoft Teams call with the insurance reps that will be on-site, or I am inviting attendees to the events. The reps are the face of the company and the ones who hold the relationships with prospects and clients. It's important that reps understand the goals of the event and they have the proper tools to position COUNTRY in a positive light.

- Multiple events are always happening at once, so then I move down my to-do list to events that will be occurring over the next few months. I may look at a sponsorship proposal and determine the best fit for COUNTRY to target our core clients or build a presentation deck to share with company leadership for approval.

- I'm constantly communicating with my colleagues across the marketing department to make sure that we are all on the same page while working toward marketing and enterprise goals.

I love what I get to do every day and am thankful for the impact I create for our clients and prospects. I have learned so much in my four years at COUNTRY Financial and know there are many more lessons to learn in the coming years.

Printed with permission from Jennifer Worth

professionals such as after-school program directors and youth sports coordinators work directly with participants. But the same sports coordinator might also provide the following services:

- They may serve as an information provider if someone is looking for a youth swim team and the agency does not offer one. The sports coordinator might be able to provide parents with information about a swim team that the local parks and recreation department offers.
- They may act as an advocate if one of their transgender youth soccer players reports concerns about the lack of gender-affirming bathroom facilities at the Y. The sports coordinator could take the issue to the administrators and the board to advocate for adequate facilities for participants of all genders.
- They may step in as a facilitator for an adult basketball league participant who is trying to think about how to stay active as they age.

Regardless of the type of position a new professional is interested in, they should be prepared to serve their participants in many ways to provide leisure and recreation opportunities.

As you see in the example above, there is no typical day for a human services professional. The two critical words are *human services*. Professionals who deal with people are in many ways engaged in professions that never sleep. Don't worry—I didn't say *professionals* who never sleep. But dealing with the public, a public that is often passionate about its recreation and leisure pursuits, is indeed a full-time job. The profession works to facilitate the public's quality of life. See the sidebar on page 384 to look at one day in the life of a professional in the field, in their own words: a marketing event specialist. With myriad responsibilities from overseeing events to managing emails to communicating with vendors to collaborating with colleagues, event specialists have to be on top of their game each and every day.

HOW TO POSITION FOR A RECREATION AND LEISURE CAREER . . . NOW!

Now that we've reassured family and friends that the field of recreation and leisure services is indeed a viable and vital profession, let's discuss how you can set yourself up for success to enter this field. Planning for a career in the profession requires taking some specific steps to ensure success. Importantly,

there are steps you can take now, while you're still getting your degree, to help position yourself advantageously when it comes time to apply for internships during your degree and for jobs after your degree. These steps to positioning yourself for a successful transition to a full-time career are outlined next, and a student benchmark checklist (see sidebar) is provided that outlines an array of activities that can help a student stand out after graduation.

Obtaining Your Degree and Other Certifications

Education is critical because it's the beginning of your path to success. You may choose to begin with a two-year degree, but a four-year degree is often preferred. Management positions sometimes require a graduate degree, particularly if you are working in higher education, such as campus recreation. Employers usually look for degrees from accredited programs in recreation and leisure services. The accreditation process, described earlier in this chapter, helps to ensure that students in a specific academic program are gaining the necessary education to be competent professionals in the field.

In addition to university education, obtaining additional certifications can be a good way to indicate to a potential employer that you have the skills and knowledge base needed to be an effective employee. For example, the certified parks and recreation professional (CPRP) is a widely known professional certification in the field and focuses on five main competencies:

1. Finance
2. Human resources
3. Operations
4. Programming
5. Communication

See the sidebar Routes to Eligibility for Sitting for the Certified Parks and Recreation Professionals (CPRP) Examination for more information. Research has found a positive link between the CPRP credential and perceptions of job performance capabilities among public park and recreation professionals (Mulvaney et al., 2015). As you talk to professionals in your specific area of interest within the field, ask them what certifications they think are most helpful for early-career professionals to pursue.

Developing Your Skills

Beyond the skill development that you'll gain in your courses, you should be developing your skills in two additional areas to help you be more competitive for jobs when you graduate:

1. Skills specific to your area of interest
2. Skills related to communication and interview ability

Kauffman (2010) suggested that students should compare the knowledge, skills, abilities, and other characteristics (KSAOCs) that they currently have with those outlined in job announcements for the types of positions they are interested in. A student with a strong set of KSAOCs that are most relevant for a specific career path will often be at the top of the applicant pool. Do some quick searching to identify a few positions similar to what you hope to apply for in the future and make a list of all the KSAOCs in the job announcements. You could even create a table to provide a visual representation of where you stand in relation to what employers are seeking. After examining the completed table, you can start to identify which KSAOCs you need to start working on to position yourself for the type of jobs that you desire. For instance, if you are interested in a position involving youth sports and every job announcement lists a requirement for first aid and CPR training, then you would want to obtain those certifications.

A second set of skills to develop as you pursue your degree are your communication and interview skills. Being able to communicate with managers and coworkers is crucial. Your communication skills are on display through nearly every aspect of the hiring and onboarding process:

- Formal writing in your résumés, portfolios, and cover letters
- Phone skills
- Email skills
- Social media presence
- Verbal and nonverbal communication during networking and interviewing

The list goes on. But don't worry! There are many steps you can take to hone your communication skills. Here are some ideas:

- Take advantage of on-campus resources, such as career centers, to get feedback on your cover letters and résumés
- Ask your professors for professional contacts in the field with whom to do practice interviews, and request their feedback

Student Benchmark Checklist

This checklist provides suggestions for activities beyond required course work that will make a student more successful and competitive when entering the job market.

- Volunteer 50 hours each semester with at least two recreation agencies.
- Create and maintain a professional LinkedIn profile.
- Find a part-time job in a sector that aligns with your career goals.
- Attend one regional professional conference.
- Visit the campus career center once a semester for seminars and mock interviews.
- Join a professional association and become active in it.
- Contact agencies you are interested in working with and familiarize them with your name.

- Review your personal social media presence to ensure information is professional.
- Complete a 10-week internship (more than one internship is recommended by graduation).
- Obtain at least one job in a recreation field.
- Job shadow for at least two recreation sectors.
- Establish at least one professional mentor in a career field of interest.
- Get to know your professors via office hours.
- Meet with three different faculty members to discuss career options in your chosen field.
- Develop your career portfolio throughout your time as a student (résumé, work samples, transcripts and degrees, awards and honors, letters of reference).

Created by Tracy Mainieri.

- Do an Internet search of your name to see what types of social media posts and other Internet results come up; then use that information to reshape your Internet presence to make it as professional as possible
- Ask a family member or friend to do some mock phone calls with you and provide feedback
- Ask trusted professors who have observed your work for feedback on your communication skills
- Video record yourself doing a mock interview and answering a few standard interview questions; then review the recording to evaluate your nonverbal communication
- Seek out volunteer, student organization, and work opportunities that consistently test your communication skills—for example, consider becoming a tour guide through your campus admissions office

Gaining Field Experience

In the field of recreation and leisure services, gaining experience is the most effective way to further your career. The recreation and leisure services field is incredibly hands on. Without practical experience, you will not have success navigating the hiring process. Faculty members recognize how important this hands-on experience is, so they build a variety of volunteer experiences into your curriculum. Further, the hands-on nature of the field is the rationale behind the internship requirement in academic programs. A typical internship is a 10-week, 40-hours-per-week experience, suggesting how important it is.

Beyond the internship, other ways to gain experience include part-time work and volunteering. Both are excellent ways to increase your experience and make additional contacts in the field. Additionally, your willingness to gain experience with organizations through part-time or volunteer experiences may allow greater access to a full-time job at those places in the future because you will already have a foot in the door. Another way to build field experience is to join student groups on campus, focusing on skills related to the field, such as a student event board, leadership clubs, volunteer clubs, or outdoor clubs. Future employers will see the field experience on your résumé as an indication of your commitment to the profession.

Growing Your Network

Networking is the process of developing a list of professional contacts who can assist with your career development. Professional networking is all about meeting the people who will

- hire you,
- introduce you to other professionals who will hire you, or
- share their knowledge with you.

Routes to Eligibility for Sitting for the Certified Parks and Recreation Professionals (CPRP) Examination

To qualify to take the CPRP examination, applicants must meet one of the following criteria by

- having just received, or being about to receive, a bachelor's degree from a program accredited by COAPRT; or
- having a bachelor's degree from an institution in recreation, park resources, or leisure services and no less than one year of full-time experience in the field; or
- having a bachelor's degree or higher in a major other than recreation, park resources, or leisure services and no less than three years of full-time experience in the field; or
- having an associate degree and four years of full-time experience in the field; or
- having a high school degree or equivalent and five years of full-time experience in the field.

For purposes of measuring years of experience, one year of part-time work experience in the field (20 hours per week or more) is equivalent to six months of full-time work experience in the field (NRPA, 2021a).

Networking can take many forms. Asking faculty, mentors, or other practitioners which avenues can be the most effective for networking is a good starting point. Attending networking events such as professional conferences, professional meetings, and job fairs can provide the right environment for meeting a wide variety of professionals. In addition, activities such as volunteering will not only build your skill set but also introduce you to professionals who are running the event or program. Career networking sites such as LinkedIn and Indeed can provide job seekers with access to an even broader network of professionals. Kauffman (2010) recommends developing a professional family. A professional family will grow over time as your career grows. If you nurture the family, it can provide you with a wide-ranging net of potential opportunities. See the sidebar for some networking tips from current professionals.

Another way to grow your professional family is by intentionally seeking out mentors in the field. Several of the professional associations in our field, and perhaps your own university, offer formal mentoring programs in which students or early-career professionals are paired with more experienced professionals in the field. For example, NIRSA: Leaders in Collegiate Recreation offers a program called NIRSA Mentor Match, a yearlong program

Networking Tips From Professionals

If you get nervous or intimidated thinking about establishing and growing your professional network, you are not alone. Many students (and even many practicing professionals!) often don't know how to start. We asked a few professionals in the field this question: What is one tip you would give to students who are unsure about how to expand their professional network? Here's what they said:

- As a queer woman, it has been really valuable to engage in spaces made for my identities—for example, a queer caucus at a conference and Facebook group for women in the challenge course industry. These spaces have helped reinforce that this field is for me and that I have a lot to offer it. (Rachel Iverson, Assistant Director of Adventure Programs, Illinois State University)

- When entering a new field, finding local or regional professional associations can help to quickly build your network. Follow them on social media to immediately see current events and best practices. Attend online or in-person events to meet professionals working with similar audiences as your organization. (Jennifer Bruggeman, Assistant Superintendent of Recreation, St. Charles Park District)

- Approach professional networking with a bird's-eye view. Think about how a short-term conversation (e.g., coffee chat, personal email, etc.) can make a lasting effect on your long-term professional goals. Don't be afraid to send that follow-up email. (Chrishaya Dixon;

Assistant Athletics Director for Equity, Diversity, and Inclusion; Illinois State University)

- Connecting with like-minded professionals is helpful for working toward common goals, but seeking out professionals that have different or even opposite points of view will broaden horizons, foster new ideas, and present new ways to do things. (Shawn Powers, Superintendent of Recreation, Pekin Park District)

- Attend state and national conferences. Volunteering to work the conference puts you in contact with professionals early, and if you are a hard worker those professionals will remember, and it could be the difference-maker in getting your first job. It also helps you to start networking with those professionals. Networking with your fellow students is important, but making connections with current professionals can be even more beneficial as you start your career. (Tom Hartwig, Executive Director, Oak Lawn Park District)

- Be open to all opportunities for development. As long as you can find one thing of value in an experience, then take opportunities that arise, even if something is not exactly what you're looking for. For example, even if you want a career in park services, a practicum at a camp can still provide valuable knowledge about how to plan programs, manage facilities, and work with diverse groups that will help you succeed in your career of choice. (Rachel Iverson, Assistant Director of Adventure Programs, Illinois State University)

that matches mentors and mentees (including students) through an application process and helps the pairs grow their relationship through monthly discussions and other supports.

The same type of mentoring can take place informally when you identify someone you feel comfortable going to with questions and who can provide insight into the hiring process. Ask your professors for recommendations of professionals you could contact, to inquire if they would be interested in starting a mentorship relationship with you. See the sidebar for a sample email you could send to a potential mentor to set up a get-to-know-each-other meeting.

Once you've set up that first meeting with a potential mentor, Horoszowski (2020) suggests a few things to help that first discussion go smoothly:

- Meet somewhere convenient for the other person
- Show up prepared
- Take time to get to know them and their career path
- Do more listening than talking

If at the end of the first meeting, you feel good about moving forward with the relationship, tell the professional you really enjoyed the conversation and ask if you could follow up with them in the future. Regardless of whether you end up wanting to move forward toward a mentor relationship after that first meeting, follow up within 48 hours with a thank-you email. Whether that person becomes a consistent mentor for you or not, you've just expanded your network!

Establishing Connections to the Field

The final step you can take to position yourself now for a career in recreation and leisure services is to establish professional connections to the field in general and your particular area of interest. One way to start establishing that connection is by joining one or more professional associations. Professional associations offer numerous opportunities for networking as well as continuing education through their sponsorship of annual meetings, schools, and

---

Sample Email to Request a Get-to-Know-Each-Other Meeting with a Potential Mentor

Subject: Meeting request from [name of your university] student

Dear [insert name of potential mentor here],

My name is [insert your name here] and I received your contact information from [name of person who recommended this potential mentor] OR I became familiar with your work [when I attended (name of conference/workshop/webinar)/when I was researching recreation organizations in my area/via my network on LinkedIn]. I was particularly excited to learn that you [insert something from their career path that connects with your own interests].

As a student in the [name of your degree program] at [name of your university] interested in [your career area of interest], I am looking for opportunities to learn from professionals in the field about what their career path has been like, what has most supported their success, and what advice they have for students like me who strive to set themselves apart.

I wonder if you would be willing to have an informal chat with me sometime in the next few weeks so I can learn from your experience. I am willing to meet at a place of your choosing that is convenient for you, in person or virtually.

I know your schedule is busy and your time is valuable so I appreciate any time you might be willing to offer. Thank you for your consideration and have a nice day.

Sincerely,
[Your Name]

conferences designed to bring together professionals with common interests.

For example, the International Festivals and Events Association offers an annual convention where practitioners from around the world meet to share ideas related to careers in festival and event planning. Another example is the National Association for Interpretation, whose annual workshop brings together more than 600 interpreters to train, network, share ideas, and enjoy a different part of the country as the conference moves from region to region. One additional reason to join professional associations while you're still in school is cost. Professional associations are committed to engaging future professionals early, so they often offer significantly reduced membership fees to students.

Beyond professional conferences, there are other ways to establish connections to the field and learn more about the big picture of the field. When you join a professional organization, you gain access to magazines, newsletters, and other publications. Sign up to receive these resources and set aside a half hour each week to review them. Some associations even have nonmember enewsletters you can subscribe to for free. For example, the National Recreation and Park Association has a free email newsletter that comes three times per week called

the NRPA SmartBrief that takes less than a minute to skim and connects you with topics and stories of importance in the field.

You can also leverage social media to connect to your field. Follow prominent leaders in your area of interest, organizations you're interested in, professional associations, and other field-related accounts to keep up with what's going on. For example, the Women in Parks and Recreation Facebook group was created in 2019 as a place for women in the field to share ideas and support, and, at the time of writing, has grown close to 10,000 members. Want to take that social media connection to the next level? Comment, react, and share posts from the accounts you follow to build your professional social media presence. Doing all these things not only builds your connection to the field, but it also ensures you are on top of the most important trends, issues, and news in your field.

CHANGES IN THE FIELD: RESPONDING TO AN EVER-CHANGING WORLD

As you get ready to embark on a career path in recreation and leisure services, a working knowl-

Attendance at professional conferences can help practitioners learn about the latest trends in the field as well as provide networking opportunities with other professional association members.

edge of current trends and issues in the field is instrumental to having a broad perspective of the field and where it is heading. Professionals in the field are working in numerous areas to increase the relevance of recreation and leisure services at all levels. All the trends are centered on the profession's overarching mission of increasing happiness and quality of life for all.

Staying on Top of Trends

The trends that affect the field at any given time will change. You should develop some skills in identifying trends as they arise. Many of the strategies you just read about to successfully position yourself for a recreation and leisure services career will allow you to stay on top of the trends that affect your profession because they will keep you engaged in the professional conversations taking place in your field. The professionals who have their fingers on the pulse of the field are the ones who regularly

- attend conferences,
- visit other agencies to see what they're doing,
- talk with other professionals, and
- read professional publications.

By regularly engaging in these activities, you will be able to pick up on patterns in what professionals are talking about. For example, by subscribing to and reading your national professional organization's listserv or email newsletter, you may see the same topic come up time and time again; usually, that points to a trend you should learn more about. Also, if you're reading the professional publications for the sectors, segments of population, and services you're interested in, you're likely to run across articles and other resources that will identify trends for you. For

OUTSTANDING GRADUATE

Background Information

Name: Andre Cobbs

Education: BS in recreation administration, Illinois State University

Credentials: Certified Parks & Recreational Professional

Affiliations: Active member of IPRA and NRPA

Career Information

Position: Program Supervisor—Athletics

Organization: Elmhurst Park District. In 1920, the residents of Elmhurst created a unit of local government to provide for the community's recreational and park interests. With boundaries that are largely coterminous with those of the city and a population of 44,722 with 15,695 households (based on the 2010 census), the park district manages 474 acres (192 ha) of parkland within 28 parks ranging in size from small neighborhood parks to large parks with playgrounds and facilities for softball, baseball, soccer, tennis, in-line skating, and basketball. Within the parks system, the district also maintains and operates the Wilder Park Conservatory and Museum and the Elizabeth Friendship Walk, which features flowers, exotic foliage, and tropical plants. The district offers a diversity of recreational opportunities including sports, specialized summer camps, environmental programs, gymnastics programs, senior programs, preschool programs, before- and after-school child activity programs, and performing art classes.

Job description: I develop and manage recreation programs in the area of athletics.

Career path: I moved along my career path pretty quickly once I buckled down and focused. I began at Elk Grove Village as a before- and after-school staff member driving a minibus to transport students to district facilities. I then took another part-time seasonal position at Winnetka Park District as an assistant athletics fields supervisor. That was followed by my position at the Elmhurst Park District in an athletics coordinator/athletics instructor position. When my supervisor at the time moved on, I was offered her position. These transitions all occurred over a two-year period.

Advice for Undergraduates

The best advice I would give to undergraduates is to focus on communication and balance. Ask questions, find out as much as you can, and try to apply what you learn when you can. As far as balance, it applies to so many different circumstances. It has been the most beneficial for me regarding humility and knowing my worth. I have no problem getting my hands dirty and doing things that no one else wants to do, but I am also aware of the skills that I have and what I am capable of doing.

Andre Cobbs

example, *Recreation Management* magazine releases an annual state of the industry report that provides insight into the trends that affect facility construction, programming, operations, and so on based on a survey it conducts each year with recreation and leisure services professionals (Tipping, 2020). In the coming sections, you will read about four trend themes that are currently capturing the attention of recreation and leisure services professionals.

Tackling the Threat of Climate Change

The global climate is changing. In Canada, annual mean temperature has increased by 1.7°C (35.1°F) for the whole country and 2.3°C (36.1°F) in northern Canada between 1948 and 2016 (Bush & Lemmen, 2019). In the United States, 8 of the top 10 warmest years on record in the contiguous United States have occurred since 1998, with the north, west, and Alaska seeing the highest rates of increased temperatures (United States Environmental Protection Agency, 2021). These temperature changes follow patterns seen across the globe, in addition to changes in

- precipitation patterns,
- natural disaster frequency and intensity,
- flooding,
- drought, and
- sea levels.

Though political debates rage about the causes of climate change and responsibility for addressing these changes, the facts of climate change are startling. During the early 21st century, professionals in recreation and leisure services took a variety of steps to mitigate the effects of climate change. Professionals will need to redouble those efforts as the rest of the century unfolds.

One way the field has been addressing the threat of climate change is through initiatives related to environmental sustainability. Sustainability refers to meeting our current needs for resources, such as food and water, without compromising the ability of future generations to meet those same needs. Many big cities in North America are taking steps to increase their sustainability, but agencies of all sizes can make intentional efforts to be more environmentally sustainable in their practices by considering things like

- the size of their carbon footprint,

- the amount of chemicals entering the water system at their facilities,
- the amount of waste they produce,
- the types of materials they use, and
- the lighting and temperatures in buildings.

For example, the National Hockey League has the NHL Green initiative, focusing on lowering emissions, conserving water, and reducing waste, among other actions. The Climate Pledge Arena in Seattle, home to the Seattle Kraken professional hockey team, uses captured rainwater to create ice, is eliminating single-use plastics by 2024, is a zero-carbon arena, and is targeting zero waste.

Event planners are increasingly looking for ways to incorporate principles of sustainability into their work as well. For example, the Great American Beer Festival, held annually in Denver, Colorado, has been recognized with the Certifiably Green Denver certification since 2016 for its sustainability efforts. Some of their initiatives have included

- switching from plastic to glass tasting cups,
- reducing overall waste by ensuring all disposable items are either recyclable or compostable,
- keeping house lights at a reduced level,
- ensuring the availability of hybrid taxis, and
- partnering with key venders to ensure those vendors are implementing sustainable practices at their event.

In addition to sustainability efforts, initiatives related to environmental stewardship are an important movement in our field. Environmental stewardship refers to cooperative planning and management that protect environmental resources and is critical to sustainability and conservation. Partnerships, often between public and private agencies, go a long way in assisting the conservation and preservation of resources. Examples such as the North Cumberland Conservation Acquisition initiative illustrate how partners can work together to protect open space for years to come. Without the cooperation of the state of Tennessee, the Nature Conservancy, and two timber companies, Conservation Forestry and Lyme Timber, it would have been difficult if not impossible to protect 127,000 acres (51,000 ha) of land that had been identified as among the most important temperate hardwoods in the world and that served as home to countless unique species (Fyke, 2009).

Parks and green space, in particular, are increasingly being seen as crucial resources to address the causes and mitigate the effects of climate change.

Parks and green spaces have a powerful role to play in slowing the consequences of climate change.

Parks and green spaces naturally help with cooling efforts in urban settings, water and air quality, and flood water management.

The Trust for Public Land's Climate Smart Cities program is founded on the idea that when intentionally planned, urban green spaces can

- act as carbon-free transportation options,
- cool heat islands,
- absorb water, and
- protect cities from rising water levels and storms.

They partner with local leaders and residents to build capacity for intentional funding and creation of "climate-smart" parks and green spaces (The Trust for Public Land, 2018). The Climate Change Response Program (CCRP) for the National Park Service in the United States released its strategic plan in 2019, which outlines the steps the program will take to

- respond to challenges of climate change,
- increase conservation efforts,
- provide scientifically sound data about climate change to their units and partners, and

- expand training for park employees on the science and related topics pertinent to climate change (U.S. Department of the Interior, 2019).

Finally, hospitality and tourism companies are increasingly recognizing the impacts their industry has on climate change. Global tourism has been documented to account for anywhere between 4 percent to 12 percent of global greenhouse gas emissions. One study found that global tourism accounted for 8 percent of global carbon emissions, with the United States having the largest carbon footprint from travelers coming into the country and citizens traveling abroad (Lenzen et al., 2018).

Many travel and tourism agencies are taking steps to reduce their carbon footprint. For example, agencies are increasingly being more transparent about their carbon footprint. Tour operators can calculate the carbon footprint of particular trips and demonstrate how travel choices in their itineraries seek out lower-impact options.

- Intrepid Travel, a tour operator with trips across the globe, has been carbon neutral since 2010 through a combination of low-impact choices for their trips and the purchase of

Ljubaphoto/E+/Getty Images

certified carbon credits for each traveler they host (Intrepid Travel US, n.d.).

- Royal Caribbean Group cruise lines reduced its emissions by 35 percent from a 2005 baseline between 2014 and 2018 and set a new target to reduce emissions by an additional 25 percent by 2025. Almost three quarters of their ships now feature a purification system that eliminates 98 percent of sulfur dioxide from their emissions. The company also intentionally designed the hulls of their ships to improve efficiency and decrease energy consumption (Royal Caribbean Group, 2021).

No area of the recreation and leisure services profession can ignore or escape the impacts of climate change. Indeed, our field can be pivotal in curbing global emissions. Future professionals must be ready to be partners and leaders in sustainability and climate-conscious service.

Embracing our Role in Public Health

Professionals both inside and outside the recreation and leisure services field are increasingly recognizing parks and recreation agencies' roles in the larger public health efforts of their communities. As communities become more complex, have fewer resources, and encounter more dynamic problems, more sectors will need to collaborate to effect change, and parks and recreation agencies' roles in public health will continue to increase. Dee Merriam (2016), with the National Center for Environmental Health's Healthy Community Design Initiative at the Centers for Disease Control, said that "public health and parks and recreation departments have many synergistic goals that could be leveraged to make both more effective." Since parks and recreation agencies are in frequent contact with the public, they are in a unique position to be part of the solution to public health issues, such as

- disease prevention,
- mental health concerns,
- obesity and lack of physical activity, and
- healthy community design.

In fact, an approach such as the Health in All Policies initiative is a perfect example of interagency collaboration (see sidebar).

An area of public health that has been in the forefront of concern for recreation and leisure agencies is preventing the spread of diseases. Prior to the COVID-19 pandemic, professionals in the tourism industry had been considering strategies to mitigate the spread of infectious diseases and invasive spe-

---

Health in All Policies Connects Sectors to Address Public Health

With the increasing complexity of public health issues, efforts are being made to formalize connections between the various sectors that can affect public health. One example of such efforts is Health in All Policies (HiAP). The Public Health Institute, the California Department of Public Health, and the American Public Health Association have created a 169-page guide for state and local governments who want to employ "a collaborative approach to improving the health of all people by incorporating health considerations into decision-making across sectors and policy areas" (Rudolph et al., 2013, p. 6).

Parks and recreation agencies are among the key community stakeholders highlighted in HiAP as potential collaborators in policies and projects related to public health. For example, the HiAP guide names promoting physical activity, contributing to livable communities via green space, and supporting social networking as three ways through which parks and recreation agencies can advance public health efforts in a community. Mesa County in Colorado has embraced the HiAP approach, bringing together a community transformation team of health industry providers, a science museum, the housing authority, public libraries, after-school programs, the humane society, and the school district to address public health concerns by focusing on building social connectedness in their communities. HiAP provides one clear indication that parks and recreation agencies will play a key role in effective public health strategies moving forward.

cies across international borders. Park professionals had been working to curb the spread of mosquito-carried viruses (e.g., Zika) or tick-related diseases (e.g., Lyme disease) by educating visitors and community citizens about insect control best practices and employing those practices themselves.

The COVID-19 pandemic accelerated the need for such a focus within our field. Every sector of the recreation and leisure services field has been involved in mitigation efforts to slow the spread of COVID-19.

- Fitness centers have overhauled their sanitation routines.
- Public parks and recreation agencies have acted as resource hubs for their communities.
- Tourism destinations have rethought their capacities.
- Outdoor parks have offered safe places to recreate.
- Recreation, sport, and park venues have hosted some of the largest vaccination sites.

The City of Toronto, for example, has an extensive resource center for parks and recreation facilities aimed to allow residents to recreate, while maintaining public health during the pandemic. They offer guidance for community gardens, fitness facilities, playgrounds, outdoor recreation venues, and recreation water facilities. They emphasize that play and recreation are vital to community health (City of Toronto, 2021). Colman (2021) explained, "From mid-March through mid-June 2020, three in five people — more than 190 million adults and children — visited a park, trail, public open space or recreation facility, and 83 percent of adults agree that those visits were essential to their mental and physical well-being" (para. 2). These types of statistics come as no surprise to professionals in our field, but the pandemic has highlighted for others the vital role that recreation and leisure services plays in the health of our communities.

Another growing area of public health initiatives that the field of recreation and leisure services can support is mental health. The statistics related to mental health show a steady increase in mental health concerns over the early 2020s. Prepandemic,

- one in five U.S. and Canadian adults reported mental illness, and
- one in six U.S. youth and one in five Canadian youth reported mental illness (Canadian Mental Health Association, 2021; National Alliance on Mental Illness, 2021).

Among causes of disability worldwide, depression tops the list. Among causes of death in the United States, suicide is second, and the rate of suicide has increased 35 percent since 1999 (National Alliance on Mental Illness, 2021). These numbers increased during the COVID-19 pandemic, with a particular focus on rates of depression and anxiety. Further, rates of mental illness and suicidal ideation are exponentially higher for people in minoritized groups, both before and since the pandemic.

Recreation and leisure services agencies are particularly well positioned to mitigate mental illness in communities, particularly through the provision of green space and parks. Lee (2020) found that having a park within walking distance was crucial to people reporting fewer poor mental health days. Other research has demonstrated that

- visits to green spaces decreased reports of stress,
- depression rates are lower in residential areas with ample green space, and
- moving from an area with low amounts of green space to greener areas can significantly improve people's mental health (NRPA, n.d.).

Recreation and leisure services professionals can also intentionally consider mental health when creating, promoting, and implementing programming. For example, as part of the National Park Service (NPS) Healthy Parks Healthy People 2018-2023 Strategic Plan, the NPS is implementing art therapy programs through partnerships with licensed art therapists to support participants' emotional health. Public, commercial, nonprofit, and campus recreation providers are increasingly incorporating practices such as

- restorative yoga,
- meditation,
- mindfulness,
- emotional freedom technique (EFT; also called tapping),
- breathing,
- gardening, and
- nature-based programming.

Providers use these practices both as stand-alone program offerings and as additions to current offerings to promote and normalize a focus on mental wellness.

In addition to addressing the increasing mental health concerns in our society, the recreation and

Recreation and leisure services professionals can incorporate programming that directly supports participants' mental health.

AzmanL/E+/Getty Images

leisure profession can be a powerful public health force in addressing rising concerns over people's physical health. Prior to the COVID-19 pandemic, obesity was a primary public health concern, and the pandemic has accelerated the issue.

- In 2020, 16 U.S. states showed an adult obesity rate at or above 35 percent, which was up from nine states in 2018, with the prevalence of adult obesity continuing to be higher for minoritized racial and ethnic groups (CDC, 2021).
- In Canada, one in four adults is living with obesity, with adults living in rural areas experiencing higher rates of obesity (31.4%) than those living in urban areas (25.6%) (Government of Canada, 2020).

The Physical Activity Alliance is an excellent example of efforts to encourage physical activity being taken by representatives from all sectors of society including

- health care,
- education,
- business,
- media,

- government, and
- nonprofits.

In fact, the overarching goal of the plan is that one day all Americans will be physically active and will live, work, and play in environments that facilitate physical activity. Community recreation, fitness and parks, and sport are three of the nine sectors identified as playing fundamental roles in the plan. Within these sectors, the plan outlines multiple strategies for improving levels of physical activity, which include

- improving existing and adding new programs and facilities,
- improving access to clean and safe facilities for physical activity,
- securing sustainable funding for services in areas of high need,
- eliminating disparities in access to sport based on diversity characteristics, and
- creating safe and inclusive environments for sports participation (Physical Activity Alliance, 2020).

To address physical inactivity, traffic issues, air quality concerns, and a range of other public health issues, communities are turning their attention to becoming more walkable and bikeable. Parks and recreation departments are lending their knowledge of recreation, physical activity, park design, and multiuse surfaces to these efforts. They can also collaborate on crucial programming initiatives to increase walking and biking as modes of transportation, such as commuting challenges, walking programs, and walking school bus days. These initiatives affect the individual, environmental, and social health of a community.

In 2021, the Canadian government announced the first National Active Transportation Strategy aimed to expand pathways and trails for active public transportation purposes. The announcement also included a fund of C$400 million over five years to support urban, rural, and Indigenous communities looking to improve their active transportation infrastructure, such as pathways, bike lanes, and pedestrian bridges. Listed among the key partners for the national strategy are Vélo Canada Bikes, Trans Canada Trails, and the Canadian Parks and Recreation Association (Minister of the Office of Infrastructure of Canada, 2021).

The public health contributions from the recreation and leisure services industry are crucial not only to community and individual wellness, but also to the economic realities communities and individuals face. For example, a study conducted by the Trust for Public Land found that physical activity via the Huron-Clinton Metroparks region of Michigan produced significant health care savings—on average, $1,250 per adult per year (Drepaul-Bruder, 2021). Emerging professionals in the field will need to be able to embrace, articulate, and leverage the role our field plays in public health.

Advocating for Inclusion, Equity, and Social Justice

The demographics in both the United States and Canada are changing. In both countries,

- the population is aging,
- immigration patterns are changing, and
- racial and ethnic makeup is diversifying.

For example, the Pew Research Center projects that no racial or ethnic group will comprise more that 50 percent of the U.S. population by 2055 (Pew Research, 2015). In Canada, the visible minority population (how Canada's Employment Equity Act labels non-Caucasian, non-Aboriginal, non-

Recreation and leisure professionals will need to implement intentionally inclusive practices to ensure participants from all backgrounds feel safe and welcome.

Neilson Barnard/Getty Images for National Park Service

white-in-color people) is projected to account for up to 36 percent of the population by 2036, up from 5 percent of the population in 1981 (Statistics Canada, 2017b). Further, the Indigenous population of Canada is projected to grow faster than the non-Indigenous population between 2011 and 2036 (Statistics Canada, 2017a).

In addition to numerical changes in the demographics in both countries, recent years have seen increasing calls for social justice in the form of protests, legislation, and public commentary. The summer of 2020 saw widespread demonstrations for racial justice in the United States in the wake of George Floyd's murder by police, and the summer of 2021 saw protest and outrage after the discovery of hundreds of children's bodies at former residential schools for Indigenous children in Canada. These singular moments in time represent a wider call in both countries to address systemic patterns of inequity, discrimination, and oppression across a wide range of diversity indicators (e.g., race, ethnicity, gender identity, sexual orientation, language, immigrant status, socioeconomic status, etc.). The larger national movements necessitate professionals in the field of recreation and leisure services to consider their role in creating inclusive spaces in their agencies and in supporting equity and social justice in their communities.

Inclusion refers to practices and policies designed to ensure access and belonging for all, with particular efforts to include people from traditionally minoritized groups. The changing demographics of society and the societal call to break down traditional power structures mean that recreation and leisure services professionals need to be intentionally inclusive in each aspect of their work, both with participants and within their agencies. With participants, professionals need to consider their programming, facilities, marketing, and customer service with an inclusive lens.

For example, recreation and leisure services agencies need to consider how they can successfully reduce barriers for people along the entire gender identity spectrum. Traditionally structured facilities (e.g., bathrooms, locker rooms), programming (male and female sports), and marketing materials can pose significant barriers to transgender, gender nonbinary, or gender expansive people who want to participate in recreation and leisure services. Because these are new and unfamiliar topics for many professionals and agencies, forward-thinking agencies are forming coalitions or work groups that

Honoring Indigenous Cultures in Recreation and Leisure Services Through Inclusive and Equitable Practices

Indigenous cultures have long experienced cultural appropriation, land loss, discrimination, and, in many cases, attempted cultural erasure within North American society, all persisting legacies of colonialism. Many recreation and leisure services agencies have, in many ways, perpetuated these legacies. Some agencies, however, are taking intentional, inclusive steps to honor Indigenous cultures, partner with local Indigenous communities, and center Indigenous voices. Some examples are

- eliminating the use of terms or imagery relating to Indigenous cultures or stereotypes of Indigenous cultures for program names, agency traditions, sports teams, mascots, and so on;

- creating Indigenous land acknowledgments, in partnership with local Indigenous groups, to honor the history of the land agencies operate on;

- partnering with local Indigenous leaders during program, facility, and strategic planning;

- amplifying and partnering with Indigenous voices in advocacy efforts;

- taking the time to listen and learn about the Indigenous cultures in an agency's specific region; and

- enacting policies that ensure consultation with local Indigenous communities occurs on a regular basis.

This list offers a sample of ways recreation and leisure services agencies are decolonizing their practices in relation to Indigenous people. Individual professionals can also take steps to be an effective ally. Want to start your own allyship journey? Check out the resources provided by the Know the Land Territories Campaign online: www.lspirg.org/knowtheland.

consist of a variety of stakeholders and topic experts to research these issues and formulate strategies that will be successful and inclusive.

The Vancouver Board of Parks and Recreation created the Trans and Gender-Variant Inclusion Working Group. After nearly a year of input gathering, community engagement, and research, this group released a final report with specific recommendations to support the needs of the trans and gender-variant community through all levels of service such as facilities, programming, human resources, and literature (Taylor, 2014). See the sidebar for a consideration of how recreation and leisure services agencies are seeking to be intentionally inclusive toward another population: Indigenous people.

Beyond being intentionally inclusive, recreation and leisure services agencies and professionals will need to question their own role in perpetuating or dismantling the larger systems of inequity within their communities. Access to parks, playgrounds, programming, and green space is increasingly being seen as a social justice issue, since data demonstrate that such access tends to be less frequent and of poorer quality in neighborhoods with high proportions of minoritized or low-income residents. The Trust for Public Land's ParkServe tool can demonstrate where "park deserts" (areas in a city where residents don't live within a 10-minute walk of a park) exist in urban areas and how they are distributed.

For example, when looking up Anaheim, California, using the tool, you'll find that the city's 2021 ParkServe ranking is number 58, with 67 percent of residents living within a 10-minute walk of a park, above the national average of 55 percent. When you delve deeper into how the parks are distributed, you find that

- residents in neighborhoods of color have access to 91 percent less park space per person than those in white neighborhoods and
- those in low-income neighborhoods have access to 85 percent less park space per person than those in high-income neighborhoods (The Trust for Public Land, 2021).

One way that public parks and recreation agencies can uncover these disparities is by conducting an equity audit of their agency to inform future funding, programming, and planning decisions. The City of San Diego Parks and Recreation Department conducted a recreation equity audit that uncovered, among other findings, that

- residents in the wealthier northern city districts have access to double the number of activities than residents in the lower-income southern districts,
- annual spending on programming in northern districts was over $60,000 more than in southern districts, and
- parks in poor condition are much more likely to be found in low- and middle-income neighborhoods.

The city has used the information from the audit to redesign their funding structure and implement a new citywide parks fee to address these areas of inequity (Garrick, 2021).

The above examples are a tiny sampling of the ways in which professionals in the field of recreation and leisure services will think about their role in inclusion, equity, and social justice moving forward. Our agencies and professionals are not separate from the society that surrounds us. Consequently, future professionals will need to

- stay attuned to the changing dynamics of society,
- advocate for inclusive practices in their agencies, and
- leverage the power of recreation, play, leisure, and sport to resist the systems of inequity at work in our society.

Leveraging Technology to Reach Expanded Audiences

How would you answer the following question: Does technology enhance or hinder people's experience of leisure? Regardless of where you land on this question, one thing is not up for debate. Recreation and leisure professionals entering the field must acknowledge the pervasiveness of technology, mobile technology, and social media in our society. In doing so, professionals will be prepared to view technology as an opportunity to leverage, rather than a barrier to overcome. Indeed, in many ways, technology can offer new ways to serve existing participants and to welcome new participants to the services our field has to offer. For example, check out the sidebar about the rise of esports as a case for technology as a way to reach new audiences. We will then explore how mobile technology, social media, and virtual programming may affect the field of recreation and leisure services moving forward.

Riding the Rising Tide of Esports to Reach New Audiences

Analysts predicted that global esport revenues would be over US$1 billion and that the global audience for esports events would be well over 400 million viewers in 2021 (Newzoo, 2021). Indeed, the esports industry has seen an unparalleled surge in popularity and growth just in the past five years. This excitement around competitive gaming offers recreation and leisure professionals a unique opportunity to leverage the power of technology to reach new audiences.

In 2018, 68 percent of teens aged 13 to 17 reported participating on a team or individual sport (Aspen Institute, 2021). In the same year, 84 percent of teens aged 13 to 17 reported having access to a game console at home and 90 percent reported playing video games in some form or fashion (Anderson & Jiang, 2018). Collegiate varsity sports and campus recreation professionals have recognized the potential of esports and gaming as a recruitment tool for universities. The first collegiate varsity esports program began in 2014; that number now exceeds 200 programs.

College campus recreation programs are increasingly offering intramural and club-level esports programming as well. For example, Red-bird Esports at Illinois State University has seen such growth since its 2019 inception that it unveiled a $4.5 million state-of-the-art gaming facility in Fall 2022 (Bersett & Emken, 2022). The program has over 1,200 students participating in its three levels of offerings, including three varsity teams and 20 esports-related registered student organizations.

Public parks and recreation agencies are also growing their esports offerings to reach new and expanded audiences. When the Bloomington, Minnesota, Parks and Recreation Department added an esports program to their offerings in 2021, in partnership with the Minnesota Esports Club, they saw it as a way to

- open doors to youth in their community;
- build discipline, social, and leadership skills in their participants; and
- include people who are not interested in traditional sports offerings (Stridsberg, 2021).

The rise in esports will undoubtedly continue, so future recreation and leisure professionals should look for ways to be early adopters and innovators in their own sector of our field.

Agencies that are not yet fully leveraging the prominence of mobile technology will continue to fall further behind in reaching and serving their target markets. In 2020, reports indicated that 85 percent of Americans and 84 percent of Canadians owned smartphones, up from 64 percent and 68 percent, respectively, in 2015. Mobile and personal technology affects a variety of sectors and services in the recreation and leisure field. Personal technology tools such as activity trackers and phone apps have changed the way participants engage with and track their activities, and fitness professionals are looking for ways to integrate these new technologies into fitness programming and equipment.

Recreation and leisure services agencies are also continually evaluating the use of apps for internal operations and participant outreach. Youth sport professionals are using apps to schedule and manage their sport leagues, event planners are using apps to plan and facilitate their events, parks are using apps to provide interpretation and information to their visitors, and the list goes on. For example, the Central Park Conservancy offers an app for visitors to Central Park that includes

- an interactive map,
- event listings,
- celebrity tours of popular locations in the park,
- an extensive list of things to see in the park,
- social media feeds for the park, and
- a souvenir shop.

Professionals are tapping into mobile technologies in sport and arena management to enhance the fan experience at and beyond professional sport events, including

- in-stadium food delivery and ordering,
- instant replays,
- electronic ticketing,
- live game statistics,

- live streaming, and
- powerful fan data collection for professionals.

Beyond enhancing fan experience and engagement, the use of mobile technology in large venue sports also has important health implications for sport engagement beyond COVID-19 because it can reduce person-to-person contact. For example, the National Football League moved entirely to paperless tickets in the 2021 season.

Recreation and leisure service agencies also need to consider the use of social media in their operations and services. Talk to a current professional in the recreation and leisure service field and they will tell you that the most successful agencies have employees who understand how to use social media to professionally market their programs, engage participants, connect staff members, and advocate for what they do.

Sport teams have been particularly keen to use social media to increase fan engagement with their teams; for example, they

- use streaming capabilities during games,
- maintain active YouTube channels,

- use Snapchat to give fans an inside look into team practices, and
- engage with fans on TikTok.

Public parks and recreation agencies are increasingly devising intentional social media marketing plans so they can engage with and lead the conversations about their agencies via social media outlets. Many times these strategies include notices about event registration, seasonal facility hours, giveaways, emergency procedures, and positive comments from users.

Finally, the COVID-19 pandemic accelerated the need for agencies in all sectors of the recreation and leisure services field to leverage technology via virtual programming.

- Public parks and recreation agencies offered "programs in a box" that participants could take home to complete, usually with linked videos created by the service providers.
- Campus recreation departments and fitness centers embraced videoconferencing software for participants to join group fitness classes from their homes.

Virtual programming, like virtual fitness classes, will remain important beyond the COVID-19 pandemic for agencies wishing to serve all of their potential participants.

FatCamera/iStock/Getty Images

- Professional sports teams offered virtual experiences to their fans while sport venues were closed to spectators.
- Therapeutic recreation professionals devised client treatment plans that utilized everyday equipment that clients had around their homes.
- Parks partnered with local libraries to do outdoor story walks for youth.

The list of pandemic adaptations using virtual programming could go on and on. While virtual programming became the only way for many agencies to offer services to their participants at the height of the pandemic, professionals in the field agree that it is here to stay, regardless of the trajectory of the pandemic. Indeed, many professionals found that virtual programming allowed them to reach new participants who did not use their services prior to the pandemic and so view the continuation of virtual programming as a vital new marketing strategy to retain and expand their audience. Regional and national professional conferences are continuing to offer virtual attendance options, even as safety restrictions relax, to allow those who cannot or prefer not to travel to the conference site to still benefit from conference offerings.

Briery (2021), the executive camp director and chief program officer for CAMP, explained the benefits of virtual programming for their participants with disabilities. He shared that after families who had been previously reluctant to send their child to camp experienced the virtual camp experience,

> they all indicated they will be ready to let their campers try traditional camp when the pandemic allows. Even beyond the pandemic, we are starting to contemplate the potential value of utilizing virtual programming to complement our in-person programs as a means of reaching campers and families who may have previously been out of reach. (para. 15)

Many of the services offered via recreation and leisure services provide a much-needed respite for participants from technology and the pressures of an ever-connected world. Additionally, access to technology is not a universal privilege, and tech literacy and access are obstacles for many. Technology-free services should continue to thrive. In order to remain viable and to connect with new audiences, however, recreation and leisure services professionals must also leverage the power of technology. Technology can offer ways to

- connect with participants,
- accomplish work more efficiently,
- provide new programs, and
- advocate for our field.

Future professionals can be on the forefront of these trends and be valuable assets to agencies looking to meaningfully leverage technology.

SUMMARY

The field of recreation and leisure services provides exciting opportunities for those who choose to make it their career path. Working in recreation and leisure services means that you are working in a field replete with possibilities, and you have the opportunity to enhance the profession through your service. Recreation and leisure services has proved its worth as a human services profession dedicated to the betterment of people. As a human services profession, the field is constantly changing. Demands for services, changing interests, enhancements in technology, and demographic shifts have all contributed to the evolution of the field. To reach their full potential, the profession and its practitioners need to constantly challenge themselves to meet the changing needs of society. Becoming part of this dynamic profession will take hard work and perseverance. Clear career positioning, as described in this chapter, will go a long way in setting the stage for an illustrious career in the field. From networking to improving communication skills, the best and brightest students and professionals set their course for success early in their careers. It's never too early to make a good impression.

Think back to that conversation with your family or friends at the start of the chapter in which they express skepticism over the value and legitimacy of your chosen career path in recreation and leisure services. We hope this chapter provides you with a number of different ways to advocate for our field. This chapter started with the quote: "We don't build bridges; we build the people who build bridges." Certainly, building bridges is important; getting to certain places would be tough without the engineers who are responsible for those bridges. The bridges are tangible representations of the hard work of engineering professionals, and the public respects that. An engineering major never has to justify their choice of profession. But what does the recreation and leisure services professional build? They build people—happier, healthier, more confident people. Those people are likely to be engineers, teachers, doctors—and the list could go on. The recreation and leisure services professional ensures that all those people are better because of what our field does to build them.

Review Questions

1. What are the seven commonly accepted markers that distinguish a profession? Which one is the most important to your reasons for becoming a recreation and leisure services professional? Why?

2. What are the four roles that recreation and leisure services professionals may take on to serve their publics? Which role are you most excited about in becoming a recreation and leisure services professional? Why?

3. The National Recreation and Park Association has identified five reasons why professional certifications are important. What are they?

4. Why is accreditation important?

5. Describe some of the steps you can take to position yourself for a career in recreation.

6. Define what is meant by a human services profession.

7. Beyond an internship, what are other ways to gain experience?

8. What are strategies professionals can use to stay on top of the most current trends?

9. What are two current trends affecting the field?

10. Why is it important to stay on top of trends as a professional?

Go to HK*Propel* to complete the activities for this chapter.

CHAPTER 19

International Perspectives on Recreation and Leisure

*Kevin J. Fink, Michael J. Bradley, Arianne C. Reis, Alcyane Marinho,
Jinyang Deng, Huimei Liu, Jian Li, Franz U. Atare*

  ❝ The bow cannot always stand bent, nor can human frailty subsist
without some lawful recreation. ❞

Miguel de Cervantes, Spanish novelist, poet, and playwright

Xinhua News Agency/Getty Images

We acknowledge Richard R. Jurin and Diane Gaede for previous contributions to this chapter.

――――――――――――― **LEARNING OUTCOMES** ―――――――――――――

After reading this chapter, you should be able to do the following:

> Understand the basis of sustainability as a concept for better living globally
> Understand how cultural interactions between more-developed countries and less-developed countries—through the former's tourism, nature travel, and leisure activities—can encourage sustainable systems in both
> Recognize how tourism, nature travel, and leisure activities are becoming increasingly global sustainability activities
> Understand the effects of social and economic issues on leisure pursuits
> Value the different ways individuals and communities socialize and enjoy leisure time in different societies
> Appreciate the similarities and differences between developed and developing countries' leisure pursuits
> Recognize how historical events, whether political, cultural, economic, or social, contribute to current leisure practices
> Describe the scope and importance of recreation and leisure in China
> Identify the characteristics of recreation and leisure pursuits among people of different walks of life
> Explain the influence of modernization and globalization on the pursuits of leisure and recreation of Chinese people
> Describe how traditional games influence leisure and recreation in Nigeria
> Explain how topography and geographic locations influence leisure preferences in Nigeria
> Characterize the effects of urbanization, economy, and social media on leisure service use

―――――――――――――――――――――――――――――――――――――――

International Perspectives: Sustainability and Ecotourism

Kevin J. Fink and Michael J. Bradley

" Recreational development is a job not of building roads into the lovely country, but of building receptivity into the still unlovely human mind. . . . A thing is right when it tends to preserve the integrity, stability and beauty of the biotic community. It is wrong when it tends otherwise. **"**

Aldo Leopold, American author, philosopher, forester, and conservationist

As people become more aware of the concept of sustainability, the opportunity arises to see how it takes shape with

- decreasing consumerism,
- increased community resilience, and
- improved positive human connections to the natural world.

At home, and especially abroad, this worldview has spawned niches that the recreation, tourism, and leisure industry is embracing. Rather than recreate in any setting, there is a drive to be in natural settings, where people are beginning to see and feel a deeper connection to natural areas. This drive toward outdoor settings increased during the COVID-19 pandemic when social distancing was encouraged and many were prohibited in their travel and daily activities due to lockdowns, temporary business closures, and other mitigation efforts. Demand for outdoor recreation equipment such as campers and RVs (Green, 2020) and bicycles (Goldbaum, 2020) increased and became, in some cases, challenging to acquire. Demand for outdoor recreation rose in the United States during 2020 as the Outdoor Industry Association (2021a, p. 3) found that at least 160 million people recreated outdoors "at least once." Common activities included walking, running or jogging, biking, and bird-watching with fewer preferring camping, backpacking, or climbing (Outdoor Industry Association, 2021b). Recreating in natural settings inevitably leads to experiences in which many visitors are eager to see how human and natural systems can coexist for mutual benefit. In many places worldwide, this transition to sustainability can be seen where natural ecological systems are now viewed as having more value when designated as biosphere reserves, and also where agricultural and living practices are more aligned with healthy natural systems.

SUSTAINABILITY

Sustainability is a word that is often used but is poorly understood. Too often it is simply used as a synonym for *being green* or *advanced environmentalism*. In fact, it is a vision of how one lives within the world and how we connect with the natural world. A simple yet all encompassing definition is to live within the limits of nature's ecosystem services and to live together in communities that are equitable, regenerative, resilient, and adaptive. Further, one should consider sustainability to include social and cultural elements of the host community alongside the environmental conditions (Butler, 1991; UNWTO, 2022). To do that, we must travel and live mindfully and consciously and think using a whole system approach.

The other major misconception about sustainability is that it is somehow about giving things up or, worse, about sacrificing lifestyle. In fact, it is about enhancing our lives to make us happier, healthier, and more prosperous. There is a focus on improving our overall well-being through rebuilding community and using resources from our ecosystems that are renewable and in harmony with the natural world. It is a positive vision, but it is one we must consciously choose. By not actively choosing this new vision, we complacently choose to accept the current, increasingly detrimental, business-as-usual model (Jurin, 2012). Sustainability means changing our worldview about ourselves and how we fit within the natural world and other cultures and customs.

The term *nature-deficit disorder (NDD)* was coined as a way of describing the apparent disconnect of modern thinking from the natural world (Louv, 2008). While it is true that natural systems are not front and center in most people's thinking, it is probably more accurate to say we are highly distracted by modern technology and lifestyles. Rideout and Robb (2020), in researching U.S. children up to age 8 before the start of the pandemic, found children spent about two and a half hours on their screens each day. As reported by parents, this time was often related to television and videos and less so by screen time related to homework and reading. Unsurprisingly, time on screens increased for older participants. In a Canadian-focused study examining behaviors of cohorts from 2009 to 2011 and 2012 to 2013, researchers estimated just over one in five children aged 3 to 4 years old met screen-time recommendations of less than one hour per day. The researchers also found just over 75 percent met the recommendation of less than two hours per day for 5-year-olds (Garriguet et al., 2016). Carson et al. (2020) in examining multiple cohorts from 2009 to 2017 found 3- to 5-year-olds averaged just under two hours of screen time for both boys and girls studied.

To emphasize how people are really connected to the natural world, consider some of the obvious indications. As biologist E.O. Wilson points out in *Biophilia* (1984), people have an innate love of living things and a natural affinity with nature.

- Chawla (2015), in a review of research from the past five decades about children and nature, shows that children seemingly want access to the outdoors, specifically to explore, play, recreate, learn about themselves, and potentially emotionally bond with outdoor spaces and places.

- It is not uncommon for park visitors to find themselves stopped in a line of cars because some large elk, moose, bison, or bears are close to the road, and visitors tend to stop, admire, and take photographs of the wildlife.

- If you find a parking area or scenic turnout with a spectacular view, it will inevitably be full of people enjoying the grandeur.

Whenever we consider nature and scenic environments, we inevitably find our feelings and emotions are much deeper than mere curiosity. This component is inherent in much of our interactions with the natural world; when we are in a location in which we feel a deep connection, we experience a feeling of being in place.

Place attachment is our attachment to geography, where we may connect to a park or trail, a lake, a store, or a school. As Scannell and Gifford (2010, p. 1) noted, this attachment is created through "person-process-place." Though dimensions and development of place attachment definitions have been hypothesized and researched, often it is described as a person's relationship to a place developed through time spent at a location where the place becomes significant to the individual through their experience within it (Scannell & Gifford, 2010; Williams & Vaske, 2003). Some dimensions of study within the place attachment literature include one's reliance on the resource for recreational or activity desires (dependence; Scannell & Gifford, 2010; Williams & Roggenbuck, 1989), the place's capacity to resonate with elements of who a person is (identity; Scannell & Gifford, 2010; Williams & Roggenbuck, 1989), and the emotional meaning of the place for the person (affect; Halpenny, 2010; Scannell & Gifford, 2010). Other dimensions of place attachment have been studied, too, such as the social aspects of experiences at a place (Kyle et al., 2004).

Notably, sense of place is often linked to

- communities where we grew up,
- places we have lived, or
- anywhere we have had profound experiences that make the place special or even sacred.

Perhaps these prior experiences of attachments may be transferable to new places. For example, studies have shown that place attachment to outdoor areas may be positively related to environmentally responsible behaviors (Halpenny, 2010; Whitburn et al., 2019). As outdoor experiences have increased due to COVID-19, investigating potential changes in environmental attitudes and stewardship behaviors will be paramount because it is conceivable that a greater inclination to become better stewards of the planet will result. It will be important to continue to cultivate this in our society moving forward.

For most of human history, Indigenous peoples lived with a profound reverence and sense of place to areas they inhabited. Jared Diamond (2012) comments on how these societies that have not yet been changed by modern living offer insights into how people can live in relative peace and harmony with one another and the natural world. He contrasts that with modern technological systems of living, and says that both have good and bad traits. He ultimately concludes the way humans used to live, coupled with some of the modern attributes of globalized living and traveling, offers us a way to live

Teaching children about nature will provide them with lifelong benefits.

kali9/E+/Getty Images

for the future. It is when we understand the global system as a human system and a natural system that we can begin to understand how a sustainable human future can exist harmoniously with the natural world (Jurin, 2012). In consideration of cultures and histories, we must be aware of and advocate for equitable access to natural places and to strive to understand our histories and experiences in nature (including lack of access, violence, and tragedy) as we move toward connections with nature and sustainability (Finney, 2014).

In many European countries, sustainability is being slowly implemented in terms of greener technology and also a return to family-based gardens. This is creating a shift in community-based living where the food is now a responsibility of the whole community and not just farmers.

- In Switzerland, many homeowners grow food in their gardens and maintain some animals. Homeowners will then barter with others to obtain various foods.

- Todmorden, England, has created an Incredible Edible project in which the whole community grows food all over the village to boost healthy eating and community building and to educate others about how urban gardening should be the way of the future. The Incredible Edible project then became the Incredible Edible Network and has spread to multiple countries and communities as more are drawn to the ideas and create new groups (Incredible Edible Limited, n.d.). Residents now encourage tourists to come experience "vegetable tourism" supported by the community of growers (Paull, 2011).

- In northeastern Scotland, Findhorn Ecovillage, with its low or zero-carbon buildings, renewable energy generation, and food gardens, is an educational destination for people and groups from all over the world who come to experience sustainable living in which the human **built environment** is as close to harmonious with the natural world as can be at this time, yet the inhabitants enjoy a modern, community-based lifestyle (Findhorn Ecovillage, n.d.).

Due to a variety of factors, travel to Cuba increased during the 2010s with international arrivals growing from 2007 to 2018 (The World Bank, 2023). When the Soviet Union dissolved and Cuba found itself embargoed and without any outside support, Cuban people were immediately forced into finding ways to be self-sufficient and sustainable. This self-sufficient and sustainable culture is, perhaps, part of the unique tourism draw. Cuba is also home

to the Caribbean's largest and best-preserved wetland area, and tourist attraction, the Ciénaga de Zapata Biosphere Reserve, and overall its protected natural areas encompass more than 1 million acres (404,686 ha) of wetlands and forests (La Ciénaga de Zapata Biosphere Reserve, 2015). Tourism to Cuba accounted for about 10 percent of the country's gross domestic product (GDP) and jobs in 2019 (ECLAC, 2020). The effect of COVID-19 on tourism in Cuba was substantial. International arrivals to Cuba decreased from over 4 million in 2019 to just over 1 million in 2020 (The World Bank, 2023).

Projects do not have to be big to attract people. Everywhere in the world there are agricultural and ecosystem-sensitive projects that have spawned whole industries with a responsible travel ethic:

- Ecotourism
- **Agricultural tourism**
- **Natural tourism and travel**

Recreation, tourism, and leisure (RTL) is big business in the global economy, and it is continually expanding. One of the fastest growing sectors of tourism is that of sustainable tourism and nature-based tourism specifically. In 1995 the United Nations World Tourism Organization (UNWTO) and the World Travel and Tourism Council (WTTC) joined forces with the Earth Council to promote an action plan to improve the environment and make the tourism industry more sustainable. Then, 20 years later, in September 2015, 154 heads of state gathered at the United Nations Sustainable Development Summit to formally adopt the 2030 Agenda for Sustainable Development (United Nations, n.d.-b) along with 17 sustainable development goals (SDGs) including the following:

- No poverty (1)
- Zero hunger (2)
- Decent work and economic growth (8)
- Climate action (13)
- Life below water (14)

With countries like Panama, Kenya, Slovakia, and many others, the UNWTO membership is a total of 159 entities. The organization acknowledges the financial importance of tourism while recognizing and working to protect against potential negative impacts on environments and cultures for those welcoming tourists. Further, the UNWTO (2022, para. 1) defines *sustainable development* in tourism as "Tourism that takes full account of its current and future economic, social and environmental impacts, addressing the needs of visitors, the industry, the environment and host communities." The relationship between tourists, the host community, local businesses and recreational activities, and the environment is interactive, complex, and interdependent. Maintaining those unique aspects of a host community and focusing on the protection of environments and wildlife, while also tapping into the economic boon offered by tourism, is a focus of UNWTO. As mentioned earlier, maintaining sustainable systems now attracts tourists worldwide; communities that use sustainable food systems are now destinations in themselves whether they are in exotic locations or simply in tourists' own backyards. A future with localized sustainable systems of food and energy production is now becoming a focus for people hopeful about new ways of living sustainably (Jurin, 2012).

WORLDWIDE IMPACT OF COVID-19 ON RECREATION, TOURISM, AND LEISURE

COVID-19 negatively impacted many industries related to recreation, tourism, and leisure (RTL).

- The American Hotel and Lodging Association (AHLA; 2021) estimated that about 700,000 workers employed by U.S. hotels lost their jobs between 2019 and 2020.
- The World Travel and Tourism Council reported an estimated worldwide travel-sector loss of 62 million jobs from 2019 (334 million jobs) to 2020 (272 million jobs), with more than 7 million travel-related jobs lost in Africa, and greater than 34 million lost in Asia–Pacific (WTTC, 2021b).
- Chinese hotels as a sector reported losses early on in pandemic with falling occupancy rates and some hotels partially or fully closing (Zhang et al., 2020).
- The International Air Transport Association (IATA; 2021), an airline industry association, reported a loss of 2.7 billion flyers during 2020, with international travel hardest hit as border closures and travel restrictions occurred to mitigate the spread of the virus.
- Serious consequences were felt by the cruise ship sector, an increasingly popular mode of tourism before the pandemic (Camilleri, 2018; ECLAC, 2020; Nhamo et al., 2020). Nhamo et al. (2020) reported cruise companies lost money because of fewer passengers booking trips and issues related to disease mitigation efforts (including passengers being temporar-

ily confined on boats because of an outbreak or ships not being allowed to dock) (Nakazawa et al., 2020).

While COVID-19 has affected the ability and willingness of many to travel and engage in domestic tourism, it has also and will continue to affect those in the international tourism sector. International tourist arrivals worldwide for 2021 were down 69 percent compared to 2019 (UNWTO, n.d.-b). The WTTC (2021b) noted a large decline of more than US$4 trillion GDP lost worldwide in tourism compared to before the pandemic.

INTERNATIONAL JOB MARKET IN RECREATION AND TOURISM

In Canada, 1 in 10 jobs is within the parks, recreation, tourism, and hospitality sector, resulting in a GDP of C$43.5 billion in 2019 (Destination Canada, 2019). In China, tourism revenue increased every year from 2010 to 2019, growing 395.68 percent over that time frame and growing 11.1 percent from 2018 to 2019 (Statista, n.d.; TravelChinaGuide, n.d.). Brazil saw a 3.12 percent decline in revenue related to tourism from 2018 to 2019; nevertheless, years of modest growth predated this decline and future growth was likely (Macrotrends, 2022). With such encouraging statistics, tourism was likely to continue its growth patterns. However, starting in early 2020, much of the world shifted into a new reality as the COVID-19 pandemic began.

Many professional sectors underwent significant reductions of positions during the COVID-19 pandemic time frame with service-related positions being more at risk of being eliminated or frozen. Ghose (2020) estimated the pandemic caused 82 million jobs to be lost internationally due to inactivity and unemployment, while noting the hardest hit areas included accommodations, food services, arts, culture, and retail. Additionally, in the last 10 to 20 years, position availability and growth in parks and recreation have been limited due to budget reductions and political shifts in municipal and state governments. Due to the nature of services offered on a more local level, the job loss or retraction in this job sector during the pandemic was not as affected as the tourism and hospitality sector. The need for employees in tourism and hospitality surely increased dramatically over the last 10 to 20 years, in which job availability is an effect of consumer behavior and demand. For example, from 2000 to 2018, international travel increased from 682.1

million to 1.4 billion. The Americas saw the smallest growth of international tourism (+69%) with the Middle East (+162%) and Asia–Pacific (+210%) seeing the highest growth (Roser, 2021). However, as previously noted, pandemic job losses significantly affected the tourism sector, with international tourism being extremely limited starting in March 2020. As the international community recovers economically from the pandemic and more future tourists feel safe, international tourism is likely to quickly improve.

While the economic recovery from the COVID-19 pandemic will be more robust in more developed nations (e.g., China, Canada), many developing countries (e.g., Sri Lanka, Niger) are likely to see a slower recovery. Many of these developing nations and regions depend on and have invested in tourism to sustain and grow their economies. While resources may be a focal point of some tourism, services and experiences are a key component in tourist travel choices. While there are a variety of factors that will affect how international tourism will recover as the world exits the pandemic, the tourism sector is likely to realize significant job growth.

INTERNATIONAL OVERVIEW

In communities around the world, RTL is undergoing a significant transformation. Technological developments as well as economic and social priorities have changed how RTL is now viewed. During the last quarter century, three aspects have accelerated changes in the RTL field.

1. The growth of the Internet has had a revolutionary impact on nearly all areas of life, such as information sharing and policy production and management, and transparency is more notable; consider how social media has transformed the world.
2. RTL is changing how governments at all levels are prioritizing community quality of life.
3. Youth participation in decision making is emerging as a key priority area in many fields, including RTL (Donohoe, 2013).

INTERNATIONAL ORGANIZATIONS

The World Leisure Organization, founded in 1952, is a worldwide, nongovernmental association dedicated to fostering conditions that allow RTL to serve as a force for human growth, development, and well-being (World Leisure Organization, n.d.). Access to meaningful RTL experiences is as important as the need for shelter, education, employment, and fundamental health care. This occurs deliberately and organically when policy makers include all stakeholders in decision making (Donohoe, 2013). Internationally, world RTL research and evaluation create essential knowledge and information about the personal and social potentialities of RTL experiences for increased benefit to human and natural systems. This collection of research and evaluation is disseminated through various print, verbal, and online formats. In addition, the organization offers scholarships to promote learning, training, and engagement.

There are several groups that regularly report on sustainable tourism developments and trends and regularly discuss current issues. For example, the founders and staff at Sustainable Travel International believe that "people's inherent wanderlust, their desire for new experiences, and concern for the places they care for most can inspire the protection of the world's natural and cultural bounty and generate economic opportunity in destinations that rely on visitors" (Sustainable Travel, n.d.). Since 2002, the organization has been charting a new course for travel and tourism that will ideally lead to a healthier environment, greater economic opportunities and social justice, and the protection of natural and cultural resources.

Like other business sectors, the tourism and hospitality industry must incorporate sustainable planning and management into their business model, because the effects of global climate change are very apparent in the tourism world (e.g., wildfires damaging natural resources and property, rising sea levels affecting beaches, less snow at ski resorts). Tourists themselves are demanding that sustainable operating practices—sometimes called *responsible tourism*—be acknowledged and followed, though demand for responsible tourism does not always meet behavior while traveling (Del Chiappa et al., 2016). Destinations must be clean and healthy, and have protected natural and cultural resources to be attractive to visitors and to compete for the tourist dollar. Whether tourists are walking a beach, hiking in the mountains, biking, boating, or otherwise enjoying outdoor recreational activities, it is the experience and the enjoyment of the activities that are marketed by the tourism industry. The tourism industry is tremendously reliant on the local environment and what the locale offers in terms of a unique tourist experience.

In the last decades, the hospitality industry has made costlier investments in their built environment including not using toxic bleaches or dyes in furniture fabric; using paint, wallpaper, carpeting, and draperies that do not have toxic chemicals; and using furniture made with wood harvested from sustainably managed forests (Edgell, 2006).

In their effort to save water and electricity, hotels are inviting guests to reuse towels and not have bedding changed daily. As sustainable tourism has evolved over time, ecotourism has also gone through a kind of metamorphosis and is viewed as a travel philosophy that is based on a set of principles. These principles were outlined in the UNWTO (n.d.-a, para. 1) definition of ecotourism:

1. It includes all nature-based forms of tourism in which the main motivation of the tourists is the observation and appreciation of nature as well as the traditional cultures that prevail in natural areas.

2. It contains educational and interpretation features.

3. It is generally, but not exclusively, organized by specialized tour operators for small groups. Service provider partners at the destinations tend to be small, locally owned businesses.

4. It minimizes negative effects on the natural and sociocultural environments.

5. It supports the maintenance of natural areas that are used as ecotourism attractions by

   - generating economic benefits for host communities, organizations, and authorities that manage natural areas with conservation purposes;
   - providing alternative employment and income opportunities for local communities; and
   - increasing awareness of the conservation of natural and cultural assets among locals and tourists.

ECOTOURISM AND NATURE TRAVEL

Ecotourism and nature travel should not be viewed as the same thing. A river-rafting trip through the jungle might be fun and educational and provide a great family vacation, but only if the trip directly promotes the protection of nature and tangibly contributes to the well-being of local people does it become ecotourism (see the previous UNWTO definition of *ecotourism*). For many purists, ecotourism is provided by nongovernmental organizations (NGOs) and governmental organizations that are dedicated to protected area land management such as those in Ecuador and the Galapagos Islands.

But the temptation to create mass island tourism by simply purchasing a boat and offering tours is constantly present. A regulated system is required, and bona fide organizations maintain expected levels of compliance to protect natural and cultural sites as well as the local people.

Of the 1,157 World Heritage sites, 900 are cultural (e.g., the Taj Mahal). The remaining 257 sites contain natural (218) and mixed natural and cultural (39) sites. These 257 sites comprise protected areas including these well-known examples (UNESCO, 2023):

- Great Barrier Reef (natural)
- The Great Wall (cultural)
- Serengeti (natural) of the United Republic of Tanzania
- Brazil's Iguaçu National Park (natural)
- Nigeria's Osun-Osogbo Sacred Grove (cultural)

Tourism's performance at those sites is rather mixed because it is a challenge to replace timber extraction as a basis for regional economy, to correct unsustainable visitor management practices, and to transfer millions of tourist dollars for the benefit of local people (Buckley, 2004).

Given the increased popularity of ecotourism prior to the COVID-19 pandemic, destinations often seek to convert mass tourism to ecotourism (Del Chiappa et al., 2016; Massi & De Nisco, 2018). Over the last decades, there has been a continuous growth of a more literate and educated public who are interested in knowing more about nature, biodiversity, wildlife, and local cultures and who are willing to pay for the conservation and protection of an area. With the growth (since 2005) of a wealthier and more educated mobile public that has grown curious about natural and cultural histories of places and people, providers have adapted their services to satisfy that curiosity; Canadian providers, for example, have focused their web efforts on highlighting "escape" (p. 173), "pleasure seeking" (p. 173), "non-consumptive use[s]" and "learning," and "experiencing nature" (Massi & De Nisco, 2018, p. 171). Conservationists and the industry see the need to invest more time, effort, and resources into educational experiences, which will ensure that the market for ecotourism will grow continuously. Ecotourism companies must re-create an interest and curiosity about nature, wildlife, and cultures through different approaches and techniques in outdoor education to continue to expand the repertoire of natural and cultural heritage that can fascinate and inspire the visitor (Buckley, 2004).

Ecotourism and its management is not without problems. Worldwide, developing countries especially struggle with how to manage everything, while still keeping their cultural and natural commons intact. Butler's Tourism Area Life Cycle (TALC; Butler, 1980, 1991, 2000) model offers an idea for how a destination might be affected by tourism. As proposed, travelers discover a destination. The destination may then try to increase tourism levels by marketing the site and developing attractions and accommodations. These efforts may entice new kinds of travelers to visit; as the site evolves, so may the types of tourists and their interests. This process, as theorized by the TALC model, proposes an initial period of a few discovering the destination followed by more discovery and an increase in travelers. This increased tourism may create a push and pull within a destination for how to maintain and sustain cultural and natural resources over time while also managing tourist-host relations as the destination perhaps becomes more mainstream (Zhang et al., 2006). As an example, prior to the pandemic, Santorini, Greece, was trying to balance large numbers of tourists and their needs against the needs of residents (e.g., places to work) within the limits of the island's resources and infrastructure. At that time, the issue became so concerning that Santorini began limiting the number of tourists able to depart from cruise ships each day (Prakash, 2017; Smith, 2018).

In a simple interactive online ecotourism game (Educational Web Adventures, n.d.), the user goes through some of the more crucial decisions of a small Amazon population attempting to cater to ecotourists while also trying to maintain the **natural environment** that defines their culture. The game is similar to a "Choose Your Own Adventure" book in which decisions made early on cascade later for your gamified Amazonian community. It can be a fine line between giving visitors a unique and selective experience, losing one's soul in becoming a mega resort, or (at least in the game) creating a stagnant economy. Large resorts have their place, but strategic decisions must address the local people and their best interests.

RECREATION, TOURISM, AND LEISURE DEVELOPMENT AND ADVOCACY

The availability of the Internet and knowledge sharing it enables has transformed the way RTL is planned and managed. Best practices can often be found by turning to the Internet and finding experts and communities that have applicable situations. The translation features of search engines now make it possible to access information in other languages in countries where RTL may be conceived and practiced in different ways. This sharing of information across geographic and cultural borders is enriching the way RTL is evolving globally. The worldwide importance of the spatial reach of the Internet is recognized by the World Bank (n.d.) as an economic driver and mechanism for change. However, the International Telecommunication Union (ITU; 2021, p. 1) estimated about 2.9 billion people are without access to the Internet; further, ITU estimated that many of those 2.9 billion people come from developing countries (i.e., an estimated 96 percent). This has immense and widespread sociocultural and economic implications. Many countries, including Estonia, Finland, and Spain, have declared access to the Internet a legal right for citizens (Donohoe, 2013).

Technological developments are changing political, economic, and social conditions, and RTL policy has also undergone transformation. Worldwide, RTL is a major income generator that acts as a stimulus to other forms of economic, social, and sustainable development. Governments are seeing this as a continuing rationale for becoming more involved. This is also seen as the impetus for more **commodification** of RTL programs, products, and services by private businesses. This joint influence is rapidly changing the global RTL landscape. Consequently, RTL policy and practice, which had changed subtly over time, are changing significantly. For example, China gained an economic presence in world markets after hosting the Olympics in 2008. International sporting events can raise the international profile of the host country, attracting tourists and foreign investment, and can leave an RTL legacy for the host communities (e.g., new RTL facilities). Consequently, as a result of hosting international events, many countries have made political commitments to begin enhancing the quality of life of their own citizens and their environments (Donohoe, 2013). Despite these perceived gains in recognition, tourism, and investment in the host country (Baade & Matheson, 2016), there may also be negative effects of hosting a massive event like the Olympics. The cost of hosting the Olympics can be steep; Flyvberg et al. estimated the average cost at US$12 billion based on their examination of the Olympic Games from 2007 to 2016 (2021). This price tag may be further compounded for the host site depending on expenses related to infrastructure installation and management of the games (Baade & Matheson, 2016; Flyvberg et al., 2021). Additionally, Flyvberg et al. analyzed over half of the Summer and Winter Games from 1960 to 2016 and found an average of

172 percent toward overspending when compared to the host's proposed budget. Advocacy for this type of investment is focused on the increase of domestic quality of life and increasing tourism for economic gain (2021).

Advocacy plays a critical role in the way that RTL is being shaped now and into the future. International organizations work tirelessly to ensure that RTL is a priority in communities around the world and sustainable development is a central focus. As we move into the future, the RTL fields will require a new generation of strong leaders and skilled professionals. As future leaders, students (typically aged 15-24 years) have a critical role in their own communities and on the world stage as advocates for sustainability, ecotourism, and agricultural tourism as well as how people perceive RTL.

For example, beginning in 1999, the United Nations declared August 12th International Youth Day, in which youth everywhere are encouraged to use the activist framework to work within their own communities (United Nations, n.d.-a). The focus for International Youth Day 2022 was "Intergenerational Solidarity." In 2021, the theme was "Transforming Food Systems: Youth Innovation for Human and Planetary Health." Previously, in 2009 and 2008 the focus was on "Sustainability: Our Future. Our Challenge" and "Youth and Climate Change: Time for Action," respectively. Similarly, the United Nations Educational, Scientific, and Cultural Organization (UNESCO) encourages the participation of young men and women by fostering partnerships with youth networks and organizations (UNESCO, n.d.). These collaborations are meant to integrate youth views and priorities into the development of projects and programs in a variety of areas including sustainable development and RTL (Donohoe, 2013).

PHYSICAL ACTIVITY, GREEN-SPACE USE, AND COVID-19

COVID-19 reduced our ability to travel with varyingly strict lockdowns, school closures, social distancing, and other disease mitigation efforts. While domestic and international travel became difficult or impossible, people were driven to outdoor spaces beyond their homes for activity and socialization. The Outdoor Industry Association (2021b), in investigating behaviors of Americans during the pandemic, reported that there was a shift toward the outdoors. The findings showed many were motivated to do so for their health and fitness, stress levels, to "get out of the house" (p. 12), and to be in nature. The inability of many to utilize indoor spaces in their communities, such

as restaurants, movie theaters, and museums due to closures, social distancing, and other mitigation efforts (Outdoor Industry Association, 2021b), coupled with guidance noting the outdoors was likely safer than indoor spaces, could be what led to increased use of outdoor spaces.

Being active and getting outdoors seemed to be an important way for people to navigate the COVID-19 pandemic. Staying and being active appeared to reduce the chances of negative health outcomes when ill with COVID-19 (Sallis et al., 2021). Psychologically, reduced physical activity in a Taiwanese sample of participants during the pandemic showed declination in mood (Chang et al., 2020), while better mental health and reduced anxiety were reported by inactive Canadians (those who were moderately or vigorously active less than 150 minutes per week) who continued their prepandemic activity or increased their prepandemic activity. Those who were inactive and reported being even less active during the pandemic had worse anxiety and mental health outcomes in comparison (Lesser & Nienhuis, 2020).

Furthermore, multiple studies found increased use of outdoor spaces during the pandemic, such as parks in the United Kingdom (Johnson et al., 2021) and Norway (Venter et al., 2020), and increased participation in outdoor recreation, like biking or walking (Venter et al., 2020). Additionally, there was more search interest (using Google Trends data) related to outdoor activities and outdoor spaces in multiple locations and multiple languages compared to similar time frames before the pandemic (Kleinschroth & Kowarik, 2020; Venter et al., 2020). Kleinschroth and Kowarik (2020) speculated that people were looking for open-air spaces where they might safely experience the world outside of their homes in alignment with knowledge and guidance about COVID-19 at the time.

SUMMARY

Globally, due to lockdowns and travel restrictions, tourism and travel were significantly and negatively affected by COVID-19. Traveling to experience different cultures and unique natural settings and to feel a sense of connection and place attachment with places different from our own is still important to many. This is more than simple recreation and leisure. It remains to be seen how travel and tourism rebound as the world begins to adjust to and exit the pandemic. There was a surge in outdoor recreation activities, such as bicycle purchases, outdoor walking, and more. Additionally, it is important to minimize impact on the places travelers are visiting and the people who live there.

The concepts and principles of sustainability are important as tourists seek authentic experiences while agencies and organizations continue to focus on sustainability of the environment, cultures, and histories of places and spaces. Likewise, ecologically conscious travelers support resources for their travels that are sustainable and that benefit the communities they visit.

Recreation and Leisure in Brazil

Arianne C. Reis and Alcyane Marinho

" All persons have a need to celebrate and share our diversity in leisure. "

São Paulo Declaration, World Leisure Association

Brazil is an exciting and diverse country. Most people have heard of at least one of these Brazilian trademarks:

- *Carnaval*
- **Samba**
- The **Amazon**
- "The Girl From Ipanema"
- **Bossa nova**
- *Caipirinha*

But these are far from what this country is all about. A nation as large and as populous as Brazil cannot possibly be summarized in a few words. This chapter intends to briefly present the **cultural diversity**, contrasting worlds, and rich history of Brazil that would certainly be better understood if experienced firsthand. Therefore, the chapter provides only a glimpse into Brazil and what its people do to have fun, relax, enjoy friends and family, and seize the day. In summary, it describes what they do for leisure and recreation.

With a total area of 8,514,877 square kilometers (about 3.2 million sq m), Brazil is the fifth largest country in the world and the largest in the Southern Hemisphere. It is also the fifth most populous country, containing more than 213 million people within its borders (IBGE, 2021). Brazil is too large to display a uniform pattern of leisure and recreation. Brazil has a colonial history that created the ideal environment for the development of regions as *silos*, which enabled cultural developments that were distinct from each other in several ways. As discussed in previous chapters, culture plays a vital role in producing leisure patterns and behaviors. Therefore, Brazil has distinct leisure practices in different parts of the country, although a few common-

alities are seen across the nation. In the following sections, these leisure patterns and behaviors will be explored in more detail. Before that, however, we provide general information about the country to build a better understanding of leisure practices and traditions in Brazil.

Brazil has an extensive coastline, which is also where most of its development has occurred since the early days of colonialism. Approximately 90 percent of its territory sits between the equator and the Tropic of Capricorn (IBGE, 2011). From this we can conclude a few things that have considerable influence on some general aspects of Brazilian leisure choices:

- Brazil has a significant beach culture on large, white sandy beaches blessed with tropical weather.
- Because most of its population resides along the coast, free coastal recreation pursuits are in high demand by tourists and locals.
- The warm weather is conducive to a variety of outdoor cultural experiences and activities all year long. In Brazil these are dominated by **folklore festivals**, popular parties (religious and pagan), and unregulated sport and physical activities (**football** played on the beach or in any open area, walking and jogging, *capoeira*, skateboarding, and so on).

Brazil's colonial history contributes significantly to its diversity. For more than 300 years, the labor force in Brazil was composed almost entirely of enslaved African people, particularly along the eastern coastline and hinterland, where sugarcane and coffee plantations predominated. This region was therefore significantly exposed to African culture, and today African cultural expressions are still predominant in music, religion, dance, and food along the coastline. In the Amazon region, where colonialism was not so present, Indigenous people left a stronger mark on the local culture, and leisure practices have been significantly influenced by their customs.

After slavery was abolished in 1888, the Brazilian government encouraged European immigration to the country. People from Germany, Italy, Japan, Turkey, and other areas were attracted to various regions of the country and particularly to the southern regions. Therefore, in the southeastern and southern regions of Brazil, visitors will feel European and Asian influences in food, dance, festivities, and general customs.

Other major aspects that affect leisure and recreation practices are the social and economic conditions of a given population. Those without financial resources will obviously have limited access to some forms of paid leisure opportunities such as cinemas, theme parks, theater, and concerts. Also, some recreation practices require the purchase of specific equipment, such as climbing gear, sailboats, or kayaks, or entrance to private spaces such as golf clubs and gyms. In addition, some leisure and recreation practices are determined in part by the local physical environment, such as easy access to green parks, open public spaces, and bars and restaurants, among others. Brazil has great differences in its social class structure and economic distribution of wealth, and these disparities influence the leisure and recreation patterns of its diverse population (Mascarenhas, 2003; Pacheco, 2016; Knuth & Antunes, 2021).

For the past 30 years, Brazil has consistently been among the 15 most powerful economies in the world. During the early 2010s, it climbed to the top 10, and it was classified as the seventh-strongest global economy in 2014 (World Bank, 2016). The political and economic turmoil of recent times have, however, severely affected the economy, and, in 2021, the country dropped out of the top 10 and is now situated 12th worldwide. But Brazil is ranked 84th in the United Nations **Human Development Index** (UNDP, 2020), which indicates that a rich country can exhibit extreme inequality and exclude many of its inhabitants from access to their most basic needs, including leisure opportunities. Indeed, approximately 25 percent of the population, or more than 40 million people, still live in poverty. In contrast, 25 percent of the population has a standard of living that is similar to that in the developed nations of North America and Europe. This contrast is apparent in leisure choices and behaviors, as we will discuss later. There is a clear difference between the leisure choices and opportunities of those who have economic power and those who do not, and

between those who live in the exclusive neighborhoods and those who live in the shantytowns, or *favelas*.

HISTORICAL DEVELOPMENT OF RECREATION AND LEISURE IN BRAZIL

Brazilian modern history is commonly divided into three main periods:

1. Colonial (1500-1824)
2. Imperial (1824-1888)
3. Republican (1889-present)

Highlighting some significant aspects of these historical moments in Brazilian life can illustrate how some leisure practices and traditions have evolved.

The colonial and imperial periods were characterized by slave labor and colonial regions that were independent from each other. The Catholic Church played a significant role in the country's cultural development because Brazil was a colony of Portugal, which was a conservative European Catholic power at the time. This context fostered the suppression of expansive manifestations of leisure; in addition to Catholics' negative views on leisure participation in general, physical recreation was associated with the labor of enslaved people and was therefore avoided by all free residents (De Jesus, 1999; Nascimento, 2020). Moreover, any joyful activity engaged in by enslaved people, such as dancing, singing, and playing, was immediately suppressed by landowners who viewed these activities as distractions from work (Gebara, 1997; Nascimento, 2020). The leisure practices of enslaved people were therefore clandestine, but fortunately they have survived and are expressed today in many forms, such as

- the hugely popular martial art *capoeira*;
- the *congado*, an annual sacred and pagan festivity; and
- the extensive use of African drums in music (*batucadas*).

The republican era, which started in the last decade of the 19th century, has been divided into various periods. In the first half of the 20th century, Brazil became a predominantly urban society, and the government pushed for industrialization and economic development. This context favored the creation of social clubs that heavily promoted the practice of sport, which was a late phenomenon compared with the European context (De Jesus, 1999).

The explanation for this was the aforementioned rejection of any physical activity by the Brazilian elite until some decades after the abolishment of slavery in the country. The general feeling was one of optimism and civic pride, which translated into

- value given to unique expressions of Brazilian culture in music, dance, theater, and other arts; and
- access to these expressions extended to the working class through the public presentation of arts and the construction of open leisure spaces in the urban environment (Almeida & Gutierrez, 2005; Melo, 2003).

In 1964, a military coup changed the cultural environment of the country again and consequently changed its leisure practices. Repression and censorship curtailed spontaneity, and fear led people to spend more of their free time at home. Mass communication networks developed during this period, and television became one of the most important forms of leisure in the country (Mascarenhas, 2003).

Soap operas were used for political propaganda and therefore were highly supported by the government. Nevertheless, they became increasingly popular. The dictatorial government also dramatically reduced the accessibility of artistic expression to the working class, which in turn increased the significance of television as a pastime for this group. The elite, on the other hand, were starting to go to the cinemas, new shopping centers, and their second homes; these phenomena increased substantially during this period. Because of the economic development experienced during this time, the Brazilian elite also started to travel more, particularly to overseas destinations, and their leisure choices became increasingly more influenced by the international trends in recreation and leisure (Almeida & Gutierrez, 2005; Almeida et al., 2013).

The rapid development of the cities, along with a political regime that repressed most forms of leisure and recreation practices, led to a decrease in public open spaces where the working class, who were increasingly marginalized economically, could freely recreate. Traditional folklore phenomena

Capoeira is a Brazilian martial art that combines dance and music that was developed as part of the leisure practices of enslaved people.

Getty Images

began to fade away, and sport became the major form of recreational pursuit. In fact, sport practices were encouraged by the government, which used them as political propaganda (Almeida et al., 2013), as did several other dictatorial regimes across the world (e.g., see Petracovschi, 2021; Shorkend, 2019).

With the fall of military power in the mid- to late 1980s, Brazil rapidly opened up to the international market. But because of the historical contingencies mentioned earlier, urban areas became extremely crowded because open spaces were not appropriately planned and developed. With the rise of poverty, violence became a problem in most urban centers, which caused people to curtail their exploration of streets, parks, and other open areas of the city. Therefore, visits to shopping centers, concerts in closed spaces, parties, restaurants, cinema, and television started to rank higher among choices of leisure activities.

The poor and working class, who could not afford to go to the same places as the elite, improvised and created their own parties, such as the *baile funk* in Rio de Janeiro (da Costa Trotta, 2016), or they went to bars in their neighborhoods where problem drinking and illegal gambling were constantly present (Mascarenhas, 2003). This scenario of segregation is still a reality as of 2022 (Pedro, 2017; Lacerda & Freitas, 2023).

This historical background helps contextualize the contemporary leisure and recreation programs and services provided by various agencies in Brazil and is, therefore, crucial to a better understanding of the current leisure practices of its citizens. In the following section, we further explore the common activities, programs, and services that are available and popular across the nation.

TYPES OF SECTORS, SEGMENTS, AND SERVICES

As in developed nations, the growth of leisure services in Brazil has been concentrated in metropolitan areas and some tourist areas. The larger cities contain the largest public recreational facilities such as the main facilities of the Serviço Social do Comércio (Social Service for Commerce, SESC), which is one of the most significant providers for leisure and recreation in the country; sports clubs with the best infrastructure; the main concert venues; the major hotel chains; and modern shopping malls.

SESC, a public–private institution whose main aim is to provide quality of life to the working class, was established in 1946 and is present in all Brazilian state capitals as well as in several midsized cities and small towns. SESC owns and operates several activity centers with large facilities and extensive infrastructure, including hotels, theaters, sport complexes, cinemas, spas, schools, and environmental protection areas.

SESC policies follow Dumazedier's (1980) understanding of leisure practices as divided into five main realms:

1. Artistic
2. Intellectual
3. Sportive or physical
4. Manual
5. Social

Programs therefore range from permanent sports programs with weekly classes to theater groups, open cinema showings, technical courses in hospitality, camping trips, and nature walks.

More broadly, the framework proposed by Dumazedier to classify leisure pursuits has been influential and has been interpreted as a set of strategies to be implemented in programs and projects for leisure at the national level in government initiatives.

Private clubs in contemporary Brazil play an important role as recreation providers, particularly with their holiday camps. The holiday camps target school-aged children and youth and are open to all members of a particular club or community. YMCAs across the country were influential in developing holiday camps as alternative leisure activities for children during their holidays and are particularly common in the southeast region of the country (Stoppa, 1999).

Sports programs are also commonly associated with clubs in Brazil, and sports such as volleyball, gymnastics, futsal, tennis, swimming, handball, and basketball are among the most popular in clubs and among youth.

The most popular organized sport in Brazil is undoubtedly football (called soccer in North America). Although it is popular in clubs, football is played, usually informally, by everyone anywhere there is a small area of dirt, grass, or pavement. Poles for the goals are made with anything available such as cans filled with small rocks, coconuts, bricks, or stones. Every kid has a football, even if it is made of old socks. Going to football games, whether in big stadia in the major cities or in open grass areas with iron stands in rural areas, is an important form of leisure in Brazil. Watching games on television at home, in a bar, or in a restaurant, or just listening to the radio broadcast, is popular in every corner of the country by rich and poor alike.

The hotel industry is also active in the provision of leisure opportunities in Brazil (Müller & Hallal, 2016). Active leisure providers in the hotel industry are usually farm-stays, hotel spas (particularly in thermal spring areas), resorts, and ecolodges (Ribeiro, 2004). In the early 1970s, Club Mediterranée on Itaparica Island, Bahia, was the first resort to implement organized leisure activities for its clients. It was run by so-called gentle organizers—trained staff whose main job was to entertain guests by providing various leisure and recreation activities. Leisure-focused hotels can be found across the country. Luxury resorts are usually found along the coast, and farm-stays are located in the hinterlands and mountain regions.

As in North America and elsewhere around the world, shopping malls in Brazil are significant spaces of leisure that provide many entertainment options such as shops, cinemas, theaters, amusement parks, skating rinks, and go-carting. The highest concentration of shopping malls is in São Paulo. Shopping malls have grown to become part of the urban fabric for Brazilian urban dwellers. Middle-class families have exchanged traditional places of recreation, such as public squares and parks, for the alleys of the malls, increasingly because of the security and convenience offered by these spaces (Ferreira, 2004; Oliveira & Mendes Silva, 2021). In Rio de Janeiro, a city surrounded by free leisure opportunities (e.g., forest parks and beaches), the proliferation of malls is oddly intense. Barra da Tijuca, a large middle-class neighborhood in the city, has the most malls per square mile in the country. Some argue that the building of malls is a result of the violence and criminality found in large Brazilian urban centers and is a means of separating the lower and poor classes, who are confined to the few open and free leisure spaces of the city, from the middle and upper classes, who increasingly "hide" in private and paid leisure spaces.

In one place, however, worlds collide harmoniously: the beach. As mentioned earlier, Brazil has a significant beach culture. Along the long coast of Brazil, the beach is one of the central spaces for leisure and recreation. From north to south, the poor and the rich share this space, and several recreation practices were born and have thrived on sandy Brazilian beaches. *Futvôlei* (an interesting mix of soccer and volleyball played on the sand) and *frescobol* (a beach paddleball game) were created on Brazilian beaches and now have been exported to beaches across the world from California to Australia. Surfing and bodyboarding are also extensively practiced along the Brazilian coast. Children who grew up in poverty might start their adventures in

the ocean with only a wooden board and later gain worldwide recognition, like Silvana Lima, two times runner-up in the World Surf League World Tour.

Another popular leisure practice in Brazil is the engagement in folk festivals as active participants or spectators. These festivals range from large folkloric parties and festivities (some of national and international reach) to small, local, traditional festivals in small towns and *vilarejos*. What they hold in common is their significance to a community's identity and history.

One of the main folkloric festivities in Brazil is the *Boi-Bumbá*, a performance influenced by the country's Portuguese culture blended with African traditions. The performance is a play in which an ox dances, dies, and is resurrected to the sound of drums and singing by all participants. The title and interpretation of the colorful play vary across the country (e.g., *Bumba-meu-boi*, *Boi-calemba*, *Bumba-de-reis*, *Reis-de-boi*, *Boi-pintadinho*, and *Boi-de-mamão*), but it is always dramatic and spectacular, involving hundreds of people in the main public squares of small towns and large cities (Cavalcanti, 2006; Watts & Ferro, 2012).

Another important Brazilian folk festival is the *Festa Junina*. These festivals, which are among the most significant Catholic festivals in the country, take place in June in honor of St. Peter, St. Anthony, and St. John. Dances around big bonfires, crafting, the launching of colorful hot air balloons, sales of typical foods in rustic stalls, and the staging of a forced-marriage play are central aspects of these festivities. Music is a main theme, and the genres played are genuinely Brazilian, such as the *forró*, *xaxado*, and *baião*, and are played with violas, accordions, triangles, and traditional instruments.

The most popular Brazilian festival, however, is certainly the *carnaval*, a blend of European traditions adapted to a tropical country with a large population that is of African descent. *Carnaval* is eagerly awaited by most of the population, rich and poor, all year-round, and it is certainly part of the country's international imagery as well as its local identity. *Carnaval* parties in clubs developed from the European masked balls of years past. Parades of floats (*escolas de samba*) are based on similar European traditions, and street music with lots of drums and percussion hails from the African influence. *Carnaval* is celebrated annually 46 days before Easter. It is officially celebrated for four days (national public holidays), but it usually goes on for an entire week. It is present in various forms in every town of the country. The cheerful and lively atmosphere is the commonality between all celebrations.

Getty Images/Vetta

Football is the most popular organized sport in Brazil, and it is also played informally anywhere there is space and a ball.

COVID-19 IMPACTS AND TRENDS

The World Health Organization declared in January 2020 that COVID-19 constituted a public health emergency due to its international dissemination, being later considered a pandemic. The first Brazilian case was confirmed in February 2020, quickly becoming one of the countries with the highest number of cases in the world (Brasil, 2020).

The closure of parks and other public and private leisure spaces led to people unexpectedly having to change their leisure-related activities in cities across the world (Stodolska, 2021; Tavares, 2021). Since then, leisure has been redefined, especially as it starts to take place in the home environment. However, although some research has started to emerge, there is still a lack of empirical data to help us fully understand the influence of the pandemic on leisure, both in terms of what has been lost but also what has been gained because of the crisis and the societal changes that emerged as a consequence.

But early studies point out that the isolation caused by COVID-19 can increase family commitments and household chores (Young, 2020; Zhou & Liu, 2020) and mental health problems (Armitage & Nellums, 2020), and decrease overall leisure engage-

ment (Bramante, 2020). According to Stodolska et al. (2021), certain groups may be more influenced by restrictions, and Tavares and Marinho (in press) argue this is the case for older persons.

Ribeiro et al. (2020) analyzed the main leisure activities experienced during the social isolation imposed by COVID-19 in Brazil. The authors identified that there was a drastic change in several leisure interests, and that sport and physical activity were particularly affected, moving from commercial or public spaces to the domestic context. Clearly, adaptations had to be made and changes in practices were evident.

- Activities such as attendance to concerts, plays, cinemas, and visiting museums began to be sought out virtually.

- Cooking for pleasure, gardening, and plant care received renewed interest during lockdowns, as did the making of decorative objects and handicrafts.

- Reading, journaling, writing, undertaking various online courses, and playing board games were also mentioned by research participants.

- Virtual activities, such as surfing the Internet and social networks, watching TV series, and participating in online games, increased during the lockdowns, seen as a way to alleviate the stress brought by the pandemic (Ribeiro et al., 2020). Montenegro et al. (2020) also identified a similar situation in their study, which the authors called "residentialization" and "virtualization" of leisure.

SUMMARY

The Brazilian elite today enjoy the leisure opportunities and practices that are available in any developed country in the world, and they engage in similar pursuits. The working class and the poor, however, have had their leisure options increasingly restricted by the unplanned and unsustainable development of the cities. These options include limited public open spaces, such as beaches and urban parks, which are usually underfunded and not always suitable for some leisure practices. Along the coast, however, beaches are enjoyed by all groups of society, and citizens value them highly.

With the COVID-19 pandemic, a variety of previously existing leisure trends seem to have gained momentum in Brazil, including movie streaming and music and video game live streaming, as well as the previously less popular but now ubiquitous online courses and virtual trips. Other leisure activities have reemerged, such as traditional board games, crafts, and leisure cooking. We hope that the creativity expressed by marginalized groups in overcoming barriers throughout the years will remain in the current and postpandemic era, and that along with this we will witness a fairer distribution of leisure and recreation opportunities across all segments of society.

Recreation and Leisure in China

Jinyang Deng, Huimei Liu, and Jian Li

" Play is one of the essential needs for people. We need to have the culture of play, do academic research in play, and master skills in and develop the arts for play. "

Guangyuan Yu, renowned economist and contributor to leisure development in China

Although leisure, recreation, and tourism are conceptually different, they are inherently interdisciplinary and practically interrelated (Smith & Godbey, 1991). A recreationist and a leisure pursuer often share the same resources, use the same facilities, and generate similar social and psychological outcomes (McKercher, 1996). Thus, as far as the scope of leisure, recreation, and tourism is concerned, drawing a distinct line between the three is difficult. In fact, recreation and leisure are usually discussed under the rubric of leisure in Western literature. This line of thought has also been followed by most Chinese tourism and leisure researchers and scholars. That is, all leisurely activities or anything meant to be enjoyed (i.e., entertainment, recreation, tourism) during free time falls into the category of the leisure industry. This understanding and classification of the leisure industry is reflected by the two most authoritative publications on China's leisure industry: the *Annual Report on China's Leisure Development*, also known as the *Green Book of China's Leisure*, which has been compiled annually since 2010 by the Tourism Research Center at the Chinese Academy of Social Science (TRC CASS), and the *Annual Report of China Leisure Development*, which has been compiled annually since 2011 by the China Tourism Academy.

The development of recreation and leisure as an industry and particularly as an academic field in China is a recent phenomenon, although the Chinese words for leisure, *xiu xian*, can be traced back at least three millennia (Liu et al., 2008). Leisure has been pursued in many forms (e.g., tai chi, mahjong) by people of different walks of life for thousands of years in China.

Although a consensus on what constitutes leisure has been achieved internationally and domestically, no common understanding of what constitutes the leisure industry has been reached among Chinese researchers and scholars. For example, Qing (2007) considers the leisure industry to be made up of three types of industries:

1. The primary leisure industry (e.g., leisure agriculture, leisure forestry, leisure husbandry, and leisure fishery sectors)

2. The secondary leisure industry (e.g., leisure food and beverage processing and manufacturing sector, leisure appliances and equipment manufacturing sector, and leisure construction sector)

3. The tertiary leisure industry (e.g., tourism leisure sector, fitness and cosmetics sector, culture and entertainment sector, hospitality sector, and others)

You and Zhen (2007) argue that the contemporary leisure industry in China can be classified into the following 11 categories:

1. Entertainment leisure (singing halls, dance halls, discotheques, concert halls, tea houses, cafés, chess houses, bars, cinemas, theaters, resorts, performing arts centers, karaoke bars, KTVs)

2. Sporting leisure (all kinds of sports and adventurous outdoor activities)

3. Health leisure (springs, forest recuperation, flower recuperation, water therapy, mud therapy, salt therapy, spas, baths, sun baths, beauty, hairdressing, massage, oxygen bars, and so on)

4. Tourism leisure (natural and historical sites, theme parks, zoos and botanical gardens, and urban scenic spots and belts)

5. Rural leisure (happy farmer inns, happy fisher inns, happy ranch inns, folk villages, and rural historical towns)

6. Educational leisure (libraries, memorial halls, galleries, all types of museums, martyr cemeteries, religious temples, college campuses, industrial parks, bookstores, and so on)

7. Food leisure (restaurants, hotels, guesthouses, flavor snack bars, and food courts)

8. Shopping leisure (shopping malls, exhibitions, wholesale markets, pedestrian streets, specialty shops, auctions, pawn shops, and so on)

9. Hobby leisure (pets, image design, gardening, stamp collecting, collecting of antiques and other items, sculpture, calligraphy, painting, knitting, flower arranging, pubs, making ceramics for fun, and phone bars)

10. Social leisure (charity, volunteering, social media and Internet cafés, festivals and events, making friends, cell phone messages, parties, and so on)

11. Leisure products manufacturing (leisure foods and beverages, leisure clothing, leisure health care, leisure books and materials, leisure equipment, and leisure facilities)

Similar to Qing's (2007) classification, Wei (2009) states that the leisure industry should consist of three subindustries:

1. Leisure foundation industry (e.g., tourism sector, sporting leisure sector, and cultural leisure sector)

2. Leisure extension industry (e.g., leisure agriculture sector, leisure commerce sector, which primarily includes business recreation areas, pedestrian streets and special shopping stores, and leisure real estates)

3. Leisure support industry (e.g., leisure manufacturing sector, leisure information technology sector, and leisure brokerage sector)

TRC CASS (2015) proposed the concept of "leisure and related industries," which involves

- the tourism leisure sector,
- the cultural leisure sector,
- the sports leisure sector, and
- other sectors (e.g., food and beverage).

Qin (2022) proposed that the leisure industry in China can be divided into three domains:

- Core domain (culture, tourism, fitness, and services)
- Peripheral domain (exhibition, retailing, landscaping, transportation, and information technology)
- Related domain (finance, real estate, environmental protection, and health care)

The aforementioned classification (Qin, 2022; Qing, 2007; You & Zhen, 2007; TRC CASS, 2015) of China's leisure industry demonstrates that China's leisure industry encompasses a wide range of sectors, many of which have emerged in the past two decades or so because of the influence of modernization and globalization. These sectors have begun to play an increasingly important role in the country's economic growth and "the construction of a harmonious society," which was a national goal proposed by the former President Jintao Hu in 2004 when he suggested, in an address to a high-level seminar at the Party School of the Central Committee of the Communist Party of China, that a high priority be placed on social harmony. This came at a time when the country was confronted with a series of social problems, such as disparity in development and distribution, inequality, injustice, and corruption, despite rapid economic growth.

During the 2010s and 2020s, the leisure industry in China has played an important role in generating revenue and jobs.

- In 2019, domestic visits reached an all-time high of 6.6 billion and generated a domestic tourism revenue of 5.7 trillion RMB (approximately US$828.5 billion), an increase of 8.4 percent and 10.0 percent, respectively, over 2018 (Xinhua, 2020).

- In the same year, 79.87 million people were directly and indirectly employed in the tourism industry, accounting for over 10 percent of the total employment of the country.

- In addition, the total gross domestic product (GDP) from tourism was estimated at 10.94 trillion RMB (or approximately US$1,590.1 billion in the same year, accounting for 11.5 percent of the national GDP.

As with many other countries in the world, the tourism industry in China was also hit hard during the COVID-19 pandemic. For example, domestic visits dropped 52.1 percent to 2.9 billion with a total revenue of 2.2 trillion RMB (approximately US $323.5 billion), a decline of 61.1 percent compared to 2019 values (Ministry of Culture and Tourism of China, 2021).

As of 2022, China's leisure industry is concentrated in urban areas, particularly in large and mid-sized cities where the leisure industry has grown quickly on a large scale and has generated considerable benefits. For example, Hangzhou, dubbed the Oriental capital of leisure, has seen a rapid development and growth of tourism and leisure in the past decade. In 2014, the total tourism and leisure revenue (both domestic and international) reached 188.6 billion RMB (approximately US$30.9 billion), accounting for 6.8 percent of the total GDP of the city (TRC CASS, 2015). In addition to the urban tourism that has been well developed in the city, rural tourism has also become increasingly popular among urban residents in the suburban areas of Hangzhou and in many other large and midsized cities in the country. For example, in 2014, there were 2.3 million rural tourists in the metropolitan area of Hangzhou, an increase of 63.3 percent over the previous year. Rural tourism brought in a total revenue of 2.7 billion RMB (approximately US$442.6 million), an increase of 157 percent over 2013. Before the outbreak of COVID-19, in 2019, Hangzhou accommodated 208 million tourists with a total tourism and leisure revenue (both

Tai chi is a traditional healthy exercise that has been practiced by people of different walks of life for thousands of years in China.

VCG/Visual China Group/Getty Images

domestic and international) of 400 billion RMB (approximately US$57.3 billion), accounting for 26 percent of the total GDP of the city in the same year (Hangzhou Municipal Administration of Culture and Tourism, 2019).

Parallel to the rapid development of the leisure industry in China is the continuing growth of tourism and leisure education at various levels. For example, in 2017, there were 2,641 tourism education institutions, including 1,694 higher education institutions, of which 608 offered tourism management undergraduate programs majoring in tourism management, hotel management, and event or exhibition economy and management, and 1,086 offered postsecondary vocational programs majoring in tourism management, tour guidance, travel agency operation and management, tourism destination development and management, hotel management, leisure service and management, and event or exhibition planning and management (Ministry of Culture and Tourism of China, 2018). In addition, 18 forestry and agriculture universities offer outdoor recreation education. The first forest recreation department was established in 1993 at the Central South University of Forestry and Technology in Hunan Province. Because *leisure* has become a buzzword among the public, 14 sport universities or schools and several other universities with tourism programs have begun to offer four-year undergraduate degrees in leisure studies. Furthermore, a doctoral degree program in leisure studies, the first and the only one in China, was approved in 2007 for Zhejiang University. Finally, several leisure research centers have been established since 2003, when the Center for Leisure Culture Study, the first leisure research center in China, was created by the Chinese Academy of Arts.

A BRIEF HISTORY OF CHINA'S LEISURE DEVELOPMENT

Contemporary recreation and leisure began to emerge as an important sector in China in the early 1980s when China began to adopt an open-door policy and make major economic reforms, which resulted in impressive economic development in the following decades. As in advanced economies, the increase of discretionary income and free time has stimulated increasing demand for leisure pursuits in China. The central government played an important role in formulating national policies for leisure industry development. For example, in 1995, China adopted a 40-hour week, and in 1999, the State Council approved three **golden weeks** (i.e.,

the Spring Festival Golden Week, the National Day Golden Week, and the Labor Day Golden Week) as national holidays. (Note: The Labor Day Golden Week was discontinued on November 17, 2007.) Along with the two-day weekends and other holidays, the golden weeks increased the free time of the country's working class to 115 days per year. In addition, the 11th Five-Year Plan placed higher priority on industry structure transformation by focusing on the tertiary sectors, or the service industry. The 12th Five-Year Plan has implemented national tourism and leisure strategies that aim to increase awareness of leisure among the public and promote leisure industry development to a higher level. Furthermore, the *Guidelines for National Tourism and Leisure (2022-2030)* promulgated by the State Council in 2022 set up goals and laid a foundation for the development of tourism and leisure.

Leisure and recreation has been an important research topic since 1993, when the first recreation research center, the Center for Forest Recreation, was established at the Central South Forestry University. Since then, many research centers on leisure and recreation have been established across the country. Table 19.1 lists the research centers that, to the best of our knowledge, are among the most academically influential. These research centers, along with many others that are not listed, have made significant contributions to leisure and recreation research in China. In addition, in 2009, topics on leisure research were included in the application guidelines of the National Social Science Fund for the first time.

Several key people have played an essential role in promoting leisure development and leisure studies and education in the country.

- The late leader Xiaoping Deng pointed out on many occasions that more emphasis should be placed on tourism development to increase national income.

- Professors Guangyuan Yu and Huidi Ma have made great contributions to leisure development and leisure education and research in the country. In addition to their own writings and talks on leisure, they also translated and published five books written by renowned leisure scholars in North America.

- Professor Chucai Wu was proclaimed a national-level expert by the State Council, and, along with Professor Zhangwen Wu, founded the country's first four-year outdoor recreation program in 1993 at Central South Forestry College (renamed as Central South University of Forestry and Technology).

Table 19.1   Selected Centers for Leisure and Recreation Research in China

Name	Year established	Affiliation
Center for Forest Recreation Research	1993	Central South University of Forestry and Technology, Hunan
Center for Leisure Studies	2000	Chinese National Academy of Arts, Beijing
China Leisure Economic Research Center	2004	Renmin University of China, Beijing
Asia-Pacific Centre for the Study and Training of Leisure	2004	Zhejiang University, Zhejiang
Research Center on Convention/Exhibition and Leisure Culture	2006	Hunan Normal University, Hunan
China Center for Leisure and Tourism Research	2008	Sichuan University, Sichuan
Research Center on Culture and Leisure Industry	2008	University of International Business and Economics, Beijing
Center for Leisure Research	2009	East China Normal University
Research Center for Leisure Sports Development	2012	Hubei University, Hubei
Sichuan Landscape and Recreation Research Center	2012	Chengdu University, Sichuan
Central China Research Center on Leisure Culture	2013	Hubei Polytechnic University, Hubei
Research Center on Leisure and Health-keeping	2016	Guilin Tourism University
Chengdu Recreation Environment Technology Research Institute	2018	Chengdu Recreation Environment Technology Research Institute
Research Center on Leisure	2021	Zhejiang Gongshang University

Note: All tourism research centers in the country, including some of the most prestigious ones, such as China Tourism Academy established in 2008 (affiliated with China National Tourism Administration) and the Tourism Research Center established in 1999 (affiliated with Chinese Academy of Social Science), are not listed in the table because the words *leisure* and *recreation* are not part of the title of the research agency.

- Professor Xuequan Pang, director of the Asia-Pacific Centre for the Study and Training of Leisure at Zhejiang University, has played an essential role in promoting leisure studies within and beyond the university.

In recent years, China has organized several international leisure conferences:

- An annual international leisure development forum held in Hangzhou since 2003
- The 9th World Leisure Congress in Hangzhou in 2006 and the 16th World Leisure Congress in Beijing in 2021
- World Leisure Expo in 2006, 2011, and 2021
- The 2009 International Sociological Association Research Committee on Leisure Study (RC 13) Mid-Term Conference
- The 2015 International Forum on Metropolitan Leisure and Tourism

National leisure forums (e.g., 2007, 2008, 2009, and 2010 National Leisure Industry Economics

Forums and the Annual Conference on Leisure Studies; and the annual China Leisure and Tourism Development Forum since 2016) and international leisure and tourism conferences organized outside of China (e.g., the biannual USA-China Tourism Research Summit since 2015; the 2020 China-International Leisure Research Association Conference) have increased public awareness of leisure and facilitated collaboration and cooperation between Chinese leisure scholars and their international counterparts.

RECREATION OPPORTUNITIES IN CHINA

China has abundant natural and cultural resources that offer great opportunities for leisure and outdoor recreation pursuits. This section introduces the settings, organizations, and structures as they relate to the provision of leisure and recreation opportunities in the country. A brief description of popular recreation and leisure activities pursued by the public follows.

Settings, Organizations, and Structures

The most popular outdoor recreation settings in China are

- scenic areas,
- nature reserves,
- forest parks, and
- national parks.

As of 2015, China had

- 3,234 forest parks, including 826 at the national level, that covered 44.5 million acres (18.02 million ha) (China State Forestry Administration, 2016), and
- 2,740 nature reserves, including 450 national ones, comprising 363.2 million acres (147 million ha).

Between 2016 and 2020, forest parks at all levels in China have accommodated 7.5 billion visits with a total gross social product value of 6.8 trillion RMB (approximately US$1.1 trillion). Since 2017, forest recreation has become one of three pillar industries for the State Forestry and Grassland Administration (Gu, 2021).

Since 2015, China has been developing a national park system that includes 10 pilot national parks. With the successful completion of the national park pilot programs, the first national parks were officially established in 2021, including Sanjiangyuan National Park, Giant Panda National Park, Northeast China Tiger and Leopard National Park, Hainan Tropical Rainforest National Park, and Wuyi Mountain National Park (China State Forestry and Grassland Administration, 2021).

As of 2021, China had established 244 national scenic areas and 807 provincial scenic areas, totaling 52.9 million acres (21.4 million ha) (China Association of National Parks and Scenic Sites, 2022).

As of 2020, China had 13,332 A-level tourist areas, an increase of 930 over 2019. Of this number,

- 302 are classified at the AAAAA level,
- 4,030 at the AAAA level, and
- 6,931 at the AAA level (Ministry of Culture and Tourism of China, 2021).

In addition, numerous urban parks, farmlands, and forest areas provide outdoor recreation opportunities for urban dwellers. Chinese people also enjoy leisure activities in indoor settings such as tea houses, mahjong houses, spas, foot massage houses, and bars of all kinds, among other places.

Forest parks such as Zhangjiajie National Forest Park (which was the original model for Hallelujah Mountain in the movie *Avatar*) are popular outdoor recreation settings in China.

VW Pics/Universal Images Group Editorial/Getty Images

Most outdoor recreational opportunities are provided by public agencies, including

- the State Forestry and Grassland Administration (forest parks at all levels);
- National Park Administration (national parks);
- the Ministry of Housing and Urban–Rural Development (scenic areas at all levels);
- the Ministry of Agriculture;
- the State Marine Bureau;
- the Geological and Mineral Bureau;
- the Ministry of Environmental Protection;
- the Ministry of Water Resources, which, along with the previous two agencies, manage nature reserves across the country; and
- the Ministry of Culture and Tourism, which manages World Heritage sites and thousands of cultural and historical sites across the country.

Popular Recreation and Leisure Pursuits

China is made up of 56 ethnic nationalities that are distinctively different from one another, culturally and historically, resulting in distinct patterns of leisure pursuits from group to group. Obviously, the scope of this chapter precludes detailed description of the leisure patterns of every nationality. Because the Han nationality accounts for 98 percent of the country's population and represents the mainstream culture of the country, the following discussion of recreation and leisure pursuits of Chinese people refers primarily to the Han nationality.

In comparison with North Americans, Chinese people tend to prefer quiet or passive leisure pursuits. For example, a comparative cross-cultural study (Jackson & Walker, 2006) found that the most frequent or most enjoyable leisure activities were passive for 84 percent of Mainland Chinese university students and active for 64 percent of Canadian students. This finding was endorsed by a survey study on leisure activities pursued by urban residents in China, which found that the most popular leisure activities were

- watching TV,
- reading books or newspapers,
- listening to the radio,
- playing mahjong, and
- chatting with family members (Yin, 2005).

This passive nature of leisure pursuits was reinforced during the pandemic with online leisure such as socializing, watching videos, live streaming, playing games, and virtual travel becoming more popular. Live streaming was especially widespread, with 560 million live-stream consumers as of March 2020, accounting for 62 percent of all Chinese Internet users (He et al., 2021).

While passive leisure pursuits still dominate in the country, China has seen a growing population who are enthusiastic to engage in active leisure activities such as walking, which has been typically studied from the Western perspective (Witte, 2021). A recent study on Chinese people's physical activities using big data from Tencent QQ (also known as QQ, one of the most popular instant messaging software services developed by Tencent, a Chinese multinational technology company) indicates that the average Chinese person walked 6,303 steps per day in 2018, increased from 5,678 steps in 2017 and 5,112 steps in 2016 (Zheng, 2019). However, this trend was reversed in 2020 with the average steps being reduced from 7,554 to 5,927 due to the COVID-19 outbreak and subsequent lockdowns, based on Zepp's health report (jksb, 2021).

As with walking, marathon running has gained popularity among Chinese across the country. For example,

- 285 cities in 31 provinces or autonomous regions held marathon events in 2019 with 7.12 million marathon participants compared to 0.4 million in 2010 (China Athletics Association, 2021).
- In 2019, a total of 1,828 large-scale events (e.g., marathon, cross-country running, 10 km running, healthy running, ultramarathon, team racing, vertical marathon) were held in China, an increase of 15.62 percent compared to 2018 (China Athletics Association, 2021).

These events led to a total consumption of 28.8 billion RMB (approximately US$4.2 billion) per year, and the annual industrial output reached 74.6 billion RMB (approximately US$11.0 billion).

Among prepandemic active leisure activities, playing golf was the least popular because of its high cost, and tennis, billiards, ice-skating, fishing, hunting, and playing bridge were also less popular than other active leisure activities (Yin, 2005). Another study (Jim & Chen, 2009) about leisure activity patterns in Zhuhai, a city situated on the south coast of Guangdong province on the banks of the Pearl River estuary and close to Macau and Hong Kong, found that residents in the city reported participating in activities in the home more frequently than in activities outside the home. Moreover, they were more likely to participate in passive activities than active ones. In-home physical exercise and sport games outside the home accounted for 10 percent of all reported leisure participation. Wei et al. (2015), in examining a nationwide survey on leisure, found that "passive leisure activities (e.g., watching TV, surfing the Internet) are related to happiness, [and] active leisure activities (e.g., exercising, socializing, shopping) do not seem to contribute to happiness in China" (p. 571).

Leisure is so highly related to culture that culture is often viewed as a synonym of leisure in the country (Ma, 1999). Leisure in China is closely related to "philosophy, aesthetics, literature and the arts, and practices of health and wellness" (Gong, 1998, as cited in Wang & Stringer, 2000, p. 35). Pursuit of such leisure activities is justified by Confucianism, which encourages a scholar or student to excel at playing the harp and chess and doing painting and calligraphy. In this way, leisure pursuits involving learning and culture could be regarded as high leisure, whereas leisure pursuits such as mahjong can be viewed as popular leisure.

China is at a crossroads of social, economic, and political transformation. During this transformation, the traditional Chinese cultural values formed in a traditional agrarian society could be changed in the process of modernization. Economic globalization could accelerate this change. In fact, globalization has already had great influence on the daily life of Chinese people. For instance, attitudes toward beauty pageants, fashion shows, sexual behavior, consumption behavior, dress, hairstyles, celebration of Western festivals, and leisure have largely changed in the past two decades because of modernization and globalization.

Western leisure pursuits and sports that are active and adventurous have been introduced to China (e.g., rock climbing, mountaineering, camping, picnicking and barbecuing, using recreational vehicles, water rafting, playing tennis, golfing). These activities are becoming increasingly popular among Chinese people, especially the youth. Another example is that cultural leisure pursuits among Chinese people have been fundamentally influenced. For instance, American movies are much more popular than local movies. Watching American movies and playing board games are rated as top leisure activities by current college students. Another cultural leisure pursuit that has been greatly influenced by globalization is the celebration of Western festivals and holidays, which

have become more popular than Chinese ones, especially among the youth. For instance, many people celebrate the Western style of Valentine's Day; *qi xi*, the traditional Chinese version of this holiday, is almost unknown among most Chinese people. Christmas is another holiday celebrated with great passion by Chinese people.

A survey study of leisure pursuits of the Chinese middle class found that the leisure patterns pursued by the youth fall into one of four leisure types:

- Tag (fashion followers) (Zhou, 2008)
- Entertainment and relaxation
- Function (utilitarianism)
- Free

Of the numerous leisure activities pursued by Chinese people, tai chi and mahjong are arguably the favorite traditional ones, particularly among middle-aged and older people. Tai chi is taught to college students in physical education classes, but because of its slow tempo, few young people like it. When people grow older, however, they realize the importance of being healthy, and they learn to practice tai chi. Although the Chinese government has favored tai chi as a healthy exercise, mahjong was once banned as a gambling activity and is not endorsed by the government today, although people of all classes, occupations, and ages are obsessed with the table game.

Another leisure activity that has recently become popular among residents in almost every city in China is public dance, or **square dance**, in which dozens to hundreds of people dance together for several hours, usually in the evening, in an urban open space (public square or plaza). Most of these dancers spontaneously stand in formation and follow one or two dancers in front who lead the dance, which has simple moves and a relatively slow tempo. A survey study conducted in Chongqing, a northwest city, found that 45 percent of the city's residents reported having participated in this group activity (Li et al., 2009). The significance of public square dance has also attracted the attention of researchers (Peng, 2010).

CHALLENGES AND TRENDS FOR THE FUTURE

Although the leisure industry in China has experienced rapid growth in recent years, there is no sign that this growth will stop if the country's economy continues to grow. However, the leisure industry faces a number of challenges.

First, attitudes toward leisure among Chinese people are generally negative (Wei et al., 2015). As recently as the 1970s, leisure (*xiu xian*) was a bad word and a symbol of pursuing the lifestyle of capitalist societies. Wang and Stringer (2000) observed that Chinese people are less likely to view leisure as an important component of their lives compared with North Americans because Chinese, in general, tend to have a stronger work ethic (see also Ap, 2002; Xiao, 1997). This view of leisure reflects the traditional values that Chinese place on hard work and achievement. But this negative attitude toward leisure has changed considerably in recent years due to rapid economic development, increasing living standards in mainland China, and the influence of globalization (Wei, 2009). In recognition of the global trends in leisure and its importance to enhancing the quality of life of Chinese people, many scholars have recently called for devoting more attention to leisure and leisure research in China, which, we contend, has led to greater awareness of leisure among the public. That said, many Chinese people still consider leisure similar to laziness.

Second, leisure education is lacking among Chinese. Chinese education is fundamentally examination and score oriented, which deprives students time for leisure. The education system is extremely competitive, which puts students under heavy pressure. As a result, leisure awareness is not well nurtured among Chinese (Deng, 2002; Liu, 2007). This situation may see improvements, since extracurricular tutoring on subjects of mathematics, English, and Chinese is being banned on weekends, public holidays, and school holidays, allowing students to have more time to engage in leisure and recreation activities (Xinhua News Agency, 2021a).

Third, China is experiencing rapid urbanization. Open spaces are shrinking, and limited facilities are available for leisure. For example, a survey (Lu & Yu, 2005) found that 37 percent of residential areas in Beijing had no sport and fitness facilities. In addition, Beijing had only 1.96 community sport and fitness centers per 10,000 people in 2003, whereas Germany had 9.08 centers per 10,000 people in 1976 (Lu & Yu, 2005). To address this issue, community sport and fitness centers are designated in most cities to provide opportunities for residents to exercise and socialize. For example, beginning in 2013, Beijing started adding outdoor fitness facilities to 97 deteriorating districts and neighborhoods. These facilities provide a variety of fitness opportunities for residents of all ages including chess and poker areas, rehabilitation areas, playgrounds, trails, tai chi areas, areas for walking with caged birds, and so on. It is estimated that more than 1,000 residents use these fitness areas every day.

To address the challenges facing public fitness and physical activities in Beijing while in line with the "National Fitness Plan" (2021-2025) (Xinhua News Agency, 2021b), "the Five-Year Action Plan for the Construction of Public Fitness Facilities in Beijing to Reduce Facilities Shortage (2021-2025)" was issued in 2022 (Beijing Bureau of Sport, 2022), aiming to increase the per capita sports space to 2.82 square meters (30.35 sq ft) from 2.69 square meters (28.95 sq ft) in 2021. Nationwide, as of 2021, there are 3.971 million sports venues in China, with a sports area of 3.41 billion square meters (36.70 billion sq ft) and 2.41 square meters (25.94 sq ft) per capita sports space, an increase of 65 percent compared with 1.46 square meters (15.72 sq ft) in 2013. Beijing's sports space per capita of 2.69 square meters (28.95 sq ft) is above the national average of 2.41 square meters (25.94 sq ft) in 2021 (Zhou & Chen, 2022).

Finally, there is inequality in leisure pursuits. Although China has experienced rapid economic development in the past two decades and has become the world's second-largest economy after the United States, the country is confronted by a number of issues, including unequal economic development across regions and a growing income gap between the wealthy and the poor, resulting in unequal leisure opportunities for the public. For example, in 2021, China had an estimated 172 million migrant workers who emigrated from the countryside to cities looking for better-paying jobs in construction sites and factories (National Bureau of Statistics, 2022). Most of these migrant workers do not pursue leisure activities because their pay is low, and they have to work long hours.

Even some middle-class people do not have time for leisure because they are busy with work and cannot fully relax. A study showed that Chinese leisure time has decreased. Specifically, urban and rural residents had an average of 1,774 hours and 1,766 hours for leisure in 2012 as opposed to 1,351 hours and 1,502 hours in 2015, respectively (China Tourism Academy, 2015). In 2017, the average Chinese spent 2.27 hours per day for leisure, which was less than that of three years prior (2.55 hours) and less than half that of their European and American counterparts. However, this number jumped to 4.9 hours for 2019 to 2020 due to the pandemic (Song et al., 2020).

According to another study (Zhou, 2008), 58.6 percent of Chinese participants were not satisfied with their leisure, and only 5 percent reported being very satisfied. The survey also showed that

- over 65 percent of the middle class had less than 20 hours per week of leisure time,
- 80 percent reported that their leisure was constrained by work,
- 80 percent felt heavy work pressure, and
- 28 percent believed that their work pressure had reached an intolerable point.

Their salaries are lower than expected given the high pressure that they are under, which further affects their leisure quality.

Although China's leisure industry faces significant challenges, it will likely continue to grow due to several trends.

- First, both domestic tourism and outbound tourism have shown a steady growth from 2011 to 2019 prior to the COVID-19 pandemic. Although COVID-19 disrupted this momentum, it is anticipated that tourism will reach the prepandemic level and resume its positive trajectory postpandemic. While no one knows when this will happen, it is only a matter of time since the demand for travel remains high (China Tourism Academy, 2020). With that said, domestic tourism may outperform outbound tourism in the short to medium term, given restrictions imposed on outbound travel due to uncertainties of COVID-19 and the negative impact of the war in Ukraine on international travel. From 2011 to 2019, domestic visits increased by 227.41 percent from 2.64 billion to 6.01 billion. Comparably during the same period, outbound visits increased by 220.11 percent from 70.25 million to 154.63 million (Ministry of Culture and Tourism of China, 2020). While domestic tourism dropped to 2.88 billion in 2020 (almost the same level as 2011), it increased to 3.25 billion in 2021, an increase of 12.8 percent over 2020 (Ministry of Culture and Tourism of China, 2022). In contrast, outbound tourism decreased to 20.23 million, down 86.9 percent over 2019 (China Tourism Academy, 2020).
- Second, unlike traditional package tours arranged by a tour operator or travel agent, various kinds of independent tours that are planned by individuals are thriving because of the rapid development of highway and railway systems and the increasing ownership of cars and recreational vehicles. For example, of the 6 billion domestic visits in 2019, 3.8 billion (63%) are independent visits made by individuals without the assistance of a travel agent (Ministry of Culture and Tourism of China, 2020).
- Third, technological developments make it possible to accomplish many more things online. More leisure activities, such as online reading and gaming as well as sharing travel or leisure experiences and activities on social media platforms, will be accomplished through Internet use. In addition, online selling and purchasing of leisure services will increase tremendously in every sector of the leisure industry.
- Finally, with increasing globalization and modernization, Western culture will continue to affect the leisure pursuits of Chinese people, which may cause the loss of local cultural traits. In other words, Chinese people's worldviews and behaviors may change over time through the pursuits of leisure activities with Western characteristics due to increasing Americanization or globalization.

SUMMARY

Traditionally, Chinese people placed less value on leisure and instead emphasized hard work and education. Although this view of leisure is still prevalent in Chinese society, it has gradually changed due to modernization and globalization. More people have come to realize that leisure is an essential part of daily life. As a result, the leisure industry has seen steady growth over the past two decades, which has caused tremendous economic and social changes in the country. The central government has played an essential role in promoting and guiding leisure pursuits of Chinese people. In addition, leisure attitudes and behaviors have been shaped by leisure researchers, particularly those who have actively promoted public leisure participation through conferences, forums, mass media, magazines, and academic publications.

Although many public agencies provide an array of outdoor recreational opportunities for the public, Chinese people tend to enjoy indoor passive leisure activities more than they do outdoor activities. Some of those indoor passive leisure activities are deeply rooted in traditional Chinese culture and are found to be significantly related to happiness.

The leisure pursuits of Chinese people, particularly the youth, have been considerably influenced by Western culture because of globalization. Leisure pursuits in China have traditionally been different from those in Western society, but cultural distance and distinctive leisure pursuits between China and Western society have diminished under the pressure of cultural diffusion resulting from economic and cultural globalization. Although cultural diffusion may bring with it some negative impacts, the concept of harmony, which is strongly rooted in Chinese culture, plays an essential role in the absorption of elements of other cultures. Moreover, the proactive policies of the Chinese government help maintain traditional Chinese culture. Thus, the negative influence of globalization on the leisure pursuits of Chinese people may be cushioned by the compatible nature of Chinese culture and the preemptive measures taken by the Chinese government.

Recreation in Nigeria

Franz U. Atare

“ The minute you lose consciousness of the need to recreate you start de-creating.   ”

Yomi Awosika, professor emeritus, University of Ibadan

Nigeria comprises 36 states and its Federal Capital Territory. Nigeria is located in West Africa and shares land borders with the Republic of Benin (west), Chad and Cameroon (east), and Niger (north); its coast to the south lies on the Gulf of Guinea in the Atlantic Ocean. Present-day Nigeria has been the site of numerous kingdoms and tribal states spanning more than 1,000 years. Nigeria is often referred to as the "giant of Africa" due to its large population and economy, with approximately 211 million inhabitants; Lagos accounts for over 15 million. The United Nations projects that the overall population of Nigeria will reach about 401.31 million by the end of the year 2050 if the current growth rate is sustained. Nigeria is the most populous country in Africa and the seventh most populous country in the world. Nigeria also has one of the largest populations of youth in the world. The country is inhabited by 500 ethnic groups, each of which has its own unique forms of recreation and leisure activities.

The country has a varied landscape. The far south is defined by its tropical rainforest climate, and annual rainfall is 60 to 80 inches (152.4 to 203.2 cm). The country has interesting natural resources that shape the recreation and leisure behavior of the inhabitants such as the Obudu plateau in Cross River, the coastal plains in Lagos, the mangrove forests in Delta and Bayelsa, the highland hills and mountains that form the Marbella plateau in Taraba (the highest in Nigeria), and Shere Hills in

Jos. The topography and climate conditions largely influence the types of recreation and leisure available in a given location. For example, swimming is popular in Lagos, Bayelsa, Delta, and Rivers due to their proximity to the Atlantic coast (Morakinyo & Atare, 2005).

Another issue that defines recreational interests is religion. Nigeria is roughly divided in half between Christians, who live mostly in the southern and central parts of the country, and Muslims, who are concentrated mostly in the northern and southwestern regions. Muslims tend to frown on the forms of recreation that come from Europe and the United States and perceive them as ploys to derail the faith and religious attitudes of their adherents. Christians are more receptive to Western forms of recreation. This division between Christians and Muslims is inconsequential when national teams engage in **competitive sports**, especially football.

In 2021, Nigeria's gross domestic product became the largest in Africa at more than US$500 billion, and it surpassed South Africa to become the world's 21st-largest economy. It is also listed among the next 11 economies set to become the biggest in the world. This is not reflected in the population, however. The poverty gap continues to widen, and most citizens live on less than US$1 per day. This development has a serious effect on the recreation patterns of a majority of the population because they cannot afford to consume leisure and recreational pursuits that are not free. This further explains why, despite its vast natural tourism potential, recreation and tourism apart from Nollywood (the Nigerian film industry) did not account for the gross domestic product. Most Nigerians continue to spend their leisure hours seeking additional sources of livelihood at the expense of leisure and recreation endeavors.

The population distribution is 51.7 percent rural and 48.3 percent urban, and the population density is 167.5 people per square kilometer (433.82 people per square mile). Modern infrastructure for recreation is located in urban areas. There is a steady increase in rural-to-urban migration, and this gradually leads to a loss of **cultural heritage** and recreation options in rural areas. Due to the population increase in major cities and high rates of unemployment, the cities have attracted criminal and gang activity, thus raising security concerns. Public recreation centers and parks are often neglected due to fear of being robbed or kidnapped for ransom, if not killed. The situation is getting worse; between July 2021 and June 2022, no fewer than 3,420 people were abducted across Nigeria, with 564 others killed in violence associated with abductions. People are now afraid to spend nights out with their families in recreation lounges and nightclubs, especially in the eastern states.

At the same time, there is a rapid expansion in the entertainment industry. Most people capitalize on this by staying home and watching movies. This contributes to the growth of the filmmaking industry. Nollywood is the second-largest producer of movies in the world. Nigerian cinema is Africa's largest movie industry in terms of value and number of movies produced per year.

HISTORICAL DEVELOPMENT OF RECREATION AND LEISURE IN NIGERIA

Sports, games, and dances in Nigeria, as in most African states, date back as far as the origin of Africans. Starting from the desire to meet basic needs, such as the provision of food and defense against hostile environments, sporting activities like hunting, wrestling, and bow shooting served as sports and recreation. In the traditional African setting, survival demanded the profitable use of available free time to do things that contributed to comfort in people's lives. Children learned to dress hides, weave clothes, shoot weapons, and play during all adult life activities. When the adults were not stalking the game, they were mending weapons, and when they were

not tilling the soil, they were repairing implements. These activities are mimicked by children as their own form of recreation and they derived fun and satisfaction from doing so. In pastoral societies, storytelling, songs, and dances were important features of recreation. In precolonial Nigeria, no organized program of recreation was deemed necessary. Very little leisure time was available, and it was not put to worthy use by the exigencies of the culture. When time permitted, people created recreation through songs, stories, and dance.

Recreation is not new to any community in Nigeria. Each has its own modes of recreation and various times or occasions for participation. The traditional lives of many Nigerians have always provided for worthy use of leisure hours. In modern times, young people and adults in all regions in Nigeria engage in recreational activities indigenous to their region (with the exception of team sports, which were introduced from Europe) that are often referred to as *games*. During the early post-independence era, Nigeria was divided into four distinct regions (North, East, West, and Midwest). These regions had different languages and cultural patterns that influenced the types of games played based on their environment. Those games served recreational, leisure, cultural, and religious functions. The games formed the basis of their everyday and cultural life (Amuchie, 2003).

Although bastardized by colonial influences, many of these games are still practiced today. Recreational activities vary between states, communities, and ethnic groups, but some are shared. Activities include traditional boxing (*dambe*), archery, canoeing (boat regatta), and dancing (*atilogwu, egwuamara, ekpe, eyo, fuji, afrojuju, awigiri, ikenike, ekong, uta, ebre, abang*, etc.). Climbing, which is recreational and used in fruit harvesting, helps develop the muscles of the trunk, arms, and legs. Hunting is done individually or communally on certain market days. In the early 1900s, very successful hunters were traditionally honored because hunting served as an occupation and a hobby. Wrestling was one of the earliest leisure activities in Nigeria, and it is practiced in all parts of the country. **Abula** and **langa** are the most popular forms to date; they are taught in schools, and there are wrestling competitions during national sports festivals.

Horse racing is a common recreational activity in the northern regions, especially Kaduna and Borno states, where it is at its peak. Good horse riders jump obstacles and use horses to play *polo*, a game that resembles hockey. Horse riding is also a popular pastime among the elite Hausas and Fulanis ethnic groups that dominate the northern region. Owning and maintaining a horse is an expensive form of recreation not open to those of low economic means.

Moonlight games are recreational games with little organization that are used as a form of relaxation after a strenuous day's work and night meals. They vary in structure, but their common feature is that they usually need no equipment and are played during the full moon. Common moonlight games include touch and run, cock fight, hide and seek, dance, storytelling, frog jump, and others. Moonlight games offer youth the opportunity to socialize, recreate, and develop mentally, physically, and emotionally, thus satisfying the World Health Organization's concept of health as a state of complete physical, mental, and social well-being, and not merely the absence of disease or infirmity. The games are popular in all states of Nigeria, especially in rural areas, and they are sometimes featured on national television.

The introduction of formal education into the country, especially physical education, changed recreation to reflect modern sports taught in schools. The British colonial masters fostered outdoor activities for recreation. Athletics, horse riding, fishing, hunting, swimming, tennis, skating, golf, football, archery, and hockey were common features of English life, and these were passed down to colonies including Nigeria. Most other foreign sports, such as gymnastics and volleyball, have common features with Nigerian traditional sports.

Before the incursion of the British colonialists in Nigeria, women were traditionally involved in several physical activities for fun and recreation even while they were performing domestic chores and agricultural duties. Dancing was a prominent recreational activity that was featured during festivals, ceremonies, and celebrations. Examples are New Yam and Argungu Fishing festivals. Ceremonies include naming, wedding, initiation, and burial. Celebrations included birthdays; housewarming; good health or recovery from illness; escape from accident, death, or robbery; safe delivery; traveling hazard; chieftaincy installation or coronation; and anniversaries (Ikulayo, 2003).

To date, dancing is highly cherished as a means of traditional and cultural recreation. It produces joy, fun, happiness, and fulfillment and is a strong means of self-expression, even among men.

Ayo is one of the oldest seed and board games in Nigeria. It has been given different names by different language groups, such as *mancala, oware, bao, onweso, oko, enkeshin, nsa,* or *isip isong.* It is played with seed and a board with 12 holes or with 12 holes dug in the ground. Each hole has four seeds.

It can be played by two to four people. Today it is included in the basic school curriculum as a recreational activity for all school children (Udomiaye & Umar, 2010).

Since independence in 1960, football has been the most popular form of recreation. It is regarded as a national obsession and is popular with male and female citizens of all ages. Watching live football matches from the English Premier League (EPL), Spanish League (*Laliga*), and German League (*Bundus liga*) is a popular pastime.

Apart from football and basketball, in which Nigeria has made a mark on the international scene, sports do not attract large crowds except during national sport festivals. As in Brazil and other football-loving nations, youth use any available space to play football, such as roads, sand banks, and beaches. Many young people have sacrificed education for a career in football; examples include international soccer stars such as Kanu Nwankwo, Austin Okocha, Mikel Obi, and Sunday Oliseh, all of whom started their football careers in the street but now play in major leagues.

Market days, which are a social and economic feature prevalent among agriculturally based groups, are held on different days in all parts of Nigeria and in many other West African countries. Traditionally, the farmers and most other craftspeople rest on important market days, some Sundays, and other special days. These special days are dedicated to local deities, and some dances and sacrifices are featured in these ceremonies. These resting days are also set aside for burial ceremonies and marriages. Apart from resting days, some ceremonial activities also take place when farmers and traders return from their farms and markets. On market days rural traders have increased leisure hours that are used for recreational purposes such as storytelling, riddles, and jokes because other strenuous daily activities are prohibited. In some communities, market day is held either weekly or fortnightly. Some youth engage in wrestling and other physical endeavors. Girls and small children participate in moonlight games, dances, songs, and jokes. It is an important day in the life of most communities because visitors from nearby communities exchange visits and cultural displays.

Each cultural group, village, or town and families or group of families are noted for some particular occupation and other cultural activities. In some cases, individuals that are gifted with some special cultural talents contribute to the recreation needs of the community. These activities help solidify families and ethnic groups.

Cinema halls and viewing centers, shopping malls, and comedy performances are also prominent leisure activities in major cities across Nigeria.

SETTINGS, ORGANIZATION, AND STRUCTURES

Agencies are responsible for recreational activities and programs, but they are also supervised by the government. An agency is a government department, business, or private organization that provides a specific service. In Nigeria, there are four types of agencies: public, private, commercial, or voluntary. Recreation areas handled by commercial agencies exist for financial profit that accrues from the provision of recreation services. Voluntary agencies seek the enrichment of individual and community life. According to Atare (2003), the structure of recreation organizations in Nigeria can be classified into five agencies based on the provision of recreation facilities, activities, and programs:

1. *Individual and home.* Recreation requires individual engagement and involvement. Many forms of recreation such as walking, artwork, hobbies, and caring for pets are essentially individual. They are, however, more enjoyable when done in a group. Modern homes devote much space to recreational use. In the backyard, pets, gardening, and toys play an important role in the lives of many families. Much of indoor play takes place at home in different forms, such as games, reading, playing with toys, playing musical instruments, or having parties. The most common forms of home recreation for young people are watching videos, listening to music, and tending gardens. Home activities tend to occupy more leisure hours than recreation provided by outside agencies.

2. *Private agencies.* These agencies usually restrict their recreational programs to members. The use of facilities might be extended to family members and close associates. These agencies do not depend on community support; rather members' payment of dues and fees helps to administer programs and build and maintain the facilities. These clubs exist in every major city (e.g., Uyo Club, founded in 1935) in Nigeria and on all university campuses (e.g., senior staff club). Some industries also have recreational clubs for their workers (e.g., Shell Petroleum Development Company, Chevron Nigeria Unlimited).

3. *Voluntary agencies.* Voluntary agencies in Nigeria provide services for varying age groups, and many require membership. Facilities and programs are usually funded through contributions from individuals, united funds, sponsorships, and membership fees. These agencies can be grouped into those that restrict participation to members and those that permit nonmembers to participate.

4. *Commercial agencies.* Commercial recreation agencies capitalize on the natural demand for recreation and the avoidance of boredom by people of different classes. The influx of commercial agencies in the provision of recreation programs reflects the inability of other agencies to meet the demand to provide adequate recreation. Although commercial agencies are profit oriented, many of them occasionally offer free and discounted services as a way to encourage those who enjoy passive forms of recreation. The most popular forms of commercial recreation are amusement parks and entertainment, travel and tourism, and athletics and sports. Ibom Icon Hotel and Golf Resort in Uyo, Akwa Ibom State, is one of the biggest tourist destinations in Nigeria due to its location, natural environment, and prevailing security.

5. *Governmental agencies.* An increasing number of government departments and bureaus (e.g., National Park Service, Forest Service, Fish and Wildlife Service, Bureau of Reclamation, Ministry of Youth and Sports) provide recreation services to the general public in cooperation with other agencies. The Nigerian government has shown remarkable concern in matters relating to recreation and sports since the end of the Nigerian Civil War in 1970. Large sums of money have been allocated and spent on sports and recreation programs. The Federal Ministry of Youth and Sports Development has changed the focus from recreation to business as contained in the Nigeria Sports Industry Policy of 2022. The implication is that government agencies will be administered as commercial agencies.

DIVERSE POPULATIONS AND THEIR INTERESTS

One of the cardinal principles of recreation is to provide ample opportunity for everyone irrespective of age, religion, sex, or social belief. Other opportunities still available for recreation are as follows.

Recreation for Those in School

Recreation in most cases is treated as a function of the family, but it is also that of the school. The schools provide programs and facilities that help children develop recreational leadership skills that will eventually be translated into adult life. Recreation facilities are not prominent in government-owned primary and secondary schools as compared to private schools. The situation is different in tertiary institutions (all states have at least four tertiary institutions) with facilities for recreation and sport. The quantity in terms of facilities and programs offered varies from institution to institution according to the need and scope of the program offered. Conventional universities have more recreational and sporting facilities than specialized institutions (Atare & Ekpu, 2014b). In all institutions of higher learning, there are no classes after noon on Wednesdays to facilitate participation in recreational opportunities. It also serves as a selection process for students who will represent the institution in the Nigerian University Games Association (NUGA), the Nigeria Polytechnic Games Association (NIPOGA), and the Nigeria Colleges of Education Games Association (NICEGA) games.

The curriculum of basic education includes dance, computer games, *ludo*, chess, draught, Scrabble, music, novel reading, table tennis, swimming, bow and arrow, *langa*, and *abula* and is designed to prepare youth to develop recreation consciousness that they will transfer to adult life.

Recreation for the Family During Holidays

A more recent trend in the industry is carnivals. In Nigeria, carnivals are held in the streets and are prevalent during national holidays. These carnivals are similar to those held in Brazil in terms of dress, number of participants, duration, age groupings, and tourist draw, and they provide families ample time away from home solely for recreation and amusement. Carnivals draw many visitors, and children and youth in particular enjoy them. Prominent among them are the Eyo Festival in Lagos, Calabar Carnival, Uyo Carnival, Durbar Festival, Kaduna, and August Meeting in Owerri (among the Ibo-speaking women, August is a time when all the women return home to take part in this carnival that has many opportunities for the leisure service and hospitality industries), Argungu Fishing Festival, Boat Regatta in Warri and Lagos, and Abuja Carnival.

STEFAN HEUNIS/AFP/Getty Images

Recreation for families takes place at the many carnivals and festivals throughout Nigeria, such as the Durbar Festival.

Recreation for Industrial Workers

Big industrial companies (e.g., Shell Petroleum Development Company, Chevron Nigeria, First Bank of Nigeria, Delta Steel Company) also provide recreation. These corporate bodies understand the integration of business and recreation and thus are expending personnel, space, and financial resources to promote recreation activities for their workers.

Recreation for Religious Adherents

Many religious groups in Nigeria are now aware of the importance of recreation in the life of their followers; hence, members are encouraged to participate in wholesome recreation activities because they contribute to the spiritual well-being of the individual. Some Christian religious organizations provide school-break camps for children, retreats, annual conventions, overnight vigils, and other programs during holidays such as Christmas, especially in the southern part of the country that is dominated by Christians. Some have provided standard recreational facilities such as a football pitch, volleyball court, swimming pool, and aerobic hall in the same premises as worship. Muslims encourage members to spend time with their families and friends in parks during holiday seasons such as *Id el Fitr* and *Id el Kabir*.

Recreation for Adults

Among adult men, draught (a highly intellectual 40-seed game played on a square board of 100 smaller square boxes, in which each player has 20 seeds evenly distributed within the first 40 boxes on each side), pet keeping, reading newspapers, and watching television are popular pastimes, especially for those who are no longer regularly employed (e.g., pensioners and retirees). For adult women, domestic chores, religious activities, and gardening rank high among pastimes. A popular leisure activity for middle-aged women is participation in social clubs and associations that meet weekly in the homes of members. Meetings are characterized by dancing, singing, and merriment, especially when humanitarian assistance is offered to members in times of need. These meetings can last three to six hours depending on the size of the group.

CHALLENGES, ISSUES, AND TRENDS

Outdoor recreation is not popular due to the country's climate. There are two seasons in Nigeria: rainy and *harmattan* (the tropical continental airmass). November to February is the harmattan season when the northeast trade wind blows across the Atlantic Ocean and causes dryness. The rainy (the tropical maritime airmass) season has heavy downpours and lasts from March to October with annual rainfall ranging from 79 inches (2,000 mm) to 185 inches (4,700 mm) with its highest peak in July. Those who engage in outdoor activities do so for economic reasons rather than for recreational interest.

Although Nigeria has a high GDP, the per capita income is low, which means many citizens live below the poverty line. As a result, expensive forms of recreation are not within reach for those in low-income groups.

Comedy shows have become increasingly popular. Ali Baba, Basket Mouth, Ay, Gordons, I Go Die, Teju Baby Face, and others have made comedy a very important form of recreation. Some individuals prefer to buy the videos and watch them at home rather than visit theaters, museums, and playhouses to watch them live. In general, the increasing demand for home video entertainment has led to a drastic decline in physical recreation activities. Most elite people prefer to visit a gym for physical activity than to engage in brisk walking or jogging; this trend is also related to security concerns. The few individuals who engage in physical recreation do so for health (e.g., prevention of obesity or diabetes), fitness, and sport competition reasons (Atare, 2014).

The number of Nigerians that visit stadiums to watch international football matches continues to increase, but the reverse is true for **local club sides** or Nigerian football clubs. Between 1990 and 2005, Nigerian local clubs enjoyed a great following: Fans traveled long distances to watch live matches, and tickets were bought in advance. Now, most clubs play in nearly empty stadiums. The situation is different with international matches: In the 2019 African Cup of Nations qualifiers held on June 10, 2017, at the Godswill Akpabio International Stadium in Uyo between Super Eagles of Nigeria and Bafana Bafana of South Africa, the stadium was filled to capacity (30,000 people). In that same stadium one week later, Akwa United Football Club played Katsina United Football Club and the attendance was less than 2,000. A September 2012 survey conducted by NOIPolls reported that 89 percent

OUTSTANDING GRADUATE

Background Information

Name: Daniel Ekomobong

Education: BS in physical education, University of Uyo

Credentials: Hostess, Ibom Icon Hotel and Golf Resort

Awards: Miss Ikono Worldwide (2018/2019), Miss Ibom Hotel (2019/2020), Award of Excellence Ibom Icon Hotel (2022).

Affiliations: Ministry of Culture and Tourism, Akwa Ibom State-Nigeria; Nigerian Association of Physical and Health Education, Recreation, Sport and Dance, University of Uyo chapter

Career Information

Position: Hostess

Organization: Ibom Icon Hotel and Golf Resort is the pride of Uyo, Akwa Ibom State. Situated amidst rich palm forest vegetation, this magnificent hotel on 174 hectares (430 acres) of land connotes peace and serenity complemented by its original atmosphere. The lush greens of the world-class 18-hole golf course create the right atmosphere for the most challenging and memorable golfing experience. Each time you visit this unique hotel in Uyo, Akwa Ibom State, discoveries await you. It is a beautiful place to behold.

Organization mission: To be a leading hospitality, leisure, recreation and tourism development and management services provider in Africa and among the best in the world

Job description: I work in the food and beverage department as a hostess, welcoming and directing guests. My responsibility as a hostess is to supervise other hosts, hostesses, and waitstaff, making sure their duties are discharged according to the hotel's established policy. With my comprehensive knowledge of the department, I also ensure that every service is attended to judiciously.

Career path: I started my career as a teacher at a nursery school. Afterward, I worked as a waitress at Le Meridien Ibom Hotel and Golf Resort as a casual staff member and was then rescheduled as a contract staff member. The experiences prompted me to further my education in a related field, which facilitated my promotion to hostess.

Likes and dislikes about the job: The job alleviated my public phobia and improved my communication skills. Prior to 2021, a hostess was not posted or assigned to the Vista Restaurant, so I pioneered the role for the Department of Food and Beverage at the restaurant. I delight in satisfying guests. The physical demands of the job, namely standing for eight hours or more, make the job challenging.

Advice for Undergraduates

Nowadays, many challenges are insurmountable for young people. I encourage them to challenge themselves—go to school, select a job, and learn good time management skills. These experiences and abilities will thrust them into the limelight and enable them to become humanitarians.

---

of Nigerians interviewed are supporters of foreign football clubs and 52 percent said they do not follow Nigerian club sides (NOIPolls, 2014).

Technology growth has also greatly influenced leisure behavior, and it seriously threatens active leisure. Many people, especially children and women, spend increasing amounts of time on their mobile devices playing games or using social media programs such as 2go, Facebook, Instagram, TikTok, WhatsApp, Badoo, BBM, and X (formerly known as Twitter).

Despite the growth in the leisure service industry, few institutions of higher learning offer degree programs in leisure and recreation. In almost all degree-awarding institutions, recreation is taught only as a course in the department of physical and health education. A few Nigerian universities offer degree programs in recreation (University of Ibadan, University of Benin, and University of Nigeria). Many universities offer programs in hospitality management and tourism.

Recreation and leisure services are now an integral part of everyday living and creating a balanced life. The number of fitness and recreational clubs, gyms, spas, stadiums, and carnivals is increasing. Apart from health concerns that have attracted many to avail themselves of recreation, the consciousness of recreational activities is great among the average Nigerian. There is also a high demand for recreational goods and products. The Nigerian market is open to manufacturers of recreational goods and products that combine traditional and modern games. This growth is likely to increase with the introduction of recreation in the secondary school curriculum and easy access to popular forms of recreation shown on television such as merry-go-rounds, computer games, rope skipping, tug-of-war, and cartoon movies.

Most rural areas are quickly evolving into urban towns due to rapid growth in settlement areas and increasing building developments. There is a concern that these new towns lack space provisions for parks or recreation centers. If this trend is sustained, people who seek recreation will have to travel long distances to participate.

COVID-19 AND LEISURE ACTIVITY

The first case of COVID-19 recorded in Nigeria was on February 27, 2020, which eventually spread to 35 states and the Federal Capital Territory. As of December 9, 2022, 5,708,974 samples were tested, 266,381 were confirmed, 3,467 were actives cases, 259,759 were discharged, and 3,155 deaths were recorded. This is marginal compared to the reports from other scientifically advanced nations.

The impact of the pandemic on recreation and sports in Nigeria was unprecedented. Sports, recreation industries, and youth organizations experienced unanticipated macroeconomic shocks because they were unable to pay wages, contracts were terminated, and livelihoods were disrupted. During the initial lockdown, the movement of people to retail and recreation centers, parks, public transportation hubs, and supermarkets declined significantly. Activity at parks, beaches, marinas, dog parks, museums, libraries, restaurants, cafés, plazas, and public gardens halted with a 24-hour curfew imposed by the government to checkmate the spread. This required the closure of all activity-based centers such as schools, hotels, clubs, and religious houses that brought a sizeable number of people together. In addition, directives such as

social distancing, the banning of congregations of more than 20 people in open and closed spaces, and compulsory use of face masks completely grounded any attempt to engage in public recreation and resulted in more sedentary behavior for many.

The availability and distribution of vaccines facilitated the quick recovery in phases from the lockdown. As of July 2022, 55,468,500 vaccines have been administered and normalcy has since resumed, but the effects of the virus still persist. Most recreation and leisure industries could not recover from the total collapse, because most individuals became attached to the mode of recreation enjoyed during the pandemic.

Social life has gradually returned to normal with some gains in the leisure and recreation industry. Some individuals now realize the need to be physically active since most of the recorded deaths from COVID-19 were people who were sedentary or had comorbidities. The importance of recreation to enhanced quality of living became more prominent. More fitness centers and groups have emerged, and there is an increased demand for fitness videos on YouTube for those who cannot use public places. Also, many have adopted cycling, squatting, weight training, and taking part in active sports or recreation as a hobby.

SUMMARY

This section examined the historical development of recreation in Nigeria and how the geopolitical distribution of the country affects recreational service delivery. Passive forms of recreation appear to be more popular than physical recreation due to security, economic reasons, and the effects of COVID-19. Recreation is administered through five agencies that meet the recreation needs of families, industrial workers, sports enthusiasts, adults, and those in school. Nigerians enjoy many forms of recreation; we hope that in the near future abundant natural and human resources that promote recreation will be properly developed and will make Nigeria a recreation, holiday, and tourist destination of choice.

Review Questions
International Perspectives: Sustainability and Ecotourism

1. Define *place attachment* as well as its elements: *dependence*, *affect*, and *identity*.

2. Identify the effects of COVID-19 on outdoor recreation and tourism.

3. Reflect on an indoor or outdoor space you are attached to. What created that attachment?

4. What sustainable efforts are the town of Todmorden, England, utilizing? What efforts are occurring in your own community?

5. How has COVID-19 affected recreation, tourism, and leisure (RTL) in your area (e.g., state, country, region)?

6. What are the potential benefits and consequences of hosting the Olympics?

Recreation and Leisure in Brazil

1. What are the influences of enslaved people in the creation and establishment of important cultural practices in Brazil?

2. What was the significance of soap operas for the Brazilian population during the military dictatorship times?

3. How have the works of Joffre Dumazedier influenced recreation and leisure in Brazil?

4. What are the main folkloric events or parties in Brazil and how are they recognized in the country?

5. How has the adventure tourism market used the unique natural resources in Brazil to offer leisure and recreation activities?

6. How have the changes in the demographic profile of the Brazilian population influenced leisure and recreation practices, particularly those related to computer use?

(continued)

Review Questions   *(continued)*

Recreation and Leisure in China

1. What are the four most popular outdoor recreation settings in China?

2. Why do Chinese people tend to prefer quiet or passive leisure pursuits, compared to their counterparts in North America?

3. To what extent has China's domestic tourism and outbound tourism been affected by COVID-19?

4. To what extent have Chinese leisure pursuits been affected by globalization and modernization?

Recreation in Nigeria

1. Explain how songs and storytelling were used as recreation in precolonial Nigeria.

2. Mention at least four names given to Ayo by different language groups in Nigeria, and briefly describe how the game is played.

3. How do the COVID-19 pandemic and economy of Nigeria influence the recreational choices of its citizens?

4. What are some of the challenges caused by urbanization, and how do those challenges affect the recreational participation of city dwellers in Nigeria?

5. Explain recreation provisions for children, adults, and industrial workers in Nigeria.

Go to HK*Propel* to complete the activities for this chapter.

Glossary

A

abula—A ball and bat game played in a rectangular court by a team of eight players with four players on the court and the other four on the bench as substitutes. The ball is played over the net and a rally is initiated until there is a default by one team. It is similar to volleyball but played with a bat.

accessibility—The extent to which a facility or activity space allows a person to navigate and engage with the surrounding environment and all its elements.

accommodation—The removal of barriers that otherwise might prevent successful participation in an activity.

accountability—Providing services that produce results as efficiently and effectively as possible.

accreditation—Assurance that a program, institution, or agency has met essential requirements or standards as set by a governing body.

active listening—The process of carefully paying attention to the information someone shares with you, and reflecting back—through questions and body language—that you heard them.

activity analysis—A systematic procedure to identify the behaviors required to participate in an activity.

activity theory—Suggests that successful aging occurs when people maintain the interests, activities, and social interactions they were involved with during middle adulthood.

adaptation—Modification of equipment, rules, or the surrounding environment directly associated with an activity to allow for successful participation.

adapted sports—Sports programs that allow rule adaptations to adjust the level of challenge and competition to meet the abilities of participants.

adolescence—One of the seven life stages, from 13 to 19 years old.

adventure recreation—A recreation experience in which risk, whether real or perceived, is a central component of the experience.

advocate—A recreation and leisure services professional who recognizes an injustice that prevents community members from engaging in recreation and leisure services and works to resolve the injustice.

aesthetics—The branch of philosophy that deals with questions of the nature of beauty, particularly in relation to the natural environment and human-made art objects. In terms of the provision of leisure services, aesthetics is an important managerial consideration for enhancing the experience of leisure in built and natural environments.

age of instruction—The period in which most learning is through basic instructions.

agricultural tourism—Any agricultural activity that draws tourists to visit, stay, or work.

Amazon—The largest rainforest in the world, covering more than one billion acres (400 million ha) of land in South America; it encompasses land in nine South American countries, and 60 percent of it is in Brazil.

American Therapeutic Recreation Association (ATRA)—The national professional organization for certified therapeutic recreation specialists (CTRSs).

amusement—A pleasure-seeking activity that Aristotle judged to be inferior to leisure.

anthropometric measurements—Quantitative techniques used to measure the human body such as size, shape, and composition.

arm's-length provider—One of the five roles that governments can take in delivering public services; the government creates a special-purpose agency, such as a museum, that operates outside the regular apparatus of government.

arts—Documented forms of expression produced by sentient beings such as opera, dance, theater, music, painting, sculpture, literature, graffiti, film, radio, television, and digital media.

arts and cultural activities—Pursuits that contribute or enhance the aesthetic, artistic, historical, intellectual, or social development or appreciation of members of the general public; examples include art and craft making; consumption of arts digitally, in live performance, or through books; learning through public programs, classes, or workshops; art sharing through digital environments; and producing or sponsoring programs.

arts and cultural sector—The individuals, entrepreneurs, and formal and informal organizations (nonprofit, private, public, and unincorporated) that create, produce, present, distribute, preserve, educate about, fund, and advocate for aesthetic, heritage, and entertainment activities, products, and artifacts.

assessment—A systematic process of gathering and synthesizing information about the client and their environment using a variety of methods, such as interviews, observation, standardized tests, and input from other disciplines and significant others, to devise an individualized treatment or service plan.

Athenian ideal—An ideal combination of soldier, athlete, artist, statesman, and philosopher that was valued in ancient Greece.

athletic sports—Participation in sport to achieve excellence through advanced skill and strategy.

attraction—A feature, facility, program, event, or natural phenomena that has the capability to attract, lure, or entice an individual to travel.

auxiliary facility—A supplementary and separate building or space that is used and managed by campus recreation but is not part of the main facility.

B

backcountry—The areas in a park or protected area that are not accessible by roads and are characterized by low use levels.

background check—A process that provides data about an individual's criminal, commercial, and financial records.

baile funk—Large dance party in a favela that plays mostly Brazilian rap, hip-hop, and electro-funk music; it originated in Rio de Janeiro, but today the concept is widespread across the country and has reached middle- and upper-class circles, although it is still mostly staged in low-income communities.

biosphere reserves—A designated geographic area where people exemplify various ways to sustain local economies and use resources while also conserving the biodiversity found in different kinds of ecosystems. As of September 2023, there were 738 biosphere reserves in 134 countries.

body mass index (BMI)—A measurement of weight divided by height that is used as a health indicator.

bossa nova—A music style developed in Brazil in the mid-1950s that became famous worldwide in the beginning of the 1960s; it evolved from samba but has a mood similar to jazz. "The Girl from Ipanema" is one of bossa nova's most famous songs, and it illustrates this style well.

bread and circuses—An ancient Roman concept that was meant to pacify unrest through pleasurable experiences that included free food and entertainment.

built environment—Human-constructed surroundings such as buildings, designed parks, or transportation systems.

businesses—Organizations that provide a service or product and charge a price that is higher than the cost of production. The difference between the cost and the price is the profit.

C

caipirinha—A Brazilian cocktail that is popular around the world, particularly in Europe; it is made with cachaça (a traditional Brazilian spirit made of sugar cane), sugar, ice, and lime.

campus recreation—A department that provides facilities and programs for campus communities to engage in recreation, sport, and wellness opportunities that contribute to the physical, social, and emotional well-being of students and the campus community.

Canadian Armed Forces (CAF)—Collectively, the Royal Canadian Navy, the Canadian Army, and the Royal Canadian Air Force.

Canadian Forces Morale and Welfare Services (CFMWS)—An organization that manages morale and welfare programs for the Canadian military community.

capoeira—The most elaborate martial art of the African diaspora. It is a spectacular combination of dance, acrobatic kicks, evasive maneuvers, slow martial arts sparring, and improvised musical performance, and it is widely practiced in Brazil as a true cultural expression.

carnaval—The most popular and famous Brazilian celebration. It is held 46 days before Easter and officially lasts for four days; it is celebrated across the country and involves music, costumes, and parades of various colors, types, and styles.

carrying capacity—The amount and type of use that an area or resource can accommodate without being unacceptably damaged.

caste system—A system of classification in which social position is ascribed at birth.

certified therapeutic recreation specialist (CTRS)—An individual who, through knowledge and experience, has met the National Council for Therapeutic Recreation Certification's CTRS certification standards.

charities—The most readily identifiable form of nonprofit that represent diverse organizations often serving the most vulnerable populations for free or for reduced fees. Charities in the United States are organized under Section 501(c)(3) of the IRS code.

class system—A system of classification in which social position is earned by wealth, power, and status.

club sports—Sport activities organized by individuals because of a common appeal or interest in a sport. Teams practice regularly, follow an organized schedule, and can be recreational or competitive; many are associated with regional and national governing bodies.

code of ethical practice—Statements outlining the ethics that an agency or organization deems critical to fulfilling its duties.

code of ethics—A written description of the established duties and obligations of the professional to protect the human rights of service recipients.

commercial recreation—Any enterprise that provides recreation or leisure experiences and has the intent of making a profit.

commodification—The process by which an object, idea, or service that historically has not been considered a commodity becomes a commodity within a society.

community—Those who are physically in a specific geographic location or region or political district or boundary; a group of people who have common interests such as social causes, gaming, or academic fields; or a group of people who hold similar identities based on affiliation, appearance, or lifestyle.

community arts—Participatory arts that can be distinguished by their nature as critical, exploratory, experimental, innovative, challenging, or even radical commentaries on society in a given moment, time, place, or cultural juncture.

community building—A set of practices and approaches developed to address the social isolation and lack of belonging and sense of community by people across the world.

community education—A concept, philosophy, and practice that focuses on community participation in planning, developing, and offering activities and programs that strengthen and benefit individuals, families, and communities.

community health—The health status of a defined group of people (e.g., grouped by proximity, gender, race, or another common factor).

commuter campus—A college or university in which students live off campus and travel to the school for class.

competitive sports—Sports competitions designed for a true champion to emerge. They can be individual or team events.

consequence-based ethics—An ethical theory that determines what is good or bad based on outcomes. It typically aims to maximize the greatest good for the greatest number of people.

conservation—Using natural resources such as trees, water, or rangeland in a wise, regulated, or planned manner so that it is not destroyed and can be used and renewed indefinitely.

constitutional monarchy—The part of the British Commonwealth with allegiance to the queen of England. In Canada, the Crown is the foundation of the executive and judicial branches of government.

constitutional republic—A form of government in which the executive branch is elected and the judicial branch is appointed by the chief executive, as in the United States.

contemplation—The highest form of leisure in ancient Greece; it involved the pursuit of truth and understanding.

continuity theory—Suggests that people need to maintain their desired levels of involvement in society to maximize their sense of self-esteem and well-being.

cooperative play—Form of play in which children work together to achieve a common goal.

cost recovery—An organizational strategy allocating funding based on operational priorities regarding services and programs.

creative placemaking—The process of identifying, supporting, and mobilizing local arts and culture toward community betterment.

credentialing—The process by which a profession or government certifies that a professional has met the established minimum standards of competency required for practice.

critical thinking—The application of the rules and principles of informal logic in evaluating arguments and inferences to distinguish good reasoning from fallacious reasoning.

cross-cultural competence—The ability to understand, respect, and communicate with diverse people.

cultural diversity—The heterogeneity encountered in the values and knowledge of various peoples, societies, or groups that share a common background.

cultural heritage—The way of life of a people that is transferred from generation to generation.

culture—The rich variety of ways that human work, thoughts, attitudes, and values of a certain time and place are communicated through practices, beliefs, behaviors, religions, institutions, and the creative arts.

D

direct provider—One of the five roles that governments can take in delivering public services; the government develops and maintains leisure facilities, operates programs, and delivers services using public funds and public employees.

direct service provider—A recreation and leisure services professional who has responsibility for a program or service from start to finish.

disability—Any restriction or lack of ability to perform an activity in the manner or within the range that is considered normal.

disability sports—Sports programs designed for people with disabilities that provide participants with a continuum of competition levels from beginner to elite that adhere to traditional rules and regulations of the sport rather than allowing individualized adaptations.

disengagement theory—Suggests that people in late adulthood start to withdraw from the world on social, physical, and psychological levels.

documentation—The written or electronic recording of a client's participation and progress in therapeutic recreation.

dual sports—Sport events that require at least one opponent (e.g., badminton, table tennis, tennis, squash, handball, racquetball).

duty-based ethics—An ethical theory that determines what is right and wrong based on what obligations must be satisfied.

E

early adulthood—One of the seven life stages; people in this stage are 20 to 39 years old.

early childhood—One of the seven life stages; people in this stage are 3 to 6 years old.

economic impact—The influence that an industry or sector has on a given economy; this is measurable in any industry or organization that spends money or has audiences spending money.

educational sports—The act of teaching or learning sport skills for the purposes of education and improvement.

emotional intelligence—The capacity to accurately perceive and understand one's own emotions and the emotions of others and to successfully manage one's emotions.

emotional labor—The ability to manage one's emotional responses when confronting work situations that are emotionally challenging, such as maintaining an appropriately professional demeanor with a rude, agitated customer.

empiricists—People who believe the philosophical thesis that knowledge is derived from observations and sensory experiences.

employee assistance program (EAP)—A work-based intervention program designed to assist employees in resolving personal problems that might adversely affect their performance.

enabler and coordinator—One of the five roles that governments can take in delivering public services; the government identifies organizations and agencies that produce leisure services and helps coordinate their efforts, resources, and activities.

entrepreneur—An individual who organizes and runs a small or medium-sized business and accepts all the financial risks and rewards of the business venture.

entrepreneurial associations—Well-established regional, national, and global organizations that focus on advancing the interests of their entrepreneurial membership.

epistemology—The branch of philosophy that examines the sources of our knowledge, the methods we use in gaining knowledge, the kinds of knowledge that are possible for us to obtain, and how certain we can be of our knowledge. Epistemology poses the philosophical question of how we really know what we think we know.

equality—The state of being equal, especially in status, rights, and opportunities.

equity—The quality of being fair and impartial.

ethical dilemma—A situation in which a basic moral choice must be made but neither option appears desirable.

ethics—The philosophical study of morality and moral justification.

ethnicity—Distinctive cultural characteristics.

evidence-based practice (EBP)—The combined use of practitioners' expertise and research findings to select the best programs and services to achieve outcomes.

evidence-based program—A program that demonstrates reliable and consistent positive changes in important health-related measures.

extramural sports—Structured sport activities between winners of various intramural sports programs.

F

facilitated leadership—This type of leadership works with groups so they can become independent and provide programs and services for themselves.

facilitator—A recreation and leisure services professional who facilitates participants' engagement in leisure in such a way that they are responsible for many of their own leisure experiences.

favelas—The Brazilian term for shantytowns.

fine motor skills—Movements of the small muscles of the body that are used for activities such as writing, cutting, and picking up small objects.

fitness programs—Instructor-led activities and classes focusing on strength, mobility, endurance, and cardiovascular health.

folklife—The ways that people assemble, work, and act together through commonplace activities for a variety of political, aesthetic, economic, familial, religious, and educational purposes.

folklore festivals—Festivals of dance, music, or any other art or cultural form that involve traditional practices of a particular cultural group or a mix of various groups.

football—The most popular team sport in the world; it is played with a ball and 11 players on each team (called *soccer* in North America).

formal operations—The ability to perform mental operations with abstract concepts, such as justice or poverty, and estimate the effect of these concepts.

formative evaluation—Evaluation that is ongoing during the implementation phase and leads to immediate changes and improvements in the treatment plan.

foundations—Nonprofits that amass resources and provide grants or direct programs for the public good. There are private foundations, operating foundations, and community foundations, among examples of such nonprofits.

front country—The parts of a park or protected area that are developed, accessed by roads, and contain primary visitor use locations.

functioning—The ability to perform specific functions in each of the five domains of health: cognitive or mental, physical, psychological or emotional, social, and spiritual.

G

gender—A social category that includes attitudes, expectations, and expressions of masculinity, femininity, and gender neutrality.

general supervision leadership—Leadership that focuses on providing facilities and areas in which people can recreate, play, and socialize independently. The participants create and control their own experiences.

goals—Broad-based intended outcomes related to the mission of the organization that help guide the types and content of programs and services offered by the agency.

golden weeks—A weeklong national holiday in China (e.g., the Spring Festival Golden Week, the National Day Golden Week, and the Labor Day Golden Week).

governmental unit—A generic term that describes a government group at any level: national, state, county, or city. It can be used to refer to one large unit (e.g., the state) or subdivisions within the unit (e.g., departments).

graduate assistantships—Positions in which full-time graduate students work part-time as paraprofessionals; they are paid a stipend for their work and the department covers their tuition.

gross national product—The sum of total goods and services manufactured or provided by all businesses, nonprofits, and government entities in a country.

gross motor skills—Movements of the large muscles of the body that are used for activities such as throwing, walking, crawling, and sitting up.

H

health—A state of complete physical, mental, and social well-being and not merely the absence of disease or infirmity, according to the World Health Organization.

health literacy—The degree to which people have the capacity to obtain, process, and understand basic health information and services needed to make appropriate health decisions.

health promotion—Engaging in healthy lifestyle practices to promote health and wellness.

health risk appraisal (HRA)—A group of screening tools used as a first step in assessing the health status of an individual or a group.

health risk assessments (HRAs)—A type of health questionnaire developed to evaluate a person's quality of life and health risks.

health status—The existence or absence of illness or disease.

hedonism—A philosophy that focuses on pleasure as the ultimate goal.

hijab—To cover, screen, or veil; the hijab is a garment (e.g., headscarf, cloak) worn by some Muslim women to cover their heads and neck to signify modesty and Muslim identity.

hosting functions—Agencies and businesses that offer accommodations and food and beverage services.

Human Development Index—A United Nations initiative that assesses and ranks nations as high, medium, or low according to their level of human development by measuring dimensions such as life expectancy, literacy, access to sewage, and clean water.

human services profession—A profession that has the objective of meeting human needs through an interdisciplinary knowledge base, focusing on prevention and remediation of problems, and maintaining a commitment to improving the overall quality of life of those they serve.

I

identity-first language—Language that puts the disability first in the wording referring to a person or persons, as in "disabled person," to reflect that disability is part of one's identity and not shameful.

inclusive recreation programs—The modification or adaptation of activities addressing needs of individuals that feel or identify the current programming does not meet their needs.

indirect leadership—A leadership option that provides the agency with an opportunity to augment programs and services for the community. It focuses on providing people with equipment or services for a fee; the only interaction between the participant and the leader occurs during the rental process.

individual health—The health status of one person.

individual sports—Events that generally allow participants to engage in the sport alone (e.g., fishing, golf, swimming, diving, trap and skeet, cycling, hunting, boxing, archery).

individual treatment plan—A written course of action to be taken by, for, and with the client based on assessment; this is part of a client's record.

infancy—One of seven life stages; people in this stage are 2 years old and younger.

informal sports—Self-directed, nonstructured participation in sport that is focused on fun and fitness.

information provider—A recreation and leisure services professional who focuses on facilitating engagement in recreation by providing information about opportunities that are available in the community.

instructional sports—Sport activity that emphasizes the learning of skills, rules, and strategies in a nonacademic credit environment.

integrated function—A combined, coordinated set of services or activities that links one or more of the key hosting, support and facilitation, or attractions functions of the recreation, event, and tourism system.

International Union for Conservation of Nature and Natural Resources (IUCN)—An international body that coordinates conservation and sustainable development activities worldwide.

intramural sports—Structured sport activity in the form of leagues, tournaments, and contests conducted within the boundaries or walls of a particular setting.

intrapreneur—A person in a large corporation who takes direct responsibility for turning an idea into a profitable finished product. This corporate management style integrates risk-taking and innovation approaches with the reward and motivational techniques that are commonly associated with entrepreneurship.

Islam—A religious faith that follows the teachings of Muhammad as laid out in the Quran and Hadith.

J

Judaism—A religious faith that follows the teaching of God as laid out in the Torah.

L

land taxes—The taxes that landowners pay, which are calculated according to the value and uses of the land and the mill rate assigned by the municipality. This is also known as a *real-estate tax*.

langa—The Hausa name for a one-legged hop game. Known by various names in other parts of Nigeria such as *kokoye*, *sapasapasingiri*, *lanka-lanka*, and *wogidija*. The game has three variations (ruwa, tureshi, and kawoshi), all played in a rectangular area with two concentric circles.

late adulthood—One of the seven life stages; people in this stage are 60 years old and older.

legislator and regulator—One of the five roles that governments can take in delivering public services; the government passes laws that leisure services providers and consumers must abide by.

leisure education—The process by which people explore their own attitudes toward leisure and recreation, understand the influence of leisure on society and in their own lives, and develop the skills to participate in the recreation activities of their choice.

life stages—The stages of growth and maturation across the life span.

local club sides—Football clubs that play in the Nigerian Premier league, such as Enyimba FC, Akwa United FC, Warri Wolves FC, and Kano Pillars FC.

logic—The branch of philosophy that examines the structure and rules of reasoning and sound argumentation. Logic is important not only for the methods of leisure research but also for the decision-making process of leisure services practitioners.

M

market days—Dedicated buying and selling days held weekly or fortnightly in Nigeria.

marketing approach—An approach in which businesses focus on the customer because the transaction between the business and the customer provides the business its lifeblood.

meet sports—Separate sport events that occur within a larger sport event and are usually conducted over a period of one or two days (e.g., swimming, gymnastics, diving, wrestling, golf, track and field).

metaphysics—The branch of philosophy that deals with the study of what really exists and the ultimate nature of reality. In the leisure research literature, the most prominent metaphysical issue concerns whether leisure is a state of mind (if you think an experience is leisurely, then it really is leisure) or a state of being (the circumstances of your life need to satisfy certain conditions for you really to be at leisure).

middle adulthood—One of the seven life stages; people in this stage are 40 to 59 years old.

middle and late childhood—One of the seven life stages; people in this stage are 7 to 12 years old.

military community—Military service members, their families, and supporting partners that sustain the military environment.

mission statement—A broad statement that defines the purpose of the organization with regard to the group of people that it serves.

Morale, Welfare and Recreation (MWR)—The key provider of recreational, fitness, family, and community services to U.S. military members and their families.

morbidity—The incidence or prevalence of a disease.

mortality—The number of deaths due to a specific cause.

multiple-use management—Managing natural areas for a variety of uses concurrently such as outdoor recreation, range grazing, timber production, watershed protection to control pollution and erosion and allocate water uses, and wildlife and fish habitat.

N

National Council for Therapeutic Recreation Certification (NCTRC)—A nonprofit, interna-

tional organization that administers the largest credentialing program in therapeutic recreation.

national park—A protected area managed mainly for ecosystem protection and recreation. It is a natural area of land or sea designated to protect the ecological integrity of one or more ecosystems for present and future generations; exclude inappropriate exploitation or occupation of the area; and provide a foundation for spiritual, scientific, educational, recreational, and visitor opportunities, all of which must be environmentally and culturally compatible.

natural environment—All the natural living and nonliving things that are not part of the built environment.

natural tourism and travel—Responsible travel to areas of natural attraction that conserves the environment and improves the welfare of local people.

nature-deficit disorder (NDD)—The consequences of the divorce between human and natural habitats.

networking—The process of developing a list of professional contacts that can assist with a person's career development.

nonprofit organization—An organization with tax-exempt status under the U.S. Internal Revenue Service code or by Revenue Canada. Contributions to them are tax deductible. A nonprofit is governed by a volunteer board of directors and is operated for public benefit, and its business is not conducted for profit. Organizations of this type are said to belong to the nonprofit sector.

nonprofit sector—The segment of society composed of organizations that are private and nongovernmental and seek to serve the public good without the motivation of profit.

North American Industry Classification System (NAICS)—A classification system employed by census agencies in Canada, the United States, and Mexico to ensure that the enumeration of businesses is collected and codified in the same way.

O

objectives—The steps that need to be taken to achieve agency and program goals. Objectives are observable and measurable and serve as the foundation to evaluate goals.

off-highway vehicle (OHV)—Vehicles such as all-terrain vehicles (ATVs), dune buggies, jeeps, motorcycles, four-wheel-drive vehicles, dirt bikes, and snowmobiles whose drivers engage in activities such as mudslinging, trail rides, rallies, hill climbs, and rock crawls.

open recreation—Unstructured use of activity spaces by drop-in users.

operational readiness and effectiveness—The mental, physical, emotional, and social conduct of military service members that steers their ability to be prepared for and perform in combat, peacekeeping, and military operational settings.

operations—The oversight, management, and maintenance of facilities and fields and the people in them; includes managing entrance and exiting processes, equipment check out, supervision and policy enforcement, and emergency response.

outcome—A measurable short- or long-term change in a client's health status or well-being as a result of receiving therapeutic recreation services.

outdoor and climbing programs—Hands-on learning opportunities for outdoor enthusiasts such as climbing and bouldering walls, outdoor clinics and education sessions, and guided outdoor adventure trips such as mountaineering, backpacking, rafting, ice climbing, mountain biking, and canyoneering.

outdoor recreation—Participation in intrinsically motivating outdoor activities that depend on human–nature interaction and an appreciation of the natural world; a subphenomenon of leisure and recreation.

P

participatory arts—Art, artists, events, and organizations that involve the public in making art.

paternalism—Performing an act you believe is in the best interest of another person without that person's consent.

person-centered planning—A process in which the client is at the center of and actively involved in choosing the life they want to live and the supports they will need in order to realize their vision of their future.

person visit—One person entering a park once.

personal health—The health status of a specific person.

Personnel Support Programs (PSP) Division—A division of the Canadian Forces Personnel and Family Support Services that delivers recreational, fitness, family, and community services to Canadian military personnel and their families.

philanthropy—Voluntary action for the public good through acts of giving (time, money, and know-how) by individuals and organizations to causes that they care about.

philosophy—Literally, lover of wisdom. In ancient times philosophy referred to all scholarly inquiry, including the natural sciences. However, in present-day scholarship the scope of the discipline of philosophy has been reduced to five subfields: metaphysics, epistemology, logic, ethics, and aesthetics.

plasticity—The ability to continue to develop skills in adulthood.

playground movement—A movement in the late 1800s aimed at improving quality of life through recreation and leisure.

population health—The health status of a defined group of people and the distribution of health outcomes within the group.

postmodern—Refers to both a time period (postmodernity) and a state of mind and associated values (postmodernism). As a period of time, postmodernity follows the recent modern era and is marked by a number of characteristics including the dissolving of boundaries between elite and mass forms of culture and the mixing of leisure and work. Though related to postmodernity, postmodernism is a skeptical outlook that questions generally accepted ideas and values of the modern era, such as the belief that scientific inquiry results in the advancement of knowledge and the improvement of the human condition.

practice model—A visual representation of the relationships between philosophy and theory and the real world that serves as a guide for practice.

preservation—Protecting a natural area, wildlife, and ecosystem in a relatively undisturbed natural state (different from conservation in that the focus is on protection rather than use).

pretend play—Form of play that incorporates conventional imaginative play (e.g., play with toys such as dolls or trucks) and symbolic play (e.g., play with unstructured objects or inanimate objects).

primary group—A group based on intimate, long-term associations, such as family and close friends.

professional and trade associations—Nonprofits organized to promote the business interests of a community, industry, or profession. They generally qualify for tax exemption under Section 501(c)(6) of the IRS tax code.

professional organizations—Formal groups that provide support, education, and resources to members who are professionals in a specific field.

professional sports—Sport events played by elite athletes that emphasize winning, entertainment, and generating money.

program classification—The designation of a program into one of 14 areas (e.g., hobby, sport, outdoor activity). Each classification area includes hundreds of opportunities for programs and services depending on the resources of the agency.

program delivery system—The system used to provide programs, services, and opportunities to a community. The system takes into consideration leadership, program classification, program format, development sequences, and characteristics of participants (e.g., age, ethnicity). The content of the program delivery system is guided by the agency's mission, goals, and objectives.

program formats—Eight program types (e.g., competition, class, outreach program) that help the recreation professional develop the program delivery system into a comprehensive plan.

project-based leisure—Clearly defined, somewhat complicated, and creative but usually short-duration activities that can be carried out in free time for a specific purpose and often as part of a group.

Protestant work ethic—The idea that work (rather than leisure) is the foundation of a worthy life and that one should diligently pursue one's calling in life.

provincial park—Parks designated and managed by a province in Canada that usually contain diverse landscapes and outdoor recreation activities. They are often classified as national parks according to the IUCN categories of national parks and protected areas.

purple leisure—Questionable activities that bring pleasure to participants but may harm society.

Q

qi xi—A traditional romantic festival in China similar to Valentine's Day in Western society. It is also called the Double Seventh Festival because it takes place on the seventh day of the seventh lunar month.

quality of life—A person's perception of satisfaction with life or feelings of general well-being based on self-assessment of one's ability to function in everyday life, relationships, mood, access to resources, and other personal and environmental factors.

quasi-public entity—A nonprofit organization that is organized privately to promote public ideals.

R

race—Physical characteristics and outward signs of cultural identity shared by a subgroup within a society.

Ramsar Convention—An international agreement and convention monitored by UNESCO to protect wetlands designated as internationally important under the Convention on Wetlands (1971). These wetlands are commonly known as Ramsar sites. Globally, in 2022, there were 172 contracting parties to the convention and 2,471 wetland sites, totaling

633 million acres (256,192,356 ha) designated for inclusion in the Ramsar List of Wetlands of International Importance.

rational recreation movement—A 19th-century movement composed of leisure reformers who were concerned with the proper use of leisure in the rapidly expanding industrial cities of England and America and who advocated for expanding the opportunities of the working classes to engage in what were perceived as ennobling, middle-class leisure activities such as visiting cultural institutions, public gardens, and urban parks.

rationalists—People who believe the philosophical thesis that knowledge is derived from the thought processes of our minds.

recreation, event, and tourism (RET) industry model—A complex and integrated model that describes the linkages between service providers, the sectors that they represent, and the primary roles that each component provides in transporting, hosting, feeding, and entertaining the consumer in recreation, event, and tourism opportunities.

recreational sports—Sport activities for the sake of fun, fitness, and participation.

relative competence—The ability to do something successfully and efficiently.

religion—Beliefs and practices that separate the profane from the sacred and develop a community of believers.

residential campus—A college or university in which most students live on campus in housing facilities that include dining services and social spaces.

S

samba—A Brazilian musical genre and dance style that has its origin in African religious traditions practiced by Brazilian slaves during colonial times; it is Brazil's most famous rhythm and is extremely popular across the country. It is characterized by the use of percussion and string instruments, such as the *cavaquinho*.

schole—Having peace and quiet, having time for oneself, and being engaged in an activity for its own sake.

secondary group—Compared with a primary group, a larger, more formal, and impersonal group based on a shared interest.

section 501(c)(3)—A U.S. Internal Revenue Service classification for qualifying nonprofits that gives such organizations tax-exempt status to operate for purposes of the public good. Most U.S.-based nonprofits operate under this tax-exempt category.

selective acculturation—A process by which one chooses to form relationships with people with similar interests, backgrounds, religious affiliations, and languages and allows this subculture to shape their values.

serious leisure—The systematic pursuit of an amateur, hobbyist, or volunteer activity that is highly substantial, interesting, and fulfilling; typically, participants find careers in acquiring and expressing a combination of its special skills, knowledge, and experience.

sexual identity discrimination—Treatment or consideration of a person in any area (e.g., work, leisure, education) based on prejudices regarding sexual orientation.

social benefits—The entirety of benefits to society from producing or consuming a good or service or participating in civic or other activities that have positive effects that extend beyond the individual to other people, groups, and organizations or a community, culture, or environment more broadly.

social capital—The network of social contacts that people develop for support in times of difficulty and to enhance the quality of their lives.

social inclusion—Shared activities and experiences that allow for mutually beneficial and respectful relationships to develop and persist regardless of disability.

social welfare organizations—Nonprofits involved in advocacy, lobbying, and political campaign activities under the U.S. 501(c)(4) IRS code.

society—People who share a culture and a territory.

solitary leisure—Activities undertaken without the physical presence of another person.

spirituality—The paths and practices that people take in their efforts to find, conserve, and transform the sacred in their lives; the quality of being concerned with the human spirit.

sport management—The study and practice of all people, activities, businesses, or organizations involved in producing, facilitating, promoting, or organizing any sport-related business or product.

sport participation—Individual physical involvement in recreational sport activities.

sport performance—The evaluation of skill in sport; also includes spectator participation in elite or professional sports.

square dance—A form of group dancing performed to popular music in public squares, plazas, or parks across China.

standards of practice—Standards that define the scope of services provided by therapeutic recreation professionals and state a minimal acceptable level of service delivery.

state park—A park that is designated and managed by the host state in the United States that usually showcases an area of historical importance or a representative natural environment for that state (e.g., prairie in Illinois, beaches in Florida).

strategic prevention framework (SPF)—A planning process created by the Substance Abuse and Mental Health Services Administration (SAMHSA) that is used to prevent substance use and misuse.

structured leadership—Leadership that is used when a program requires face-to-face instruction. This approach is used in all types of classes, and the participant's experience is controlled, guided, and facilitated by the leader.

student affairs—A department or division within the university or college structure that provides students with support outside of their academic pursuits.

summative evaluation—Evaluation that occurs at the completion of a program to determine whether it was effective in helping the client reach their goals and whether changes in the program are needed before implementing it in the future.

support and facilitation functions—Diverse key business activities that support the ability of a person or group to travel to desired destinations or that provide the knowledge, information, and contacts that allow travelers to make informed decisions.

supporter and patron—One of the five roles that governments can take in delivering public services; the government provides support to existing organizations that produce public leisure services.

sustainability—Living within the limits of nature's ecosystem services and living together in communities that are equitable, regenerative, resilient, and adaptive.

T

team sports—Events that require a specific number of players who play as a team of either men, women, or mixed intramural or extramural sport divisions (e.g., baseball, basketball, softball, kickball, lacrosse, field hockey, rowing, soccer, volleyball, wallyball, water polo, flag football).

three-sector model—Nonprofits (the social sector), businesses (the economic/market sector), and government (the public, political sector) are ways in which individuals and organizations are organized to provide services and products in society. Recreation organizations are found in all three sectors.

Title IX—Legislation enacted in the United States in 1972 that directed educational institutions to develop parity for men's and women's sports.

tourism association—A nonprofit group of professionals within the travel and tourism industry, or a specialized subsection of it, whose mission is to educate its members and advocate for the industry.

transparency—Being clear and open with information.

U

U.S. Armed Forces—Collectively, the U.S. Army, U.S. Marine Corps, U.S. Navy, U.S. Air Force, and U.S. Coast Guard.

V

value added—The amount by which the value of an article is increased at each stage of its production, exclusive of initial costs.

virtue-based ethics—An ethical theory that focuses on the character of the individual rather than on moral rules or principles.

visitor day—One day of recreation for one person.

visitor studies—A field of study and professional practice that examines and evaluates the leisure motivations, behaviors, and informal learning experiences of attendees at cultural venues.

W

wellness—The subjective perception of a person's relative holistic health status and fitness level across all domains (social, emotional, physical, intellectual, occupational, and spiritual) and the absence or management of disease.

wilderness—Large areas left in an entirely natural condition, usually without roads or motorized vehicles, with no buildings or utilities. This is also a formal designation of land use and protection in the United States.

wildlife refuge—Lands, wetlands, and waters that are primarily managed as wildlife or fish habitats or protected areas (although some allow regulated hunting and fishing) by fish and wildlife agencies, usually at the state or federal level. Limited recreational use compatible with wildlife management is permitted in most refuges.

wise-use philosophy—A philosophy that holds that the earth's resources were meant to be exploited for human gain and profit, typically with more of a short-term focus. Wise use tends to be promoted by the extractive industries such as mining and lumber companies who lobby politicians to influence multiple-use agencies such as the Forest Service and the Bureau of Land Management toward a so-called wise-use orientation.

work—A productive, purposeful activity that was disliked by the ancient Greeks but that has great importance in modern societies.

World Heritage site—A specific site (such as a forest, mountain range, lake, desert, building, complex, or city) that has been designated within the international World Heritage Convention administered by UNESCO. The World Heritage list in 2023 included 1,157 properties that the World Heritage Committee considered as having outstanding universal value. These include 900 cultural sites, 218 natural sites, and 39 mixed properties in 167 countries.

Y

youth and family programs—Activities that serve the entire family and foster development in a safe and energetic campus environment.

Bibliography

CHAPTER 1

Alas, H. (2021). *U.S. ranks last among 11 wealthy nations for health care, study says*. U.S. News & World Report. https://www.usnews.com/news/best-countries/articles/2021-08-09/us-ranks-last-among-11-wealthy-nations-for-health-care-study-says

Alberta Community Development. (n.d.). *Look at Leisure #42: Desired Activities and Barriers to Participation* . Open Government Program. https://open.alberta.ca/dataset/0715-2361/resource/a4439992-ab4f-49d2-a432-393c4d30fad4

American Heart Association. (n.d.). *Breaking down barriers to fitness*. www.heart.org/en/healthy-living/fitness/getting-active/breaking-down-barriers-to-fitness

The American Institute of Stress. (n.d.). *Workplace stress*. The American Institute of Stress. https://www.stress.org/workplace-stress

American Marketing Association. (n.d.). Definition of marketing. www.ama.org/the-definition-of-marketing-what-is-marketing

British Columbia Recreation and Parks Association. (2008). The Way Forward - A Strategic Plan for the Parks, Recreation and Culture Sector of BC. https://www.bcrpa.bc.ca/media/43524/strategicplan_complete.pdf

California Park & Recreation Society (CPRS). (1999). *VIP Project: Creating Community in the 21st Century - An Action Plan for Parks & Recreation in California*. California Park & Recreation Society.

Canadian Internet Registration Authority. (2022). Canada's Internet Factbook 2022. https://www.cira.ca/resources/state-internet/report/canadas-internet-factbook-2022

Canadian Mental Health Association, National. (2021). *Fast facts about mental health and mental illness*. CMHA National. https://cmha.ca/brochure/fast-facts-about-mental-illness/

Cantor, C. (2019). *Why being bored can be hazardous to your health*. Columbia News. https://news.columbia.edu/news/why-being-bored-can-be-hazardous-your-health

Carlson, S. A., Adams, E. K., Yang, Z., & Fulton, J. E. (2018) Percentage of deaths associated with inadequate physical activity in the United States. Preventing Chronic Disease, 15, DOI: http://dx.doi.org/10.5888/pcd18.170354

Carlson, S. A., Fulton, J. E., Pratt, M., Yang, Z., & Adams, E. K. (2015). Inadequate physical activity and health care expenditures in the United States. Progress in cardiovascular diseases, 57(4), 315–323. https://doi.org/10.1016/j.pcad.2014.08.002

Chubb, M., & Chubb, H. R. (1981). One third of our time?: An introduction to recreation behavior and resources. Wiley.

City of Tampa. (2022). *#happyathometpa with TPR*. Tampa.gov. https://www.tampa.gov/parks-and-recreation/tprvirtualrec

City Parks Alliance. (n.d.). *Case Studies - Share Your City Parks Story*. City Parks Alliance. https://cityparksalliance.org/resources/case-studies/

Clement, J. (2021). *Global in-game spending 2025*. Statista. https://www.statista.com/statistics/558952/in-game-consumer-spending-worldwide/

Dean, N. (2019). *The importance of novelty*. Brain World. https://brainworldmagazine.com/the-importance-of-novelty/

ESRI. (2022). Recreation Expenditures. https://downloads.esri.com/esri_content_doc/dbl/us/sample_reports/cex_recreation.pdf Fantasy Sports and Gaming Association. (n.d.). Industry demographics. Retrieved from https://thefsga.org/industry-demographics/.

FairForce Consulting. (2021). *Why building community is so important?*. Medium. https://fairforceberlin.medium.com/why-building-community-is-so-important-6f1a3953c1d7

Flowers, L., Houser, A., Noel-Miller, C., Shaw, J., Bhattacharya, J., Schoemaker, L., & Farid, M. (2017). *Medicare spends more on socially isolated older adults*. AARP. https://www.aarp.org/content/dam/aarp/ppi/2017/10/medicare-spends-more-on-socially-isolated-older-adults.pdf

Government of Canada. (2022). *Social isolation of seniors - Volume 1: Understanding the issue and finding solutions*. Canada.ca. https://www.canada.ca/en/employment-social-development/corporate/partners/seniors-forum/social-isolation-toolkit-vol1.html

International Telecommunication Union World Telecommunication/ICT Indicators Database. (n.d.). *Individuals using the internet (% of population) - North America*. World Bank Open Data. https://data.worldbank.org/indicator/IT.NET.USER.ZS?locations=XU

Ipsos-Reid. (2000). Stress becoming a way of life for Canadians. https://www.ipsos.com/en-ca/stress-becoming-way-life-canadians

Ireland, S. (2021). Revealed: Countries with the best health care systems, 2021. Retrieved from https://ceoworld.biz/2021/04/27/revealed-countries-with-the-best-health-care-systems-2021/

Iso-Ahola, S. E., & Weissinger, E. (1987). Leisure and boredom. *Journal of Social and Clinical Psychology, 5*(3), 356–364. https://doi.org/10.1521/jscp.1987.5.3.356

Knickmeyer, E., Swanson, E., & Ellgren, N. (2021). *Majority in US concerned about climate: AP-Norc/Epic Poll*. AP NEWS.

https://apnews.com/article/climate-joe-biden-science-environment-and-nature-only-on-ap-1e48e3315d2e0b618ccaa4a8d466e057

Knueven, L. (2021). *How much does a wedding cost?*. Business Insider. https://www.businessinsider.com/personal-finance/how-much-does-a-wedding-cost

Louv, R. (2012). *The nature principle: Reconnecting with life in a virtual age*. Algonquin Books.

Merriam-Webster. (n.d.). Essential. *Merriam-Webster Dictionary*. Retrieved July 17, 2023, from www.merriam-webster.com/dictionary/essential

Peter G. Peterson Foundation. (2020). *Why are Americans paying more for healthcare?*. Blog. Retrieved from https://www.pgpf.org/blog/2020/04/why-are-americans-paying-more-for-healthcare. Archived at https://web.archive.org/web/20200502103429/https://www.pgpf.org/blog/2020/04/why-are-americans-paying-more-for-healthcare

Piercy, K. L., Troiano, R. P., Ballard, R. M., Carlson, S. A., Fulton, J. E., Galuska, D. A., George, S. M., & Olson, R. D. (2018). The Physical Activity Guidelines for Americans. *JAMA*, 320(19), 2020–2028. https://doi.org/10.1001/jama.2018.14854

Reinert, M, Fritze, D. & Nguyen, T. (2021). "The State of Mental Health in America 2022" Mental Health America, Alexandria VA

Riehm KE, Feder KA, Tormohlen KN, Crum RM, Young AS, Green KM, Pacek LR, La Flair LN, Mojtabai R. Associations Between Time Spent Using Social Media and Internalizing and Externalizing Problems Among US Youth. JAMA Psychiatry. 2019 Dec 1;76(12):1266-1273. doi: 10.1001/jamapsychiatry.2019.2325. PMID: 31509167; PMCID: PMC6739732.

Ross University School of Medicine. (2021). *US vs. Canadian Healthcare: What is the difference?*. Ross University School of Medicine. https://medical.rossu.edu/about/blog/us-vs-canadian-healthcare

Ruffner, B. (2022). Short cactus league season takes bite out of AZ economy. *Daily Independent*. Retrieved July 17, 2023, from https://www.yourvalley.net/stories/short-cactus-league-season-takes-bite-out-of-az-economy,291914.

Selyukh, A. (2020). Amazon doubles profit to $5.2 billion as online shopping spikes. NPR. https://www.npr.org/sections/coronavirus-live-updates/2020/07/30/897271729/amazon-doubles-profit-to-5-8-billion-as-online-shopping-spikes

Solomon, J. (2019). Staying in the Game: Progress and Challenges in Youth Sports. https://www.aspeninstitute.org/blog-posts/staying-in-the-game-progress-and-challenges-in-youth-sports/

Sports Management Degree Hub. (n.d.). Fantasy-Football. Sports Management Degree Hub. https://www.sports-managementdegreehub.com/fantasy-football-industry/fantasy-football/

Statistics Canada. (2021). *Canadian health measures survey: Activity Monitor Data, 2018-2019*. The Daily. https://www150.statcan.gc.ca/n1/daily-quotidien/210901/dq210901c-eng.htm

Taylor, P. (2023). *Forecast number of Mobile Users Worldwide 2020-2025*. Statista. https://www.statista.com/statistics/218984/number-of-global-mobile-users-since-2010/

Thomas, L. (2020). Peloton says recent spike in covid-19 cases, lockdowns are boosting sales. CNBC. https://www.cnbc.com/2020/11/05/peloton-says-recent-spike-in-covid-19-cases-lockdowns-boosting-sales.html

U.S. Bureau of Economic Analysis. (2022). *Outdoor Recreation Satellite Account, U.S. and States, 2021*. News Release. https://www.bea.gov/news/2022/outdoor-recreation-satellite-account-us-and-states-2021

U.S. Department of Health and Human Services, Office of the Surgeon General. (2023). Our Epidemic of Loneliness and Isolation: The U.S. Surgeon General's Advisory on the Healing Effects of Social Connection and Community. https://www.hhs.gov/sites/default/files/surgeon-general-social-connection-advisory.pdf

U.S. Census Bureau. (n.d.). *Quick facts: Waukegan City, Illinois*. www.census.gov/quickfacts/waukegancityillinois

Wiles, K. (2021). *The U.S. again ranks last in health care compared with other high-income countries: Report*. MarketWatch. www.marketwatch.com/story/the-u-s-again-ranks-last-in-health-care-compared-with-other-high-income-countries-report-11628110844

World Health Organization. (n.d.). *Social isolation and loneliness*. World Health Organization. https://www.who.int/teams/social-determinants-of-health/demographic-change-and-healthy-ageing/social-isolation-and-loneliness

World Health Organization. (2020). *Zoonoses*. World Health Organization. https://www.who.int/news-room/fact-sheets/detail/zoonoses

Worldometer. (n.d.). *Life expectancy of the World Population*. Worldometer. https://www.worldometers.info/demographics/life-expectancy/

CHAPTER 2

American Alliance for Health, Physical Education, Recreation and Dance (AAHPERD). (n.d.). *About*. www.aahperd.org/about

Barry, J. M. (2004). *The Great Influenza*. Penguin.

Byrd, J. A. (2011). The transit of empire: Indigenous critiques of colonialism. University of Minnesota Press.

Canadian Parks and Recreation Association (CPRA). (n.d.). *What is CPRA*. www.cpra.ca/what-is-cpra

Canadian Parks and Recreation Association (CPRA). (2015). *A framework for recreation in Canada: Pathways to well-being*. www.cpra.ca/about-the-framework

Coulthard, G. S. (2014). Red skin, white masks: Rejecting the colonial politics of recognition. University of Minnesota Press.

Cross, G. (1990). *A social history of leisure since 1600*. Venture.

Dare, B., Welton, G., & Coe, W. (1987). *Concepts of leisure in Western thought: A critical and historical analysis*. Kendall/Hunt.

Dave, D., Friedson, A. I., McNichols, D., & Sabia, J. J. (2020). *The Contagion Externality of a Superspreading Event: The Sturgis Motorcycle Rally and COVID-19*. IZA Institute of Labor Economics - Discussion Paper Series. https://docs.iza.org/dp13670.pdf

Davis, K. C. (2018). *Philadelphia threw a WWI parade that gave thousands of onlookers the flu*. Smithsonian.com. https://www.smithsonianmag.com/history/philadelphia-threw-wwi-parade-gave-thousands-onlookers-flu-180970372/

DeGraff, J., Wann, D., & Naylor, T.H. (2001). *Affluenza: The all-consuming epidemic*. Berrett-Koehler.

Edgington, C., Jordan, D., DeGraff, D., & Edgington, S. (1998). *Leisure and life satisfaction: Foundational perspectives*. WCB/McGraw Hill.

Forsyth, J. (2013). Bodies of meaning: Sports and games at Canadian residential schools. In J. Forsyth & A. Giles (Eds.), *Aboriginal peoples & sport in Canada: Historical foundations and contemporary issues*. UBC Press.

Francis, R.D., Jones, R., & Smith, D. (1988). *Origins: Canadian history to confederation*. Holt, Rinehart and Winston of Canada.

Goodale, T., & Godbey, G. (1988). *The evolution of leisure*. Venture.

Harrington, M. (1996). Women's leisure and the family in Canada. In N. Samuel (Ed.), *Women, leisure and the family in contemporary society: A multinational perspective* (pp. 35-48). CAB International.

Hokowhitu, B. (2014). If you're not healthy, then what are you? Healthism, colonial disease and body-logic. In K. Fitzpatrick & R. Tinning (Eds.), *Health education: Critical perspectives* (pp. 31–47). Routledge.

Horna, J. (1994). *The study of leisure: An introduction*. Oxford University Press.

Ibrahim, H. (1979). Leisure in the ancient world. In H. Ibrahim & J. Shivers (Eds.), *Leisure: emergence and expansion* (pp. 45-78). Hwong.

Ibrahim, H. (1991). *Leisure and society: A comparative approach*. Brown.

Illinois State Museum. (n.d.). *The Illinois: Society, recreation*. www.museum.state.il.us/muslink/nat_amer/post/htmls/soc_rec.html

Interprovincial Sport and Recreation Council (ISRC). (1987). *National recreation statement*. www.lin.ca/resource/html/statemen.htm

Karlis, G. (2004). *Leisure and recreation in Canadian society: An introduction*. Thompson.

Karlis, G. (2016). *Leisure and recreation in Canadian Society: An introduction* (3rd ed.). Thompson.

Kim, J., & Van Puymbroeck, M. (2011). Providing culturally competent therapeutic recreation for East Asian immigrant clients. *Annual in Therapeutic Recreation, 19,* 114-124.

Kim, K., Compton, D.M., & McCormick, B. (2013). The relationship among motivational environment, autonomous self-regulation and personal variables in refugee youth: Implications for mental health and youth leadership. *Journal of Leisure Research, 16*(3), 230-251.

Kraus, R. (1971). *Recreation and leisure in modern society*. Scott Foresman.

Kraus, R. (1990). *Recreation and leisure in modern society* (4th ed.). Scott Foresman.

Kraus, R. (2001). *Recreation and leisure in modern society* (6th ed.). Jones and Bartlett.

LaPierre, L. (1992). *Canada, my Canada: What happened?* McLelland & Stewart.

Lavallée, L., & Lévesque, L. (2013). Two-eyed seeing: Physical activity, sport, and recreation promotion in Indigenous communities. In J. Forsyth & A. Giles (Ed.) *Aboriginal peoples & sport in Canada: Historical foundations and contemporary issues* (pp. 206-228). UBC Press.

MacNeil, R., & Gould, D.L. (2012). Global perspectives on leisure and aging. In H. Gibson & J. Singleton (Eds.), *Leisure and aging: Theory and practice* (pp. 3-26). Human Kinetics.

Markham, S. (1992). Our leaders speak up. *Recreation Canada, 50*(2), 15-19.

Markham, S. (1995). The early years: 1944 to 1951. *Recreation Canada, 53*(3), 6-16.

McFarland, E.M. (1970). *The development of public recreation in Canada*. Canadian Parks and Recreation Association.

McLean, A.D., Hurd, A.R., & Rogers, N.B. (2005). *Kraus' recreation and leisure in modern society*. Jones and Bartlett.

Meier, A. C. (2019). *The 1918 parade that spread death in Philadelphia - Jstor Daily*. The 1918 Parade That Spread Death in Philadelphia. https://daily.jstor.org/the-1918-parade-that-spread-death-in-philadelphia/

Mendelsohn, D. (2004). What Olympic ideal? *New York Times Magazine*, 11-13.

Missouri State Parks and Historic Sites. (n.d.). *The history of Missouri's state park system*. http://mostateparks.com/page/59044/history-missouris-state-park-system

National Alliance for Youth Sports (NAYS). (n.d.). *Mission and history*. www.nays.org/about/about-nays/mission

National Recreation and Park Association (NRPA). (n.d.). *About*. www.nrpa.org/About-National-Recreation-and-Park-Association

Paraschak, V. (2013). Aboriginal peoples and the construction of Canadian sport policy. In J. Forsyth & A. R. Giles (Eds.), *Aboriginal peoples & sport in Canada: Historical Foundations and contemporary issues* (pp. 95-123). UBC Press.

Parks and Recreation Ontario (PRO). (n.d.). *Who we are*. www.prontario.org/index.php?ci_id=3669

Parks Canada. (n.d.). *The Parks Canada mandate and charter*. www.pc.gc.ca/en/agence-agency/mandat-mandate

ParticipACTION. (n.d.). *About: Leading Canada towards sitting less and moving more*. www.participaction.com/en-ca/about

The ParticipACTION Archive Project. (n.d.-a). *The early years: TV, radio and print media*. http://scaa.sk.ca/gallery/participaction/english/motivate/theearlyyears.html

The ParticipACTION Archive Project. (n.d.-b). *Historic timeline*. http://scaa.sk.ca/gallery/participaction/english/structure/timeline.html

PHE Canada. (n.d.-a). *Our history*. www.phecanada.ca/about-us

PHE Canada. (n.d.-b). *Our vision and mission*. www.phecanada.ca/about-us/vision/mission

Poliakoff, M. (1993). Stadium and arena: Reflections on Greek, Roman and contemporary social history. *Olympika: The International Journal of Olympic Studies, 2*, 67-78.

Pruchno, R. (2012). Not your mother's old age: Baby boomers at 65. *The Gerontologist, 52*(2), 149-152.

Rainwater, C. (1992). *The play movement in the United States*. University of Chicago Press.

Recreation Nova Scotia. (n.d.). *Discover RNS*. www.recreationns.ns.ca/discover-rns

Reimann, N. (2020). *Coronavirus hospitalizations have more than tripled in South Dakota after Sturgis Motorcycle Rally*. Forbes. https://www.forbes.com/sites/nicholasreimann/2020/09/27/coronavirus-hospitalizations-have-more-than-tripled-in-south-dakota-after-sturgis-motorcycle-rally/?sh=639f60a87f7e

Reimann, N. (2021). *Covid cases Spike after Sturgis Motorcycle Rally-Again*. Forbes. https://www.forbes.com/sites/nicholasreimann/2021/08/24/covid-cases-spike-after-sturgis-motorcycle-rally-again/?sh=cfd540569154

Saskatchewan Parks and Recreation Association (SPRA). (n.d.). *About*. www.spra.sk.ca/spra

Searle, M., & Brayley, R. (1993). *Leisure services in Canada: An introduction*. Venture.

SHAPE America. (n.d.). *About SHAPE America*. www.shapeamerica.org/about

Shivers, J., & deLisle, L. (1997). *The story of leisure: Context, concepts and current controversy*. Human Kinetics.

South Dakota Department of Health. (n.d.). *South Dakota COVID-19 Updates. South Dakota COVID-19 Dashboard*. Retrieved February 1, 2023, from https://doh.sd.gov/COVID/Dashboard.aspx

Sperazza, L., & Bannerjee, P. (2010). Baby boomers and seniors: Understanding their leisure values enhances programs. *Activities, Adaptation, and Aging, 34*(3), 196-215.

Truth and Reconciliation Canada. (2015). *Honouring the truth, reconciling for the future: Summary of the final report of the truth and reconciliation commission of Canada*. Winnipeg, Manitoba: Truth and Reconciliation Commission of Canada.

United Nations. (2015). *Population facts: Trends in international migration, 2015*. www.un.org/en/development/desa/population/migration/publications/populationfacts/docs/MigrationPopFacts20154.pdf

United Nations General Assembly. (2007). *United Nations (UN) Declaration on the Rights of Indigenous Peoples*.

United States Bureau of Labor Statistics. (2021). https://www.bls.gov/

Vennum, T., Jr. (n.d.). *The history of lacrosse*. www.uslacrosse.org/about-the-sport/history

Virginia State Parks. (n.d.). *History of Virginia state parks*. www.dcr.virginia.gov/state-parks/history

Westland, C. (1979). *Fitness and amateur sport in Canada—government's programme: An historical perspective*. Canadian Parks/Recreation Association.

Wetherell, D.G., & Kmet, I. (1990). *Useful pleasures: The shaping of Alberta 1896-1945*. Canadian Plains Research Centre.

Willman, C. (2020). *Smash mouth singer says "F- that covid S-!" as band plays Sturgis Biker rally*. Variety. https://variety.com/2020/music/news/smash-mouth-sturgis-biker-rally-concert-1234730887/

World Health Organization. (n.d.). *WHO coronavirus (COVID-19) dashboard*. Retrieved February 1, 2023, from https://covid19.who.int

Wright, J.R. (1983). *Urban parks in Ontario, part I: Origins to 1860*. Ministry of Tourism and Recreation.

CHAPTER 3

Alexander, E., Alexander, M., & Decker, J. (2017). *Museums in motion: An introduction to the history and functions of museums* (3rd ed.). Rowman & Littlefield.

Borgmann, A. (1984). *Technology and the character of contemporary life: A philosophical inquiry*. University of Chicago Press.

Cross, G. (1990). *A social history of leisure since 1600*. Venture Publishing.

Cuno, J. (2004). The object of art museums. In J. Cuno (Ed.), *Whose muse? Art museums and the public trust*. Princeton University Press; Harvard University Art Museums.

de Grazia, S. (1963). *Of time, work and leisure*. Doubleday.

Falk, J., & Dierking, L. (2000). *Learning from museums: Visitor experiences and the making of meaning*. AltaMira Press.

Featherstone, M. (1991). *Consumer culture & postmodernism*. Sage Publications.

Gerbner, G. (1999). The stories we tell. *Peace Review, 11*(1), 9-15.

Groarke, L. (2017). Informal logic. In E.N. Zalta (Ed.), *Stanford encyclopedia of philosophy*. Stanford University. https://plato.stanford.edu/entries/logic-informal

Haughwout, A., Lee, D., Scally, J., & van der Klaauw, W. (2017). *Household borrowing in historical perspective*. http://libertystreeteconomics.newyorkfed.org/2017/05/household-borrowing-in-historical-perspective.html

Hein, G. (1998). *Learning in the museum*. Routledge.

Hemingway, J. (1988). Leisure and civility: Reflections on a Greek ideal. *Leisure Sciences, 10*, 179-191.

Hemingway, J. (1996). Emancipating leisure: The recovery of freedom in leisure. *Journal of Leisure Research, 28*(1), 27-43.

Hunnicutt, B. (1990). Leisure and play in Plato's teaching and philosophy of learning. *Leisure Sciences, 12*, 211-227.

Jackson, A., Fawcett, G., Milan, A., Roberts, P., Schetagne, S., Scott, K., & Tsoukalas, S. (2000). *Social cohesion in Canada: Possible indicators—highlights*. Canadian Council on Social Development.

Johnson, R., & McLean, D. (1994). Leisure and the development of ethical character: Changing views of the North American ideal. *Journal of Applied Recreation Research, 19*(2), 117-130.

Kubey, R., & Csikzentmihalyi, M. (1990). *Television and the quality of life: How viewing shapes everyday experience*. Lawrence Erlbaum.

Nash, R. (1982). *Wilderness and the American mind* (3rd ed.). Yale University Press.

Neulinger, J. (1974). *The psychology of leisure: Research approaches to the study of leisure*. Charles C Thomas.

Pieper, J. (1998). *Leisure: The basis of culture* (R. Scruton, Trans.). St. Augustine's Press.

Putnam, R. (2000). *Bowling alone*. Simon & Schuster.

Rojek, C. (1995). *Decentering leisure: Rethinking leisure theory*. Sage Publications.

Rojek, C. (2010). *The labour of leisure*. Sage Publications.

Russell, B. (1960). *In praise of idleness: And other essays*. George Allen & Unwin.

Schor, J. (1998). *The overspent American*. Basic Books.

Sylvester, C. (1991). Recovering a good idea for the sake of goodness: An interpretive critique of subjective leisure. In T.L. Goodale and P.A. Witt (Eds.), *Recreation and leisure: Issues in an era of change* (pp. 441-454). Venture.

Veblen, T. (1998). *The theory of the leisure class*. Prometheus Books. (Original work published 1899)

Weber, M. (1958). *The Protestant ethic and the spirit of capitalism* (T. Parson, Trans.). Scribner's. (Original work published 1930)

CHAPTER 4

Beaubier, D. (2004). Athletic gender equity policy in Canadian universities: Issues and possibilities. *Canadian Journal of Educational Administration and Policy, 34*, 49-59.

Beauregard, A. (1996). *Running feet*. www.lehigh.edu/~dmd1/art.html

Bell, C.M., & Hurd, A.R. (2006). Research update: Recreation across ethnicity: People of different races often seek contrasting recreation opportunities. *Parks & Recreation, 41*(10), 27-36.

Bureau of Labor Statistics. (2022). Highlights of women's earnings in 2020. Retrieved from https://www.bls.gov/opub/reports/womens-earnings/2020/home.htm.

Byrne, J.A. (2007). *The role of race in configuring park use: A political ecology perspective* [Unpublished doctoral dissertation]. University of Southern California, Los Angeles.

Central Intelligence Agency. (2023). *World factbook*. https://www.cia.gov/the-world-factbook/field/gini-index-coefficient-distribution-of-family-income/country-comparison\

Chubb, M., & Chubb, H. R. (1981). *One third of our time?: An introduction to recreation behavior and resources*. Wiley.

Clark, W. (2008). Kids' sports. *Canadian Social Trends, 85*(3), 54-61.

Clinton, W. J. (2013). *Howard University commencement address*. [Video]. C-SPAN. www.c-span.org/video/?312699-1/howard-university-commencement-address

Countries and Their Cultures. (n.d.). *Pakistan*. www.everyculture.com/No-Sa/Pakistan.html

Crawford, D., Jackson E., & Godbey, G. (1991). A hierarchical model of leisure constraints. *Leisure Sciences, 9*, 119-127.

Curtis, J. (1979). *Recreation: Theory and practice*. Mosby.

Edwards, H. (1973). *Sociology of sport*. Dorsey Press.

Eshleman, J., Cashion, B., & Basirico, L. (1993). *Sociology: An introduction* (4th ed.). Harper Collins College.

Federation of Gay Games. (n.d.). *Mission & Vision. Promoting equality through sport & culture*. Retrieved March 13, 2023, from https://gaygames.org/Mission-& -Vision

Floyd, M. (1998). Getting beyond marginality and ethnicity: The challenge for race and ethnic studies in leisure research. *Journal of Leisure Research, 30*(1), 3-22.

Fredriksen-Goldsen, K.I., Kim, H.J., Shiu, C., Goldsen, J., & Emlet, C.A. (2015). Successful aging among LGBT older adults: Physical and mental health-related quality of life by age group. *The Gerontologist, 55*(1), 154-168.

Gruneau, R. (1999). *Class, sports, and social development*. Human Kinetics.

Henderson, K. (1997). A critique of constraints theory: A response. *Journal of Leisure Research, 29*(4), 453-458.

Henderson, K. (2010). Leisure studies in the 21st century: The sky is falling? *Leisure Sciences, 32*(4), 391-400.

Henslin, J.M. (1993). *Sociology: A down-to-earth approach*. Allyn & Bacon.

Human Rights Campaign. (n.d.). *The wage gap among LGBTQ+ workers in the United States*. Retrieved February 10, 2023, from www.hrc.org/resources/the-wage-gap-among-lgbtq-workers-in-the-united-states

Human Rights Campaign. (2018). *A workplace divided: Understanding the climate for LGBTQ workers nationwide*. Human Rights Campaign Foundation.

Johns, M.M., Lowry, R., Haderxhanaj, L.T., Rasberry, C.N., Suarez, N.A., Stone, D., Scales, L., & Robin, L. (2020). *Trends in violence victimization and suicide risk by sexual identity among high school students: Youth risk behavior survey, United States, 2015–2019*. Centers for Disease Control and Prevention. Retrieved February 28, 2023, from www.cdc.gov/mmwr/volumes/69/su/su6901a3.htm

Kelly, J.R. (1987). *Freedom to be: A new sociology of leisure*. Macmillan.

Kelly, J.R. (2012). *Leisure* (4th ed.). Sagamore.

Lenski, G., & Lenski, J. (1987). *Human societies: An introduction to macrosociology* (5th ed.). McGraw-Hill.

Lenski, G., Nolan, P., & Lenski, J. (1995). *Human societies: An introduction to macrosociology* (7th ed.). McGraw-Hill.

McChesney, J., Gerken, M., & McDonald, K. (2005). Reaching out to Hispanics. *Parks & Recreation, 40*(3), 74-78.

Mill, R. (1986). Tourist characteristics and trends. *Literature review: The President's Commission on Americans Outdoors.* Government Printing Office.

Morton, M.H., Dworsky, A., Matjasko, J.L., Curry, S.R., Schlueter, D., Chávez, R., & Farrell, A. F. (2018). Prevalence and correlates of youth homelessness in the United States. *The Journal of adolescent health: Official publication of the Society for Adolescent Medicine, 62*(1), 14-21. https://doi.org/10.1016/j.jadohealth.2017.10.006

Nash, J. (1953). *Philosophy of recreation and leisure.* Brown.

National Federation of State High School Associations. (2011). *High school athletic participation survey.* Author.

National Federation of State High School Associations. (2019). High school athletic participation survey. Indianapolis, IN: Author.

Phillip, S. (2000). Race and the pursuit of happiness. *Journal of Leisure Research, 32*(1), 121-124.

Prebish, C. (1993). *Religion and sport: The meeting of sacred and profane.* Westport, CT: Greenwood Press.

Roberts, K. (2010). Sociology of leisure. *Sociopedia.isa.* https://doi.org/0.1177/205684601371

Robinson, J.P., & Godbey, G. (1997). *Time for life: The surprising ways Americans use their time.* Penn State University Press.

Sage & National Resource Center on LGBT Aging. (n.d.). *Facts on LGBT aging.* Retrieved February 10, 2023, from www.sageusa.org/wp-content/uploads/2021/05/sage-lgbt-aging-final-2021.pdf

Shinew, K.J., Floyd, M.E., & Parry, D. (2004). Understanding the relationship between race and leisure activities and constraints: Exploring an alternative framework. *Leisure Sciences, 26,* 181-199.

U.S. Census Bureau. (2010). *United States census 2010.* www.census.gov/2010census

U. S. Census Bureau. (2020). United States census 2020. Retrieved from https://www.census.gov/programs-surveys/decennial-census/decade/2020/2020-census-main.html

Veblen, T. (1998). *The theory of the leisure class.* Prometheus Books. (Original work published 1899.)

Youth.gov. (n.d.). *Homelessness and housing.* Youth.gov. https://youth.gov/youth-topics/lgbtq-youth/homelessness

CHAPTER 5

Bureau of Labor Statistics. (2022). *Leisure and hospitality.* www.bls.gov/iag/tgs/iag70.htm

Internal Revenue Service. (n.d.). *Charitable purposes.* www.irs.gov/charities-non-profits/charitable-purposes

Internal Revenue Service. (2023). Exempt Organizations Business Master File Extract. Internal Revenue Service. Retrieved from https://www.irs.gov/charities-non-profits/exempt-organizations-business-master-file-extract-eo-bmf

National Recreation and Park Association. (1997). *The legends of parks and recreation administration* [Video]. Author.

CHAPTER 6

Adirondack State Park Agency. (n.d.). *About the Adirondack park.* www.apa.state.ny.us/about_park/index.html

Alabama State Parks. (2005). *Welcome to Cheaha State Park.* Retrieved June 4, 2005, from http://cheahastpark.com

Alberta Wilderness Association. (2021). *An essential piece of the Alberta's ecological puzzle, the Castle offers outstanding wilderness values and crucial connectivity within the Crown of the Continent.* Retrieved August 25, 2021, from https://albertawilderness.ca/issues/wildlands/areas-of-concern/castle/#parentHorizontalTab2

America's State Parks. (n.d.). *State park facts.* www.stateparks.org/about-us/state-park-facts

American Planning Association. (2007). *How cities use parks to help children learn.* www.planning.org/cityparks/briefingpapers/helpchildrenlearn.htm

Balmford, A., Beresford, J., Green, J., Naidoo, R., Walpole, M., & Manica, A. (2009). A global perspective on trends in nature-based tourism. *PLoS Biology, 7*(6), Article e1000144. https://doi.org/10.1371/journal.pbio.1000144

Belasco, W.J. (1979). *Americans on the road: From autocamp to motel 1910-1945.* Johns Hopkins Press.

Boogman, S. (2021). *New travel research shows 2020 camping interest, activity exceeded Spring predictions.* Retrieved August 25, 2021, from www.prnewswire.com/news-releases/new-travel-research-shows-2020-camping-interest-activity-exceeded-spring-predictions-301143804.html

British Columbia Ministry of Forests. (2022). *Impacts of 2021 fires on forests and timber supply in British Columbia.* Retrieved November 29, 2022, from www2.gov.bc.ca/assets/gov/farming-natural-resources-and-industry/forestry/stewardship/forest-analysis-inventory/tsr-annual-allowable-cut/impacts_of_2021_fires_final.pdf

Brown, D. (1970). *Bury my heart at Wounded Knee: An Indian history of the American West.* Henry Holt.

Bureau of Land Management. (n.d.-a). *About the BLM.* www.blm.gov/about

Bureau of Land Management. (n.d.-b). *The Bureau of Land Management's outdoor recreation and visitor services accomplishments report 2006-2008.* www.blm.gov/wo/st/en/prog/Recreation.html

Bureau of Reclamation. (2005). *Bureau of Reclamation.* Retrieved June 6, 2005, from www.usbr.gov

Canada. (2020). *Sixth national report.* Retrieved November 29, 2022, from https://chm.cbd.int/database/record/C54338B1-F853-7542-B2AD-34985A78BE08

Cavallo, D. (1981). *Muscles and morals: Organized playgrounds and urban reform, 1880–1920.* University of Pennsylvania Press.

CBC. (2020). *Documents reveal doubts on Alberta plans to close, deregulate parks.* Retrieved August 25, 2021, from www.

cbc.ca/news/canada/edmonton/documents-reveal-doubts-on-alberta-plans-to-close-deregulate-parks-1.5660069

Chape, S., Blyth, S., Fish, L., Fox, P., & Spalding, M. (Compilers). (2003). *2003 United Nations list of protected areas.* IUCN; UNEP-WCMC.

Chavez, D.J. (2002). Adaptive management in outdoor recreation: Serving Hispanics in southern California. *Western Journal of Applied Forestry, 17*(3), 129-133.

Cordell, H.K., Betz, C.J., Green, G., & Owens, M. (2005). *Off-highway vehicle recreation in the United States, regions and states: A national report from the national survey on recreation and the environment (NSRE).* U.S. Forest Service Southern Research Station. www.fs.fed.us/recreation/programs/ohv/OHV_final_report.pdf

Defend Alberta Parks. (2020). *Alberta government announces parks will no longer be delisted or closed.* Retrieved August 25, 2021, from https://defendabparks.ca/december-update

Eagles, P.F.J. (2014). Fiscal implications of moving to tourism finance for parks: Ontario Provincial Parks. *Managing Leisure, 19*(1), 1-17.

Eagles, P.F.J., McLean, D., & Stabler, M.J. (2000). Estimating the tourism volume and value in parks and protected areas in Canada and the USA. *George Wright Forum, 17*(3), 62-76.

Eagles, P.F.J., Novosel, A., Skunca, O., & Vukadin, V. (2021). Developing targets for visitation with sustainable tourism. In A. Spenceley (Ed.), *Handbook of sustainable tourism.* Edward Elgar Publishing.

Ehrlich, G. (2000). *John Muir: Nature's visionary.* National Geographic.

Environment and Climate Change Canada. (n.d.). *National wildlife areas across Canada.* https://ec.gc.ca/ap-pa/default.asp?lang=En&n=2BD71B33-1

Fisheries and Oceans Canada. (2021). *Canada's 2025 marine conservation targets.* Retrieved August 19, 2021, from www.canada.ca/en/fisheries-oceans/news/2021/07/canadas-2025-marine-conservation-targets.html

Foster, J. (1978). *Working for wildlife: The beginning of preservation in Canada.* University of Toronto Press.

Glendening, J. (1997). *The high road: Romantic tourism, Scotland, and literature, 1720-1820.* St. Martin's Press.

Government of Canada. (2021). *Government of Canada announces $340 million to support Indigenous-led conservation.* Retrieved August 25, 2021, from https://www.canada.ca/en/environment-climate-change/news/2021/08/government-of-canada-announces-340-million-to-support-indigenous-led-conservation.html

Harnick, P. (2000). *Inside city parks.* Urban Land Institute.

Hill. B. (2021) A decade of broken promises: How Canada failed to meet it goal for protecting land and water. Retrieved June 10, 2023 from https://globalnews.ca/news/8146846/a-decade-of-broken-promises-canada-land-and-water/

Hudson, B.J. (2001). Wild ways and paths of pleasure: Access to British waterfalls, 1500-2000. *Landscape Research, 26*(4), 285-303.

Johnson, C.Y., Bowker, J.M., English, D.B.K., & Worthen, D. (1997). *Theoretical perspectives of ethnicity and outdoor recreation: A review and synthesis of African-American and European-American participation.* General Technical Report SRS-11. USDA Forest Service, Southern Research Station.

Jones, K.R., & Wills, J. (2005). *The invention of the park.* Polity Press.

Keene, A. (1994). *Earthkeepers: Observers and protectors of nature.* Oxford University Press.

Kentucky State Parks. (n.d.). *Lake Barkley.* Retrieved from http://parks.ky.gov/parks/resortparks/lake-barkley/default.aspx

Kentucky State Parks. (2005). *The Lake Barkley State Resort Park.* Retrieved June 6, 2005, from http://parks.ky.gov/resortparks/lb/index.htm

Killan, G. (1993). *Protected places: A history of Ontario's provincial park system.* Dundurn Press.

Klag, G. (2020). *Biosphere reserves of the United States of America.* Retrieved August 19, 2021, from https://storymaps.arcgis.com/stories/a341b7d2012345f3a61ad46710256b6c

Landrum, N.C. (2004). *The state park movement in America: A critical review.* University of Columbia Press.

Leduc, J. (2009). *The Canadian Heritage Rivers System.* Canadian Heritage Rivers Board.

Lovgren, S. (2004). *U.S. national parks told to quietly cut services.* National Geographic. http://news.nationalgeographic.com/news/2004/03/0319_040319_parks.html

Lysenko, I., Besançon, C., & Savy, C. (2007). *2007 UNEP-WCMC global list of transboundary protected areas.* www.tbpa.net/docs/78_Transboundary_PAs_database_2007_WCMC_tbpa.net.pdf

Manning, R. (2007). *Parks and carrying capacity: Commons without tragedy.* Island Press.

Manning, R., Lawson, S., Newman, P., Hallo, J., Monz, C., & Barber, J. (in press). *Natural quiet and natural darkness: Managing the "new" resources of the national parks.* University Press of New England.

Marty, S. (1984). *A grand and fabulous notion: The first century of Canada's parks.* NC Press.

McFarland, E. (1982). The beginning of municipal park systems. In G. Wall & J. Marsh (Eds.), *Recreational land use: Perspectives on its evolution in Canada.* Carleton University Press.

McNamee, K. & Finkelstein, M.W. (2021). National Parks in Canada. In *The Canadian Encyclopedia.* Retrieved August 19, 2021, from www.thecanadianencyclopedia.ca/en/article/national-parks-of-canada

McWilliam, W., Eagles, P., Seasons, M., & Brown, R. (2010). Assessing the degradation effects of local residents on urban forests in Ontario, Canada. *Journal of Arboriculture and Urban Forestry, 36*(6), 253-260.

Miller, C. (2004). *Gifford Pinchot and the making of modern environmentalism.* Island Press.

Minister of Environment and Climate Change. (2021). *Progress on mandate letter commitments: Appearance before the Standing Committee (March 10, 2021)*. Retrieved August 25, 2021, from www.canada.ca/en/environment-climate-change/corporate/transparency/briefing-materials/appearance-before-standing-committee-march-10-2021/progress-mandate-letter-commitments.html

Nash, R. (1982). *Wilderness and the American mind* (3rd ed.). Yale University Press.

National Park Service. (n.d.-a). *How many areas are in the National Park System?* www.nps.gov/aboutus/faqs.htm

National Park Service. (n.d.-b). *National Park Service visitor use statistics*. https://irma.nps.gov/Stats

National Park Service. (n.d.-c). *Protecting lands and giving back to communities*. www.nps.gov/subjects/lwcf/index.htm

National Park Service. (n.d.-d). *Work with us*. www.nps.gov/aboutus/workwithus.htm

National Park Service. (2003). *A brief history of the National Park Service: National Park Service created*. www.nps.gov/parkhistory/online_books/kieley

National Wild and Scenic Rivers System. (n.d.). *About the WSR Act*. www.rivers.gov/wsr-act.php

Nebraska Game and Parks Commission. (n.d.). *Eugene T. Mahoney state park*. http://nebraskastateparks.reserveamerica.com/campgroundDetails.do?topTableIndex=CampingSpot&contractCode=ne&parkCode=0273

Office of National Marine Sanctuaries. (n.d.). About your National Marine Sanctuaries. https://sanctuaries.noaa.gov/about/

Parks Canada. (n.d.). *Parks Canada attendance 2011-12 to 2015-16*. www.pc.gc.ca/eng/docs/pc/attend/index.aspx

Parks Canada. (2017a). *National Parks List*. www.pc.gc.ca/en/pn-np/recherche-parcs-parks-search

Parks Canada. (2017b). *World Heritage sites in Canada*. www.pc.gc.ca/en/culture/spm-whs

Parks Canada. (2021a). Government of Canada invests $130 million to work with partners to create a network of national urban parks. Retrieved August 19, 2021, from www.newswire.ca/news-releases/government-of-canada-invests-130-million-to-work-with-partners-to-create-a-network-of-national-urban-parks-887305875.html

Parks Canada. (2021b). *State of Canada's Natural and Cultural Heritage Places 2021 Report*. Retrieved November 29, 2022, from www.pc.gc.ca/en/docs/pc/rpts/elnhc-scnhp.

Parks Canada. (2023). *Historical information on Post-Tropical Storm Fiona and PEI National Park*. Retrieved June 10, 2023, from https://parks.canada.ca/pn-np/pe/pei-ipe/Principal-Main-Fiona/fiona-archive

Pergams, O.R.W., Czech, B., Haney, J.C., & Nyberg, D. (2004). Linkage of conservation activity to trends in the U.S. economy. *Conservation Biology, 18*(6), 1617-1623.

Pergams, O.R.W., & Zaradic, P.A. (2006). Is love of nature in the US becoming love of electronic media? 16-year downtrend in national park visits explained by watching movies, playing video games, Internet use, and oil prices. *Journal of Environmental Management, 80*, 387-393.

Protected Planet. (2022). *Canada*. Retrieved November 29, 2022, from www.protectedplanet.net/country/CAN

Ramsar. (2022). *Ramsar sites information service*. Retrieved November 30, 2022, from https://rsis.ramsar.org

Ritvo, H. (2003). Fighting for Thirlmere: The roots of environmentalism. *Science, 300*(5625), 1510-1511.

Runte, A. (2010). *National parks: The American experience* (4th ed.). University of Nebraska Press.

Rybczynski, W. (1999). *A clearing in the distance: Frederick Law Olmsted and America in the nineteenth century*. Scribner.

Saunders, A. (1998). *Algonquin story* (3rd ed.). Friends of Algonquin Park.

Sears, J. (1980). *Sacred places: American tourist attractions in the nineteenth century*. University of Massachusetts Press.

Seibel, G.A. (1995). *Ontario's Niagara parks, Niagara Falls*. Niagara Parks Commission.

Sellars, R.W. (1999). *Preserving nature in the national parks*. Yale University Press.

Shaffer, M.S. (2001). *See America first: Tourism and national identity, 1880-1940*. Smithsonian Institution Press.

Sheail, J. (2010). *Nature's spectacle: The world's first national parks and protected areas*. Earthscan.

Smith, C. & Greshko, M. (2017). *UN Announces 23 New Nature Reserves while US removes 17*. National Geographic. http://news.nationalgeographic.com/2017/06/unesco-new-biosphere-reserves-us-withdraws-reserves

Tate, A. (2001). *Great city parks*. Routledge.

Taylor, A.F., Kuo, F.E., & Sullivan, W.C. (2001). Views of nature and self-discipline: Evidence from inner city children. *Journal of Environmental Psychology, 22*, 49-63.

Tennessee Valley Authority. (n.d.). *Recreation*. www.tva.gov/river/recreation/index.htm

Trans Canada Trail (TCT). (2021). *About the Trans Canada Trail*. Retrieved August 19, 2021, from https://tctrail.ca/media

Trudeau, J., & Obama, B. (2016). *U.S.-Canada joint statement on climate, energy, and Arctic leadership*. http://pm.gc.ca/eng/news/2016/03/10/us-canada-joint-statement-climate-energy-and-arctic-leadership

U.S. Army Corps of Engineers. (n.d.). *Recreation overview*. www.usace.army.mil/Missions/Civil-Works/Recreation

U.S. Department of the Interior. (n.d.). *Bureau of Indian Affairs*. www.bia.gov

U.S. Fish and Wildlife Service. (2013). *National Wildlife Refuge System overview*. www.fws.gov/refuges/about/pdfs/NWRSOverviewFactSheetApr2013revNov032013.pdf

UNEP-WCMC (2023a). Protected Area Profile for Canada from the World Database on Protected Areas, July 2023. Available at: www.protectedplanet.net

UNEP-WCMC (2023b). Protected Area Profile for United States of America from the World Database on Protected Areas, July 2023. Available at: www.protectedplanet.net

United Nations Educational, Scientific and Cultural Organization (UNESCO). (n.d.). *World Heritage list*. http://whc.unesco.org/en/list

United Nations Educational, Scientific and Cultural Organization (UNESCO). (2017a). *Biosphere reserves in Canada*. http://unesco.ca/home-accueil/biosphere%20new/biosphere%20reserves%20in%20canada-%20reserves%20de%20la%20biosphere%20au%20canada

United Nations Educational, Scientific and Cultural Organization (UNESCO). (2017b) *Biosphere reserves in the USA*. www.unesco.org/mabdb/br/brdir/europe-n/USAmap.htm

United Nations Environment Programme. (2004). *Protected area and world heritage programme: parks for peace*. Retrieved June 12, 2005, from www.unep-wcmc.org/protected_areas/transboundary/somersetwest/somersetwest-24.html

USDA Forest Service. (2017). *By the Numbers*. www.fs.fed.us/about-agency/newsroom/by-the-numbers

Virden, R.J. & Walker, C.J. (1999). Ethnic/racial and gender variations among meanings given to, and preferences for, the natural environment. *Leisure Sciences, 21*(3), 219-239.

Wals, A.E.J. (1994). Nobody planted it, it just grew! Young adolescents' perceptions and experiences of nature in the context of urban environmental education. *Children's Environment, 11*(3), 1-27.

Wetlands International. (2023). *Introduction to Ramsar Sites Information Service*. Retrieved June 10, 2023 from https://rsis.ramsar.org/.

Young, T. (2004). *Building San Francisco's parks, 1850–1930*. Johns Hopkins University Press.

Zaslowsky, D., & Watkins, T.H. (1994). *These American lands: Parks, wilderness and the public lands*. Island Press.

Zinser, C.I. (1995). *Outdoor recreation: United States national parks, forests and public lands*. Wiley.

CHAPTER 7

Americans With Disabilities Act of 1990, Public Law No. 101-336, 104 Stat. 328 (1990).

Broadway Neighbourhood Centre. (n.d.). *About*. www.thebnc.ca/about

Burton, T.L., & Glover, T.D. (1999). Back to the future: Leisure services and the reemergence of the enabling authority of the state. In E.L. Jackson & T.L. Burton (Eds.), *Leisure studies: Prospects for the twenty-first century*. Venture Publishing.

Canadian Heritage. (n.d.). *Mandate*. http://canada.pch.gc.ca/eng/1461064135424/1461064244449

Canadian Parks and Recreation Association. (2023). *What is CPRA*. www.cpra.ca/what-is-cpra

Davis, R. (2010). Inclusive sports. In Human Kinetics (Ed.), *Inclusive recreation* (pp. 193-207). Human Kinetics.

Hironaka-Juteau, J.H., & Crawford, T. (2010). Introduction to inclusion. In Human Kinetics (Ed.), *Inclusive recreation* (pp. 3-18). Human Kinetics.

Indigenous and Northern Affairs Canada. (2016). *Urban indigenous peoples*. www.aadnc-aandc.gc.ca/eng/1100100014265/1369225120949

Interprovincial Sport and Recreation Council (ISRC). (1987). *National recreation statement*. http://lin.ca/resource-details/4467

Justice Canada. (2017). *Table of public statutes and responsible ministers*. http://laws-lois.justice.gc.ca/eng/TablePublicStatutes/index.html

MacIntosh, D., Bedecki, T., & Franks, C.E.S. (1988). *Sport and politics in Canada: Federal government involvement since 1961*. McGill-Queen's University Press.

McFarland, E.M. (1970). *The development of public recreation in Canada*. Canadian Parks and Recreation Association.

National Center on Health, Physical Activity and Disability (NCHPAD). (n.d.). *What to know before you go: The big questions to ask before arriving at your "accessible" recreation destination: Park and recreation departments*. www.nchpad.org/277/1758/What~to~Know~Before~You~Go~~The~Big~Questions~to~Ask~Before~Arriving~at~Your~~Accessible~~Recreation~Destination

Parks and Recreation Association of Canada. (1947). *Charter*. Author.

Peters, M. (1913). Annual report of the committee on vacation schools and supervised playgrounds. In National Council of Women of Canada (Ed.), *The yearbook containing the report of the twentieth annual meeting of the National Council of Women of Canada* (pp. 43-48). National Council of Women of Canada.

Rutherford, P. (Ed.). (1974). *Saving the Canadian city: The first phase, 1880-1920*. University of Toronto Press.

Schrodt, B. (1979). *A history of Pro-Rec: The British Columbia provincial recreation programme: 1934-1953* [Unpublished dissertation]. University of Alberta, Edmonton.

Social Planning Toronto. (2016). *Newcomer youth access to recreation in Toronto: Relationships, resources, and relevance* https://d3n8a8pro7vhmx.cloudfront.net/socialplanningtoronto/pages/419/attachments/original/1472010169/Newcomer-Youth-Recreation-FINAL.pdf?1472010169

Special Olympics. (n.d.). *2021 Global Reach Report*. Reach Report. https://media.specialolympics.org/resources/reports/reach-reports/2021-Global-Reach-Report.pdf

Stanton, T., Markham-Starr, S., & Hodgkinson, J. (2013). Public recreation. In Human Kinetics (Ed.) *Introduction to recreation and leisure* (pp. 109-142). Human Kinetics.

Statistics Canada. (2017). *Population size and growth in Canada: Key results from the 2016 Census*. www.statcan.gc.ca/daily-quotidien/170208/dq170208a-eng.pdf

Statistics Canada. (2021). *Census of population*. www12.statcan.gc.ca/census-recensement/index-eng.cfm

Statutes of Canada. (1943). *The National Physical Fitness Act*. S.C. 1943, c. 29. King's Printer.

Statutes of Canada. (1982). *Constitution Act*. http://laws-lois.justice.gc.ca/eng/const/page-15.html#h-38

Bibliography 461

Statutes of Canada. (2003). *Physical Activity and Sport Act*. S.C. 2003, c. 2. http://laws-lois.justice.gc.ca/eng/acts/P-13.4/FullText.html

Strong-Boag, V.J. (1976). *The parliament of women of Canada, 1893-1929*. National Museums of Canada.

Sunset Community Association. (2016). *2016 Annual general report*. www.mysunset.net/wp-content/uploads/Sunset-Community-Association-AGM-Report-2016.pdf

Vancouver. (n.d.). *Sunset census data*. http://vancouver.ca/files/cov/Sunset-census-data.pdf

Westland. (1979). *Fitness and amateur sport in Canada: The federal government's programme: An historical perspective*. Canadian Parks and Recreation Association.

CHAPTER 8

American Automobile Association. (n.d.). *AAA fact sheet*. http://newsroom.aaa.com/about-aaa/aaa-fact-sheet

Bureau of Labor Statistics. (2009). *U.S. Department of Labor, wages in the nonprofit sector: Management, professional, and administrative support occupations*. www.bls.gov/opub/mlr/cwc/wages-in-the-nonprofit-sector-management-professional-and-administrative-support-occupations.pdf

Bureau of Labor Statistics. (2018) *U.S. Department of Labor, the economics daily* (2018). https://www.bls.gov/opub/ted/2018/nonprofits-account-for-12-3-million-jobs-10-2-percent-of-private-sector-employment-in-2016.htm

Center for Association Leadership. (2022). *Association FAQ*. www.asaecenter.org/about-us/newsroom/association-faq

Frumkin, P. (2002). *On being nonprofit*. Harvard University Press.

Giving USA Foundation. (2020). *Giving USA 2020: The annual report on philanthropy for the year 2019*. Giving USA Foundation. https://givingusa.org/giving-usa-2020-charitable-giving-showed-solid-growth-climbing-to-449-64-billion-in-2019-one-of-the-highest-years-for-giving-on-record/

Hansmann, H. (1987). Economic theories of non-profit organizations. In W.W. Powell (Ed.), *The nonprofit sector: A research handbook*. Yale University Press.

Imagine Canada. (2022) *Canada's charities & nonprofits*. www.imaginecanada.ca/sites/default/files/Infographic-sector-stat-2021.pdf

Independent Sector. (2016). *Threads: Insights from the charitable community*. www.independentsector.org/resource/threads

Johns Hopkins Center for Civil Society Studies. (2019). *Nonprofit economic data project (1999-2021)*. Retrieved March 14, 2023, from http://ccss.jhu.edu/research-projects/nonprofit-economic-data

Mason, D. (1999). Address on accepting ARNOVA's Award for Distinguished Lifetime Achievement. Speech presented to the Association for Research on Nonprofit Organizations and Voluntary Action, Washington, DC.

Nanus, B., & Dobbs, S.M. (1999). *Leaders who make a difference: Essential strategies for meeting the nonprofit challenge*. Jossey-Bass.

National Center for Charitable Statistics. (2015). *The Nonprofit Sector in Brief 2015: Public Charities, Giving and Volunteering*. www.urban.org/research/publication/nonprofit-sector-brief-2015-public-charities-giving-and-volunteering

National Center for Charitable Statistics. (2019). *The Nonprofit Sector in Brief 2019*. https://nccs.urban.org/publication/nonprofit-sector-brief-2019#highlights

O'Neill, M. (2002). *Nonprofit nation: A new look at the third America*. Jossey-Bass.

Ott, J. S. and Dicke, L.(Eds.). (2021). The Nature of the Nonprofit Sector. Routledge.

Payton, R.L. (1988). *Philanthropy: Voluntary action for the public good*. American Council on Education and Macmillan.

Points of Light Global Network. (n.d.). *Our Global Network*. The Points of Light Global Network. Retrieved March 14, 2023, from www.pointsoflight.org/global-network

Powell, W., & Bromley, P. (2020). *The nonprofit sector: A research handbook* (3rd ed.). Stanford University Press.

Revenue Canada. (2021). *Definition of a nonprofit organization*. https://www.canada.ca/en/revenue-agency/services/charities-giving/giving-charity-information-donors/about-registered-charities/what-difference-between-a-registered-charity-a-non-profit-organization.html

Salamon, L. (1999). *America's nonprofit sector* (2nd ed.). Foundation Center.

Salamon, L. (2012). *America's nonprofit sector: A primary* (3rd ed.). Foundation Center.

Salamon, L.M., & Anheier, H.K. (1996). The international classification of nonprofit organizations: ICNPO-revision 1. *Working Papers of the Johns Hopkins Comparative Nonprofit Sector Project* (Vol. 19). Johns Hopkins Institute for Policy Studies.

Statistics Canada. (2021). Volunteering counts: Formal and informal contributions of Canadians in 2018. https://www150.statcan.gc.ca/n1/pub/75-006-x/2021001/article/00002-eng.pdf

United Nations. (2003). *Handbook on Non-Profit Institutions in the System of National Accounts*. Author.

YMCA. (n.d.). *Facts & figures*. www.ymca.net/organizational-profile

CHAPTER 9

Asian American Hotel Owners Association. (n.d.). *About AAHOA*. www.aahoa.com/about-AAHOA

Baldanza, B. (2022). *Hotel and car supply chain challenges are pressuring package travel*. Forbes. www.forbes.com/sites/benbaldanza/2022/10/14/higher-hotel-and-car-supply-chain--pressuring-package-travel-options/?sh=af89f8279121

Branson, R. (2006). *Screw it, let's do it: Lessons in life*. Virgin Books.

Covey, S.R. (1992). *Principle-centered leadership*. Simon and Schuster.

Covey, S. (2020). *The 7 habits of highly effective people* (30th anniversary ed.). Simon and Schuster.

Economic Intelligence Unit. (2022). *Tourism outlook 2023*. Retrieved December 2, 2022, from www.eiu.com/n/campaigns/tourism-in-2023

Flory, Kate. (2015). *Richard Branson quotes—starting your day on a high*. LinkedIn. Retrieved December 3, 2022, from www.linkedin.com/pulse/richard-branson-quotes-starting-your-day-high-kate-flory?trk=portfolio_article-card_title

GrowThink Consulting. (2021). *Tip: Marketing truths you must understand*. Retrieved December 3, 2021, from www.growthink.com/marketing-truths-you-must-understand

International Panel on Climate Change. (2022). *IPCC sixth assessment report*. Retrieved November 29, 2022, from www.ipcc.ch/report/ar6/wg2

IPL. (n.d.). *The importance of entrepreneurships in tourism*. Retrieved December 3, 2022, from www.ipl.org/essay/The-Importance-Of-Entrepreneurships-In-Tourism-PKMPVU74AJPR

Layne, D. (2017). Impacts of climate change on tourism in the coastal and marine environments of Caribbean small island developing states. *Science Review*, 174-184.

Mind Body Business. (2021). *Ten spa and wellness business trends, 2021*. Retrieved November 29, 2022, from www.mindbodyonline.com/business/education/blog/10-spa-and-wellness-business-trends-2021

Murphy, B., Jr. (2015). *20 great quotes about finding happiness (Richard Branson edition)*. Retrieved December 3, 2022, from www.inc.com/bill-murphy-jr/20-great-quotes-about-finding-happiness-richard-branson-edition.html

Nahavandi, A. (2021). *The art and science of leadership* (7th ed.) Person India.

National Park Service. (2022). *Annual visitation highlights, 2021*. Retrieved December 2, 2022, from www.nps.gov/subjects/socialscience/annual-visitation-highlights.htm

O'Regan, M. (2022). *Ukraine war: International tourism hit as Russian travellers disappear*. Retrieved December 3, 2022, from https://theconversation.com/ukraine-war-international-tourism-hit-as-russian-travellers-disappear-187121

Outdoor Industry Association. (n.d.). *Increase in outdoor activities due to COVID-19*. Outdoor Industry Association. https://outdoorindustry.org/article/increase-outdoor-activities-due-covid-19/

Outdoor Industry Association. (2021). *2021 special report. The new outdoor participant (COVID and beyond)*. Outdoor Industry Association. https://outdoorindustry.org/resource/2021-special-report-new-outdoor-participant--covid-beyond/

Pinchot, G., & Pellman, R. (1999). *Intrapreneuring in action: A handbook for business innovation*. Berrett-Koehler.

Rizzi, C. (2023). Turkiye stays open for tourist despite earthquake tragedy. Euronews.net. Retrieved August 9, 2023 from https://www.euronews.com/next/2023/02/27/turkiye-stays-open-for-tourists-despite-earthquake-tragedy#:~:text=Travelling%20in%20T%C3%BCrkiye%20

%2D%20as%20long,Havas%20Voyages%20and%20Selectour%2C%20confirm.

Sheel, A. (2008). US economy, recession and its impact on the US tourism, hotel and restaurant business: A brief review. *Journal of Hospitality Financial Management*.

Tedlow, R.S. (2021). *The emergence of charismatic business leadership*. RosettaBooks Publisher.

Tierney, P., Hunt, M., & Latkova, P. (2011). Do travelers support green practices and sustainable development? *Journal of Tourism Insights*, 2(2), 1-2.

U.S. Census Bureau. (2021) *North American industry classification system*. Retrieved December 1, 2022, from www.census.gov/naics

U.S. Travel Association. (2022). *U.S. travel answer sheet*. Retrieved December 1, 2022, from www.ustravel.org/research/us-travel-answer-sheet

United Nations World Tourism Organization. (2021). *International travel and COVID*. UNWTO Tourism Data Dashboard. Retrieved October 13, 2021, from www.unwto.org/unwto-tourism-dashboard

Volenec, Z., Abraham, J.O., Becker, A.D., & Dobson, A.P. (2021). Public parks and the pandemic: How park usage has been affected by COVID-19 policies. *PLOS One*. Retrieved October 12, 2021, from https://doi.org/10.1371/journal.pone.0251799

Weston, S. (2019). *Leadership: A critical text* (3rd ed.). Sage Publications.

Wolff-Mann, E. (2015). *15 Richard Branson quotes to start your week*. Thrillist. Retrieved December 3, 2022, from www.thrillist.com/vice/best-richard-branson-quotes-virgin-gallactic-billionaire

World Travel and Tourism Council. (2022). *Economic impact reports*. Retrieved December 2, 2022, from https://wttc.org/research/economic-impact

Zou Y., & Yu, Q. (2022). Sense of safety toward tourism destinations: A social constructivist perspective. *Journal of Destination Marketing & Management*, 24, 1-9.

CHAPTER 10

American Therapeutic Recreation Association. (n.d.). *What is RT/TR?* www.atra-online.com/what/FAQ

American Therapeutic Recreation Association. (2015). *Who we are*. Retrieved November 26, 2022, from www.atra-online.com/page/WhoWeAre

Anderson, L., & Heyne, L. (2012). Flourishing through leisure: An ecological extension of the leisure and well-being model in therapeutic recreation strengths-based practice. *Therapeutic Recreation Journal*, 46(2), 129-152.

Austin, D. (2018). *Therapeutic recreation process and techniques: Evidence-based recreational therapy* (4th ed.). Sagamore-Venture.

Bullock, C., & Mahon, M. (2017). *Introduction to recreation services for people with disabilities: A person-centered approach* (4th ed.). Sagamore-Venture.

Bureau of Labor Statistics. (2015). *Occupational outlook handbook: Recreational therapists.* www.bls.gov/ooh/healthcare/recreational-therapists.htm

Bureau of Labor Statistics. (2021). Occupational employment and wages, May 2020: 29-1125 recreational therapists. Washington, DC: U.S. Department of Labor www.bls.gov/oes/current/oes291125.htm

Canadian Therapeutic Recreation Association. (2022). *About recreation therapy: What is recreation therapy.* https://canadian-tr.org/about-recreation-therapy

Colman, A. (2020). An agent of public health. *Parks and Recreation Magazine.* National Recreation and Park Association. www.nrpa.org/parks-recreation-magazine/2020/june/an-agent-of-public-health

Dattilo, J., Kleiber, D., & Williams, R. (1998). Self-determination and enjoyment enhancement: A psychologically-based service delivery model for therapeutic recreation. *Therapeutic Recreation Journal, 32*(4), 258-271.

Devine, M., & Bennett, J. (2020). Person-first philosophy in therapeutic recreation. In T. Long & T. Robertson (Eds.), *Foundations of therapeutic recreation* (2nd ed., pp. 51-62). Human Kinetics.

Dieser, R. (2020). History of therapeutic recreation. In T. Long & T. Robertson (Eds.), *Foundations of therapeutic recreation* (2nd ed., pp. 15-32). Human Kinetics.

Hawley, E. (2020). *Person-first and identity-first language choices.* National Aging and Disability Transportation Center. Retrieved November 26, 2022, from www.nadtc.org/news/blog/person-first-and-identity-first-language-choices

Heintzman, P. (2008). Leisure-spiritual coping: A model for therapeutic recreation and leisure services. *Therapeutic Recreation Journal, 42*(1), 56-73.

Heyne, L., & Anderson, L. (2012). *Therapeutic recreation practice: A strengths approach.* Venture.

Hoffman, J., & Long, T. (2020). Models and modalities of practice. In T. Long & T. Robertson (Eds.), *Foundations of therapeutic recreation* (2nd ed., pp. 63-81). Human Kinetics.

Hood, C., & Carruthers, C. (2007). Enhancing leisure experience and developing resources: The leisure and well-being model, part II. *Therapeutic Recreation Journal, 41*(4), 298-325.

Kunstler, R., & Stavola Daly, F. (2010). *Therapeutic recreation leadership and programming.* Human Kinetics.

Long, T. (2020). The therapeutic recreation process. In In T. Long & T. Robertson (Eds.), *Foundations of therapeutic recreation* (2nd ed., pp. 85-108). Human Kinetics.

McCormick, B., Crawford, M., & Austin, D. (2020). Trends and issues. In D. Austin, M. Crawford, B. McCormick, & M. Van Puymbroeck (Eds.), *Recreational therapy: An introduction* (5th ed., pp. 333-350). Sagamore-Venture.

National Council for Therapeutic Recreation Certification. (2020). *2019 professional profile NCTRC demographics and psychographics survey of Certified Therapeutic Recreation Specialists.* NCTRC.

National Council for Therapeutic Recreation Certification. (2021). *2019 professional profile: Diversity and inclusion data.* NCTRC.

Negley, S. (2010). Therapeutic recreation. In C. Bullock, M. Mahon, & C. Killingsworth (Eds.), *Introduction to recreation services for people with disabilities: A person-centered approach* (3rd ed., pp. 335-377). Sagamore.

Ross, J., & Ashton, C. (2017). Therapeutic recreation practice models. In N. Stumbo, B. Wolfe, & S. Pegg (Eds.), *Professional issues in therapeutic recreation: On competence and outcomes* (3rd ed., pp. 257-331). Sagamore-Venture.

Snethen, G., & Mitchell, J. (2019). RT: Harnessing the environment: A response to Haun's ecological ideology in modern day healthcare environments. *Therapeutic Recreation Journal 53*(4), 440-446.

Stumbo, N., & Peterson, C. (2021). *Therapeutic recreation program design: Principles and procedures* (6th ed.). Sagamore-Venture.

CHAPTER 11

Agergaard, S. (2016) Religious culture as a barrier? A counter-narrative of Danish Muslim girls' participation in sports, *Qualitative Research in Sport, Exercise and Health, 8*(2), 213-224. https://doi.org/10.1080/2159676X.2015.1121914

Air Force Installation & Mission Support Center. (n.d.). Air Force Services Center. www.afimsc.af.mil/Units/Air-Force-Services-Center

Ambrosini, M. (2016). Protected but separate: International immigrants in the Italian Catholic church. In D. Pasura & M. Erdal (Eds.), *Migration, transnationalism and Catholicism.* Palgrave Macmillan. https://doi.org/10.1057/978-1-137-58347-5_13

American Camping Association. (2010). Serving diverse populations: A profile of three camps. *Camping Magazine, 83*(6), 58-63.

American-Israeli Cooperative Enterprise (AICE). (n.d.). *Jews in Sports: The Maccabiah Games.* Jewish Virtual Library. https://www.jewishvirtuallibrary.org/the-maccabiah-games#:~:text=The%20Maccabiah%20is%20a%20series,is%20held%20every%20four%20years

Angus Reid Institute. (2017). *A spectrum of spirituality: Canadians keep the faith to varying degrees, but few reject it entirely.* https://angusreid.org/religion-in-canada-150

Arcan, C., Kulhane-Pera, K.A., Pergament, S., Rosas-Lee, M., & Xiong, M.B. (2017). Somali, Latino and Hmong parents' perceptions and approaches about raising healthy-weight children: A community-based participatory research study. *Public Health Nutrition, 21*, 1079-1093.

Armed Forces Recreation Center Resorts. (n.d.). *AFRC resorts.* www.armymwr.com/travel/armed-forces-hotels-resorts

Army MWR. (n.d.). *History.* www.armymwr.com/about-us/history

Army One Source. (2017). Armed forces recreation centers. Retrieved from www.myarmyonesource.com/Recreation-

TravelandBOSS/ArmedForcesRecreationCenters/Default. aspx

Army Study Guide. (2017). *Better opportunities for single soldiers*. www.armystudyguide.com/content/army_board_study_guide_topics/army_programs/about-better-opportunitie.shtml

Association of Church Sports & Recreation Ministries, Inc. (CSRM). (n.d.). *About CSRM*. Association of Church Sports & Recreation Ministries, Inc. https://www.csrm.org/about.html

Baykara, C., Baykara, S., & Yaman, C. (2021). An investigation of recreation in terms of Islamic Religion. 10(1), 24-56.

Bhatnagar, P., & Foster, C. (2021). Barriers and facilitators to physical activity in second-generation British Indian women: A qualitative study. *PLoS One*, 16, Article e0259248.

Bibby, R.W., & Grenville, A. (2016). What the polls do show: Toward enhanced survey readings of religion in Canada. *Canadian Review of Sociology*, *53*(1), 123-136.

Blizzard. 2022. *About Blizzard*. www.blizzard.com/en-us/company/about

Borish, L. (1999). Athletic activities of various kinds: Physical health and sports programs for Jewish American women. *Journal of Sport History*, *26*(2), 240-270.

Bountie Gaming. (2018). *The history and evolution of e-sports*. https://bountiegaming.medium.com/thE-history-and-evolution-of-E-sports-8ab6c1cf3257

Brinkley, A., McDermott, H., & Munir, F. (2017). What benefits does team sport hold for the workplace? A systematic review. *Journal of Sports Sciences*, *35*(2), 136-148. https://doi.org/10.1080/02640414.2016.1158852

Brown, N. (2009). Accommodating the recreation needs of Muslims is especially challenging to public aquatics providers. *Athletic Business*, *33*(4), 86-88.

Burks, M., (2012). YMCA offers women-only swim hours for Muslim women. KPBS. www.kpbs.org/news/2012/jun/26/ymca-offers-women-only-swim-hours-muslim-women-and

Buttorff, C., Ruder, T., & and Bauman, M. (2017). *Multiple chronic conditions in the United States*. RAND Corporation. www.rand.org/pubs/tools/TL221.html

Bynum, M. (2003). The little flock: Church rec ministries connect with youths through an innovative sports-based day camp. *Athletic Business*, *27*(5), 36-40.

Canadian Army. (2017a). *About the army*. Retrieved from www.army-armee.forces.gc.ca/en/about-army/organization.page

Canadian Army. (2017b). *History and heritage*. www.army-armee.forces.gc.ca/en/about-army/history.page

Canadian Army. (2022). *Canadian army*. www.canada.ca/en/army.html

Canadian Forces Morale and Welfare Services (CFMWS). (n.d.). Policies within the Context of Non-Public Property. www.cfmws.com/en/AboutUs/Library/PoliciesandRegulations/Corporate/Pages/Historical-Context.aspx

Canadian Forces Morale and Welfare Services (CFMWS). (2016). CFMWS celebrates its 20th anniversary. www.cfmws.com/en/AboutUs/Library/MediaCentre/Archive/Pages/CFMWS-20th-Anniversary-.aspx

Canadian Forces Morale and Welfare Services (CFMWS). (2017). About CFMWS. www.cfmws.com/en/AboutUs/CFPFSS/Pages/default.aspx

Canadian Forces Morale and Welfare Services (CFMWS). (2022). *About Canadian Forces Morale and Welfare Services*. https://cfmws.ca/about-us

Centers for Disease Control and Prevention (CDC). (2021). COVID-19 *Overview and Infection Prevention and Control Priorities in non-US Healthcare Settings*. www.cdc.gov/coronavirus/2019-ncov/hcp/non-us-settings/overview/index.html#background

Centers for Disease Control and Prevention (CDC). (2022). *About Chronic Diseases*. www.cdc.gov/chronicdisease/about/index.htm

Columbus Recreation and Parks Department. (2022). ESports. Columbus Recreation and Parks Department. Retrieved March 20, 2023, from https://columbusrecparks.com/wellness/athletics/esports

Cooke, H. (2022). Global ambition: Saudi Arabia wants to be a gaming and esports hub. Is it ready for major international human rights pushback? *Sports Business Journal*. www.sportsbusinessjournal.com/Journal/Issues/2022/10/10/Upfront/Esports.aspx

Cornelissen, L. (2021). *Religiosity in Canada and its evolution from 1985 to 2019*. Statistics Canada. https://www150.statcan.gc.ca/n1/pub/75-006-x/2021001/article/00010-eng.htm

Cross, G. (1990). *A social history of leisure since 1600*. Venture.

Deloitte. (n.d.). The rise of eSports investments. www2.deloitte.com/us/en/pages/advisory/articles/the-rise-of-esports-investments.html

Epp, M. (2019). *Cookbook as Metaphor for A People of Diversity: Canadian Mennonites after 1970*.

Ghoshal, A. (2019). Ethics in esports. *Gaming Law Review*, *23*(5), 338-343.

Google (n.d.-a). *About Google*. https://about.google

Google (n.d.-b). *Benefits at Google*. https://careers.google.com/benefits

Gordon, K. (2014). Hilliard sisters build confidence in Muslim girls through karate, soccer. *The Columbus Dispatch*. www.dispatch.com/content/stories/life_and_entertainment/2014/09/30/goal-tenders.html

Government of Canada. (n.d.). *Royal Canadian navy*. www.canada.ca/en/navy.html

Government of Canada. (2021). *Evaluation of Military Housing*. www.canada.ca/en/department-national-defence/corporate/reports-publications/audit-evaluation/eval-military-housing.html

Hamzeh, M., & Oliver, K.L. (2012). "Because I am Muslim I cannot wear a swimsuit": Muslim girls negotiate participation opportunities for physical activity. *Research Quarterly for Exercise and Sport*, *83*, 330-339.

Influencer Marketing Hub. (2022). *The incredible growth of esports*. https://influencermarketinghub.com/esports-stats

Jewish Community Center Maccabi Games. (n.d.). *About.* www.jccmaccabigames.org/about

Jiwani, N., & Rail, G. (2010). Islam, hijab and young Shia Muslim Canadian women's discursive constructions of physical activity. *Sociology of Sport Journal, 27,* 251-267.

Jowers, K. (2020). Military exchange, MWR operations hit hard by effects of pandemic. *Military Times.* www.militarytimes.com/pay-benefits/2020/06/05/military-exchangE-mwr-operations-hit-hard-by-effects-of-pandemic

Karlis, G., Karadakis, K., & Makrodimitris, P. (2014). Recreation and Christian youth ministries: The Ottawa chapter of the Greek Orthodox Youth of America. *International Journal of Sport Management Recreation & Tourism, 14,* 21-37.

Khiabany, G. (2007). Is there an Islamic communication? The persistence of "tradition" and the lure of modernity. *Critical Arts, 21*(1), 61, 106-124.

Kim, Y.H., Nauright, J., & Suveatwatanakul, C. (2020). The rise of E-Sports and potential for Post-COVID continued growth. *Sport in Society, 23*(11), 1861-1871. https://doi.org/10.1080/17430437.2020.1819695

Knez, K., Macdonald, D., & Abbott, R. (2012). Challenging stereotypes: Muslim girls talk about physical activity, physical education and sport. *Asia-Pacific Journal of Health, Sport and Physical Education, 3,* 109-122.

LaGrone, S. (2021). Navy plans to cut 1,000 civilian jobs, close U.S. base libraries in $280M cost savings drive. *U.S. Naval Institute News.* https://news.usni.org/2021/09/22/navy-plans-to-cut-1000-civilian-jobs-close-u-s-base-libraries-in-280m-cost-savings-drive

Maccabi Canada. (n.d.). *About Us.* Maccabi Canada. Retrieved June 1, 2023, from https://www.maccabicanada.com/about-us

MacLean, J., Peterson, J., & Martin, W.D. (1985). *Recreation and leisure: The changing scene* (4th ed.). Macmillan.

Marine Corps Community Service. (n.d.). *Marine Corps Family Programs Division campaign plan, 2021-2024.* https://usmc-mccs.org/about/2021-mf-campaign-pdf

Marine Corps Community Service Careers. (n.d.). *MCCS careers.* https://careers.usmc-mccs.org

Marshall, C. (2020). Analysis of a comprehensive wellness program's impact on satisfaction in the workplace. *International Hospitality Review, 34,* 221-241. www.emerald.com/insight/2516-8142.htm

Merriam-Webster. (n.d.). *Esprit de corps Definition & Meaning.* Merriam-Webster. Retrieved August 9, 2023, from https://www.merriam-webster.com/dictionary/esprit%20de%20corps

Miles, C., & Benn, T. (2014). A case study on the experiences of university-based Muslim women in physical activity during their studies at one UK higher education institution. *Sport, Education and Society, 21*(5). https://doi.org/10.1080/13573322.2014.942623

Military 4 Life. (2017). *Military MWR.* www.military4life.com/military-mwr-morale-welfare-recreation-list-of-mwr-facilities-worldwide

Military Benefits. (2017). *Morale, welfare, and recreation (MWR) benefits.* http://militarybenefits.info/morale-welfare-and-recreation-mwr-benefits

Military Health Service. (n.d.) *Support and resources for single service members.* https://health.mil/Military-Health-Topics/Centers-of-Excellence/Psychological-Health-Center-of-Excellence/Real-Warriors-Campaign/Articles/Support-and-Resources-for-Single-Service-Members

Military.com. (2017). What are the branches of the US military? www.military.com/join-armed-forces/us-military-overview.html

Mohamed, B. (2018). New estimates show U.S. Muslim population continues to grow. https://www.pewresearch.org/short-reads/2018/01/03/new-estimates-show-u-s-muslim-population-continues-to-grow/

Moore, E., Ali, M., Graham, E., & Quan, L. (2010). Responding to a request: Gender-exclusive swims in a Somali community. *Public Health Reports, 125,* 137-140.

MWR. (n.d). *MWR employment.* www.defensemwr.com/resources/mwr-employment

My Jewish Learning. (n.d.). *Types of Jews.* My Jewish Learning. https://www.myjewishlearning.com/article/types-of-jews

MYNA (n.d.) *MYNA spring camps are here!* Retrieved December, 2022, from www.myna.org/camps

National Academies of Sciences, Engineering, and Medicine. (2019). Strengthening the military family readiness system for a changing American society. *National Academies Press.*

National Governors Association. (2020). Summary of public health criteria in reopening plans. www.nga.org/coronavirus-reopening-plans

Navy MWR Careers. (n.d.). www.navymwr.org/careers

Navy MWR Great Lakes. (2021). Naval station Great Lakes COVID-19 update. www.navymwrgreatlakes.com/covid-19

Navy MWR Pax River. (n.d.). Covid-19 update. www.navymwrpaxriver.com/covid-19-update

New International Version Bible. (2011). Zechariah 8 NIV. https://biblehub.com/niv/zechariah/8.htm

NIRSA. (n.d.-a). *NIRSA history.* https://nirsa.net/nirsa/about/history

NIRSA. (n.d.-b). *NIRSA's Mission & Vision.* About NIRSA. https://nirsa.net/nirsa/about/mission-vision/

NIRSA. (2004). *The value of recreational sports in higher education: Impact on student enrollment, success, and buying power.* Human Kinetics.

NIRSA. (2016). *About NIRSA.* https://nirsa.net/nirsa/about

Nordland, J. (2021, Feburary 17). *E-sports 5 years on: Where is the industry headed in the future?* Esport News UK. https://E-sports-news.co.uk/2021/02/17/E-sports-5-years-on-wherE-is-thE-industry-headed

Parry, J. (2019). E-sports are not sports. *Sport, ethics and philosophy, 13*(1), 3-18.

Pew Research Center. (2009). *Mapping the global Muslim population: A report on the size and distribution of the world's Muslim population.* Author.

Pew Research Center. (2011). *Muslim Americans: No signs of growth in alienation or support for extremism.* www.people-press.org/2011/08/30/muslim-americans-no-signs-of-growth-in-alienation-or-support-for-extremism

Pew Research Center. (2015). *America's changing religious landscape.* www.pewforum.org/2015/05/12/americas-changing-religious-landscape

Pew Research Center. (2021). *The size of the U.S. Jewish population.* Pew Research Center's Religion & Public Life Project. https://www.pewresearch.org/religion/2021/05/11/the-size-of-the-u-s-jewish-population/

PSP. (2017). Recreation. www.cfmws.com/en/AboutUs/PSP/recreation/Pages/default.aspx

Qian, T.Y., Wang, J.J., Zhang, J.J., & Lu, L.Z. (2020). It is in the game: Dimensions of esports online spectator motivation and development of a scale. *European sport management quarterly, 20*(4), 458-479.

Ratey, J. (2008). *Spark: The revolutionary new science of exercise and the brain.* New York, NY: Little, Brown and Company.

Riot Games. 2022. *Who We Are.* www.riotgames.com/en/who-we-are

Robertson, B.J. (1993). *The roots of at risk behaviour. Recreation Canada, 41*(4), 21-27.

Rothman, D. J. (1971). *The discovery of the asylum.* Toronto, ON: Little, Brown.

Royal Canadian Air Force. (2017). *Welcome to the Royal Canadian Air Force.* www.rcaf-arc.forces.gc.ca/en/index.page

Royal Canadian Navy. (2017). *Welcome to the Royal Canadian Navy.* www.navy-marine.forces.gc.ca/en/index.page

Saini, N. (2021). *The Future of E-sports, as influenced by streaming TV.* TV Tech. www.tvtechnology.com/opinion/thE-futurE-of-E-sports-as-influenced-by-streaming-tv

Schutz, M. (2016). *Science shows that eSports professionals are real athletes.* DW. www.dw.com/en/science-shows-that-esports-professionals-are-real-athletes/a-19084993

Sessoms, H.D., Meyer, H., & Brightbill, C.K. (1975). *Leisure services: The organized recreation and park system* (5th ed.). Prentice Hall.

Sheskin, I.M., & Hartman, H.J. (2019) Religious diversity and religious participation in U.S. Jewish communities. *The Professional Geographer, 71*(1), 39-51. https://doi.org/10.1080/00330124.2018.1455520

Shoemaker, T. (2019). Deconversion, Sport, and Rehabilitative Hope. Religions, 10(5), 341; https://doi.org/10.3390/rel10050341

Society for Human Resource Management. (2019). *2019 employee benefits.* www.shrm.org/hr-today/trends-and-forecasting/research-and-surveys/pages/benefits19.aspx

Soltani, N., Botticello, J., & Watts, P. (2021). Exploring the physical activity of Iranian migrant women in the United Kingdom: A qualitative study. *International Journal of Qualitative Studies of Health and Well-being, 16,* 1963111.

Statistics Canada. (2022). *Religion by visible minority and generation status: Canada, provinces and territories, census metropolitan areas and census agglomerations with parts.* https://www150.statcan.gc.ca/t1/tbl1/en/tv.action?pid=9810034201

Stride, A. (2016). Centralising space: the physical education and physical activity experiences of South Asian, Muslim girls. *Sport, Education and Society, 21*(5), 677-697. https://doi.org/10.1080/13573322.2014.938622

Stutteville, S. (2015). B-ball unites, uplifts a new generation of East Africans. *The Seattle Times,* B1, B7.

Substance Abuse and Mental Health Services Administration. (n.d.) *Applying the strategic prevention framework (SPF).* www.samhsa.gov/capt/applying-strategic-prevention-framework

Substance Abuse and Mental Health Services Administration. (2019). *A guide to SAMHSA's strategic prevention framework.* Center for Substance Abuse Prevention.

Upward Sports. (n.d.). *Our mission is promoting the discovery of jesus through sports.* Upward Sports. Retrieved June 1, 2023, from https://www.upward.org/about/

U.S. Coast Guard. (n.d.) *MWR. Taking care of those who protect and defend.* www.dcms.uscg.mil/Our-Organization/Assistant-Commandant-for-Human-Resources-CG-1/Community-Services-Command-CSC/MWR/#:~:text=The%20mission%20of%20the%20Coast,driven%20MWR%20programs%20and%20services

U.S. Department of Defense. (2020). *HPCON: Understanding health protection condition levels.* DOD News. www.defense.gov/News/InsidE-DOD/Blog/article/2128863/hpcon-understanding-health-protection-condition-levels

U.S. Department of Defense. (2023). Coronavirus: Timeline. Retrieved from https://www.defense.gov/Spotlights/Coronavirus-DOD-Response/Timeline/

U.S. Department of Health and Human Services (2023). Covid-19 public health emergency. Retrieved from https://www.hhs.gov/coronavirus/covid-19-public-health-emergency/index.html

U.S. Navy. (n.d.). Serving the fleet, fighter and family. www.navymwr.org/programs

USA Government. (2017). Military history and museums. www.usa.gov/history#skiptarget

Vergun, D. (2021). *Secretary of Defense mandates COVID-19 vaccinations for service members.* U.S. Department of Defense News. www.defense.gov/News/News-Stories/Article/Article/2746111/secretary-of-defensE-mandates-covid-19-vaccinations-for-servicE-members

WHO. (n.d.). *Timeline: WHO's COVID-19 response.* www.who.int/emergencies/diseases/novel-coronavirus-2019/interactivE-timeline

Wieland, M.L., Tiedje, K., Meiers, S., Mohamed, A.A., Formea, C.M., Ridgeway, J.L., Asiedu, G.B., Boyum, G., Weis, J.A., Nigon, J.A., Patten, C.A., & Sia, I.G. (2015). Perspectives on physical activity among immigrants and refugees to a small urban community in Minnesota. *Journal of Immigrant and Minority Health, 17,* 263-275.

Wikipedia. (n.d.). *Valve Corporation.* https://en.wikipedia.org/wiki/Valve_Corporation

CHAPTER 12

Administration on Aging. (2014). *A profile of older Americans.* U.S. Department of Health and Human Services.

Baltes, P. B. (Guest Ed.). (2005). Theoretical approaches to life span development: Interdisciplinary perspectives [Special issue]. *Research in Human Development, 2(1/2)*

Baltes, P.B., Lindenberger, U., & Staudinger, U. (2006). Life span theory in developmental psychology. In W. Damon & R. Lerner (Eds.), *Handbook of child psychology* (6th ed.). Wiley.

Cochran, L.J., Rothschadl, A.M., & Rudick, J.L. (2009). *Leisure programming for baby boomers.* Human Kinetics.

Edginton, C.R., DeGraaf, D.G., Dieser, R.B., & Edginton, S.R. (2006). *Leisure and life satisfaction: Foundational perspectives.* McGraw-Hill.

Edginton, C.R., Hudson, S.R., Dieser, R.B., & Edginton, S.R. (2004). *Leisure programming: A service-centered and benefits approach* (4th ed.). McGraw-Hill.

Edginton, C.R., Kowalski, C.L., & Ranall, S.W. (2005). *Youth work: Emerging perspectives in youth development.* Sagamore.

Epstein, R. H. (2019). Why more kids are starting puberty earlier than ever before. Psychology Today. https://www.psychologytoday.com/us/articles/201908/why-more-kids-are-starting-puberty-earlier-ever.

Erikson, E.H. (1950). *Childhood and society.* Norton.

Fryar CD, Carroll MD, Afful J. Prevalence of overweight, obesity, and severe obesity among children and adolescents aged 2–19 years: United States, 1963–1965 through 2017–2018. NCHS Health E-Stats. 2020.

Godbey, G. (2008). *Leisure in your life: New perspectives.* Venture Publishing.

Howe, N., & Strauss, B. (1997). *The fourth turning: What the cycles of history tell us about America's next rendezvous with destiny.* Broadway Books.

Howe, N., & Strauss, B. (2000). *Millennials rising.* Vintage Books.

Kagan, J. (2002). Behavioral inhibition as a temperamental category. In R.J. Davidson, K.R. Scherer, & H.H. Goldsmith (Eds.), *Handbook of affective sciences.* Oxford University Press.

Kagan, J. (2010). Emotions and temperament. In M.H. Burnstein (Ed.), *Handbook of cultural developmental science.* Psychology Press.

Kelly, J.R., & Godbey, G. (1991). *The sociology of leisure.* Venture Publishing.

Kleiber, D. A., & McGuire, F. A. (2016). Leisure and human development. Sagamore Publishing.

Larson, R.W., & Ham, M. (1993). Stress and storm and stress in early adolescence: the relationship of negative events with dysphoric affect. *Developmental Psychology, 29,* 130-140.

Larson, R.W., & Verma, S. (1999). How children and adolescents spend their time across the world: Work, play and developmental opportunities. *Psychological Bulletin, 125,* 701-736.

Leitner, M.J., & Leitner, S.F. (2004). *Leisure in later life* (3rd ed.). Haworth Press.

Levinson, D. (1978). *The seasons of man's life.* Alfred A. Knopf.

Louv, R. (2005). *Last child in the woods: Saving our children from nature-deficit disorder.* Algonquin Books.

Liu, S., Caneday, L., & Tapps, T.N. (2013). The relationship between lifestyle and serious leisure of amateur volleyball players in a rural community. *The Journal of Applied Leisure and Recreation Research, 16*(4), 23-36.

Neulinger, J. (1974). *The psychology of leisure.* Charles C. Thomas.

Nied, R., & Franklin, B. (2002). Promoting and prescribing exercise for the elderly. *American Academy of Family Physician, 65*(3), 419-426.

Piaget, J., 1970. Science of education and the psychology of the child. New York: Orion Press.

Pittman, K.J. (1991). *Promoting youth development: Strengthening the role of youth serving community organizations.* Center for Youth Development and Policy Research.

Schaie, K. W., & Willis, S. L. (2016). Handbook of the psychology of aging (8th ed.). Academic Press.

Stebbins, R.A., (1992). *Amateurs, professional and serious leisure.* McGill-Queen's University Press.

Sutton-Smith, B. (1971). Children at play. *Natural History, 80*(1), 55.

Tapps, T.N. (2012). *Diversity and the college experience: Workbook.* Kendall Hunt.

Tapps, T.N., & McKenzie, E. (2014). The importance of young professional's involvement with community organizations. *Parks and Recreation Magazine, 49*(10), 44-45.

Tapps, T.N., Passmore, T., Lindenmeier, D., & Bishop, A. (2013). An investigation into the effects of resistance physical activity participation on depression of older adults in a long-term care facility. *Annual in Therapeutic Recreation, 21*(1), 63-72.

CHAPTER 13

DeGraff, D. & Jordan, D. (2019). *Programming for parks and leisure services: A servant leadership approach* (4th ed.). Venture.

Human Kinetics (Ed.). (2006). *Introduction to recreation and leisure.* Human Kinetics.

Human Kinetics (Ed.). (2019). *Introduction to recreation and leisure.* (3rd. ed.) Human Kinetics.

Maryland National Capital Park and Planning Commission. (2022) *Mission, vision, values.* www.pgparks.com/176/Mission-Vision-Value-Statements

Moiseichik, M. (Eds.). (2016). *Management of parks and recreation agencies* (4th ed.) National Recreation and Park Association.

Mulvaney, M., & Hurd, A. (2022). *Official study guide for the certified park and recreation professional* (6th ed.). Sagamore.

Rossman, J.R., & Schlatter, B. (2011). *Recreation programming* (6th ed.). Sagamore.

Toronto Canada. (n.d.) Parks, forestry and recreation. www.toronto.ca/city-government/accountability-operations-customer-service/city-administration/staff-directory-divisions-and-customer-service/parks-forestry-recreation

CHAPTER 14

Active Healthy Kids Global Alliance (n.d.). *Global matrix 4.0*. Retrieved February 20, 2023, from www.activehealthykids.org

Al-Kahteeb, Z. (2023). *How much are Super Bowl tickets 2023?* The Sporting News. Retrieved February 20, 2023, from www.sportingnews.com/us/nfl/news/super-bowl-tickets-2023-cheapest-expensive-seats/nqlbarx9gyqb2xozospdrfkf

Alamar, B., & Mehrotra, V. (2011). *Beyond Moneyball: Rapidly evolving world of sports analytics, Part I.* Retrieved from https://pubsonline.informs.org/do/10.1287/LYTX.2011.05.05/full/

Amateur Athletic Association. (2021). *About AAU.* Lake Buena Vista: FL. Retrieved from http://aausports.org

Barcelona, R., Wells, M., & Arthur-Banning, S. (2016). *Recreational sport: Program design, delivery and management.* Human Kinetics.

Boys and Girls Clubs of America. (2021). *About us: Careers.* www.bgca.org/about-us/careers

BGC Canada (2020). *Opportunity changes everything: 2020 annual report.* Retrieved from https://www.bgccan.com/wp-content/uploads/2021/07/BGC-Canada-2020-Annual-Report.pdf

Bureau of Labor Statistics. (2021). *Recreation workers: Job outlook.* www.bls.gov/ooh/personal-care-and-service/recreation-workers.htm

Delaney, T. & Madigan, T. (2015). *The sociology of sports: An introduction* (2nd ed). McFarland & Company.

DeSensi, J. & Rosenberg, D. (2010). *Ethics and morality in sport management, 4th Edition.* Morgantown, WV: Fitness Information Technology.

Employee Morale and Recreation Association. (2023). *Employee morale & recreation programs. EMRA.* Retrieved February 20, 2023, from https://esmassn.wildapricot.org/page-372979

Fleming, D., Dorsch, T., Serang, S., Hardiman, A., Blazo, J., Farrey, T., Lerner, J., & Solomon, J. (2023). The association of families' socioeconomic and demographic characteristics with parents' perceived barriers to returning to youth sport following the COVID-19 pandemic. *Psychology of Sport and Exercise, 65.* https://doi.org/10.1016/j.psychsport.2022.102348

Forney, C.A. (2010). *The holy trinity of American sports: Civil religion in football, baseball, and basketball.* Mercer University Press.

Fry, M.J., & Ohlmann, J.W. (2012). Introduction to the special issue on analytics in sports, Part I: General sports applications. *Interfaces, 42*(2), 105-108.

Gould, D. (2016). Quality coaching counts. *Phi Delta Kappan, 97*(8), 13-18.

Government of Canada. (2021). *Sport organizations.* Retrieved from https://www.canada.ca/en/canadian-heritage/services/sport-organizations/national.html

Hashemi, F., Tojari, F., Sajjadi Hezave, H., & Amirtash, A. (2021). Analysis of the effect of recreational sports development on health and participation of students in sports activities. *Jorjani Biomedical Journal, 9*(1), 32-43.

Hedlund, D.P. (2021). A typology of esports players. *Journal of Global Sport Management, 8*(2), 460-477.

Hwang, Y., Deng, Y., Manninen, M., Waller, S., Evans, E.M., Schmidt, M.D., Chen, S. & Yli-Piipari, S. (2023) Short- and longer-term psychological and behavioral effects of exergaming and traditional aerobic training: A randomized controlled trial. *International Journal of Sport and Exercise Psychology, 21*(1), 120-137. https://doi.org/10.1080/1612197X.2021.2025135

Ibisworld. (2023). *Gym, health & fitness clubs in the US: Market size 2004–2029.* Retrieved February 20, 2023, from www.ibisworld.com/industry-statistics/market-size/gym-health-fitness-clubs-united-states

International Health, Racquet & Sportsclub Association. (2021). *About IHRSA.* www.ihrsa.org/about

Mull, R.F., Forrester, S.A., & Barnes, M.L. F (2019). *Recreational sport management* (6th ed.). Human Kinetics.

National Congress of State Games. (2021). *About.* http://stategames.org/about

National Recreation and Park Association. (2022). Marketing and promoting your recreation programs. *Open Space: The Official Blog and Podcast of NRPA.* www.nrpa.org/blog/marketing-and-promoting-your-recreation-programs

National Survey of Children's Health (2019). *The Child and Adolescent Health Measurement Initiative.* Retrieved February 20, 2023, from www.childhealthdata.org/browse/survey/results?q=8071&r=1

Navy MWR. (n.d.). *Navy MWR fleet recreation.* Retrieved from www.navymwr.org

Nielsen.com. (2016). *The year in sports media report: 2015.* www.nielsen.com/us/en/insights/reports/2016/the-year-in-sports-media-report-2015.html

NIRSA. (n.d.). *About NIRSA.* Retrieved February 20, 2023, from https://nirsa.net/nirsa/about

North American Society of Sport Management. (n.d.). *NASSM home.* www.nassm.com

Physical Activity Council. (2022). *2022 Physical activity council's overview report on participation.* Retrieved March 14, 2023, from www.physicalactivitycouncil.org/_files/ugd/286de6_292481f0e76443d4b0921fbb879f8cfc.pdf

Pitts, B., & Stotlar, D. (2013). *Fundamentals of sport marketing, 4th edition.* Morgantown, WV: Fitness Information Technology.

SIGNA Sports United and Boston Consulting Group (2021). *New study from SIGNA Sports United and Boston Consulting Group reports $1.1 trillion global sports market and predicts $3.5 billion in global sports participation by 2025.* Retrieved from https://www.businesswire.com/news/home/20210511005210/en/New-Study-from-SIGNA-Sports-United-and-Boston-Consulting-Group-Reports-1.1-Trillion-Global-Sports-Market-and-Predicts-3.5-Billion-in-Global-Sports-Participation-by-2025.

Solutions Research Group Consultants, Inc. (2023). Canadian youth sports rebound after pandemic disruptions, but rising costs raise concerns about affordability. Retrieved from https://www.srgnet.com/2023/06/26/canadian-youth-sports-rebound-after-pandemic-disruptions-but-rising-costs-raise-concerns-about-affordability/

Sport England (2020). *Active lives data tables.* Retrieved from https://www.sportengland.org/research-and-data/data/active-lives/active-lives-data-tables

Statista. (n.d.). Total number of viewers of the most watched television shows in the United States in the 2021/2022 season. Retrieved February 20, 2023, from www.statista.com/statistics/804812/top-tv-series-usa-2015

Szymanski, M., Wolfe, R., Danis, W., Lee, F., & Uy, M. (2020). Sport and international management: Exploring research synergy. Retrieved from https://onlinelibrary.wiley.com/doi/10.1002/tie.22139.

YMCA (2021). *Who we are: By the numbers.* Retrieved from https://www.ymca.org/who-we-are/our-impact

YMCA Canada. (2017). *About Us.* Retrieved from https://www.ymca.ca/who-we-are/about-us

CHAPTER 15

American Psychological Association. (2011). *Mind/body health: Did you know?* www.apa.org/helpcenter/mind-body.aspx

Canadian Mental Health Association, National. (2021). *Fast facts about mental health and mental illness.* CMHA National. https://cmha.ca/brochure/fast-facts-about-mental-illness/

Centers for Disease Control and Prevention (CDC). (2017). *Healthy communities program (2008-2012).* www.cdc.gov/nccdphp/dch/programs/healthycommunitiesprogram/index.htm

Centers for Disease Control and Prevention (CDC). (2020). *CDC release 2019 youth risk behavior survey results.* www.cdc.gov/healthyyouth/data/yrbs/feature

Centers for Disease Control and Prevention (CDC). (2021a). *About mental health.* www.cdc.gov/mentalhealth/learn/index.htm

Centers for Disease Control and Prevention (CDC). (2021b). *Mortality in the United States, 2020.* www.cdc.gov/nchs/products/databriefs/db427.htm

Centers for Disease Control and Prevention (CDC). (2022a). *Adult obesity causes and consequences.* www.cdc.gov/obesity/adult/causes.html

Centers for Disease Control and Prevention (CDC). (2022b). *Overweight and obesity: Childhood obesity facts.* www.cdc.gov/obesity/data/childhood.html

Centers for Disease Control and Prevention (CDC). (2022c). *Overweight and obesity: Obesity, race/ethnicity, and COVID-19.* www.cdc.gov/obesity/data/obesity-and-covid-19.html#Increasing

Czeisler, M.É., & Czeisler, C.A. (2022). Shifting mortality dynamics in the United States during the COVID-19 pandemic as measured by years of life lost. *Annals of Internal Medicine.* https://doi.org/10.7326/M22-2226

The Global Health Observatory. (n.d.). Infant mortality. WHO. www.who.int/data/gho/data/themes/topics/indicator-groups/indicator-group-details/GHO/infant-mortality

Grad, F.P. (2002). The preamble of the constitution of the World Health Organization. 80(12): 982. Retrieved from www.who.int/bulletin/archives/80(12)981.pdf

Hancock, T., & Duhl, L. (1988). *Promoting health in the urban context.* WHO Healthy Cities Paper, 1. FADL.

Hudson, A (2020). Bowling Alone at Twenty. National Affairs, Number 55, https://www.nationalaffairs.com/publications/detail/bowling-alone-at-twenty"

International Living. (2022). *Quality of life index.* https://internationalliving.com

Irvin, V.L., & Kaplan, R.M. (2016). Effect sizes and primary outcomes in large-budget cardiovascular-related behavioral randomized controlled trials funded by NIH since 1980. *Annals of Behavioral Medicine,* 50(1), 130-146. https://doi.org/10/1007/s12160-015-9739-7

Kochanek, K.D., Xu, J., & Arias, E. (2020). *Mortality in the United States, 2019.* U.S. Department of Health and Human Services, National Center for Health Statistics. www.cdc.gov/nchs/data/databriefs/db395-H.pdf

National Institutes of Health. (2015). *Positive emotions and your health, developing a brighter outlook.* News in Health. https://newsinhealth.nih.gov/issue/aug2015/feature1

National Wellness Institute. (2011). *A definition of spiritual wellness.* www.nationalwellness.org/general.php?id_tier=2%20&%20id=684

Putnam, R. D. (2000). *Bowling alone: The collapse and revival of American community.* Touchstone Books/Simon & Schuster. https://doi.org/10.1145/358916.361990

Roser, M., Ortiz-Ospina, E., & Ritchie, H. (2019). *Life expectancy.* Our World in Data. https://ourworldindata.org/life-expectancy

Sanders, L.M., Perrin, E.M., Yin, H.S., Delamater, A.M., Flower, K.B., Bian, A., Schildcrout, J., Rothman, R.L, & Greenlight Study Team. (2021). A health-literacy intervention for early childhood obesity prevention: a cluster-randomized controlled trial. *Pediatrics,* 147(5).

Statistics Canada. (2015). *Canada's population estimates: Age and sex, July 1, 2015.* Author.

Statistics Canada. (2018). *Mortality overview.* www150. statcan.gc.ca/n1/pub/91-209-x/2018001/article/54957-eng.htm

World Health Organization (WHO). (2020). *The top 10 causes of death.* www.who.int/en/news-room/fact-sheets/detail/the-top-10-causes-of-death

World Health Organization (WHO). (2021). *Obesity and overweight.* www.who.int/news-room/fact-sheets/detail/obesity-and-overweight

World Health Organization (WHO) (2022a). *Newborn mortality.* www.who.int/news-room/fact-sheets/detail/levels-and-trends-in-child-mortality-report-2021

World Health Organization (WHO). (2022b). *Physical activity.* www.who.int/news-room/fact-sheets/detail/physical-activity

World Leisure Organization. (2020). *Charter for leisure.* www.worldleisure.org/wlo2019/wp-content/uploads/2021/07/Charter-for-Leisure_en.pdf

Xu, J., Murphy, S.L., Cochanek, K.D., Arias, E. (2021). Deaths: Final data for 2019. *National Vital Statistics Reports, 79,* 8.

CHAPTER 16

Alagona, P.S., & Simon, G.L. (2012). Leave No Trace starts at home: A response to critics and vision for the future. *Ethics, Policy and Environment, 15*(1), 119-124.

American Camp Association. (2022). *Mission and vision.* www.acacamps.org/about/mission-vision

Bernard, M. (1999). The camping movement takes shape. *Camping Magazine, 72*(6), 20.

Bryson, B. (2006). *A walk in the woods: Rediscovering America on the Appalachian Trail.* Broadway Books.

Bunyan, P. (2011). Models and milestones in adventure education. In M. Berry & C. Hodgson (Eds.), *Adventure education: An introduction* (pp. 5-23). Routledge.

Campbell, C.E. (2011). Governing a kingdom: Parks Canada, 1911-2011. In C.E. Campbell (Ed.), *A century of Parks Canada 1911-2011* (pp. 1-19). University of Calgary Press.

Carson, R. (1962). *Silent spring.* Houghton Mifflin Company.

Cordes, K., & Hutson, G. (2015). *Outdoor recreation: Enrichment for a lifetime* (4th ed.). Sagamore.

DeMerritte, E. (1999). The emergence of the camping movement. *Camping Magazine, 72*(6), 18-19.

Dennis, S. (2012). *Natural resources and the informed citizen.* Sagamore.

Dustin, D., Bricker, K., & Schwab, K. (2010). People and nature: Toward an ecological model of health promotion. *Leisure Sciences, 32*(1), 3-14. https://doi.org/10.1080/01490400903430772

Duvall, J., & Kaplan, R. (2014). Enhancing the well-being of veterans using extended group-based nature recreation experiences. *Journal of Rehabilitation Research and Development, 51*(5), 685-696.

Ewert, A.W. (1989). *Outdoor adventure pursuits: Foundations, models, and theories.* Publishing Horizons.

Ewert, A., Mitten, D., & Overholt, J. (2021). *Health and natural landscapes: Concepts and applications.* CABI.

Gelles, D. (2022). Billionaire no more: Patagonia founder gives away the company. *New York Times.* www.nytimes.com/2022/09/14/climate/patagonia-climate-philanthropy-chouinard.html

Goldenberg, M., & Soule, K. (2014). A four-year follow-up of means-end outcomes from outdoor adventure programs. *Journal of Adventure Education and Outdoor Learning, 15*(4), 1-12.

Government of Canada. (2021). Truth and reconciliation commission of Canada. www.rcaanc-cirnac.gc.ca/eng/1450124405592/1529106060525#chp1

Hitchner, S., Schelhas, J., Brosius, J.P., & Nibbelink, N.P. (2019) Zen and the art of the selfie stick: Blogging the John Muir Trail thru-hiking experience. *Environmental Communication, 13*(3), 353-365. https://doi.org/10.1080/17524032.2019.1567568

Huddart, D., & Stott, T. (2019). *Outdoor recreation: Environmental impacts and management.* Palgrave Macmillan.

The International Ecotourism Society. (2022). *Our mission.* www.ecotoruism.org/our-mission

Lemelin, R.H., Dawson, J., & Stewart, E.J. (Eds.). (2012). *Last chance tourism: Adapting tourism opportunities in a changing world.* Routledge.

Mammoth Mountain Ski Area. (n.d.). *Mammoth Bike Park.* www.mammothmountain.com/things-to-do/activities/bike-park

Manning, R.E. (2007). *Parks and carrying capacity: Commons without tragedy.* Island Press.

Martin, B., Breunig, M., Wagstaff, M., & Goldenberg, M. (2017). *Outdoor leadership: Theory and practice* (2nd ed.). Human Kinetics.

Martin, P., & Priest, S. (1986). Understanding the adventure experience. *Journal of Adventure Education, 3*(1), 18-21.

McClean, D.D., Hurd, A.R., & Anderson, D.M. (2017). *Kraus' recreation and leisure in modern society* (11th ed.). Jones & Bartlett Learning.

Nash, R. (2014). *Wilderness and the American mind* (5th ed.). Yale University Press.

National Outdoor Leadership School (NOLS). (2022). *About NOLS.* www.nols.edu/en/about/mission

National Park Service. (2022). *Great American Outdoors Act.* www.nps.gov/subjects/legal/great-american-outdoors-act.htm

National Recreation and Park Association (NRPA). (2022). *About NRPA.* www.nrpa.org/About-National-Recreation-and-Park-Association

Newland, B. (2022). Federal Indian boarding school initiative investigative report. www.bia.gov/sites/default/files/dup/inline-files/bsi_investigative_report_may_2022_508.pdf

Olmstead, L. (2013). *Martis camp: Possibly the best four-season private community in the U.S.* Forbes. www.forbes.com/sites/larryolmsted/2013/10/02/the-best-four-season-private-community-in-the-us/#795abecc7f1d

Outdoor Industry Foundation. (2021). *Outdoor participation trends report 2021.* https://outdoorindustry.org/wp-content/uploads/2015/03/2021-Outdoor-Participation-Trends-Report.pdf

Ozier, L. (2018). Learning landscapes: The education spectrum from camps to classrooms. *Journal of Youth Development*, *13*(1-2), 4-13. https://doi.org/10.5195/jyd.2018.612

Parks Canada. (2021). *Parks Canada attendance 2019-2020.* www.pc.gc.ca/en/docs/pc/attend#summary

Plummer, R. (2009). *Outdoor recreation: An introduction.* Routledge.

Priest, S., & Gass, M. (2018). *Effective leadership in adventure programming* (3rd ed.). Human Kinetics.

Ripper, F. (2023). Why have there been so many deaths on Mount Everest this spring climbing season. *Australian Broadcasting Corporation.* https://www.abc.net.au/news/2023-05-26/spring-2023-one-of-the-deadliest-climbing-season/102381296

Simon, G.L., & Alagona, P.S. (2013). Contradictions at the confluence of commerce, consumption and conservation; or, an REI shopper camps in the forest, does anyone notice? *Geoforum*, *45*, 325-336. https://doi.org/10.1016/j.geoforum.2012.11.022.

Strayed, C. (2013). *Wild: From lost to found on the Pacific Crest Trail.* Vintage Books.

Turner, J.M. (2002). From woodcraft to "Leave No Trace": Wilderness, consumerism, and environmentalism in twentieth-century America. *Environmental History*, *7*(3), 462-484.

U.S. Army MWR. (2022). *Outdoor recreation.* https://italy.armymwr.com/programs/outdoor-recreation

U.S. Bureau of Economic Analysis. (2022). *Outdoor recreation satellite account, U.S. and States, 2021.* www.bea.gov/news/2022/outdoor-recreation-satellite-account-us-and-states-2021

Welser, H.T. (2012). The growth of technology and the end of wilderness experience. In B. Martin and M. Wagstaff (Eds.), *Controversial issues in adventure programming* (pp. 147-155). Human Kinetics.

Woosman, K.M., Denly, T.J., Foley, B.B., Ribeiro, M.A., & Hehir, C. (2022). Psychological antecedents of intentions to participate in last chance tourism: Considering complementary theories. *Journal of Travel Research*, *61*(6), 1342-1357. https://doi.org/10.1177/00472875211025097.

YMCA. (2022). *YMCA history: The founding years.* www.ymca.org/who-we-are/our-history/founding-years

CHAPTER 17

110%. (n.d.). The smart approach to cost recovery. www.110percent.net/services/cost-recovery

Abilene (Texas) Public Library. (n.d.). Cosplay contest information. https://www.abilenetx.gov/295/Cosplay-Contest

American Assembly. (1997). The arts and the public purpose. http://americanassembly.org/publications/arts-and-public-purpose

Americans for the Arts. (2010). *Arts and economic prosperity: The economic impact of nonprofit arts and culture organizations and their audiences.* www.americansforthearts.org/sites/default/files/pdf/information_services/research/services/economic_impact/aepiv/NationalStatisticalReport.pdf

Americans for the Arts. (2017). Creative industries: Business & employment in the arts. www.americansforthearts.org/by-program/reports-and-data/research-studies-publications/creative-industries

Andina, T. (2017). What is art: The question of definition reloaded. *Art and Law 1*(2), 1-88. https://doi.org/10.1163/24684309-12340002

Animating Democracy. (2022). *Aesthetic perspectives: Attributes of excellence in arts for change.* Americans for the Arts. Retrieved from www.animatingdemocracy.org/aesthetic-perspectives

Arnold, N.D. (1976). *The interrelated arts in leisure: Perceiving and creating.* C.V. Mosby Company.

Arnold, N.D. (1978). Pop art: The human footprint in infinity. *Journal of Physical Education, Recreation and Dance*, *49*(8), 56-57.

Arts Consulting Group. (2017). *The economic impact of America's nonprofit arts and culture industry.* https://artsconsulting.com/arts-insights/the-economic-impact-of-americas-nonprofit-arts-and-culture-industry

Bachman, J.R., Feng, F. & Hull, J.S., (2022). Resident impacts for queer film festivals: Assessing benefits and loyalty in Vancouver, British Columbia, Canada. *Event Management*, *26*(1), 107-126.

Bhatt, N. (2020). *Park and recreation in a post-pandemic world.* National Recreation and Park Association. www.nrpa.org/parks-recreation-magazine/2020/july/parks-and-recreation-in-a-post-pandemic-world

Blandy, D. (2008). Cultural programming. In G. Carpenter & D. Blandy (Eds.), *Arts and cultural programming: A leisure perspective* (pp. 173-184). Human Kinetics.

Blandy, D. (2019). Art education *qua* civic preparation. Paper presented at Constitutional Democracy Under Stress: A Time for Heroic Citizenship. www.section1.ca/constitutional-democracy-under-stress

Blandy, D. & Congdon, K. (Eds.). (1987). *Art in a democracy.* Teachers College Press.

Blandy, D. & Congdon, K. (Eds.). (1991). *Pluralistic approaches to art criticism.* Bowling Green State University Popular Press.

Bosse, R. (2015). *The impact of music festivals.* Donald W. Reynolds National Center for Business Journalism. https://businessjournalism.org/2015/06/entertaining-business-tournalism.org

Canada Review Agency. (1991). *Festivals and the promotion of tourism: Policy statement.* www.cra-arc.gc.ca/chrts-gvng/chrts/plcy/cps/cps-005-eng.html

Canadian Parks and Recreation Association. (2022). *CPRA briefing note: Federal budget.* https://cpra.ca/2022-cpra-briefing-note-federal-budget

Canadian Parks and Wilderness Society. (2020). Healthy nature, healthy people: A call to put nature protection at the heart of Canada's COVID-19 recovery strategies. https://cpaws.org/2020parksreport/Canadian Parks Council. (2011). *The economic impact of Canada's national, provincial and territorial parks in 2009.* www.parks-parcs.ca/english/pdf/econ_impact_2009_part1.pdf

Canadian Tourism Commission. (2022). National tourism indicators: 2021 Q2 highlights. www.destinationcanada.com/en/research#tourismreports

Carpenter, G. (2008). Overview of arts and cultural programming. In G. Carpenter & D. Blandy (Eds.), *Arts and cultural programming: A leisure perspective* (pp. 3-23). Human Kinetics.

Carpenter, G. (2013). Arts & culture. In *Introduction to recreation and leisure* (2nd ed.). Human Kinetics

Carpenter, G., & Howe, C.Z. (1985). *Programming leisure experiences: A cyclical approach.* Prentice-Hall, Inc.

Cascone, S. (2020). *New York City's 2021 budget slashes already modest funding for public-school arts education by 70 percent.* Americans for the Arts. www.americansforthearts.org/news-room/new-york-citys-2021-budget-slashes-already-modest-funding-for-public-school-arts-education-by-70

Chang, K-C., & Hsieh, T. (2017). From having fun to applause: The study of relationships among festival benefits, festival identify, and festival support by viewpoints of the hosts and guests. *Sustainability, 9*(12), 2240. doi:10.3390/su9122240Chapman, L.H. (1978). *Approaches to art in education.* Harcourt Brace Jovanovich.

Chapman, L.H. (2003). Studies of the mass arts. *Studies in Art Education, 44*(3), 230-245.

Chartrand, H.H. (2000). Toward an American arts industry. In J.M. Cherbo & M.J. Wyszormirski (Eds.), *The public life of the arts in America* (pp. 22-49). Rutgers University Press.

Cherbo, J.M. (2007). On valuing the arts. *The Journal of Arts Management, Law, and Society, 37*(2), 170-172. https://doi.org/10.3200/JAML.37.2.170-172

Cherbo, J.M., Stewart, R.A., & Wyszomirski, M.J. (Eds.). (2008). *Understanding the arts and creative sector in the United States.* Rutgers University Press.

City of Paducah, Kentucky. (n.d.). *Lowertown artist program.* http://paducahky.gov/lowertown-artist-program

City Parks Forum. (2008). *How cities use parks for arts and cultural programming.* American Planning Association. https://w1.planning.org/publications/document/9148684

Coleman, J.S. (1988). Social capital in the creation of human capital. *American Journal of Sociology, 94,* 95-120.

Conference Board of Canada. (2008). Valuing culture: Measuring and understanding Canada's creative economy. www.conferenceboard.ca/e-library/abstract.aspx?DID=2671

Congdon, K.G., & Blandy, D. (2003). Administering the culture of everyday life: Imaging the future of arts sector administration. In V.B. Morris & D.B. Pankratz (Eds.), *The arts in a new millennium* (pp. 177-188). Praeger.

Corbin, H.D., & Williams, E. (1987). *Recreation: Programming and leadership* (4th ed.). Prentice Hall.

Csikszentmihalyi, M. (1990). *Flow: The psychology of optimal experience.* Harper & Row.

Cuyler, A. (2007). *The career paths of non-European American opera administrators in the United States* [Dissertation]. Dissertation Abstracts International.

Cuyler, A. (2013). Affirmative action and diversity: Implications for arts management. *The Journal of Arts Management, Law, and Society, 43,* 98-105.

Darts, D. (2004). Visual culture jam: Art, pedagogy, and creative resistance. *Studies in Art Education, 45*(4), 313-327.

Davies, K. (2020). Festivals post Covid-19. *Leisure Sciences: An Interdisciplinary Journal, 43*(1-2), 184-189. https://doi.org/10.1080/01490400.2020.1774000

Dehner, M. (2021). *2021 annual report: The state of art education 2021.* The Art of Education University.

Delamere, T.A., Wankel, L.M., & Hinch, T.D. (2001). Measuring resident attitudes toward the social impact of community festivals. Pretesting and purification of the scale. *Festival Management and Event Tourism, 7*(1), 11-24.

DeLaure, M. & Fink, M. (Eds.). (2017). *Culture jamming : activism and the art of cultural resistance.* New York University Press.

Deshays, T. (Director). (2022). *You, myself and art: What is art for?* [Film]. TMW Media/Ulloa Films.

Discover Clearview. (2021). *Virtual recreation experiences.* www.discoverclearview.ca/recreation-leisure/virtual-recreation-experiences

Dissanayake, E. (2008). The universality of the arts in human life. In J.M. Cherbo, R.A. Stewart, & M.J. Wyszomirski (Eds.), *Understanding the arts and creative sector in the United States.* Rutgers University Press.

Dissanayake, E. (2018). From play and ritualisation to ritual and its arts: Sources of Upper Pleistocene ritual practices in Lower Middle Pleistocene ritualised and play behaviors in ancestral hominins. In C. Renfrew, I. Morley, & M. Boyd (Eds.), *Ritual, play and belief, in evolution and early human societies.* Cambridge University Press.

Dropinski, C. (2020). Can cost recovery and social equity be compatible in public parks & recreation? https://www.amilia.com/blog/cost-recovery-social-equity

Edin, K., & Kefalas, M. (2011). *Promises I can keep: Why poor women put motherhood before marriage* (3rd ed.). Berkeley: University of California Press.

Elsabagh, H., Bashandy, S., Abd Elaziz, N., & Abd El Aziz, N. (2022). The impact of 3D public art on improving visual image and identity of urban spaces. *Journal of Urban Research, 46*(1), 76-102.

Farrell, P., & Lundegren, H. (1978). *The process of recreation programming: Theory and technique.* Wiley.

Farrell, P., & Lundegren, H. (1983). *The process of recreation programming: Theory and technique* (2nd ed.). Wiley.

Farrell, P., & Lundegren, H. (1991). *The process of recreation programming: Theory and technique* (3rd ed.). Wiley.

Florida, R. (2002). *The rise of the creative class.* Basic Books.

Fraley, J. (2022). *Washington National Opera brings "Carman" to Audi Field.* WTOP News. https://wtop.com/entertainment/2022/09/washington-national-opera-brings-carmen-to-audi-field

Freedman, K., & Stuhr, P. (2004). Curriculum changes for the 21st century: Visual culture in art education. In E. Eisner & M. Day (Eds.), *Handbook of research and policy in art education* (pp. 815-828). National Art Education Association.

Friedenwald-Fishman, E., & Fraher, D. (2016). Creating connection through creative expression. *CultureWork: A Periodic Broadside for Arts & Culture Workers, 20*(2). https://culturework.uoregon.edu/2016/04/12/april-2016-vol-20-no-2-creating-connection-through-creative-expression-eric-friedenwald-fishman-and-david-fraher

Goldberg-Miller, S.B.D., & Heimlich, J.E. (2017). Creatives' expectations: The role of supercreatives in cultural district development. *Cities, 62,* 120-130.

Graham, D. (2020). *Arts and culture in parks and recreation.* National Recreation and Park Association. www.nrpa.org/parks-recreation-magazine/2020/october/arts-and-culture-in-parks-and-recreation

Gray, D. (1984). *The great simplicities.* J.B. Nash Scholar Lecture, Anaheim, CA.

GreenPlay, LLC. (n.d.) *Parks, recreation, and libraries consulting.* https://greenplayllc.com/time-for-appropriate-cost-recovery-now-more-than-ever

Guinard, P., & Margier, A. (2018). Art as a new urban norm: Between normalization of the city through art and normalization of art through the city in Montreal and Johannesburg. *Cities, 77,* p.13-20.

Hall, C., & Thomson, P. (2021). Making the most of school arts education partnerships. *Curriculum Perspectives, 41*(1), pp. 101-106.

Hetland, L., Winner, E., Veenema, S., & Sheridan, K. (2007). *Studio thinking: The real benefits of arts education.* Teachers College Press.

Hill Strategies. (2019). *Estimates of the direct economic impact of culture in Canada in 2017.* www150.statcan.gc.ca/n1/daily-quotidien/190425/dq190425b-eng.htm

Hogan, J., Hetland, L., Jaquith, D. B., Winner, E. & Nelson, D.P. (2018). *Studio thinking from the start: The K–8 art educator's handbook.* Teachers College Press.

Holladay, L., & Loewenthal, T. (2014). Growing a lotus in Indiana/Lotus World Music & Arts Festival: Developing a volunteer cohort (Fenn. J. Guest Ed.). *CultureWork: A Periodic Broadside for Arts and Culture Workers, 18*(3). https://culturework.uoregon.edu/2014/07/17/july-2014-vol-18-no-3-growing-a-lotus-in-indianalotus-world-music-arts-festival-developing-a-volunteer-cohort-luanne-holladay-and-tamara-loewenthal-john-fenn-guest/3

Indiana Arts Commission. (n.d.). *Arts in the parks and historic sites 2018 guidelines for organizations.* www.in.gov › arts › files › CY18-APHS-guidelines_org.pdf

International Labor Organization. (2013). *Sustainable tourism for development.* www.ilo.org/Search5/search.do?sitelang=en&locale=en_EN&consumercode=ILOHQ_STELLENT_PUBLIC&searchWhat=Sustainable+tourism+for+development.&searchLanguage=en

Ione, A. (2016). *Art and the brain: Plasticity, embodiment, and the unclosed circle.* Brill Academic Publishers.

Iso-Ahola, S.E. (1980). *The social psychology of leisure and recreation.* Brown.

Karwowski, M., & Kaufman, J.C. (2017). *The creative self: Effect of beliefs, self-efficacy, mindset, and identity.* Elsevier Science & Technology.

Kelly, J.R. (1996). *Leisure* (3rd ed.) Allyn and Bacon.

Kelly, J.R., & Freysinger, V.J. (2000). *Twentieth century leisure: Current issues.* Allyn and Bacon.

Kirkpatrick, K. & Romens, A. (2015). Creating connection: Research findings and proposed message framework to build public will for arts and culture. Minneapolis, MN: Arts Midwest & Metropolitan Group.

Kleiber, D.A. (1999). *Leisure experience and human development.* Basic Books.

Knight Foundation. (n.d.). *About Knight: Soul of the community.* www.knightfoundation.org/sotc/about-knight-soul-community

Kraus, R. (1966). *Recreation today: Program planning and leadership.* Appleton-Century-Crofts.

Kraus, R. (1979). *Social recreation: A group dynamics approach.* Mosby.

Kraus, R. (1985). *Recreation program planning today.* Scott Foresman.

Lanier, V. (1969). The teaching of art as social revolution. *Phi Delta Kappa, 50*(G), 314-319.

Leroux, K. & Bernadska, A. (2014). Impact of the arts on individual contributions to US civil society. *Journal of Civil Society, 10*(2), pp. 144-164.

Litwiller, F. (2021). Youth perspectives on genderplay recreation programming: Insights and critiques on identity development theories. *Leisure Sciences* (ahead-of-print), pp. 1-18.

Loden, M. & Rosener, J. (1990). Workforce America! Managing employee diversity as a vital resource. McGraw-Hill Professional Publishing. Retrieved from Cultural Competence Learning Institute, https://community.astc.org/ccli/resources-for-action/group-activities/diversity-wheel

Lotus Education & Arts Foundation. (2022). *Lotus blossoms world bazaar virtual resources.* www.lotusfest.org/2022/2021bazaar

Lynch, R.L. (2017). The arts mean business. *Arts & economic prosperity 5 summary report: The economic impact of nonprofit arts & cultural organizations and their audiences.* Americans for the Arts. www.americansforthearts.org/by-program/reports-and-data/research-studies-publications/ arts-economic-prosperity-5/use/download-the-report

Mandala Research, LLC. (2013). *The cultural and heritage traveler.* http://mandalaresearch.com/downloads/2013-cultural-heritage-traveler-report

Markusen, A., & Gadwa, A. (2010). *Creative placemaking.* www.arts.gov/sites/default/files/CreativePlacemaking-Paper.pdf

Mauldin, B., Laramee Kidd, S., Ruskin, J., & Agustin, M. (2016). *Executive summary: Los Angeles County Arts Commission cultural equity and inclusion initiative literature review.* Los Angeles County Arts Commission.

McCarthy, K.F., & Jinnett, K. (2001). *A new framework for building participation in the arts.* Rand.

McFee, J.K. (1961). *Preparation for art.* Wadsworth Publishing Company.

McFee, J.K. (1978). Art abilities in environmental reform. *Art Education, 31*(4), 9-12.

Meyer, H.D., & Brightbill, C.K. (1956). *Community recreation: A guide to its organization.* Prentice-Hall.

Miller, R.K. (2021). *Travel & tourism market research handbook 2021-2022* (17th ed.). Richard K. Miller & Associates.

Moffit, K. (2017). *Redrawing boundaries—real and imagined—with digital artist Jer Thorp at the St. Louis Map Room.* St. Louis Public Radio. https://news.stlpublicradio.org/show/st-louis-on-the-air/2017-02-14/redrawing-boundaries-real-and-imagined-with-digital-artist-jer-thorp-at-the-st-louis-map-room#stream/0

Mowen, A.J., Barrett, A.G., Graefe, A.R. and Roth, K. (2017). *Local government officials' perceptions of parks and recreation.* National Recreation and Park Association.

MTC-ABAG Library. (n.d.). *Bay Area census: San Francisco city and county.* www.bayareacensus.ca.gov/counties/SanFranciscoCounty.htm

Nathan, M., Kemeny, T., Pratt, A., & Spencer, G. (2016). *Creative economy employment in the US, Canada and the UK.* Nesta.

National Assembly of State Art Agencies. (2022). *Percent for art policy brief.* https://nasaa-arts.org/nasaa_research/state-percent-art-programs

National Council for the Traditional Arts. (2022). *National folk festival tallies 400,000 attendees over 4 years.* https://ncta-usa.org/national-folk-festival-tallies-400000-attendees-over-4-years

National Endowment for the Arts. (2011a). *Arts education in America: What the declines mean for arts participation.* www.arts.gov/sites/default/files/2008-SPPA-ArtsLearning.pdf

National Endowment for the Arts. (2011b). *Beyond attendance: A multi-modal understanding of arts participation.* www.arts.gov/sites/default/files/2008-SPPA-BeyondAttendance.pdf

National Endowment for the Arts. (2019). *U.S. patterns of arts participation: A full report from the 2017 survey of public participation in the arts.* www.arts.gov/impact/research/publications/us-patterns-arts-participation-full-report-2017-survey-public-participation-arts

National Endowment for the Arts. (2020a). *Why we engage: Attending, creating, and performing art.* www.arts.gov/sites/default/files/Why-We-Engage-0920_0.pdf

National Endowment for the Arts. (2020b). *Paths to participation: Understanding how art forms and activities intersect.* www.arts.gov/impact/research/publications/paths-participation-understanding-how-art-forms-and-activities-intersect

National Endowment for the Arts. (2021). *NEA offers relief funds to help arts and culture sector recover from pandemic: Doors open for applications for American Rescue Plan funding.* www.arts.gov/news/press-releases/2021/nea-offers-relief-funds-help-arts-and-culture-sector-recover-pandemic

National Governors Association. (n.d.). *Arts and the economy: Using arts and culture to stimulate state economic development.* www.nga.org/files/live/sites/NGA/files/pdf/0901ARTSANDECONOMY.PDF

National Recreation and Park Association. (n.d.). *NRPA agency performance review.* www.nrpa.org/publications-research/research-papers/agency-performance-review

National Recreation and Park Association. (2015). *The economic impact of local parks: An examination of the economic impacts of operations and capital spending on the United States economy.* www.nrpa.org/uploadedFiles/nrpa.org/Publications_and_Research/Research/Papers/Economic-Impact-Study-Summary.pdf

National Recreation and Park Association. (2016). *Annual report.* National Recreation and Park Association.

National Recreation and Park Association. (2017a). *Community-based, summertime events survey results.* www.nrpa.org/publications-research/park-pulse/Park-Pulse-Survey-Results-Community-Based-Events

National Recreation and Park Association. (2017b). *The economic impact of parks: An examination of the economic impacts of operations and capital spending by local park and recreation agencies on the U.S economy.* www.nrpa.org/publications-research/research-papers/the-economic-impact-of-local-parks

National Recreation and Park Association. (2020). *Annual report.* www.nrpa.org/about-national-recreation-and-park-association/leadership/annual-report/2020-nrpa-annual-report

National Recreation and Park Association. (2021). *Equity.* www.nrpa.org/our-work/Three-Pillars/equity

National Recreation and Park Association. (2022). *2022 NRPA agency performance review.* https://www.nrpa.org/parks-recreation-magazine/2022/may/delving-into-the-2022-agency-performance-review/

Nelson, G.M., & Rich, K.A. (2022). Community context and therapeutic recreation programming in rural long-term care: A socio-ecological examination. *Leisure = Loisir, 46*(1), 97-122.

Niagara Folk Arts Festival (NFAF). (n.d.). *Welcome.* http://folk-arts.ca/festival

Ontario Ministry of Heritage, Sport, Tourism and Culture Industries. (2021). Tourism Economic Recovery Ministerial Task Force Report.

Orend, R.J. (1989). *Socialization and participating in the arts.* Princeton University Press.

Parks and Recreation Federation of Ontario. (1992). *The benefits of parks and recreation: A catalogue.* Canadian Parks/Recreation Association.

Polley, M., & Sabey, A. (2022). The health benefits of arts, cultural and community

Portes, A. (1998). Social capital: Its origins and applications in modern sociology. *Annual Review Sociology, 24,* 1-24.

Powell Hanna, G. (2016). Arts, health and aging. In P. Dewey Lambert (Ed.), *Managing arts programs in healthcare* (pp. 189-201). Routledge.

Prince George's County Department of Arts and Recreation. (n.d.). *About us.* www.pgparks.com/1732/About-Us

Putnam, R.D. (2000). Bowling alone: The collapse and revival of American community. Simon & Schuster.

Rennie, B. (2020). *An ethology of religion and art.* Routledge.

Rollins, R., & Delamere, T. (2007). Measuring the social impact of festivals. *Annals of Tourism Research, 34*(3), p.805-808.

Rosewall, E. (2014). *Arts management: Uniting arts and audiences in the 21st century.* Oxford University Press.

Rosewall, E. (2021). *Arts management: Uniting arts and audiences in the 21st century* (2nd ed.). Oxford University Press.

Rossman, J. R. (1995). Recreation programming: Designing leisure experiences. Champaign, IL: Sagamore Publications.

Rossman, J.R., & Schlatter, B.E. (2009). *Recreation programming: Designing leisure experiences.* Sagamore Publications.

Roth, K. (2020) *How COVID-19 impacts parks and recreation funding.* National Recreation and Parks Association. https://www.nrpa.org/parks-recreation-magazine/2020/may/how-covid-19-impacts-park-and-recreation-funding/

Roth, K. (2021). *Diversity, equity and inclusion in parks and recreation.* National Recreation and Park Association. www.nrpa.org/parks-recreation-magazine/2021/june/diversity-equity-and-inclusion-in-parks-and-recreation

Seibel, S. & Volmer, J.A. (2021). Diary study on anticipated leisure time, morning recovery, and employees' work engagement. *International Journal of Environmental Research and Public Health, 18*(8). https://doi.org/10.3390/ijerph18189436

Sheridan, K.M., Feenema, S., & Winner, E. (2022). *Studio thinking 3: The real benefits of visual arts education* (3rd ed.). Teachers College Press.

Sherman A., & Morrissey C. (2017). What is art good for? The socio-epistemic value of art. *Frontiers in Human Neuroscience, 11*(411), 1-17. https://doi.org/10.3389/fnhum.2017.00411

Simonds, L. (Executive Producer). (2020). *Corey Newhouse: A shift from monitoring and evaluation, to learning and quality improvement* [Audio podcast]. Lindsay Simonds. https://lindsaysimondsconsulting.com/a-shift-from-monitoring-and-evaluation-to-learning-and-quality-improvement

Stack, C.B. (1975). *All our kin: Strategies for survival in a black community.* Basic Books.

Statistics Canada. (2017). *Income and expenditure accounts technical series: Provincial and territorial culture indicators, 2010 to 2014.* www.statcan.gc.ca/pub/13-604-m/13-604-m2016081-eng.htm

Stebbins, R.A. (1992). *Amateurs, professionals, and serious leisure.* McGill-Queen's University Press.

Stebbins, R.A. (2005a). Project-based learners: Theoretical neglect of a common use of free time. *Leisure Studies, 24*(1), pp. 1-11.

Stebbins, R.A. (2005b). Choice and experiential definitions of leisure. *Leisure Sciences, 27*(4), 349-352.

Stebbins, R.A. (2017). *The idea of leisure: First principles.* Taylor and Francis.

Stebbins, R.A., & Graham, M. (2004). *Volunteering as leisure/leisure as volunteering: An international assessment.* CABI.

Steele, R. (2019). *Western Kentucky & Jingdezhen, China, enhance creative connection with ceramics and craft breweries.* Paducah Arts Alliance. www.paducahartsalliance.com/news-announcements/western-kentucky-jingdezhen-china-enhance-creative-connection-with-ceramics-and-craft-breweries

Stein, T. (2000). Creating opportunities for people of color in performing arts management. *Journal of Arts Management, Law, and Society, 29,* 304-318.

Stern, M.J., & Siefert, S. (2002). *Culture builds community evaluation: Summary report.* University of Pennsylvania Libraries. https://repository.upenn.edu/siap_culture_builds_community/2

Stern, M.J., & Seifert, S. (2015). Communities, culture, and capabilities: Preliminary results of a four-city study. *Grantmakers in the Arts Reader, 26*(2). https://repository.upenn.edu/cgi/viewcontent.cgi?referer=&httpsredir=1&article=1000&context=siap_ccc

Stern, M.J., & Seifert, S. (2018). Culture and the new geography of social exclusion: The New York experience. *Social work & Society, 16*(2), p. 1-9.

Stern M.J., & Seifert, S. (2022). Cultural ecology and social wellbeing in urban California: Los Angeles and the Bay Area, with particular attention to neighborhoods of color and lower income. Philadelphia PA: Social Impact of the Arts Project, University of Pennsylvania. Sternberg, R.J., Grigorenko, E.L., & Singer, J.L. (Eds.). (2004). *Creativity: From potential to realization.* American Psychological Association.

Sternberg, R.J., Kaufman, J.C., & Pretz, J.E. (2002). *The creativity conundrum.* Psychology Press.

Tavin, K. (2003). Wrestling with angels, searching for ghosts: Toward a critical pedagogy of visual culture. *Studies in Art Education, 44*(3), 197-213.

Taylor, S. & Littleton, K. (2012). *Contemporary identities of creativity and creative work*. Routledge, Taylor and Francis Group.

Tennessee State Library and Archives. (n.d.). Tennessee State Parks folklife project. Retrieved from https://teva.contentdm.oclc.org/customizations/global/pages/collections/parksfolklife/parksfolklife.html

Tennessee State Museum. (2022). *Lunch and learn: Tennessee folklife with Bob Fulcher and Jay Orr*. Tennessee State Museum Lunch and Learn, Zoom. https://tnmuseum.org/calendar-of-events/event/2662133

Thorp, J. (2017). St. Louis Map Room. www.jerthorp.com/stlmaproom

Township of Esquimalt. (2021). *Virtual recreation: Arts*. www.esquimalt.ca/node/6839

Traditional Arts Indiana. (n.d.). *2021-2022 apprenticeships* https://traditionalarts.indiana.edu/Programs/Apprenticeships/Current%20Recipients/index.html

Traditional Arts Indiana. (n.d.). *What is traditional arts Indiana?* www.traditionalartsindiana.org/about/what-is-traditional-arts-indiana

U.S. Bank. (n.d.). *Community possible grant program—play*. www.usbank.com/community/community-possible-grant-program-play.aspx

U.S. Travel Association. (2022). *U.S. travel answer sheet/fact sheet*. www.ustravel.org/research/us-travel-answer-sheet

UNESCO. (2021). *Cultural and creative industries in the face of COVID-19: An economic impact outlook*. https://unesdoc.unesco.org/ark:/48223/pf0000377863

United Nations World Tourism Organization. (1997). The social impacts of tourism. https://www.e-unwto.org/doi/book/10.18111/9789284410965

Van Deursen, A.J., & Van Dijk, J.A. (2014). The digital divide shifts to differences in usage. *New Media & Society, 16*(3), 507-526.

Van Wyk, N., McCallum, N.T., Katz, L. (2022). Developing an intentionally designed physical activity model of programming for children's structured recreation in Canada. *Journal of Park and Recreation Administration, 40*(3), 69.

Wallace Foundation. (n.d.). *Knowledge center: Arts education*. www.wallacefoundation.org/knowledge-center/arts-education/Pages/default.aspx

Walsh, P. (2018). *Five reasons why public art matters*. www.americansforthearts.org/2018/08/30/five-reasons-why-public-art-matters

WDVX. (n.d.). *Cumberland trail*. https://wdvx.com/program/the-cumberland-trail

Weissman, S.E., St. John, L.R., Khalil, A., Tamminen, K.A., Cowie Bonne, J., Kitchener, L., & Arbour-Nicitopoulos, K. P. (2022). An evaluation of quality participation experiences in inclusive recreation programming for adults who have an intellectual disability. *Leisure = Loisir, 46*(2), 197-230.

White, M. (2009). *Arts development in community health: A social tonic*. Radcliffe Publishers.

Wilson Chamber of Commerce. (n.d.). *World's largest Czech egg*. https://wilsonkschamber.com/worlds-largest-czech-egg

Wolff, B. (2022). *The 2022 midterms were a billion dollar win for the arts in America*. Forbes. www.forbes.com/sites/benjaminwolff/2022/11/29/the-2022-midterms-were-a-billion-dollar-win-for-the-arts-in-america/?sh=4273c00b631b

Wyszomirski, M.J. (2002). Arts and culture. In L.M. Salamon (Ed.), *The state of nonprofit America* (pp. 187-218). Brookings Institution Press.

Youth Art Exchange (2022). *Mission and vision*. www.youthartexchange.org/mission

Zakaras, L., & Lowell, J.F. (2008). *Cultivating demand for the arts: Arts learning, arts engagement, and state arts policy*. Rand.

Zuidervaart, L. (2011). *Art in public: Politics, economics, and a democratic culture*. Cambridge University Press.

Zhang, S-N, & Deng, F. (2022). Innovation and authenticity: Constructing tourists' subjective well-being in festival tourism. Frontiers in Psychology, 13, p.950024-950024. DOI: 10.3389/fpsyg.2022.950024

CHAPTER 18

Association of Outdoor Recreation and Education. (n.d.). *Association of Outdoor Recreation and Education*. Retrieved March 13, 2023, from www.aore.org

Bersett, K., & Emken, T. (2022). *Redbird esports is here: Nationally recognized program continues growth with new facility*. https://news.illinoisstate.edu/2022/11/esports-is-here

Canadian Camping Association. (n.d.). *Canadian Camping Association*. Retrieved March 13, 2023, from https://ccamping.org

Fyke, J. (2009). Connecting the Cumberlands: A public lands success story in Tennessee reveals the benefits of cooperative partnering. *Parks & Recreation. 44*(2).

Henderson, K.A. (2014). *Introduction to recreation services: Sustainability for a changing world*. Venture Publishing.

Kauffman, R.B. (2010). *Career development in recreation, parks, and tourism*. Human Kinetics.

McGuire, F.A., Boyd, R.K., & Tedrick, R.E. (2009). *Leisure and aging: Ulyssean living in later life* (4th ed.). Sagamore.

Merriam, D. (2016). Parks: An opportunity to leverage environmental health. *Journal of Environmental Health, 78*(6), 112-114.

Mulvaney, M A., Beggs, B.A., Elkins, D.J., & Hurd, A.R. (2015). Professional certifications and job self-efficacy of public park and recreation professionals. *Journal of Park and Recreation Administration 33*(1), 93-111.

Murphy, J.F., Niepoth, E.W., Jamieson, L.M., & Williams, J.G. (1991). *Leisure systems: Critical concepts and applications*. Sagamore.

National Organization for Human Services. (n.d.). *What is human services?* www.nationalhumanservices.org/what-is-human-services

Rudolph, L., Caplan, J., Ben-Moshe, K., & Dillon, L. (2013). *Health in all policies: A guide for state and local governments*. www.phi.org/uploads/files/Health_in_All_Policies-A_Guide_for_State_and_Local_Governments.pdf

Taylor, D. (2014). Park for all: Parks in Vancouver seek to welcome and serve people all along the gender spectrum. *Parks & Recreation, 49*(7), 34-35.

CHAPTER 19

Akinlabi, A., Oyejide, A.J., Atoyebi, E.O., Awonusi, A., Herbert, E., Oyedele, C. & Abolade, M. (2022). Desk review of COVID-19 pandemic in Sub-Sahara Africa: The challenges and proffered solutions. *African Journal of Empirical Research, 3*(1), 250-262.

Almeida, M.A.B., & Gutierrez, G.L. (2005). O lazer no Brasil: Do nacional-desenvolvimentismo à globalização. *Conexões, 3*(1), 36-57.Almeida, M.A.B.D., Gutierrez, G.L., & Marques, R.F.R. (2013). Leisure in Brazil: The transformations during the military period (1964-1984). *Revista Brasileira de Educação Física e Esporte, 27*, 101-115.

American Hotel & Lodging Association (AHLA). (2021). *AHLA'S midyear state of the hotel industry: Top findings. AHLA research*. www.ahla.com/ahla-research-reports

Amuchie, F.A. (2003). Pre-colonial sports in Nigeria: Their influence on contemporary sports development in Nigeria. In L.O. Amusa & A.L. Toriola (Eds.), *Sports in contemporary African Society: An anthology* (pp. 47-64). Technikon Pretoria: Africa Association for Health, Physical Education recreation sports and Dance.

Ap, J. (2002). *Inter-cultural behavior: Some glimpses of leisure from an Asian perspective*. Invited paper presented at the Leisure Futures Conference, April 11-13, 2002, Innsbruck, Austria.

Armitage, R., & Nellums, L.B. (2020). COVID-19 and the consequences of isolating the elderly. *The Lancet Public Health, 5*(5), e256.

Atare, F.U. (2003). *Introduction to leisure and recreation education*. COEWA.

Atare, F.U. (2014). The health benefit of walking: A Nigerian reflection. *World Leisure Journal, 56*(2), 164-167. https://doi.org/10.1080/16078055.2014

Atare, F.U., & Ekpu, F.S. (2014). Status of recreation facilities in health-promoting tertiary institutions in Akwa Ibom state: Nigeria. *International Journal of Humanities Social Sciences and Education. 1*(4), 69-74. www.arcjournals.org

Baade, R.A., & Matheson, V.A. (2016). Going for gold: The economics of the Olympics. *Journal of Economic Perspectives, 30*(2), 201-218. http://dx.doi.org/10.1257/jep.30.2.201

Beijing Bureau of Sport. (2022). Notice on printing and distributing the five-year action plan for the construction of public fitness facilities in Beijing to reduce the facilities shortage (2021-2025). http://tyj.beijing.gov.cn/bjsports/zcfg15/ghjh/21235253/index.html

Bramante, A.C. (2020). Leisure and COVID-19 in Brazil: Brief impressions. *World Leisure Journal, 62*(4), 300-302.

Brasil. (2020). Coronavírus. Manual de Comunicação da Secom. Senado Federal. www12.senado.leg.br/manualde-comunicacao/redacao-e-estilo/coronavirus-1

Buckley, R. (2004). *Environmental impacts of ecotourism*. CABI.

Butler, R.W. (1980). The concept of tourism-area cycle of evolution and implications for management. *The Canadian Geographer, 24*, 5-12.

Butler, R.W. (1991). Environment, and sustainable development. *Environmental Conservation, 18*(3), 201-209.

Butler, R.W. (2000). The resort cycle two decades on. In B. Faulkner, G.M., & E. Laws (Eds.), *Tourism in the 21st Century: Reflections on Experience* (pp. 284-299). Continuum.

Camilleri, M.A. (2018). The planning and development of the tourism product. In M.A. Camilleri (Ed.), *Tourism planning and destination marketing*. Emerald Publishing.

Carson, V., Langlois, K., & Colley, R. (2020). Associations between parent and child sedentary behaviour and physical activity in early childhood. *Health Reports, 31*(2), 3-10.

Cavalcanti, M.L.V.D.C. (2006). Tema e variantes do mito: sobre a morte e a ressurreição do boi. *Mana, 12*, 69-104.

Chang, Y.K., Hung, C.L., Timme, S., Nosrat, S., & Chu, C.H. (2020). Exercise behavior and mood during the COVID-19 pandemic in Taiwan: Lessons for the future. *International Journal of Environmental Research and Public Health, 17*(19), 7092- 7109. https://doi.org/10.3390/ijerph17197092

Chawla, L. (2015). Benefits of nature contact for children. *Journal of Planning Literature, 30*(4), 433-452. https://doi.org/10.1177/088541221559441

China Association of National Parks and Scenic Sites. (2022). *Report of the high-quality development of China scenic areas: A big data analysis*. http://heritap.whitr-ap.org/themes/370/userfiles/download/2022/4/11/xlpigf6sdsl-gdit.pdf

China Athletics Association. (2021). *2019 China marathon big data analysis report*. https://lujuba.cc/en/559029.html

China State Forestry Administration. (2016). *China forest parks in 2015*. http://zgslgy.forestry.gov.cn/portal/slgy/s/2452/content-862765.html

China State Forestry and Grassland Administration. (2021). *China will establish its first national parks in 2021*. www.forestry.gov.cn/main/5497/20210320/212554338998134.html

China Tourism Academy. (2015). *Annual report of China leisure development (2013-2014)*. Tourism Education Press.

China Tourism Academy. (2020). *China Outbound Tourism Development Report 2020*. https://finance.sina.com.cn/tech/2020-11-12/doc-iiznezxs1371940.shtml

da Costa Trotta, F. (2016). O funk no Brasil contemporâneo: uma música que incomoda. *Latin American Research Review*, 86-101.

De Jesus, G.M. (1999). Do espaço colonial ao espaço da modernidade: Os esportes na vida urbana do Rio de Janeiro. *Scripta Nova, 45*(7). www.ub.edu/geocrit/sn-45-7.htm

Del Chiappa, G., Grappi, S., & Romani, S. (2016). Attitudes toward responsible tourism and behavioral change to practice it: A demand-side perspective in the context of Italy. *Journal of Quality Assurance in Hospitality & Tourism, 17*(2), 191-208. https://doi.org/10.1080/1528008X.2015.1115254

Deng, R. (2002). Leisure education and the strategy of Chinese higher education. *Studies in Dialectics in Nature, 18*(6), 46-48.

Destination Canada. (2019). *2019: Another record-breaking year for Canada.* www.destinationcanada.com/en/news/canada-experiences-third-consecutive-record-breaking-year-tourism-2019

Diamond, J. (2012). *The world until yesterday: What can we learn from traditional societies?* Viking.

Donohoe, H. (2013). *Introduction to recreation and leisure* (2nd ed.). Human Kinetics.

Dumazedier, J. (1980). *Valores e conteúdos culturais do lazer.* SESC.

ECLAC. (2020). COVID-19 reports: Recovery measures for the tourism sector in Latin America and the Caribbean present an opportunity to promote sustainability and resilience. www.cepal.org

Edgell, D.L. (2006). *Managing sustainable tourism: A legacy for the future.* Haworth Hospitality Press.

Educational Web Adventures. (n.d.). *Amazon interactive: The ecotourism game.* www.eduweb.com/ecotourism/eco1.html

Ferreira, R.F. (2004). Shopping center. In C.L. Gomes (Org.), *Dicionário crítico do lazer* (pp. 211-213). Autêntica.

Findhorn Ecovillage. (n.d.). *Findhorn ecovillage: New frontiers for sustainability.* Homepage. Ecovillage Findhorn https://www.ecovillagefindhorn.com/

Finney, C. (2014). *Black faces, white spaces: Reimagining the relationship of African Americans to the Great Outdoors.* University of North Carolina Press.

Flyvberg, B., Budzier, A., & Lunn, D. (2021). Regression to the tail: Why the Olympics blow up. *Economy and Space, 53*(2), 233-260. https://doi.org/10.1177/0308518X20958724

Frank, M. (2022). *Cuban tourism industry flounders as sunseekers look elsewhere.* Reuters. www.reuters.com/world/americas/cuban-tourism-industry-flounders-sunseekers-look-elsewhere-2022-02-18

Garriguet, D., Carson, V., Colley, R.C., Janssen, I., Timmons, B.W., & Tremblay, M.S. (2016). Physical activity and sedentary behaviour of Canadian children aged 3 to 5. *Health Reports, 27*(9), 14-23.

Gebara, A. (1997). Considerações para a história do lazer no Brasil. In H.T. Bruhns (Ed.), *Introdução aos estudos do lazer* (pp. 61-81). Unicamp.

Ghose, A.K. (2020). The pandemic, lockdown and employment. *The Indian Journal of Labour Economics, 63*(1), 67-71. https://doi.org/10.1007/s41027-020-00258-x

Goldbaum, C. (2020). Thinking of buying a bike? Get ready for a very long wait. *The New York Times.*

Gu, Z. (2021). Forest recreation visits reached to 7.5 billion between 2016 and 2020. www.gov.cn/shuju/2021-01/19/content_5580910.htm

Halpenny, E.A. (2010). Pro-environmental behaviours and park visitors: The effect of place attachment. *Journal of Environmental Psychology, 30*, 409-421.

Hangzhou Municipal Administration of Culture and Tourism. (2019). *An overview of Hangzhou's cultural, radio, TV and tourism sectors.* https://zjjcmspublic.oss-cn-hangzhou-zwynet-d01-a.internet.cloud.zj.gov.cn/jcms_files/jcms1/web3039/site/attach/0/055a818f10a24db49cb269ef55965d10.pdf

He, D., Yan, K., Xia, J., Zhang, J., Liu, D., Song, R., Jin Z., Li, W., & Wu, J. (2021). Tourism Development in China: Analysis and Forecast (2020-2021). Social Sciences Academic Press.

IBGE. (2011). *Sinopse do Censo Demográfico 2010.* Rio de Janeiro, Brazil: IBGE.

IBGE. (2021). *População do Brasil.* www.ibge.gov.br/apps/populacao/projecao/box_popclock.php

Ikulayo, P.B. (2003). Women in sports: An historical Perspectives. In L.O. Amusa & A. L. Toriola (Eds.) *Sports in contemporary African Society: An anthology* (pp 77-87). Technikon Pretoria: Africa Association for Health, Physical Education Recreation Sports and Dance.

Incredible Edible Limited. (n.d.). *Our story.* Incredible Edible Network. https://www.incredibleedible.org.uk/our-story/

International Air Transport Association (IATA). (2021). *Airlines struggle through worst year on record.* Economics. https://airlines.iata.org/analysis/airlines-struggle-through-the-worst-year-on-record

International Telecommunication Union (ITU). (2021). *Measuring digital development: Facts and figures 2021.* www.itu.int/en/ITU-D/Statistics/Documents/facts/FactsFigures2021.pdf

Jackson, E.L., & Walker, G.J. (2006). *A cross cultural comparison of leisure styles and constraints experienced by Chinese and Canadian university students.* Abstracts of the 9th World Leisure Congress, Hangzhou, China.

Jim, C.Y., & Chen, W.Y. (2009). Leisure participation pattern of residents in a new Chinese city. *Annals of the Association of American Geographers, 99*(4), 657-673.

Jksb. (2021). *Chinese health report 2020: average steps were decreased.* www.jksb.com.cn/index.php?m=wap&a=show&catid=27&id=168581

Johnson, T.F., Hordley, L.A., Greenwell, M.P., & Evans, L.C. (2021). Associations between COVID-19 transmission rates, park use, and landscape structure. *Science of the Total Environment, 789*, 1-11. https://doi.org/10.1016/j.scitotenv.2021.1148123

Jurin, R.R. (2012). *Principles of sustainable living: A new vision of health, happiness, and prosperity.* Human Kinetics.

Kleinschroth, F., & Kowarik, I. (2020). COVID-19 crisis demonstrates the urgent need for urban greenspaces. *Frontiers in Ecology and the Environment, 18*(6), 318-319. https://doi.org/10.1002/fee.2230

Knuth, A.G., & Antunes, P.D.C. (2021). Práticas corporais/atividades físicas demarcadas como privilégio e não escolha: análise à luz das desigualdades brasileiras. *Saúde e Sociedade, 30*, e200363.

Kyle, G., Graefe, A., Manning, R., & Bacon, J. (2004). Effect of activity involvement and place attachment on recreationists' perceptions of setting density. *Journal of Leisure Research, 36*(2), 209-231.

La Cienaga de Zapata.com. (2015). La Cienaga de Zapata Biosphere Reserve. http://www.lacienagadezapata.com/en/biosphere-reserve/

Lacerda, I., & Freitas, R. F. (2023). Baile encerrado, pancadão silenciado: a ação policial no baile de Paraisópolis (São Paulo). *Lumina, 17*(1), 195-209.

Lesser, I.A., & Nienhuis, C.P. (2020). The impact of COVID-19 on physical activity behavior and well-being of Canadians. *International Journal of Environmental Research and Public Health, 17*(11), 3899-3911. http://dx.doi.org/10.3390/ijerph17113899

Li, S., Zhou, Z., & Chen, Y. (2009). The functions, problems and strategies of group dance in squares in the establishment of community culture. *Science & Technology Information, 19*, 491.

Liu, H. (2007). The education of leisure loses the position, the dislocation and turns over to the position. *Studies in Dialectics in Nature, 23*(4), 67-70.

Liu, H., Yeh, C.K., Chick, G.E., & Zinn, H.C. (2008). An exploration of meanings of leisure: A chinese perspective. *Leisure Sciences, 30*, 482-488.

Louv, R. (2008). *Last child in the woods: Saving our children from nature-deficit disorder.* Algonquin Books.

Lu, Y., & Yu, Y. (2005). Investigation on sport facilities in Beijing residential areas. *Sport Science Research, 26*(5), 20-24.

Ma, H. (1999). *Call for leisure studies in China.* www.chineseleisure.org/onatheory.htm

Macrotrends. (2022). *Brazil tourism statistics 1995-2022.* www.macrotrends.net/countries/BRA/brazil/tourism-statistics#:~:text=Data%20are%20in%20current%20U.S.,a%206.62%25%20decline%20from%202016

Mascarenhas, F. (2003). O pedaço sitiado: Cidade, cultura e lazer em tempos de globalização. *Revista Brasileira de Ciências do Esporte, 24*(3), 121-143.

Massi, M. & De Nisco, A. (2018). The internet-based marketing of ecotourism: Are ecotourists really getting what they want? In M.A. Camilleri (Ed.), *Tourism planning and destination marketing* (pp. 161-182). Emerald Publishing Limited. https://doi.org/10.1108/978-1-78756-291-220181008

McKercher, B. (1996). Differences between tourism and recreation in parks. *Annals of Tourism Research, 23*(3), 563-575.

Melo, V.A. (2003). Lazer e educação física: Problemas historicamente contruídos, saídas possíveis—um enfoque na questão da formação. In C.L.G. Werneck & H. F. Isayama (Eds.), *Lazer, recreação e educação física* (pp. 57-80). Autêntica.

Ministry of Culture and Tourism of China. (2018). *2017 China tourism statistical bulletin.* www.ctaweb.org.cn/cta/gzdt/202103/066d7a05e0f244f5a5acc8d9287e487e.shtml

Ministry of Culture and Tourism of China. (2020). *Statistical bulletin of the Ministry of Culture and Tourism of the People's Republic of China on cultural and tourism development in 2019.* www.mct.gov.cn/whzx/ggtz/202006/t20200620_872735.htm

Ministry of Culture and Tourism of China. (2021). *Statistical bulletin of the Ministry of Culture and Tourism of the People's Republic of China on cultural and tourism development in 2020.* http://zwgk.mct.gov.cn/zfxxgkml/tjxx/202107/t20210705_926206.html

Ministry of Culture and Tourism of China. (2022). *Statistical bulletin of the Ministry of Culture and Tourism of the People's Republic of China on cultural and tourism development in 2021.* https://zwgk.mct.gov.cn/zfxxgkml/tjxx/202206/t20220629_934328.html

Montenegro, G.M., da Silva Queiroz, B., & Dias, M.C. (2020). Lazer em tempos de distanciamento social: impactos da pandemia de COVID-19 nas atividades de lazer de universitários na cidade de Macapá (AP). *Licere, 23*(3), 1-26.

Morakinyo, E.O., & Atare, F.U. (2005). Ecological constraints of outdoor recreation participation among municipal workers in Delta state, Nigeria. *Journal of ICHPER.SD, 3*(Summer), 51-55

Müller, D., & Hallal, D.R. (2016). A história dos meios de hospedagem no Brasil nos periódicos científicos brasileiros de turismo. *Revista Hospitalidade, 13*(2), 304-320.

Nakazawa, E., Ino, H., & Akabayashi, A. (2020). Chronology of COVID-19 cases on the Diamond Princess cruise ship and ethical considerations: A report from Japan. *Disaster Medicine and Public Health Preparedness, 14*(4), 506-513. https://doi.org/10.1017/dmp.2020.50

Nascimento, A.F. (2020). As origens históricas do lazer no seio de uma sociedade de natureza escravocrata: do Brasil colônia a Getúlio Vargas. *Revista Brasileira de Estudos do Lazer, 7*(2): 114-133.

National Bureau of Statistics. (2022). *2021 migrant worker monitoring survey report.* www.stats.gov.cn/tjsj/zxfb/202204/t20220429_1830126.html

National Primary Health Care Development Agency (NPHCDA). (2022). *COVID-19 vaccine update.* www.nphcda.gov.ng

Nhamo, G., Dube, K., & Chikodzi, D. (2020). Counting the cost of COVID-19 on global cruise ship industry. In *Counting the cost of COVID-19 on the global tourism industry* (pp. 135-158). Springer.

NOIPolls. (2014). *Reforming the Nigeria premier leagues.* www.noi-polls.com/root/index.php?pid=143&rptid=1&rparentid=14

Oliveira, C.A. de, & Mendes Silva, D. (2021). Os impactos do medo do crime sobre o consumo de atividades de lazer no Brasil. *Revista Brasileira De Segurança Pública, 15*(1), 156-173.

Outdoor Industry Association. (2021a). *2021 outdoor participation trends.* Outdoor Industry Association. https://outdoorindustry.org/wp-content/uploads/2015/03/2021-Outdoor-Participation-Trends-Report.pdf

Outdoor Industry Association. (2021b). *2021 special report. The new outdoor participant (COVID and beyond)*. Outdoor Industry Association. https://outdoorindustry.org/resource/2021-special-report-new-outdoor-participant--covid-beyond/

Pacheco, R.T.B. (2016). Lazer e cidades: protagonismos e antagonismos nas lutas por espaço. *Revista do Centro de Pesquisa e Formação, 2*, 92-103.

Paull, J.V. (2011). Incredible edible Todmorden: Eating the street. *Farming Matters, 27*(3), 28-29.

Pedro, T.M.G. (2017). É o fluxo: "baile de favela" e funk em São Paulo. *PROA: Revista de Antropologia e Arte, 2*(7), 115-135.

Peng, W. (2010). *Square Leisure culture and the construction of a harmonious, healthy and civilized lifestyle*. Proceedings of the 11th World Leisure Congress (pp. 189-190), Chuncheon, Korea.

Petracovschi, S. (2021). Daciada and mass sport during communism in Romania as reflected in the Sport Magazine: A propaganda tool. *The International Journal of the History of Sport*, 1-19.

Prakash, A. (2017). *Santorini's tourism numbers are growing, but is that actually a good thing?* News.com.au. https://www.news.com.au/travel/destinations/europe/santorinis-tourism-numbers-are-growing-but-is-that-actually-a-good-thing/news-story/058a52d0a38409f370af652ed37150b9

Qin, H. (2022). A comprehensive assessment of the development level of the leisure industry in Heilongjian Province using the entropy weight-TOPSIS method. *Think Tank of Science & Technology, 2*, 38-45.

Qing, Q. (2007). Leisure industry: Concepts, scopes and statistical issues. *Tourism Tribune, 22*(8), 82-85.

Ribeiro, O.C.F. (2004). Hotéis de lazer. In C.L. Gomes (Org.), *Dicionário crítico do lazer* (pp. 107-112). Belo Horizonte: Autêntica.

Ribeiro, O.C.F., de Santana, G.J., Tengan, E.Y.M., da Silva, L.W.M., & Nicolas, E.A. (2020). Os impactos da pandemia da COVID-19 no lazer de adultos e idosos. *Licere, 23*(3), 391-428.

Rideout, V., & Robb, M.B. (2020). *The common sense census: Media use by kids age zero to eight, 2020*. Common Sense Media.

Roser, M. (2021). *Tourism*. OurWorldInData. https://ourworldindata.org/tourism

Ryfield, F., Cabana, D., Brannigan, J., & Crowe, T. (2019). Conceptualizing 'sense of place' in cultural ecosystem services: A framework for interdisciplinary research. *Ecosystem Services, 36*. https://doi.org/10.1016/j.ecoser.2019.100907

Salau, S.J. (2021). Time to grow Nigeria Football league. *Business Day Newspaper*. Dec 28. www.businessday.org

Sallis, R., Rohm Young, D., Tartof, S.Y., Sallis, J.F., Sall, J., Li, Q., Smith, G.N., & Cohen, D.A. (2021). Physical inactivity is associated with higher risk for severe COVID-19 outcomes: A study in 48,440 adult patients. *British Journal of Sports Medicine, 55*(19), 1-8. https//doi.org/10.1136/bjsports-2021-104080

Scannell, L., & Gifford, R. (2010). Defining place attachment: A tripartite organizing framework. *Journal of Environmental Psychology, 30*, 1-10.

Shorkend, D. (2019). Nazism and sport: The dangers of art aesthetics. *International Journal of Innovative Studies in Sociology and Humanities, 4*(7), 22-32.

Smith, J. (2018). *Greece tourism at record high amid alarm over environmental cost. The Guardian*. https://www.theguardian.com/world/2018/jun/03/greece-tourism-at-record-high-amid-alarm-over-environmental-cost

Smith, S.L.J., & Godbey, G.C. (1991). Leisure, recreation, and tourism. *Annals of Tourism Research, 18*(1), 85-100.

Song, R., Jin, H., Li, W., Wu, J., He, D., Ming, K., Xia, J., & Liu, D. (2020). *Annual report of China's leisure development (2019-2020)*. Social Sciences Academic Press (China).

Statista. (n.d.). *China's revenue from tourism from 2011 to 2021*. Retrieved December 6, 2022, from www.statista.com/statistics/236040/revenue-from-tourism-in-china

Stodolska, M. (2021). #QuarantineChallenge2k20: Leisure in the time of the pandemic. *Leisure Sciences, 43*(1-2), 232-239.

Stoppa, E.A. (1999). *Acampamentos de férias*. Campinas, Brazil: Papirus.

Sustainable Travel. (n.d.). *About us*. Sustainable Travel International. http://sustainabletravel.org

Tavares, L.M. (2021). *Parques públicos urbanos como possibilidade de lazer para idosos em Florianópolis*. [Masters Dissertation, Universidade Federal de Santa Catarina].

Tavares, L.M.; Marinho, A. (in press). Leisure and COVID-19: Reflections on Brazilian elderly people who frequent urban public parks. *World Leisure Journal*.

Tourism Research Center of the Chinese Academy of Social Sciences. (2015). *Annual report on China's leisure development (2013-2015)*. Social Sciences Academic Press (China).

TravelChinaGuide. (n.d.). *2019 China tourism facts and figures*. www.travelchinaguide.com

Udomiaye, M. & Umar, Z. (2010). *Understanding physical and health education for junior secondary school*. Waka Fast.

United Nations. (n.d.-a). *International youth day: August 12*. International Youth Day | United Nations. https://www.un.org/development/desa/youth/what-we-do/international-youth-day.html

United Nations. (n.d.-b). *Sustainable development knowledge platform: Sustainable development goals*. https://sdgs.un.org/goals

United Nations. (2010). *International year of youth*. www.un.org/esa/socdev/unyin/documents/iyy/guide.pdf

United Nations Development Programme (UNDP). (2020). *Human development report 2020. The next frontier: Human development and the anthropocene. Briefing note for countries on the 2020 Human Development Report*. http://hdr.undp.org/sites/all/themes/hdr_theme/country-notes/BRA.pdf

United Nations Educational, Scientific, and Cultural Organization (UNESCO). (n.d.). *Youth: Because youth matter*. UNESCO. https://www.unesco.org/en/youth

United Nations Educational, Scientific, and Cultural Organization (UNESCO). (2023). *World Heritage list.* World Heritage Centre. https://whc.unesco.org/en/list

United Nations World Tourism Organization (UNWTO). (n.d.-a). *Ecotourism and protected areas.* UNWTO Tourism Data Dashboard. Ecotourism and Protected areas | UNWTO https://www.unwto.org/sustainable-development/ecotourism-and-protected-areas

United Nations World Tourism Organization (UNWTO). (n.d.-b). *The first global dashboard for tourism insights.* UNWTO Tourism Data Dashboard. UNWTO Tourism Data Dashboard | UNWTO https://www.unwto.org/tourism-data/unwto-tourism-dashboard

United Nations World Tourism Organization. (UNWTO). (2022). *Sustainable development.* www.unwto.org/sustainable-development

Venter, Z.S., Barton, D.N., Gundersen, V., Figari, H., & Nowell, M. (2020). Urban nature in a time of crisis: Recreational use of green space increases during the COVID-19 outbreak in Oslo, Norway. *Environmental Research Letters, 15*(10), 104075.

Wang, J., & Stringer, L.A. (2000). The impact of Taoism on Chinese leisure. *World Leisure, 42*(3), 33-41.

Watts, M.W., & Ferro, S.L. (2012). The coexistence of folk and popular culture as vehicles of social and historical activism: Transformation of the Bumba-meu-boi in Northeast Brazil. *Journal of Popular Culture, 45*, 883-901.

Wei, X. (2009). *China leisure industry: Review and prospect.* http://weixiaoan.blog.sohu.com/144349753.html

Wei, X., Huang, S., Stodolska, M., & Yu Y. (2015). Leisure time, leisure activities, and happiness in China. *Journal of Leisure Research, 47*(5), 556-576.

Whitburn, J., Linklater, W.L., & Milfont, T.L. (2019). Exposure to urban nature and tree planting are related to pro-environmental behavior via connection to nature, the use of nature for psychological restoration, and environmental attitudes. *Environment and Behavior, 51*(7), 787-810. https://doi.org/10.1177/0013916517751009

Williams, D.R., & Roggenbuck, J.R. (1989). Measuring place attachment: Some preliminary results. Paper presented at the Paper presented at the Session on Outdoor Planning and Management NRPA Symposium on Leisure Research. San Antonio, TX.

Williams, D.R., & Vaske, J.J. (2003). The measurement of place attachment: Validity and generalizability of a psychometric approach. *Forest Science, 49*(6), 830-840.

Wilson, E.O. (1984). *Biophilia.* Harvard University Press.

Witte, A. (2021). "Chinese don't walk?" The emergence of domestic walking tourism on China's Ancient Tea Horse Road. *Journal of Leisure Research, 52*(4), 424-445.

World Bank. (n.d.). *Connecting for inclusion: Broadband access for all.* www.worldbank.org/en/topic/digitaldevebrief/connecting-for-inclusion-broadband-ac

World Bank. (2016). Annual Report 2016. World Development Indicators Database. Retrieved from https://thedocs.worldbank.org/en/doc/596391540568499043-0340022018/original/worldbankannualreport2016.pdf

World Bank. (2023). *International tourism, number of arrivals -Cuba.* Data. https://data.worldbank.org/indicator/ST.INT.ARVL?end=2020&locations=CU&start=2019

World Leisure Organization. (n.d.). *Description.* www.worldleisure.org/about

World Travel and Tourism Council (WTTC). (2021a). *EIR 2021 global infographic.* Economic Impact Reports. https://wttc.org/Research/Economic-Impact

World Travel and Tourism Council (WTTC). (2021b). *Travel and tourism economic impact: Global economic impact and trends 2021.* Economic Impact Reports. https://wttc.org/Portals/0/Documents/Reports/2021/Global%20Economic%20Impact%20and%20Trends%202021.pdf?-ver=2021-07-01-114957-177

Xiao, H. (1997). Tourism and leisure in China: A tale of two cities. *Annals of Tourism Research, 24*(2), 357-370.

Xinhua News Agency. (2020). *Chinese tourists make over 6 bln domestic trips in 2019.* https://global.chinadaily.com.cn/a/202003/11/WS5e683b54a31012821727e085.html

Xinhua News Agency. (2021a). *The general office of the central committee of the Communist Party of China and the general office of the State Council issued the "Opinions on further reducing the homework burden and off-campus training burden of students in compulsory education."* www.gov.cn/zhengce/2021-07/24/content_5627132.htm

Xinhua News Agency. (2021b). *The State Council issued the "National fitness plan (2021-2025).* www.gov.cn/xinwen/2021-08/03/content_5629234.htm

Yin, X. (2005). New trends of leisure consumption in China. *Journal of Family and Economic Issues, 26*(1), 175-182.

You, B., & Zhen, X. (2007). *On the leisure society and the leisure industry of China.* www.gogoplay.cn/html/xiuxianlilun/200711/20071110164526733.html

Young, M.E. (2020). Leisure pursuits in South Africa as observed during the COVID-19 pandemic. *World Leisure Journal, 62*(4), 331-335.

Zhang, C., Cui, R., Xu, C., & Wang, J. (2020). *COVID-19 and the Chinese hotel sector.* www.hospitalitynet.org/file/152008810.pdf

Zhang, J., Inbakaran, R. J., & Jackson, M. S. (2006). Understanding community attitudes towards tourism and host-guest interaction in the urban-rural border region. *Tourism Geographies, 8*(2), 182-204. DOI: 10.1080/14616680600585455

Zheng, Z. (2019). *2018 report of Chinese physical activities: Average Chinese walked over 6000 steps per day.* http://it.people.com.cn/n1/2019/0109/c1009-30511370.html

Zhou, B., & Chen, Y. (2022). Research on the high-quality development of national fitness venues and facilities in China in the new era. *Sports Culture Guide, 8*, 50-57.

Zhou, L.J., & Liu, L. (2020). COVID-19 pandemic in China: Observation and reflections. *World Leisure Journal, 62*(4), 315-318.

Zhou, X. (2008). *Survey of Chinese middle class.* Social Science Academic Press.

Index

Note: The italicized *f* and *t* following page numbers refer to figures and tables, respectively.

D

dance 356, 428, 433
dark skies 139
death, leading causes of 324, 324*t*
debt levels 60
decision making, logic and 52
deductive inferences 52
De Grazia, Sebastian 48
demand 137
demographic trends 40, 153-154, 156, 182, 397-398
Deng, Xiaoping 424
Denver, Colorado 392
depression 9, 15, 395. *See also* mental health
destination marketing organizations (DMOs) 195-196
developer roles 18
developing nations 411
Dewdney, Edgar 112
dietary practices 326
direct provider role of government 148
direct service providers 383
disabilities. *See also* inclusive recreation
  inclusive language for 209
  legislation on 159, 208-209, 208*t*
  population statistics 204
  sports programs 162
disadvantaged groups 15
discrimination 75, 78
disease
  chronic 245, 246, 321, 326
  leading causes of death 324, 324*t*
  prevention 246, 250, 394-395
  risk 9, 245
disengagement theory 279
Disney 6, 18, 21, 22
dispositional barriers 19, 20
diversity
  arts and culture accessibility and 372-375
  in leisure 72, 196
  population 40-41, 78, 139, 397-398
Dix, Dorothea 206
DMOs (destination marketing organizations) 195-196
documentation, in TR 217
Dominion Parks Branch 112
donations 95, 96, 123
Don't Get Caught With the Cookie activity 272
drug use 85, 138
dual sports 303
duty-based ethics 64-65

E

early adulthood (20s and 30s) 276-277
early childhood 269-270
Eastern Wilderness Act 128
economics
  arts and cultural industry 366-367
  in Brazil 416
  challenges 33, 40, 41, 122-123, 183

of China's recreation and leisure 423-424
disposable income and 33
of experience making 22
household debt 60
by industry 14
leisure services delivery and 91-92
obesity impact on 321
in postpandemic era 13-14, 17-18
recreation expenditures 13-14
ecotourism 122, 137, 347-348, 412-413
Edmonton Mall 21
education
  academic programs 98, 379, 385
  for careers in parks 135
  international programs 424, 429, 437
  for RET industry 197-198
  for therapeutic recreation professionals 218
educational sports 301
educators (facilitator roles) 384-385
Egyptians 206
Ekomobong, Daniel 437
electronic sports. *See* esports
Ellis, Nicki 49
Elora Prescription 18
emerging professional roles 17-22
Emerson, Ralph Waldo 54, 341, 342
emotional intelligence 59
emotional labor 59
emotional wellness 328
empiricists 50
employee assistance programs 248, 249
employee recreation. *See* worksite wellness
employees
  aging populations and 139
  background checks 311-312
  contingent 314-315
  private sector 94
  public sector 99
  technology use by 101, 311
employment. *See* career areas; jobs
enabler and coordinator roles 18, 148
encroachment 137-138
Endangered American Wilderness Act 121
enewsletters 195, 382, 390, 391
England, parks 107, 109
enslaved people 26, 27, 28, 31, 47, 56, 416
entertainment 28, 200, 432, 436
entrepreneurial associations 193
entrepreneurs 187, 192, 193, 196, 197, 372
environment
  aesthetic value of 54-55
  impact assessments 54
  interaction with resources 330*f*
  nature 54, 341-342, 407, 413
  stewardship 244, 392
  sustainability 10, 15-16, 21-22, 199-200, 407-410
  threats to parks 138
environmental nonprofits 170, 179

environmental QOL indicators 332
environmental wellness 329-330
environment migration 15-16
Epcot Center 18
epistemology 50-51
equality, versus equity 15
equity 8
  advocating for 397-399
  in arts and culture 372-375
  versus equality 15
  ethnic and racial 77-78, 182
  gender equity 75
  in postpandemic era 15
  usage fees and 19
Erikson, Erik 267
esports
  in Asian Games 310
  in campus recreation 234
  career opportunities in 236
  future of 237-238
  history of 234-236
  organizations in 236
  in parks and recreation 236
  reaching new audiences with 400
  sponsorships in 237
  as sports 237, 309-310
  viewership of 236, 237
ESRI 13
essential, term 10-11
essential human needs 9-10
ethical dilemmas 63-65
ethics
  bioethical principles 219
  codes of 219, 381, 382
  leisure and 55-57
  in nonprofit sector 183
ethnicity 77-79, 397-398
ethos 56
Eugene T. Mahoney State Park (Omaha, NB) 125
evaluation
  in TR process 216-217
  in worksite wellness 248
event specialists 384
Everglades National Park 129
Everson, Christin 228
evidence-based practice 220, 246
exergaming 309
experience makers 22
extramural sports 302, 304
Eyquem de Montaigne, Michel 29

F

facilitated leadership 292, 294
facilitation functions in RET 190-191
facilitator roles 18, 384-385
facilities
  accessibility 159-161
  in Armed Forces recreation 258
  in campus recreation 229
  community-based 149, 181
  for community education 155
  environmental wellness and 329-330
  for recreational sport 305-306, 309

About the Editors

Tyler Tapps, PhD, is the assistant vice president for health and well-being at Northwest Missouri State University and was formerly an associate professor and the assistant director for health sciences. He received his PhD in health, leisure, and human performance from Oklahoma State University in 2009. In 2015, he was certified as a park and recreation professional by the National Recreation and Park Association (NRPA), from which he also received the Robert W. Crawford Young Professional Award. Tapps is a military veteran with recreation programming experience in the military. He is a past president of the Leisure Educators section of the Missouri Park and Recreation Association.

Mary Sara Wells, PhD, is an associate professor in the department of parks, recreation, and tourism at the University of Utah, where she serves as the director of undergraduate studies. She teaches courses in youth development, community recreation, and sport management. She has been a member of The Academy of Leisure Sciences (TALS), the National Recreation and Park Association (NRPA), and Society of Park and Recreation Educators (SPRE) since 2004. Wells has researched issues of sporting conduct in youth sport. She has published her research in numerous journals, presented at several national and international conferences, and conducted trainings and evaluations for multiple municipal youth sport agencies across the country.

Contributors

Robert F. Ashcraft, PhD
Arizona State University

Franz U. Atare, PhD
University of Uyo

Robert J. Barcelona, PhD
Clemson University

Rhonda Cross Beemer, PhD, ATC
Northwest Missouri State University

Diane C. Blankenship, EdD
Frostburg State University

Michael J. Bradley, PhD
Arkansas Tech University

John Byl, PhD
Redeemer University College, Professor Emeritus

Frances Stavola Daly, EdD
Kean University

Jinyang Deng, PhD
West Virginia University

Paul F. J. Eagles, PhD
University of Waterloo, Professor Emeritus

David N. Emanuelson, PhD
President and CEO, Impact Planning and Polling;
  Partner, The Public Research Group

Kevin J. Fink, PhD
University of Central Oklahoma

Marni Goldenberg, PhD
California Polytechnic State University, San Luis
  Obispo

H. Joey Gray, PhD
North Carolina Agricultural and Technical State
  University

Nicole Green, MEd
Assistant Director, Facilities Operations,
  University of Michigan

Augustus W. Hallmon, PhD
James Madison University

Jeffrey C. Hallo, PhD
Clemson University

Tristan Hopper, PhD
University of Regina

Garrett Hutson, PhD
Brock University

David Kahan, PhD
Coastal Carolina University

Douglas Kennedy, EdD
Virginia Wesleyan University

Rachel Kollasch, MS, CTRS
Richcroft, Inc.

Robin Kunstler, ReD
Lehman College

Jian Li, PhD
Zhejiang A&F University

Yating "Tina" Liang, PhD
Missouri State University

Huimei Liu, PhD
Zhejiang University

Terry Long, PhD
Northwest Missouri State University

Kim Lyddane, MS
Director, Albany Parks & Recreation

Tracy L. Mainieri, PhD
Illinois State University

Alcyane Marinho, PhD
Santa Catarina State University

Bruce Martin, PhD
Ohio University

Juan Tortosa Martínez, PhD
University of Alicante

Donald J. McLean, PhD
Western Illinois University

Ellen O'Sullivan, PhD
President, Leisure Lifestyle Consulting

Mary Parr, PhD
Kent State University

Robert E. Pfister, PhD
Vancouver Island University, Retired

Arianne C. Reis, PhD
Western Sydney University

Kelsie N. Roberts, PhD
Northern State University

Terrance Robertson, PhD
California State University, Long Beach

Jerome F. Singleton, PhD
Dalhousie University

Jill Sturts, PhD
Virginia Wesleyan University

Matthew Symonds, EdD
Northwest Missouri State University

Patrick T. Tierney, PhD
San Francisco State University

Julie Voelker-Morris, MS, WPCC
University of Oregon

Daniel G. Yoder, PhD
Western Illinois University